HANDBOOK
OF
HUMAN
SEXUALITY

HANDBOOK OF HUMAN SEXUALITY

Benjamin B. Wolman
editor

John Money
consulting editor

PRENTICE-HALL, INC., Englewood Cliffs, New Jersey 07632

Library of Congress Cataloging in Publication Data
Main entry under title:
Handbook of human sexuality.

    Bibliography: p.
    Includes index.
    1.   Sex—Handbooks, manuals, etc.   2. Sexual
disorders—Handbooks, manuals, etc.   3. Sex
(Psychology)—Handbooks, manuals, etc.   4. Sex
customs—Handbooks, manuals, etc.   I. Wolman,
Benjamin B.   II. Money, John William
HQ12.H36   612.6   79–16907
ISBN 0–13–378422–3

© 1980 *by* PRENTICE-HALL, INC., Englewood Cliffs, N.J. 07632

Printed in the United States of America

10 9 8 7 6 5 4 3 2 1

editorial/production supervision and interior design: CATHIE MICK MAHAR
cover design: ELAINE REICHERT
manufacturing buyer: HARRY P. BAISLEY

PRENTICE-HALL INTERNATIONAL, INC., *London*
PRENTICE-HALL OF AUSTRALIA PTY. LIMITED, *Sydney*
PRENTICE-HALL OF CANADA, LTD., *Toronto*
PRENTICE-HALL OF INDIA PRIVATE LIMITED, *New Delhi*
PRENTICE-HALL OF JAPAN, INC., *Tokyo*
PRENTICE-HALL OF SOUTHEAST ASIA PTE. LTD., *Singapore*
WHITEHALL BOOKS LIMITED, *Wellington, New Zealand*

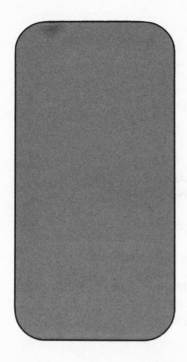

CONTENTS

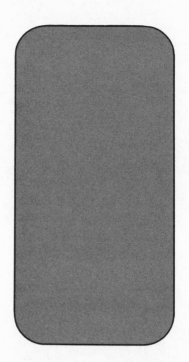

PREFACE

This Handbook describes three salient areas of human sexuality. The first part analyzes developmental and behavioral aspects of sexuality from the onset of human life to its end. Part two deals with social, cultural, and legal aspects of sexual behavior viewed in historical perspective and contemporary social relations. Sexual aberrations and dysfunctions and their various treatment methods are the subject matter of the third part.

I am fully aware of the diversity of views and approaches of the authors of the respective chapters of this Handbook. No effort was made to attain any degree of uniformity; to the contrary, we have been fortunate to secure the cooperation of experts in various areas of research and theory, and to put together this broadly conceived survey of the field. Biology and psychology, sociology and anthropology, psychoanalysis and behavior modification, are represented in the pages of this Handbook.

I am profoundly grateful to Dr. John Money, the consulting editor, and to Dr. Helen S. Kaplan and Dr. Raymond W. Waggoner for their kind and efficient help and guidance.

Benjamin B. Wolman

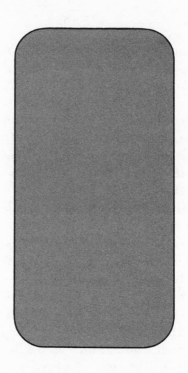

CONTRIBUTORS

ROBERT ATHANASIOU (Chapter 13), Ph.D., M.D. is a medical psychologist and Assistant Professor of Psychiatry at the Albany Medical College, Albany, New York. He is a certified sex therapist (AASECT), and a member of the American College of Sexologists and the International Academy of Sex Researchers. He has authored numerous articles and contributed to several books on human sexuality. His current interests include sexual function therapy, research on erotica, psychosomatic medicine, and the training of medical students and residents in sexuality.

BARBARA L. DOLGIN (Co-author Chapter 11), J.D., Columbia Law School, is a practicing attorney in New York City.

JANET L. DOLGIN (Co-author, Chapter 11), Ph.D., Princeton University, has most recently taught anthropology at Teachers College, Columbia University and at the Hebrew University of Jerusalem. She is author of *Jewish Identity and the JDL* (Princeton University Press) and co-editor of *Symbolic Anthropology* (Columbia University Press). She is presently studying law at the Yale Law School.

HERBERT FENSTERHEIM (Chapter 16), is a clinical associate professor of psychology at Cornell University Medical College. He is co-director of the Behavior Therapy Training and Research Unit, Payne Whitney Clinic of the New York Hospital.

LAWRENCE E. FISHER (Chapter 9), Ph.D., Northwestern University; former Postdoctoral Fellow, University of Chicago, is Assistant Professor of Anthropology at the University of Illinois, Chicago Circle. During 1979–80 he is Visiting Assistant Professor at University of Michigan, Ann Arbor. He has conducted research in areas of mental health, social organization, language, and sexuality in the British Caribbean, his major ethnographic area.

MADELINE E. HEILMAN (Chapter 12), Ph.D., Columbia University, is an Associate Professor of Administrative Sciences and Psychology at the School of Organization and Management, Yale University. Currently serving on the editorial boards of *The Journal of Conflict Resolution* and *The Journal of Applied Behavioral Science*, she has published widely in such journals as *Organizational Behavior and Human Performance, Journal of Applied Psychology,*

Journal of Experimental Social Psychology, and *Journal of Personality and Social Psychology.* Dr. Heilman's principal area of interest is the dynamics and consequences of occupational sex bias.

EILEEN HIGHAM (Chapter 2), Ph.D., University of California, Los Angeles, is an assistant professor of Medical Psychology at The Johns Hopkins Hospital and Medical Institutions. She is Coordinator of Psychological Services for Gender Identity Disorders at the Psychohormonal Research Unit and is engaged in private practice. Her main interests are human sexology, and behavioral endocrinology.

JERRY S. KANTOR (Chapter 16), M.D., University of Texas Medical Branch, Cornell University Medical College; Board Certified in Adult Psychiatry and AASECT certified in Sex Therapy. He is a member of the adjunct faculty at the Graduate School of Applied Psychology, Rutgers University, and is presently developing a phobia clinic at Rutgers Medical School. He is a contributor to various professional journals and practices psychiatry in Princeton. His major fields of interest are in the etiology, and treatment of sexual disorders and phobic anxiety syndromes.

HELEN SINGER KAPLAN (Co-author, Chapter 18), M.D., New York Medical College, Ph.D., Columbia University, is director of Human Sexuality Program, Payne Whitney Clinic at New York Hospital-Cornell Medical Center. She developed and now directs clinic for the study, evaluation and treatment of sexual disorders, and responsible for course on Human Sexuality for medical students and staff. She is responsible for post-graduate training program in psychosexual therapy.

FLOYD M. MARTINSON (Chapter 3), Ph.D., University of Minnesota, is Professor of Sociology at Gustavus Adolphus College. Most of his research and writing has been in the areas of family, marriage, and sexuality, with primary emphasis recently on infant and child sexuality. He has written *Marriage and the American Ideal* (Dodd Mead, 1960), *Family in Society* (Dodd Mead, 1970), and is at present co-editing a book on *Perspectives and Research in Child Sexuality* (Little, Brown). He has also published numerous articles in professional journals and as chapters in books. He has spent a year each in Norway and Sweden as visiting professor engaged in teaching and research. He was Director of the International Seminar on The Child and The Family sponsored by the Committee on Family Research of the International Sociological Association and the International Section of the National Council on Family Relations in August 1979. He also organized and chaired the first International Symposium on Infant and Child Sexuality at University College of Swansea, Wales, in September 1977.

TOM MAZUR (Co-author, Chapter 1), Psy.D., Baylor University, is a Medical Psychologist in the Department of Psychiatry and Behavioral Sciences, The Johns Hopkins University School of Medicine and Hospital. Among his special professional interests are psychoendocrinology, and behavioral sexology, especially childhood sexuality.

WILLIAM W. MEISSNER (Chapter 15), M.D., is engaged in the practice of psychiatry and psychoanalysis. He is Associate Clinical Professor of Psychiatry at Harvard Medical School and a Faculty Member at the Boston Psychoanalytic Institute. He is also Staff Psychiatrist at the Massachusetts Mental Health Center. In addition to publishing numerous articles, he co-authored a basic psychoanalytic text with Dr. Elizabeth Zetzel and in 1978 published *The Paranoid Process.* He has been actively involved in the study of various aspects of clinical psychoanalysis.

HEINO F. L. MEYER-BAHLBURG (Chapter 4), Dr. rer. nat., University of Dusseldorf, Germany, is Associate Clinical Professor of Medical Psychology in Psychiatry, College of Physicians & Surgeons of Columbia University, New York City, Research Scientist at the New York State Psychiatric Institute, and Co-director of the Psychoendocrine Clinic at Babies Hospital, New York City. His major research interest is developmental psychoendocrinology, particularly the area of sex and gender.

TAGHI MODARRESSI (Chapter 8), M.D., is Associate Professor of Psychiatry, Director of Children's Residential Service, Division of Child and Adolescent Psychiatry, Department of Psychiatry, University of Maryland Hospital. He has investigated and published in the area of early mother-child relationship, the development of body image during infancy, and severe developmental arrests in children.

JOHN MONEY (Co-author, Chapter 1), Ph.D., Harvard University, is Professor of Medical Psychology and Associate Professor of Pediatrics, The Johns Hopkins University School of Medicine and Hospital. He is the director of the Psychohormonal Research Unit and co-founder of the Johns Hopkins Gender Identity Clinic, the first such clinic in the United States. He is the author of *Sex Errors of the Body*, a co-author of *Man & Woman, Boy & Girl*, and a co-editor of *Transsexualism and Sex Reassignment* and the *Handbook of Sexology*. In 1972 he received the annual award of the Society for the Scientific Study of Sex.

FARIDA K. SHAH (Co-author, Chapter 5), M.S., The Johns Hopkins University, Baltimore, is Research Associate in the Department of Population Dynamics, The Johns Hopkins University, School of Hygiene and Public Health. Her research interests are factors associated with infant mortality, fertility differentials in some developing countries and fertility of young women in the United States.

ANN JOHNSON SILNY (Chapter 7), Ph.D., University of California, Berkeley, in experimental/biological psychology, is a vice president at ASI Market Research in Los Angeles. Her professional work deals with advertising research with a strong emphasis on experimental design, methodology and analysis. She is involved as a primary investigator in a study to develop a predictive model relating copytest scores and market variables to real world brand performance. She taught experimental psychology, statistics, learning theory and human sexuality on the undergraduate and graduate levels before leaving academia to enter the private sector. Biological mechanisms of social behavior and human sexuality remain strong outside interests.

RAYMOND W. WAGGONER (Chapter 9), M.D., University of Michigan is Professor and Chairman Emeritus at the University of Michigan. He is Psychiatric Consultant to Reproductive Biology Research Foundation at St. Louis, Missouri. He serves on the Ethics Committee for the American Psychiatric Society, is Chairman of Stanley Dean Awards Committee. He is an advisor to the Department of Mental Health for the State of Michigan. Dr. Waggoner has published numerous articles which contribute significantly to the field of Psychiatry. He is also on the Editorial Board for *Behavioral Science* and *Psychiatry Digest*.

CLAUS WIEDEKING (Co-author, Chapter 14), M.D., Ph.D., University of Ruhr, West Germany. He is currently involved in research in human genetics and joint training in psychiatry at Gottingen University, West Germany. He is published in genetics and sexology.

JUANITA H. WILLIAMS (Chapter 6), Ph.D., University of South Florida, is professor of women's studies and psychology. She is the author of *Psychology of Women: Behavior in a Biosocial Context*, and has published extensively in the area of psychology of women, sexuality, the female life cycle, and sex roles. She is in private practice in Temple Terrace, Florida.

MILDRED HOPE WITKIN (Co-author, Chapter 18 and Chapter 19), Ph.D. is Assistant Clinical Professor, Department of Psychiatry, Cornell University Medical College in New York, and Associate Director of the Human Sexuality Program at the Payne Whitney Psychiatric Clinic of The New York Hospital-Cornell Medical Center, New York. She serves on the Accreditation Board and the Regional Board of the American Association of Sex Educators, Counselors, and Therapists, and is a Certified psychosex therapist and Certified sex educator. Her major fields of professional interest are in marriage and family therapy, and psychosex therapy. Dr. Witkin has published numerous articles on dyadic and family therapy, ethical issues and sex therapy, and the psychological effects of cancer of the breast based upon her clinical observations and research. She is currently continuing research on the psychosexual factors in the psychological recovery of the mastectomy patient.

BENJAMIN B. WOLMAN (Chapter 10), Ph.D., 1935, University of Warsaw, Clinical Psychologist and Assistant Director, Centos Institute for Disturbed Children, 1932–33; Chief Psychologist and Director, Mental Health Clinic, Tel-Aviv, Israel, 1935–42; Director, Educational Services for Jewish Servicemen's Families in World War II, 1942–45; Lecturer in Psychology, Teachers College, Tel-Aviv, Israel, 1945–48;

Visiting Lecturer, Columbia University, 1949–53; Visiting Associate Professor of Psychology, Yeshiva University, 1953–57; Clinical Lecturer in Psychiatry and Supervisor of Psychotherapy, Post Doctoral Program, Albert Einstein College of Medicine, 1958–62; Clinical Professor in Psychoanalysis and Psychotherapy, Post Doctoral Program, Adelphi University, 1963–65; Professor Emeritus, Doctoral Program in Clinical Psychology, Long Island University; private practice of psychoanalysis and psychotherapy since 1939. Author of over 190 scientific papers and eighteen books in psychology and related fields. Among the books, *Contemporary Theories and Systems in Psychology*, Harper & Row, 1960; *Vectoriasis Traecox or the Group of Schizophrenias*, Thomas, 1966; *The Unconscious Mind*, Prentice-Hall, 1967; *Children Without Childhood*, Grune and Stratton, 1970; *Call No Man Normal*, International Universities Press, 1973; *Victims of Success*, Quadrangle/New York Times, 1973; Editor-in-chief, *International Encyclopedia of Psychiatry, Psychology, Psychoanalysis, and Neurology*, Aesculapius, 1977; and others.

MELVIN ZELNIK (Co-author, Chapter 5), Ph.D., Princeton University, is a Professor in the Department of Population Dynamics, School of Hygiene and Public Health, The Johns Hopkins University. He has published a number of articles based on two national probability sample surveys of young women 15–19 years of age. He is currently principal investigator of a study on contraceptive use that involves young males and young females sponsored by the National Institute of Child Health and Human Development.

1

DEVELOPMENTAL PHASES

ONE

Prenatal Influences and Subsequent Sexuality

TOM MAZUR

JOHN MONEY

TERMINOLOGY AND DEFINITIONS *

Gender identity/role is a relatively new term in sexology. Obviously sex and gender overlap, but the two are not synonymous. Gender encompasses sex but conceptually is more all-inclusive. That is to say, gender extends beyond genital sex to include those aspects of male and female dimorphism, behavior included, that do not pertain directly to the organs of generation and the erotic and procreative process itself. Thus, gender dimorphism applies to male/female differences in legal status, vocation, recreation, grooming, manners, and cosmetics, but it does not exclude sexual status, psychosexual status, sexuality, erotic practice, and erotic imagery.

Gender identity/role signifies the unity of gender identity and gender role. According to Money (1965), gender identity and gender role are defined as follows:

> *Gender identity* is the sameness, unity, and persistence of one's individuality as male, female, or ambivalent, in greater or lesser degree, especially as it is experienced in self-awareness and behavior; gender identity is the private experience of gender role, and gender role is the public expression of gender identity.
>
> *Gender role* is everything that a person says and does to indicate to others or to the self the degree that one is either male or female, or ambivalent; it includes but is not restricted to sexual arousal and response; gender role is the public expression of gender identity, and gender identity is the private experience of gender role (p. 240).

The differentiation and development of gender identity/role is best conceptualized as a program that involves diverse variables interacting sequentially during critical periods of prenatal and postnatal development (Figure 1).

* Supported by USPHS grants HD-00325 and HD-07111.

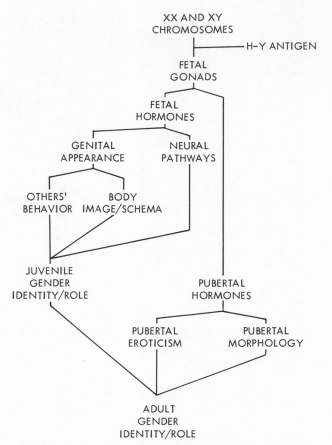

Fig. 1 *Sequential and cumulative components of the program of gender identity/role.*

X AND Y CHROMOSOMES

The program of gender identity/role commences with the sex chromosomes. Nature's plan is that the X or Y sex chromosome of the male parent, when added to the one X sex chromosome invariably supplied by the female parent, determines the genetic sex of the offspring. Should a Y chromosome be added, the chromosomal pattern is XY and, provided prenatal development goes according to plan, male differentiation occurs. Should an X chromosome be added, the chromosomal pattern is XX and, provided all goes according to plan, female differentiation occurs.

Nature's regular plan for the X and Y chromosomes is not always the one carried out. Among human beings, the known chromosomal anomalies include the loss of either the X or Y chromosome, the addition of one or more, or the combination of more than one chromosomal pattern in the same individual. The term for this latter type of genetic anomaly is mosaicism. When mosaicism occurs, one or more supernumerary chromosomes may be present or a chromosome may be missing in some cells but not in others. An example of the latter type of mosaicism is the 45,X/46,XX pattern found in some girls with Turner's syndrome.

Concerning chromosomal loss, it is possible for one of the X chromosomes from the XX pair or for the Y from the XY pair to be lost without lethal effect. When either occurs, the result is a phenotypic female, minus fertility, with a 45,X chromosomal pattern (Turner's syndrome). Girls with Turner's syndrome have gonadal streaks in the place of ovaries. Consequently, hormonal replacement is necessary for them to have a feminizing puberty. Psychosexually, they are assigned and reared as girls, and they develop a stereotypically feminine gender identity/role. By contrast, the loss of an X chromosome from the XY combination is lethal, whereas the addition of one or more X or Y chromosomes is not. Examples of two chromosomal patterns with an extra sex chromosome are 47,XXY (Klinefelter's syndrome) and the 47,XYY. Individuals with Klinefelter's syndrome are morphologic males who have a small penis. The testes are small and sterile. Such individuals are greatly susceptible to severe mental retardation or psychopathology which may be of almost any type, including the sexual psychopathology of transsexualism or transvestism (Money, 1975). The occurrence of psychopathology and mental retardation is sporadic and not a consistent concomitant of the supernumerary X chromosome.

In morphologic phenotype, 47,XYY individuals are male. They are usually tall, many over six feet. Sterility is not uncommon. Money and associates (1974) compared 47,XYY individuals and 47,XXY individuals for behavioral disability, sexuality, and social interaction. Those 47,XYY individuals with behavioral disability often were found to be characterized by impulsive acting out (e.g., destruction of property) and poor long-term planning. By contrast, 47,XXY individuals often were found to be characterized by deficiency or inhibition of action (e.g., phobia). With regard to sexuality, the 47,XYY individuals showed a diversity of sexual experience, whereas the 47,XXY individuals were sexually rather inert (hyposexual). Socially, both 47,XYY individuals and 47,XXY individuals preferred being alone to being with a group.

There also exists a 47,XXX condition which occurs with a female morphology and a female gender identity/role. Fertility may or may not be diminished in this condition, and there may or may not be behavioral disability.

H-Y ANTIGEN

The Y chromosome programs the differentiation of the undifferentiated cells of the primitive gonads into testes, beginning at around the sixth week of gestation. Differentiation of the undifferentiated gonads into ovaries does not begin until the twelfth week and requires the presence of two X chromosomes and no Y.

The Y chromosome programs the undifferentiated gonads toward testicular development via a plasma membrane protein, the Y-linked histocompatibility (H-Y) antigen (Silvers and Wachtel, 1977). Exactly how the undifferentiated gonads in XX individuals are programed into ovaries is not clear. Ohno (1978) suggests the possibility of an ovarian-organizing antigen similar to that of the H-Y antigen. This ovarian-organizing antigen has not yet been identified.

Having programed the differentiation of the gonads, the sex chromosomes have no other known direct influence on subsequent sexual behavior and psychosexual (gender identity/ role) differentiation. The program of gender identity/role differentiation and development is now carried forward by the presence or absence of secretions of the newly differentiated fetal testes. Without the secretions of the testes, morphologic differentiation is female.

ADAM–EVE PRINCIPLE

Prenatally, the program of gender identity/role is carried forward specifically by the determinants of masculine morphologic differentiation, namely, mullerian inhibiting substance (see below) and androgen, secreted by the testes. Present knowledge of embryology indicates that fetal ovarian hormones are not essential to female morphologic differentiation. Whether or not maternal and placental hormones are essential is not known. Nature is predisposed first to make a female and only with the addition of testicular secretions does it make a male. The embryological fact that nature's preference is female is epitomized as the Eve principle. The fact that something must be added to make a male is epitomized as the Adam principle.

MORPHOLOGIC DIFFERENTIATION OF THE GENITALIA

The internal genitalia differentiate ahead of the external genitalia. Prenatal hormones, their presence or absence, control the differentiation of both.

Figure 2 illustrates that the male and female internal genital structures differentiate from two separate primordia, the wolffian and mullerian ducts, respectively. In normal male development, the fetal testes first secrete their two hormones, androgen and mullerian inhibiting substance (MIS) at around the sixth week of gestation. Androgen ensures that the wolffian ducts proliferate into the vas deferens, seminal vesicles, and the ejaculatory ducts of the male internal genitalia. MIS ensures that the mullerian ducts vestigiate. In the absence of MIS, the mullerian ducts proliferate into a uterus, fallopian tubes, and the upper vagina of the female internal genitalia. In normal female development, the fetal ovaries do not, so far as is

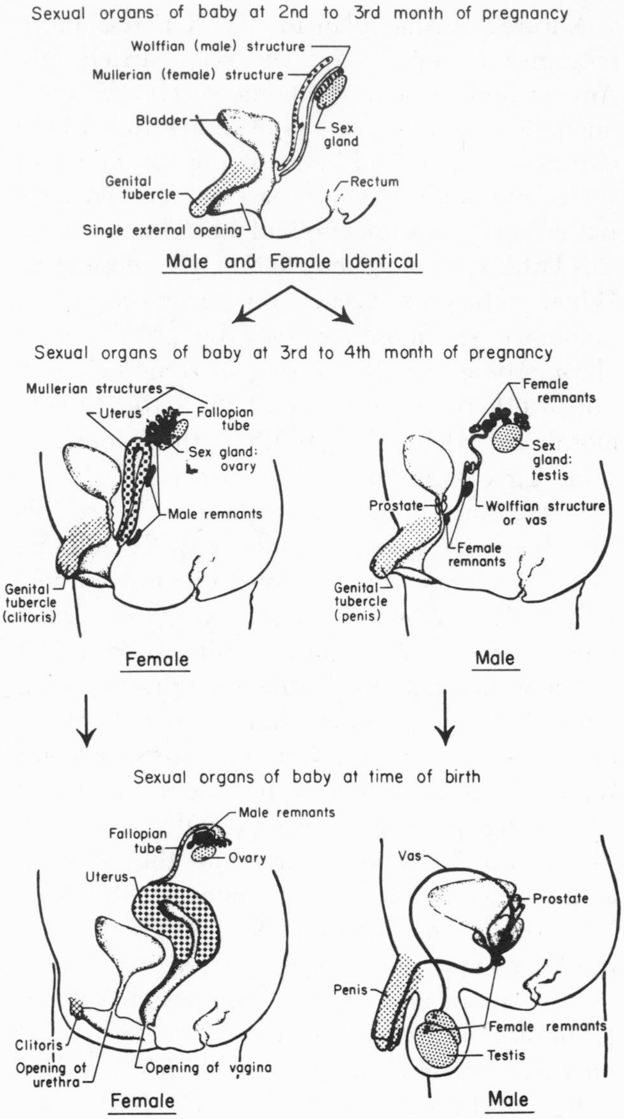

Fig. 2 *Three stages in the differentiation of internal genital organs. They are dually represented at the outset.*

known, secrete hormones prenatally, and if maternal or placental hormones play a role in female differentiation, it has yet to be demonstrated.

Whereas the male and female internal genital structures differentiate from two separate primordia, the external genitalia develop from the same primordia (Figure 3). These structures remain undifferentiated until approximately the eighth week of fetal life, at which time androgen secreted from the fetal testes begins to masculinize them. It is possible that testoster-

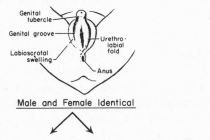

Sexual appearance of baby at 2nd to 3rd month of pregnancy

Genital tubercle
Genital groove
Urethro-labial fold
Labioscrotal swelling
Anus

Male and Female Identical

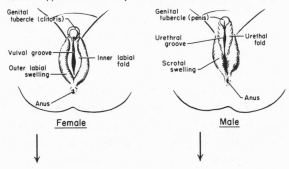

Sexual appearance of baby at 3rd to 4th month of pregnancy

Genital tubercle (clitoris)
Vulval groove
Inner labial fold
Outer labial swelling
Anus

Female

Genital tubercle (penis)
Urethral groove
Urethal fold
Scrotal swelling
Anus

Male

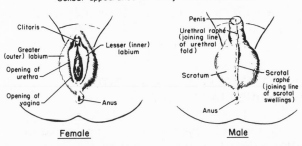

Sexual appearance of baby at time of birth

Clitoris
Greater (outer) labium
Lesser (inner) labium
Opening of urethra
Opening of vagina
Anus

Female

Penis
Urethral raphé (joining line of urethral fold)
Scrotum
Scrotal raphé (joining line of scrotal swellings)
Anus

Male

Fig. 3 *Three stages in the differentiation of the external genital organs. The male and female organs have the same beginnings and are homologous with one another.*

one is converted to 5α-dihydrotestosterone (DHT) before masculinization of the external genitalia is effected. In any event, in the presence of androgen, the genital tubercle differentiates into a penis. The skin that becomes the hood of the clitoris and labia minora in the female wraps around the penis to cover it and to form the foreskin. The labioscrotal swellings fuse and form the scrotum. In the absence of androgen, the genital tubercle remains small and becomes the clitoris. What in the male is the foreskin and outer covering of the penis becomes the hood of the clitoris and the labia minora in the female. The labioscrotal swellings remain separate and form the labia majora.

MORPHOLOGIC DIFFERENTIATION OF THE BRAIN

Fetal androgen programs not only the differentiation of the internal and external genitalia but also the differentiation of sex-related pathways in the brain. Exactly how androgen affects brain differentiation is not known. It is probable that it acts on neural substrates which in turn regulate thresholds for the expression of sexually dimorphic behavior. Cyclic secretion of gonadotropins is sexually dimorphic. Hormonally, females cycle and males do not. In female rats, the ventromedial and preoptic areas of the hypothalamus regulate the cyclic secretion of gonadotropins. If female rat fetuses or neonates receive androgen, then, in adulthood, they are acyclic. (For a review of the literature of the effects of hormones on animals see Reinisch, 1974).

Regarding sexual behavior on mating tests, prenatally androgen-treated female rats behave more like males than do untreated females. They also resemble control males on various dimorphic nonmating tests, including tests for some forms of aggressive behavior, wheel running, and open-field behavior. Exposure to androgen after the critical period does not produce these masculinizing effects.

The experimental opposite of fetal androgenization of the female is not estrogenization but deandrogenization by fetal castration or antiandrogenization of the male. Male rat pups castrated immediately after birth are cyclic, like females, in gonadotropin release. The use of antiandrogen (cyproterone acetate) is even more dramatic in its effect. When injected into the pregnant female at the critical period in fetal development, the fetal testes of the XY fetuses become dormant and fail to supply androgen to the primordia of the external genitalia. Consequently, these chromosomally male pups are born with completely normal-appearing female genitals. By castrating them to eliminate all further influence of their own androgenic hormone and by giving replacement doses of female hormone at puberty, it is possible to obtain female mating behavior from these treated males. The stud males of the colony do not distinguish them from normal females.

ANDROGENIZED FEMALE MONKEYS

Rhesus monkeys, if pregnant with a daughter fetus and if injected with testosterone during a critical period, give birth to a baby with female internal reproductive organs (two ovaries, uterus, and fallopian tubes) and male external reproductive organs (a well-developed empty scrotum and a clitorine penis). These masculinized female (hermaphroditic) monkeys have been extensively studied over the last twenty years by various researchers in different laboratories (see reviews by Goy, Wolf, and Eisele, 1977; and Télégdy, 1977).

Prenatal androgen does not render such monkeys acyclic, as it does the female rat. There is, however, a delay in menarche associated with prenatal androgen, though subsequent ovarian function can be entirely normal and ovulation occurs. Whether the incongruency between rodents and primates on this variable is due to timing, dosage, or species differences is not known. Possibly there is a mechanism in the primate that protects the brain-pituitary systems which regulate ovulation from the damaging effects of steroid hormones present in fetal life.

The behavior of masculinized female monkeys resembles that of normal male monkeys and deviates from that of normal female monkeys. Specifically, masculinized females in the juvenile period resemble males in frequency of mounting and thrusting behavior, rough-and-tumble play, and threat and dominance behavior. Only those androgenized females whose mothers have been injected with testosterone for a long period during gestation persistently retain the spontaneous display of mounting behavior through adolescence. However, when hermaphroditic females are ovariectomized in adulthood and injected with testosterone, they mount stimulus females and can even achieve intromission and the equivalent of ejaculation with emission. Apparently, the degree of behavioral masculinization in rhesus monkeys depends in part on the total duration and amount of fetal exposure to androgen. Although prenatal exposure to androgen is one variable associated with masculinized behavior, it is not the only one. Goldfoot (1977), in a review of the literature on nonhuman primate (primarily rhesus) sexual behavior, makes it clear that the expression of sexual behavior is determined by an intricate and as yet unexplained balance of hormonal and social environmental variables which act throughout the animal's life cycle.

There has not yet been reported in primates a counterpart to the XY male rat fetally deandrogenized by the antiandrogen, cyproterone acetate. In human beings, however, there are several syndromes of fetal deandrogenization and of androgenization as well. In the interest of space, only two syndromes, the adrenogenital syndrome and the androgen-insensitivity syndrome will be used here, since they illustrate all of the principles involved.

ANDROGENIZED XX HUMAN FETUS: ADRENOGENITAL SYNDROME

For obvious reasons one cannot experimentally manipulate the prenatal environment of human beings to produce cases of hermaphroditism or intersexuality as can be done with rodents or nonhuman primates. However, there are cases of human hermaphroditism (intersexuality) produced by nature, similar to those produced experimentally in animals.

One such form of human intersexuality occurring in XX females is the adrenogenital syndrome. This is a genetic autosomal recessive condition in which the adrenal cortex of the fetus fails to synthesize one of its proper hormones, cortisol. Instead, it secretes an excess of androgen. In some cases, there is an associated deficit in salt retention. Affected females are born with a hypertrophied clitoris (Figure 4). In some cases masculinization is so complete that instead of an enlarged clitoris, there is a penis and empty scrotum.

In some instances, an XX adrenogenital baby

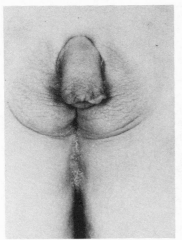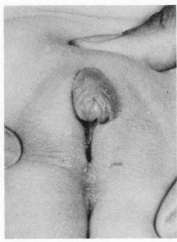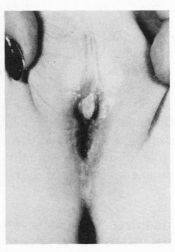

Fig. 4 *Left and center: two degrees of urogenital fusion and clitoral enlargement in the adreno-genital syndrome; right: genital appearance following clitoridectomy and exteriorization of the vagina.*

is assigned and reared as a boy. But the more common practice, once the diagnosis has been established, is to institute a program of surgical feminization consistent with assigning and rearing the baby as a girl—even if a sex reannouncement is necessitated.

The endocrine treatment for all babies with the adrenogenital syndrome, discovered in 1950, is therapy with a synthetic form of cortisol, the missing adrenocortical hormone. This therapy, if begun neonatally and continuously maintained, suppresses excessive postnatal androgen production. Then, at the expected time of puberty, girls with the adrenogenital syndrome develop a feminine physique. Their menses may be late, the time of onset being variable. They will ovulate in adulthood and can expect to conceive pregnancies.

Adrenogenital girls treated since infancy are of special interest to gender identity/role theory because of their history of prenatal androgenization subsequently corrected. Their psychosocial and psychosexual development has been followed longitudinally at The Johns Hopkins Hospital and at Children's Hospital at Buffalo. The evidence to date is that fetal androgenization does influence subsequent development of behavior, though only to a limited degree (Money and Ehrhardt, 1972; Ehrhardt, 1977).

Behaviorally, girls with the adrenogenital syndrome are described as having a high level of athletic energy as demonstrated by their interest and participation in organized group competitive sports, usually with boys. For example, they become involved in boys' neighborhood football, basketball, or baseball. They are accepted by the boys because of their superior athletic skills. They do not assert themselves to obtain a high rank in the dominance hierarchy of boys.

Adrenogenital girls do not display much interest in dolls or stereotypic girls' games. During childhood, they do not show much interest in babies, romance, and marriage, as compared to their unaffected sisters.

Girls with the adrenogenital syndrome show an interest in boys and dating much later in adolescence than do their peers. Divergent from their age-mates in this respect, they often become relatively isolated from them.

Recently it has been possible to obtain the first followup information on the psychosexual status of adrenogenital girls, now young adults, who have a history of being hormonally normal as the consequence of cortisone therapy started in infancy. Money and Schwartz (1976) and Schwartz (unpublished Sc.D. dissertation) report findings suggesting a greater incidence of bisexual and homosexual imagery than would be expected by chance. A replication study is needed.

Not all of the 46,XX infants with the adrenogenital syndrome are assigned and reared as girls. In the past, some were assigned and reared as boys, especially those born with a completely formed penis and fused scrotum as a result of extreme fetal androgenization. Although their counterparts who are reared as girls differentiate a female gender identity/role, these boys differentiate a male gender identity/role, performing sexually as men with women partners (Money and Daléry, 1977).

DEANDROGENIZED XY HUMAN FETUS: ANDROGEN-INSENSITIVITY SYNDROME

In human beings, not only do XX fetuses become androgenized, but also XY fetuses become deandrogenized. The term for the latter type of hermaphroditism is the androgen-insensitivity syndrome (see review by Money, 1977). The primary pathognomonic feature of the androgen-insensitivity syndrome is the genetically transmitted insensitivity of the target tissues of the body to androgen.

The effect of androgen insensitivity in fetal life is that the external genital structures differentiate as female. There is a lack of development of the wolffian ducts and failure of masculinization of the external genitalia. When androgen insensitivity is total, the external appearance of affected individuals is indistinguishable from the external appearance of normal females (Figure 5). Internally, the fallopian tubes, uterus, and upper vagina fail to differentiate and develop, since responsiveness to mullerian inhibiting substance (MIS), in contrast to androgen, is unaffected. When androgen insensitivity is partial, as sometimes happens, the affected individuals are born with ambiguous-looking sex organs. Some such babies have been assigned and reared as females and some as males.

Since totally androgen-insensitive individuals at birth look like normal females, they are invariably assigned and reared as females. Although such females are occasionally detected in infancy or childhood because of the presence of inguinal hernias or labial masses which are

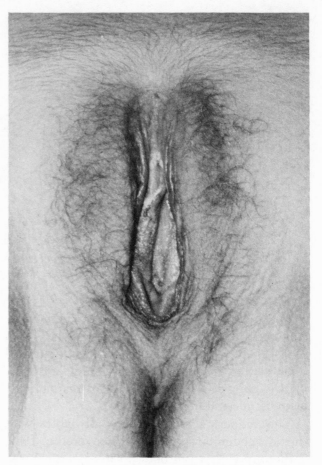

Fig. 5 *Appearance of the external genitalia in a woman with androgen-insensitivity syndrome.*

the gonads (defective testes), the majority are not recognized until puberty. At puberty the patients consult physicians because of primary amenorrhea, secondary to absence of the uterus.

With the exception of amenorrhea, girls with the androgen-insensitivity syndrome have a feminizing puberty. Feminization is the result of estrogen secreted noncyclically by the gonads (testes) and unopposed by androgen.

Once puberty is complete, physicians usually advise gonadectomy because it is a widely held, though poorly documented doctrine, that there is an increased risk in adulthood of potentially malignant gonadal tumors. Having had a gonadectomy, androgen-insensitive girls require replacement estrogen, preferably combined with progestin, to maintain hormonal femininity.

Since the upper one-third of the vagina fails to differentiate, the vagina usually requires lengthening. This lengthening may be achieved by a self-dilatation technique or by surgery (vaginoplasty).

Psychosexually, individuals diagnosed as androgen insensitive who are assigned and reared as girls, differentiate and develop an unequivocal feminine gender identity/role.

Viola G. Lewis (unpublished M.A. thesis) recently compared a group of androgen-insensitive women with a group of women diagnosed as having Rokitansky's syndrome. Women with Rokitansky's syndrome resemble women with the androgen-insensitivity syndrome anatomically and physiologically, but have XX instead of XY chromosomes, ovaries instead of testes, and are hormonally cyclic instead of acyclic. Results of the comparison indicate no statistical differences between the findings on the two groups of women on the following variables: psychosexual orientation, acceptance of sexual status, self-rating of sexual frequency and interest, masturbation, orgasm, attitude toward infant care, and attitude toward marriage. All of the women had differentiated an unequivocal female gender identity/role.

In partial androgen insensitivity, also known as Reifenstein's syndrome, there is partial masculinization of the external genitalia in fetal life. Consequently, the baby is born with ambiguous-looking, hermaphroditic external genitalia and may be assigned and reared as either a male or female. Money and Ogunro (1974) compared partially androgen-insensitive hermaphrodites discordant for sex assignment and rearing.

Behaviorally, the individuals reared as boys tried to compensate for their relative inferiority in competitive sports. Because of their unvirilized, beardless appearance, and extremely small, surgically repaired genitalia, they had great difficulty in establishing a sex life, even though they had differentiated a male gender identity/role.

Individuals reared as females differentiated a female gender identity/role, and for them an adequate sex life was feasible.

In partial androgen insensitivity, as in the adrenogenital syndrome, it is possible to match patients in pairs concordant for diagnosis and prenatal history but discordant for assigned sex and postnatal history. This matched-pair method demonstrates the relative importance of postnatal history in differentiating gender identity/role. The method is applicable also to the syndrome of micropenis.

MATCHED PAIR WITH MICROPENIS

In micropenis, the penile corpora are underdeveloped. They may be so small that the penis looks like a clitoris (Figure 6). Unlike a clitoris, however, the micropenis has a median raphe, a covered urethra, a foreskin, and a glans in which the urethral meatus is normally placed. It may or may not be erectile, dependent upon the

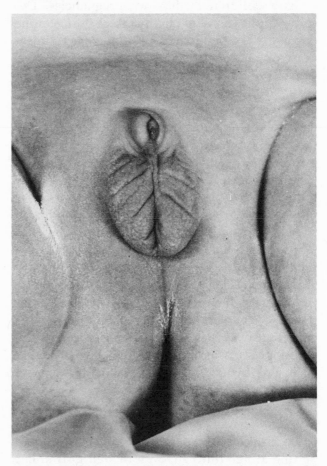

Fig. 6. *An example of micropenis in a five-month-old 46,XY infant. Though the organ looks like a clitoris, it is a fully formed penis with a urethral tube and meatus in the normal male position.*

amount of corpora cavernosa and corpus spongiosum present. The scrotum is present and fused. The testes may be descended or either unilaterally or bilaterally cryptorchid. The etiology of micropenis is unknown.

In the two cases of micropenis compared here, the sex of assignment, rearing, and rehabilitation (surgical and hormonal, as required) was male and female respectively. In the male case, the boy differentiated a masculine gender identity/role, but not without difficulty. As a child, he did not join in rough-and-tumble play. He played more with girls than he did with boys. At the age of ten, he revealed to an interviewer that he had often thought about changing his sex. He already had made up his mind, however, that he would not bother with a change of sex unless he could be guaranteed to have children by his own pregnancies. Despite application in childhood of testosterone cream to his penis and, in adolescence, injections of androgen (given primarily to induce a masculinizing puberty since his testes were vestigial and defective) the micropenis remained excessively minute. Consequently, its use in both heterosexual and homosexual relationships was grossly impaired. Maintenance of intromission was, in fact, impossible.

At the present time, despite surgical and/or hormonal treatments for micropenis, there is no evidence that such treatments produce a fully functioning penis of adult size.

The other micropenis infant was surgically rehabilitated as a girl during the fourth month after birth. This consisted of bilateral gonadectomy and feminization of the external genitalia. At age twelve, feminizing puberty was exogenously induced by means of oral estrogen. Vaginoplasty was performed at age seventeen.

In childhood, this girl played with boys and girls. Although she did prefer outdoor activities, it was not to an intense or one-sided degree. With adolescence, she began to be interested in boys and had experiences with necking and petting at age thirteen, even though girls in her family were not officially permitted to date. At age eighteen and a half, she had intercourse for the first time with her steady boyfriend.

Three years later they married. Her gender identity/role is unquestionably female.

The fact that the testes of the infant assigned and reared male were defective and did not produce pubertal androgen, and that the testes of the infant assigned and reared female were removed before the age of six months, might eventually prove important in relationship to the differentiation of their erotic gender identity/role. In normal XY infants there is an increase in plasma testosterone from birth until the second or third month of life, followed by a gradual decrease (Forest, Cathiard, and Bertrand, 1973). By the seventh month, the level of plasma testosterone diminishes and stays at the low, prepubertal level of boyhood. Perhaps the high postnatal level of plasma testosterone is needed to complete the job, initiated prenatally, of setting in the brain thresholds for the release of certain types of sexually dimorphic behavior later in life. This hypothesis is currently only speculative. In any event, the lesson of the matched pair of micropenis individuals teaches the same lesson taught by individuals matched for various diagnoses of hermaphroditism. It is that, in the differentiation of an individual's gender identity/role, the determinants are prenatal as well as postnatal. It is possible for postnatal determinants to override prenatal ones, just as it is possible for prenatal determinants to intrude on postnatal ones. The various possible permutations and combinations still need to be clarified.

SEX DIFFERENCES: ABSOLUTE, SEX-SHARED/THRESHOLD-DIMORPHIC, AND ARBITRARY

There are absolute sex differences, but they pertain to reproduction. Females menstruate, gestate, and lactate. Males impregnate. Other behavior which is hormonally primed prenatally is shared by both sexes. The difference lies in the threshold for its elicitation. This is sex-shared/threshold-dimorphic behavior. There is also sex-different behavior of a purely arbitrary type. Some of the arbitrary differences may be traced historically to an association with the absolute sex differences. For example, it is not too difficult to recognize that breast feeding of infants historically came to include the preparation of food for all members of the family, except on special or ceremonial occasions when the men might prepare a feast. Today, many sex differences, such as those pertaining to work, play, and cosmetics, are purely arbitrary and are a product of cultural and historical caprice. Sex difference in legal status is equally arbitrary. These arbitrary differences are built into the individual, developmentally, according to the principles of identification and complementation.

REFERENCES

EHRHARDT, A. A. 1977. Prenatal androgenization and human psychosexual behavior. In *Handbook of sexology*, ed. J. Money and H. Musaph. Amsterdam/New York: Excerpta Medica.

FOREST, M. G.; CATHIARD, A. M.; and BERTRAND, J. A. 1973. Evidence of testicular activity in early infancy. *Journal of Clinical Endocrinology and Metabolism* 37: 148–51.

GOLDFOOT, D. A. 1977. Sociosexual behavior of nonhuman primates during development and maturity: social and hormonal relationships. In *Behavioral primatology: advances in research and theory*, vol. 1, ed. A. M. Schrier. Hillsdale, N.J.: Lawrence Erlbaum Association.

GOY, R. W.; WOLF, J. E.; and EISELE, S. G. 1977. Experimental female hermaphroditism in rhesus monkeys: anatomical and psychological characteristics. In *Handbook of sexology*, ed. J. Money and H. Musaph. Amsterdam/New York: Excerpta Medica.

LEWIS, V. G. 1978. Vaginal atresia in the 46,XY androgen-insensitivity (testicular feminizing) syndrome and the 46,XX Rokitansky syndrome: female gender identity/role compared. Master's thesis, Loyola College, Baltimore, Maryland.

MONEY, J., ed. 1965. *Sex research: new developments*. New York: Holt, Rinehart, and Winston.

———. 1975. Human behavior cytogenetics: review of psychopathology in three syndromes—47,XXY; 47,XYY; and 45,X. *Journal of Sex Research* 11: 181–200.

———. 1977. Prenatal deandrogenization of human beings. In *Handbook of sexology*, ed. J. Money and H. Musaph. Amsterdam/New York: Excerpta Medica.

———; ANNECILLO, C.; VAN ORMAN, B.; and BORGAONKAR, D. S. 1974. Cytogenetics, hormones and behavior disability: comparison of XYY and XXY syndromes. *Clinical Genetics* 6: 370–82.

———, and DALÉRY, J. 1977. Hyperadrenocortical 46,XX hermaphroditism with penile urethra: psychological studies in seven cases, three reared as boys, four as girls. In *Congenital adrenal hyperplasia*, ed. P. A. Lee, L. P. Plotnick, A. A. Kowarski, and C. J. Migeon. Baltimore: University Park Press.

———, and EHRHARDT, A. A. 1972. *Man and woman, boy and girl: the differentiation and dimorphism of gender identity from conception to maturity*. Baltimore: Johns Hopkins University Press.

———, and OGUNRO, C. 1974. Behavioral sexology: ten cases of genetic male intersexuality with impaired prenatal and pubertal androgenization. *Archives of Sexual Behavior* 3: 181–205.

———, and SCHWARTZ, M. F. 1977. Dating, romantic, and nonromantic friendships and sexuality in 17 early-treated adrenogenital females, ages 16 to 25. In *Congenital adrenal hyperplasia*, ed. P. A. Lee; L. P. Plotnick; A. A. Kowarski; and C. J. Migeon. Baltimore: University Park Press.

OHNO, S. 1978. The role of H-Y antigen in primary sex determination. *Journal of the American Medical Association* 239: 217–20.

REINISCH, J. M. 1974. Fetal hormones, the brain and human sex differences: a heuristic, integrative review of the recent literature. *Archives of Sexual Behavior* 3: 51–90.

SCHWARTZ, M. F. 1977. Athletics, friendships, dating, romance, and sexuality in adreno-genital females aged 17–27, compared with females with androgen-insensitivity and Rokitansky syndromes. Sc.D. dissertation, The Johns Hopkins University School of Hygiene and Public Health.

SILVERS, W. K., and WACHTEL, S. S. 1977. H-Y antigen: behavior and function. *Science* 195: 956–60.

TÉLÉGDY, G. 1977. Prenatal androgenization of primates and humans. In *Handbook of sexology*, ed. J. Money and H. Musaph Amsterdam/New York: Excerpta Medica.

TWO

Sexuality in the Infant and Neonate: Birth to Two Years

EILEEN HIGHAM

INTRODUCTION *

When a child is born, the program of sexual development and differentiation, previously controlled by genetic, hormonal, and constitutional events, passes to the behavior environment. There, social and cultural influences govern the continuing development and differentiation of psychosexual functioning. The principle of sexual bipotentiality, which pertains to reproductive anatomy and to the neurosexual centers located in the hypothalamus, applies also to psychosexual and sociosexual behavior. The social program of rearing resolves behavioral bipotentiality as masculine or feminine in early life (Money and Ehrhardt, 1972).

In the first two years of life, behavioral components of adult sexual behavior begin to emerge, and the sociosexual and psychosexual components of adult eroticism are initiated. Childhood constitutes a period of preparation and rehearsal of the part-responses that are eventually chained together into adult sexual pair-bonding. It is characteristic of mammals for behavior segments to appear and to be rehearsed and practiced prior to their functional integration into the life cycle. Sexual behavior is no exception to this rule, judging from observations of animals, from accounts of primitive societies in which childhood sex play and sex rehearsals are permitted, and from the retrospective accounts of human adults (Bateson and Mead, 1942; Kinsey, Pomeroy, and Martin, 1948; Kinsey, Pomeroy, Martin, and Gebhard, 1953; Ford and Beach, 1951; Money, 1976).

SEXUAL REHEARSALS
IN THE NEONATE AND INFANT

There are three phases of psychosexual development in the neonatal and infancy period. The first, common to both sexes, is related to pair-bonding of the infant and the parent; it begins in the delivery room with parental participation in childbirth. The second comprises genital activity rehearsals, also present at or even before birth, and clearly observed in the genitopelvic responses of the male neonate. The third is a masculine and feminine differentiation phase which begins in the delivery room with the announcement of the infant's sex.

PAIR-BONDING AND SEX REHEARSALS

The earliest or haptic phase of sexual and affectional development comprises body proximity and skin contact, the sensuous closeness of mother and infant through holding, clinging, and cuddling. It foreshadows the later phase of adolescent and adult sexual pair-bonding in which sensuous skin contact and bodily proximity are paramount. Between infancy and adulthood, childhood rehearsals with toys, games, and peers are part of the gradual evolution of "affectional systems" (Harlow and Harlow, 1965).

The haptic phase begins during childbirth, especially with an awake and participating mother who experiences the delivery of the infant and sees and holds the child immediately thereafter. Hormonal changes during childbirth lower the threshold for maternal behavior when appropriate perceptual stimulation is present (Rossi, 1977). When the father is also present in the delivery room, is prepared to participate in childbirth, and is able to see and hold the newborn child, a three-bond of mother, father, and infant is established. Soon thereafter, the initial sensual/haptic phase is expanded to include the oral phase of development in connection with feeding and thumb- and finger-sucking. With shared parenting, both the mother and the

* Dr. John Money and Mr. Russell Jobaris made suggestions for the organization of this chapter.

16

father are associated with the haptic-oral phase of infant development, although breast-feeding inevitably establishes a strong mother-child attachment.

The oral stage of infantile sexuality, set forth in psychoanalytic theory, is now seen as part of a broader developmental phase of pair-bonding and attachment, which includes all aspects of body contact, cuddling, clinging and touching, and also rhythmic rocking movements. The "contact-comfort" accompanying sucking and feeding in early life has an importance for socioemotional and sociosexual development beyond that of obtaining adequate nutrition and oral gratification. As the infant develops, clinging and cuddling is expanded to include soft and furry blankets and toys. Bonding to a favorite blanket, stuffed animal, or doll is part of normal development in infancy and childhood. The comfort of a soft cloth or toy, thumb-sucking, and rhythmic rocking are the customary stimuli employed during physical or psychological stress and also to facilitate the release into sleep.

By two years of age, children begin to respond affectionately to each other by touching, hugging, and kissing, and sometimes touching the genitals, when free expression of sexuality is permitted (Spiro, 1965; Kleeman, 1966; see also Martinson, 1973). Affectionate behavior in two-year-olds growing up in a kibbutz illustrates the haptic phase in pair-bonding:

Ofer (male) and Pnina (female) sit side by side on chamber pots. . . . Ofer puts his foot on Pnina's foot, she then does the same—this happens several times . . . finally, Pnina shifts her pot away, then moves back, then away . . . they laugh . . . Pnina stands up, lies on the table on her stomach, says "ADINA." Ofer pats her buttocks. Nurse comes in, and Pnina stands up, sits on the table . . . Ofer puts his foot on her leg. She offers him a piece of bread, and he eats it . . . this is repeated twice . . . Ofer kicks Pnina gently, and they laugh . . . Pnina touches and caresses Ofer's leg with her foot . . . says "more more" . . . Ofer stands, then Pnina stands, both bounce up and down . . . both children are excited, bounce, laugh together . . . Pnina

grabs Ofer's penis, and he pushes her away . . . she repeats, he pushes her away, and turns around . . . Pnina touches his buttocks (Spiro, 1965, p. 225).

Affectionate behavior between boys and between girls was also observed in the two-year-old and three-year-old groups:

Mirav (female) hugs Sara (female) and both grin. . . .
    Avinoam (male) and Amikam (male) sit side by side on chamber pots. Avinoam clutches Amikam's chest and nipples, and they both laugh (Spiro, 1965, p. 226).

The appearance of prolonged attachments and of falling in love customarily occurs at a later age in relation to social experiences and cognitive development. The child's love affair with the opposite sex parent, the Oedipal phase of psychoanalytic theory, is the first rehearsal of falling in love. Bell (1902) dates the first stage of "sex-love" between children as beginning at the same age:

The presence of the emotion in children between three and eight years of age is shown by such action as the following: hugging, kissing, lifting each other, scuffling, sitting close to each other; confessions to each other and to others, talking about each other when apart; seeking each other and excluding others, grief at being separated; giving of gifts, extending courtesies to each other that are withheld from others, making sacrifices such as giving up desired things or foregoing pleasures; jealousies, etc. (p. 330).

Bell's findings, based upon accounts of adults and observations of children, include the following examples: *

Case 3. B. 3, g. 3½. Have been deeply in love since their third week in kindergarten. Rose not so jealous as Russel. She always watches for his coming, and runs to meet him the moment he enters the room. They sit together at the table and in the circle, and cry if sep-

* The absence of more recent accounts of love between children is an indication of the degree to which childhood sexuality is a taboo subject of study. See also Noll, A. 1912. *The sexual life of the child*. E. Paul (translated edition), London: George Allen.

arated. They are very free and unrestrained in showing their love by kissing, hugging, and by many little attentions.

Case 4. B. 3, g. 3. My little nephew of three and a little neighbor girl of the same age had a most affectionate love for each other, and were not at all shy about it. They would kiss each other when they met, and seemed to think it all right. The little boy used to tell me that they would marry when grown. This continued about two and a half years; then the girl's parents moved away, much to the grief of both children. The little boy would often climb up and take the girl's photograph from the mantle and kiss it (p. 335).

The importance of the haptic, contact-comfort phase of neonatal development, is shown in studies of human infants separated from their caretakers (Bowlby, 1969; 1973; Spitz, 1946) and in experimental primatology (Harlow and Harlow, 1962; Harlow, Dodsworth, and Harlow, 1965; Harlow, Harlow, Dodsworth, and Arling, 1966; McKinney, 1975).*

Monkeys reared in isolation develop severe social and sexual disabilities. In later life, these monkeys continue to be isolated; rocking, huddling and self-clasping, self-mouthing, and self-aggression are common. Play and grooming responses, which are part of normal social interaction with peers, are absent. In adulthood, males reared in isolation are unable to approach and appropriately mount a normal female. Similarly, a female reared in isolation is unable to reciprocate with appropriate positioning even when approached by an experienced, nor-

* See also Goldfoot, D. 1977. Sociosexual behaviors of nonhuman primates during development and maturity: social and hormonal relationships. In *Behavioral Primatology Advances in Research and Theory*, vol. 1, A. Schreier, ed., Hillsdale, N.J.: Lawrence Erlbaum, Assoc. Goldfoot concludes his exceptionally detailed and lucid account of the development of sociosexual behavior in nonhuman primates, in part, as follows: "Prenatal hormonal influences, interacting with the genetic substrate, predispose animals to behave along certain dimensions, *but the postnatal social system, depending upon its particular characteristics, almost immediately modifies, limits, or permits full expression of the biologically set predespositions* (p. 176). (author's italics)." In early life, the postnatal social factors regulating sociosexual expression in monkeys include the opportunity for social interaction with the mother, with same and opposite sex peers, and a positive emotional environment, i.e., an environment in which the infant monkeys are not fearful of one another.

mal male. Both male and female monkeys reared in isolation are deprived of the neonatal, infant and childhood rehearsals of pair-bonding and of social and sex play with peers. The sociosexual impairments stemming from early isolation also affect maternalism in the female monkey who reproduces after being artificially inseminated. The social-isolate mothers either are indifferent to the offspring or brutalize them.

The human infant is rarely, if ever, subjected to the pervasive isolation imposed on infant monkeys. The relative deprivation of institutional care following parental separation, or from birth, in the first two years of life, affects social, emotional, and intellectual development adversely (see review by Rutter, 1972). In rare instances of child abuse without parental separation, statural, behavioral, and psychosexual impairments occur (Money, 1977). The "affectionless character," described by Bowlby, illustrates the long-term consequences of the absence of early parent-infant bonding on affectional development. The effect of pair-bonding impairments or disruptions on psychosexual development currently is speculative (Rutter, 1971). Clinical investigative studies of individuals with sexual disabilities suggest that the loss of a parent or grandparent in the critical early years may disrupt the psychosexual developmental program.

GENITAL PLAY AND SEX REHEARSALS

At birth and perhaps even before, the sensory, motor, and neurologic systems are sufficiently mature to permit genitopelvic functioning. The male infant may be born with a penile erection, and erections are observed in the majority of them in the early weeks of life (Halverson, 1940). The parallel phenomenon, vaginal lubrication in the female infant, is more difficult to establish, but it also may occur (Martinson, 1976). Both male and female infants respond to genital stimulation with behavior indicating an increased sense of well-being—quieting and relaxation and smiling; boys may have an erection.

When it is not prohibited, genital self-touching begins between six and twelve months, somewhat earlier in boys than in girls, as part of the exploration of one's own body (Spitz, 1949; Levine, 1951; Galenson, 1975; Bieber, 1975). Spitz reported genital play in 21 of the 170 infants studied throughout their first year. The majority of infants, whether male or female, began genital play after eight months of age. He also reported that genital play was common in children reared in private homes in which mother-child contact was rated as "normal" but was virtually absent in children reared in a foundling home by nurses. Genital self-touching appears to be more frequent in infants reared in circumstances promoting healthy psychosocial development and continuing mother-infant pair-bonding.

In the second half of the second year, infants typically are interested in their own genitals, appear to experience sexual feelings, and to recognize anatomical differences when the opportunity to do so exists. This "early genital phase" (Roiphe, 1968) occurs a year or two before the psychoanalytic genital phase, which is accompanied by the sexual competition and rivalry of the Oedipal period. The genital discovery phase may occur earlier when there are less severe constraints on body exploration. Kleeman (1965; 1966) describes a boy's discovery of his penis, and the gradual evolution from exploratory touching to pleasurable masturbation from eight months into the second year:

(8 mos.) He was just eight months to the day. There he sat in the bathtub playing with the rubber mat beneath himself as the water ran out of the tub. Looking down, he spied a small object between his chunky, little thighs. He reached down and gently felt it in his fingers (his initial approach to anything new was usually a gentle one). He moved it and squeezed it with interest several times. He released his hand and reached again for the bathmat and then for the drain plug and, as if he were suddenly reminded, once again he lowered his eyes and put his hand down to discover anew his penis.
(10 mos.) William played with his genitals again, for the first time in two months. It also occurred this time in the bath. He had an erection. I am not certain whether this preceded, or was the result of, his manipula-tion. He played with one hand and then with both, talking in a quiet jabber as he did. He then got on all fours and "peeked" as if to check if his penis was still there, but his pendulous belly made viewing difficult. He sat down and checked. He felt himself a little more. That was that!
(11 mos.) During most of the bath he played with a washcloth. As the water was draining out, William grabbed at his penis and held it with one hand. He released the penis shortly thereafter, and pressed his genitalia with a plastic bottle he was holding in the other hand. He rubbed the bottle against his penis. He again put his free hand back on his penis and pulled back and forth on the foreskin, in fine movements with his fingers. He squeezed the penis and testicles together and moved them around. The penis became erect. The mother (who frankly acknowledged her interest in his budding masculinity) said, "Do you like it, Billy?" Shortly he let go; the mother did not focus any more attention on his genitalia. The erection gradually subsided (1965, pp. 240–244).
(16 mos.) In the bath William carried on active and rather absorbed manipulations and stimulation of his genitals for approximately five minutes. This resulted in a 3+ erection, which had been occurring frequently but not invariably with less concentrated stimulation. He lifted the penis upward, rolled the testicles and scrotum up toward the penis, squeezed the scrotum and penis together, and tugged on the foreskin and the glans. He was "talking" and chortling as he stimulated himself. Clearly this directed behavior brought him localized sensation and pleasure. There was no evidence of orgasm (1966, p 363).
(19 mos.) Several times the following was observed: After he was undressed for his bath, William would sit on the floor stimulating his penis with his fingers. It quickly became fully erect and he tugged on his penis with excitement of considerable intensity. He would bob his erect penis up and down with his fingers. The degree of absorption in self-stimulation was still such that he could be readily distracted. Whenever his mother said it was time for his bath or nap, he turned to his mother at once. (1966, p. 368)

An account of the parallel phenomenon of a girl's discovery of her clitoris and vagina has not been recorded. Existing accounts of a girl's interest in her own and other's genitals and in the initiation of masturbation tend to emphasize the pathological aspects of the genital play (Roiphe and Galenson, 1973).

In some children, the recognition of anatomical differences produces fear of genital loss. Such fears are more likely to occur in children who have experienced a disturbance in body image through illness or pain, or who have experienced parental loss or detachment (Klein, 1928; Sachs, 1962; Roiphe, 1968). Normal, healthy children also express concern. Providing a small child with names for his genital organs as they are discovered and clarifying confusions about genital loss, promotes healthy psychosexual development and pride in one's own body image. Kleeman (1966) describes a small boy and his mother's perceptive responses to his inquiries:

(18 mos.) In his bath at the end of the day he was standing and bent way over, looking at his genitals. He pushed the penis aside and pointed to his scrotum and testicles, uttering "Oooh, oooh" with concern. When his mother named them, "Those are your ballies," he repeated, "Ballies," and seemed relieved.

(21 mos.) At twenty-one months William's awareness of his scrotum and testicles became more definite. Before his bath he was sitting nude on the floor. Looking down at his genitalia, he pointed to his scrotal sac and asked: "Dat is?" His mother replied, "Those are your ballies." He then named them: "Ballies."

(21 mos.) Today William watched his mother empty his bowel movement from the diaper into the toilet. The feces were brownish and ball-shaped. When she flushed the toilet, William commented: "Billy's other penis down the toidet." His mother explained very carefully: "Billy's penis and ballies are right here (she had already put on fresh diapers and pointed to the genital area through them) and they don't come off!" On the previous day, while sitting on the toilet, he had leaned over, pointed to his scrotal sac and testicles, and asked: "Dis is?" His mother had explained: "Those are your ballies" (1966, pp. 365, 371).

In boys, masturbation is defined as genital self-touching associated with erection and increasing excitement moving rhythmically to-

ward a climax (Kleeman, 1966; Kinsey, Pomeroy, and Martin, 1948). In girls, masturbation also comprises rhythmical self-stimulation with indications of pleasure and climax. It may begin as early as the first or second year, but more commonly occurs after the third year (Martinson, 1973). Kinsey and his coworkers reported orgasm in both boy and girl infants in the first six months of life. They based their conclusions on adult observations of a sample of children being sexually stimulated and achieving a climax. Approximately half the sample of twenty-two boys achieved climax by age two, with gradual increases in successive years. Similar findings are reported for girls, but the data are based on both observation and adult recall. Orgasm is reported for twenty-three girls under age three, four of them less than one year of age. A composite account of climax in the infant male follows:

the behavior involves a series of gradual physiologic changes, the development of rhythmic body movements with distinct penis throbs and pelvic thrusts, an obvious change in sensory capacities, a final tension of muscles, especially the abdomen, hips, and back, a sudden release with convulsions, including rhythmic anal contractions—followed by the disappearance of all symptoms. A fretful babe quiets down under the initial sexual stimulation, is distracted from other activities, begins rhythmic pelvic thrusts, becomes tense as climax approaches, is thrown into convulsive action, often with violent arm and leg movements, sometimes with weeping at the moment of climax. After climax the child loses erection quickly and subsides into the calm and peace that typically follows adult orgasm. It may be some time before erection can be induced again after such an experience (Kinsey, Pomeroy, and Martin, 1948, p. 177).

Masturbation to orgasm in a girl, age three, the youngest reported by Kinsey and his associates is described by the child's mother:

Lying face down on the bed, with her knees drawn up, she started rhythmic pelvic thrusts, about one second or less apart. The thrusts were primarily pelvic, with the legs tensed in a fixed position. The forward components of the thrusts were in a smooth and perfect rhythm which was unbroken except for momentary pauses during which the genitalia were readjusted against the doll on which they were pressed; the return from each thrust was convulsive, jerky. There were 44 thrusts in unbroken rhythm, a slight momentary pause, 87 thrusts followed by a slight momentary pause, then 10 thrusts, and then a cessation of all movement. There was marked concentration and intense breathing with abrupt jerks as orgasm approached. She was completely oblivious to everything during these later stages of the activity. Her eyes were glassy and fixed in a vacant stare. There was noticeable relief and relaxation after orgasm. A second series of reactions began two minutes later with series of 48, 18, and 57 thrusts, with slight momentary pauses between each series. With the mounting tensions, there were audible gasps, but immediately following the cessation of pelvic thrusts there was complete relaxation and only desultory movements thereafter (Kinsey, Pomeroy, Martin, and Gebhard, 1953, pp. 104–105).

Masturbation to orgasm, by various techniques, was also reported in younger female infants (Bakwin, 1973). A seven-month-old girl masturbated by pressing her body against her rag doll: ". . . from time to time would throw the doll on the floor, lie down on top of it, and rhythmically press her body against it . . ." (p. 52). Another infant, at five months, "would press her legs together, lift them and bear down, and her face became flushed" (pp. 52–53). Still another, at fourteen months, "would cross her legs, grunt, and get red in the face. After some seconds or minutes she would relax, break out in perspiration, and appear exhausted" (p. 53). The follow-up data on these girls indicated that masturbation in early infancy was not associated with behavioral disability later. In two of the infants, masturbation gradually diminished, but in the third who was routinely punished for self-stimulation, it continued and apparently increased.

Pelvic thrusting movements begin in the first year, mainly when the infant is held close and cuddled. The majority of infants respond recip-

rocally to holding and cuddling, sometimes with pelvic thrusting. Since sex play is rarely permitted in our society, the continuing occurrence of pelvic thrusting rehearsals is not known. In a society which permits sexual play in children, as the Yolunga of Arnhem Lane in Australia do, pelvic thrusting may occur as children are falling asleep together (Money and Ehrhardt, 1972).

GENDER DIFFERENTIATION AND SEX REHEARSALS

It is a social and cultural imperative to assign an infant as male or female, in accord with external genital status. The regularity with which infants are assigned as male or female masks the social importance of that event for the child, the parents, and the family. Only when an infant is born with a defect of the sex organs, and sex of assignment must be delayed, or sex must be reannounced, are the social consequences easily observed. Uncertainty of gender status characteristically produces distress and anxiety in medical caretakers as well as in family members, who may presuppose that sexual development and sexual functioning stems from chromosomal, hormonal, or gonadal status, rather than from the program of upbringing. Without parent counseling, a child may then grow up sensing ambiguity about the self, feeling freakish or queer, neither male nor female, reflecting parental attitudes, anxieties, and misconceptions. Sex reannouncements are successful only when the parents are able to rear the child convincingly in the reassigned gender; parents cannot ordinarily bring up a child as a girl, if they continue to believe the child to be a boy, genitalia notwithstanding.

The genitalia of the newborn act as a releasing stimulus that initiates the program of rearing considered culturally, socially, and personally appropriate to a male or female child. Once set into motion, the program of rearing tends to be fixed and resistant to change. The gender status of the baby may be imprinted on the family in the critical period at childbirth, just as gender identity is imprinted on the child in the following eighteen to twenty-four months.

Different expectations and responses toward girl and boy infants and children often are so automatic as to go unnoticed by the parents as well as by others. In rare instances of sex-reannouncement, the dimorphism of rearing practices employed with the same child, living first as a boy, then as a girl, is strikingly illustrated. Money and Ehrhardt (1972) report the comments of several articulate parents. The observant mother of a child who was sex-reassigned from male to female at age eleven months, after ablation of the penis, reported:

> "I started dressing her not in dresses but, you know, in little pink slacks and frilly blouses . . . and letting her hair grow." A year and six months later, the mother wrote that she had made a special effort at keeping her girl in dresses almost exclusively, changing any item of clothes into something that was clearly feminine. "I even made all her nightwear into granny gowns and she wears bracelets and hair ribbons." The effects of emphasizing feminine clothing became clearly noticeable in the girl's attitude towards clothes and hairdo another year later, when she was observed to have a clear preference for dresses over slacks and to take pride in her long hair.
>
> Related to being dressed nicely is the sense of neatness. The mother stated that her daughter by four and a half years of age was much neater than her brother, and in contrast with him, disliked to be dirty: "She likes for me to wipe her face. She doesn't like to be dirty, and yet my son is quite different. I can't wash his face for anything. . . . She seems to be daintier. Maybe it's because I encourage it" (p. 119).

Similarly, parents of a baby boy with a microphallus, reassigned to live as a girl at seventeen months, noted changes in their behavior and parallel changes in the child:

> The night she came home from the hospital, she was dancing to music. Father caught himself thinking as he danced around with her: imagine dancing at her wedding; what a culmination of events. Wife said she was think-ing same. I imagine that's an indication of how we've accepted it (John Money, personal communication).
>
> The first change was related to different clothes. The baby received a completely new set of female clothing and her hair was allowed to grow long. Another recent immediate change was a completely new set of girl's toys (Money and Ehrhardt, 1972, p. 124).

Two months after the sex reassignment, the mother reported that she and her husband thought the girl had really changed in her ways and had become much more feminine. They allowed that it may have something to do with their own perception, but that they thought it was a clear-cut objective observation. The father described at that time his own feelings: "It's a great feeling of fun for me to have a little girl. I have completely different feelings towards this child as a girl than as a boy." He had noticed a change in his behavior towards his daughter compared to his son: "I treat my son quite differently—wrestling around, playing ball." He said that he had done the same with the second child before sex reassignment. Now he avoided such things with the girl. He attempted to distinguish between "things you associate with fun for boys and things for girls" (Money and Ehrhardt, 1972, p. 124).

At age three, the girl also had clearly feminine wishes. For Christmas, she wanted glass slippers, so that she could go to the ball like Cinderella, and a doll. The parents were delighted. The girl continued to receive typically girlish toys from her parents. She continued more and more to show feminine interests, as in helping her mother (Money and Ehrhardt, 1972, p. 125).

The father gave an example, when the girl was three years old, of how girls and boys are differently treated with respect to rehearsal of their adult roles as a female or male romantic partner. The family had established the habit of dancing together to the record-player, after the father arrived home from work. The father usually picked his daughter up, or danced with her, holding her close to him, while the boy was doing rock and roll dancing of a more solo type, maybe including his mother as a partner. At first, the girl wanted to copy her brother, but then she began to enjoy the favoritism of dancing with her father (Money and Ehrhardt, 1972, p. 125).

Shortly after the sex reassignment, the parents noted a marked change in the brother who was about three and a half years of age at that time. The parents had explained to the boy that his baby brother really was a baby sister and that the doctors had made a mistake. Subsequently, they showed him the surgically feminized genitalia and he had no difficulty in accepting the sex reassignment. The father reported: "My wife tells me, she has noticed a marked difference in his behavior towards his new sister . . . she sees a very evident degree of protectionism, now, on his part towards his sister, and a marked tendency to treat her much more gently. Whereas, before he was just as likely to stick his foot out and trip her as he went by, he now wants to hold her hand to make sure she doesn't fall." The parents were not aware of making a special point that their son should treat his sister differently from the time she had been a boy. The only reason they could think of for the change in his behavior was that he copied other boys' behavior towards their sisters (Money and Ehrhardt, 1972, p. 124).

In addition to differential parental expectations and responses for girl versus boy infants, parents provide models for identification and complementation. Identification with or copying the parent of the same sex, and complementation or reciprocation to the parent of the opposite sex are dual processes essential to the establishment of gender identity and gender role. Developmentally, the emergence of gender identity/role parallels the emergence of language at eighteen months to two years. The gender designations of language, the gender dimorphism of upbringing, and the body image jointly contribute to the imprinting of core gender identity, much as native language itself is imprinted. Once established, core gender identity is resistive to change and likely to be associated with psychopathology (Hampson, 1955). In the ensuing years of childhood, gender identity/role is elaborated and consolidated as the child interacts with adult models for identification and complementation, and rehearses both sex-coded roles and sex roles in play and in fantasy.

ENDOCRINE FUNCTION AND GENDER DIFFERENTIATION

NEONATAL HORMONES

In neonatal life, sex hormones circulating in the bloodstream are at a high level compared to that of later infancy and childhood. Prior to birth, hormone function depends upon maternal and placental endocrine activity, and upon the endocrine activity of the fetus itself. The period after birth is one of rapid transition from maternal and placental dependence to autonomous functioning (Mitchell and Shackleton, 1969).

From birth until the first seven to twelve months of age, there are sex differences in hormone concentrations (Forest, Saez, and Bertrand, 1973; Forest, Cathiard, and Bertrand, 1974; Forest, Sizonenko, Cathiard, and Bertrand, 1974). Testosterone levels are high in both boys and girls but higher in boys. In boys, there is a testosterone peak by the second or third month, followed by a gradual decrease to prepubertal levels by one year. In girls, the testosterone level rapidly declines to the prepubertal level by the second week of life. There is an increase in lutenizing hormone (LH) and follicular stimulating hormone (FSH) in both sexes during the first year, but girls have higher levels of FSH and boys of LH. Estrogen levels have not yet been ascertained for boys or girls.

Differences in endocrine function present at birth and in the neonatal period are not known to be related to psychosexual differentiation or to any aspect of behavioral development. Precise methods of measuring steroid levels by radioimmunoassay determinations are relatively recent; behavioral correlation studies have not been undertaken.

PRENATAL HORMONES

In contrast, the prenatal hormones affect the sexually dimorphic pathways in the brain during the early months of fetal development, altering the threshold for behavior traits defined as boyish or girlish. The prenatal program does not preordain psychosexual differentiation as masculine or feminine but instead establishes a predisposition for behavior traits that are gender-shared but threshold-dimorphic.

The readiness with which some behavior traits are evoked in males is associated with boyishness and built into a masculine gender-identity; the same principle applies to girlishness and a feminine gender-identity. A listing of the behavior traits, obtained from the study of animals and of human clinical syndromes with a known history of prenatal androgenization and deandrogenization is presented by Money (in press):

First, is general kinesis, a high level of energy expenditure, not in the disorganized way of a hyperkinetic child, but in outdoor athletic or team-sport activities, or in muscular work. It is more prevalent in males than females.

Second, is competitive rivalry and assertiveness to elevate one's rank in the dominance hierarchy. It is more transparently evident in childhood than adulthood when it may take more covert and symbolic form as a power struggle. It is more prevalent in males than females. It is associated with preference for utility clothing and lack of adornment.

Third, is roaming which appears to be related to territory mapping or marking which, in many lower species is done with special scent glands that under the influence of androgen, secrete pheromones. It is more prevalent in boys than girls, and may, by a stretch of the scientific imagination, indirectly have something to do with space-form perception and praxic ability.

Fourth, is defense of the troop against intruders and predators which is also related to boundary maintenance. It is more prevalent in males than females. It does not mean that males are more aggressive than females, but only that the stimulus that triggers aggression in the two sexes is threshold different.

Fifth, is guarding and defense of the young. It is more prevalent in females than males, and demonstrates the potential aggressiveness of females as well as males.

Sixth, is nesting and homemaking, which is explicitly under hormonal, especially progestinic, control in lower species. It is more prevalent in females than males, but even in lower species can also be evoked in the hormonally untreated male.

Seventh, is parental care of the young, including the rehearsal of parentalism in doll play and other play of childhood. It is more prevalent in females than males. It may be associated with a more sensitive threshold for detecting distress sounds of the young, especially in sleep. Thus, by another stretch of the scientific imagination, it may indirectly have something to do with the linguistic achievement of girls, especially in reading.

Eighth, is sexual mounting and thrusting, more prevalent in males, versus spreading and containing, more prevalent in females. Observation of the play of juveniles among lower primates suggests that there may be some degree of prenatal programming of these sexual positionings in human beings.

Ninth, especially with respect to initiating an erotic engagement, is dependence on visual stimuli for erotic arousal, more prevalent in the male, versus dependence on tactual or haptic stimuli, more prevalent in the female.

These behavior traits emerge slowly in the years between birth and adolescence. In the first two years of life, few of the items on this list are included in an infant's behavioral repertoire. General kinesis and roaming or exploration are reported as more common in males by numerous investigators (Korner, 1969, 1973; Goldberg and Lewis, 1969; Hutt, 1972; Graves, 1978). Rehearsals of parentalism also may begin in the second year; they differentiate from the earlier common haptic phase of clinging to and cuddling with soft toys and blankets. Infants of both sexes hug, cuddle, and feed their teddy bears and dolls, but baby care rehearsals gradually become more prominent in girls. The majority of the threshold-dimorphic behavior traits emerge in succeeding years, in relation to physical, mental, and social maturation.

Sex of assignment and sex of rearing exert their respective influences upon an organism which already contains behavioral predispositions deriving from the prenatal program. Presumably, gender-dimorphic behavior traits affect the responses of parents and other caretakers, confirming sex of assignment and the program of upbringing. Similarly, sex of assignment is likely to evoke differential parenting responses which exert a feedback effect on the infant. For example, mothers are reported to vocalize to and smile more frequently at female infants and to employ nonverbal arousal stimuli more frequently with boys. Boys also are fed more often, held upright more frequently and discouraged from touching (Thoman, Leiderman, and Olson, 1972, Korner, Lewis, and Weinraub, 1974). The interaction of differential parental expectations and of the daily practices of rearing in relation to psychosexual differentiation and infant behavior, is only beginning to be investigated and the findings to date are tentative (Moss, 1974, Lewis, 1975).

In the first weeks and months of life, when infant behavior is characteristically variable, efforts to discover gender differences are extraordinarily difficult. Moreover, differences attributed to gender may stem from social and cultural practices which are overlooked unless cross-cultural comparisons are made. One recent investigation showed that the early gender differences reported in American studies were not replicated in European studies, possibly because of variations in circumcision practice on the two continents (Richards, Bernal, and Brackbill, 1975). An intrusive physical procedure, circumcision, affected the male infant's behavior by increasing irritability which, in turn, affected parenting practices. In the neonate and infant, variations in state of arousal, in temperament, and in sensorimotor capacities may have a more pervasive effect on socioemotional behavior than gender status or parenting practices do. The possibility is not surprising since interaction with the behavior environment appears to be essential to the differentiation of gender-dimorphic behavior. The effect of learning, from stimulus and response, from reward and punishment or neglect, and from observation and copying, is a cumulative phenomenon, visible only after the passage of time.

In the first two years of life sexuality is expressed mainly in the sensuous attachment of the child to the parents and is common to both boys and girls. Sociosexual differentiation as male or female is initiated in the discovery and exploration of one's own body and in the gender-dimorphic patterns of rearing. These events are precursors of the sexually erotic partnerships which will emerge in adolescence and adulthood.

REFERENCES

BAKWIN, H. 1973. Erotic feelings in infants and young children. *American Journal of Diseases of Children* 126: 52–54.

BATESON, G. and MEAD, M. 1942. *Balinese character: a photographic analysis*, vol. 2. New York: New York Academy of Sciences.

BELL, S. 1902. A preliminary study of the emotions of love between the sexes. *American Journal of Psychology* 13: 325–54.

BIEBER, I. 1975. Biosocial roots of childhood sexuality. In *Sexuality and psychoanalysis*, ed. E. Adelson. New York: Brunner/Mazel.

BOWLBY, J. 1969. *Attachment and loss*, vol. 1, Attachment. New York: Basic Books.

———. 1973. *Attachment and loss*, vol. 2, Separation. New York: Basic Books.

FORD, C., and BEACH, F. 1951. *Patterns of sexual behavior*. New York: Harper.

FOREST, M.; CATHIARD, A.; and BERTRAND, J. 1973. Evidence of testicular activity in early infancy. *Journal of Clinical Endocrinology and Metabolism* 37: 148–50.

———; SAEZ, J.; and BERTRAND, J. 1973. Assessment of gonadal function in children. *Paediatrician* 2: 102–28.

———; SIZONENKO, P.; CATHIARD, A.; and BERTRAND, J. 1974. Hypophyso-gonadal function in humans during the first year of life. I. Evidence for testicular activity in early infancy. *Journal of Clinical Investigation* 53: 819–28.

GALENSON, H. 1975. Discussion (Early sexual differences and development, P. B. Neubauer). In *Sexuality and psychoanalysis*, ed. E. Adelson. New York: Brunner/Mazel.

GOLDBERG, S., and LEWIS, M. 1969. Play behavior in the year-old infant: early sex differences. *Child Development* 40: 21–32.

GRAVES, P. 1978. Infant behavior and maternal attitudes in West Bengal, India: early sex differences. *Journal of Cross-Cultural Psychology* 9: 45–60.

HALVERSON, H. 1940. Genital and sphincter behavior of the male infant. *Journal of Genetic Psychology* 56: 95–136.

HAMPSON, J. 1955. Hermaphroditic genital appearance, rearing, and eroticism in hyperadrenocorticism. *Bulletin of The Johns Hopkins Hospital* 96: 265–73.

HARLOW, H., and HARLOW, M. 1962. The effect of rearing conditions on behavior. *Bulletin of the Menninger Clinic* 26: 213–24.

———. 1965. The affectional systems. In *Behavior of non-human primates*, vol. 2, ed. A. Schrier, H. Harlow, and F. Stollnitz. New York and London: Academic Press.

———; DODSWORTH, R.; and HARLOW, M. 1965. Total social isolation in monkeys. *Proceedings of the National Academy of Science* 54: 90–96.

———; HARLOW, M.; DODSWORTH, R.; and ARLING, G. 1966. Maternal behavior of rhesus monkeys deprived of mothering and peer associations in infancy. *Proceedings of the American Philosophical Society* 110: 58–66.

HUTT, C. 1972. Sex differences in human development. *Human Development* 15: 153–70.

KINSEY, A.; POMEROY, W.; and MARTIN, C. 1948. *Sexual behavior in the human male*. Philadelphia: W. B. Saunders.

———; POMEROY, W.; MARTIN, C.; and GEBHARD, P. 1953. *Sexual behavior in the human female*. Philadelphia: W. B. Saunders.

KLEEMAN, J. 1965. A boy discovers his penis. *Psychoanalytic Study of the Child* 20: 239–66. New York: International Universities Press.

———. 1966. Genital self-discovery during a boy's second year: a follow-up. *Psychoanalytic Study of the Child* 21: 358–91. New York: International Universities Press.

KLEIN, M. 1928. *Early stages of the oedipus conflict. Contributions to psycho-analysis*. London: Hogarth Press.

KORNER, A. 1974. The effect of the infant's state, level of arousal, sex and ontogenetic stage on the caregiver. In *The effect of the infant on its caregiver*, ed. M. Lewis and L. Rosenblum. New York: Wiley.

———. 1969. Neonatal startles, smiles, erections, and reflex sucks as related to state, sex and individuality. *Child Development* 40: 1039–53.

———. 1973. Sex differences in newborns with special reference to differences in the organization of oral behavior. *Journal of Child Psychology and Psychiatry* 14: 19–29.

LEVINE, M. 1951. Pediatric observations on masturbation in children. *Psychoanalytic Study of the Child* 6: 117–24. New York: International Universities Press.

LEWIS, M. 1975. Early sex differences in the human: studies of socioemotional development. *Archives of Sexual Behavior* 4: 329–35.

LEWIS, M., and WEINRAUB, M. 1974. Sex of parent and sex of child: socioemotional development. In *Sex differences in behavior*, ed. R. Friedman; R. Richart; and R. Vande Wiele. New York: Wiley.

MARTINSON, F. 1973. *Infant and child sexuality*. St. Peter, Minn.: The Book Mark.

McKINNEY, W. 1975. Experimental primatology. In *Sexuality and psychoanalysis*, ed. E. Adelson. New York: Brunner/Mazel.

———. 1976. Eroticism in infancy and childhood. *Journal of Sex Research* 12: 251–62.

MITCHELL, F., and SHACKLETON, C. 1969. Investigation of steroid metabolism in early infancy. *Advances in Clinical Chemistry* 12: 141–215.

MONEY, J. 1976. Childhood: the last frontier in sex research. *The Sciences* 16: 12–15, 27.

———. In press. Endocrine influences and psychosexual status spanning the life cycle. In *Handbook of biological psychiatry*, ed.

H. van Praag; O. Rafaelsen; H. Lader; and E. Sachar. New York: Marcel Dekker.

———. 1977. The syndrome of abuse-dwarfism (psychosocial dwarfism or reversible hyposomatotropinism): behavioral data. *American Journal of Diseases of Children* 31: 508–12.

———, and EHRHARDT, A. 1972. *Man and woman, boy and girl: the differentiation and dimorphism of gender identity from conception to maturity.* Baltimore: Johns Hopkins University Press.

MOSS, H. 1974. Early sex differences and mother-infant interaction. In *Sex differences in behavior,* ed. R. Friedman, R. Richart, R. Vande Wiele, and L. Stern. New York: Wiley.

RICHARDS, M.; BERNAL, J.; and BRACKBILL, Y. 1975. Early behavioral differences: gender or circumcision. *Developmental Psychobiology* 9: 89–95.

ROIPHE, H. 1968. On an early genital phase, with an addendum on genesis. *Psychoanalytic Study of the Child* 23: 348–65. New York: International Universities Press.

———, and GALENSON, E. 1973. The infantile fetish. *The Psychoanalytic Study of the Child* 28: 147–66.

ROSSI, A. 1977. A biosocial perspective on parenting. *Proceedings of the American Academy of Arts and Sciences* 106: 1–31 (*Daedalus, The Family*: Spring, 1977).

RUTTER, M. 1972. *Maternal deprivation reassessed.* Baltimore: Penguin Books.

———. 1971. Normal psychosexual development. *Journal of Child Psychology and Psychiatry* 11: 259–83.

SACHS, L. 1962. A case of castration anxiety beginning at eighteen months. *Journal of the American Psychoanalytic Association* 10: 329–37.

SPIRO, M. E. 1965. Children of the kibbutz. New York: Shocken Books.

SPITZ, R. 1946. Anaclitic depression: an inquiry into the genesis of psychiatric conditions in early childhood. *Psychoanalytic Study of the Child* 2: 313–42. New York: International Universities Press.

———. 1949. Autoerotism: some empirical findings and hypotheses on three of its manifestations in the first year of life. *Psychoanalytic Study of the Child* 3, 4. New York: International Universities Press.

THOMAN, E.; LEIDERMAN, P.; and OLSON, J. 1972. Neonate-mother interaction during breast-feeding. *Developmental Psychology* 6: 110–18.

THREE

Childhood Sexuality

FLOYD M. MARTINSON

INFANCY (0–3 YEARS)

There are few human activities about which there is greater curiosity, greater social concern, and less knowledge than child sexuality. To understand it, we must improve on its theoretical and conceptual base, develop testable hypotheses from the different theoretical systems, and carry out the designated research, including theoretical alternatives to the psychoanalytic theory of infant and child sexuality. We have left the explanation of sexuality of the young to psychoanalysis alone. Freud (1915) had no intention that it should be so. He insisted that his conclusions were based on psychoanalytic investigations alone and that these needed to be amplified by studies in other spheres. Freud himself turned to a sociology of sex in his latter years when he gave much attention to the opposition between civilization and the freedom of sexual expression (Jones, 1955).

There are currently several theories as to how and when human beings develop sexually and arrive at patterns of sexual behavior. From a physiological point of view, it has been said that preadolescent boys and girls do not desire each other sexually because certain glands are not functioning. The testes, for example, after a period of prenatal activity, enter a period of hormonal quiescence until the onset of puberty (Money, 1973). At puberty, when the glands secrete their hormones, boys and girls awaken sexually and have an urge to engage in sexual activities. According to this hormone theory, it is only because of social restraints that they do not indulge in sexual license (Udry, 1966, p. 104). Also according to this theory, sexual inadequacy, frigidity, and impotence are the result of too few sex hormones, too many, or the wrong kind (Broderick, 1964). Hence, most persons develop this sex urge at puberty, but some develop it abnormally early and some develop it abnormally late or not at all.

According to psychoanalytic theory, the libido, the basic life force, is present from birth, and even the infant has sex needs which are met in sucking, eliminating, or manipulating the sex organs. The ages seven to eleven are seen as a period of relatively decreased intensity of the biological drive and are referred to as latency. Relieved from the internal stress and conflict occasioned by the severe internal pressure of the drive, the latency child supposedly busies itself with learning about the outer world. The period from eleven to thirteen years of age is seen as one of relative peace. But it is short-lived; indeed in some cases it may not be distinguishable at all. Preadolescence then anticipates the onrush of intensified sexual drive for the second time.

In recent years, the emphasis on latency as well as a general disregard of sexuality in infancy and childhood has brought both hormone theory and psychoanalytic theory into question by social scientists. Anthropologists had earlier questioned latency theory because of the sexual activity observed among children in permissive primitive societies. Social scientists suggest that the conception of a latency period, a time of life without passion, may be something of a myth (Douvan and Adelson, 1966). This period is more complex than we have realized; the contrasts between this and other periods of development are impressive. Relative to what precedes and follows it, the preadolescent period is indeed low in drive and conflict; the child is absorbed in the quiet growth of ego capacities.

During late preadolescence friends focus on activity, on what they are doing together, and not on each other as persons (Douvan and Adelson, 1966). There appears to be little interest in a friend's personality as such. Sexually precocious children are no more advanced in general personality development than are other children (Maccoby, 1966). Friendship is not yet rational; it is an adjunct to something else, the partnership in work and play. Basically, the preadolescent's emotional commitment is to his or her family rather than to his or her friends.

If there is a latency period, it can be modified, for the notion of an innate predetermined psychological sexuality does not correspond with existing evidence. According to a social learning theory of sexual development, the individual begins life with a biological capacity for sexual maturity and a psychosexual plasticity capable of developing along a variety of lines depending upon the definition of social roles in his or her particular culture and community as well as upon his or her unique learning, especially during the formative periods of life (Brown and Lynn, May 1966).

Rather than passing through a set series of sexual stages determined by physical growth, children develop at different rates in a wide variety of directions depending upon how they are raised. In some communities they may go through the classic series of stages in attitude toward the opposite sex, preschool friendships, elementary school dislikes, followed by junior high school awakening and high school attraction and involvement. In other communities, perhaps only a few miles away, the series of stages may be quite different. Broderick found communities in the United States in which there were well established romances going on in kindergarten class and a great deal of giggling and gossiping over couples. Among these five year olds, who-is-going-to-marry-whom was a common subject of conversation. By eight and nine years of age, children played kissing games at their parties. By ages ten and eleven nearly half had begun to date and most had a series of crushes on adults and other children. Ninety percent of the fifth grade boys in one community were involved in what Broderick referred to as "special" relationships with girl-friends (Broderick, 1966).

Anthropologists have complained for years

that both the hormone and the psychoanalytic theories failed to account for the sexual activities of young children in certain primitive societies. United States data have shown that romantic interest in the opposite sex begins in infancy or early childhood, depending on the degree of permissiveness and stimulation in the social environment. This is not to deny the marked impact of puberty upon sexual attitudes and experiences.

Psychoanalytic theory of sexual development has had more emphasis in the human sexuality literature than it deserves, particularly the literature on infant and child sexuality. This is so, first because psychoanalytic theory, though rich in insights, has not produced many empirically verifiable hypotheses (Chodoff, 1966). Second, psychoanalytic theory has drawn what empirical support it does have largely from observations of small samples of clinical populations rather than from broad representative samples of children and adults and particularly disturbed adults. Children and adults who have been brought to a therapist or clinic because of some behavior problem have provided the major source of samples in the past. Psychoanalytic theory, though inadequately tested, has been utilized as a source and justification for after-the-fact casual explanations of various manifestations of sexual behavior.

Psychoanalytic theorists must continue to derive and test hypotheses using psychoanalytic concepts. To complement this, other behavioral scientists with other theoretical and conceptual orientations, should test social theories of sexual development using large (rather than small) and representative (rather than clinical) populations.

The human infant, here defined as being between the ages from birth up to but not including three years of age, is a creature of potential. The development of that potential, whether related to mental, physical, or sexual-erotic aspects of growth, occurs at a very rapid rate during the first two years of life. Actually the sensing mechanism is at work much earlier than that, by about the eighth week of gestation (Liley, 1972). Until recently the human fetus *in situ* was not accessible for study. It was thought that quickening (when the fetus begins moving limbs and trunk) did not take place until the sixteenth to twentieth week of gestation. Fetal movement is necessary to the development of bones and joints, but the fetus apparently also moves to make itself comfortable in the uterus. The fetus is responsive to pressure and touch, for instance, tickling the scalp and stroking the palm to elicit reactions (Langworthy, 1933). It is possible that the fetus is also experienced in sucking before birth. It is not uncommon to detect the fetus sucking thumbs, fingers, or toes. We can conclude that at least habituation and perhaps even some sensate learning can take place during the gestation period.

That sensate learning is possible before or outside of the achievement of self-awareness also is at least tangentially supported in studies of infant "socialization" among other mammals. Harlow's report (Harlow and Zimmerman, 1959; Harlow, 1962) on affectional patterns of rhesus monkeys deprived of interaction with a mother figure is an example. These monkeys were deprived of the learning opportunity provided in normal dependency-affectional and sexual behavior patterns as monkeys grow older.

The human infant, a pliable but nonambulatory bundle of soft and spongy boney tissue with a resultant uncanny ability to achieve unusual postures both prenatally and postnatally, can interact with people only as they come to him or her. At a rapid rate, however, the infant develops the capacity to locomote, thereby facilitating the development of the ability to initiate encounters with others. The newborn's whole body of impulse and potential can be viewed as an undifferentiated potential for physical, emotional, and social experience (Comfort, 1963). Sexual-erotic development, like all development, takes place at different rates and in different ways in different individuals; development in the affectional-sexual-erotic area is not separable from development in other areas. As an infant develops, every aspect of his or her life experience is capable of affecting every other part. This is markedly evident in the case of the infant whose motor development has progressed to the stage at which it no longer must await but can actively seek encounters with others, whether they be running to hug daddy hello or opening his or her arms as an indication of the desire to be held.

The earliest encounters of infant and mother can hardly help but contribute to the sensory and affectional awakening of the infant, arousing sensitivity in the body and stimulating the growth of sexual consciousness. Evidence of a child's capacity for sensory pleasure in the first year of life can be observed. From birth to one year of age the mouth is the chief pleasure zone of the infant, but infants also respond to total body contact (Renshaw, 1971). The chief pleasurable activity in the first year is sucking the mother's breast or the thumb. The progressive development and orderly shift of sexuality from the mouth to other parts of the body (feet, thighs, abdomen) is evidenced in the activities of the infant when naked or when being bathed. Fingers wander searchingly over other parts of the body exploring the ears, the navel, the nipple region, and the genital area. Whether the infant is free to explore and stimulate its own body depends largely upon the parental acceptance of the infant's nakedness and freedom of bodily activities.

Both before and after birth the human begins to develop a system of tensional outlets. These include changing positions in the womb, rocking to sleep in the crib, bed shaking, head banging, as well as handling the genitals and possibly some masturbating. Removal of clothes and attempts to run around naked occur between one and two years (Ilg and Ames, 1955). By two years the infant has already incorporated some of these impulses into forms of expression permitted by society, and although rocking, head banging, and some masturbating occur (Gesell and Ilg, 1946, p. 271), much of the two-year-old's release of tension is manifested by displays of strong affection toward parents, kissing, for example (Gesell and Ilg, 1946, p. 322). Dolls and teddy bears also receive much attention. Being fed, taken to the toilet, dressed, and taken for rides are characteristic of things that occupy the two-year-old's attention (Gesell and Ilg, 1946, p. 366). The evidence of underlying sexual development is exhibited in the infant's other achievements. Naming of the genitals with the use of a word for urination, distinguishing boys from girls even before the age of two (*Behavior Today*, January 3, 1977, pp. 2–3), and differentiating adults by such words as "lady" or "man" are among these achievements (Gesell and Ilg, 1946, p. 322).

At two and one-half years of age, the infant has still more understanding of the sociosexual scene. Differentiation of male and female roles has increased markedly. The child is aware of his or her gender and the fact that it is like the parent of the same gender and different from the other parent and his or her opposite-gender peers. The child can now differentiate the gender of children by the terms boy and girl. The two-and-a-half-year-old may well have incorporated a nonverbal generalization that boys and fathers have distinct genitalia and stand when they urinate, but girls and mothers do not. This age marks the beginning of interest in the physiological differences between sexes. The infant is very conscious of its own sex organs and may handle them when undressed. Inquiries concerning mothers' breasts are common. All in all, the child has reached a point at which, because gender distinctions are possible, socialization into a male or female identity can and does occur (Gesell and Ilg, 1946, p. 322; Ilg and Ames, 1955, p. 203).

In early childhood, erotic feelings become centered on the genitalia, and definite periods of sex play can be observed (Ribble, 1955, p. 26). Sex interest increases with age and varies in that some infants and children are much more interested than others in the subject of sex.

THE SEXUAL CAPACITY OF INFANTS

Boy babies are sometimes born with erections, and girls demonstrate vaginal lubrication almost at the start. In a study of nine male babies of ages three to twenty weeks, tumescence (penile erection) was observed at least once daily in seven of the nine (Halverson, 1940). Individual responses varied greatly from five to forty erections per day. Tumes-

cence often was accompanied by restlessness, fretting, crying, stretching, and flexing the limbs stiffly. The behavior following the detumescence was in the nature of playful activity or relaxation. Parents often report having observed erections in infant boys (Conn, 1940).

Pelvic thrust movements in male and female infants eight to ten months old appear to occur as an expression of affection in which the baby holds onto the parent, nuzzles the parent, and rapidly thrusts and rotates the pelvis for a few seconds (Lewis and Kagan, 1965). It appears to be more an evidence of pleasure, an ecstatic rather than an erotic mood. This kind of behavior diminishes when holding the infant closely decreases as the infant becomes ambulatory. Pelvic thrusts have also been observed among primate infants; infantile sexual behavior in all mammals is perhaps the rule (Bowlby, 1969, p. 158).

A newborn infant is responsive to external stimulation of the genital area (Sears, Maccoby, and Levin, 1957, p. 176). A gentle touch, or the rubbing of clothes or bed coverings, seems to attract attention. If the infant has been active or restless or is having a crying spell, genital stimulation appears to quiet and relax. In the third or fourth month of life, genital stimulation is sometimes accompanied by smiling and making a few soft sounds. The boy baby from birth is likely to have an erection on such occasions. Girls show similar responsiveness. Internal sources of stimulation, such as a full bladder or a full bowel, also produce sensory reactions (Sears and others, 1957, pp. 175–217). These reactions are less likely to be accompanied by signs of pleasure and relaxation than are reactions to external stimulation.

Orgasm has been reported for a four-month-old female baby and has been observed in boys as young as five months (Kinsey, 1953, pp. 104–5).

GENITAL PLAY—MASTURBATION

Spitz (1962) makes an important distinction between genital play and masturbation in infancy. He observes that infants in the first year of life generally are not capable of the direct, volitional behavior required for what we call the masturbatory act or masturbation. Any more or less random play with various parts of the body, including the genitals, is nonspecific activity and should be labeled as genital play and not as masturbation.

Yet some infants do specifically stimulate themselves sexually. Kinsey (1953, p. 142) reports one record of a seven-month-old infant and records of five infants under one year who were observed to masturbate. Twenty-three girls, three years or younger, appeared to reach orgasm through self-stimulation. Kinsey's unpublished interview data contains notations from interviews with a small sample of two-year-olds and their mothers. One mother reported that her son had the habit of rubbing against a doll's head to masturbate. Another reported that her son's masturbating was deliberate, prolonged, and accompanied by an erection. Cuddling and kissing parents and others was reported for both boys and girls.

Kinsey reported more records of small girls than of small boys masturbating to orgasm at an early age. This does not agree with the finding of Levy (1928). Levy reports that direct stimulation of the genitals in over half of a group of boys under three years of age whose mothers were interviewed by him, as contrasting with only four out of twenty-six girls. Koch (1935), like Levy, reports more masturbation among infant boys than among infant girls.

It cannot be assumed that behavior that appears to be erotic to adults is actually erotic in the consciousness of the infant, since the infant lacks the well developed erotic imagery available and so important to adult sexual activity. Also in the sexual realm, sociocultural influences come to modify and interpret biological influences so that a straight-line developmental continuity from infancy to maturity cannot be assumed (Simon and Gagnon, March, 1969). In societies with a tolerant and permissive attitude toward erotic expression in infancy, fingering the genitals becomes an occasional but established habit (Ford and Beach, 1951, p. 188). One example is that of the Marquesa. Sex play was common practice from the earliest ages among the Marquesa and not only tolerated but encouraged (Kardiner, 1939, pp. 205–6). They recognized the erotic impulse in childhood and accorded it the right of free exercise. They eroticized the child by masturbating it to keep it quiet. In the case of the girls, labia were manipulated as a placebo and also to encourage the growth of large labia, which to the Marquesans were a mark of beauty. Such activity was, no doubt, also erotically stimulating. There was social recognition of all sexual activity in childhood, and there were no restrictions against engaging in it freely; it was allocated the same place in the child's world as it occupied in the adult's.

INFANT-OTHER INTERACTION

During the first several years of life, the infant's relationship to others centers mostly on relationships with the mother (or a mother substitute) and having physiological needs met, especially the need for food. Feeding is necessary for survival, but it is also an occasion for intimate contact with other persons as a part of the infant's exploration of the environment. Objects are experienced by putting them in the mouth, by sucking, touching, eating, and biting. This basically autoerotic stage lasts for the first five or six months of life (Hurlock, 1950, p. 485). From as early as two months of age onward and increasingly through the first year of life, infants are not so much passive and receptive as active in seeking interaction. Most infants show the need for the proximity of others sometime during the first quarter of the first year (Ainsworth, 1963).

Attachment is a two-way process. Attachment behavior between mother and infant consolidates the affectional relationship. In studying the interaction of twenty-eight babies with their mothers, Ainsworth (1964) catalogued thirteen patterns of attachment besides those associated with feeding—the rooting response, sucking, and search for the breast. On the infant's side, the thirteen include differential crying, smiling and vocalizing, visual-motor orientation, crying when the mother left, following, scrambling, burying the face, exploring from a secure base, clinging, lifting the arms and clapping the hands in greeting, and approaching through locomotion.

Preference for the mother is not present at birth; it must develop out of the feeding and caring experience. The infant's earliest posture is one of undiscriminating responsiveness. In the first few weeks of life it can be assumed that the infant experiences the mother, and particularly her breast, as part of itself (Spitz, 1962). The first few weeks of life can be characterized as an around-the-clock time of sleep alternating with waking periods in which the infant's contact with the mother is directed by hunger rather than by any other drive or appetite. But the mother and the infant are two independent psycho-physiological systems. They interact through specific mechanisms of stimulation and pacification (Segal, 1971, p. 203). In the process, circular social interaction becomes more discriminating, and the relations between the two become numberless and infinitely varied (Spitz, 1962).

Most mothers in the nuclear family do not share the intimate care of their offspring with another adult (although more and more fathers are becoming involved) and are in a position to develop an unusually close relationship with their babies. Caldwell and Hersher (1964) found that such mothers, in contrast to mothers who shared care of the infant with others, were less intellectualized in their relationships with the baby, were more sensuous in their touching and handling, were more likely to vocalize, were more active and more playful with their six-month-old babies. At one year of age they were rated as more dependent upon their babies for the achievement of their own need gratifications. In general, the data suggests a comfortable relationship between infant and mother in the cases in which the mother had exclusive responsibility for the child.

Infants show differing personality traits, strengths in their aggressive instincts, for example. Some are placid. Some are quiet. Some are noisy and active. These temperaments stay with them as they grow (Finch, 1969). There are also male-female behavioral differences present at birth, though research findings are still sparse (Korner, 1973). The male infant has greater muscular strength at birth, but the female is in no way less active or expressive. The female infant from birth shows more oral sensitivity, engages in more frequent mouth-dominated approaches, and is a more frequent and more persistent thumb-sucker. Newborn females also exhibit greater cutaneous sensitivity than do males.

Parents treat male and female infants differently right from the start, hence there is constant parental reinforcement, not only of innate differences but also of differences in what society regards as gender-appropriate behavior. In other words, the infant's unique male or female characteristics, as well as cultural expectations, may affect the nature of parent-infant interaction from the day of birth and onward. Moss (Segal, 1971) found, for instance, that mothers had significantly more contact with infant boys than with girls on such variables as "attends" and "stimulates-arouses."

Infants also can be divided into two categories based on the extent to which they seek close personal contacts—noncuddlers and cuddlers. (Schaffer and Emerson, 1964b). Noncuddlers reach this developmental stage somewhat later than do cuddlers. Noncuddlers show displeasure at being restricted and contained from the early weeks, initially through restlessness. At nine or ten months, when they can crawl or walk away, resistance to handling becomes still more pronounced. This does not mean the noncuddlers show a lack of orientation toward the mother; she is still treated as a "haven of safety" and when frightened, the noncuddler seeks her proximity. Their means of establishing proximity is, however, different from that of cuddlers. Instead of the close physical contact which other infants seek, the noncuddler either makes visual contact with its mother, establishes a physical contact such as holding onto her skirt, or hides his or her face against her knee. Apparently it is not contact per se that is avoided by noncuddlers but the restriction of movement involved in cuddling and holding. In motor development the noncuddlers are ahead of the cuddlers, reaching such milestones as the ability to sit unsupported, to stand holding on, and to crawl, considerably sooner than the cuddlers.

Resistance to close physical contact does not appear to be primarily a social phenomenon but an expression of an innate, more general aspect of the infant's personality. Nor is the noncuddling pattern bad; it is not a deterrent to development.

Since the encounters with mother in the normal course of infant-mother relations are numberless and infinitely varied, each requires a different adaptive response. Self-stimulation in the form of thumb-sucking has been observed prenatally. The first somato-sensory encounter of the newborn infant and mother is the birth experience itself. Male babies are sometimes born with erections; whether this is due to internal stimulation or the birth experience itself has not been determined. It is reasonable to assume that it is in part due to the tactile stimulation of the birth experience. It is now understood that although the birth experience may result in some pain for both mother and infant, some mothers have reported erotic experience during the delivery, including sexual climax (Ziegler and Rodgers, 1968, p. 186).

The major tactile and potentially erotic encounter between infant and mother is the sucking relationship. The mechanisms of sucking are simple. The infant is born with a sucking reflex which is stimulated by the touch of an object on the cheek or lips. The infant turns its head toward the object (in this case the nipple), opens its lips, and starts to suck when the nipple is placed in the mouth. Though sucking is a reflex action, practice helps. As the control of neck muscles improves, the infant becomes more and more efficient at getting into place and finding the nipple (Sears and others, 1957, pp. 64, 66).

The sucking encounter is a cooperative venture of infant and mother. From the infant's side, behavior problems can occur because of inefficient sucking, apparent dislike of nursing, and lack of responsiveness. The infant can be fickle and demanding. The situation has to be "right" or the infant may refuse to participate. Robinson observed that many infants whose mothers fed them strictly by the clock refused "point-blank" to take the breast after the age of three months and had to be bottle-fed (Robinson, 1968, p. 123). The breast was not refused if the mother was "easy-going" and fed her infant by "instinct" rather than by the clock. On the other hand, scheduling infrequent feedings causes the breast to become too full, so that when nursing begins the milk may spurt out and choke the infant. This interference with the infant's breathing, although only temporary, may instill fear or ambivalence toward the nursing process. Ejection-reflex failures also are related to the infant's dislike of breast feeding, since it responds to a consistent supply of milk. Breast feeding is significantly more successful when the amount of milk obtained from one feeding to another does not fluctuate (Newton and Newton, 1967, p. 1182). Active, satisfied infants establish the sucking reflex and rhythm quickly and seek the nipple when it is withdrawn. The satisfaction received is likely to increase the infant's desire to suckle its mother frequently and fully, thus stimulating the secretion of milk. The reaction of older infants is even more pronounced than that of newborn infants. The total body may show alertness and motion—rhythmic motions of hands, fingers, feet, and toes along with the rhythm of sucking. After feeding, there is a relaxation that has been compared to the relaxation characteristic of the conclusion of satisfactory sexual response (Newton and Newton, 1967).

Though the sucking experience may give the infant pleasure, especially orally, and though penile erections are observed in conditions related to the sucking experience, we must be cautious in attributing penile erections to stimulation resulting from the sucking experience. In some cases it may be so, but in others it is not. It has been reported that vigorous sucking by active infants is accompanied by penile erection which may last throughout the sucking period and continue for several minutes after the breast is removed (Baliassnikova and

Model, as reported in Halverson, 1940; and Newton and Newton, 1967). On the other hand, Halverson (1940) from his experiments on infant sucking, reports that although infants like to suck at the breast, preferring it to the bottle, penile erection never occurred during sucking at the breast. It is possible that the experiment itself served to deter from the full pleasurable response, since during this period the breast-fed infants lay on the mother's lap while the mother leaned forward so that her breast was above the baby's mouth. To remove the nipple from the infant's mouth the mother merely assumed an upright position. In other words, the stimulation was severely restricted, being limited to the presence of the nipple in the infant's mouth. No caressing, no fondling by the mother, no eye-to-eye contact, no opportunity for the infant to touch the mother's face, to place its fingers in her mouth apparently existed. The question left unanswered is how many of these infant boys would have responded with penile erections under normal nursing conditions. Some older infants in the Halverson experiment thumped the nipple vigorously with the tongue and rolled it about in the mouth in what Halverson regarded as purely playful activity, but these things occurred only with bottle feeding; none of the breast-fed babies exhibited this reaction. Halverson concluded that so-called pleasure-sucking activities have little or no connection with penile erection. Penile erection did occur during the observation period but never while sucking at the breast. Instead, erection occurred when infants encountered a difficult or irritating situation. Halverson interprets the erections as related to abdominal pressure, for when thwarting was introduced (such as removing the nipple or giving the infant a difficult nipple) the resulting movements were conspicuously characterized by severe contractions of the abdominal walls. Although other motor patterns varied during the onset of penile erection, marked abdominal pressure was always present. The fact that marked abdominal pressure is probably the most effective stimulus for penile erection, as observed in the Halverson experi-

ment, does not rule out other possible stimulants, such as the stimulation received in a normal satisfying nursing experience.

The mother's physiological responses to sucking and coitus are very similar. Uterine contractions occur during sucking as they do during sexual stimulation. Nipple erection occurs during both (Masters and Johnson, 1966). Milk ejection has been observed to occur in both, and the degree of milk ejection appears to be related to the degree of erotic response. The nipple-erection reflex may lead to more efficient nursing, increasing the satisfaction for the sucking infant as well as for the mother. Marked breast stimulation occurring during sucking or through fondling and caressing induces orgasms in some women.

Mothers who choose to suckle their babies have a higher general level of sexual interest than do nonsuckling, postpartum women. This is borne out in two studies in which mothers who suckled their babies were compared with those who did not (Sears, Maccoby, and Levin, 1957, p. 74; Masters and Johnson, 1966, pp. 161–63). Mothers with positive attitudes toward suckling gave more milk and were more successful in breast feeding than those with negative feelings. Uteri of suckling mothers returned to normal size sooner. Many mothers (25% in one study) felt erotic arousal during suckling—to the point of orgasm for a few of them. Suckling mothers not only reported erotic stimulation from the suckling experience, they were interested in as rapid a return to coitus as possible. Suckling mothers engaged in coitus sooner after birth than did nonsuckling mothers. They were more interested in sex and placed more importance on the exchange of affection with others than did mothers who chose to bottle-feed their babies. Suckling mothers were also more tolerant toward erotic behavior of their offspring, such as masturbation and sex play with others (Sears and others, 1957, p. 549).

Some of the mothers experienced fear of a perverted sexual interest from the amount of eroticism stimulated by the nursing process, and several nonnursing mothers who had nursed previous babies refused to nurse again because of concern and guilt over their erotic feelings. If the husband felt that nursing was disgusting or harmful, it discouraged many women from nursing, and they had little erotic interest for months. Ironically, these men were denied sex relations longer than if their wives had suckled their babies. The closeness and the pleasurable feelings from the relationship in the long run may benefit infant, mother, and husband, too.

Not only the amount but also the nature of stimulation between the infant and mother is important. When the infant is suckling, it reciprocates by putting fingers into the mother's mouth; she responds by moving her lips on the baby's fingers. The baby moves its fingers; she responds with a smile. All the while the baby studies her face with rapt attention (Spitz, 1949, p. 291). Infants pat the mother's breast while sucking, pat her face, turn a cheek to be kissed, clasp her around the neck, lay a cheek on hers, hug, and bite. "Such little scenes can be observed in endless variations in any mother-child couple" (Spitz, 1949, p. 291). Some of the expressions of affection through patting and hugging may be spontaneous, while others are learned in the infant's encounters with mother and other adults (Shirley, 1933).

If a responsive woman is the mother of a noncuddling infant, there is considerable challenge to her adaptability, as with a cuddly baby and a nonresponsive mother. Some mothers make it clear that breast feeding is at best a duty and is not physically nor emotionally pleasurable. If the suckling experience seems unworthy or shameful to her, the mother may not be able to acknowledge it or may feel the need to find acceptable excuses. In the United States, illness or physical inadequacy are commonly accepted as "good" reasons for not suckling infants.

In contemporary American culture, the breasts play a more prominent part in the erotic encounters of adults than they do in suckling experiences with infants. In societies in which suckling is generally accepted, infant-mother separation is not easily tolerated by either participant. In speaking to Ganda women, Ains-worth (1963) relates that a number of mothers said they enjoyed breast feeding, and one confessed with embarrassment that it was so satisfactory to her that though her child was over twelve months of age she was reluctant to wean him. Matthews, in describing the infant-mother sensory contact among the Yorubas of Nigeria (as reported in Newton and Newton, 1967), reports that a strict breast-feeding routine would be difficult to attain because the mothers, determined and obstinate, were not easily separated from their babies for long. The baby remains from birth until about the second year of life almost constantly in close physical contact with the mother who feeds it at irregular intervals, usually determined by the infant's crying.

Among the Dahomey, mothers regularly carry their infants about with them, and the infants seldom have other nurses. Close bodily contact and suckling are continued for two to three years. There is no cohabiting between husband and wife during this period if the man has other wives (Herskovits, 1952, p. 259). To what extent the infant becomes a "lover" surrogate in such long absences from marital coitus is a moot question. Infant and mother frequently stay in continuously close sensory contact in many societies characterized by late weaning.

Besides the suckling encounters, in a few primitive societies adults participate actively in the erotic stimulation of infants and young children. Among the Kazak, adults who are playing with small children, especially boys, excite the young one's genitals by rubbing and playing with them. Autogenital stimulation by the young child is accepted also as a normal practice (Ford and Beach, 1951, p. 188). Among the Balinese, playing and teasing with the genitals is common. A mother will pat her baby girl on the vulva and exclaim, "Pretty! Pretty!" (Bateson and Mead, 1942, pp. 26, 32, 131). A boy's penis will be stroked and rubbed. After he has urinated, he will be dried by a flick of his penis. As he grows older, his penis will be pulled and stretched and ruffled, and often he will attempt to keep his balance when learning to walk by holding on to it. Babies are comforted and quieted by manipulating the genital organs. In fact, in Bali, a baby, especially a baby's genitals, are toys with which to play. There is much delight taken in stimulating and playing with the baby to watch it respond.

There has been a strong taboo in the United States on suckling an infant in public or even on including photographs in magazines of infants suckling, whereas bottle feeding in public and pictures of bottle-feeding infants are acceptable. In America, a young mother often starts suckling her infant without having once observed another woman suckling an infant. Lactation failure, or the inability to suckle infants, fluctuates greatly over short periods of time, suggesting that it is triggered by psychological rather than by physiological factors. For instance, national surveys indicate that the rate of breast-feeding infants in the United States fell by almost half during a ten-year period. Likewise, during twenty years in Bristol, England, the number of three-month-old breast-fed infants dropped from seventy-seven to thirty-six percent. In an obstetric clinic in France the proportion of babies not suckled increased from thirty-one to fifty-one percent in five years. This change is so rapid that it cannot be attributed to hereditary factors and major physiological changes in function would be unlikely in the absence of radical stresses such as starvation or epidemic disease (Newton and Newton, 1963).

It is reasonable to assume that there is in the United States a preoccupation with words and articulated culture rather than with touch. There has been a prudery and anxiety about physical contact and erotic matters. With this assumption in mind, Clay (1968) observed the behavior of forty-five children and their mothers at three public beaches patronized by persons of different social classes. One of the patterns he observed was the lack of contact between infant and mother on the beach. The majority of encounters between infant and mother were of two kinds: first, taking care of the infants and, second, controlling their behavior. Far less frequent were intimate contacts expressing love and attachment. Parents rewarded "desexual-ized" motor performance that kept the infant away from the mother. Girl children received more physical touches than did boys, and they were in physical contact with their mothers longer than were the boys. For mothers of young children, having a good time at the beach did not appear to include mothers enjoying their offspring in a direct, personal, affective, tactile, and sensual encounter. Upper- and working-class mothers were more inclined to comfort their children with tactile contacts; middle-class mothers offered distractions, mostly food. Middle-class mothers seemed more interested in meeting friends at the beach than in relating to their children. Small children were expected to play alone away from the parents. These observations and conclusions, however, must be regarded as suggestive rather than definitive.

An area of infant-adult encounter with great potential for educating the child in sexual matters is toilet training. There are important adult values, attitudes, and behavior patterns which the infant learns in connection with toilet training. In the United States, one of these is the value placed on cleanliness. The infant is expected to keep itself and its clothes from being soiled when it urinates or defecates. Waste matter must go into the proper container, and the child must "wipe" itself so that no spots or odors remain. The mother may instruct the child to wash its hands after urinating or defecating to get rid of the "germs." Children's attitudes of disgust toward the texture, color, and odor of feces develop only after socialization by a parent who expresses such attitudes (Sears and others, 1957, pp. 106–7).

In looking for relationships between toilet-training patterns and the mother's sexual anxiety or strictness toward control of sexual behavior, Sears (Sears and others, 1957, p. 111) found that toilet training and control of sexual behavior were frequently linked by the mothers. If eliminating had sexual implications for mothers, one can hypothesize that her degree of sexual anxiety might influence her toilet-training patterns. The assumption is all the more reasonable since high sexual anxiety has been found to be associated with the decision not to suckle. If the mother had sexual anxiety over toilet training, she might consciously or unconsciously try to get it over with as early and as quickly as possible.

Mothers who chose to start toilet training before the infant was five months old had the lowest average rating on a sexual permissiveness scale. That is, they expressed strong rejection of sex and strict attitudes about prohibiting sexual play in their children. This tendency was more pronounced among the mothers of girl infants than among boy infants.[1] Early starts on training tended to require longer periods for completion than late starts, yet the mothers who started early and had high sexual anxiety completed the task more rapidly than did those with low sexual anxiety who started later. The difference was statistically significant (Sears and others, 1957, p. 112). The evidence seems clear that the mother's level of sexual anxiety—her strictness of attitude toward sex—played some role in her decision to start toilet training at an early age and to complete it quickly. Mothers who were tolerant of the infant's dependent behavior were also warmer toward the child, gentler about toilet training, lower in their use of physical punishment for aggression toward parents, and higher in esteem for both self and husband (Sears and others, 1957, p. 166).

Has there been any change in permissiveness in mothers, and has there been any increase or decrease in infant-mother intimacy over the years? The evidence is indirect and superficial at best. Several students of child behavior have examined the child guidance literature and report a change in attitudes (Stendler, 1950; Sears and others, 1957, pp. 9–10; Gordon, 1968). The 1890s and 1900s were characterized by a highly sentimental approach to child rearing as demonstrated in popular periodicals; 1910 through the 1930s saw a rigid, disciplinary approach; and the 1940s emphasized self-regulation and

understanding of the child. Over the sixty years there was a swing from emphasis on character development to emphasis on personality development. In the 1914 edition of *Infant Care,* masturbation by infants was treated very severely. It was thought that masturbation would "wreck" a person for life, and it was to be stopped by tying the infant's limbs to opposite sides of the crib. In subsequent editions there was a fairly continuous decline in the degree of severity recommended. By the 1951 edition of *Infant Care* masturbation was treated as a rather petty nuisance that might be ignored. Along with permissiveness went a distinct devaluing of the satisfaction a child gets from such stimulation. For thumb-sucking, the curve of severity also showed a distinct decline. In fact, by the 1940s, instructions regarding the handling of the infant in all areas became very gentle. This tendency continued and was carried further in later editions. By 1963, parents were counseled to treat masturbation casually.

INFANT-INFANT SEXUAL ENCOUNTERS

Infant-infant sexual encounters are fairly uncommon, partly because of the infant's lack of mobility. However, the older infant who is one or two years of age and old enough to crawl or walk is capable of initiating various encounters. It was reported of Louis XIII's carefully observed permissive infancy, for instance, that "he throws down little Marguerite, kisses her, throws himself on her . . ." (as reported in Hunt, 1970, p. 167). The Israeli kibbutz is a setting which allows for intimate encounters (Kaffman, 1972). The kevutza is a bisexual children's peer group that has common living and sleeping quarters—boys and girls who are one through five years of age sleep in the same room, shower together, go to the toilet together, and often run around together before getting dressed in the morning or after being undressed in the evening. Intimate encounters include different activities. In a group of children with a mean age of two years, it was found that the most frequent expression consisted in a simple embrace of one child by another, fol-

[1] Rejection of the suckling infant also may be selective by sex. In a Swedish study (Dahlstrom, p. 65) of eighteen families, girl babies were suckled on an average of only three months after birth; boy babies were suckled for an average of six months.

lowed in frequency by stroking or caressing, kissing, and touching the genitals (Spiro, 1958, p. 221). In some previously unpublished data, Kinsey records instances of cuddling and kissing encounters between infants two years of age or less.

Infant Encounters with Children and Adolescents

Infant encounters with children (three to seven years old) do occur, but they have not been systematically observed or if observed they have not been recorded. Kinsey observed in some of his unpublished interviews that embracing and kissing among young siblings is much in evidence. It is reasonable to speculate that such behavior is not uncommon in unsupervised intimate play of siblings within the family.

Survey data on the infant's sexual encounters with preadolescents and adolescents is also sparse, though isolated cases are frequently reported in the psychoanalytic literature. This should not be understood as implying that such encounters do not occur among infants and children not referred for treatment. For example, in a recent survey of a large, self-selected United States sample of adults, approximately three hundred (one percent of the females and two percent of the males) reported that they had had their first sexual intercourse with a relative (Athanasiou, Shaver, and Tavis, 1970). If this is true of coitus, intimacy among young siblings, short of incest, can be assumed to be much more prevalent. No researcher has systematically studied such encounters, however, and in a sexually repressive society adolescents and preadolescents are careful not to be caught in such play.

Results of Infant Sexual-Affectional Encounters

An infant will not form intimate relationships with anyone if no one forms intimate relationships with him or her (Landreth, 1967). In the first eighteen months of life, autoerotic activity, in the form of genital play, has been shown to be an indicator of whether or not the infant is having adequate affectional encounters with others. If the infant-mother encounters are positive and at a maximum, infants engage in autoerotic activities occasionally when by themselves. Among children reared in families, Spitz (1949) found that sixteen out of seventeen infants manifested genital play within the first year, at ages which were on the average two months earlier than those of infants cared for in nurseries. If intimate encounters were inadequate, rocking—rhythmic movements back and forth or from side to side commonly in a sitting position and commonly involving head banging —results. When personal encounters are normal, genital play results. If the encounters between mother and infant were "optimal" in the first year of life, genital play was present in all cases, and general development surpassed that of the average infant in all respects. If the encounters between mother and infant were problematic, genital play was much rarer, and other activities tended to replace it. Finally, when infant-mother encounters were absent, genital play was completely missing. These findings support the assumption that during the first year of life, autoerotic activities vary with the nature of the relationship between the infant and those with whom it has intimate, affectional encounters.

Prescott (1969, 1972) hypothesizes that it is reasonable to assume that affectional deprivation can have neurobiological consequences produced by the absence of physical touching. Neurostructural, neurochemical, and neuroelectrical measurements document abnormal development and functions of the sensory system resulting from sensory deprivation during the formative periods (Prescott, 1972). Infants deprived of touch—holding, caressing, fondling— exhibit more than their share of violent-aggressive behavior and social-emotional disorders in later years (Prescott, September 8, 1970).

Prescott and McKay (1973) reason that human societies characterized by enrichment or impoverishment of the stimulation that comes from touching during the formative years of development would produce predominantly peaceful or violent adult behavior. In an ingenious though at best partial test of the hypotheses, Prescott and McKay examined published data on forty-nine societies. It was assumed that high, physical, intimate affection would presage permissive and tolerant sexual behavior in adulthood, and that low, physical, intimate affection would produce punitive and repressive sexual behavior in adulthood. The data, however, did not indicate a significant relationship between early infant affection and later permissive sexuality.

Prescott and McKay returned to the data and asked if it could be possible that deprivation of affection imposed during the later formative period (denial of the right to premarital intercourse, for example) contributed to high adult violence despite the presence of high infant affection. In an examination of seven societies that did not provide a high level of infant affection and yet had a record of low adult violence, all freely permitted premarital sexual behavior. Prescott and McKay suggest that the effects of early affectional deprivation might be compensated for by adolescent affectional permissiveness. According to Prescott and McKay, premarital sexual relations may constitute an effective prophylactic against later destructive and violent interpersonal behavior. When both early (infant) and later (adolescent) affectional permissiveness or the lack of it were considered together, it was possible to predict accurately adult interpersonal behavior in forty-seven of the forty-nine societies studied. Prescott and McKay conclude that this data validates the effects of affectional enrichment or deprivation on human behavior. The data also indicate that a two-stage developmental theory of affectional stimulation, the first in infancy and the second in adolescence, is necessary to account accurately for the development and expression of peaceful or destructive-violent interpersonal behavior in adulthood.

Affectional-sexual development, in comparison with other aspects of development, motor and language, for example, has been more often repressed than encouraged by most families in the United States and throughout most of the Western world. In the United States, sex is seldom treated as a strong and healthy force in the positive development of personality (Ribble, 1955). Infant sexual behavior, in the eyes of many, is negative, perverse, and destructive. Some see infant sexual-affectional potential as related to excesses—addictions that control the individual and weaken reason. That infants have erotic capacity has been pointedly ignored or overlooked. After an asexual infancy and childhood, sex is supposed to burst out in full bloom at puberty or, better, later. Sexual innocence has been assumed to be normal and appropriate. Still earlier, infants were considered depraved if they masturbated, asked sex-related questions, or showed any sexual interest or curiosity. Ignorance was and is deemed best to keep dormant any precocious sexual feelings. It has been taken for granted that other aspects of physical and mental growth would proceed gradually from birth to full maturity, but knowledge about sexual capacity and interest has been either consciously or unconsciously suppressed even in the community of social and behavioral scientists. This is an enigma, for as early as the turn of the century, Bell (1902), Freud (1905), and Moll (1909) were reporting that in infants of suckling age, various parts of the body could give pleasurable sensation and romances did develop in childhood, and it was known that "unscrupulous nurses" had found that they could calm crying babies by stroking their genitals. Freud observed that sexual behavior of the infant and child not only was ignored but "the educators consider all sexual manifestations of the child as an 'evil' in the face of which little can be accomplished" (Freud, 1962, p. 41). To find sexuality suppressed in the schools is perhaps understandable; to find it largely overlooked in the behavioral and social sciences is more difficult to understand and to accept.

What would be the outcome of a concerted effort to give infants the opportunity to develop fully their capacity for sensory and affectional response? We do not know because we have not wanted to know. Those who argue that the individual, to be fully human, must have the opportunity to develop all his or her capacities argue that this principle should apply to sexual capacity as well as to intellect and motor skills. Those who argue for discipline, self-control, and the curbing of harmful or socially disruptive human tendencies, argue that only the minimum of stimulation and no erotic experience should characterize the personal encounters of infants. Those who opt for restriction of erotic expression in infancy and childhood are in the majority in the United States at the present time.

EARLY CHILDHOOD (3—8 YEARS)

The early childhood years (here defined as ages three through eight) witness a marked intensification of sexual interest (Group, 1965, p. 137), and capacity for erotic response. Kinsey reports (1948, p. 176) an increase in the percentage of individuals able to reach a sexual climax, from thirty-two percent of boys two to twelve months of age, and fifty-seven percent of those two to five years of age, to nearly eighty percent of preadolescent boys ten to thirteen years of age. The genitals supercede other organs as a main source of bodily pleasure. The Child Study Association of America in its publication "When Children Ask About Sex," (1969) treats sex play as so integral to childhood as to say that masturbation is a necessary phase of sex maturing, and that parents would do well to think of masturbation as part of the growing up process instead of as a dangerous habit.

In interviewing three- and four-year-olds and their parents, Kinsey found that at three they were showing awareness of genital differences between male and female. Handling of their own genitals, cuddling, kissing mother and father, touching, and kissing others were common. Three-year-olds enjoyed a great deal of kissing. Among four-year-olds there was kissing, some homosexual and heterosexual play, mild masturbation, cuddling with family members, touching, and tickling. According to Bell (1902) relationships between the sexes or the "emotion

of sex-love" may appear in the life of the child as early as the middle of the third year. The presence of the emotion in children between three and eight years of age is characterized by "hugging, kissing, lifting each other, scuffling, sitting close to each other; confessions to each other and excluding others, grief at being separated; giving of gifts, extending courtesies to each other that are withheld from others, making sacrifices such as giving up desired things or foregoing pleasures; jealousies, etc."

In American society, at four years of age the child shows interest in sex questions pertaining to where babies come from and how babies get out of their mothers. The attitudes they find associated with elimination and the genital area as a portion of the excretory rather than reproductive system are influential in the period following toilet training. The game of "show" is common and often contains verbal play about elimination. Interest in other people's bathrooms is high, and while the child may demand privacy for itself, the four-year-old child is extremely interested in the bathroom activities of others. Under social stresses the young child reacts by grasping the genitals and experiencing a need to urinate.

Five-year-old American children commonly behave in ways quite contrary to those demonstrated only one year earlier. They appear to be more self-contained, serious about themselves, and impressed with their ability to imitate grown-up behavior. Their interests lie in immediate experiences. They are more realistic than younger children, undertaking those things they know they can do. An interest in babies in general, as well as an interest in having a baby of one's own is present and may be dramatized. Both boys and girls relate to when they were in mother's stomach or to the future when they will have a baby of their own. Despite this interest in pregnancy, they often do not make the connection between the appearance of a pregnant woman and the presence of a baby. Sex play and games of "show" decrease in frequency at this age as children become more modest and less apt to expose themselves. Less bathroom play and interest in strange bathrooms is characteristic of five year olds. They are familiar with, but not as much interested in, the physical differences between the sexes, although they may wonder as to why the father does not have breasts or a sister does not have a penis. In play, boy-girl pairs occur frequently. Domestic play continues with imitative attempts at playing house, store, and hospital. Boys may reject girls' roles but still take part in house play, imitating adult male activities. Dolls are given roles as babies and cared for appropriately, especially by girls (Gesell and Ilg, 1946, pp. 320, 323, 367).

At six years there are a greater awareness of and interest in the differences between sexes in body structure. Questioning and mutual investigation by both sexes reveal practical answers to questions about sex differences. Interest in the origin of babies, pregnancy, and birth continues. If the child is told of intercourse by older playmates, it may question its mother about it. The six-year-old commonly accepts the idea that the baby grows in the mother's stomach and starts from a seed. The six-year-old has some sort of vague notion that in sequence babies commonly follow marriage. How the baby comes out of the mother's stomach and whether it hurts are favorite topics for questions. The six-year-old wants a new baby in the family and wants to hold it after it is born. Mild sex play or exhibitionism in play or in school toilets occurs. Simultaneously, one finds frequent name-calling and giggling about words dealing with the elimination function. Games of "show" and hospital (in which rectal temperatures are taken) are common. Some children are subjected to sex play by older children and some six-year-old girls are bothered by older men. Strong interest by older boys in younger girls begins to appear among the children themselves. Some confusion in the differentiation of the male and female exists. The child may dress up in the attire of the opposite sex but when thinking of marriage, the child thinks in terms of a person of the opposite sex, often a relative. Domestic play continues with games of house, school, and library. Girls, reared in the traditional ways, enjoy elaborated doll play with dolls' accessories as well as dressing up in adult clothes (Gesell and Ilg, 1946, p. 320, 323, 324, 368; Ilg and Ames, 1955, p. 204).

At seven years some mutual exploration, experimentation, and sex play continues but in some aspects less than earlier. Intimate behavior, including coitus, can occur but is not generally permissible in American society outside some "counter-culture" communes and other "liberated" groups (Berger, Deischer, and Johnson; Martinson, 1977). Any interest in male-female differences is more apt to relate to the sex roles of boys and girls rather than to physical differences. The topic of birth is still quite popular. Seven-year-olds seem satisfied to know that babies come from two seeds, one from the father and one from the mother. They associate the appearance of pregnant women with the presence of a baby and ask details of birth. Where the mother will be at time of delivery and how the baby gets out are frequent questions. Intense longing for a new baby in the family is usually for one of the same sex and a mother's pregnancy is met with excitement. The baby's growth, how it is fed, its size, and how much it costs all are questions raised. Meanwhile, the seven-year-old's world is broadening and includes his or her place in the social and physical world. Seven-year-olds are ashamed of their fears, mistakes, and tears. They are self-conscious about their own bodies and sensitive about body exposure. They may not like to be touched and have become quite modest about using the toilet. Strong and persistent boy-girl love affairs with the idea of marriage occur. Among traditionally reared children, play activities center on playing house with the use of elaborate adult costumes for girls, while boys enjoy building and playing in tree houses, forts, huts, and tents (Gesell and Ilg, 1946, p. 320, 324, 368; Ilg and Ames, 1955, p. 204).

Masturbation is common during childhood, but not all children between the ages of three and seven masturbate. We have no accurate count as to the number who do, nor the frequency for those who do. Based on data from pre-1955 interviews conducted with boys (upper-white-collar class) with an average age of 7.2 years (age range was 4 to 14 years), Elias and Gebhard (1969) report that thirty-eight percent reported having masturbated, with more beginning in the three to seven-year-age range than at any subsequent time. Miller and Swanson (1958) asked parents if, at or before age five, their children had "touched" their sex organs. About fifty-eight percent of the mothers said that they had not, while some thirty-four percent said that they had. In the Sears study (Sears, Maccoby, and Levin, 1957, p. 200), only two-fifths of the mothers said that they had never noticed their children doing anything that could be referred to as masturbation. In a study of 284 boys, Ramsey reports that five percent in the age group six or less had had masturbatory experience, and ten percent of those seven-year-olds (Ramsey, 1943, p. 224).

Touching or holding the genitals is not necessarily associated with erotic pleasure; it appears to be a source of security for some infants when learning to walk or doing other things.

The child's initial attempt at masturbation often is inspired by the observation of other children engaging in such activity or through deliberate instruction given by some older child or adult. According to Kinsey, these are the first sources of information for most males (Kinsey, 1953, p. 107). The great majority of females who masturbate, on the other hand, learn to masturbate by discovering by themselves the possibility of such activity.

Often siblings, close to each other in age, engage in sex play with each other. This is most likely to be true when they share a bedroom, and the rate is higher when they share the same bed (Finch, 1969, p. 65). Cuddling, fondling, and handling the genitals of others of the same or opposite sex occurs frequently during unsupervised play. Other forms of sexual activity occasionally include oral-genital contacts and attempted copulation with another child. If begun early, masturbation may continue at varying intervals throughout childhood. The child learns that in our society masturbation is not done in public.

Erotic awakening is of two kinds, autoerotic and sociosexual or interpersonal erotic. Since Freud and Kinsey, if not before, we have been aware that autoeroticism—erotic gratification obtained from the self without the participation of another person—can be present from the first year of life. Interpersonal awakening comes at different ages for different persons depending on biological-response capacity and maturation, temperamental tendencies (cuddler or noncuddler, for instance), and experience.

Erotic awakening is a vague and mystical concept. What it means is that someone who previously lacked the capacity for erotic experience now possesses that capacity. One has "new life" so to speak; something is there that was not there before. Puberty is sometimes looked upon as establishing the biological-response base for the first erotic event. But we know that the capacity for at least the rudiments of erotic awakening is present from birth or shortly thereafter. Erotic awakening comes when that which is "dormant" or "asleep" is aroused to action. The experience may be feeding at the breast of the mother, being handled or caressed at a tender age, a first kiss, or later "falling in love," first coitus, or first coitus with orgasm. Some parents consciously or unconsciously treat their offspring as though the erotic capacity were present from birth, as indeed it is. Such parents act as though what they do to and with the infant or child will affect the time at which they experience their erotic awakening and that after awakening they will in fact be different. This belief no doubt explains much of the style of infant and child care that mothers give their offspring, starting with the decision to suckle or not to suckle the infant.

Besides direct erotic encounters with peers, there are many events which stimulate the growth of sexual curiosity and aid in sexual awakening of the infant or child. Among these events are the presence of a puppy in the home, seeing a litter of kittens for the first time, seeing members of the family in the nude, noticing the differences in men's and women's bodily characteristics, seeing the changes that occur in a pregnant woman, the presence of a new baby, or a chance bit of information concerning the coming of babies or other sexual events.

Despite such apparent sexual precocity, children aged three to four have some difficulty learning that there are genital differences between the sexes. They do not appear to form clear concepts of genital differences until ages five to seven. From a sample of children mostly from a lower socioeconomic level, whose parents indicated that many of them had not been told about basic anatomical differences, Conn (1940), and Conn and Kanner (1947), were able to elicit knowledge of genital differences from only fifty percent of children ages four to six years and from seventy-two percent of children ages seven to eight. Among children of parents with more formal education, Butler (1952) found a similar degree of ignorance among children of four to five years of age. Although fifteen of seventeen children had been informed by their parents of anatomical differences, Butler was able to elicit awareness of genital differences from only five of the fifteen children. Ketcher (1955) found in a study of 226 three- to nine-year-olds that children most easily make sex differentiations based on the clothing worn by each sex, followed by differentiation based on hair styles, and lastly by observing differences in genitalia and breasts. Age seemed to be the most important factor in ability to differentiate between the sexes, and younger girls were better than younger boys in this regard. Children report that before their first witnessing they had assumed that the genitals of all people were alike.

The young child who has been told which male and female attributes are used in producing a baby still remains perplexed as to how the elements come together (Conn, 1948). Even children who have observed parental coitus do not find this sufficient to create an articulated sexual image of the mother or father, whatever else it might do (Gagnon, 1965).

By age five, children are easily aware of most of the noncoital content of the marital relationship—cooking, cleaning house, caring for children, going to work. They practice many of the marriage and family roles through "playing house." They also have a good idea of the field of future eligible mates, opposite-sex peers of the same generation but not of the same family (Broderick, 1966). Broderick found that the majority of five-year-olds he studied were already committed to their own eventual marriages. This majority increases through each age group throughout childhood.

SEXUAL ENCOUNTERS WITH PEERS IN EARLY CHILDHOOD

We now turn to a systematic account of a young child's sexual and erotic encounters, first of all with peers and later with preadolescents, adolescents, and adults. Many children "experiment" with one another sexually. Approximately half of the mothers in the Sears study (1957) reported some activity that could be identified as sex play. Some play was between brothers and sisters, some with neighbor children, some with children of the same sex, and some with the opposite sex. This exploration is often carried to what could be dangerous extremes, such as the insertion of unclean or rusty objects into body orifices. "Doctor games" are popular, serving as an excuse for examining the sex organs of the child's playmates (Hurlock, 1950, p. 493). It would be wrong to assume that all of the activity in "playing doctor" such as taking temperatures rectally is erotic play. It would also be wrong to assume that all children who play doctor are erotically awakened. On the other hand, it is clear that "playing doctor" can have erotic overtones beyond the mere desire to play with other children and to satisfy curiosity about the nature of others' genitals. Sex play can produce mixed emotions for the child as he or she tries to understand and sort out feelings of curiosity, fear of the unknown, erotic desire, and even guilt. The child's guilt often is reinforced by the mother or someone else who discovers the children in sex play (Martinson, 1973, pp. 35–36).

It is well known that during childhood, romances sometimes develop between boys and girls. The romance may contain the traditional elements of respect and affection on the part of the boy, accompanied by the desire to serve his beloved. He carries her books to and from school and may protect her from the teasing and torments of other boys. Traditionally reared girls are more tolerant of the romances of other children than are boys. Girls may snicker at and make jokes about the girl who is having a romance, but they do not exclude her from their group, as a boy might be excluded from the boys' gang. There is evidence that girls are envious of the girl who has a boy to accompany her to school and who receives thoughtful attention instead of the annoyances that they have been accustomed to receive from boys (Hurlock, 1950, p. 489).

HOMOSEXUAL ENCOUNTERS WITH PEERS IN EARLY CHILDHOOD

Because caresses sometimes are exchanged with children of both sexes, this behavior could be labeled as bisexual. Actually, during late childhood and early adolescence, sexual play with members of the same sex is probably more common than with members of the opposite sex (Comfort, 1963, p. 42). Homosexual play in childhood includes handling of the genitals of a person of the same sex. In a smaller number of cases it also involves oral or anal contact and occasionally urethral or vaginal insertions (Broderick, 1966). Sometimes homosexual activity takes the form of "show it" such as a group of boys urinating together outdoors. The activity is mildly competitive and perhaps low in erotic intent or satisfaction.

Both heterosexual and homosexual encounters occur in early childhood. The demarcation between what is erotic behavior and what is not is not segregated in the mind of the child as it is in the mind of an adult observer. This could be why children often feel that adults overreact to childhood sex play.

In homosexual encounters, a young child, usually a boy, is frequently propositioned by an older boy. A boy aged seven may suggest sexual activity in which his partner (a boy aged four) is unwilling to cooperate. This can result in the older boy exhibiting himself to his own obvious satisfaction and at least interest by the younger boy.

SEXUAL ENCOUNTERS IN EARLY CHILDHOOD WITH PREADOLESCENTS AND ADOLESCENTS

In sex, as in most other aspects of life, the older teach the younger. In the vast majority of cases such encounters are with someone close to the child, a family member, another relative, a neighbor, or a "babysitter." If the "teaching" is sexual, it most often is fondling or oral relations; attempted intercourse is relatively uncommon (Mohr and others, 1964). If intercourse is attempted, it is often exploratory and becomes part of the initiator's learning experience rather than being purposeful, aggressive, or violent.

Since the preadolescent or adolescent who initiates a sexual encounter with a child is usually known by the child and by the child's parents, he or she does not dare to be too aggressive but feels the need to be devious so as not to be exposed, embarrassed, and perhaps punished.

The need to ejaculate can be very compelling in an adolescent boy who approaches a child. For example, a boy of sixteen was babysitting for a young girl of seven at her home while her parents were out of town. While the girl was taking a bath, with the excuse of making sure that she got clean, the boy stripped and entered the tub. He then proceeded to wash the girl's genitals, and suggested that she do the same to him. After a little protest she obliged. She was surprised when the boy's penis became erect. With urging from her "babysitter," she continued washing and he had an ejaculation.

These different encounters contribute more to a child's sexual knowledge and experience than do physiological readiness or sex interest. Interest in coitus and knowledge and acceptance of premarital coitus is well established among seven-year-old boys in some communities, and in some instances as early as four years old (Kinsey, 1948, p. 377). Much of this sexual sophistication comes from associating with older companions. Children overhear adolescent boys talking to one another about naked women and couples who have had sex relations (Rogler and Hollingshead, 1965, p. 135). The size and shape of a woman's vagina are topics of conversation among boys and men, and younger boys learn from older males that women are objects of sexual gratification. As a consequence, they orient their thoughts and behavior in accordance with what other males expect of them as young, on-the-make *machos*. Kinsey found that the boy from the comparatively sheltered, upper-socioeconomic level home was not exposed to such experiences and was likely to confine his sex play to exhibition and manual manipulation of the genitalia. He does not attempt coitus because, in many instances, he has not learned that there is such a possibility. In spite of their limited contact with coitus or information about coitus, children raised in homes of educated parents have often seen genitalia at an earlier age, primarily because of the greater acceptance of nudity in their homes than in lower-class homes (Kinsey, 1953, p. 112).

Before leaving the subject of sexual encounters of children with preadolescents and adolescents, we must say a little more about fraternal incest, sexual encounters with siblings. If siblings share the same home, in some cases the same room or even the same bed, the possibilities of sexual encounters are always present. They occur even in families in which the children are supervised closely and in which such behavior is not acceptable. Fraternal incest usually stops short of coitus. More often it is limited to disclosure, fondling, or perhaps oral-genital relations.

Most cases of a young child in a sexual encounter with a preadolescent or adolescent could be lumped under an emotionally laden label—child molestation. But when we take a close look at the encounters we find that the content of the interaction is different in each case. To say that a preadolescent or adolescent is "molesting" a younger child is neither a fair nor precise definition in many cases.

SEXUAL ENCOUNTERS WITH PARENTS IN EARLY CHILDHOOD

There are societies, excluding the United States, in which no effort or only limited effort is made to conceal parental sexual encounters from children. Among the Melanesians to whom a certain amount of parental privacy is considered desirable, if a child becomes too curious and bold, it is told to mind its own business and is instructed not to look (Brecher and Brecher, 1966, p. 188). But among the Alorese, by the age of five children are informed of the details of the reproductive act. Members of Pukapukan households sleep in the same room and although parents may wait until the children are asleep, there are opportunities for youngsters to observe adult sexual activity and sexual matters are discussed. Lesu children are free to observe adult coitus, although they are not to watch their own mothers having coitus. On Ponape, children are given instruction in coitus after the fourth or fifth year. Trukese children receive no formal education, but they learn by watching adults at night and by asking their elders about sexual matters (Ford and Beach, 1951, pp. 188–89).

A high proportion of adults in the United States (the Kinsey sample) rather precisely recalled the age at which they had first seen the genitalia of the opposite sex. This, according to Kinsey, emphasizes the importance that the experience has for the child in a culture that has gone to such lengths to conceal the anatomic differences between the sexes. In searching for some characteristic trait that would distinguish nonmarital sexual behavior in primitive societies from that in other societies, Maxwell (1967) looked to differences in the structure of dwellings. He based his work on the thesis that restrictions placed upon contact—the maintenance of social distance—can generate and sustain such awe. He assumed that sex was most likely to be private in societies in which houses had substantial opaque walls.

On the other hand, attitudes toward sex probably would be more casual if people lived in houses made of lattice work or grass or if the houses had no walls. Maxwell made a cross-culture check of his theory using information on wall material and norms of premarital sex behavior for ninety-three societies. The data supported the hypothesis. The more opaque the walls, the stricter the sex norms. Homes in the United States almost always have opaque walls.

The child can be traumatized if he or she has been sheltered and is suddenly exposed to an unusual adult genital-related experience without receiving an adequate explanation of the behavior.

It is quite rare that parents in the United States show sexual and erotic attachment for each other in the presence of their children and in ways which a child can comprehend. As a result children show little awareness of the sexual relationship between their parents. Parents who have good relations with each other are likely to be seen as associates rather than as lovers by their children (Mead and Wolfenstein, 1955). The general taboo on child-parent sexual encounters in the United States makes any specifically sensory-affectional socialization of the child by parents awkward and out of character. This greatly minimizes the amount of intimacy learning that the child receives directly in the home.

Though children in the United States have little opportunity to learn the intimate sexual aspects of sensory-affectional relations from watching their parents, they do base their sexual behavior on general observation of parental behavior and their own experience of affection or the lack of it in interaction with their parents. Bandura and Walters (1963) report that sexually anxious parents have sons who are both guilty about sex and exhibit anxieties about relating dependently to people. Parents of inhibited boys showed a constellation of general emotional inhibition, sex anxiety, and relatively infrequent dependency responses directed toward other adults. Bandura and Walters conclude that social training of sex is accomplished mainly through the transmission to children of parental anxiety reactions to their exploratory, manipulative, and inquisitive behavior. Because of prolonged negative conditioning at home, young people may respond to their initial sexual experiences with anxiety and guilt and especially fear that their parents might learn of their activities.

There are changes taking place, however, and one must not overlook the cases in which extreme reserve and anxiety do not prevail, though these are in the minority. Some parents in the United States do not attempt to mask completely their own sexual activity, and a few even engage in sexual encounters with their own children (Martinson, 1977). Some of the new life styles do not take advantage of the privacy that opaque walls and locked doors can give. It is too soon to know the effects of such upbringing on children in contemporary society since we have no longitudinal research data.

The child's first ideas about marriage are based upon what he or she observes in the parents' behavior and on the encounters with the parents. He or she is aware that emotion and affection are or are not displayed, that sharing does or does not take place, and that thoughtfulness and concern are or are not shown. Later on, he or she seeks to emulate or reject their patterns of behavior. On the other hand, most children do not learn much about sexual behavior even from parents who accept their own sexual activity and enjoy it, if the parents desire privacy and need to keep their sexuality secret from the child (Gagnon, August 1965, p. 225). Children often contribute to the parents' felt need of secrecy by showing disgust or rejection of the sex displays of their parents. Young people often report that any sight of their parents showing affection toward each other embarrassed them as children.

From survey data and from case histories we must conclude that usually whenever a young child in the United States engages verbally or physically in a sexual encounter with a parent, the situation is usually one of conflict rather than accommodation, cooperation, and affection. Most sexual encounters between children and their parents are with the parent not as a participant in the encounter but as an observer of a sexual encounter between the child and a peer. The parent often makes his appearance unexpectedly and puts a stop to the activity (Litin and others, 1956).

The child also learns what the prevailing adult attitudes are toward sex even without parental interference in direct encounters. The tone of voice in which gossip is relayed warns him to avoid becoming a subject for similar gossip. The care and circumlocution with which certain matters of sex are avoided in books, in the press, and in other public communications subtly reminds the child of the state of public opinion on these matters. Discussions of such things as divorce, marital discord, sexual scandals in the community and gossip about public figures probably have more influence in controlling the child's behavior than any specific action that society may take or any legal penalties (Kinsey, 1948, p. 446). Given a framework of repression and avoidance by parents and other adults and by adult-sponsored agencies, the child receives the bulk of its sexual information, though not attitudes, but through peer relationships. The parents do not provide cognitive information about sexuality for the child, but they create attitudes and orientations through which information from other children is filtered (Gagnon, August 1965, p. 223).

Both traditional parents in Western societies with their Victorian morality and parents in some nonliterate societies may repress their children's sexual activity. Susii parents, for instance, do not tolerate their children's sex play, and beat boys and girls for indulging in it. Nevertheless, children find opportunities to escape parental supervision and engage in heterosexuality. Adults are aware that children "in general" do such things, but they become upset on learning that a child of their own has done so. If the parent seems undecided as to what his or her own response should be, the response is commonly ambiguous or it is postponed to some not clearly defined later time.

Likewise, the average child of five or six who has not been openly and positively socialized about sexual matters and who has had an opportunity to observe genital differences, can say that "a boy's sticks out and a girl's doesn't." The child is very reluctant to divulge the name or label by which the organ is known. The name for the organ may be as innocuous as the term "dewdrop," "teddy bear," "dicky bird," "train," or "piece of string." Nevertheless, the child becomes restless, bites his lip, or hangs his head and refuses to speak when he is requested to utter the word which refers to that part of the body. Conn and Kanner (1947) reported no less than sixty-one different names for the sex organs in the vocabularies of two hundred children. Many had two or three terms for the sex organs which they could use interchangeably. Most of these served for both the male and female genitals. The great majority of children had something to say about how bad, naughty, or "not nice" it was to talk about genitality, genitals, to see others undressed, and to be seen in the nude. Sex talk was generally regarded as a great offense. This attitude was especially strong when it came to naming the genitals. A girl six years old said, "That's a bad word." When she was asked why, she said "Because it's really bad." A five-year-old boy said, "A girl has a different thing. I don't want to say it because it might be a bad word."

This phenomenon of not labeling or mislabeling the sex organs and their functions, encouraged by many parents, leaves the child without a vocabulary with which to think properly about or to describe human physical attributes and physical or psychic experiences. Because he or she lacks a definitive sexual vocabulary, it is possible that fantasy will overrun sex life. The mysterious penis that supposedly exists behind the female pubic hair, the feeling that females have been castrated, and other childhood fantasies are possible because there is no naming of parts and functions which could guide the child's nascent interest in its own or other's bodies (Gagnon, 1965). Nevertheless, innocuous misinformation given rationally is apt to have a less negative effect on the child than if the parent handles the situation by going "into a rage."

Generally speaking, the schools have been little better than the parents when it comes to sex education. Ambiguity, misinformation, mislabeling, and excessive idealism often characterize sex instruction in the schools as well as at home. But it is not that simple. Some parents object to sex education in the school, not because it goes "too far" but because it does not go far enough (Athanasiou, and others, 1970). A school principal told me that his school felt that it was being very progressive and was doing the right thing when they told children that every child born is the result of an act of love on the part of the parents. In this case, some progressive parents called in as consultants on the school's sex education curriculum objected to such instruction, pointing out that such instruction was too idealistic.

Sex Questions Children Ask of Parents

If the home atmosphere is sexually repressive, the children do not ask many questions. Conn (1948) reports that twenty-nine percent of 128 boys and thirty percent of 72 girls in one of his studies had inquired about sexual topics. As a group, the more intelligent children offered more questions. But even in superior groups (I.Q. 111–140) the average number of sex inquiries did not rise above two questions for each child. The children (four to six years of age) used such information as they had received at home, and combining this information with their limited experiences, were able to produce naive explanations of, for example, where babies come from. The child of this age thinks of "being born" in such terms as: "the baby is little," "they grow out of the ground," "they grow and then they buy them," "the baby comes from the hospital," "God put 'em in. God makes 'em" (Conn, 1948). Of twenty-five children of preschool age (four to six years of age), God was frequently referred to as the source of babies. Children also spoke of babies as being bought from stores. In about one-third of the cases they mentioned the hospital as a place from which babies are obtained. The idea of the doctor as the person who brings the baby

to the mother was introduced by only two children. There was no reference to the mother's role in the coming of the baby, and the concept of the birth process was foreign to these children. Many children twenty years later were not giving better answers than were the children in 1948.

Parental Permissiveness

To get some perspective on the degree of permissiveness or repressiveness of parents, Sears (Sears and others, 1957) tabulated mothers' reported evaluations of their reactions to sex play among children and the severity of the pressure put on children. Only two percent rated themselves as "entirely permissive" and an additional fourteen percent of the mothers reported that they had made no attempt to stop sex play when they encountered it. Miller and Swanson (1958) found in Detroit that about the same number of mothers said they had done something about the child touching his or her genitals as those who said they had not done anything. Of the seventeen percent of the population who said that their children had touched their genitals and that they had done something about it, five percent diverted the child's attention, seven percent used gentle physical prevention or talked to the child, two percent punished the child physically, and two percent used shame or ridicule. In a recent interview study (Lindahl, 1973), a small random sample of mothers in Minnesota were asked what they had done when they noticed their child "handling his/her genitals—playing with himself/herself." The answers ranged from complete permissiveness to complete restrictiveness. Except for five percent of the responses that could not be categorized, twenty-nine percent were completely restrictive, although sixty-six percent gave answers that could be categorized as slightly to entirely permissive, with twenty-four percent falling in the entirely permissive category.

A permissive attitude is taken toward autogenital stimulation of children and adolescents in most societies, while adult masturbation is generally disapproved. In some societies masturbation is condemned regardless of the individual's age, but in many societies it is believed that masturbation is a natural and normal activity for the young boy or girl. Among the Hopi and Sirion, masturbation passes practically unnoticed during early childhood, with adults taking a tolerant and permissive attitude toward all sexual behavior at least until the age of puberty (Ford and Beach, 1951, p. 188). Among the Pukapukans of Polynesia, where parents simply ignore the sexual activity of young children, boys and girls masturbate freely and openly in public. Among the Nama Hottentot, no secret is made of autogenital stimulation in early childhood. Young Trobriand children also engage in a variety of sexual activities. In the absence of adult control, typical forms of amusement for Trobriand girls and boys include manual and oral stimulation of the genitals and simulated coitus. Young Seniang children publicly simulate adult copulation without being reproved; older boys masturbate freely and play sexual games with little girls, but the boys are warned not to copulate on the grounds that it would weaken them. Lesu children playing on the beach give imitations of adult sexual intercourse, and adults regard this as a natural and normal game. On Tikopia, small boys induce erections in themselves through manual manipulation, and this is ignored or mildly reproved by adults. Little girls also masturbate without being punished (Ford and Beach, 1951, p. 189).

Sexual Encounters in Early Childhood with Adults other than Parents

Encounters involving sexual intimacy between child and adult can be overhearing adult sex talk, innocent and accidental encounters, loving and affectionate relations, or sensationally aggressive and violent child molestation.

It is common in the United States to debase nonmarital sexual activity, especially that involving adults and children. Incest, pedophilia, exhibitionism, and child-molestation have become pejorative terms. In the United States, we usually use the general term pedophilia to define sexual behavior in which adults derive erotic pleasure from encounters with children. Such pedophilic practices include exposure of the genitals to a child, manipulation of a child, and possible penetration of a child, though the latter is not common. Adults who expose themselves to children are almost always males. Such exhibitionists usually do not pursue the child or aggressively seek involvement beyond exposure.

Contrary to common assumptions, old men relatively seldom are child molesters, and their approaches to children might be judged as quite harmless. The middle to late thirties, and the late fifties, are the main age groups from which so-called molesters come (Mohr, 1964).

An excellent account of the ambivalent attitudes of a child toward molestation by an adult is that by Maya Angelou (1970, pp. 94–98). She provides a graphic and moving account of a child's response to the tenderness, as well as to the violence, that can accompany intimate, sexual encounters with an adult. In good faith the child cooperates and receives certain satisfactions only later to be deeply hurt by rape, extreme feelings of guilt, and the threat of violence by the molester should she tell of the experience to anyone. The events following child molestation can be as traumatic or more traumatic for both parties than the precipitating event itself. Intimacy is a normal part of the maturational process of children, and pedophilia, if no violent aggression or physical harm accompanies the activity, need not create sexual trauma for the child. The child sometimes even has pleasant memories of such encounters (Brongersma, 1977). Parental distress, anger, and anxiety, a police investigation, and a court trial may have a more traumatic effect on the child than the sexual experience itself. A major difference between the child and the adult in a child-adult intimate encounter is that the adult is more aware of possible criminal penalties. But the child's experiences are over before he or she has any comprehension of the legal proscriptions of adult sex codes (Kinsey, 1948, p. 447).

RESULTS OF SEXUAL ENCOUNTERS IN CHILDREN THREE TO EIGHT YEARS OF AGE

More and more authorities on child development are accepting intimate and even sexual encounters as a normal part of the maturational process (Katzman, 1972). No longer do we feel that early discovery of genital differences, child-child sex play, or even a single occurrence of sexual molestation will have lasting ill effects on a child in a stable pattern of family-community experiences. Healthy children are not as easily upset by sexual experiences as some theorists would have us believe. Feeling the genitals of another child, getting a glimpse of the parent undressed, or a look at a "girly" magazine does not seriously disturb the average child (Finch, 1969).

There is no one reaction, for instance, to the discovery of genital differences of the sexes. Children generally accept the differences between the sexes with composure though some have a feeling of strangeness, surprise, curiosity, disappointment, or humor. There are children who are somewhat disturbed; they feel that something is "wrong" with what they have seen, something that should not be. Acceptance is mingled with the feeling that reality has somehow not come up to expectations. Some boys, thinking in terms of the external genitalia in the male and their absence in the female, assume that girls have lost an existing penis. Some girls also think that "something is wrong" with what they see (Conn, 1940).

Young people today generally recall their childhood sexual encounters, including their sex education, as having been almost totally inadequate in preparing them for experiences with the opposite sex during adolescence and adulthood. If the child received any formal sex education from parents or from the school, it usually consisted of a certain amount of cautious information about anatomy and the mechanisms of reproduction. It is too early to say if the programs of sex education for children being introduced in the schools today are effective.

Parents who go to great effort to protect their child from the normal intimate, sexual experiences of childhood may unconsciously do the very things that are designed to defeat their purposes. Frustration or the withholding of positive reinforcement of intimacy needs may result in an increase rather than a decrease in the motivation to satisfy such needs (Bandura and Walters, 1963). It is a moot question. Is it the repressive rather than the permissive parents who contribute most to the high level of interest in sex and the high sexual-erotic content of our culture? Those who support the repressive sexual socialization of children do so largely out of fear that children will misbehave sexually if sensory, affectional, and sexual appetites are not repressed from infancy. It is true also that the clinical literature provides ample evidence of unwise or disturbed parents who willingly or unwillingly encourage and reinforce deviant and antisocial sexual behavior in their offspring. It is true also that because of varying types of upbringing, individuals differ in the extent to which they are able through self-restraint to tolerate delay of reward. The child learns whether taught or not. If not presented with models, he or she will find models. Attempts to postpone sexual socialization will only be partially successful and the models chosen could be less than adequate. Given the nature of human personality, the socialization process will continue in some manner or other from birth to maturity. One can conclude from Broderick's research on intimacy patterns of children that intimate associations and attachments at all ages in infancy and childhood are necessary to sensory, affectional, and sexual maturity (Broderick, 1961, 1964, 1966, 1968).

REFERENCES

ABELSON, H.; COHEN, R.; HEATON, F.; and SUDER, C. 1970. "Public attitudes toward and experience with erotic materials." *Technical reports of the commission on obscenity and pornography,* vol. 6. Washington, D.C.: U.S. Government Printing Office.

AINSWORTH, M. D. 1963. The development of infant-mother interaction among the Ganda, pp. 67–104. In *Determinants of infant behavior*, vol. 2, ed. Brian Foss. London: Methuen.

———. 1964. Patterns of attachment behavior shown by the infant in interaction with his mother. *Merrill-Palmer Quarterly*, 10: 57–58.

ALPERT, A. 1941. The latency period. *American Journal of Orthopsychiatry*, 2: 126–32.

ANGELOU, M. 1970. I know why the caged bird sings. *Harper's Magazine*, 240: 86–98.

ARNOW, P. 1977. Pomeroy on children. *Multi Media Resource Guide*, 2: 4–5, 52–53.

ATHANASIOU, R.; SHAVER, P.; and TAVIS, C. 1970. Sex. *Psychology Today*, (July 1970), 39–52.

AVERY, C. E. 1964. Family life education: its philosophy and purpose. *The Family Life Coordinator*, 13: 27–37.

BALIASSNIKOWA, N. J., and MODEL, M. M. 1931–32. Zur neurologie des saugens. *Zsch. f. Kinderhk.*, 39: 1–16.

BANDURA, A., and WALTERS, R. H. 1963. *Social learning and personality development*. New York: Holt, Rinehart & Winston.

BATESON, G., and MEAD, M. 1942. *Balinese character: a photographic analysis*, vol. 2. The New York Academy of Sciences Inc.

BEACH, F. A. 1956. Characteristics of masculine sex drive, pp. 1–32. In *Nebraska Symposium on Motivation*. Lincoln: University of Nebraska Press.

BELL, S. A preliminary study of the emotion of love between the sexes. 1902. *The American Journal of Psychology*. 13: 325–54.

BENDER, L., and BLAU, A. 1937. The reaction of children to sexual relations with adults. *American Journal of Orthopsychiatry*, 7: 500–18.

BEREST, J. J. 1970. Report on a case of sadism. *The Journal of Sex Research*, 6: 210–19.

BERGER, B. 1977. The sexuality of children. Talk delivered at international conference on love and attraction, Swansea, Wales, U.K.

———, and HACKETT, B. 1974. On the decline of age grading in rural hippie communes." *Journal of Social Issues*, 30: 163–83.

BLAIR, A. W., and BURTON, W. H. 1951. *Growth and development of the preadolescent*. New York: Appleton Century Crofts.

BOSOCK, T. N. 1973. Effects of fluid delivery in the sucking response of the human newborn. *Journal of Experimental Child Psychology*, 15: 77–85.

BOWLBY, J. 1969. *Attachment and loss*, vol. 1, p. 158. New York: Basic Books, Inc.

BRECHER, R., and BRECHER, E., eds. 1966. *An analysis of human sexual response*. New York: Signet Books.

BRODERICK, C. B. 1964. How the sex drive develops. *Sexology*, 30: 780–84.

———. 1966. Sexual development among preadolescents. *The Journal of Social Issues*, 22: 6–21.

———, and FOWLER, S. E. 1961. New patterns of relationships between the sexes among preadolescents. *Marriage and Family Living*, 23: 27–30.

———, and ROWE, G. P. 1968. A scale of preadolescent heterosexual development. *Journal of Marriage and The Family*, 30: 97–101.

BRONGERSMA, E. 1977. On loving relationships human and humane. *Children's Rights*, 1.

BROWN, D. G., and LYNN, D. B. 1966. Human sexual development: an outline of components and concepts. *Journal of Marriage and The Family*, 26: 155–62.

BURCH, B. 1952. Sex and the young child. *Parents Magazine*, 27: 36–37.

BUTLER, C. 1952. The influence of parents' emotional attitudes concerning sex on the sex education of their children. Masters Thesis, University of Chicago, Committee on Human Development.

CALDWELL, B. M., and HERSHER, L. 1964. Mother-infant interaction during the first year of life. *Merrill-Palmer Quarterly*, 10: 119–28.

CAMERON, W. J., and KENKEL, W. F. 1960. High school dating: a study in variation. *Marriage and Family Living*, 22: 74–76.

CAMPBELL, E. H. 1939. The social-sex development of children. *Genetic Psychology Monograph*, 21: 461–552.

CAPLAN, G., and LEBOVICI, S. 1969. *Adolescence: psychological perspectives*, pp. 27–49. New York: Basic Books, Inc.

CHODOFF, P. 1966. A critique of Freud's theory of infantile sexuality. *American Journal of Psychology*, 123: 507–18.

CLAY, V. S. 1968. The effects of culture on mother-child tactile communication. *The Family Coordinator*, 17: 204–10.

COLEMAN, J. S. 1961. *The adolescent society*. New York: Free Press of Glencoe.

COMFORT, A. 1963. *Sex in society*. London: Duckworth.

CONN, J. H. 1948. Children's awareness of the origins of babies. *Journal of Child Psychiatry*, 1: 140–76.

——. 1940. Children's reactions to the discovery of genital differences. *The American Journal of Orthopsychiatry*, 10: 747–55.

CONSTANTINE, L. 1977. The sexual rights of children. Paper presented at the international conference on love and attraction, Swansea, Wales, U.K.

CRIST, J. R. 1953. High school dating as a behavior system. *Marriage and Family Living*, 15: 23–28.

Curiosities. 1964. *Sexology*, 30: 466.

DAHLSTROM, E. 1967. *The changing roles of men and women*. London: Duckworth.

DICKINSON, R. L., and BEAM, L. 1931. *A thousand marriages*. Baltimore: The Williams and Wilkins Co.

DOUVAN, E., and ADELSON, J. 1966. *The adolescent experience*. New York: John Wiley and Sons, Inc.

ELIAS, J., and GEBHARD, P. 1969. Sexuality and sexual learning in children. *Phi Delta Kappan*, 50: 401–05.

ERIKSON, E. H. 1950. *Childhood and society*. New York: W. W. Norton & Co.

FINCH, S. M. 1969. Sex play among boys and girls. *Medical Aspects of Human Sexuality*, 58–66.

FISCHER, V. E. 1947. Obsessive compulsive neuroses, pp. 221–34. In *Case histories in clinical and abnormal psychology*, ed. A. Burton and R. E. Harris. New York: Harper and Row.

FORD, C. S., and BEACH, F. A. 1951. *Patterns of sexual behavior*. New York: Harper and Row.

FOX, J. R. 1962. Sibling incest. *British Journal of Sociology*, 13: 128–50.

FREUD, S. 1962. *Three contributions to the theory of sex*, pp. 35–64. New York: E. P. Dutton.

FRIEDMAN, S. M. 1952. An empirical study of the castration and oedipus complexes. *Genetic Psychology Monographs*, 61–130.

FURFEY, P. H. 1930. *The growing boy*, p. 101. New York: The Macmillan Co.

GAGNON, J. H. 1965. Sexuality and sexual learning in the child. *Psychiatry*, 28: 212–28.

——, and SIMON, W. 1967. The sociological perspective on homosexuality. *The Dublin Review*, 512, pp. 96–114.

GESELL, A., and ILG, F. L. 1946. *The child from five to ten*. New York: Harper and Row.

GORDON, M. 1968. Infant care revisited. *Journal of Marriage and The Family*, 30: 578–83.

GREENACRE, P. 1950. Special problems of early female sexual development. *The Psychoanalytic Study of the Child*, 5: 122–38.

HALLECK, S. L. 1962. The physician's role in management of victims of sex offenders. *Journal of the American Medical Association*, 180: 273–78.

HALVERSON, H. M. 1940. Genital and sphincter

behavior of the male infant. *Journal of Genetic Psychology*, 43: 95–136.

———. 1938. Infant sucking and tensional behavior. *The Journal of Genetic Psychology*, 53: 365–430.

HARLOW, H. F. 1962. The hetero-sexual affectional system in monkeys. *American Psychologist*, 17.

———, and ZIMMERMAN, R. 1959. Affectional responses in the infant monkey. *Science*, 130.

HARTLEY, R. E. 1964. A developmental view of female sex-role definition and identification. *Merrill-Palmer Quarterly*, 10: 3–16.

HATTENDORF, K. W. 1932. A study of the questions of young children concerning sex: a phase of an experimental approach to parent education. p. 3. *Journal of Social Psychology*.

HENDRICK, I. 1942. Instinct and the ego during infancy. *Psychoanalytic Quarterly*, 2: 33–58.

HERSKOVITZ, M. J. 1952. *Man and his works*. New York: Alfred A. Knopf.

HOLLINGSHEAD, A. B. 1949. *Elmtown's youth*. New York: Wiley.

HUNT, D. 1970. *Parents and children in history: The psychology of family life in early modern France*. New York: Basic Books.

HURLOCK, E. B. 1950. *Child development*. New York: McGraw-Hill.

ILG, F. L., and AMES, L. B. 1955. *Child behavior*. New York: Dell.

JOHNSTON, C., and DEISCHER, R. 1973. Contemporary communal child rearing: A first analysis. *Pediatrics*, 52: 319–26.

JONES, E. 1950. The early development of female sexuality. pp. 438–51. *Papers on Psychoanalysis*. London: Bailliere, Tindahl, and Cox.

———. 1955. *The life and works of Sigmund Freud*. New York: Basic Books.

KAFFMAN, M. 1972. Toilet-training by multiple caretakers: Enuresis among kibbutz children. *Israel Annals of Psychiatry and Related Disciplines*, 10: 341–64.

KANNER, L. 1939. Infantile sexuality. *Journal of Pediatrics*, 4: 583–608.

KARDINER, A. 1939. *The individual and his society*, pp. 197–250. New York: Columbia University Press.

KARLSSON, G. 1964. Sexuella vanor och attityder bland folkhogskoleelever. *Sociologisk Forskning*, pp. 55–63, 105–11.

KATZMAN, M. 1972. Early sexual trauma. *Sexual Behavior*, 13–17.

KENNY, J. A. 1973. Sexuality of pregnant and breastfeeding women. *Archives of Sexual Behavior*, 2: 215–29.

KETCHER, A. 1955. The discrimination of sex differences by young children. *Journal of Genetic Psychology*, 87: 131–43.

KINSEY, A. C.; POMEROY, W. B.; and MARTIN, C. E. 1948. *Sexual behavior in the human male*. Philadelphia: W. B. Saunders.

KIRKENDAL, L. A., and RUBIN, I. 1969. Sexuality and the life cycle: a broad concept of sexuality. SIECUS Study Guide, no. 8, Sex information and education counsel of the United States.

KLAUS, M.; JERAULD, R.; and KREGER, N. C. 1972. Maternal attachment: importance of the first post-partum days. *New England Journal of Medicine*.

KLEEMAN, J. A. 1966. Genital self-discovery during a boy's second year: a follow-up. *Psychoanalytic Study of the Child*, 21: 358–91.

KOCH, H. L. 1935. Analysis of certain forms of so-called 'nervous habits' in young children. *Journal of Genetic Psychology*, 46: 139–70.

KORNER, A. 1973. Sex differences in newborns with special reference to differences in the organization of oral behavior. *Journal of Child Psychology and Psychiatry*, 14: 19–29.

LANDRETH, C. 1967. *Early childhood: Behavior and learning*. New York: Alfred A. Knopf.

LANGWORTHY, O. R. 1933. Development of behavior patterns and myelinization of the nervous system in the human fetus and infant. *Contributions to Embryology*, 24: 1–57.

LANSKY, L. M. 1963. The family structures also affects the model: sex-role attitudes in parents of preschool children. *Merrill-Palmer Quarterly*, 10: 39–50.

LEHMAN, H. C., and WITTY, P. A. 1927. *The psychology of play activities*. New York: Barnes & Noble.

LEVITT, E. E., and KLASSEN, A. 1973. Public attitudes toward sexual behavior: the latest investigation of the institute for sex research. Fiftieth anniversary meeting, American Orthopsychiatric Association.

LEVY, D. M. 1928. Finger sucking and accessory movements in early infancy. *American Journal of Psychiatry*, 7: 881–918.

LEWIS, G. M. 1958. *Educating children in grades four, five and six*. Washington, D.C.: U. S. Office of Education, U.S. Department of Health, Education, and Welfare.

LEWIS, M., and KAGAN, J. 1965. Studies in attention. *Merrill-Palmer Quarterly*, 2: 95–127.

LEWIS, O. 1961. *The family of Sanchez: autobiography of a Mexican family*. London: Secker and Wartburg.

LILEY, A. W. 1972. The foetus as a personality. *Australian and New Zealand Journal of Psychiatry*, 6: 99–105.

LINDAHL, J. A. 1973. The sexual socialization of children: four-five year olds in a Minnesotan community. Unpublished.

LITIN, E. M.; GIFFIN, M. E.; and JOHNSON, A. M. Parental influence in unusual sexual behavior in children. *The Psychoanalytic Quarterly*, 25: 37–55.

LOWRIE, S. H. 1956. Factors involved in the frequency of dating. *Marriage and Family Living*, 18.

LOWRY, T. P. 1970. How breast feeding arouses women. *Sexology*, 37: 46–49.

McCANDLESS, B. R. 1967. *Children: behavior and development*. pp. 382–414. New York: Holt, Rinehart & Winston.

MACCOBY, E. E., ed., 1966. *The development of sex differences*. Stanford, Calif.: Stanford University Press.

MARTINSON, F. M. 1976. Eroticism in infancy and childhood. *The Journal of Sex Research*, 2: 251–62.

——. 1977. Infant and child sexuality: capacity and experience—A conceptual framework. Paper read at symposium on infant and child sexuality, international conference on love and attraction, Swansea, Wales, U.K.

——. 1960. *Marriage and the American ideal*. New York: Dodd Mead.

——. 1966. Sexual knowledge, values, and behavior patterns. A report based on a study conducted by the Department of Sociology, Gustavus Adolphus College in conjunction with the Lutheran Social Service of Minnesota, 1966.

MASTERS, W. H., and JOHNSON, V. 1966. *Human sexual response*. Boston: Little, Brown.

MAXWELL, R. J. 1967. *Cornell Journal of Social Relations*, as reported in *Transaction*, 5: 4.

MEAD, M., and WOLFENSTEIN, M. 1955. *Childhood in contemporary cultures*. Chicago: University of Chicago Press.

MEEK, L. H. 1940. *Your child's development and guidance*. New York: J. B. Lippincott.

MILES, F. F., and ASSOCIATES OF THE E. C. BROWN TRUST FOUNDATION. 1967. Children's art and the human beginnings: analyzing the E. C. Brown collection of children's art. *The family life coordinator*.

MILLER, D. R., and SWANSON, G. E. 1958. *The changing American parent*. New York: Wiley.

MOHR, J. W.; TURNER, R. E.; and JERRY, M. B.

Pedophilia and exhibitionism. Toronto: University of Toronto Press.

MOLL, A. 1913. *The sexual life of the child.* New York: Macmillan.

MONEY, J. 1973. Sexology: Behavior, cultural, hormonal, genetic, etc. *The Journal of Sex Research,* 9: 1–10.

NEWSON, J., and NEWSON, E. 1963. *Infant care in an urban community.* London: Allen and Anwin.

NEWTON, N., and NEWTON, M. 1967. Psychologic aspects of lactation. *The New England Journal of Medicine,* 277: 1179–88.

Normal Adolescence. 1968. Group for the advancement of psychiatry committee on adolescence. New York: Group for the advancement of psychiatry.

PELLER, L. 1965. Sex education of the young child. *The Journal of Sex Research,* 1: 17–23.

PRESCOTT, J. W. 1970. A developmental neural-behavioral theory of socialization. American Psychological Association Symposium.

——. 1972. Developmental neuropsychophysics. (draft), National Institute of United Health and Human Development.

——. 1970. Early somatosensory deprivation as an ontogenetic process in the abnormal development of the brain and behavior. *Medical Prematology.*

——, and McKAY, C. 1973. Human affection, violence and sexuality: A developmental and cross-cultural perspective. Society for cross-cultural research, Philadelphia.

——, and McKAY, C. 1972. Somatosensory deprivation and the pleasure principle: neurobiological and cross-cultural perspectives of sexual, sadistic, and affectional behavior. Society of Biological Psychiatry, Dallas, Texas.

RAINWATER, L. 1970. *Behind ghetto walls: Black families in a federal slum.* Chicago: Aldine.

RAMSEY, G. V. 1943. The sex information of younger boys. *The American Journal of Orthopsychiatry,* 13: 347–52.

——. 1943. The sexual development of boys. *American Journal of Psychology,* 56: 217–33.

RATH, R. A., and McDOWELL, D. J. 1971. Coming up hip; child rearing perspectives and life style values among counter culture families. *Sociological Symposium,* 7: 49–60.

REEVY, W. R. 1967. Child sexuality. *The Encyclopedia of Sexual Behavior,* pp. 258–67, ed. A. Ellis and A. Abarbanel. New York: Hawthorn Books.

RENSHAW, D. C. 1971. Sexuality in children. *Medical Aspects of Human Sexuality,* 63–74.

RIBBLE, M. A. 1955. *The personality of the young child.* New York: Columbia University Press.

ROBINSON, I. E.; KING, K.; DUDLEY, C. J.; and CLUNE, F. J. 1968. Change in sexual behavior and attitudes of college students. *Family Coordinator,* 17: 119–23.

ROGLER, L. H., and HOLLINGSHEAD, A. B. 1965. *Trapped: families and schizophrenia.* New York: Wiley.

SCARR-SALAPATIK, S., and WILLIAMS, M. 1973. The effects of early stimulation on low-birth-weight infants. *Child Development,* 44: 94–101.

SCHAFFER, H. R., and EMERSON, P. E. 1964. Patterns of response to physical contact in early human development. *Journal of Child Psychology and Psychiatry,* 5: 1–13.

——. 1964b. The development of social attachment in infancy. Monograph of social research and child development, 29: 1–77.

SEARS, R. R.; MACCOBY, E. E.; and LEVIN, H. 1957. *Patterns of child rearing.* Evanston, Illinois: Row, Peterson.

SEGAL, J. ed., 1971. *The mental health of the child: program reports of the national institute of mental health,* pp. 193–99. Washington, D.C.: Public Health Service Publication no. 2168.

SEWELL, W. H. 1953. Infant training and the personality of the child. *American Journal of Sociology,* 58: 150–91.

SHIPMAN, G. 1968. The psychodynamics of sex education. *The Family Coordinator,* 17, 3–12.

SHIRLEY, M. M. 1933. *The first two years,* vol. 1. Minneapolis: University of Minnesota Press.

SIMON, W., and GAGNON, J. 1969. Psychosexual development. *Transaction,* 6: 9–17.

SMITH, E. A. 1962. *American youth culture: group life in teen-age society.* New York: The Free Press.

SMITH, W. M., JR. 1952. Rating and dating: a re-study. *Marriage and Family Living,* 14, 312–17.

SPIRO, M. E. 1965. *Children of the kevutza.* New York: Schocken Books.

SPITZ, R. A. 1949. Autoerotism: some empirical findings and hypotheses on three of its manifestations in the first year of life, pp. 85–120. *The psychoanalytic study of the child,* 3/4, New York: International Universities Press.

STENDLER, C. B. 1950. Sixty years of child training practices. *Journal of Pediatrics,* 3–15.

STERN, W. 1930. *Psychology of early childhood up to the sixth year of age.* New York: Holt, Rinehart & Winston.

TAYLOR, W. S. 1933. A critique of sublimation in males: a study of forty superior single men. *Genetic psychology monographs,* 1–115.

TULKIN, S. R. 1973. Social class differences in attachment behaviors of ten-month-old infants. *Child development,* 44, 171–74.

UDRY, R. J. 1966. *The social context of marriage.* New York: J. B. Lippincott.

ULLERSTAM, L. 1966. *The erotic minorities.* New York: Grove Press.

WALLON, H. 1973. The psychological development of the child. *International Journal of Mental Health,* 1: 29–39.

When children ask about sex, revised edition. 1969. Child Study Association of America.

WINICK, C. 1968. *The new people: desexualization in American life.* New York: Pegasus.

WOODY, J. D. 1973. Contemporary sex education: Attitudes and implications for child-rearing. *The Journal of School Health,* 63: 241–46.

ZIEGLER, F. J., and RODGERS, D. A. 1968. Vasectomy, ovulation suppressors, and sexual behavior. *The Journal of Sex Research,* 4: 169–93.

FOUR

Sexuality
in
Early Adolescence

HEINO F. L. MEYER-BAHLBURG

INTRODUCTION

Early adolescence, the ages from twelve through sixteen, is marked by two major changes in most teenagers' lives: pubertal maturation and the transition from elementary to high school. Both processes have profound and often stressful effects on the adolescent's environment and personality in general (Hamburg, 1974), and both are intimately interwoven with psychosexual development. The purpose of this chapter is to focus on the biological aspects of early adolescence and to delineate the probable role of hormones and somatic maturation in psychosexual development—"probable" because the psychoendocrinology of puberty is a highly complex, interdisciplinary area in which research encounters tremendous logistical and methodological difficulties and in which, consequently, very little has been done. Although it seems obvious that puberty marks the attainment of full reproductive as well as of sexual capacity, the latter aspect is by no means clearly established. Part of the problem is that we know relatively little about childhood sexuality, with which we have to contrast pubertal and adult sexuality if we want to assess these changes. Also, because there are so many social pressures exerted on sexual behavior, it is difficult to disentangle the biologic from the social influences, particularly since both are likely to exert their effects interacting with each other.

Systematic correlative studies of somatic-endocrine and psychosexual development in normal puberty have yet to be done. Currently, the major evidence for a role of biologic factors in psychosexual development comes from three indirect sources: (1) the data on the role of sex hormones in adult sexuality, (2) puberty studies on other mammals, and (3) sexual behavior in children and adolescents with pubertal abnormalities.

SOMATIC AND ENDOCRINE CHANGES

The biologic marker of early adolescence is puberty, defined as the developmental phase of physical maturation to full reproductive capacity. It is a time of rapid conspicuous changes in body size and appearance, which are associated with the maturation of internal reproductive structures and based on major alterations of endocrine function. The most visible somatic changes include the pubertal growth spurt and the development of secondary sex characteristics.

THE GROWTH SPURT

Most early adolescents experience a transient increase of growth velocity or growth rate of the body, which results in the attainment of adult size (Tanner, 1975). From infancy on, the annual rate of growth falls steadily throughout childhood, picks up again rather suddenly at the time of puberty (this is the "growth spurt") and declines to zero in later adolescence, when skeletal maturation is completed and the growth potential exhausted. There are wide interindividual variations in the slope of the growth curve, the age at onset of the pubertal spurt, the shape of this spurt, and its peak growth velocity. Some of the variability is due to socioeconomic differences: generally, children and adolescents from higher socioeconomic levels provided with better nutrition, tend to grow more rapidly (Tanner, 1962; Takahashi, 1966). There are also marked sex differences. Whereas both boys and girls are of comparable stature until the end of childhood, their growth curves diverge in puberty. Boys

This work was supported in part by NIMH Center Grant, MH 30906–01A1.

start their growth spurt about two years later than girls do. Thus, at the onset of their own growth spurt, boys are already taller (on the average, by 10 cm) than girls usually are when they start growing faster. In addition, boys have, on the average, a higher peak growth velocity than girls do. Girls who are in the midst of their pubertal growth spurt tend to be taller than boys of the same age, but when the boys catch up in pubertal development, the girls fall behind and end up with a shorter adult stature than the boys.

The growth spurt is not restricted to body size. Practically all muscular and skeletal components of the body are included (Tanner, 1975). Bone and muscle diameters increase, with boys showing a considerably greater increase in number and size of muscle cells than girls do. Consequently, physical strength increases rapidly in both sexes with boys significantly surpassing girls. Subcutaneous fat decreases in most boys and in some girls. All these changes combined result in the characteristic adult sex differences in body build: most conspicuously, the relatively greater height and broader shoulders of men, and the relatively wider hips of women. There are many internal sex differences (for instance, in blood chemistry) that develop in puberty (Tanner, 1975), but they will not be discussed here.

SECONDARY SEXUAL CHARACTERISTICS

The major accentuation of the sex differences in external appearance is brought about by the development of secondary sexual characteristics. The typical sequence of events has been described by Marshall and Tanner (1969, 1970). In girls, the first sign of puberty is usually the appearance of "breast buds," that is, an elevation of the breast and nipple as a small mound, with the areolar diameter enlarging over the infantile status. In some girls, the appearance of pubic hair precedes breast budding, but in the majority it follows. Axillary hair typically appears about two years after the start of pubic hair growth. More or less concurrently with the external changes, internal sexual

structures, including the uterus, grow and mature also. Uterine development probably will have reached a definitive stage for menarche, the first menstrual period, to occur, usually after the peak of the height spurt has been passed. However, menarche by itself does not signify the attainment of full reproductive capacity. Early menstrual cycles are often anovulatory, that is, do not produce fertile eggs, and postmenarcheal "adolescent sterility" may last from one year to eighteen months.

On the average, pubertal changes in boys begin only about six months later than in girls. The general impression of an overall, considerably earlier maturation of girls is largely due to the fact that the growth spurt (with its concomitant somatic changes) is placed earlier in the sequence of pubertal changes in girls than in boys; the average boy has his growth peak two years later than the average girl. The earliest sign of pubertal changes in boys is a growth acceleration of testes and scrotum, often accompanied by the thinning and reddening of the scrotal skin. Simultaneously or shortly after, pigmented pubic hairs start to appear. About a year later, spurts in penile growth and height begin. Coinciding with the penile growth spurt, the male internal sexual structures, for instance, the seminal vesicles and the prostate, enlarge and develop. Their maturation is the prerequisite for the first ejaculation of seminal fluid which tends to occur about a year after the beginning of accelerated penile growth (Tanner, 1975). Approximately one-third of all boys show a distinct enlargement of the breasts around the middle of puberty, which usually regresses after about a year. About two years after the onset of pubic hair growth, axillary hair appears; there is also an increase in axillary sweating due to an enlargement of axillary sweat glands. At about the same time, facial hair starts to grow. It usually begins at the corners of the upper lip, then spreads out to form the mustache, later extends to the upper part of the cheeks, and finally forms the beard. More toward the end of the growth spurt, the voice breaks and deepens, often very gradually. Starting in adolescence, the hairline above the forehead recedes; this process becomes more marked in adulthood.

For clinical and research purposes, several scales for the normative characterization of pubertal status have been developed. Most widely used are Tanner's photographic and descriptive standards of breast and pubic hair development in girls, and genital and pubic hair development in boys (see Tanner, 1975; colored standards are available in van Wieringen and others, 1971). The standards comprise five stages. (There is a sixth stage of pubic hair development in 80% of the males and 10% of the females.) Stage 1 is always prepubertal, stage 5 (and 6) adult. Tanner (1975) has published centile standards for age ranges of pubertal developmental stages.

The average timing of pubertal events in European and North American girls and boys has been graphically depicted by Marshall and Tanner (1969, 1970). Even within this relatively homogeneous group, there are wide age variations: in girls, for instance, the onset of breast budding varies from age 8 to 13 years, and menarche ranges from age 10 to 16.5 years. In boys, the acceleration of testicular growth may start anywhere from age 9.5 to 13.5. The penile growth spurt starts between age 10.5 and 14.5 and the penis reaches adult size between age 12.5 and 16.5. The development of pubic hair may continue into adulthood. In contrast to the age at which the pubertal events occur, the sequence of events is much less variable. However, the sequence is not identical for all boys or all girls; also the rate of passing through the whole sequence varies considerably between individuals, and some sexual characteristics may mature relatively faster than others. Both adolescent girls (especially between the ages of 11 and 14 years) and boys (particularly the age group from 13 to 16 years) show a tremendous variation in somatic developmental status, which is one of the important factors explaining the typical problems of adolescent self-image and behavior.

The age at onset of puberty varies because of many factors, genetic as well as environmental (Tanner, 1975). There are differences even between Western European countries. For example, the current mean age at menarche is 12.5 years in Germany, 13.0 years in England, and 13.4 years in Switzerland (Bierich, 1975). Socioeconomic status also has a strong influence (Tanner, 1966): menarche occurs several months earlier in girls of a higher social class than in girls of a lower social class. This has been demonstrated in as different geographic regions and racial groups as Danes or African Bantu (Burrell and others, 1961), Indians (Israel, 1959) or Rumanians (Stukovsky and others, 1967). Higher social class usually implies better living conditions, including nutrition, sleep, and exercise, and these may be the major factors accounting for class differences in rates of growth in childhood as well as in timing of the growth spurt and of menarche.

Increased growth in childhood and early onset of menarche may be tied together by the critical weight hypothesis according to which menarche occurs in females who have reached a "critical weight," associated with a decline in metabolic rate and with achievement of a characteristic body composition (Frisch and Revelle, 1970). More recent studies have shown that menarche correlates more closely with body composition than with the critical weight (e.g., Frisch and others, 1973) which suggests that menarche requires a critical level of fat stored in the body. There are corresponding standards for predicting the minimum weight, at a given height which is necessary for menarche to occur (Frisch and McArthur, 1974). The theory is not yet generally accepted, however. The direction of the causal relation between body composition and menarche is under investigation (Crawford and Osler, 1975); the validity of the findings and conclusions have been questioned on statistical and other grounds (e.g., Johnston and others, 1975; Billewicz and others, 1976; Frisch, 1976).

A particularly interesting phenomenon is the acceleration of puberty. In Western countries, the onset of puberty seems to have gradually dropped in age over the last 150 years (Tanner, 1962, 1975). For example, the age of menarche has fallen from seventeen to thirteen years during this period. Acceleration of puberty has also been demonstrated in non-Caucasian populations, for instance, in China (Tanner, 1968) or in Japan (Asayama, 1976). Most likely, this secular trend is due to the complex changes in nutrition, social conditions, and public health, brought about by the technological development of the modern industrialized society.

HORMONES

Underlying the conspicuous changes of puberty in growth and sexual maturation are changes in the hypothalamic-pituitary-gonadal and -adrenal systems which lead to an increased secretion of male and female sex hormones. Since reliable methods for the measurement of pituitary, gonadal, and adrenal hormones have been developed only recently, our knowledge of the complex endocrinology of puberty is still limited. (For overviews see Grumbach and others, 1974; Tanner, 1975). Some representative findings follow.

For girls, Winter and Faiman (1973) found in a cross-sectional study that systematic changes in hormone levels coincided with the first signs of puberty. The first appearance of labial hair or of a subareolar breast bud (thelarche) was accompanied by rises in the mean plasma concentrations of FSH, estradiol and testosterone, whereas levels of serum LH did not become significantly elevated over prepubertal values before pubertal stage 3. It is not until several months after menarche that adult levels of estradiol appear as well as its cyclical variation which, in association with LH peaks of ovulatory magnitude and a normal luteal rise in serum progesterone levels, is the prerequisite of the final attainment of reproductive capacity. It is noteworthy that hormonal changes predate the onset of conspicuous pubertal changes. Mixed cross-sectional/longitudinal data of the same authors (Faiman and Winter, 1974) showed small increments of gonadotropins in prepubertal girls between ages six and ten, and a steep rise thereafter, whereas serum estradiol did not change noticeably before age ten.

Analogous data are available for boys. Cross-sectional studies (August and others, 1972) show that serum gonadotropins in males rise gradually between ages six and ten—again, in the prepubertal period—whereas significant rises in plasma testosterone tend to occur after this period. These findings have been confirmed basically in a mixed cross-sectional/longitudinal study by Lee and coworkers (1974). LH levels rose throughout puberty, the initial rise of LH occurring before testosterone concentrations were significantly increased. Testosterone levels rose progressively from before the appearance of sexual hair until an adult distribution was achieved. Noticeable genital growth started before testosterone concentrations increased and continued after elevations of testosterone were no longer detectable. The question of which hormone or hormone combination causes which pubertal event cannot yet be answered in satisfactory detail except for the well established fact that testosterone has a major role in the development of male sexual characteristics and estrogens a major role in female puberty. There are numerous gonadal hormones in both sexes and some of the pubertal changes cannot be explained without taking into account adrenal androgens whose secretion shows significant increases already well before the gonadal changes of puberty in both sexes (Parker and others, 1978). Pubertal changes in other than sex hormones are reviewed by Hays (1978).

An important methodological question for psychoendocrine research is whether hormone measures contribute valuable information above and beyond the assessment of physical development during puberty. The answer is that they probably do. One argument is the previously mentioned finding that several puberty-related hormones rise before puberty becomes visible. Some more arguments follow.

Compared over the total span of pubertal development in normal children, indices of physical maturation (Tanner stages) and endocrine measures averaged over individuals are well correlated in both boys and girls (e.g., Lee and Migeon, 1975; Collu and Ducharme, 1975; Gupta and others, 1975), but the slope of the regression of interindividual means of hormone measures on Tanner stages varies from hormone to hormone between the sexes. Tanner stages constitute ordinal scales of only five to six points whereas hormones are measured on a ratio scale and thereby much more precisely. Thus, for each Tanner stage, there exists a tremendous variability of plasma hormone levels (e.g., August and others, 1972).

Intraindividually, considerable increases in hormone secretion occur during one or two Tanner stages of pubertal maturation. A particularly dramatic example of this is the longitudinal study of boys by Knorr and others (1974), which shows steep intraindividual rises in plasma testosterone levels from 40 to 240 ng/100 ml (i.e., from the average adult female range to the lower limit of the adult male range) within ten months; the gradients were surprisingly uniform across individuals, irrespective of chronological age at the onset of this rise. Lee and others (1974) found that individual plasma testosterone levels rose from prepubertal to adult levels within two years. These findings imply that pubertal subjects with similar Tanner ratings may, in fact, show considerable differences in hormone secretion which are likely to be relevant to behavior effects. This is a particularly important consideration for the lower ranges of testosterone values characteristic of the early stages of male puberty in which dose-response relationships between hormones and sexual behavior appear to be more likely than later (Davidson, 1977).

Apparently Tanner stages are only very crude indicators of pubertal development and are far from sufficient in elaborating the role of hormones in behavioral development at puberty. The hormones in question have to be assessed directly. Tanner staging will be useful, however, for the systematic assessment of pubertal changes in body build and their relationships to body image and perception by others.

For humans as well as other mammals, the biologically active fraction of total testosterone is believed to be free testosterone, testosterone not bound to sex-hormone binding globulin, SHBG (Vermeulen and Verdonck, 1972). Horst and others (1977) have shown in boys that the increase of total plasma testosterone levels in puberty is associated with a sharp decline of SHBG binding capacity (especially for ages nine to fifteen years) and of the percentage of bound testosterone, so that free testosterone is increasing at a relatively faster rate than total testosterone (see also Vermeulen and others, 1974). The situation for girls is slightly different; although the SHBG binding capacity increases from prepubertal age to adulthood, free (unbound) estradiol rises from prepubertal age until stage 3 of puberty at which it plateaus (Radfar and others, 1976). Thus, it is probably not even sufficient to measure total plasma concentrations; at least for certain key hormones, one may have to analyze the unbound fraction in order to arrive at valid relationships between hormones and behavior.

The mechanism by which the timing of puberty is regulated is not yet fully understood. Much available evidence points to the assumption that it is not primarily the peripheral glands nor the pituitary but the brain itself, especially the hypothalamus, which is responsible. The currently most widely shared theory is the one proposed originally by Hohlweg and Dohrn (1932) on the basis of rat experiments, according to which puberty is induced by a change in sensitivity to circulating sex steroids of a sexual center in the central nervous system which regulates gonadotropin secretion. In its present form, the theory states that the hypothalamic gonadotropin-regulating mechanism in the prepubertal individual is much more sensitive to the negative feedback effects of circulating androgens and estrogens than in the adult. Thus, the low levels of sex hormones in the prepubertal individual are sufficient to suppress the release of gonadotropin-releasing factor from the hypothalamus and thereby the secretion of FSH and LH. With the approach of puberty, the hypothalamic negative feedback receptors show a progressive decrease in sensitivity to the sex steroids. Consequently, the secretion of pituitary gonadotropins increases, stimulating an increased production of sex hormones which, in turn, leads to the development of the secondary sex characteristics (Grumbach and others, 1974). During mid- to late puberty, a second and positive feedback mechanism matures which provides the capacity for an estrogen-induced LH surge to effect ovulation in the female.

Another pubertal event is the establishment of an episodic or pulsatile secretion of gonadotropins which, during puberty only, is associated with an augmentation of secretion synchronous with sleep (Boyar and others, 1972; Boyar, 1978). When children approach and enter (physically visible) puberty, they show more and more consistently episodes of LH secretory bursts at night as compared to daytime, and the amplitudes of these bursts increase (Boyar and others, 1972; Kulin and others, 1976; Judd and others, 1977; Lee and others, 1976). With advancing puberty, the amplitude (not the number) of the secretory episodes increases further (Kulin and others, 1976; Penny and others, 1977), and late in puberty, the daytime secretion is also elevated. Similar findings have been described for FSH (Lee and others, 1978). Since this phenomenon appears to be independent of gonadal activity, it underlines the active role of the central nervous system in the initiation of puberty.

A competing theory of the initiation of puberty has been proposed by Odell and Swerdloff (1976), on the basis of extensive experiments in the rat and corroborating evidence from other animals. They believe that sexual maturation, at least in male rats, and probably in pigs and cattle, is predominantly due to maturation at the gonadal level as a result of FSH induction of LH receptors in the gonads, resulting in increasing gonadal steroid secretion. They conclude from certain endocrine data on children that this mechanism also may be a contributing factor in the onset of human puberty.

SURVEY DATA ON SEXUAL BEHAVIOR

The term "sexual behavior" covers a great variety of distinct behavioral variables, including covert behavior such as sexual dreams and fantasies; measures of psychophysiological arousal such as acid phosphatase excretion; autosexual behavior such as self-stimulation and genital masturbation; and overt sociosexual behavior such as dating, kissing, or sexual intercourse. Animal-behavior research has provided a useful classification scheme for observable patterns of hormone-influenced sociosexual interaction (Beach, 1976): attractivity, proceptive behavior, and receptive behavior. Attractivity denotes those aspects of the sexually mature individual—in lower mammals mainly odor cues, in nonhuman primates both odor and visual cues—which elicit the sexual approach or proceptive behavior of a potential mating partner. Receptive behavior is a term used for postural compliance with a partner who initiates the copulatory sequence. Although originally defined for female mammals, these terms seem applicable to male mammals as well. It is fairly easy to point out analogous patterns of sociosexual interaction for humans. Any human study, however, also has to take into consideration covert and autosexual behavior, since they constitute major aspects of human sexual behavior.

To what extent the various aspects of sexual behavior are intercorrelated in development and influenced by somatic-endocrine factors has not been sufficiently investigated. Heterosexual attractivity seems to be brought about primarily by the development of the secondary sex characteristics in puberty. Evidence for this conclusion comes from ample but undocumented sex-clinical experience, from systematic rating studies of sexual attractivity (e.g., Wiggins and others, 1968; Lerner and Karabenick, 1974; Lavrakas, 1975) and from studies of men's arousal response, measured by penile plethysmography, to pictures or films of nude females of varying degrees of sexual maturation (Freund and others, 1973), although longitudinal studies of attractivity changes in early adolescence have not been done. Flirting, dating, and related proceptive behaviors also are of major importance in adolescence and play only a minor role in childhood (Broderick, 1966; Douvan and Adelson, 1966; Douvan and Gold, 1966).

Particularly detailed data are available on genital sexuality. The reports by Kinsey and others (1948, 1953) have documented that many aspects of sexual behavior, including orgasm, can occur well before puberty, but sexual activity in childhood usually is only sporadic and lacks the regularity of adolescent and adult life (for a summary of the Kinsey data on childhood, see Meyer-Bahlburg, 1977). It is in most cases not before puberty that sexual concerns and behavior in its various aspects become a major part of everyday life.

Using orgasm as the behavioral criterion, Kinsey and others (1948, 1953) demonstrated striking differences between the sexes during puberty. Boys showed a sudden upsurge in sexual activity which could begin a year or more before the onset of puberty was noticeable; they usually reached their life peak in terms of orgasmic frequency within a year or two after the onset of puberty. Most of this early activity was masturbation. For two-thirds (68%) of the boys in the Kinsey sample, masturbation provided the first ejaculation; for the remaining ones, nocturnal emissions and heterosexual coitus provided the first ejaculation. By age fifteen, 82% of the boys were experienced in masturbation to orgasm.

In girls, by contrast, the gradual and steady increase in the accumulative incidence of erotic arousal and orgasmic response which was observed before puberty continued into puberty and beyond; typically, women did not reach their maximum rate of orgasm until their middle twenties to thirties. Of the relatively small percentage of girls in the Kinsey sample who experienced orgasm during puberty (20% by age fifteen), the majority (84%) used masturbation as the most important outlet. For the average male, adolescence was the age of highest orgasmic frequency, with 3.4 outlets per week, whereas the corresponding figure for sexually active females (including masturbation) was around 0.5 orgasms per week.

The occurrence of the first ejaculation—Levin (1976) introduced the appropriate term thorarche (from Greek *thorós*, sperm, and *arché*, beginning)—is brought about by masturbation in the majority of North American males. Asayama (1976) has demonstrated the same for Japanese males. Thus, there appears to be a relatively close relationship of puberty, thorarche, and autosexual activity for most males, while masturbation to orgasm by females is a relatively late event. In both Kinsey and others' (1953) and Asayama's (1976) reports, masturbation was practiced by only a minority of female adolescents; it developed later than the somatic markers of puberty in the majority of those who ever practiced it.

Most survey data available on psychosexual development in adolescence concern the onset of coital behavior. In the Kinsey studies, the majority of adolescents had their first coital experience years later than their first ejaculation or menarche, and the average female had this experience later than the average male: by fifteen years of age, 24% of the males and 3% of the females were coitally experienced. Surveys of young American teenagers have been provided more recently by Sorensen (1972), Miller and Simon (1974), and Vener and Stewart (1974). For the age group thirteen to fifteen, the incidence of coitus ranged from 9 to 44% in males and from 7 to 30% in females. The methodological problems that may account for the discrepancies have been discussed by Hopkins (1977). Similarly low rates have been published by Schofield (1965) on English teenagers, by Schmidt and Sigusch (1972) for German samples, and by Asayama (1976) for Japanese adolescents. These data, together with the report by Jessor and Jessor (1975) on late adolescents and the numerous studies on college students (summarized by Hopkins, 1977) make it clear that for most white populations studied, the initiation to coital activity occurs after age sixteen, after the major somatic-endocrine changes of puberty have occurred and well after reproductive capacity has been attained.

Many factors other than gender have been shown to affect age at first coitus. In North America, the most influential one seems to be race: for instance, Zelnik and Kantner (1977) found that of fifteen-year-old women, 38.4% of blacks but only 13.8% of whites were coitally experienced. The authors had shown in an earlier sample (Kantner and Zelnik, 1972) that the difference remains largely the same when the socioeconomic level is controlled. Socioeconomic level has a less consistent effect on coital initiation. It seems that adolescents from lower socioeconomic strata are sexually active earlier than others (e.g., Kinsey and others, 1948, 1953; Miller and Simon, 1974). However, recent data on late adolescent or college student samples (Kantner and Zelnik, 1972; Simon and others, 1972; Miller and Simon, 1974) showed conflicting results which have been critically discussed by Hopkins (1977).

More pertinent to psychoendocrine research are data on acceleration. As mentioned earlier, the age at puberty in terms of menarche has consistently regressed over the last 150 years. Is there a similar shift in coital activity? Within the last two decades or less, such shifts have been demonstrated by Vener and Stewart (1974), Zelnik and Kantner (1977), Schmidt and Sigusch (1972) for Germany, and Asayama (1976) for Japan. More of a shift seems to have occurred in females than in males so that the sex difference is shrinking. Such changes, however, appear to be of relatively recent origin (Hopkins, 1977). Nothing suggests that there has been a consistent regular decline of age at first coitus which would parallel the acceleration of puberty over the last 150 years mentioned before.

Although it is obvious that strong social pressures have influenced and are still influencing coital initiation during adolescence, sexual behavior that is less subject to interference may be more closely related to puberty. One example is masturbation in males. If masturbation is closely related to physical maturation, age at onset should follow the acceleration of puberty, and this was shown by Asayama (1976) for Japanese adolescents. Romantic love is another variable that is generally less prohibited than (premarital) coitus. Broderick (1966) surveyed 1,000 middle-class children and adolescents from age five to eighteen years. He found that from the fifth grade (ages ten to eleven) on between 40% and 60% of both boys and girls reported having been in love or being in love. Kephart (1973) made a recall study of 1,079 young people. Males reported their first infatua-

tion at age thirteen and a half, their first love affair at seventeen and a half; the corresponding figures for females were thirteen and seventeen years. The age range from eleven to thirteen years coincides with Tanner stages 2 through 4 in typical girls and Tanner stages 2 and 3 in boys. It is tempting to speculate that the association of the development of romantic love with pubertal stages may be more than accidental.

HORMONES THAT INFLUENCE SEXUAL BEHAVIOR

The body produces a great variety of hormones and metabolites, the functions of which are often poorly understood. Delineation of the effects of individual hormones is difficult; one of the major problems is that hormones do not operate in isolation but are part of a complex endocrine system in which many components influence each other's production, release, target tissue effects, and metabolism. Nevertheless, systematic experimental and clinical observation make it possible to identify certain physiologic or behavioral events that are influenced greatly, although usually not exclusively, by a given individual hormone. With regard to sexual behavior, it seems obvious that all hormones of the hypothalamic-pituitary-gonadal axis need to be screened for behavioral effects. Sex steroids produced by the adrenals also must be considered. Although many other hormones have been shown to interact with sex steroids, their respective influences on sexual behavior are largely unknown and will not be discussed here.

Evidence from Animal Research

Testosterone of gonadal origin appears to be the major hormone in both the pre- and perinatal organization as well as the pubertal activation and adult maintenance of male sexual behavior in subhuman mammals (Beach, 1977, chap. 9). A major, continuing controversy concerns the mechanism of action that is important to the choice of androgen metabolites to be measured in psychoendocrine studies. In the rat, 5-alpha-reduced metabolites, especially dihydrotestosterone, appear to be effective mainly in peripheral target tissues and in the hypothalamic-pituitary regulation of gonadotropin release (negative feedback) but not in brain systems which regulate sexual behavior (Davidson and Trupin, 1975). The latter is believed by some researchers to depend on the aromatization of androgens to estradiol on the target cell level (McEwen, 1976). However, findings in other lower mammals (Luttge and others, 1975) and in rhesus monkeys (Phoenix, 1974) negate such a simple dichotomy, and recent data suggest that even in the rat not aromatization but 19-hydroxylation of androgens may be the decisive metabolic step for behavioral effects (Johnston and others, 1975). In contrast to testosterone, adrenal androgens seem to have a negligible role in male sexual behavior: in several lower mammalian species, adrenal hormones do not account for the persistence of sexual behavior after castration (see references in Phoenix, 1974). LH–RH, the hypothalamic polypeptide hormone that stimulates pituitary gonadotropin (especially LH) secretion and thereby regulates gonadal steroid production, has been shown to facilitate sexual behavior in lower mammals (Moss, 1978), but the effects are clearly weaker than those of the gonadal steroids.

For the major components of female sexual behavior, i.e. attractiveness, proceptivity, and receptivity, the estrogens, especially estradiol, are clearly the most important hormones in lower mammals (Beach, 1977). In some species, progesterone is needed in addition to optimize female sexual behavior, but under certain conditions progesterone has inhibitory effects. Testosterone increases components of male behavior (e.g., mounting) in females of lower mammalian species. In female primates (Herbert, 1974; Johnson and Phoenix, 1976), estrogens increase all aspects of sexual behavior, while progesterone lowers them. Testosterone has also been shown to have facilitory effects. There are a few reports showing a positive effect of adrenal androgen therapy on sexual behavior in

adrenalectomized monkeys: Everitt and Herbert (see Herbert, 1974) found that dehydroepiandrosterone was ineffective, while androstenedione had marked effects. It is unclear if the latter's effects are mainly due to the adrenal androgen itself or to its conversion product, testosterone. As in males, females of some mammalian species exhibit facilitory effects of LH–RH on sexual behavior (Moss, 1978).

EVIDENCE FROM HUMAN CLINICAL STUDIES

On the basis of clinical experience, surprisingly little of which has been systematically documented (Davidson, 1977), testosterone has long been the treatment of choice to induce or restore sexual functioning and drive in hypogonadal or castrated men. Estrogens (Meyer-Bahlburg, 1978) and certain progestogens (e.g., Money, 1970; Laschet and Laschet, 1975) which suppress testicular testosterone production and/or compete with testosterone at the target-organ level, typically interfere with male libido and sexual functioning. The clinical data on the effects of other androgens on sexual behavior are too scanty to permit any reasonable conclusion. There is an increasing number of clinical studies (reviewed in Moss, 1978), that show a beneficial effect of LH–RH administration on libido and potency in impotent, hypogonadal, and normal men. Although the data are suggestive, one has to reserve judgment at this point because the sample sizes are usually small, the methodology sometimes inadequate and the results inconsistent.

High-dose androgen treatment as it is used in estrogen-dependent cancer in women, is known to have a strong, positive impact on sexual drive in many such patients. Analogously, female patients with abnormally high androgen levels due to adrenal tumors or other abnormalities, also show an increased sexual drive (Money and Ehrhardt, 1972). A new report on endocrinologically normal women (Persky and others, 1978a) presented sizable correlations between their plasma testosterone levels, averaged over the menstrual cycle, and their "self-gratification scores" (a more appropriate label might be "self-rated sexual arousal"). Testosterone has been used successfully in the treatment of sexually unresponsive women (Carney and others, 1978). It has been shown (Waxenberg and others, 1959)—although without replication—that adrenalectomy, not ovarectomy, will decrease female sexual drive. Therefore, Money (1961) has called adrenal androgen the female "libido hormone." It appears likely, however, that it is not the weak adrenal androgens, but the much more potent testosterone itself (which, in the female, is largely a conversion product of adrenal androstenedione) that is responsible for such effects. The role of female ovarian hormones, estrogens and progesterone, on female sexuality is even less clear, and menstrual-cycle studies of female sexual activity and desire have not produced a consistent body of data (McCauley and Ehrhardt, 1976). Estrogens clearly affect female attractivity to males via their effects on the secondary sex characteristics and facilitate female receptivity, at least indirectly, through their effect on the vaginal mucosa. However, Persky and others (1978b) failed to show any relationship of plasma estradiol level to sexual behavior in young women. Data on the role of progesterone in female sexual behavior are not yet conclusive (McCauley and Ehrhardt, 1976), and data on behavioral LH–RH effects are not available.

In conclusion, the evidence described above names testosterone as the major hormone for sexual motivation and behavior in human males and possibly in females, while hardly anything is known in humans about a facilitory or contributing role of adrenal androgens, and there is only inconsistent but suggestive evidence for such a role of LH–RH in males. Estrogens and progestogens inhibit male sexual behavior, at least when used in pharmacologic dosage. Their role in female sexual motivation is not well established; it is probably much less prominent than in the case of lower mammals, but the available studies on women are not sufficient for ruling out facilitory effects of estrogens or inhibiting effects of progestogens as they have been observed in nonhuman primates.

PUBERTY AND SEXUAL BEHAVIOR IN SUBHUMAN MAMMALS

Although the dependence of sexual behavior on gonadal hormones has been demonstrated in numerous experiments involving gonadectomy and hormonal replacement, there are very few research data available on the emergence of sexual behavior during spontaneous pubertal development. The most comprehensive studies on lower mammals have been reported by Södersten and others (1977) who assessed sexual behavior and plasma testosterone concentrations in developing normal male rats and tested the effectiveness of various steroid hormone implants in inducing precocious mating behavior in prepubertal males. The results of the first part of the experiment showed no marked changes of testosterone levels in the majority of cases on the day before or after the first mount, intromission, or ejaculation was observed, although it appears from the graphs in their publication that the onset of mating behavior coincided with the beginning of a systematic gradual elevation of plasma testosterone levels. Their finding makes it unlikely that an increase of testosterone production was primarily responsible for the onset of mating behavior. Testosterone treatment, however, of prepubertal rats resulted in precocious onset of mating behavior, as had been shown previously by other authors. To explain the onset of mating behavior in spontaneous puberty without marked changes in testosterone levels, the authors suggested an alteration of the sensitivity of the sex-regulating systems of the central nervous system to testosterone. This hypothesis was supported by the demonstration that castrated immature male rats displayed less sexual behavior than castrated adult male rats without prior sexual experience, although the immature rats were exposed to equal or higher testosterone concentrations. Moreover, the immature males needed more mounts and intromissions prior to ejaculation and displayed longer response latencies which also may be linked to their lower behavioral sensitivity to testosterone. In both groups, higher testosterone levels induced higher levels of sexual performance. The results by Södersten and others seem to indicate that both increased behavioral sensitivity to testosterone and increased testosterone levels determine the development of sexual behavior during puberty in the male rat. It is conceivable that the increase of behavioral sensitivity to testosterone early in puberty is mediated by LH–RH increases which probably predate the enhancement of gonadal testosterone production. The same reasoning applies to the sensitivity difference between adult and immature rats, since LH–RH production must be assumed to remain elevated above prepubertal levels throughout adulthood.

There are no similarly comprehensive studies on sexual behavior in pubertal primates, but some hormone-behavior correlations have recently been presented by Rose and others (1978). This team followed five adolescent male rhesus monkeys longitudinally from age two through age four with the collection of monthly testosterone levels and observations of behavior. These animals were part of a larger social group of rhesus monkeys of varying ages. Typically, adult rhesus males show strong elevations of both testosterone and sexual behavior during the breeding season and relatively low levels during the remainder of the year. In the adolescent males, testosterone levels showed initial seasonal rises by age three but did not show the adult male seasonal pattern until age four years. Sex behavior demonstrated (gradual) seasonal increases in both year two and three prior to the rise in testosterone. These results appear to be quite similar to the ones in the rat, but whether or not the same explanations apply, needs to be clarified in future investigations. Social learning is an additional potential factor which must be considered in these group-reared animals. Another noteworthy finding by Rose and coworkers was that the extent of the increase of testosterone levels during the third year depended on the number of adult males present in a given social group, probably affecting the relative rank of the adolescents in the dominance hierarchy. Similar delays of pubertal maturation caused by

the presence of intact adult males have been described for rodents (e.g., McKinney and Desjardins, 1973).

In summary, the animal literature suggests that pubertal rises in male sexual behavior can be caused both by increases in testosterone production and by increased behavioral sensitivity to testosterone. The latter may be due to early LH–RH production or, independently, to CNS maturation. Comparable data on female puberty and sexual behavior have not been described.

PUBERTAL DISORDERS AND SEXUAL BEHAVIOR IN MAN

Deviations from the usual timetable of pubertal development lead to discrepancies of several variables that are usually highly correlated: chronological age, physique age, and psychosocial age (Money and Ehrhardt, 1972). When physique age is advanced or retarded in relation to chronological age, it depends to some extent on the particular environment, for example, social pressures from peers and adults, whether or not and to what extent the psychosocial age will coincide with or deviate from the physique age on the one hand and the chronological age on the other. Usually, the child or adolescent will be aware of these discrepancies. The degree of his or her emotional response and the quality of coping will depend largely on support from the outside. Principles of psychological management of disorders in puberty have been described in detail elsewhere (Ehrhardt and Meyer-Bahlburg, 1975; Money, 1968; Pinch and others, 1974). The general social impact of differential maturation has been reviewed by Clausen (1975).

To the extent that the hormonal changes of puberty are causally involved in human psychosexual development, variations of the timing of puberty should correlate with differences in the onset of mature sexual behavior. For normal variations of puberty, such correlations are suggested by the classical Kinsey reports: early-normal maturing boys started sexual activity earlier, became involved in more types of sexual activity, had higher frequency rates in each type of activity, and subsequently remained at higher rates of total orgasmic outlet (Kinsey and others, 1948). Early-normal maturing girls, however, showed only a slight tendency to start their orgasmic sexual activity (including masturbation) earlier than their peers, and there was also a trend for earlier onset of petting experiences (Kinsey and others, 1953) which might reflect the response of males to the mature-looking young girl as well as the girl's own sexual motivation.

More extreme variations of pubertal timing can be found in clinical syndromes such as precocious or delayed puberty or in hypogonadism in which puberty must be induced artificially. The examination of such syndromes permits a quasi-experimental separation in time of the hormonal from some of the institutionalized social changes; they serve as "experiments of nature." For instance, a boy in mid-puberty at age seven years—with an almost adult-size penis, marked pubic hair, and testosterone levels in the (low) adult male range—will usually not be able to share his sexual feelings and interests, if any, with a pubertal teenage peer group in junior high school; instead he will be with second graders who do not have much understanding of his advanced development. Thus, whatever effects his raised hormone levels may have on his sexual motivation and behavior will manifest themselves relatively independent of social entraining of sexuality.

PRECOCIOUS PUBERTY

The line drawn between "early normal" and pathologically early or precocious puberty is somewhat arbitrary. In the leading American handbook of pediatric endocrinology, van der Werft ten Bosch (1975, p. 621) refrains from giving a definition of sexual precocity other than "the appearance of symptoms and signs of puberty earlier than is to be expected in a child with a particular genetic and environmental background." He finds it desirable that a child of either sex who begins pubertal

changes before age nine years have detailed medical investigation. By contrast, some endocrinologists agree with Bierich's (1975) definition by which the term sexual precocity is used for girls, and if they show signs of sexual maturity before their sixth birthday (menarche before their eighth birthday), and for boys, if signs of sexual maturity appear before their eighth birthday. Precocious puberty can be secondary to a variety of more general medical abnormalities, including a lesion in the brain or the peripheral endocrine glands. It also can be idiopathic or spontaneous without any other physical disorder. Children with idiopathic precocious puberty show a hormonal pattern similar to that of normal children during puberty (Radfar and others, 1976), including the pubertal pattern of sleep-associated LH release (Boyar and others, 1973), and in girls, an enhanced (in some cases even exaggerated) gonadotropin response to LH–RH administration (Reiter and others, 1975). It is not yet quite clear, however, if idiopathic precocious puberty can simply be equated with an early timed but otherwise completely normal puberty: for instance, Bidlingmaier and others (1977) found considerably lower basal gonadotropin and estrogen levels in girls with precocious puberty than in normally maturing girls of the same developmental stage, although those patients who were examined repeatedly at short intervals, showed an almost cyclic pattern of their estradiol levels similar to the pattern of normal pubertal girls before menarche. The authors speculate that enhanced receptor sensitivity or changes in the concentration of sex-hormone binding globulin may play a role in idiopathic precocious puberty, in addition to the premature neural activation of the hypothalamic-pituitary-gonadal system. Clarification of this issue is obviously important to the interpretation of future behavioral studies on such children.

A girl with precocious puberty typically has to cope with an early growth spurt putting her on the growth level of other children who are two or three years older than her chronological age, so that a six-year-old girl may be as tall as one who is eight or nine years old. At the same time, she will begin to show pubic and axillary hair, breast enlargement, and menstruation. The psychosexual development of girls with precocious puberty is not well researched. In an early medical review, Reuben and Manning (1922, 1923) cited eighty-three cases of pregnancy below age fifteen years—thirty of those below age twelve years—and claimed that the majority of the young women had a history of precocious puberty; they screened their own eight female cases of precocious puberty without pregnancy and noticed "sexual desire" only in one, mentally defective girl. Kinsey and others (1953, p. 746), in examining cases of precocious puberty, "have rarely found sexual activities which exceeded those ordinarily found among normal children of the same age." In a follow-up study of fifteen girls with idiopathic precocious puberty (ages ten to twenty-five years) by Money and Walker (1971), apart from case reports the only more recent study that deals with this particular issue, masturbation and sex play did not appear to be increased. Normal sexual curiosity occurred more or less consistent with age and independent from the precocious puberty. Premarital intercourse did not occur earlier than normally expected (age seventeen years and up), with the exception of one girl who became pregnant at age eleven and was the only mother in the sample. Contrary to the typical fears of parents and teachers, precocious sexual behavior did not seem to be a frequent concomitant of precocious puberty in these girls. We do not know, however, how representative the sample was for such patients in general.

Precocious puberty occurs less frequently in boys than in girls. The overall somatic effects in boys with precocious puberty are analogous to the ones in girls. Parental fear is even higher than with girls that their sexual behavior will become a problem at an early age; however, this fear seems to be largely unwarranted. Money and Alexander (1969) studied eighteen boys with precocious puberty; four of them had the idiopathic condition and fourteen were virilized as a result of congenital adrenal hyperplasia. In the latter condition, the adrenal is de-

fective and produces high amounts of androgens leading to the typical signs of male pubertal maturation except for testicular development, since the hypothalamic-pituitary-gonadal axis is not involved. Onset of the corrective glucocorticoid treatment may occasionally induce true precocious puberty. The authors found that sociosexual behavior typically was only moderately ahead of chronological age. Erotic fantasies and masturbation occurred considerably earlier than usual, but the fantasy content was often very immature and reflected the age-typical lack of adequate sex information. Homosexuality and paraphilias did not develop. Unfortunately, the two diagnostic groups were not compared to each other.

In summary, the clinical studies of precocious puberty provide some evidence for hormonal effects on sexual behavior, more so in boys than in girls. In most cases, the effects are usually not very dramatic and do not involve uncontrollable overt sexual behavior.

DELAYED PUBERTY

The diagnosis of idiopathic delayed puberty is as much a matter of convention as the definition of idiopathic precocious puberty (Prader, 1975). Most clinicians seem to agree that the onset of puberty two or three years after the median age justifies concern and the label "delayed puberty." Many boys aged fifteen or sixteen who are not yet in puberty are unhappy, and many of them seek professional help. Just by statistical definition, there must be the same percentage of girls with delayed puberty, but relatively fewer of them seek medical attention, because they do not seem to suffer as much as boys do. Although there are many physical conditions that may cause delayed onset of puberty, the most common is idiopathic or constitutional. Again it is not quite clear whether the hormonal pattern of constitutionally delayed puberty is identical with normal puberty, except for timing, or whether there are also some characteristic endocrine differences.

The delayed adolescent boy has many disadvantages. Compared with his peers, he falls behind in size and strength, and faces teasing and sometimes physical harassment by peers. If he is not able to keep up with his peers in some way, he may withdraw, which usually implies missing out on all the typical experiences of one's age group and having less of an opportunity of acquiring the teenage skills of same-sex socializing and heterosexual contact and bonding. These transient developmental deficiencies may have long-term effects. Several longitudinal studies in which late maturers were compared to early (not precocious) or normal maturers, like the classical California Adolescent Growth Study, found not only the described disadvantages of late pubertal development during adolescence (Jones and Bayley, 1950) but also relative delays in their career status and "organizational leadership" (Ames, 1957) as well as in marriage (Peskin, 1967; Kiernan, 1977) and number of children (Peskin, 1967) in adulthood. Unfortunately, information on the sexual behavior of these subjects was not published. Clinical studies of severe forms of delayed puberty show both psychological and psychosexual delay to be present (Lewis and others, 1977; Money and Wolff, 1974), though it is difficult to disentangle the influence of pubertal delay per se from other contributing factors, especially the short stature resulting from the delayed growth spurt.

FAILURE OF PUBERTY

In the case of idiopathic delayed puberty, mainly timing is in error. The hypothalamic-pituitary-gonadal system matures late but appears to function largely normally thereafter. In other cases, the gonads, the pituitary, or the hypothalamus, are defective so that puberty will never occur spontaneously. For those patients, it becomes of utmost importance for their psychological growth and development that puberty is induced by a sex-appropriate hormone regimen. Our clinical experience has been that there are no dramatic, uncontrollable psychosexual effects of sex hormone treatment. Usually, for both boys and girls, sex hormone

treatment constitutes a boost to morale, especially when the body begins changing visibly. Often there is an upswing in mood and assertiveness and later also in sexual feelings, sexual fantasies, and interests.

Hypopituitary or hypogonadal patients usually do not show full psychosexual development without hormone treatment. Particularly important is the timing of the induction of puberty. If the appropriate sex hormone treatment can be started when the patient's peers go into puberty, both psychosocial and psychosexual development may be mostly normal. The longer treatment is delayed, the greater is the chance of maldevelopment. The evidence for this comes from studies of Turner's syndrome in females (Money and Mittenthal, 1970; Perheentupa and others, 1974), hypogonadism in males (Money and Alexander, 1967; Bobrow and others, 1971), and hypopituitarism (Huffer, 1964; Meyer-Bahlburg, 1975; Money and Clopper, 1975; Clopper and others, 1976). Induction of puberty after age twenty often does not lead to normal psychosexual development. A number of older (hypopituitary) patients have even refused to start sex hormone treatment or have ceased taking it later. It is unclear if this negative reaction toward treatment is due to a generally poorer physiological response to exogenous sex hormones (Zachman and Prader, 1970) or to a psychological rigidity and contentment with the patient's particular status at that age. Generally, the patient groups described showed low sexual arousability, motivation, and activities, as well as deficiencies in sexual pair-bonding, the latter possibly related to decreased socializing with peers. In part, this must be because many of the patients started adequate endocrine treatment later than desirable and/or showed very slow or incomplete somatic maturation. Moreover, it is likely that current treatment regimens do not create an internal hormonal milieu comparable to the one of normal adolescents which may have behavioral consequences of its own. In addition, several syndromes involve hypogonadotropinism of hypothalamic origin; here, behavioral deficiencies may be linked to the deficiency of LH–RH or to additional undiagnosed hypothalamic dysfunctions.

Methodologically, the clinical studies of pubertal disorders available can be considered only preliminary. No control groups have been employed, hormone measures at the time of psychosexual assessment are usually missing, and the effects of the timing and dosage of hormonal treatment regimens on behavioral changes have not been analyzed. The assessment of social influences also is usually incomplete. Nevertheless, the data suggest an interactive view in the theory of psychosexual development: physical and hormonal changes are necessary for normal psychosocial and psychosexual development in adolescence, but even if they are present, normal psychosexual development is dependent on the social integration of the individual in society and especially in his or her peer group. More detailed theoretical formulation would require much methodologically refined investigation.

CONCLUSIONS

A comprehensive psychoendocrine theory of sexual behavior in early adolescence would specify the hormones involved, their behaviorally effective blood levels or dose-response curves, hormone-receptor interactions, sensitive periods of development, differential effects of hormones on the various components of sexual behavior, and the interactions of hormones, physical appearance, and social factors. Although the recent advances in endocrinology make this approach feasible, our current data base is obviously much too limited for establishing such a theory and is sufficient only to answer the question of whether hormones play any role at all in psychosexual development during puberty. The correlation between age at first intercourse and pubertal development is far from impressive. The developmental data on masturbation are suggestive, at least for males, but there are no studies of direct assessments of somatic development and hormones. The same is true of the data on romantic love. On the other hand,

clinical studies of patients with pubertal failure strongly support the notion that untreated hormonal deficiencies in adolescent development are incompatible with full psychosexual maturity. Thus, puberty seems to be a necessary condition for normal psychosexual development but by no means sufficient by itself. This conclusion is supported by the clinical findings on delayed puberty and pubertal failure which show that the exposure to endogenous or exogenous hormones per se does not bring about normal psychosexual development unless the timing of hormonal exposure is adequate.

An important facet of psychosexual development that is clearly hormone-dependent is attractivity. For coital behavior, hormones seem to have a permissive role which must be partly mediated through their effects on the genital apparatus, but the separation in time of puberty from the initiation of intercourse for most adolescents demonstrates the importance of non-hormonal factors. Pubertal hormones may have a particularly important role for the development of sexual attractions, imagery, and arousability, but supportive data on humans are minimal.

As for the hormones important to psychosexual development, estrogens and androgens play a major role in the development of secondary sex characteristics and the resulting attractivity, as well as in genital development, although many details still have to be clarified. Direct effects of specific pubertal sex hormones or their metabolites on brain systems controlling distinct aspects of sexual behavior are likely, since hypothalamic and limbic systems in man seem to be very similar to those of other mammals, but the demonstrations of such effects require more comprehensive and sophisticated investigations than are available to date.

The theoretical position advocated here is an interactionist one. A deterministic-biologic concept of an "activation" of sexual behavior as a consequence of neuroendocrine processes is a necessary component of a theory of sexual behavior development in lower mammals but even there is not sufficiently comprehensive. A purely sociological theory in which the development of adolescent sexuality is described exclusively in such terms as role theory and social learning, neglects the available clinical evidence on the role of hormones. The interactionist viewpoint, albeit unsatisfactorily vague in its current formulations due to the paucity of the data available, is the only one that can adequately take into account both the somatic-endocrine and the social influences.

REFERENCES

AMES, R. 1957. Physical maturing among boys as related to adult social behavior. *Calif. J. Educat. Res.* 8: 69–75.

ASAYAMA, S. 1976. Sexual behavior in Japanese students: comparisons between 1974, 1960 and 1952. *Arch. Sex. Behav.* 5: 371–90.

AUGUST, G. P.; GRUMBACH, M. M.; and KAPLAN, S. L. 1972. Hormonal changes in puberty: III. Correlation of plasma testosterone, LH, FSH, testicular size, and bone age with male pubertal development. *J. Clin. Endocrinol. Metab.* 34: 319–26.

BEACH, F. A. 1977. Hormonal control of sex-related behavior. In *Human sexuality in four perspectives*, ed. F. A. Beach, pp. 247–67. Baltimore: Johns Hopkins University Press.

—— 1976. Sexual attractivity, proceptivity, and receptivity in female mammals. *Hormones and Behavior* 7: 105–38.

BIDLINGMAIER, F.; BUTENANDT, O.; and KNORR, D. 1977. Plasma gonadotropins and estrogens in girls with idiopathic precocious puberty. *Pediatric Research* 11: 91–94.

BIERICH, J. R. 1975. Sexual precocity. In *Disorders of puberty; Clinics in Endocrinology and Metabolism*, vol. 4, ed. J. R. Bierich, pp. 107–42. Philadelphia: W. B. Saunders.

BILLEWICZ, W. Z.; FELLOWES, H. M.; and HYTTEN, C. A. 1976. Comments on the critical metabolic mass and the age of menarche. *Annals of Human Biology* 3: 51–59.

DAVIDSON, J. M. 1977. Neurohormonal bases of

1971. Delayed puberty, eroticism and sense of smell: a psychological study of hypogonadotropinism, osmatic and anosmatic (Kallmann's syndrome). *Arch. Sex. Behav.* 1: 329–44.

BOYAR, R. M. 1978. Control of onset of puberty. *Annual Review of Medicine* 29: 509–20.

——; FINKELSTEIN, J. M.; DAVID, R.; ROFFWARG, H.; KAPEN, S.; WEITZMAN, E. D.; and HELLMAN, L. 1973. Twenty-four hour patterns of plasma luteinizing hormone and follicle stimulating hormone in sexual precocity. *New England Journal of Medicine* 289: 282–286.

——; FINKELSTEIN, J.; ROFFWARG, H.; KAPEN, S.; WEITZMAN, E.; and HELLMAN, L. 1972. Synchronization of LH secretion with sleep during puberty. *New England Journal of Medicine*, 287: 582–86.

BRODERICK, C. B. 1966. Socio-sexual development in a suburban community. *Journal of Sex Research* 2: 1–24.

BURRELL, R. J. W.; HEALY, M. J. R.; and TANNER, J. M. 1961. Age at menarche in South African Bantu schoolgirls living in the Transkei Reserve. *Hum. Biol.* 33: 250–61.

CARNEY, A., BANCROFT, J., and MATHEWS, A. 1978. Combination of hormonal and psychological treatment for female sexual unresponsiveness: a comparative study. *British Journal of Psychiatry* 133: 339–346.

CLAUSEN, J. A. 1975. The social meaning of differential physical and sexual maturation. In *Adolescence in the life cycle*, ed. S. E. Dragastén and G. H. Elder, pp. 25–47. New York: Wiley.

CLOPPER, R. R., JR.; ADELSON, J. M.; and MONEY, J. 1976. Postpubertal psychosexual function in male hypopituitarism without hypogonadotropinism after growth hormone therapy. *Journal of Sex Research* 12: 14–32.

COLLU, R., and DUCHARME, J. R. 1975. Role of adrenal steroids in the regulation of gonadotropin secretion at puberty. *Journal of Steroid Biochemistry* 6: 869–72.

CRAWFORD, J. D., and OSLER, D. C. 1975. Body composition at menarche: the Frisch-Revelle hypothesis revisited. *Pediatrics* 56: 449–58.

DAVIDSON, J. M. 1977. Neurohormonal bases of male sexual behavior. In *International review of physiology. Reproductive physiology II*, vol. 13, ed. R. O. Greep, pp. 225–54. Baltimore: University Park Press.

——, and TRUPIN, S. 1975. Neural mediation of steroid-induced sexual behavior in rats. In Sandler, M., and Gessa, G. L. *Sexual behavior—pharmacology and biochemistry*, pp. 13–20. New York: Raven Press.

DOUVAN, E., and ADELSON, J. 1966. The adolescent experience. New York: Wiley.

——, and GOLD, M. 1966. Modal patterns in American adolescence. In *Child development research*, ed. L. W. Hoffman and M. L. Hoffman, pp. 469–528. New York: Russell Sage Foundation.

EHRHARDT, A. A., and MEYER-BAHLBURG, H. F. L. 1975. Psychological correlates of abnormal pubertal development. In *Disorders of puberty; Clinics in Endocrinology and Metabolism*, vol. 4, ed. J. R. Bierich, pp. 207–22. Philadelphia: W. B. Saunders.

FAIMAN, C., and WINTER, J. S. D. 1974. Gonadotropins and sex hormone patterns in puberty: clinical data. In *The control of the onset of puberty*, ed. M. M. Grumbach, G. D. Grave and F. E. Mayer, pp. 32–61. New York: Wiley.

FREUND, K., LANGEVIN, R.; CIBIRI, S.; and ZAJAC, Y. 1973. Heterosexual aversion in homosexual males. *British Journal of Psychiatry* 122: 163–69.

FRISCH, R. E. 1976. Critical metabolic mass and the age at menarche. *Annals of Human Biology* 3: 489–92.

——, and McARTHUR, J. W. 1974. Menstrual cycles: fatness as a determinant of minimum weight for height necessary for their maintenance or onset. *Science* 185: 949–51.

——, and REVELLE, R. 1970. Height and weight at menarche and a hypothesis of critical body weight and adolescent events. *Science* 169: 397–98.

——; REVELLE, R.; and COOK, S. 1973. Components of weight at menarche and the initiation of the adolescent growth spurt in girls: estimated total water, lean body weight and fat. *Hum. Biol.* 45: 469–83.

GRUMBACH, M. M.; GRAVE, G. D.; and MAYER, F. E., eds. 1974. *The control of the onset of puberty*. New York: Wiley.

GUPTA, D.; ATTANASIO, A.; and RAAF, S. 1975. Plasma estrogen and androgen concentrations in children during adolescence. *Journal of Clinical Endocrinology and Metabolism* 40: 636–43.

HAMBURG, B. A. 1974. Early adolescence: a specific and stressful stage of the life cycle. In *Coping and adaptation*, ed. G. V. Coelho, D. A. Hamburg; and J. E. Adams, pp. 101–24. New York: Basic Books.

HAYS, S. E. 1978. Strategies for psychoendocrine studies of puberty. *Psychoneuroendocrinology* 3: 1–15.

HERBERT, J. 1974. Some functions of hormones and the hypothalamus in the sexual activity of primates. In *Integrative hypothalamic activity. Progress in Brain Research*, vol. 41, ed. D. F. Swaab and J. P. Schade, pp. 331–48. Amsterdam: Elsevier Scientific Publishing Co.

HOHLWEG, W., and DOHRN, M. 1932. Über die Beziehungen zwischen Hypophysenvorderlappen und Keimdrüsen. *Klin. Wochenschr.* 11: 233–35.

HOPKINS, J. R. 1977. Sexual behavior in adolescence. *Journal of Social Issues* 33: 67–85.

HORST, H. J.; BARTSCH, W.; and DIRKSEN-THEDENS, I. 1977. Plasma testosterone, sex hormone binding globulin binding capacity and percent binding of testosterone and 5 alpha-dihydrotestosterone in prepubertal, pubertal and adult males. *Journal of Clinical Endocrinology and Metabolism* 45: 522–27.

HUFFER, V.; SCOTT, W. H.; CONNER, T. B.; and

LOVICE, H. 1964. Psychological studies of adult male patients with sexual infantilism before and after androgen therapy. *Ann. Intern. Med.* 61: 255–68.

ISRAEL, S. 1959. The onset of menstruation in Indian women. *J. Obstet. Gynecol. Br. Emp.* 66: 311–16.

JESSOR, S., and JESSOR, R. 1975. Transition from virginity to nonvirginity among youth: a social-psychological study over time. *Developmental Psychology* 11: 473–84.

JOHNSON, D. F., and PHOENIX, C. H. 1976. Hormonal control of female sexual attractiveness, proceptivity, and receptivity in rhesus monkeys. *Journal of Comparative and Physiological Psychology* 90: 473–83.

JOHNSTON, F. E.; ROCHE, A. F.; SCHELL, L. M.; and WETTENHALL, H. N. B. 1975. Critical weight at menarche. *Am. J. Dis. Child.* 129: 19–23.

JOHNSTON, J. O.; GRUNWELL, J. F.; BENSON, H. D.; KANDEL, A.; and PETROW, V. 1975. Behavioral effects of 19-hydroxytestosterone. In *Sexual behavior: pharmacology and biochemistry*, ed. M. Sandler, and G. L. Gessa, pp. 227–40. New York: Raven Press.

JONES, M. C., and BAYLEY, N. 1950. Physical maturing among boys as related to behavior. *J. Educat. Psychol.* 41: 129–48.

JUDD, H. L.; PARKER, D. C.; and YEN, S. S. C. 1977. Sleep-wake patterns of LH and testosterone release in prepubertal boys. *Journal of Clinical Endocrinology and Metabolism* 44: 865–69.

KANTNER, J. F. and ZELNIK, M. 1972. Sexual experience of young unmarried women in the United States. *Fam. Plan. Perspect.* 4: 9–18.

KEPHART, W. M. 1973. Evaluation of romantic love. *Medical Aspects of Human Sexuality* 7: 92; 98; 100; 106–8.

KIERNAN, K. E. 1977. Age at puberty in relation to age at marriage and parenthood: a national longitudinal study. *Annals of Human Biology* 4: 301–8.

KINSEY, A. C.; POMEROY, W. B. and MARTIN, C. E. 1948. *Sexual behavior in the human male.* Philadelphia: W. B. Saunders.

——; POMEROY, W. B.; MARTIN, C. E.; and GEBHARD, P. H. 1953. *Sexual behavior in the human female.* Philadelphia: W. B. Saunders.

KNORR, D.; BIDLINGMAIER, F.; BUTENANDT, O.; FENDEL, H.; and EHRT-WEHLE, R. 1974. Plasma testosterone in male puberty, I. Physiology of plasma testosterone. *Acta Endocrinologica* 75: 181–94.

KULIN, H. E.; MOORE, R. G., JR.; and SANTNER, S. J. 1976. Circadian rhythms in gonadotropin excretion in prepubertal and pubertal children. *Journal of Clinical Endocrinology and Metabolism* 42: 770–72.

LASCHET, U., and LASCHET, L. 1975. Antiandrogens in the treatment of sexual deviations of men. *Journal of Steroid Biochemistry* 6: 821–26.

LAVRAKAS, P. J. 1975. Female preference for male physique. *Journal of Research in Personality* 9: 324–34.

LEE, P. A.; JAFFE, R. B.; and MIDGLEY, A. R. 1974. Serum gonadotropin, testosterone and prolactin concentrations throughout puberty in boys: a longitudinal study. *Journal of Clinical Endocrinology and Metabolism* 39: 664–72.

——, and MIGEON, C. J. 1975. Puberty in boys: correlation of plasma levels of gonadotropins (LH, FSH), androgens, (testosterone, androstenedione, dehydroepiandrosterone and its sulfate), estrogens (estrone and estradiol) and progestins (progesterone and 17-hydroxyprogesterone). *Journal of Clinical Endocrinology and Metabolism* 41: 556–62.

——; PLOTNICK, L. P.; MIGEON, C. J.; and KOWARSKI, A. A. 1978. Integrated concentrations of follicle stimulating hormone and puberty. *Journal of Clinical Endocrinology and Metabolism* 46: 488–90.

——; PLOTNICK, L. P.; STEELE, R. E.; THOMPSON, R. G.; and BLIZZARD, R. M. 1976. Integrated concentrations of luteinizing hormone and puberty. *Journal of Clinical Endocrinology and Metabolism* 43: 168–72.

LERNER, R. M., and KARABENICK, S. A. 1974. Physical attractiveness, body attitudes, and self-concept in late adolescents. *Journal of Youth and Adolescence* 3: 307–16.

LEWIS, V. G.; MONEY, J.; and BOBROW, N. A. 1977. Idiopathic pubertal delay beyond age fifteen: psychologic study of twelve boys. *Adolescence* 12: 1–11.

LEVIN, R. J. 1976. Thorarche—a seasonal influence but no secular trend. *Journal of Sex Research* 12: 173–79.

LUTTGE, W. G.; HALL, N. R.; and WALLIS, C. J. 1975. Physiologic and pharmacologic actions of hormonal steroids in sexual behavior. In *Sexual behavior: pharmacology and biochemistry*, ed. M. Sandler and G. L. Gessa, pp. 209–17. New York: Raven Press.

MCCAULEY, E., and EHRHARDT, A. A., 1976. Female sexual response: hormonal and behavioral interactions. In *Health care for women, I. Current social and behavioral issues. Primary Care*, vol. 3. ed. D. D. Youngs and A. A. Ehrhardt, pp. 455–76. Philadelphia: W. B. Saunders.

MCEWEN, B. 1976. Interactions between hormones and nerve tissue. *Scientific American* 235: 48–58.

MCKINNEY, T. D., and DESJARDINS, C. 1973. Intermale stimuli and testicular function in adult and immature house mice. *Biology of Reproduction* 9: 370–78.

MARSHALL, W. A., and TANNER, J. M. 1970. Variations in the patterns of pubertal changes in boys. *Arch. Dis. Child.* 45: 13–23.

———. 1969. Variations in pattern of pubertal changes in girls. *Arch. Dis. Child.* 44: 291–303.

MEYER-BAHLBURG, H. F. L. 1978. Behavioral effects of estrogen treatment in human males. Pediatrics 62, No. 6, Part 2, Supplement "Estrogen Treatment of the Young", 1171–1177.

———. 1977. Puberty: physical maturation and sexual behavior. In *Handbook of sexology*, ed. J. Money and H. Musaph, pp. 351–72. Excerpta Medica (Elsevier/North Holland Biomedical Press).

———, and ACETO, T. JR. 1976. Psychosexual status of adolescents and adults with idiopathic hypopituitarism. Paper presented at the 33rd Annual Meeting of the American Psychosomatic Society, Pittsburgh, Pa., March 26–28.

MILLER, P. Y., and SIMON, W. 1974. Adolescent sexual behavior: context and change. *Social Problems* 22: 58–76.

MONEY, J. 1961. Components of eroticism: I. The hormones in relation to sexual morphology and sexual desire. *Journal of Nervous and Mental Disease* 132: 239–48.

———. 1968. *Sex errors of the body.* Baltimore: Johns Hopkins Press.

———. 1970. Use of an androgen-depleting hormone in the treatment of male sex offenders. *Journal of Sex Research* 6: 165–72.

———, and ALEXANDER, D. 1969. Psychosexual development and absence of homosexuality in males with precocious puberty. *J. Nerv. Ment. Dis.* 148: 111–23.

———, and CLOPPER, R. R. 1975. Postpubertal psychosexual function in post-surgical male hypopituitarism. *J. Sex Res.* 11: 25–38.

———, and EHRHARDT, A. A. 1972. *Man & woman, boy & girl.* Baltimore: Johns Hopkins University Press.

———, and MITTENTHAL, S. 1970. Lack of personality pathology in Turner's Syndrome: relation to cytogenetics, hormones and physique. *Behav. Genet.* 1: 43–56.

———, and WALKER, P. A. 1971. Psychosexual development, maternalism, nonpromiscuity, and body image in 15 females with precocious puberty. *Arch. Sex. Behav.* 1: 45–60.

———, and WOLFF, G. 1974. Late puberty, retarded growth and reversible hyposomatotropinism (psychosocial dwarfism). *Adolescence* 9: 121–34.

Moss, R. L. 1978. Effects of hypothalamic peptides on sex behavior in animal and man. In *Psychopharmacology: a generation of progress,* ed. M. A. Lipton, A. Dimascio, and K. F. Killam, pp. 431–40. New York: Raven Press.

Odell, W. D., and Swerdloff, R. S. 1976. Etiologies of sexual maturation: a model system based on the sexually maturing rat. *Recent Progress in Hormone Research* 32: 245–88.

Parker, L. N.; Sack, J.; Fisher, D. A.; and Odell, W. D. 1978. Adrenarche—prolactin, gonadotropins, adrenal androgens, and cortisol. *Journal of Clinical Endocrinology and Metabolism* 46: 396–401.

Persky, H., Charney, N., Lief, H. I., O'Brien, C. P., Miller, W. R., and Strauss, D. 1978b. The relationship of plasma estradiol level to sexual behavior in young women. *Psychosomatic Medicine* 40: 523–535.

Penny, R.; Olambiwonnu, N. O.; and Frasier, S. D. 1977. Episodic fluctuations of serum gonadotropins in pre-pubertal and post-pubertal girls and boys. *Journal of Clinical Endocrinology and Metabolism* 45: 307–11.

Perheentupa, J.; Lenko, H. L.; Nevalainen, J.; Niittymäki, M.; Söderholm, A.; and Taipale, V. 1974. Hormonal therapy in Turner's Syndrome: growth and psychological aspects. *Pediatria XIV,* (XIV (1974) Int. Congr. Pediat.) vol. 5, *Growth and development. Endocrinology,* pp. 121–27. Buenos Aires: Editorial Medica Panamericana, S. A.

Persky, H.; Lief, H. I.; Strauss, D.; Miller, W. R.; and O'Brien, C. P. 1978. Plasma testosterone level and sexual behavior of couples. *Archives of Sexual Behavior* 7: 157–73.

Peskin, H. 1967. Pubertal onset and ego functioning. *J. Abnorm. Psychol.* 72: 1–15.

Phoenix, C. H. 1974. The role of androgens in the sexual behavior of adult male rhesus monkeys. In *Reproductive behavior,* ed.

W. Montagna and W. A. Sadler, pp. 249–58. New York: Plenum Press.

Pinch, L.; Aceto, T., Jr.; and Meyer-Bahlburg, H. F. L. 1974. Cryptorchidism. In *Pediatric urology; The Urologic Clinics of North America,* vol. 1, ed. L. C. King, pp. 573–92. Philadelphia: W. B. Saunders.

Prader, A. 1975. Delayed adolescence. In *Disorders of puberty; Clinics in Endocrinology and metabolism,* vol. 4, ed. J. R. Bierich, pp. 143–55. Philadelphia: W. B. Saunders.

Radfar, N.; Ansusingha, K.; and Kenny, F. M. 1976. Circulating bound and free estradiol and estrone during normal growth and development and in premature thelarche and isosexual precocity. *Journal of Pediatrics* 89: 719–23.

Reiter, E. O.; Kaplan, S. L.; Conte, F. A.; and Grumbach, M. M. 1975. Responsivity of pituitary gonadotropes to luteinizing hormone-releasing factor in idiopathic precocious puberty, precocious thelarche, precocious adrenarche, and in patients treated with medroxyprogesterone acetate. *Pediatric Research* 9: 111–16.

Reuben, M. S., and Manning, G. R. 1922. Precocious puberty. *Archives of Pediatrics* 39: 769–85.

———. 1923. Precocious puberty. (ctd.). *Archives of Pediatrics* 40: 27–44.

Rose, R. M.; Bernstein, I. S.; Gordon, T. P.; and Lindsley, J. G. 1978. Changes in testosterone and behavior during adolescence in the male rhesus monkey. *Psychosomatic Medicine* 40: 60–70.

Schmidt, G., and Sigusch, V. 1972. Changes in sexual behavior among young males and females between 1960–1970. *Arch. Sex. Behav.* 2: 27–45.

Schofield, M. 1965. *The Sexual Behavior of Young People.* London: Longmans, Green.

Simon, W.; Berger, A. S.; and Gagnon, J. H. 1972. Beyond anxiety and fantasy: the coital experiences of college youth. *Journal of Youth and Adolescence* 1: 203–22.

SÖDERSTEN, P.; DAMASSA, D. A.; and SMITH, E. R. 1977. Sexual behavior in developing male rats. *Hormones and Behavior* 8: 320–41.

SORENSEN, R. 1973. *Adolescent sexuality in contemporary America.* New York: World Publishing.

STUKOVSKY, R.; VALSIK, J. A.; and BULAI-STIRBU, M. 1967. Family size and menarcheal age in Constanza, Roumania. *Hum. Biol.* 39: 277–83.

TAKAHASHI, E. 1966. Growth and environmental factors in Japan. *Hum. Biol.* 38: 112–30.

TANNER, J. M. 1975. Growth and endocrinology of the adolescent. In *Endocrine and genetic diseases of childhood and adolescence,* 2d ed., ed. L. I. Gardner, pp. 14–64. Philadelphia: W. B. Saunders.

———. 1968. Earlier maturation in man. *Sci. Am.* 218: 21–26.

———. 1966. Growth and physique in different populations of mankind. In *The biology of human adaptability,* ed. P. T. Baker and J. J. Weiner, pp. 45–66. Oxford: Clarendon Press.

———. 1962. *Growth at adolescence,* 2d ed. Oxford: Blackwell Scientific Publications.

VAN DER WERFF TEN BOSCH, J. J. 1975. Isosexual precocity. In *Endocrine and genetic diseases of childhood and adolescence,* 2d ed., L. I. Gardner, pp. 619–39. Philadelphia: W. B. Saunders.

VAN WIERINGEN, J. C.; WAFELBAKKER, F.; VERBRUGGE, H. P.; and de HAAS, J. H. 1971. *Growth diagrams 1965, Netherlands.* Groningen, Netherlands: Wolters-Noordhoff.

VENER, A. M., and STEWART, C. S. 1974. Adolescent sexual behavior in middle America revisited: 1970–1973. *Journal of Marriage and the Family* 36: 728–35.

VERMEULEN, A., and VERDONCK, L. 1972. Some studies on the biological significance of free testosterone. *Journal of Steroid Biochemistry* 3: 421–26.

———; VERDONCK, L.; and COMHAIRE, F. 1974. Rhythms of the male hypothalamo-pituitary-testicular axis. In *Biorhythms and human reproduction,* ed. M. Ferin, F. Halberg, R. M. Richart, and R. L. Vande Wiele, pp. 427–45. New York: Wiley.

WAXENBERG, S. E.; DRELLICH, M. G.; and SUTHERLAND, A. M. 1959. The role of hormones in human behavior 1. Changes in female sexuality after adrenalectomy. *Journal of Clinical Endocrinology* 19: 193–202.

WIGGINS, J. S.; WIGGINS, N.; and CONGER, J. C. 1968. Correlates of heterosexual somatic preference. *Journal of Personality and Social Psychology* 10: 82–90.

WINTER, J. S. D., and FAIMAN, C. 1973. The development of cyclic pituitary-gonadal function in adolescent females. *Journal of Clinical Endocrinology and Metabolism* 37: 714–18.

ZACHMANN, M., and PRADER, A. 1970. Anabolic and androgenic effect of testosterone in sexually immature boys and its dependency on growth hormone. *J. Clin. Endocrinol. Metab.* 30: 85–95.

ZELNIK, M., and KANTNER, J. F. 1977. Sexual and contraceptive experience of young unmarried women in the United States, 1976 and 1971. *Family Planning Perspectives* 9: 55–71.

FIVE

Sexuality in Adolescence

FARIDA SHAH

MELVIN ZELNIK

INTRODUCTION

Adolescence in American society is generally viewed as a period of change, friction, and problems. It is a period during which the individual is no longer a child and yet not quite an adult. The adolescent is encouraged to be independent and to be assertive, but with regard to sexual expression there are varying degrees of prohibition depending on gender and social status. More restrictive sexual standards are applied to women than to men, blacks are more sexually permissive than whites, and lower social class people are generally more permissive than other social groups.[1] The sexual restrictions imposed by society on adolescents at a stage when the physiological need for sexual expression increases creates many conflicts. The period of conflicts is now longer than it ever has been, because there has been a prolongation of adolescence both biologically and socially. The mean age at menarche in the Western European populations declined from about age sixteen in 1870 to age fourteen by around 1930 and went down to about age thirteen years during the 1950s (Tanner, 1968). The present mean age at menarche in the United States is about age twelve. Socially, there have been changes in the life cycle. The median age at marriage for United States women increased from 20.3 years in 1960 to 21.6 years in 1977, and the proportion of unmarried adolescent women has increased dramatically. In 1960, 60 percent of nineteen-year-old women were single compared to 74 percent in 1977 (Current Population Reports, 1978). Also, adolescents are exposed to sex to a much greater degree than ever before, both through the mass media and through personal experiences. Under these circumstances, the restrictive standards of society with respect to sexual behavior are likely to be violated. There seems to be a greater tolerance now of the violators of the sexual code than there was a few decades ago, but this tolerance is not usually extended to the young woman who becomes pregnant before marriage. The social, psychological, and economic consequences of an out-of-wedlock birth are grim for both the young mother and her child.

Most earlier studies on adolescent sexual behavior have dealt not with the consequences of sexual behavior but with different types of sexual outlets in the context of sexual standards, interpersonal relationships, attainment of orgasm, and marital happiness. For example, Kinsey (1953) studied the correlation between premarital patterns of various types of sexual behavior and subsequent sexual adjustments in marriage, based on the sexual histories of females of all ages; Reiss (1961, 1967) analyzed premarital sexual standards and premarital sexual permissiveness: Ehrmann (1959) examined premarital sexual behavior in terms of sex codes of conduct and the love relationship; Burgess and Wallin (1953) analyzed factors influencing engagement and marriage adjustments; Kirkendall (1961) studied premarital intercourse and interpersonal relationships based on experiences of 200 college-level males; and Locke (1951) dealt with premarital sexual intercourse and marital sexual adjustment among 525 divorced and 404 happily married persons.

In this chapter we will examine adolescent sexual behavior from the viewpoint of the consequences of sexual behavior, for example, out-of-wedlock pregnancy. Our focus will be on premarital sexual behavior and more particularly on the social aspects of premarital intercourse (heterosexual coitus) among women fif-

---

[1] For a fuller discussion of permissiveness in premarital sex, see I. L. Reiss, *The Social Context of Premarital Sexual Permissiveness* New York: Holt, Rinehart and Winston, 1967.

teen to nineteen years of age. Our findings are based largely on data from two national surveys of women aged fifteen to nineteen. In the first study, conducted in the spring and early summer of 1971, interviews were obtained from a national probability sample of 4,611 adolescent women fifteen to nineteen years of age living in households and in college dormitories in the continental United States. The sampled population included young women of all marital statuses and races (Zelnik, 1972). A similar but independent study was carried out in the spring and summer of 1976, with a national probability sample of 2,193 adolescent women fifteen to nineteen years of age, who lived in households in the continental United States. Again, the sampled population covered women of all marital statuses and races (Zelnik, 1977).[2] In this article we will deal mainly with the unmarried women and when comparisons are made between 1971 and 1976, we will use data only on women living in households.

TRENDS IN PREMARITAL INTERCOURSE

There seems to be a consensus of opinion that in the early part of the twentieth century and especially in the 1920s, there was a "sexual revolution" (Terman, 1938; Ehrmann, 1964; McCary, 1973). However, there is some debate

[2] Other published articles based on data from these two national surveys are: Probability of Premarital Intercourse, *Social Science Research*, I(1972), 335; "Sex and Contraception among Unmarried Teenagers," in C. F. Westoff, *Toward the End of Growth*, (Englewood Cliffs, N.J.: Prentice-Hall, Inc., 1973, p. 7; "The Resolution of Teenage First Pregnancies," *Family Planning Perspectives*, 6(1974), 74; "Attitudes of American Teenagers toward Abortion," *Family Planning Perspectives*, 7(1975), 89. "Sexual Experience of Young Unmarried Women in the United States," *Family Planning Perspectives*, vol. 4, no. 4 (1972), 9; "Contraception and Pregnancy: Experience of Young Unmarried Women in the United States, *Family Planning Perspectives*," 5(1973), 21; "Unprotected Intercourse among Unwed Teenagers," *Family Planning Perspectives*, 7(1975), 39; "Sexual and Contraceptive Experience of Young Unmarried Women in the United States, 1976 and 1971," *Family Planning Perspectives*, vol. 9, no. 2 (1977); "First Pregnancies to Women, Aged 15–19: 1976 and 1971," *Family Planning Perspectives*, vol. 10, no. 1 (1978); and "Contraceptive Patterns and Premarital Pregnancy among Women Aged 15–19 in 1976," *Family Planning Perspectives*, vol. 10. no. 3 (1978).

about the trend between 1930 and 1960. Udry et al. (1975) report "sharp increases" in the coital experience of unmarried women at ages fifteen through nineteen in cohorts born in the 1920s through the 1950s. Other investigators (Bell, 1966; Vener, 1972) believe that between the 1920s and the 1960s there was little change in the proportions of women having premarital intercourse. Reiss (1969) contends that there has not been a real increase in premarital activity and that reported increases in premarital intercourse are a result of liberalized attitudes toward sexual behavior which make people more willing to talk. This view has not held true since the 1960s when evidence presented by several studies—especially those that examined similar groups at two or more points in time—revealed a steady increase in rates of premarital intercourse. Bell and Chaskes (1970) compared the sexual behavior of female students in the same college in 1958 and in 1968 and found an increase in the rate of premarital coitus for each category of dating relationship. Similar findings were reported by Christensen and Gregg (1970) in their comparison of college students from three different social settings in 1958 and 1968. More recently, Vener and Stewart (1974) and King and others (1977) have found the trend of increase in premarital intercourse continuing in the 1970s.[3] These studies were all based on select groups such as volunteers, college students, and unwed mothers, and therefore do not provide accurate estimates of the trend in prevalence of premarital intercourse among United States adolescent women.

The data from the two national surveys show that there has been an increase in sexual activity among unmarried fifteen- to nineteen-year-old women between 1971 and 1976 in the United States and permit an estimation of this increase. As Table 1 shows, thirty-five percent of the unmarried adolescents interviewed in 1976 had experienced coitus compared to twenty-seven percent of those interviewed in

[3] Vener and Stewart compared behavior of students in a Michigan community in 1970 and in 1973. King et al. compared the behavior of university students in 1965, 1970, and 1975.

Table 1. PERCENT OF NEVER-MARRIED WOMEN AGED 15–19 WHO HAVE EVER HAD INTERCOURSE, BY AGE AND RACE, 1976 AND 1971.

	PERCENT SEXUALLY ACTIVE											
	1976						1971					
	Total		Black		White		Total		Black		White	
AGE	%	N	%	N	%	N	%	N	%	N	%	N
15–19	34.9	1886	62.3	654	31.7	1232	26.8	3972	52.4	1339	22.7	2633
15	18.0	409	38.4	133	13.8	276	13.8	986	31.9	344	10.8	642
16	25.4	436	52.6	135	22.6	301	21.2	982	46.4	320	17.5	662
17	40.9	416	68.4	139	36.1	277	26.6	942	56.8	296	21.7	646
18	45.2	363	74.1	143	43.6	220	36.8	624	59.6	228	32.8	396
19	55.2	262	83.7	104	48.7	158	46.8	438	79.2	151	41.2	287

Note: All percentages are computed from weighted data. The Ns, however, are unweighted totals from the interview sample.

1971. This represents an increase of thirty percent in the prevalence of intercourse among unmarried fifteen- to nineteen-year-old women between 1971 and 1976. Even if an allowance is made for a possible increase in candor, this change clearly indicates that more young women now are engaging in premarital intercourse than did in the past. Sexual activity has increased both among black and white women, with a higher percent increase among whites than among blacks. Within each race group sexual activity has increased at each age. By age nineteen, eighty-four percent of the black and forty-nine percent of the white unmarried women had experienced intercourse in 1976 compared to seventy-nine percent of blacks and forty-one percent of whites in 1971.

Not only are more adolescent women having intercourse, but the age at which young unmarried women initiate intercourse is dropping: the median age at first intercourse was 16.2 in 1976, down from 16.5 years in 1971. This decline in the median age at first intercourse, although small, is consistent with the general relaxation in sexual behavior evident in the increased proportion of young unmarried women who have had intercourse. The earlier initiation of sexual intercourse does not seem to be related to the earlier maturation of young white women. However, black women who begin menstruation early tend to have intercourse at an earlier age.

There are socially accepted and expected patterns of sexual behavior extending over several stages of increasingly deeper commitments to interpersonal relations. Within a stable relationship, such as an engagement, the societal restrictions on premarital intercourse seem to be relaxed. These norms appear to apply more to whites than to blacks. Among older black adolescents (eighteen- to nineteen-year-olds), coitus is almost universal. About eight out of ten unmarried black eighteen- to nineteen-year-olds had experienced coitus including both those who were engaged to be married in 1976 and those without this commitment. Among whites, a higher proportion of engaged women had had coitus than did those with no marriage plans. Even among whites, the commitment of engagement as a condition for engaging in premarital intercourse has become less important than it used to be. Between 1971 and 1976 the increase in the proportion having intercourse was greater among those who had no marriage plans than among those who were engaged. Bell and Chaskes (1970) also have reported that between 1958 and 1968 the commitment of engagement as a prerequisite for premarital intercourse among college girls had decreased. Along with the general relaxation in attitudes toward sexual behavior has been the increased opportunity available to adolescents. Most first coital experiences (about 80%) for young unmarried women take place in homes of either the partner, a friend or relative, or the young woman herself.

FREQUENCY OF INTERCOURSE
AND NUMBER OF PARTNERS

Although intercourse among unmarried adolescent women is not rare, young women are, generally speaking, not promiscuous. This is seen both by their frequency of intercourse as well as by the number of partners with whom they have ever had intercourse. About four out of ten sexually experienced women in the 1971 survey had not had intercourse for at least one month prior to interview. Young women interviewed in 1976 appear to have intercourse even less frequently; about half of the sexually experienced women interviewed in 1976 had not had intercourse in the preceding month (Table 2). The decline in frequency of intercourse was true for each age group and for both blacks and whites. In 1971 as well as 1976, white women who had had intercourse in the month preceding interview had a higher frequency of intercourse than did comparable black women (Table 2).

Most sexually experienced unmarried women in the 1971 survey tended to confine themselves to one male partner. Six out of ten unmarried adolescent women had had only one partner. Whites and blacks were quite similar, except that whites were more likely than blacks to to have had six or more partners. By 1976 the proportion of young unmarried women who had had intercourse with only one partner had dropped to five out of ten. The increase in number of partners was true for each age group and was greater for blacks than for whites.

However, even in 1976 a higher proportion of whites had had six or more partners than did blacks.

Thus, it appears that proportionately more unmarried adolescent women are having intercourse, they are initiating sex earlier, and on the average they have had more partners, but there has not been an increase in frequency of intercourse. An explanation for the apparent decline in coital frequency could be that having more partners is indicative of relations not being well established and females tend to have "greater sexual intimacies with a steady than a nonsteady or with a lover than a nonlover" (Ehrmann, 1964, p. 602).

RELATIONSHIP TO SOCIAL FACTORS
TO PREMARITAL INTERCOURSE

Thus far we have seen that there has been an increase in sexual activity among adolescent women in the United States. This increase has occurred at all ages for both races and is not restricted to those who are engaged. We now shall examine the relationship between some social factors and premarital intercourse.[4]

"Of all sexual behaviors . . . none is more influenced than coitus by cultural influences, such as those reflected particularly in social level and social class upbringing" (Reevy, 1967, p. 58). The influence of social status on the sexual

---

[4] The analyses relating to social factors in premarital intercourse is based mainly on data from the 1971 national survey.

Table 2. PERCENT DISTRIBUTION OF SEXUALLY EXPERIENCED, NEVER-MARRIED WOMEN AGED 15–19, BY FREQUENCY OF INTERCOURSE IN THE FOUR WEEKS PRECEDING INTERVIEW AND BY RACE, 1976 AND 1971.

FREQUENCY OF INTERCOURSE	1976			1971		
	Total	Black	White	Total	Black	White
	(N = 782)	(N = 404)	(N = 378)	(N = 1169)	(N = 641)	(N = 528)
0	48.9	49.5	48.8	39.6	41.3	39.0
1–2	22.9	29.2	20.8	30.2	32.8	29.2
3–5	12.7	14.0	12.3	17.4	17.9	17.3
≥ 6	15.4	7.4	18.1	12.8	8.1	14.5

Note: See Table 1.

behavior of white adolescent women differs from that on blacks. Premarital intercourse among black adolescent women was inversely associated with family income (Table 3); the higher the family income of the black unmarried adolescent, the less likely she was to have had coitus. This inverse relationship between social status and premarital intercourse was true for all the measures of social status used, namely, poverty status, education of the male parent or guardian, and education of the female parent or guardian, and was true for every age group.

For whites the relationship between social status and premarital intercourse was more complex. Unmarried adolescent white women from the lower and upper social classes were more likely to be sexually experienced than those from the middle class. Although the proportions of sexually experienced whites do not show too much variability by family income (Table 3), this pattern—middle-class unmarried white women having the lowest rates of sexual experience—was found consistently for each of the indices of social status. According to theory, the lower class groups were the most permissive and hence were expected to have high rates of premarital intercourse. Why do the high-status groups have higher rates of premarital

intercourse than do the middle-class group? Perhaps higher-status groups tend to be more liberal and "in the higher status groups, liberal individuals are much more permissive than conservative individuals." (Reiss, 1967, p. 65). At each social class level, for each age, blacks experienced coitus at a higher rate than whites. The only social group with similar rates of coital experience for both black and white adolescents was the group whose male parents or guardians were college graduates. The percent sexually experienced among blacks in this social group was 28.6 percent compared to 26.6 percent among whites in a similar social group. This convergence of rates of sexually experienced black and white women occurs because high-status whites are more permissive whereas high-status blacks are the most conservative.

There was no consistent difference in premarital sexual behavior by affiliation to the major religious groups. Burgess and Wallin (1953), and Kinsey et al. (1953) also found no consistent relationship between the three major religious groups and premarital sexual behavior. However, the degree of religious devotion, that is religiosity, was clearly related to premarital intercourse. Within each religious group (with the exception of Jews), young unmarried women who attended church most frequently were the least likely to have coitus, whereas those who attended church infrequently or not at all were the most likely to have coitus. Unmarried women fifteen to nineteen years of age who had no religious affiliation had the highest rates of premarital intercourse—almost half of them were sexually experienced. The inverse relationship between religiosity and premarital intercourse was true for both whites and blacks. As with social class, in each category of religiosity blacks had higher proportions of sexually experienced unmarried women than did whites. In other words, neither social class nor religiosity explains the difference in the proportion who are sexually experienced among blacks and whites.

The place of residence seems to have an influence on sexual behavior. Young unmarried women who once lived on a farm but have

Table 3. PERCENT OF UNMARRIED YOUNG WOMEN AGED 15–19 WHO HAVE EVER HAD INTERCOURSE, BY FAMILY INCOME AND RACE, 1971.

| FAMILY INCOME $ | PERCENT SEXUALLY ACTIVE | | | | | |
| | Total | | Black | | White | |
	%	N	%	N	%	N
≤3000	42.2	385	60.0	265	28.5	120
3001–6000	31.2	749	53.9	400	23.4	349
6001–10,000	26.4	997	56.3	321	22.1	676
10,001–15,000	25.6	964	49.3	196	23.6	768
>15,000	26.6	817	44.7	116	25.6	701

Note: See Table 1.

Source: Kantner, J. F. and Zelnik, M. 1972. Sexual Experience of Young Unmarried Women in the United States, *Family Planning Perspectives*: Vol. 4, No. 4, pp. 9–18.

moved away have the highest proportion having had coitus, whereas those who have always lived on a farm have the lowest rates. As for metropolitan-nonmetropolitan residence, the proportions who have ever had intercourse generally are highest for those who live in the central cities of metropolitan areas. The size of the metropolitan area does not seem to matter. Those who live in nonmetropolitan areas have levels of experience which generally fall between those of central cities and their suburbs. Similar patterns of sexual experience were found for both blacks and whites by place of residence.

Family structure also was found to be related to adolescent sexual behavior. Most young women interviewed in 1971 lived in families headed by their natural fathers. While this was the case for seven out of ten white adolescent women, it was true for only four out of ten blacks. Nearly a third of the black women lived in households headed by their mothers. The lowest proportion with coital experience was found among young women living in families headed by their natural fathers. This pattern is much more evident among whites than among blacks. Young women living in families headed by stepfathers had coital rates similar to those of women in families headed by fathers. The stepfather seems to be a fair substitute for the natural father. The important consideration, perhaps, is the integrity of the family, with its full complement of members to fill the essential roles. Unaided, the mother—especially the white mother—appears to have more difficulty maintaining "control" over her daughter. Three out of ten white adolescent women from households headed by the mother were sexually experienced compared to two out of ten from households headed by the father or stepfather. Other women acting as family heads and perhaps lacking the mother's claim to authority, appear to be even less successful. Four out of ten white adolescents from families headed by women other than their natural mothers were sexually experienced. The comparable rates for black adolescents were forty-six to forty-eight percent when the head of household was the father or stepfather, fifty-four percent for households headed by the mother, and seventy-three percent for households headed by other women.

CONTRACEPTIVE PRACTICE AND PREGNANCY

Since our interest in sexual behavior is in the context of its consequences for adolescent women, a pertinent question is: To what extent do sexually experienced adolescent women attempt to avoid pregnancy through use of contraception?

Although most sexually experienced unmarried adolescent women interviewed in 1971 had used contraception at some time, they took many chances. Over half of them had not used any contraception at their most recent coitus, and only two out of ten used contraception consistently. Younger sexually experienced women (fifteen- and sixteen-year-olds) were more likely to have never used contraception than older adolescents (seventeen- to nineteen-year-olds). Those adolescents who did use contraception generally began using it sometime after the first coitus. The earlier the age was at the first coitus the wider the gap was between first intercourse and first contraception. For most adolescent women, sex is a sometime thing and this may be an important factor in the low levels of consistent use of contraception. Sex is either unanticipated or it is not proper to go "prepared." The data on the use of contraception as well as on the methods of contraception by frequency of intercourse were consistent with this line of interpretation. About forty-six percent of the women who had intercourse less than three times a month had used contraception at last intercourse compared to two-thirds of those who had intercourse six or more times a month. The choice of contraceptive methods also depended a great deal on the frequency of intercourse. Among the women who had not had intercourse in the month prior to interview, over half had used either the condom or withdrawal at their most recent experience, and only fourteen percent used the pill. In contrast, half the women with the highest frequencies of intercourse (six or more times a month) had used the pill at their last intercourse.

There is also considerable misconception about the risks of pregnancy. Seven out of ten sexually experienced women did not use contraception because they did not think they could become pregnant, because they had intercourse at a time of the month when they could not become pregnant, because they were too young to become pregnant, or because they had sex too infrequently to become pregnant. Some who believed they could not become pregnant because of the time of the month were correct in their judgement, but many were clearly misinformed about the risk of unprotected coitus.

One in ten of all fifteen- to nineteen-year-old women (married as well as unmarried) interviewed in 1971 had become pregnant before marriage. The overwhelming majority (about three-fourths) of the women indicated that the pregnancy was unintended. Yet, about nine out of ten of those who did not intend the pregnancy had not used contraception at the time of conception. A premarital pregnancy very often precipitates marriage, at least among whites. Over half the white young women who became pregnant premaritally married before the outcome of the pregnancy.[5] The divorce

rate among such marriages is reported to be much greater than among other marriages of young people (Schofield, 1973).

A comparison of the contraceptive use of sexually experienced, never-married women interviewed in 1971, with those interviewed in 1976 (Table 4) shows a dramatic increase in the proportion using contraception both consistently and at last intercourse. The increased use was seen for adolescent women of all ages and among both blacks and whites. In 1976, the younger respondents, those aged seventeen and under were more likely to have used contraception at last intercourse than were those over seventeen in 1971. Moderating this picture of improved contraceptive practice is the fact that there was also an increase in the proportion who never used contraception.

Along with the increased use of contraception there was a change in the methods of contraception. The pill was the most commonly used method by both blacks and whites and for all groups. About half the sexually experienced women in the 1976 survey named the pill as the method most recently used compared to less than a fourth in 1971. The condom, withdrawal, and douche, popular in 1971, were not as much in demand in 1976.

The increased permissiveness in sexual behavior has been paralleled by the increased effort at avoiding a premarital pregnancy, both by greater use of contraception and also by use of more effective methods. In 1976 the sporadic engaging in sex did not seem to be as great a

[5] By 1976 a premarital pregnancy was less likely to lead to a "shotgun" marriage—about a third of the white women who were premaritally pregnant married before the outcome of the pregnancy. This is probably due to the increased tendency of young women to seek abortion rather than to get married.

Table 4. PERCENT OF SEXUALLY EXPERIENCED NEVER MARRIED WOMEN AGED 15–19 BY CONTRACEPTIVE USE, STATUS, AND RACE, 1976 AND 1971.

USE STATUS	1976			1971		
	Total	Black	White	Total	Black	White
	(N = 786)	(N = 408)	(N = 378)	(N = 1217)	(N = 669)	(N = 548)
Never	23.8	25.2	23.3	17.0	16.1	17.4
Sometimes	46.4	45.9	46.6	64.6	68.9	62.9
Always	29.8	28.9	30.1	18.4	15.0	19.7
Last Time *	63.7	58.2	65.5	45.4	41.5	46.9

* "Last Time" includes always-users and sometimes-users who used contraception at the time of last intercourse.
Note: See Table 1

deterrent to the use of contraception as it did in 1971. The greater use of oral contraception also suggests an increased willingness by adolescent women to be "prepared" for the occasion. Another factor in the greater use of birth-control pills may be that they are more readily available to young unmarried women now than they were in 1971.

Although the use of contraception has increased considerably, about half the sexually experienced adolescent women interviewed in 1976 had not used contraception at their first intercourse, and the gap between age at first intercourse and age at first contraception was wider in 1976 than it was in 1971. However, those who do not use contraception the first time but do so subsequently, tend to use more sophisticated methods like the pill and the IUD. In 1976, of the women who had not used contraception at their first intercourse but did so subsequently, six out of ten used the pill or IUD as their first method, and only three out of ten used the condom or withdrawal. In contrast, six out of ten women who used contraception at their first intercourse used the condom or withdrawal. This difference in the quality of contraception between those who delayed first use and those who did not was not a matter of age at the time contraception was first used or of experience with pregnancy, although pregnancy was frequently an incentive to more effective contraception.

Although the increasing use of the pill and the IUD among adolescent women should help prevent undesired pregnancy, the desirability of early and continued use of these contraceptives is questionable because of known and suspected risks of serious side effects. A question may also be raised about the increased prevalence of venereal diseases among adolescents which seems to coincide with the decline in use of the condom. The detrimental effects of the present contraceptive practices of adolescents, combined with the likelihood that the prevalence of sexual intercourse will continue to increase, suggest a need for the development of contraceptives suitable for young adolescents.

REFERENCES

BELL, R. R. 1966. *Premarital sex in a changing society.* Englewood Cliffs, N.J.: Prentice-Hall.

———, and CHASKES, J. B. 1970. Premarital sexual experience among coeds, 1958 and 1968. *Journal of Marriage and the Family* 32.

BURGESS, E. W., and WALLIN, P. 1953. *Engagement and marriage.* Philadelphia: Lippincott.

CHRISTENSEN, H. T., and GREGG, C. F. 1970. Changing sex norms in America and Scandinavia. *Journal of Marriage and the Family* 32.

Current population reports. 1978. Population characteristics: marital status and living arrangements: March 1977. Series P-20, no. 323, April.

EHRMANN, W. 1959. *Premarital dating behavior.* New York: Holt, Rinehart & Winston.

———. 1964. Marital and Nonmarital Sexual Behavior. In *Handbook of marriage and the family,* ed. H. T. Christensen. Chicago: Rand McNally.

KING, K.; BALSWICK, J. O.; and ROBINSON, I. E. 1977. The continuing premarital sexual revolution among college females. *Journal of Marriage and the Family* 39.

KINSEY, A. C.; POMEROY, W. B.; and MARTIN, C. E. 1948. *Sexual behavior in the human male.* Philadelphia: W. B. Saunders.

———; and GEBHARD, P. H. 1953 *Sexual behavior in the human female.* Philadelphia: W. B. Saunders.

KIRKENDALL, L. A. 1961. *Premarital intercourse and interpersonal relationships.* New York: Matrix House.

LOCKE, H. J. 1951. *Predicting adjustment in marriage: a comparison of a divorced and a happily married group.* New York: Holt, Rinehart & Winston.

McCARY, J. L. 1973. *Human sexuality: physiological, psychological and sociological fac-*

tors, 2d ed. New York: Van Nostrand Reinhold.

REEVY, W. R. 1967. Adolescent sexuality. In *Encyclopedia of sexual behavior,* ed. Albert Ellis and Albert Abarbanel, Hawthorne Books, Inc., New York, p. 52–68.

REISS, I. L. 1961. Standards of sexual behavior. In *Encyclopedia of sexual behavior,* ed. A. Ellis and A. Abarbanel. New York: Hawthorne.

REISS, I. L. 1967. *The social context of premarital sexual permissiveness.* New York: Holt, Rinehart & Winston.

REISS, I. R. 1969. Premarital sexual standards. In *The individual, sex, and society,* ed. C. B. Broderick and J. Bernard. Baltimore: Johns Hopkins Press.

SCHOFIELD, M. 1965. *The sexual behavior of young people.* Boston: Little, Brown.

———. 1973. *The sexual behavior of young adults.* Boston: Little, Brown.

TANNER, J. M. 1968. Earlier maturation in man. *Scientific American* Vol. 218, No. 1, p. 21–27.

TERMAN, L. M. 1938. *Psychological factors in marital happiness.* New York: McGraw-Hill.

UDRY, J. R.; BAUMAN, K. E.; and MORRIS, N. M. 1975. Changes in premarital experience of recent decade of birth cohorts of urban American women. *Journal of Marriage and the Family* 37.

VENER, A. M., and STEWART, C. S. 1974. Adolescent sexual behavior in middle America revisited: 1970–1973. *Journal of Marriage and the Family* 36.

———; and HAGER, D. L. 1972. The sexual behavior of adolescents in middle America: generational and American-British comparisons. *Journal of Marriage and the Family* 34.

ZELNIK, M., and KANTNER, J. F. 1972. Sexuality, contraception and pregnancy among young unwed females in the United States. In *Demographic and Social Aspects of Population Growth,* ed. C. F. Westoff and R. Parke. Washington, D.C.: Government Printing Office.

———. 1977. Sexual and contraceptive experience of young unmarried women in the United States, 1976 and 1971. *Family Planning Perspectives,* vol. 9.

SIX

Sexuality in Marriage

JUANITA H. WILLIAMS

INTRODUCTION

The sexual behavior of women and men in the marriage relationship probably has just as much variety as any other behaviors. Affected by deeply ingrained attitudes, themselves determined by cultural and idiosyncratic histories, sexual behavior also reflects the quality of the relationship, situational variables, and personal characteristics such as age, health, and equality. Biological, psychological, cultural, and historical determinants interact to produce similarities and differences, fascinating mosaics within which patterns can be discerned, some stronger and more pervasive than others.

Currently, both marriage and sexuality are the subjects of examination, commentary, and criticism by social scientists and those in a variety of other disciplines. Sexual permissiveness, along with other contemporary phenomena such as the availability of birth control and abortion, declining birth rates, and the increasing incidence of divorce, is seen by some as threatening the survival of marriage. At the same time the new permissiveness is seen to encourage marital happiness by disavowing old inhibitions and taboos and by stimulating new practices to banish boredom, expand experiment, and enhance consciousness.

Sexual behavior in marriage today can be observed, studied, and understood by the conventional methods of social science. But to fully appreciate its importance, its relation to its sociocultural context at any given time, and its sensitivity to sex roles and the power relationship of women and men, historical beliefs, attitudes, and practices must be studied.

The discussion will begin by reviewing sexuality and marriage historically, examining normative attitudes and values as they were formulated, promoted, and supported by religious and secular leaders.

During the first half of the twentieth century, sexual behavior first was studied seriously by investigators in such disciplines as anthropology, medicine, and psychology. For the first time, objective studies using interviews, questionnaires, and direct observation began to appear. These data required the conventional wisdom to be modified and sanctioned the emergence of more open attitudes toward and greater freedom in sex in and out of marriage.

Publication of such scholarly studies as those of Kinsey and later of Masters and Johnson, facilitated subsequent inquiry, and sex research became a respectable discipline. At the same time, other social movements, such as the counter-culture movement of the sixties and the women's liberation movement, demanded freedom from authoritarian teachings about role and place. There was a serious examination of the old institution of marriage and its place in the new society. Sexual behavior in marriage, its norms and variety, emerged from the Victorian shadows as a topic fit for science and the public media.

Sexual activity outside of marriage always has been legally and morally proscribed in our society. Sexual activity outside of marriage always has had vastly different meanings for women and men, a double standard which persists today. Even so, the heterosexual monogamous pattern is being eroded by experiments in group marriage, communal living arrangements, and casual physical exchanges. The long-term effects of these as competitors with conventional sexual monogamy are not yet known.

The renaissance of the feminist movement of the past decade has had a significant impact on all the institutions of our society, including marriage. As the old power relationships in which man was dominant and woman submissive began to shift, so did the sexual relationships, and women began to express their needs and to make their demands in this most private encounter between the sexes. Reports of the effects of the new female consciousness on marital sexuality are just beginning to appear, and while so far unsystematic, they suggest a new pattern of expectations, especially for the educated young.

There is human diversity in this area of behavior as in all others. Variability is the rule, and what is normative in one culture is deviant in another. It is both healthful and humbling to realize, as Havelock Ellis pointed out long ago, that not everyone is like us.

HISTORICAL PERSPECTIVE

Marriage is older than recorded history, and its origins are unknown, though the question has stimulated several theories. These include the sexual promiscuity-matriarchy theory (Bachofen, 1967); the theory that monogamy has always been characteristic of human groups, as it is of other primates with whom we share common ancestors (Westermarck, 1921); and theories of ubiquitous patriarchy, in which the formal institution of marriage arose from the reciprocal exchange of women (e.g., Levi-Strauss, 1969). Although each of these has had its supporters and detractors (Murstein, note 1), the last is the most influential today and is worth a closer look because of its implications for the history of relations between women and men and of the development of attitudes about sexuality.

It is Levi-Strauss's contention that the universally observed incest taboo served to promote exogamy, whose functional value was the formation of alliances between groups through the elaboration of kinship systems. Such alliances were based on reciprocity, the ceremonial exchange of gifts, property, and especially women.

> Such is the case with exchange. Its role in primitive society is essential because it embraces material objects, social values and women. But while in the case of merchandise this role has progressively diminished in importance . . . as far as women are concerned, reciprocity has maintained its funda-mental function, on the one hand because women are the most precious possession . . . but above all because women are not primarily a sign of social value, but a natural stimulant; and the stimulant of the only instinct the satisfaction of which can be deferred, and consequently the only one for which, in the act of exchange, and through the awareness of reciprocity, the transformation from the stimulant to the sign can take place, and defining by this fundamental process the transformation from nature to culture, assume the character of an institution (Levi-Strauss, 1969, pp. 62–63.)

The systematic exchange of women greatly strengthened the original family, bringing it into a cultural kinship system, and ensuring its existence as a group. The giving away of sisters and daughters became an insurance against extinction.

The significance of this theory for our discussion is that an important sex difference is made: it is men who are exchanging women. The opposite, as far as we know, has never occurred in any human society (Mitchell, 1974). Levi-Strauss wrote: "The reciprocal bond basic to marriage is not set up between men and women, but between men and men by means of women, who are only the principal occasion for it" (cited in Mitchell, 1974, p. 373).

Marriage, then, was an important link between kinship groups and permitted the establishment of kin lines through which property and power were transmitted from one generation to the next. This being the case, marriages had to be arranged carefully to provide the maximum advantage to all parties. Such a serious matter could not be left to the young, and arranged marriages were the norm until recent times. Such marriages included the payment of a bride price to the bride's father or, in some cases, the custom of the dowry, valuable goods, which went with the bride to her new home.

Attitudes toward sex and marriage revealed in the Old Testament indicate a sensual and earthy consciousness of sex with an accompanying double standard and devaluation of women. The Song of Solomon is essentially a hymn of appreciation for the sexual potential of the human body. Women as sexual beings were, however, regarded as property, and there were strict sanctions against such trespasses as violating a virgin and adultery. The unchaste maid was no longer marriageable, thus worthless to her father; the violator had to marry her and pay money to her father (Exodus 22: 17). Adulterers could be put to death (Leviticus 20: 10), the woman for her sin, the man for violating the property of another man. The sexual behavior of women was carefully prescribed and guarded in order to ensure that legal offspring would inherit property. Women were unclean and required ritual purification in connection with the natural events of their bodies, such as menstruation and childbirth. If a woman gave birth to a son, the period required for her purification was thirty-three days. If the child was a daughter, the time required was sixty-six days (Leviticus 12: 4–5).

Although sexual behavior was carefully regulated, especially for women, and fornication and adultery were serious crimes, marriage itself was an important institution, and everyone was expected to marry and produce children (Kennett, 1931). The good wife, described in the Book of Proverbs, had a price "above rubies," and the impression in that account is that she was a respected companion in the marital enterprise, though subservient (Proverbs 31: 10–26). Sexual desire was an accepted characteristic of humans, and chastity was valued only before marriage.

With the advent of Christianity, beliefs and values about marriage and sexuality began to change. Chastity and asceticism became synonomous with holiness; marriage was a sorry state, to be contracted only in direst need or for procreation, and the status of women declined accordingly. At best, the woman was a silent submissive wife; at worst, she was the instrument of damnation, exciting lust and luring man from his holy mission. Paul wished that all men could be celibate as he was. "But if they cannot contain, let them marry; for it is better to marry than to burn" (I Corinthians 7: 7–9). The man was not made for the woman, but the woman for the man. "Wives, submit yourselves unto your own husbands, . . . as unto the Lord. For the husband is the head of the wife, even as Christ is the head of the church" (Ephesians 6: 22–23). "Let the woman learn in silence with all subjection . . . I suffer not a woman to teach, nor to usurp authority over the man, but to be in silence" (I Timothy 2: 11–12).

The doctrine of asceticism was largely responsible for the low esteem to which marriage fell during this period:

> "It would be difficult to conceive of anything more coarse or more repulsive than the manner in which (the ascetics) regarded it. . . . Even when the bond had been formed, the ascetic passion retained its sting. . . . Whenever any strong religious fervor fell upon a husband or wife, its first effect was to make a happy union impossible The more religious partner desired to live a life of solitary asceticism, or at least, if no ostensible separation took place, an unnatural life of separation in marriage" (Lecky, 1905, vol. 2, 117–18).

During the Middle Ages the equation of chastity and abstinence with sanctity and superior virtue continued to be prominent in the writings of the theologians. The Penitentials of Theodore, seventh-century archbishop of Canterbury, described various punishments for transgressions. A man who had intercourse with his wife must take a bath before entering the church. Newly married persons or women who had given birth were likewise barred from the church for a period, followed by a set penance. Even the more liberal St. Thomas Aquinas thought that marriage was inferior to virginity. Sexual intercourse, even in marriage, partook of the profane connotations of the body. One who indulged would never be as high on the ladder of sanctity as one who abjured the devilments of the flesh in favor of the spiritual life and its promised rewards.

If this was the approved model, however, it appears that in many cases practices in real life were less elevated and more corporeal. Between the sixth and the eleventh centuries the clergy were noted for their sexual excesses and license. Consort with women as wives or concubines was common, and friars, monks, and priests were the main clientele of prostitutes. Suggestions that some women appreciated the pleasures of sex appear in the love letters of Héloise to Abelard, and in the frank sensuality of Chaucer's Wife of Bath. In general, however, women and their sexuality continued to be devalued, and there is little evidence that sexual gratification and emotional satisfaction were normally expected to be part of marriage (Murstein, 1974).

Attitudes toward marriage and sex became somewhat more positive during the Reformation, even though women, their bodies, minds, and functions continued to be denigrated. Martin Luther in his *Table Talk* (Luther, 1890) said that women had narrow chests and broad hips because they were destined to "remain at home, sit still, keep house, and bear and bring up children" (p. 299). Even so, he was a strong advocate of marriage; knowing that celibacy was an elusive goal for most, including the clergy, he saw it as a gift approved by God and a prevention of graver sins. His contemporary, John Calvin, also favored marriage over its inevitable alternatives. He thought that one should refrain from marriage in favor of celibacy as long as possible, however, and recommended restraint and modesty in this activity as in all others. The renunciation of pleasure and worldliness was a strong theme of his, and their equation with sin and the evocation of guilt continued to permeate Western ideas about sex and morality until recent times (Rugoff, 1971).

During the eighteenth and nineteenth centuries, the romantic movement began, with its emphases on nature, freedom, defiance of traditional mores, and the ascendancy of the individual. Sexual love was imbued with divinity; and emotion, rather than cool reason, was the guide to truth and happiness. Romanticism was the antithesis of conventional bourgeois marriage, arranged for practical reasons of family and patrimony. The romantic might marry, but only for love and its passion. Leaders of the romantic movement were such literary figures as Shelley, Byron, and Keats, who themselves exemplified this life style. George Sand, though married, had many lovers, and her public flouting of conventional norms provided an unusual model of assumed sexual equality. The romantic tradition waned with the influence of the Victorian era, but its thematic ideas of the relationships among love, sex, and marriage continue to be important, and its rejection of traditional values echoed through the Victorian counter-culture, the bohemian ethos, and the emergence of the widespread acceptance of sexual freedom in modern times.

The arrival of the Victorian era with its attitudes toward sexuality and marriage linked many of these antecedent themes and integrated a system of morals and values which became a powerful arbiter of behavior for our society. Abolition of slavery, woman suffrage, and labor unions were among the reforms reflecting ideological change as the political and social environment became more and more complex. As Strong (1973) observed, "The comforting security derived from a sense of hierarchy and order appeared to be crumbling with the advent of the new democracy" (p. 457). Opposing this was the vision of the family, united in the sacred and secular bonds of love and marriage, as a refuge from the swirling uncertainties of the world and as a conservatory of traditional values.

The Victorian model of the family relied upon rigid role segregation of the sexes, the husband as head of the household and economic provider and the wife as keeper of the home, maintaining domestic serenity and inculcating spiritual and moral values in the young—the "angel in the house." The idealized notion of the moral superiority of women in this role meant that she was to regulate the display of human passions, including sex. The repressive control of sexual passions was the major motif of Victorian morality, and physicians, preachers, and moralists of all persuasions, male and female, inveighed against the horrors of its abuse, citing disease, mania, and death. (For a detailed review of this literature, see Haller and Haller, 1974.)

Chastity until marriage was valued by both sexes, but its loss for women had far more sinister implications: "Preeminence has its perils—those who fall from it fall farthest, and a female who lost her virtue was, if anything, more reprehensible than a male who did; she went against her nature, while he only obeyed his" (Walter, 1974, p. 68). Marriage was seen as a means for containing and restraining the sexual urges of men, even more the victims of their power than women were. It was part of nature's plan that women have little sexual passion and that to restrain man's ardor, it was both necessary and natural for her to be passive and indifferent to his sexual impulses.

> It should also be pointed out that woman was not advised to experience the same pleasures as the male in the sexual union. As a passive creature, she was to endure the attentions of her husband in a negative sense, if only to deter the greater weakening of the "vital forces" in the male. Writers also believed that if women experienced "any spasmodic convulsion" in coition it would interfere with the possibility of conception—the primary function of the marriage act (Haller, 1972, p. 56).

Married couples were advised to avoid undressing in each others' presence and to sleep in separate beds if possible. The ideal was continence in the marital relationship, the principle being that indulgence of the sexual impulses was not only debilitating and degrading but ran counter to the development and strengthening of character, will, and social responsibility (Haller, 1972).

Given the Victorian status of the parameters of male hegemony, sex role segregation, differential valuing of male and female sexuality, and the role of sex in human arrangements, it was inevitable that sex in marriage was paradoxical, loaded with conflicts and contradictions, and at the same time, invested with feelings of love and responsibility.

Expectations for marriage and the sexual relationship had to be based on the obscure and highly sentimentalized teachings of the times. It was not uncommon for a bride to experience her wedding night totally unprepared for the realities of sexual intercourse, her first experience with sex being closer to rape than to her romantic dreams of sanctioned closeness. What she knew was fiction, gathered from casual talk, overheard conversations, romantic stories and novels, sermons, what her parents and teachers taught her, and her own integration of all these resulting in an utterly unrealistic expectation of what her future as a wife and a sexual partner would be like.

Advice on sexual matters for the married couple was plentiful (Walters, 1974; Haller and Haller, 1974). Unlike the contemporary emphases on both quantity and quality of sexual experience, nineteenth-century authorities, almost to a man, laid down spartan rules for permissible frequency of intercourse and discussed its quality not at all. Dr. Sylvester Graham, for example, thought that once a month was just about right, and Dr. John Cowan advised complete abstinence during pregnancy, lactation, and for an additional year after weaning. "This may not be required in a perfectly healthy woman, but healthy women being an exception, the rule holds good" (in Walter, 1974, p. 89). Since women were held to be asexual (except in rare and pathological cases), there was no obligation to arouse her or to be concerned for her satisfaction.

Because a pretentious and repressive morality was the official position of family, school, and church, it is still not possible to know the extent of its influence on married couples. That even the educated were often ignorant and uninformed about sex is doubtless true. When one considers the hold that fear, guilt, and shame of sex continues to have, it seems likely that most conventional marriages of the time were affected by the prevalent attitudes.

It is worthwhile to note, however, that the Victorian era had another side, less often mentioned in chronicles of the times. Prostitution flourished, as did the institution of the mistress, at least in Europe (Pearsall, 1969). Pornography, the organized sexual use of children, and ritual flagellation all were common. There existed, too, a free love movement which flourished briefly toward the end of the century, a harbinger of the loosening of restraints which would appear again in the 1920s. Finally, the era brought forth the most scholarly and progressive work on sex yet to appear, the classic six-volume *Studies in the Psychology of Sex*, by Havelock Ellis. Appearing between 1898 and 1910, this monumental work covered a panorama of human sexuality and demolished most of the myths cherished by the proper Victorians. Ellis's work will be discussed in a later section.

Nineteenth-century Experiments in Sex and Marriage

Although the family, founded in monogamous marriage, was considered the basis of society in the nineteenth century, its sanctity and its assumption of sexual exclusivity of husband and wife, were not unchallenged. Utopian communities, with missions of economic, religious, or social reform, sought to change or exclude marriage as antagonistic to the communal spirit. Some of these were celibate, some adopted polygyny, and some had a system of "complex marriage," in which every man was married to every woman, and vice versa (Muncy, 1973). The most important of these was the Oneida community in New York, founded by John Humphrey Noyes in 1848.

Exclusive attachments were not permitted at Oneida. Any man could approach any woman, but she was under no obligation to accept his proposal, even if he were her legal husband. The young did not mate exclusively with the young but were introduced into the system of complex marriage by older persons of the opposite sex. Thus, virgins learned about sex from the skilled attentions of older men, and boys were taught to give and receive pleasure by experienced women. Noyes regarded the amative function of sex as superior to the procreative function, knowing that children were expensive and childbirth dangerous. He developed the art of what he called "male continence," the restraint of ejaculation through self-control. The female orgasm was the objective, and when the male became skilled at the technique, intercourse could last for an hour or more and pregnancy could be avoided. Though not foolproof, male continence was highly regarded at Oneida, and careless or unskilled men were avoided by the women of the community (Muncy, 1973).

EARLY RESEARCH ON MARITAL SEX

The intellectual climate which made sex research possible appeared during the 1890s with the work of Freud and Ellis. A major contribution of theirs was to remove sexuality from its status of alienation and discontinuity in other areas of life, bringing it into the cultural consciousness of the late nineteenth-century—an act of inclusion, as Gagnon (1975) described it.

> They exposed and brought forward deeply held cultural beliefs about sexuality. The act of including the sexual into life not only as a pathological manifestation but also as it informed and shaped conventional lives was a profound challenge to that elite for whom the sexual existed outside the normal social order (Gagnon, 1975, p. 116).

Although sexuality was a central concern for both Freud and Ellis,[1] neither gave marital sex a special place separate from sex in general. Freud was more interested in psychosexual development and its effect on personality than he was in the sexual lives of married people. Ellis, less interested in distinctions between pathologies and normal behavior, was an unsparing and exhaustive observer of sex in natural settings— what real people really do, all over the world.

Although Freud himself had a conventional marriage in the patriarchal tradition, he was quite aware of its typical constraints, particularly as they affected women. In a 1908 paper, " 'Civilized' Sexual Morality and Modern Nervousness," he showed how the double standard of morality, the Victorian ideal of abstinence, and women's sexual frustrations in marriage brought about neurosis:

[1] The two, however, were utterly different in their cultural backgrounds, approaches and appreciations, and in intellectual and research styles.

Marriage under the present cultural standard has long since ceased to be a panacea for the nervous sufferings of women; even if we physicians in such cases still advise matrimony, we are nevertheless aware that a girl must be very healthy to "stand" marriage. . . . Marital unfaithfulness would . . . be a much more probable cure for the neurosis resulting from marriage; the more strictly a wife has been brought up, the more earnestly she has submitted to the demands of civilization, the more does she fear this way of escape, and in conflict between her desires and her sense of duty she again will seek refuge in a neurosis (p. 177).

Ellis was highly progressive in his attitudes about sexuality. He favored sex education, birth control, trial marriage, and lifting legal and social restrictions against sexual acts of all kinds between consenting adults, and opposed the rigid and narrow definition of marriage in his time. His studies, drawing on anthropological data, case histories and correspondence with friends and other scholars, and his own observations and enormous erudition are unmatched examples of the cultural relativism of sexual behavior and sexual standards. The first essay in the *Studies,* "The Evolution of Modesty," was named by Brecher (1971) as "the best introduction I have found to the scientific study of sex" (p. 26).

Ellis (1937) had no illusions about the state of sexual knowledge and of the art of love in his society. "At times one feels hopeless at the thought that civilization in this supremely intimate field of life has achieved so little" (p. 121). In an essay on "The Play-Function of Sex" (1937), he wrote that the average man had two ideals regarding sex: his wish to prove himself a man, to experience his virility, and to enjoy the pleasurable relief from sexual tension. Both of these, said Ellis, are essentially self-regarding. But "love is not primarily self-regarding. It is the intimate, harmonious, combined play . . . of two personalities" (p. 123–24). Because of these male values, the woman typically attains neither pride in her womanliness nor physical satisfaction. Though she may appear in her role as wife and mother to be playing her proper part in the home and in the world, she remains as emotionally immature and virginal as a schoolgirl (Ellis, 1937).

The influence of Freud's and Ellis's ideas interacted with other cultural phenomena, setting the stage for a new kind of research on sexuality which adopted the quantitative methods and techniques of the natural sciences. (For a detailed analysis of this evolution, see Gagnon, 1975.) Before the publication of *Sexual Behavior in the Human Male* (Kinsey and others, 1948), however, only a few such studies had appeared, dealing mostly with students and patients. Of the few whose samples were normal married persons, three deserve mention: *Factors in the Sex Life of 2200 Women,* (Davis, 1929); *A Research in Marriage* (Hamilton, 1929); and *One Thousand Marriages* (Dickinson and Beam, 1932). The first two were based on questionnaire data, and the last relied on cases in Dickinson's files on his gynecological patients.

It becomes clear from these early studies that ignorance and frustration among married persons was commonplace, as they tried to work out their sexual lives in an era when accurate information was not readily available and when the prevailing mores and attitudes still reflected what Brecher (1972) called the debilitating disease of Victorianism. Dickinson, for example, reported that eighteen of his one thousand patients remained virgins for an average of four years after marriage, because neither the husband nor the wife knew how to have intercourse. Characteristically, he said, the marital coitus of his patients was brief and male-oriented, the wife remaining passive and unaroused. Intercourse occurred once or twice a week, usually without foreplay. Intromission lasted about five minutes, after which the husband had an orgasm and the wife did not.

Hamilton, in his study of one hundred married persons of each sex, felt that the institution of marriage had "fared rather better than had been expected" (p. 553), when 48% of his sample had been rated as reasonably satisfied with their marriage. Of the one hundred women, only thirty-six had had orgasm during the first year of their marriages, though this number had increased to fifty-four by the time of the study. Hamilton thought that his study gave evidence that in many families the children "are so affected by their parents that when adult life is reached no conceivable mode of prolonged and intimate relationship with a person of the opposite sex is likely to end otherwise than disastrously" (p. 554).

During the same period, there appeared a noteworthy attempt to change this dismal picture, to give to physicians and married men the knowledge they needed to introduce satisfaction and joy into marital sex for both the man and the woman, and to dispel the tedium and misery of the sexual side of marriage which seemed to be so typical of the time. *Ideal Marriage,* by Dutch gynecologist Theodoor Van de Velde (1930), was an explicit manual whose intention was to dispel ignorance, to teach men how effectively and lovingly to introduce their brides to the marriage bed, and, by describing in detail many possible variations and techniques, to help couples to keep their sex lives alive and interesting through their lives. One of Van de Velde's most important contributions was to emphasize the mutuality of sex, of the reciprocal giving and receiving of pleasure between the partners. He insisted throughout the work on the importance of the wife's satisfaction and described the typical sex act consisting of brief or no foreplay, intromission, and ejaculation as a parody of how sex could be. Though himself a Victorian who believed that sex should be expressed only within the context of marriage, Van de Velde provided a popular and knowledgeable antidote to the prevailing climate of ignorance and inhibition about sex.

SEXUAL BEHAVIOR IN MARRIAGE

There are few studies of sexual behavior in marriage which meet even minimal criteria for scientific acceptability. The most important attempts to get a representative picture of sexual behavior in the United States were those of Kinsey and others (1948, 1953). Two more recent large-scale surveys (Hunt, 1974; Tavris and Sadd, 1977) have looked at marital sexual behavior, and both have reported remarkable changes in the thirty years since Kinsey and his colleagues collected their data. We shall consider the nature of each of these studies as they pertain to marital sex.

The Kinsey studies consist of samples of 5,300 males and 5,940 females of a wide range of ages, educational levels, and geographical distribution, and are based on data collected in structured interviews and statistically analyzed to reveal what Gagnon (1975) called social bookkeeping: who does what with whom, how, and how often. Each of the volumes contains a chapter on marital intercourse, as well as numerous references to it throughout the books. The studies do not claim to be representative, since some groups in the population are underrepresented (e.g., less educated and rural groups) or not represented at all (e.g., blacks). Besides methodological problems in the studies, we can be sure that much of the data are now obsolete. Nevertheless, they do provide a framework for sexual behavior and a reference for comparison with later studies.

The Hunt study, *Sexual Behavior in the 1970s,* was based on a sample of 982 males and 1,044 females, supposedly representative of the adult U. S. population in such variables as race, marital status, education, occupation, and urban-rural background. The data for the statistical analyses were gathered by self-administered questionnaires; an additional sample of 100 males and 100 females were interviewed in depth for the book's narrative material. The intention was to collect data paralleling that of Kinsey's so as to compare his sample with the present generation. The study does not claim to be truly representative of the American population. One problem is that only one in five of those persons originally contacted agreed to participate. Another is that the material was presented in *Playboy* magazine (October 1973–February 1974) and in book-form (Hunt, 1974) for the general public, and the analyses are not nearly as comprehensive or detailed as Kinsey's. Even so, despite shortcomings of the data presentation, it is a study of adult sexual behavior in our society, it looks at many of the same variables that Kinsey used, and it, too, has a chapter on marital sex.

The third study, by Tavris and Sadd (1977), is based on a sample of 2,278 married women, whose questionnaire responses were scientifically selected from 100,000 such responses by women readers of *Redbook* magazine. The sample was claimed to be "virtually parallel" (p. 20) to the national distribution of married women in geographical area, religious belief, and percentage who work outside the home. They are, however, younger, better educated, and more affluent than are married women in general.

The problem in discussing marital sexual behavior, then, is obvious: not enough up-to-date, reliable, methodologically sound data. Despite these limitations, this section will deal with frequency of marital intercourse, coital techniques, orgasm, masturbation, pregnancy, and satisfaction with marital sex.

FREQUENCY

The increase in reported sexual activity over the past decade or so is reflected in the data on marital intercourse. Tables 1 and 2 show the weekly frequencies of marital intercourse reported by husbands and wives in the Kinsey and Hunt studies. There are increases for all age groups, though they are greater for males than for females. Hunt makes the interesting observation that the smaller increase for females may mean that women are perceiv-

Table 1. MARITAL COITUS: FREQUENCY PER WEEK AS ESTIMATED BY HUSBANDS, 1938–1946 AND 1972 [a]

| *1938–1946 (Kinsey)* | | | *1972 (Present Survey)* | | |
Age	Mean	Median	Age	Mean	Median
16–25	3.3	2.3	18–24	3.7	3.5
26–35	2.5	1.9	25–34	2.8	3.0
36–45	1.8	1.4	35–44	2.2	2.0
46–55	1.3	.8	45–54	1.5	1.0
56–60	.8	.6	55 & over	1.0	1.0

[a] Reprinted from Morton Hunt, *Sexual Behavior in The 1970s*. Chicago: Playboy Press, 1974. By permission.

Table 2. MARITAL COITUS: FREQUENCY PER WEEK AS ESTIMATED BY WIVES, 1938–1949 AND 1972 [a]

| *1938–1949 (Kinsey)* | | | *1972 (Present Survey)* | | |
Age	Mean	Median	Age	Mean	Median
16–25	3.2	2.6	18–24	3.3	3.0
26–35	2.5	2.0	25–34	2.6	2.1
36–45	1.9	1.4	35–44	2.0	2.0
46–55	1.3	.9	45–54	1.5	1.0
56–60	.8	.4	55 & over	1.0	1.0

[a] Reprinted from Morton Hunt, *Sexual Behavior in The 1970s*. Chicago: Playboy Press, 1974. By permission.

ing the frequency of their sexual intercourse more accurately today. If frequency of intercourse were tied more to the male's desire than to the female's, so that she had to meet his needs rather than her own, she might tend to overestimate the incidence of such events. By contrast, if we assume that wives today have more control over the frequency of intercourse, then their estimates should be closer to reality. If this hypothesis is valid, then the smaller increase in females' reported frequency is related to subjective factors.

Frequencies reported by the *Redbook* wives are shown in Table 3. Though not directly comparable to the data from the Hunt study, the median frequency is calculated at 8.5 times per month, or about twice a week. This is nearly identical with the medians which Hunt obtained for the twenty-five to thirty-four and thirty-five to forty-four age groups. Since three out of four women in the *Redbook* sample were under thirty-five, the frequencies for the two groups appear to be very similar.

Obviously median frequencies are only one kind of indication of how often married people have intercourse. Individual variation, as one would expect, was considerable in all the stud-

Table 3. FREQUENCY OF INTERCOURSE PER MONTH [a]

0	1–5	6–10	11–15	16–20	20+
2%	26%	32%	21%	11%	8%

[a] Reprinted from Carol Tavris and Susan Sadd, *The Redbook Report on Female Sexuality*. New York: Delacorte Press, 1977. By permission.

ies. For example, even in Kinsey's younger groups, a few individuals had marital coitus less often than once in two weeks, while in every age group, from the youngest to age forty, some persons were having marital coitus on an average of four times a day, seven days a week (Kinsey and others, 1953).

Neither Kinsey nor Hunt found a relationship between frequency of coitus in marriage and either education or occupational status. Religion, however, was related to frequency in both studies. Kinsey and others (1948) reported that less religious husbands had intercourse 20% to 30% more often than did religious mates; such an effect was not found for women, however, leading Kinsey and others (1953) to remark that the wife's coital rate was more likely to be tied to her husband's desires than to her level of devotion. Hunt (1974) found the opposite effect: churchgoing females reported a lower frequency of marital coitus than did churchgoing males or non-churchgoing males and females. Hunt thought that this, too, might reflect the greater influence that wives now have over marital sexual activity. The frequency of sex for married women now might reflect more closely their own wishes than their husbands' desires.

Although intercourse with the spouse is the chief sexual outlet for married people, it falls far short of being their only outlet. Kinsey and others (1948) found an interesting relationship between social level and percent of the total outlet which the married male derived from intercourse with his spouse. For the lower group, marital intercourse accounted for 80% of the outlet during the early years of marriage, increasing to 90% by age fifty. College-educated males on the other hand derived 85% of their total outlet from their wives during the early years, but only 62% by age fifty-five. Kinsey thought that one explanation for this dramatic decline was an increasing dissatisfaction "with the relations which are had with restrained upper level wives" (p. 568).

Wives, likewise, derived only part of their sexual outlet from marital coitus. The maximum part of the sexual outlet derived from marital

intercourse was 89%, reached between the ages of twenty-one and twenty-five, after which the percentage steadily dropped. By age sixty, only 72% of the total outlet of the married women was derived from marital coitus (Kinsey and others, 1953, p. 354, note 2).

A recent study (Edwards and Booth, 1976b) provides evidence that marital intercourse tends to be discontinuous for a sizeable segment of the population. Their stratified probability sample consisted of 144 men and 221 women who had been married between one and twenty years. As part of a two-hour interview, subjects were asked whether intercourse had ever stopped for any reason other than pregnancy, and if so, why and for how long. One-third of the respondents indicated that they had experienced such a cessation, the median length of which was eight weeks. Significant differences emerged between the men and women reporting such cessation: for the men, social background factors such as recent emigration from Europe, being non-Catholic, and lack of employment for the wife were important; for the women, avoidance of intercourse was related to factors in the marriage: perception of the husband as dominant, as not affectionate, or as threatening to leave home. The only common factor for the two sexes was perception of a lack of privacy. Self-reported causes, however, were the same for both men and women: surgery, illness, marital discord, and type of birth control used were some of them. The incidence of discontinuity in marital sex for this sample suggests that the phenomenon is by no means uncommon and enhances, as the authors point out, the sense of intercourse as a symbolic communication between spouses who are otherwise distant from each other's true feelings.

INTERCOURSE: FOREPLAY,
DURATION, AND TECHNIQUES

Not only has the frequency of marital intercourse increased in this generation, but its other parameters also appear to have been affected by attitudinal and behavioral changes in the direction of greater freedom and permissiveness. Both foreplay and coitus are reported to last longer and to include acceptance and use of a greater variety of techniques by more people. These increases have occurred in all age groups and across educational levels but are greatest among the young and the noncollege population.

Kinsey found that precoital activities such as mouth-breast contact, manual stimulation of the genitals, and cunnilingus and fellatio were more characteristic of the college-educated persons in his samples, and that at any educational level, they were more often reported by younger individuals (1948, p. 368; 1953, p. 399). For example, the percentages of males using cunnilingus in marital foreplay were 4%, 15%, and 45% for grade school, high school, and college levels respectively. Manual stimulation of the female genitalia was utilized by 95% of the under-twenty-five age group, compared to 83% of the over-forty-six group.

Hunt (1974) found striking increases in the use of certain techniques in marital foreplay. In general, the increases were greatest for those activities which had been most strongly tabooed. The increase in breast play, for example, was small, since this activity was common in Kinsey's time. The biggest changes were in oral-genital acts, which have long been not only morally tabooed but legally forbidden as well in most states. In contrast to the 15% of high school males whom Kinsey found had used cunnilingus, Hunt's study revealed that 56% of his sample at that educational level had done so. Corresponding data for college males in the two studies were 45% and 66% (p. 198). Among the *Redbook* wives, (Tavris and Sadd, 1977) 87% reported experience with cunnilingus. The fact that this group was younger and better educated fits with the observations of both Kinsey and Hunt on the greater incidence of such behavior in these populations.

Duration of foreplay has also increased, especially among the less educated. Kinsey's histories for his lower-level sample suggested that precoital play in marriage was often quite perfunctory, consisting of a kiss or two, while his college men might extend such play to five minutes or more. Hunt found no difference by educational level. Foreplay averaged about fifteen minutes for both college and noncollege married men.

Married people today report using a greater variety of positions in actual intercourse than did their counterparts a generation ago. Kinsey reported that nearly all coitus in our culture occurs with the partners face-to-face and the man on top. As many as 70%, he said, had never used any other position (1948, p. 578). By contrast, Hunt found that the female-above position is used by three-fourths of all married couples at least some of the time. Likewise, rear-entry vaginal intercourse was used by only a tenth of Kinsey's sample, compared to four-tenths of Hunt's (Hunt, 1974, p. 202).

Finally, the duration of coitus has increased dramatically among married people. Kinsey reported that three-fourths of all males probably reached orgasm within two minutes after intromission. In an interesting discussion of the pros and cons of the speedy orgasm for males, Kinsey revealed his belief that the male who responded so quickly, far from being "impotent" as some had labeled him, was in fact normal or even superior, "however inconvenient and unfortunate his qualities may be from the standpoint of the wife" (1948, p. 580). Today prolongation of the sexual act is the goal for many. Hunt found that the median duration of marital intercourse, as reported by both males and females, was ten minutes—not long, but an improvement (from the female view) over the hasty performance reported by a generation past. Moreover, differences owing to such factors as education, occupation, religious and political attitudes were either nonexistent or quite small. Younger people, however, spend more time on their marital love-making than older ones do. Given the greater urgency associated with youthful libido, this must reflect subjective differences in values as a function of age.

It is not difficult to identify at least some of the factors responsible for these changes: lifting of old sanctions against sex for nonprocreative purposes; increase in premarital sex; availability of birth control, with increasing acceptance of sterilization and abortion; disinhibiting effects of media presentations: explicit movies, books, and magazines; greater availability of information about sex, with emphasis on sex as valuable and pleasurable in and of itself; and the contemporary women's movement, which has informed women and men that the sexual needs of women are just as important as are those of men and has taught women to ask and to expect that their needs will be met in the sexual relationship. In any case, the shifts in marital sexual behavior are remarkable: "We stand convinced that a dramatic and historic change has taken place in the practice of marital coitus in America" (Hunt, 1974, p. 206).

Orgasm

The experience of orgasm by the female has been variously valued, even during the present century. Kinsey, for example, commented on the "post-Victorian" development of the idea that respectable women should enjoy marital coitus. Even so, he cited a 1951 study which found evidence in the British working class that responsiveness in the wife was hardly expected and if too marked, was disapproved (1953, p. 373). Kinsey's research suggested to him that orgasm was not nearly as important to the female as it was to the male. Without orgasm, she could still feel pleasure in the "social aspects" of a sexual relationship: "Whether or not she herself reaches orgasm, many a female finds satisfaction in knowing that her husband or other sexual partner has enjoyed the contact, and in realizing that she has contributed to the male's pleasure" (p. 371). Even so, "persistent failure of the female to reach orgasm in her marital coitus, or even to respond with fair frequency, may do considerable damage to a marriage" (p. 371).

About 36% of the married females in Kinsey's sample had never experienced orgasm from any source before marriage. By contrast, over 99% of the late adolescent male sample were responding sexually to orgasm more than twice a week. While almost all marital intercourse of his male sample resulted in orgasm, the average female reached orgasm in only 70% to 77% of her marital sexual experiences. The longer the women were married, however, the more likely they were to experience orgasm. For example, the percent of females who never had orgasm in marital coitus decreased from 25% by the end of the first year to 11% by the end of the twentieth year. Likewise, the percent of those having orgasms more than 60% of the time increased from 51% in the first year to 64% in the twentieth.

In addition to length of marriage, some factors which were strongly related to occurrence of orgasm in Kinsey's sample were decade of birth and premarital experience in orgasm, whether through coitus, petting, or masturbation. For example, 33% of women born before 1900 were unresponsive in the first year of marriage, compared to only 22% of those born after 1909. As for experience, no factor showed a higher correlation with the frequency of orgasm in marital coitus than the presence or absence of premarital experience in orgasm. Among those women with no premarital experience of orgasm, 44% failed to have orgasm during their first year of marriage. Among those with even limited experience only 19% failed to reach orgasm in the first year.

Neither the Hunt nor the *Redbook* data can be directly compared with Kinsey's figures, since neither is broken down by length of marriage. Hunt did, however, compare his females with fifteen-years-median-duration of marriage with Kinsey's females in their fifteenth year of marriage. Of the Kinsey wives, 45% reported having orgasm 90% to 100% of the time, compared to 53% of the Hunt wives who had orgasm "all or almost all of the time" (p. 212). Of the same Kinsey group, 12% never had orgasm, compared with 7% of the Hunt group.

Figures for the *Redbook* sample show that 63% of these wives have orgasm all or most of the time, 7% never. These data are more recent than Hunt's and as we have noted, the sample consists of younger, more educated individuals, all of which could account for the higher orgasmic figure.

Hunt collected some interesting data on the incidence of orgasm among married men. Contrary to Kinsey's assertion that married men achieved orgasm in nearly 100% of their marital coitus, Hunt found that 8% of the husbands aged forty-five and up did not have orgasm anywhere from occasionally to most of the time; 7% of the men between twenty-four and forty-four did not have orgasm at least a quarter of the time; and 15% of the under-twenty-five husbands failed to have orgasm a quarter or more of the time.

Kinsey's stress on the relationship between length of marriage and sexual responsiveness in his married sample was challenged in part by Clark and Wallin (1965). Proposing that women's responsiveness is influenced by the quality, not just the duration, of their marriages, they did a twenty-year longitudinal study which began with 1,000 engaged couples, 602 of whom were studied after a "few years" of marriage, and the 428 remaining couples again after sixteen or more years of marriage. They found a strong relationship across time between positive ratings of the quality of the marriage and sexual responsiveness. Sexual responsiveness increased from 65% to 91% among those wives who rated their marriages as positive, and from 61% to 69% among those rating them negative. The authors suggest that increased responsiveness does not inevitably follow as a function of length of marriage, but rather is interdependent with the perceived quality of the marital relationship.

MASTURBATION

Although masturbation is used less frequently by married than by unmarried people, it continues to be an outlet for many. Among Kinsey's married males between the ages of twenty-six and thirty-five, almost half masturbated occasionally, along with about one-third of the female sample in that age range (1948, p. 241; 1953, p. 178). Hunt found about 72% of his married male sample in that age range still masturbating, along with two-thirds of the wives, a quite remarkable increase (1974, p. 86).

Consistent with Hunt's data, the *Redbook* study found 68% of their sample, all married women, masturbating often or occasionally (p. 96). Reasons given included husband absent (38%), relaxation of tensions (31%), and enjoyable addition to intercourse (31%).

A recent Danish study (Hessellund, 1976) of thirty-eight couples married a mean of 10.7 years found that 60% of the men and 37% of the women masturbated at least occasionally. Analysis of the relationship between intercourse and masturbation for this sample led the authors to conclude that, since intercourse frequency was determined by the wife and was generally not more than twice a week, masturbation functioned as a supplement to the sexual activity of the men and as a substitute for the women.

PREGNANCY AND SEXUALITY

Taboos against intercourse with a pregnant woman are very common in undeveloped countries and have been observed historically as a religious rule among some people. A study of sexual behavior in sixty preliterate societies found that twenty-one of them forbade sexual intercourse during most or all of the pregnancy (Ford & Beach, 1951). Among a Ghana group, the Ashanti, the taboo begins with the discovery of the pregnancy, and husbands, tiring of abstinence, often take another wife (Saucier, 1972).

In our society the continuation of sexual activity by pregnant women is not only common practice but is generally sanctioned by physicians. For example, a study of sexual attitudes and behavior in pregnancy (Tolor and Di-Grazia, 1976) noted that the subjects' physicians placed no restrictions whatever on their sexual activity from conception to delivery, unless complications such as bleeding, occurred. After delivery the women were advised to refrain from intercourse for four weeks and then to let their own preferences and comfort be their guide.

A study of 101 women revealed an increase in sexual tension and performance during the second trimester, attributed by the authors to the increased pelvic vascularity associated with pregnancy (Masters and Johnson, 1966). But other studies are in general agreement that sexual interest and activity fall off during pregnancy, especially during the last trimester (Kenny, 1973; Morris, 1975; Solberg and others, 1973). An example is a study (Tolor and Di-Grazia, 1976) of a sample of 216 women who were patients of a group of obstetricians. The women comprised four groups: first trimester, second trimester, third trimester, and six weeks postpartum. The median frequency of sexual intercourse for all groups combined was 2.10 per week. Separately, the median reported frequencies for the first, second, and third trimesters and for the postpartum period were 2.25, 2.39, 1.08, and 2.65, respectively. Except for the third trimester group, about two-thirds of each group expressed satisfaction with the frequency of intercourse they were having. The third trimester group, however, had the strongest preference for less intercourse than they were having.

In a study of a large sample of Thai women, Morris (1975), reporting similar findings of marked decline in frequency of intercourse with advancing pregnancy, suggested that the cross-cultural consistency of this phenomenon raises the question of a biological reason. This would be difficult to test because of cultural norms, perhaps medical advice, and psychological factors which no doubt also play a part in such behavior.

Coital techniques and positions also are affected by the course of pregnancy. The preferred sexual practice for the first trimester women in the Tolor and DiGrazia (1976) study was vaginal stimulation, whereas the later pregnancy groups preferred breast and clitoral manipulation. These women also reported a very strong need for physical contact, for wanting to be held. Given a choice of alternatives when they did not wish to have intercourse, most of them wanted just to be held. As for positions in coitus, Solberg and others (1973) found that side-by-side or rear entry became the preferred modes as pregnancy advanced.

Women who reported a change in their sexual behavior during pregnancy gave these reasons: physical discomfort, 46%; fear of injury to the baby, 27%; and loss of interest, 23%. Less frequently reported reasons included awkwardness and loss of attractiveness (Solberg and others, 1973). Of the 260 women in this study, 29% were instructed by their physicians to abstain from coitus from two to eight weeks before the delivery date. Ten percent were advised about positions that might be more comfortable than the male superior position, and only two percent received suggestions about sexual activities that could be substituted for coitus (hand stimulation for both partners in all cases). This finding suggests a notable paucity of discussion between doctor and patient of sexuality in pregnancy.

The resumption of coitus after the woman has given birth follows no particular pattern, and its regulation and prescription vary widely from culture to culture. Ford and Beach (1951) reported postpartum taboos in sixty-six societies ranging in length of time from a few weeks to the end of lactation, sometimes three years. When there are no religious or cultural taboos against postpartum intercourse, abstention may be practiced for a few weeks for a variety of reasons relating to the woman's health and comfort (Saucier, 1972). Four out of six women in one study (Masters and Johnson, 1966) experienced erotic arousal four to five weeks after delivery, but their physiological responses—vasocongestion of the labia, lubrication, and orgasmic contractions—were reduced in degree and intensity. About half of this large sample reported a low level of sexual response; their reasons included fatigue, fear, pain, and vaginal discharge. By three months, however, most of the women had returned to their prepregnancy level of activity.

SATISFACTION WITH MARITAL SEX

Because of the attention in our professional literature given to problem sexuality, its causes and treatment, it is interesting to find that significantly high percentages of married people find their sex lives to be pleasurable and satisfying. Though Kinsey's studies did not report data on satisfaction with marital sex, Hunt (1974) presented some findings which indicate the extent to which his sample viewed the sexual part of their marriage as positive. Among the youngest married male cohort, 99% termed their marital coitus "mostly" or "very" pleasurable, as did at least 94% of the older cohorts. The married women in this sample presented a somewhat different picture. The percentage rating their marital coitus "very pleasurable" rose from 57% for the under-twenty-five cohort to a high of 63% for the thirty-five to forty-four age group. Thereafter, the highly positive appraisal dropped, with only 45% of the forty-five to fifty-four group and 38% of the fifty-five and over group giving their marital sex such a rating. Adding the "mostly pleasurable" responses to these resulted in 88% for the under-twenty-five women, 93% for those between thirty-five and forty-four, followed by a decline to 91 and 83%, respectively, for women in the next two decades (p. 215).

The Tavris and Sadd (1977) *Redbook* study found that happiness and sexual satisfaction were related to religiosity and freedom of communication with husbands. The more religious the wives, the more likely they were to report their marital sex as good or very good. Even so, two-thirds of the nonreligious or moderately religious wives rated their sex lives good to very good, compared with 88% of the very religious wives (p. 99).

The strongest indicator of sexual and marital satisfaction for the *Redbook* wives was the ability to discuss sex with their husbands. "The more they talk, the better they rate their sex lives, their marriages, and their overall happiness" (p. 106). For example, of the 47% who "always" or "often" discuss sex with their husbands, 56% and 43%, respectively, rated their sex lives as "very good."

Meanwhile, a survey of British wives recently reported in *Sexuality Today* (February 27, 1978) concluded that 54% of them are contented with their sex lives. The "average woman" in this sample of 836 wives makes love about twice a week; more than a fourth consider themselves "pretty sexy."

EXTRAMARITAL SEXUAL RELATIONS

Extramarital sexual relations, sexual intercourse of a married person with someone other than the spouse, have been considered sinful, criminal, and immoral throughout the history of Western society. Theologians of all times and creeds have treated adultery as a heinous act, and as late as the seventeenth century the penalty for adultery in most of the New England colonies was death. Although few courts enforced such laws, whippings, fines, and brandings were common. During the nineteenth century, adultery came to be viewed more casually—for males—and upper-class men might have mistresses or meet their surplus sexual needs with servants, as long as they were discreet (Murstein, 1974).

A double standard for adultery traditionally has been recognized and rationalized. A trenchant example was provided by the British literary figure, Dr. Samuel Johnson:

> Confusion of progeny constitutes the essence of the crime; and therefore a woman who breaks her marriage vows is much more criminal than a man who does it. A man, to be sure, is criminal in the sight of God; but he does not do his wife a very material injury . . . if he steals privately to her chambermaid. Sir, a wife ought not greatly to resent this (Boswell, 1956, p. 160).

The reasons for the double standard are not difficult to identify: the long tradition with legal sanction of the view of woman as property, in which a man who committed adultery with a married woman was violating the property of another man; and as noted by Dr. Johnson, the possibility of uncertain parentage, clouding matters of ownership of property and inheritance.

Although the double standard may have lost ground in recent years, condemnation of extramarital sex continues to be very strong in our society. In studies conducted during the past twenty years reviewed by Hunt (1974), all reported that the "great majority" of their respondents disapproved of extramarital sex. In

Hunt's own sample, from 80% to 98% said that they or their mates would object to extramarital affairs. In a recent study of a national sample of 1,044 registered voters representing various regions, races, ages, and religious groups in the United States, 76% of the respondents said that it is "morally wrong" for a man to be unfaithful to his wife, while 79% believed that it is wrong for a woman to be unfaithful to her husband. Female respondents were somewhat more conservative than male, and both male and female were more disapproving of unfaithful wives than of unfaithful husbands (*Time*, November 21, 1977).

Our discussion here will be on a distinction proposed by Smith and Smith (1974) between conventional adultery and consensual adultery. The former is characterized by secrecy and deception, unknown and uncondoned by the spouse. The latter is characterized by openness and consent of the spouse. Consensual adultery may take the form of a spousal agreement for such activity for one or both mates.

CONVENTIONAL ADULTERY

Comparison of the various data sources on the incidence of adultery is difficult because of differences in the collection and presentation of data. Even so, results of the few studies we do have are consistent enough to tell us something about trends and to reveal some surprises.

Kinsey and others (1948) provided an interesting essay on extramarital sex among males, but very little data. A major reason for this, explained by the authors, was the inability to get adequate representation in the male sample of older married men from upper educational and social levels: "We have every reason for believing that extramarital intercourse is the source of the hesitance of many of the individuals in such groups to cooperate" (p. 585). Frequency figures given are thus held to be a minimum, the truth perhaps being 10% to 20% higher.

From available data and allowing for the "cover-up," Kinsey estimated that about half of all married males had intercourse with women other than their wives, at some time while they were married. Age, social level, and religion were important variables for this sample, the first two, especially, introducing some interesting differences. Among lower-level males, 45% of the youngest married cohort reported having had extramarital intercourse, whereas only 27% did so by age forty and not more than 19% by age fifty. On the other hand, among college-level males, the lowest frequencies were found among the youngest group, in which only 15% to 20% had, the incidence increasing steadily to age fifty, when about 27% was having extramarital relations. Kinsey suggested that lower-level males were more likely to have a great deal of premarital intercourse, with some carry-over into marriage followed by a slowing down, which he did not attempt to explain, among the older males. By contrast, upper-level males had a history of greater restraint in the premarital years which continued to be characteristic for some years after marriage, loosening up as they grew older. Though not nearly as great as the differences among social levels, a difference was found between church and nonchurch related males, the more devout having significantly less experience with extramarital sex.

The data for Hunt's (1974) most closely comparable group revealed that only 41% of the males had ever had extramarital sex. Hunt thought that the lifetime accumulative incidence for the entire sample would be somewhat higher, but still not more than 50%, since the data showed no rise after the age of forty-four. Though Hunt found a slight increase among the youngest cohort, it was small compared to the increases in other types of sexual outlets for this group. Likewise, he found little change compared to the Kinsey data for educational level and religion.

Kinsey and others (1953) presented much more data on extramarital activity among females than in the earlier volume on males. His female sample, however, had a much higher ratio of previously married to married women, than is the case in the general population. Since previously married women have a much higher incidence of extramarital relations than do women who have been married only once (Bohannon, 1971), this had the effect of inflating Kinsey's figures. When Hunt "rebalanced" Kinsey's figures to account for this and compared them with his own sample, he concluded that there was no difference in the accumulative incidences up to age forty-five for the two groups. By age forty-five, 20% of Kinsey's sample had had extramarital intercourse, compared to 18% of Hunt's sample. Broken down by age groups, however, a remarkable change was found in the group of women below age twenty-five. Whereas only 8% of Kinsey's group had had such experience, 24% of Hunt's had. Comparisons between the generations sampled in these two studies, then, suggest that, in spite of widespread beliefs to the contrary, the incidence of extramarital intercourse has changed little if any among male and female groups in general; it has increased slightly among under-twenty-five males, and greatly among under-twenty-five females, bringing them nearly to the level of their male cohorts. Extramarital sex is increasing in the direction of equality, with the greater increase being among females.

The figures on the *Redbook* wives who had had extramarital sex by different ages are somewhat different, as one would expect, given the nature of the sample. Twenty-nine percent of the total sample had had extramarital sex, the accumulative incidence rising from 20% of the under-twenty-five wives to 40% by age forty and over. A very important variable not mentioned in the other studies was employment of the wife. Full-time employed wives were far more likely to have had extramarital relations than were stay-at-home wives. Among wives in their late thirties, for example, 53% of those employed had had extramarital sex, compared to only 24% of the housewives. Religion was also a factor, with more than twice as many non-religious women as devout women reporting such activity.

Other findings in these studies, which we will briefly summarize, relate to number of partners, frequency of orgasm, and overall pleasure of extramarital sex compared to marital sex, reported by those with both kinds of experience.

Kinsey did not report on any of these variables for his male sample. The data for the number of extramarital partners for both the Kinsey and the Hunt females are almost identical: about 40% in each had had only one partner, and more than 80% had had five or fewer. For the *Redbook* women, the corresponding percents are 50% and 40%.

The only data comparing marital and extramarital frequency of orgasm are from the Hunt female sample. These women who had had extramarital sex reported that they had orgasm all or almost all the time in 53% of their marital coitus, compared to only 39% of their extramarital coitus, and that they had orgasm almost none or none of the time in 7% of their marital coitus but in 35% of their extramarital coitus. These data suggest that extramarital intercourse is considerably less satisfying than marital intercourse. It is likely that factors such as guilt, haste, anxiety, and inexperience with the partner enter to some extent in these findings.

Related to the figures on orgasm are some data from Hunt's survey on overall pleasure of marital and extramarital relations. Males rated both marital and extramarital sex more pleasurable than females did, and both sexes gave their marital sex higher ratings than their extramarital experiences.

While adultery seems to be an enduring and intimate aspect of marriage, the data are skimpy, indeed, to support a conclusion that it is increasing, compared to other forms of sexual experience such as premarital or postmarital sex. The exception is its rather dramatic rise among young married women, and this may portend a trend for future observations. As for the other parameters, though one must be very cautious in generalizing from the research, it appears that women, at least, who have extramarital experiences tend to have few partners rather than many and share with men the experience of being less orgasmic and getting less pleasure from their extramarital encounters than from their sexual relations at home.

Why do people seek sex outside of marriage? Edwards and Booth (1976a) looked for correlates of the frequency of extramarital involvement among a stratified probability sample of Toronto families among both subject-background variables and marital variables. Unlike previous research, they found no effects from education, occupation, employment of the wife, or religion. Age was the strongest predictor of the demographic variables, with reported involvement being greater among the younger members of the sample. The frequency of extramarital relations was related more to contextual variables in the marriage: the more negative was the perception of the marriage, the greater was the sexual deprivation in the marriage; as the latter increased, the more probable was extramarital sex to occur.

Although most of the studies in this area support the plausible expectation that having an unhappy marriage increases the probability of having an extramarital relationship, there still remains the observation by Tavris and Sadd (1977), Hunt (1974) and others of a stable minority of happily married persons who have other sexual partners, some of them of long duration. This suggests that variables other than marriage rating are important in some cases. In looking at female extramarital coital behavior, Bell, Turner, and Rosen (1975) were able to identify four groups of women in their sample of 2,262, to show how ratings of the marriage interacted with sexual values to predict extramarital coitus. These groups were labeled Traditional, Modern, Uptight, and Experimenting, and were characterized respectively by the following combinations of marriage ratings and sexual values: high rating, conservative values; high rating, liberal values; low rating, conservative values; and low rating, liberal values. Examination of some aspects of life styles and sexual preferences of these groups led the authors to propose that the general set most predictive of a high rate of extramarital sex for women would be a low rating of their marriage with sexually liberal views and a liberal life style. The set most predictive of a low rate would include women with highly rated marriages and with sexually conservative views and conventional life styles.

Finally, Johnson (1970) examined sixty case histories from a Family Service Agency for actual reasons given by clients for engaging in sex outside of their marriages. As one would expect, they tended to blame the spouse. He or she was: physically handicapped, unfaithful, unloving, physically unattractive or unclean, absent, or an unwilling or uninterested sex partner. Murstein (1974) added other factors, including curiosity, need for variety, uncertainty about one's sexuality, unusual opportunity, need for escape, fear of aging, and relative lack of inhibitions and guilt for unconventional behavior.

A number of writers on the subject have concluded that for many an extramarital experience or relationship can have beneficial effects on both the participant and her or his marriage. One of the strongest supporters of this view is Albert Ellis (1977), who believes that adultery has its distinct advantages even in a society such as ours, which makes it difficult and hazardous. Ellis's views include these benefits:

• Sexual variety. Humans have a biological need for sexual variety. With the emergence of alternative marriage forms and more liberal values, more people will meet their needs for sexual variety in nonmonogamous activities.

• Desire for freedom. Marriage can be confining and boring, and outside affairs can add to a feeling of freedom by breaking up the routine.

• Frustration reduction. "Exclusive" marriage leads to the limiting of one's experiences and to frustration when sexual appetites differ. Affairs can drain off these frustrations and help the person to cope with marital problems better.

•Improved marriages. Clinical evidence suggests to Ellis that married people are less resentful and more open with each other after an affair. Sex may improve because of increased knowledge and/or greater appreciation of the partner.

Ellis would like to see the removal of legal and social sanctions against adultery, the encouragement of open marriage, and moves toward educating people to cope better with feelings of jealousy and other emotional problems that accompany adultery today.

Consensual adultery occurs with the knowledge and consent of the spouse. Smith and Smith (1974) have described three forms: adultery toleration, comarital relations, and group marriage. Adultery toleration is similar to conventional adultery except that the spouses extend to each other the freedom to engage in extramarital sex, relieving the partners of the requirement of sexual exclusivity and of the need for secrecy and deception. Such liberal arrangements are by no means new. Havelock Ellis had such an agreement with his wife, and the gynecologist, Robert L. Dickinson in 1932 described such a case among his series (Brecher, 1971). Others have been reported by Hamilton (1929) and by Lindsey and Evans (1929). On a more contemporary level, the open marriage model proposed by the O'Neills (1972) includes absence of sexual exclusivity.

Comarital relations incorporate extramarital relations into the marital relationship. Both partners participate as a dyad, both on a couple-to-couple basis and sometimes a group basis, which is popularly called mate swapping or swinging. Although such relations may be quite impersonal and transient, the Smiths (1974) say that their studies suggest that some couples "succeed in establishing basic friendship relations which yield more enduring and more rewarding social networks" (p. 89).

Group marriage does not include, strictly speaking, extramarital relations, since it consists of members of a group all of whom consider themselves married to each other. Rarer than the other two forms, it is ideologically the same as the Oneida model discussed earlier, with unrestricted sexual access of the individual members to each other.

Such forms of extramarital sex with the knowledge, consent, and sometimes the participation of the spouse are phenomena which have attracted much more attention than their prevalence in the population seems to justify. Their deviance from traditional norms in an area of behavior which more than any other has historically been rigidly defined and pre-scribed has attracted a high level of attention in the popular media.

Recent estimates agree that the numbers of persons participating in any of the forms of consensual adultery are quite small. No reliable data exist on adultery toleration but if they did, they would probably be higher than figures for the other two forms, simply because "toleration" is less deviant from conventional norms than is mate swapping or group marriage. Hunt found that about two percent of the husbands and wives in his sample had ever engaged in mate swapping, but Tavris and Sadd (1977) reported that four percent of the *Redbook* wives, a less representative sample, had tried swapping at least once. A stratified probability sample of 579 married adults drawn from a midwestern community of 40,000 found that less than two percent of the respondents had ever participated in swinging (Spanier and Cole, 1975). Smith and Smith (1974) state that the incidence of group marriage is far lower than either of the other forms. Ramey (1974) provides an interesting account of eighty upper-middle class couples who explored over a three-year period the various problems and possibilities of communal and group marriage arrangements. Only eighteen of these couples did, in fact, have any experience in such living arrangements.

Finally, in an analysis of some moral and social implications of infidelity, Bernard (1974) speculates that the conditions of exclusivity and permanence required in traditional marriage may now be incompatible: "It may be that we will have to choose. . . . If we insist on permanence, exclusivity is harder to enforce; if we insist on exclusivity, permanence may be endangered. The trend . . . seems to be in the direction of exclusivity at the expense of permanence in the younger years but permanence at the expense of exclusivity in the later years" (p. 138).

Bernard reveals in this same paper that she has changed her views on the significance for women of extramarital relations. A few years ago she thought that women could not be casual about such relations. She sees now that there is a new kind of woman who can be casual about sex and can accept the idea of sex-as-fun without conflict. She believes that the increasing economic independence of women plays some part in this change. We have seen already that working women were more likely than nonworking (outside the home) women to have affairs, certainly in part because of more opportunities and contacts with men. At the same time, such a woman, less dependent on her husband for economic security, might be less fearful of the consequences of discovery. She also might be less frightened at the prospect of her husband's involvement with another woman although, as Bernard rightly pointed out, economic independence is far from the whole story. The threat to one's psychological needs can be more terrifying than the threat to one's material security.

THE WOMAN'S MOVEMENT AND MARITAL SEX

The changing roles and status of women are rooted in the renaissance of feminism, the women's movement which re-emerged in the late 1960s. These changes generally are toward greater equality for women, through the removal of historic oppression. Shifts toward greater power and participation for women now can be seen in the personal, social, political, and economic sectors of their lives. These changes affect sexuality in marriage either directly or indirectly.

1. Availability of birth control and abortion means that women now control their reproductive functions and can limit their fertility. Birth control also frees women to participate in and to enjoy sexual experiences without the fear of pregnancy.

2. Sex research, such as that of Masters and Johnson (1966), Sherfey (1973), and Hite (1976), have brought to women a new awareness and appreciation of their own sexuality and its potential. The dissemination of such information to large numbers of the population has reduced inhibitions and changed expectations and behavior (Humphrey, 1975).

3. Opportunities for education and employment have brought women into contact with the outside world more than ever before and have provided them with the means for economic independence. Women are exposed to a greater number and variety of possible sex partners, increasing both their level of sophistication and the probability of extramarital sex experiences. Economic independence removes one source of inequality in marriage, as well as the need to remain in an incompatible situation.

4. The availability of alternative life styles— deferred marriage, staying single, nonmarital cohabitation—again suggests options to a traditional marriage, which was until recently the most desirable and socially acceptable outcome for women.

5. The women's movement has provided an intellectual and experiential framework within which women can find self-esteem, respect for other women, and supportive relations with others, both women and men, outside the old exclusive bonds of marriage.

6. Finally, the goal of egalitarian relationships between women and men promises to free both from old power and dominance roles, with their inherent components of exploitation and deceit, and to substitute more humane and satisfying relationships.

SEXUALITY AND AGING

The sexuality of older people has only recently begun to receive attention. The prevalent view has seemed to be that sex is the prerogative of the young, that older people do not participate in or enjoy sex and if they do, such activity is ridiculous, embarrassing, or downright obscene. In May 1974, however, the *SIECUS Report* published a policy statement on sex and aging: "Aging people are too often deprived of opportunities for sexual companionship and expression, which they need despite unscientific beliefs to the contrary. Society has an obligation to create conditions conducive to the fulfillment of these needs" (p. 1). In a recent issue of the *SIECUS Report*, Alex

Comfort (1976) expanded on that statement, presenting some facts about sexuality in older people along with some suggestions for alleviating problems, many of which are the result of ignorance, superstition, and prejudice against the elderly.

Changes in sexual physiology occur with aging in both sexes. Some of these are in common and are related to the general effects of aging: strength and energy are reduced, and body responses are generally slowed and attenuated. However, both men and women continue to respond as before, though frequency and intensity of sexual response are reduced. Both remain capable of orgasm. Exceptions to this are produced by factors other than normal physiology, that is, loss of orgasmic capacity is not an inevitable part of aging.

Most studies support the idea that women have a more stable sex drive than men have and that it is less susceptible to the effects of aging. Although many men remain potent and sexually active into their eighties, impotence is a common problem after middle age. Studies of sexual inadequacy revealed that 83% of the impotent males were past forty years of age, and 75% were past fifty (Masters and Johnson, 1968). There are a number of reasons for male impotence, such as the ego-shattering "fear of failure" which sometimes leads men to seek newer or younger partners to reassure them of their virility. Since women often marry men who are older than they are, it is inevitable that some who are still as interested as ever in sex will find themselves with a husband who has withdrawn from sexual activity or is directing it elsewhere. Also, some husbands in the older age groups may have physical problems or disabilities associated with advancing age which may make their accustomed form of sexual activity impossible. Still, Comfort reports studies showing that as many as one-third of men past seventy are still sexually active. It appeared that those most active as youths continued to be active longer in their later years, but those with a low sex drive in their younger years were less likely to be having sex as they grew older.

Most important to sexual behavior in older women are the availability of a partner and the opportunity for regular sexual expression (Williams, 1977). With these, many women in their fifties and sixties have an increased interest in their sexuality for a number of reasons. The cessation of the menses brings a freedom from fear of pregnancy, so that the woman, perhaps for the first time, can abandon herself to the enjoyment of sex without apprehension. This release from "pregnancy phobia" is probably one of the most plausible reasons for increased sexual interest given by postmenopausal women who did not have effective birth control methods available to them in their reproductive years. The problems which may beset a young marriage, such as finances, in-laws, and adjustment to the marital relationship, all may be in the past. For both members of the couple the draining demands of having and rearing children, and of establishing and succeeding in a job or career, may no longer exhaust and preoccupy them, leaving more time and energy for the renewal of interest in each other.

Sviland (1976) has described a "sexual liberation" program for elderly couples with basically sound marriages who want to get rid of their inhibitions and to increase their repertoire of sexual behavior. The program focuses on attitude restructuring and relationship enhancement. The therapist gives permission for sexual curiosity and exploration, and gives exercises designed to replicate the fun of dating, such as candlelight dinners, love notes, and making love by the fireplace. She reports that the program has changed attitudes and behavior within weeks, helping couples to communicate, to increase intimacy, and to enjoy without guilt sexual pleasures usually restricted to youth.

CROSS-CULTURAL OBSERVATIONS

Anthropology has shared with the other social sciences a Victorian reticence to include investigation of sexual behavior among its interests in diverse cultural groups. Little more than a decade ago, an analysis (Marshall, 1967) of ten leading anthropology textbooks concluded that sexual behavior was accorded neither space nor attention in the basic formulations of anthropological knowledge. This lack of attention in the profession did not come from lack of either interest or knowledge; indeed, Suggs and Marshall (1971) noted that researchers might be interested in and know quite a bit about the sexual behavior of "their people," without ever including such information in their scholarly books and articles. Scientists who violated the taboo on writing about sex risked their reputation, or at least the onus of being thought too interested in "pornography," or too ready to violate the privacy of their subject groups. Stimulated by the work of Masters and Johnson, however, papers and monographs have begun to appear, and there is now a knowledge base sufficient to inform us of the diversity of sexual practices among earth's people.

Patterns of sexual behavior among people do not arise independently or quixotically in some random fashion. Rather, they are part of society and culture, and reflect patterns of sex roles, beliefs about men and women, religious beliefs, notions of modesty and socialization practices, population and ecological factors, and other characteristics of a particular group. As Rostand (1961) said, in the joining of two human bodies, all society is the third presence.

An example of the interrelationship between sexual and nonsexual phenomena is an analysis by Friedl (1975) of sex roles in foraging and horticultural societies. She suggests that the universality of a degree of male dominance is the male monopoly on hunting game and their power to distribute it. If male hunting is minimal, and both sexes collect the plants which comprise most of the diet, women's status is more equal to that of men. Women have the lowest status in groups whose main food is big game hunted entirely by the men. The importance of variations in patterns of male dominance is especially noted in marital sex relations. If woman has a more equal status, because of her role in providing a large share of the food, she has considerable autonomy in sexual matters. She may initiate sex and expect satisfaction. She may divorce, and her adultery is not more serious than is the husband's. If her status is very low, the male being sole provider of all food, she may have no control over sexual relations in or out of marriage. Among the Eskimo, for example, who subsist on big game or sea mammals hunted by men only, the sexual services of women are considered a commodity that men can take at will, or give or exchange to another man. Pubertal girls are fair game for any man, and wives are freely exchanged among men who wish to make alliances with one another or to repay favors (Friedl, 1975).

FREQUENCY

Average frequencies of marital coitus among groups vary from about two to five times per week (Gebhard, 1971). The Ecuadorian Cayapa Indians described by Altschuler (1971) thought that twice a week was an occasion for bragging by new husbands. This group has an exceptionally low level of sexuality, accompanied by avoidance of women, anxiety, inhibition about sexual matters, and much homoerotic behavior among the men. Even the more virile and forward men can go for long periods with little sexual activity. Male sexual inadequacy is the norm, resulting apparently from high-anxiety socialization practices in the weaning and toilet training of children. The Inis Beag, an Irish folk community studied by Messenger (1971) have very strict rules of modesty and separation of the sexes from childhood on. Frequency of marital coitus is not known but is probably low. Men believe that intercourse is debilitating and drains energy needed for other work. Sexual inhibitions extend to avoidance of nudity at all times and shunning of sexual innuendoes and jokes, even with the most pallid content. Asked to compare the sexual desires of men and women, a married woman said, "Men can wait a long time before wanting it, but we can wait longer" (p. 16).

Other people described by Davenport (1965),

Marshall (1971), and Merriam (1971), value sex highly, frequent copulation being an important part of their life styles. The Mangaians (Marshall, 1971) of central Polynesia engage in a high level of sexual activity before marriage, valuing frequent coitus, many partners, and multiple orgasms for their women. After marriage the male wishes to copulate with his wife every night, beginning to skip nights only after a decade or so of marriage. Davenport's East Bay Melanesian group (1965) expects that sexual excitement will remain high during the early years of marriage, and it is usual for couples to have intercourse each day while they are in their garden and again at night after going to bed. Frequencies of three times in a twenty-four-hour period were not uncommon. Merriam (1971), in his study of the Bala, a people of the Congo, collected data on frequency of intercourse by asking men, each morning, how many times they had had intercourse in the preceding twenty-four hours. Although the data may be less than reliable, the average over a ten-day period ranged from 1.2 to 1.9 acts of marital coitus per day. Even the men in their fifties and sixties reported having intercourse more than seven times per week.

These examples only suggest the variability of frequency of marital coitus among human groups. Obviously, it depends on factors such as attitudes toward sex, availability (as when the men are absent for long periods), restrictions and taboos, and the woman's right of refusal. In general, if teachings are repressive with many negative sanctions and taboos, and if sex is thought to be dangerous and tinged with evil, frequency is low. But if attitudes are permissive, children's exploratory activity indulged or encouraged, and people are rewarded for sexual interest and exploits, frequency is high.

FOREPLAY AND COITAL TECHNIQUES

Foreplay, precoital sexual activity directed toward arousing the partner for intercourse, is widely observed among both literate and nonliterate groups of people. Its duration and techniques vary greatly. The puritannical Inis Beag men limit foreplay to brief kissing and some fondling of the buttocks. Underclothes are not removed. Only the male superior position is used; intercourse is quite brief, the orgasm quickly achieved for the male, after which he immediately falls asleep. Davenport's Melanesians, by contrast, consider foreplay to be the indispensable "root" of intercourse, to be prolonged until both partners are close to orgasm. Techniques include kissing, fondling the woman's breasts, and mutual manual manipulation. Mouth-genital contact does not occur. Coital positions include the male superior and side-by-side, with little or no experimenting reported. After prolonged foreplay, coitus is brief, culminating in orgasm for both partners. The male, apparently, feels a responsibility for his partner's orgasm, though it need not occur simultaneously with his. Gebhard (1971), summarizing foreplay and coital practices in groups for whom data exist, said that foreplay is usually initiated by males, with female reciprocity varying from little to great. Kissing is absent in a minority of societies. Male fondling of the female breasts and genitalia is universal, and female handling of the penis is common nearly everywhere. Cunnilingus and fellatio are similarly distributed; where the former is practiced, the other is likely to be also, although the reverse is not necessarily true. Though anthropological data are scant, mouth-genital techniques are widely used in parts of Oceania, in the higher civilizations of Asia, and in North Africa, where it is said to be an Arabic invention.

Coital positions common in one group may be quite uncommon in another. Among the Bala, the usual position is with the man on his right side and the woman on her left, facing each other. The male superior position is known, but the female superior position is considered odd. Other varieties are not practiced.

The male superior position, with the female supine and the male prone on top of her, is very common, and where it is the preferred position, other positions may not be used at all, or only when conditions of time or place require a modification. In Melanesia, Australia, and parts of India, the favored position is the female supine with the male squatting between her outspread legs (Gebhard, 1971). Side-by-side is also common, especially during the later months of pregnancy.

ORGASM

According to available data, male orgasm in marital intercourse is a universal norm. For males, the correlation between incidence of intercourse and incidence of orgasm is positive and nearly perfect. The female experience of orgasm is far more variable, not only in our own society but cross-culturally as well, and its occurrence is highly influenced by cultural values and norms, and socialization practices. As Mead (1949) pointed out, "There seems therefore to be a reasonable basis for assuming that the human female's capacity for orgasm is to be viewed much more as a potentiality that may or may not be developed by a given culture" (p. 217).

Messenger reported of the Inis Beag that "there is much evidence to indicate that the female orgasm is unknown—or at least doubted, or considered a deviant response" (p. 16). In the Tepoztlan village in Mexico, wives are not expected to be passionate, and husbands refrain from arousing their wives sexually, assuming that the passive and frigid wife will be faithful (Lewis, 1960).

Mangaian women, by contrast, have a great deal of premarital experience and develop orgasmic response as a matter of course. Female orgasm is highly valued: "The really important aspect of sexual intercourse for either the married man or the more experienced unwed male is to give pleasure to his wife or woman or girl—the pleasure of the orgasm" (Marshall, 1971, p. 123). Davenport's East Bay Melanesian group likewise took for granted the woman's experience of orgasm in marital coitus. They believed firmly that, once engaged in foreplay, there was nothing to prevent a woman from having orgasm if intercourse followed (Davenport, 1965).

The evidence suggests that, in general, young females take longer in coitus to reach orgasm than young males do. Therefore, in repressive societies, in which even marital sex is furtive and hurried, characterized by attitudes antagonistic to sensuality and pleasure, the incidence of female orgasm is predictably low. If sexuality is openly valued and enjoyed, emphasizing prolongation and satisfaction for both partners, the orgasmic potential of women is more likely to be realized.

SEXUAL TABOOS IN MARRIAGE

Many societies forbid sexual relations between marital partners during menstruation, pregnancy, and the postpartum period. In general, these taboos reflect fear of the woman's power to contaminate at these times, though the postpartum taboos also serve as a control on fertility by spacing births. Such spacing serves as a protective health measure for both the lactating mother and the nursing child, and also assures that she will not be burdened with two children needing to be carried, an important consideration in foraging societies (Friedl, 1978).

Menstruating women historically have been held to have the power to pollute and to contaminate food, utensils, and livestock, and to harm men by weakening them or bringing them bad luck in hunting or war. Among the Baganda, for example, a menstruating wife may not touch anything belonging to her husband, nor may she cook his food. Were she to handle any article of his, he would fall ill; if she touched his weapons, he would be killed in the next battle. She also has the power to dry up wells and spoil milk (Frazer, 1951). Among the East Bay Melanesian in Davenport's group, intercourse was avoided during the woman's menstrual period because the flow was extremely repulsive. Women were not secluded during their periods, a common practice elsewhere, but they did not cook for their husbands.

Pregnancy and postpartum taboos also are very common. The Mangaians, however, can have intercourse with their wives up until the onset of labor. In East Bay, there is no post-partum taboo, although husbands are supposed to give their wives at least a month to recuperate from giving birth.

Such taboos and practices seem to be less related to attitudes toward sex than to attitudes toward women. Their prevalence is widespread among both literate and nonliterate groups, and there is much literature describing them (e.g., Delaney and others, 1976).

Attitudes Toward Marital Sex

Among groups, with few exceptions, men regard marital sex as a natural right, to be sampled regularly and enjoyed. As with orgasm, the data for women are more variable. Rainwater (1971), in his study of marital relations in four cultures of poverty, found a range of responses to questions on interest and enjoyment of marital sex by women. The gamut went from, "If God made anything better he kept it to himself," to "I would be happy if I never had to do that again; it's disgusting" (p. 188). The norm among his four groups, however, was closer to the latter attitude. Sex was generally considered to be a man's pleasure and a woman's duty. Women were believed not to have sexual desires at all or to have much weaker needs than men had. In Tepoztlan respectable women were expected also to have strong negative attitudes toward sex. Women who needed men sexually were called *loca* (crazy) and perhaps bewitched (Lewis, 1960).

Although data are scant, the women of Mangaia, Bala, and East Bay appear to have more positive attitudes toward the sexual parts of their marriages, if frequency is any indication. Even so, a high normative interest and positive regard for sex by married women is not frequently encountered in the cross-cultural literature. Reasons for this are not hard to find: emphasis on virginity for girls, with lack of premarital experience; the cultural/experiential factor in women's orgasmic response, typically observed to be more important to women than to men; the characteristic male domina-

tion of marital sex, in that males initiate sexual activity and direct it to their satisfaction (with some exceptions as previously noted); the consequences for women of pregnancy and child care; the fairly widespread regard for women as sexual property, to be used, bartered, and exchanged; and rules of modesty, religious sanctions, and taboos which are directed more against women's participation in sex than against men's.

Extramarital Sexual Relations

In most societies, marital intercourse accounts for most of the sexual activity of adults. Even so, extramarital coitus is very common and is even institutionalized and sanctioned under certain conditions and regulations. Although wives everywhere are more restricted than husbands are, it is estimated that from two-fifths to three-fifths of nonliterate societies permit some kind of extramarital coitus for wives (Gebhard, 1971). Variables include the double standard, the knowledge and/or permission of the spouse, the choice of partner, the occasion and place where intercourse may occur, and the risks and penalties involved. Often, as Gebhard (1971) noted, the concern is less with the act itself than with its social implications, such as degradation of the spouse, implications of pregnancy, and effects on kinship ties and loyalty.

A typical example of the way adultery is viewed and managed is described in Davenport's account of the East Bay people. Before marriage, control of the right of sexual access to a young woman belongs to her father. When the bride price is paid to him at her marriage, the controlling right passes to her husband and any kin who contributed to the bride price. Adultery, then, with a married woman is an offense against the husband and the other contributors. Although a wife has some of the same rights in her husband, she, as a woman, has no recourse to law. Therefore, any offense by her, as the accused or the accuser, immediately affects those close male kin who are her legal representatives. If the offense goes into litigation, it affects the men of several families and may become very complex, as all the offended ones must finally be compensated in money. Although most of the concern seems to be for the violation of the rights of the men with an investment in the woman, the moral culpability rests more heavily on the man in the adulterous relationship. In this society, in which women are trained to serve and to be obedient to the men with legitimate authority over them, it is expected that they are unable to refuse the request of a male for sexual services, especially if he offers presents.

Another widespread pattern includes the expectation that husbands will stray, but wives will be faithful. In Tepoztlan sexual promiscuity is for males only, and married men are expected to prove their masculinity by having affairs, usually with widows, unmarried women, or prostitutes. Husbands are anxious about their wives' fidelity in the early months of marriage and feel most secure when they are pregnant or caring for an infant (Lewis, 1960).

In horticultural societies there is often an option according to which adults can have sex with someone other than a spouse (Friedl, 1975). Even so, adultery is thought to be risky for both partners and may be punishable by penalties or divorce. Men have firmer entitlements to their wives' sexual services than do wives to their husbands'. An adulterous man may be required to pay a penalty to the husband of his lover or to her father if she is unmarried. A wife, however, cannot usually extract a penalty from the woman with whom her husband is involved.

Finally, Schneider (1971) described an institutionalized form of adultery among the Turu of Tanzania. The lover relationship, called *mbuya*, is compared to romantic love in the West, with the same components of courtship, mooning, and jealous, possessive behavior. Love songs are composed and gifts exchanged. The furtiveness of the relationship adds to its delights, so that its clandestine nature may be preserved even when the affair is well known to everyone and tacitly approved by the husband. A husband may forbid such a relationship but may have difficulty doing so, since others will not cooperate with him. His wife may point out to him that he, himself, has a mistress, or she may go to her father and request an annulment of her marriage on the grounds that her husband is treating her shabbily.

SUMMARY

Marriage is the only human relationship within which sexual intercourse is universally sanctioned. We have seen, however, how variable are individuals within groups. Among some people, marital intercourse is proscribed at certain times, as during menstruation and pregnancy. Among others, provision is made routinely for extramarital liaisons, as among the Turu, and in Western countries which have institutionalized the mistress-lover relationship. Within groups data also testify to individual variation in needs, tastes, and behavior. Even within an individual's historical repertoire, changes over time may be observed as a life style evolves and new behaviors emerge.

Generalizations about sex in marriage seem possible only for carefully defined samples, the results qualified by attention to the sources of variation and their effects. Currently in our society, we can describe the scene of marital sexuality only as pluralistic, providing many models, each with adaptations and variants. From one couple's brief, once-a-week encounter, never deviating from the male superior position, to another's daily, highly sensual, experimenting adventure, to yet another's exploration of swinging and group sex, and many others closer to and farther from the norm, we gain a sense of the plasticity of human sexual experience as it occurs in the old institution of marriage.

REFERENCE NOTES

[1] The theory of primitive matriarchy, in which women were family heads, bequeathing their names and goods to their children until they were finally vanquished and subdued by the physical superiority of males, is no longer considered viable by theorists of the origin of the family.

B. L. Murstein, *Love, Sex, and Marriage through the Ages.* (New York: Springer, 1974).

² All page numbers for quotations from Kinsey and others, (1953) are from the 1965 Pocket Book edition.

REFERENCES

ALTSCHULER, M. 1971. Cayapa personality and sexual motivation. In *Human sexual behavior,* ed. D. S. Marshall and R. C. Suggs. New York: Basic Books.

BACHOFEN, J. J. 1967. *Myth, religion, and mother-right,* trans. R. Manheim. Princeton, N.J.: Princeton University Press.

BELL, R. R.; TURNER, S.; and ROSEN, L. 1975. A multivariate analysis of female extramarital coitus. *Journal of Marriage and the Family* 37: 375–84.

BERNARD, J. 1972. *The future of marriage.* New York: World Publishing.

——. 1974. Infidelity: some moral and social issues. In *Beyond monogamy,* ed. J. R. Smith and L. G. Smith. Baltimore: Johns Hopkins University Press.

BOHANNON, P., ed. 1971. *Divorce and after.* Garden City N.Y.: Doubleday Anchor.

BOSWELL, J. 1956. *In search of a wife.* New York: McGraw-Hill.

BRECHER, E. M. 1971. *The sex researchers.* New York: New American Library.

CLARK, A. L., and WALLIN, P. 1965. Women's sexual responsiveness and the duration and quality of their marriages. *American Journal of Sociology* 71: 187–96.

COMFORT, A. 1976. Sexuality and aging. *SIECUS Report* 4: 7–9.

DAVENPORT, W. 1965. Sexual patterns and their regulation in a society of the Southwest Pacific. In *Sex and behavior,* ed. F. A. Beach. New York: Wiley.

DAVIS, K. 1929. *Factors in the sex life of 2200 women.* New York: Harper.

DECKARD, B. 1975. *The women's movement: political, socioeconomic, and psychological issues.* New York: Harper & Row.

DELANEY, J.; LUPTON, M. J.; and TOTH, E. 1976. *The curse: a cultural history of menstruation.* New York: Dutton.

DICKINSON, R. L., and BEAM, L. 1932. *One thousand marriages.* London: Williams and Northgate.

EDWARDS, J. N., and BOOTH, A. 1976a. The cessation of marital intercourse. *American Journal of Psychiatry* 133: 1333–36.

——. 1976b. Sexual behavior in and out of marriage: an assessment of correlates. *Journal of Marriage and the Family* 38: 73–81.

ELLIS, A. 1977. Pros and cons of extramarital sexual relations. In *the Densen-Gerber Crusade and ongoing developments in contemporary sexuality.* New York: ATCOM.

ELLIS, H. 1937. *On life and sex.* New York: Garden City Publishing Co.

FORD, C., and BEACH, F. 1951. *Patterns of sexual behavior.* New York: Perennial (Harper & Row).

FRAZER, J. G. 1951. *The golden bough.* New York: Macmillan.

FREUD, S. 1947. "Civilized" sexual morality and modern nervousness. In *On war, sex, and neurosis,* ed. S. Katz. New York: Arts and Sciences Press.

FRIEDL, E. 1975. *Women and men: an anthropologist's view.* New York: Holt, Rinehart & Winston.

——. 1978. Society and sex roles. *Human Nature* 1: 68–75.

GAGNON, J. H. 1975. Sex research and social change. *Archives of Sexual Behavior* 4: 111–41.

GEBHARD, P. 1971. Human sexual behavior: a summary statement. In *Human sexual behavior,* ed. D. S. Marshall and R. C. Suggs. New York: Basic Books.

HALLER, J. S. 1972. From maidenhood to menopause: sex education for women in Victorian America. *Journal of Popular Culture* 6: 49–69.

——, and HALLER, R. M. 1974. *The physician*

and sexuality in Victorian America. Urbana, Ill.: University of Illinois Press.

HAMILTON, G. V. 1929. *A research in marriage.* New York: Lear.

HESSELLUND, H. 1976. Masturbation and sexual fantasies in married couples. *Archives of Sexual Behavior* 5: 133–47.

HITE, S. 1976. *The Hite report.* New York: Macmillan.

HUMPHREY, F. G. 1975. Changing roles for women: implications for marriage counselors. *Journal of Marriage and Family Counseling* 1: 219–27.

HUNT, M. 1974. *Sexual behavior in the 1970s.* Chicago: Playboy Press.

JOHNSON, R. E. 1970. Some correlates of extramarital coitus. *Journal of Marriage and the Family* 32: 449–56.

KATCHEDOURIAN, H. A., and LUNDE, D. T. 1975. *Fundamentals of human sexuality,* 2d ed. New York: Holt, Rinehart & Winston.

KENNETT, R. H. 1931. *Ancient Hebrew social life and custom.* London: Oxford University Press.

KENNY, J. A. 1973. Sexuality of pregnant and breastfeeding women. *Archives of Sexual Behavior* 2: 215–29.

KINSEY, A.; POMEROY, W.; and MARTIN, C. 1948. *Sexual behavior in the human male.* Philadelphia: W. B. Saunders.

———; and GEBHARD, P. H. 1965. *Sexual behavior in the human female.* New York: Pocket Books.

LECKY, W. E. H. 1905. *History of European morals.* 2 vols. New York: Appleton.

LEVI-STRAUSS, C. 1969. *The elementary structures of kinship.* London: Eyre & Spottiswoode.

LEWIS, O. 1960. *Tepoztlan: village in Mexico.* New York: Holt, Rinehart & Winston.

LINDSEY, B. B., and EVANS, W. 1929. *The companionate marriage.* New York: Garden City.

LUTHER, M. 1890. *The table talk of Martin Luther.* London: George Bell & Sons.

MARSHALL, D. S. 1967. General anthropology: strategy for a human science. *Current anthropology* 8: 61–66.

———. 1971. Sexual behavior on Mangaia. In *Human sexual behavior,* ed. D. S. Marshall and R. C. Suggs. New York: Basic Books.

MASTERS, W., and JOHNSON, V. 1966. *Human sexual response.* Boston: Little, Brown.

———. 1968. Human sexual response: the aging female and the aging male. In *Middle age and aging,* ed. B. Neugarten. Chicago: University of Chicago Press.

MEAD, M. 1949. *Male and female.* New York: William Morrow.

MERRIAM, A. P. 1971. Aspects of sexual behavior among the Bala (Basongye). In *Human sexual behavior,* ed. D. S. Marshall and R. C. Suggs. New York: Basic Books.

MESSENGER, J. C. 1971. Sex and repression in an Irish folk community. In *Human sexual behavior,* ed. D. S. Marshall and R. C. Suggs. New York: Basic Books.

MITCHELL, J. 1974. *Psychoanalysis and feminism.* New York: Pantheon.

MORRIS, N. M. 1975. The frequency of sexual intercourse during pregnancy. *Archives of Sexual Behavior* 4: 501–7.

MUNCY, R. L. 1973. *Sex and marriage in utopian communities.* Bloomington, Ind.: Indiana University Press.

MURSTEIN, B. I. 1974. *Love, sex, and marriage through the ages.* New York: Springer.

O'NEILL, G. C., and O'NEILL, N. 1972. *Open marriage: a new life style for couples.* New York: M. Evans & Co.

PEARSALL, R. 1969. *The worm in the bud: the world of Victorian sexuality.* Toronto: Macmillan.

RAINWATER, L. 1971. Marital sexuality in four "cultures of poverty." In *Human sexual behavior,* ed. D. S. Marshall and R. C. Suggs. New York: Basic Books.

RAMEY, J. W. 1974. Communes, group marriage, and the upper-middle class. In *Beyond monogamy,* ed. J. R. Smith and L. G.

Smith. Baltimore: Johns Hopkins University Press.

ROSTAND, J. 1961. The evolution of the species. In *The Orion book of evolution*. New York: Orion Press.

RUGOFF, M. 1971. *Prudery and passion*. New York: Putnam.

SAUCIER, J. F. 1972. Correlates of the long postpartum taboo: a cross-cultural study. *Current Anthropology* 13: 238–49.

SCHNEIDER, H. K. 1971. Romantic love among the Turu. In *Human sexual behavior*, ed. D. S. Marshall and R. C. Suggs. New York: Basic Books.

SHERFEY, M. J. 1973. *The nature and evolution of female sexuality*. New York: Vintage Books.

SIECUS Report. 1976. Sexuality and the aging: a selective bibliography 4.

SMITH, L. G., and SMITH, J. R. 1974. Co-marital sex: the incorporation of extramarital sex into the marriage relationship. In *Beyond monogamy*, ed. J. R. Smith and L. G. Smith. Baltimore: Johns Hopkins University Press.

SOLBERG, D. A.; BUTLER, J.; and WAGNER, N. N. 1973. Sexual behavior in pregnancy. *New England Journal of Medicine* 288: 1098–103.

SPANIER, G. B., and COLE, C. L. 1975. Mate swapping: perceptions, value orientations, and participation in a midwestern community. *Archives of sexual behavior* 4: 143–59.

STRONG, B. 1973. Toward a history of the experiential family: sex and incest in the nineteenth-century family. *Journal of Marriage and the Family* 35: 457–66.

SUGGS, R. C., and MARSHALL, D. S. 1971. Anthropological perspectives on human sexual behavior. In *Human sexual behavior*, ed. D. S. Marshall and R. C. Suggs. New York: Basic Books.

SVILAND, M. A. P. 1976. Helping elderly couples attain sexual liberation and growth. *SIECUS Report* 4: 3–4.

TAVRIS, C., and SADD, S. 1977. *The Redbook report on female sexuality*. New York: Delacorte Press.

TOLOR, A., and DIGRAZIA, P. V. 1976. Sexual attitudes and behavior patterns during and following pregnancy. *Archives of Sexual Behavior* 5: 539–51.

VAN DE VELDE, T. 1930. *Ideal marriage*. New York: Random House.

WALTER, R. G. 1974. *Primers for prudery: sexual advice to Victorian America*. Englewood Cliffs, N.J.: Prentice-Hall.

WESTERMARCK, E. 1921. *The history of human marriage*. 3 vols. London: Macmillan.

WILLIAMS, J. H. 1977. *Psychology of women: behavior in a biosocial context*. New York: Norton.

SEVEN

Sexuality
and
Aging

ANN JOHNSON SILNY

Changes in sex-related characteristics which occur in humans with advancing age include both physiological changes and behavioral changes. The latter are the result of physiological or psychological causes or both. It generally is true that aging, per se, is only one of a number of variables which interact to reduce sexuality in older people. Aging, although it has powerful physiological effects, cannot be viewed as the primary cause of changes in sexuality. Most research suggests that aging produces many general physical changes which combined with sociopsychological variables influence sexuality.

It is difficult, if not impossible, to isolate those aspects of human sexuality which only physiology (or age-related physiological change) influences. The relationship between biology and sexual behavior in humans is not fully understood. Many correlational studies point to the importance of endocrine structures as they support reproductive functioning, but since sexuality in humans involves more than reproductive capacity, isolating physiological mechanisms cannot tell the whole story. Much less is known about specific psychological mechanisms (for example, early experience and learning, cognitive style) as they affect sexuality and certainly the complex interaction of these variables is not known.

This essay will outline the principle differences between sexually mature humans and their elderly counterparts in terms of physiological factors, sexual capacity, activity, and attitudes.

ENDOCRINE AND REPRODUCTIVE TRACT CHANGES IN FEMALES

The most striking change in the aging human female is a drop in circulating levels of estrogen and progesterone. These changes in hormone levels are directly tied to the aging ovary's inability to produce its principle steroid hormones. The structural changes in the ovary are thought to be an intrinsic result of the aging process itself, because no specific causal agents for structural change have been found.

Total estrogen levels in females are stable throughout the thirties (or until menopause), decline steadily until about the mid-sixties and remain at low levels thereafter (Pincus, 1954). Measured urinary excretion of estrogens in women at ages fifty through sixty-five are 40% of the levels found at ages eighteen to thirty-four, and at age sixty-five and above are 20% of the earlier values (Pincus, 1954). Urinary excretion of prenanediol in women about age eighty was found in one study to be about half the value for women in their early thirties (Timeras, 1972). Changes in estrogen secretion do not occur because of lowered anterior pituitary activity; there is evidence that the pituitary increases production and release of gonadotropins as ovarian estrogen secretion slows down. Johnsen (1959) demonstrated that gonadotropin release increased slightly in premenopausal women (compared with those under forty) and then increased dramatically at menopause, to over ten times the values at ages eighteen to thirty-four. Paschkis (1967) reports that 4 to 40 mouse weight units (measure of gonadotropins extracted from urine) is characteristic of young females, depending upon the phase of the menstrual cycle, whereas menopausal and postmenopausal women show values of from 92 to 300 m. w. units. Gonadotropin levels remain high well into advanced age and drop off after about age eighty (Albert, 1956). These elevated gonadotropin levels suggest that the pituitary is attempting to compensate for reduced ovarian production. Talbert (1968) has shown that the number of anterior pituitary basophil cells producing gonadotropins is higher in menopausal women than in younger women.

124

There is a moderate age-related decrease in female androgens as measured by urinary 17–ketosteroids. In females, the principle source of nonphenolic (neutral) 17-ketosteroids is thought to be the adrenals. Paschkis (1967) reported urinary androgen levels in premenopausal females at 5 to 15 mg/day. In postmenopausal women (ages fifty to sixty), these values were as low as 3 mg/day. At menopause, some women show a moderate increase of urinary androgens, which could represent adrenal hyperfunction.

With age, the ovary shows definite structural changes. There is a progressive decline in the number of primordial follicles from puberty until menopause (Block, 1952). The number of follicles in the human ovary is about 6,000 at ages forty-one to forty-five compared with 50,000 at ages thirty-one to thirty-five. The number of follicles seen in the early thirties represents a 70% drop from the number present before age twenty (Timeras, 1972). The direct causes of this decline are unknown. Since estrogen production before menopause is relatively constant, changes in the ovary are thought to be unrelated initially to hormonal levels and are probably intrinsic to the ovary itself. Maturing follicles are the principle source of estrogen production, although the specific part of the follicle responsible has yet to be identified. In the aging female, the reduction in number of maturing follicles is accompanied by a decrease in the number of functional corpus lutea following ovulation and lowered progesterone levels. Changes in progesterone levels are implicated in the increasing number of anovulatory cycles seen in women just before menopause.

Because the reproductive tract and the external genitals require estrogens and progesterones for their maintenance, lowered levels of these hormones produce morphological changes. The most general effect of estrogens is tissue growth, and female reproductive structures are highly sensitive to estrogens. The uterus reaches its maximum weight at about age thirty; by age fifty, uterine weight can drop as much as 50%. Collagen and elastin content of the uterus also decline (Timeras, 1972). The uterine endometrium in menopausal and postmenopausal women shows changes ranging from mild atrophy to marked hypertrophy (Paschkis, 1967). Estrogen withdrawal also results in a thinning and shrinking of the vaginal wall with the epithelium reduced to a single row of cells. In premenopausal women, vaginal smears show the typical cornified cells of the preovulatory phase of the menstrual cycle. In menopausal women, only precornified cells and transitional epithelial cells are seen in the smear. The normally alkaline pH of vaginal secretions, which are thought to neutralize the more acidic vaginal canal, becomes more alkaline. Fallopian tubes shrink in size and secretory activity is severely diminished.

At menopause, the external genitals change their appearance as a result of estrogen slowdown. The subcutaneous fat of the labia majoris is lost, resulting in a "flattening" of this structure. The labia minoris and the clitoris decrease in size. A reduction in the size and firmness of breast tissue is often seen, and pubic and axillary hair thin slightly. Beginning at menopause, all of these changes occur rather gradually but become quite marked later in senescence. Some of the initial changes (thinning of vaginal wall, shrinking of major labia) can be reversed by administering steroids (Masters, 1957), but the evidence suggests that most of these changes are more directly related to the aging process itself and only secondarily to estrogen/progesterone reductions. A finding that seems to support the hypothesis that aging tissues become less sensitive to circulating steroids is the fact that when estrogen therapy is discontinued in postmenopausal women, withdrawal bleeding is less frequent than in younger premenopausal women (Talbert, 1968).

Female menopause represents tangible evidence of waning reproductive capacity and is signaled by the cessation of menstrual cycles. Menopause is a function of the aging ovary and the accompanying hormonal changes. It comes for most women in the mid- to late forties. Industrialized societies report a slightly earlier average age (48) than do some nonindustrialized cultures—a New Zealand sample reports average age as fifty to fifty-one (Burch and Gunz, 1967). When menopause occurs in the late forties, it is thought to be a result of normal ovarian aging; when it occurs substantially earlier, nutritional, health, and stress factors may be implicated (Timeras, 1972). The classic menopausal symptoms include autonomic and vasomotor changes (increased heart rate, hypertension, "hot flashes"), bone and joint discomfort, and psychological disturbances such as depression, irritability, and emotional instability.

"Hot flashes" are the most common vasomotor manifestation. Paschkis (1967) states that estrogen deprivation is not the cause of this disturbance, because it is relatively unknown in patients with estrogen deprivation secondary to pituitary hypofunction. Hot flashes in menopausal women are invariably accompanied by high FSH titers in blood and urine. Gonadotropin administration, however, will not induce hot flashes, and estrogen administration in doses which do not affect gonadotropin titers can suppress them.

There are many degrees to which menopausal women suffer these symptoms of menopause. Only about one-fourth of all menopausal women suffer "distressful" menopausal symptoms (Riedman, 1961). Paschkis reports a study conducted by the Women's Medical Federation in which 179 subjects, five or more years past menopause, were interviewed for the occurrence of menopausal symptoms: 15.8% reported that they had had no symptoms whatsoever, and 10.3% had been incapacitated for various amounts of time. For those women who had experienced any symptoms, flushing (or hot flashes) was the most frequent (62.3%) with headaches (44.6%) and nervous instability (30.9%) less common. Paschkis states that in his experience of treating menopausal women, loss of libido or increase in libido is the least frequent of his patients' complaints. Although estrogen administration can frequently alleviate physical symptoms, there is no evidence that the psychological problems attendant at menopause are directly a result of hormone imbalance.

There is some evidence that a woman's attitude towards menopause may affect the occurrence and/or severity of symptoms (Kelly, 1961; Sharman, 1962). Women who are mentally well adjusted before the climacteric tend to have fewer unpleasant symptoms at menopause (Coleman, 1972). However, Neugarten (1963; 1967) was unable to detect any consistent relationship between severity of symptoms and negative attitudes. In interviews with one-hundred white females, ages forty-five through fifty-five, the majority saw menopause as disagreeable. The worst aspects of menopause were seen as not knowing what to expect and recognizing it as tangible evidence of aging. About 50% of the sample said they felt the menopause was detrimental to a woman's appearance. Premenopausal women were more fearful of the climacteric than those who had experienced it. Premenopausal females also had more negative attitudes about the experience and more fears and misunderstandings about what postmenopausal sexuality would be like.

ENDOCRINE AND REPRODUCTIVE TRACT CHANGES IN MALES

Changes in endocrine function and reproductive structures are more gradual, less pronounced, and seem to occur somewhat later for males than for females. Unlike females, males have no abrupt change of life.

Circulating androgens in males are relatively constant after puberty, showing only gradual declines until about age forty or forty-five. After the mid-forties, androgen levels are about 55 to 60% of what they were earlier. After age sixty-five, values are about 30% of those in the thirties. In advanced age, about seventy-five, androgens have dropped 85 to 90% compared with levels before thirty. Paschkis (1967) reported 8 to 20 mg/day total urinary 17-ketosteroids in sexually mature males; values of less than 5 mg/day were not uncommon among elderly men. The fact that aging affects testicular cells known to produce androgen and correlates in time with declining androgen levels is taken as evidence that declining androgen levels are primarily a result of testicular decline. Because androgen levels decrease in both males and females (Dorfman and Shipley, 1956), it suggests that the adrenals may also be involved (Gherondache, 1967).

Conclusions about pituitary activity in males parallel those for females. Although gonadotropin levels are not as high in aging men as in aging women, there is evidence of increased anterior pituitary activity. Paschkis (1967) reported 4 to 24 mouse weight units of urinary gonadotropins as typical of his sample of sexually mature males under fifty. In subjects in their sixties and seventies, amounts up to 96 m.w. units have been found.

It is debatable whether there are significant changes in estrogen levels in males. Pincus (1954) reported no change in total estrogen levels, although specific estrogen groups showed some decline. Gherondache (1967) has reported that total estrogen output in aging men is reduced by about 30% and progesterone output declines about 60%.

Compared with young men, testicles of males fifty-five and older seem smaller and less firm (Rubin, 1965). Although there is little change in testicular weight with age, there are marked changes in testicular tissue. The number of Leydig cells decreases progressively with age and changes as early as twenty-five or thirty years have been observed in some men (Tillinger, 1957). The reduced number of secretory cells follows rather closely the lowered levels of androgen, suggesting a functional relationship. The lipid content of Leydig cells decreases after the fourth decade (Lynch and Scott, 1950). However, the lipid content of Sertoli cells increases with age. The functional significance of this is unknown.

Spermatogenesis which occurs continuously in sexually mature males is reduced in older men, although total inability to produce sperm is rarely found even in very old men. Molnar (1965) reported that the number of sperm in the ejaculate of men in their sixties was about 30% lower than at previous ages and in much older men, this percentage decrease was even greater. Reduced spermatogenesis is thought to be related to changes in the seminiferous tubules and to decreased androgen levels. Aging males display a proliferation of connective tissue along the basement membrane of the seminiferous tubules (Engle, 1952; Molnar, 1965) which may interfere with effective sperm production. Alterations in the size and shape of sperm are more frequently seen in aging men.

Genital tract and duct systems require androgens for maintenance. Lowered androgen levels contribute to age-related changes. The seminal vesicles show weight reduction after age sixty and display decreased secretory activity. The prostate gland often follows a predictable sequence of change beginning as early as the forties and ending in the mid-fifties with muscular atrophy and fibrosis (Moore, 1952; Steward and Brandes, 1961). There often is dramatic enlargement in the seventies and eighties. This sequence of prostate changes is not inevitable but occurs with a high relative frequency in aging men. Enzyme and secretory activity of the prostate is reduced. Since the prostate contributes 20% and the seminal vesicles 60% to the total volume of seminal fluid, reduced secretory activity of these accessory structures results in lower amounts of ejaculate as well as a change in the composition of semen in older males.

There is no male analogue for female menopause, although reports of "menopausal" symptoms in middle-aged males crop up in the clinical literature from time to time. Since male reproductive capability shows only gradual changes and since there are no abrupt hormonal alterations, the analogy is a loose one at best. Benjamin (1959) has reported male patients with symptoms of irritability, insomnia, depression, and hot flashes. These symptoms tended to occur in the sixties and seventies. Other reports (see Walker, 1964) suggest that they may come earlier with the onset of prostate difficulties. Rubin (1965) cited a study of 273 men with menopausal complaints. In that sample, 90% complained of nervousness with a similar proportion claiming impotence. Eighty-one percent said they experienced a loss of libido, and the same percentage experienced irritability and fatigue. Libido and sexual capability, although the least frequent of female menopausal complaints, were much more common in this male sample. Lowered androgen levels may have been responsible for libidinal changes in these men. Menopausal women who experience abrupt estrogen (but not androgen) changes do not show these libidinal changes (or at least do not report them as frequently). In fact, Masters and Johnson (1966) report increases in libido in some segments of their postmenopausal sample. Since androgens underlie libido in both males and females, it is reasonable to suppose that the relatively greater androgen decline in older males (compared with older females) should lead to more pronounced libidinal changes in males. The degree to which physical condition and sexual expectations affect libido for both males and females is unknown, so libidinal changes cannot be tied solely to hormonal shifts.

Endocrine and reproductive tract changes also are accompanied by altered abilities in sexual capacity. The most comprehensive work on the changes in physical functioning with age has been done by Masters and Johnson and is reported in their publication *Human Sexual Response* (1966).

SEXUAL CAPACITY IN THE MALE

Although age-related endocrine and reproductive tract changes in males are less obvious than those in females, aging males demonstrate more pronounced declines in sexual functioning.

When compared with younger men, males fifty-five and older show decreases in the amount of precoital mucus secreted in the urethral canal. The source of this mucus is generally believed to be the Cowpers glands which become less active with age. The Kinsey self-report data (1948) showed relative amounts of mucus secreted by males at various ages. The average amount for males in their twenties and

thirties was slightly more than three times as much as for men in their fifties and sixties. Although there were individual differences in the amounts of these secretions at every age, Kinsey suggested that the amount of mucus secreted was related to the intensity of erotic stimulation and that lowered secretions in older men represented increased thresholds for stimulation and declining arousal levels as well as glandular changes themselves. Older men generally have reduced amounts of ejaculate and the force of ejaculation as measured by expelled distance and subjective report is diminished (Masters and Johnson, 1966). Declining volume of ejaculate can be tied to declining secretory activity of reproductive accessory structures (primarily the prostate and seminal vesicles), but force of ejaculation is influenced by the changing character of penile contractions. Young males were observed to expel seminal fluid twelve to twenty-four inches from the urethral meatus; in men over fifty, the maximum distances were from six to twelve inches (Masters and Johnson, 1966). Instead of the usual recurrent, expulsive penile contractions which forcefully propel the ejaculate, older males tend to develop spastic contractions. Although contractions occur at the same intervals (0.8 seconds), older men have fewer of them and with protracted penile erection, ejaculate often "seeps out." The viscosity of ejaculate from older males is generally lower than that found in younger men.

There are a number of behavioral changes in male sexual activity. Penile erection is typically slower for older men. For males under forty, ten seconds is the typical reaction time; young men can demonstrate full erection in from three to five seconds of sexual stimulation. The reaction time is doubled or tripled for men in their fifties and above (Masters and Johnson, 1966). Older men also show a decline in the number of ejaculations per fixed unit of time; the number of ejaculations declines from its peak in late adolescence (four to eight per day are not unusual) to an average of slightly less than two per week in the fifties to less than one per week in the sixties and thereafter (Kinsey, 1948). Kinsey reported that the number of males capable of multiejaculation decreased with age. In his sample, 15 to 20% of the sample reported the occurrence of multiple ejaculations in the teens. Only 3% of men in their sixties and older reported this behavior. The greatest proportional decline in Kinsey's sample occurred in the late thirties and early forties.

The erectile refractory period following ejaculation increases progressively from minutes in the teens (Kaplan and Sager, 1971) to about a half hour in the thirties to eight to twenty-four hours in the fifties. Many males in their fifties and sixties experience paradoxical refractory periods in which loss of erection in protracted sexual encounters results in a wait of from twelve to twenty-four hours before erection can be attained again. This "refractory period" resembles that following ejaculation although ejaculation did not take place.

Penile erection under coital stimulation can be maintained longer by older men (Masters and Johnson, 1966). This age-related increase in latency to ejaculate may be a function of both previous coital experience and decreased sensitivity to erotic stimulation.

Both morning erections and nocturnal emissions occur less frequently with age. Kinsey reported the median frequencies of morning erections at two per week in the thirties, one per week by age sixty-five and two per month in the late sixties. In a *Sexology* study reported by Rubin (1963), 57% of a sample of sixty-five to sixty-nine-year-old males who were being treated for impotence claimed to have some morning erections. Rubin used these data to suggest that in many of these men the etiology of impotence was psychological. Kinsey reported that 71% of single males in their early twenties had nocturnal emissions. For both married and single men, emissions declined in frequency after age thirty. By fifty, about 30% of males interviewed had emissions but less frequently than in earlier years. Maximum frequencies per week recorded by Kinsey were twelve in the teens, three in the thirties, and

less than one (.5) in the fifties. Only 14% of the men over sixty were still having any nocturnal emissions.

Scrotal elevation which occurs for younger males in the late excitement or early plateau phase of the sexual response cycle is attenuated for men over fifty-five. Full scrotal elevation prior to ejaculation is not always observed, and testicular descent following ejaculation may be extremely rapid. Past age fifty-five, the testicles often do not show the usual 50% increase in size due to vasocongestion. Penile detumescence during the resolution phase often occurs extremely rapidly following ejaculation rather than in the two stages typical of younger men (Masters and Johnson, 1966).

Erectile impotence is quite rare in males under age thirty-five. In Kinsey's sample less than .005% under twenty-five and 1% under thirty-five suffered from erectile failure. For these young men, the condition frequently was transitory. However, Kinsey observed an increasing proportion of erectilly impotent males at ages above fifty. These proportions at fifty, seventy, and seventy-five years were 8%, 27%, and 55%, respectively. The degree to which generally poor health and other physical factors contribute to the rising proportions of impotence is unknown.

A number of behavioral changes in sexual activity (increased latency to ejaculate, increased reaction time for penile erection, decreases in precoital mucus) suggest that aging males lose sensitivity to stimulation or that their thresholds for erotic stimulation increase with age. Alterations in collagen and elastic tissues of the skin may contribute to increases in the threshold of cutaneous sensitivity (Magladery, 1959). The loss of accessory structures' ability to maintain recurring penile contractions probably contributes to a diminished sense of satisfaction at ejaculation. Kinsey's erotic responsiveness ratings by age showed that with advancing years responsiveness (or sensitivity) decreased. The average indexed responsiveness figure for males thirty to thirty-five was about fourteen; this figure fell to six by the mid-fifties, to four by the late sixties, and went to zero for persons over seventy.

SEXUAL CAPACITY IN THE FEMALE

Past age fifty, vaginal lubrication in response to sexual excitement is slower and more scanty than in premenopausal women. The vaginal walls themselves are the source of most vaginal lubrication. Although the vagina possesses no known secretory cells, a thick mucoid substance has been observed to seep or "sweat" through the walls until the entire vaginal barrel is moistened (Masters and Johnson, 1966). The thinning of the vaginal wall as a result of estrogen withdrawal correlates with the reduced ability to produce lubricant. The amount of vaginal lubrication can be increased with estrogen administered at menopause. In women under forty, vaginal lubrication occurs as quickly as ten to thirty seconds following stimulation (Masters and Johnson, 1966). This latency increases with age; by sixty, one to three minutes may be required for any obvious lubrication. (There are individual differences—Masters and Johnson observed a few women over sixty who showed lubrication responses characteristic of women thirty years younger. The most plausible explanation, they felt, was that these women had had very regular sexual activity throughout their adult years.) Well after menopause, the Bartholin glands decrease their secretory activity but even in young females they contribute very little to full vaginal lubrication.

Following menopause, the vaginal barrel shortens in length and width and loses some of its elasticity (Masters and Johnson, 1966). The thinning of the vaginal wall often results in uncomfortable side effects following coitus— burning and irritation during urination. In premenopausal women, the normally thick vaginal walls serve as a buffer against bladder irritation.

Nipple erection remains unchanged with age, but the typical vasocongestive size increase of the breasts during the plateau phase of the sexual response cycle diminishes (Masters and Johnson, 1966). In postmenopausal women, a significant amount of elasticity in breast tissue is lost, causing sagging and/or flattening. The more pendulous and slack the breasts at any age, the more resistant they are to the vasocongestive size increase. In older women the absence of this response is more obvious (Masters and Johnson, 1966).

There is relatively little vasocongestive enlargement in the shrunken postmenopausal uterus. Uterine elevation in the response cycle often does not occur in older women; when it does, it is later in the cycle than usually observed for younger women.

Older women do not show the characteristic flattening (for nulliparous females) or thinning (for multiparous females) response of the labia majoris to sexual stimulation, nor do they show size increases. The characteristic deep coloration of the labis minora seen in young women is attenuated or absent. Vasocongestion, however, occurs at every age.

There are a number of differences in the sexual response cycle when women past menopause are compared with their younger counterparts. Pelvic platform contractions in the orgasmic phase are fewer in number and less intense. The average number of contractions at age thirty ranges from a minimum of three to five to a maximum of ten to fifteen. The average number of postmenopausal women is about three to five. The clitoris does not show a decrease in responsiveness with age; however, clitoral tumescence in the excitement phase occurs less frequently in older women. In a sample of women over age forty, only 23% showed tumescence compared with 40% of younger women (Masters and Johnson, 1966). The resolution phase of the response cycle occurs more rapidly for older women. The inner two-thirds of the vagina shrinks back to its unstimulated size more quickly and more uniformly than in younger women. The rapid vaginal wall collapse is related to the decreasing elasticity of the vaginal barrel.

There is very little change in the typically short (one minute or less) refractory period. Women who have had a history of being multiorgasmic continue this behavior well into advanced age. In terms of frequency of orgasm, a woman of eighty has the same potential as she had in her early twenties (Kaplan & Sager, 1971).

SEXUAL CAPACITY IN MEN AND WOMEN

In summarizing age-related changes in sexual capacity, Masters and Johnson (1966, p. 262) state that "there is no question of the fact that the human male's sexual responsiveness wanes as he ages." The variables affecting this change, are both physiological and psychosocial. This is also true for females, who Masters and Johnson contend, have no time limit with regard to sexuality. With the obvious exception of reproduction per se, age-related changes in sexual capacity are not as severe for females as for males. The components of female sexual behavior are not as "obvious," and female sexuality has traditionally not been as "performance-oriented" as has male sexuality. For example, the inability of a male to achieve a rapid erection is an obvious sign of waning sexual function; the female analogue of this, the inability to lubricate readily, is not as obvious and can be alleviated more easily, either endogenously or exogenously. The male's signal of sexual responsiveness is external and evident. The female's is much less overt. Sexual capability is a principle part of most males' roles and self-concepts; capability per se is not the stereotyped badge of femininity. Previous experience and availability of appropriate sexual partners are important influences on sexuality for both men and women. Within the constraints set by physical changes, experience and attitudes towards self and sexuality are probably the most important determinants of sexual functioning and satisfaction in later years—but this is probably as true in young and middle adulthood.

LEVELS OF SEXUAL ACTIVITY

The Kinsey self-report survey data (1948, 1953) are still considered to be the most comprehensive picture of sexuality across the life span. Although Kinsey did not adequately represent older people in his sample (he had only 126 males and 56 females over sixty) and although he drew some of his conclusions by extrapolating patterns in younger subjects, most of his conclusions have stood up remarkably well in view of later research (for example, Masters and Johnson on sexual capacity, 1966; Pfeiffer and Verwoerdt on activity and interest, 1969).

The Kinsey data indicate that males are most sexually active in their teens. It is at this age that frequency of sexual behavior (all types) and number of sexual outlets are greatest. Sexual activity in males diminishes gradually with age, but changes across age groups do not represent differential rates of decline (Kinsey, 1948, p. 235). Average corrected U.S. population frequencies of sexual activity (total outlet) were 3.3/week at age twenty with relatively little change to age thirty. By age forty-five, this average was 2/week and declined to .8/week at age sixty and .2/week by age seventy-five. Married and single males showed differences in maximum average frequencies in their teens—4.8/week and 3.2/week, respectively. The differences in average frequencies by marital status, however, leveled and were comparable by age fifty. Age-related declines in sexual activity can be observed by referring to the maximum reported frequencies per week of various types of sexual activities across representative age groups. Masturbatory frequencies per week in single males declined from 15 in the late teens to 7 in the late thirties to .5 in the late fifties. The maximum frequencies per week for marital intercourse at these age groups were 25, 20, and 5, respectively. Extramarital intercourse frequencies per week were 18 in the late teens, 4 in the thirties, and 2 in the fifties.

Kinsey's data (1953) on female sexual activity showed that women on the average were less sexually active than males. In frequency of total outlet, single women (active incidence) had a median frequency of orgasm per week which did not significantly decline with age. At twenty, this frequency was about .3; at forty and at fifty, frequencies were .5 and at age fifty-five, it was .35. The active median frequency for married women showed some age-related decline, going from 2 per week at twenty to 1.5 per week at 35 to .8 at age fifty. By age fifty-five, this average frequency was .6 per week. Variability in frequency of female behavior was much greater than in males. For example, although females on the average have much lower frequencies per unit time in total outlet, 1% of the single females from sixteen to thirty reported having from seven to twenty-nine orgasms per week. Slightly less than 1% of single females from forty-six to fifty reported frequencies in the range of seven to eighteen per week. There were slightly higher percentages of married females reporting these frequencies in their respective age groups.

MASTURBATION

According to the Kinsey data, masturbation is chiefly a phenomenon of young unmarried men, although it occurs to some extent among both sexes at every age and marital status level. Eighty-eight percent of the single males from sixteen to twenty in the Kinsey sample masturbated; the proportion of married males at this age level was considerably less (39%), presumably because marital intercourse was a preferred substitute. For young single males, masturbation represented the highest proportion of total outlet (60%). After age forty, masturbation was a relatively lower percentage of the total outlet (about 40% for the active sample). The average frequency of masturbation in the active single male sample dropped from 1.7 times per week in the teens to once a week or less by age forty. Kinsey did not report masturbation data for single males over fifty. Masturbation accounted for a lower proportion of the total outlet for married males than single males at every age. The average frequencies per week were from four to five times lower for married men.

Sixty-two percent of Kinsey's total female sample reported that they had masturbated at some time, and 58% of these women had masturbated to orgasm. Among the single active sample, the average frequency of masturbation was .3 to .4 per week; for married females the mean was directionally lower (.2 per week). There was very little change in the active median frequencies for single and married women from the late teens through the fifties. Masturbation represented the highest percentage of total sexual outlet for single women; for married women, it accounted for 10% of the total outlet. Average frequencies of masturbation for single women showed virtually no decline with age (about 1 per week from the late teens through the fifties). For married women, average frequencies per week went from 1 in the teens, to .60 at age forty, to .2 at age fifty. For every age group, the percentage of total outlet was from three to seven times as great for single as for married women. Based on their clinical experience, Masters and Johnson (1966) suggest that both married and single women who masturbated during their adult years continue to masturbate in old age, although the frequency declines after age sixty. Christenson and Gagnon (1965) reported that 25% of a sample of postmarital women in their seventies were masturbating.

MARITAL COITUS (MC)

The Kinsey data indicated that the proportions of males and females engaging in MC decreased gradually as they aged. Comparable proportions of men under forty and females in this age group (98%) reported some outlet from MC. By age sixty, 94% of the males and 84% of the females were still active.

Among young married males, 85% of the average 4.8 per week outlet was accounted for by MC. Although each successive five-year period reflected a drop in average frequency, MC accounted for roughly the same percentage of total outlet over the years.

Females from sixteen to twenty reported a mean frequency of MC of about 4 per week. This average dropped to 2 per week at age forty and to 1.5 per week at age fifty. By age sixty, the average frequency was nearly 1 per week. The percentage of women with maximum frequencies of MC of 7 or more per week declined steadily from 5% at age thirty to 0% at age fifty-five. Within each age group, the average frequencies of orgasm closely paralleled frequencies of MC.

Bell and Bell (1972) looked at average frequencies of MC among a sample of nearly 2,400 women who had been married on the average for thirteen years. The frequencies reported were extremely close to those reported by Kinsey. In another study, Pearlman (1972) reported data from 2,600 married males on the frequency of intercourse. Among subjects in their twenties, 45% had engaged in MC from three to four times per week. For subjects in their forties, only 14% reported these frequencies. By the fifties, the incidence was 5% and past age sixty, less than 1%. By ages sixty to seventy, 25% of the men were engaging in MC one or fewer times per month, and 33% were not having MC at all. By age seventy, 20% were having MC with a frequency of two or more times per month.

Extramarital Coitus (EMC)

From 23 to 37% of married males within each age group surveyed by Kinsey had engaged in EMC. Twenty-six percent of the married women in his sample also reported having had EMC by the age of forty. Active incidence in males tended to remain about the same across all age groups, whereas the active incidence in females was low in the teens, increased through the thirties and decreased thereafter. Only 6% of women in their fifties were active. Again, the average male frequencies were higher than the average female frequencies at all ages sampled. For men under twenty-five, the average frequency in the active sample was 1.3 per week and decreased to 1 per month by age sixty. For active females, these frequencies increased from .5 per week in the teens to .8 per week in the forties. After age thirty, EMC accounted for a relatively con-

stant proportion of total outlet among males. For females, EMC as a percentage of total increased steadily from 3% in the teens to 13% in the late forties.

SEXUAL ACTIVITY LEVELS AND PATTERNS

Researchers at Duke University have published results of an extensive longitudinal study on sexuality in old age (Pfeiffer, 1968, 1969a, 1969b, 1972; Verwoerdt, 1969). This study used interviews with individuals ranging in age from sixty to ninety-four over a six-year period of time. Study I was conducted in 1957; a second set of observations on the same subjects was made four years later (Study II) and again in 1964 (Study III). The investigators, therefore, had cross-sectional age data for each of the three studies and longitudinal data across the six-year period. There is a series of publications on various aspects of sexuality and aging based on these studies which will be referred to in the following paragraphs. In order to study middle-age antecedents of old age sexuality, special augments of middle-aged people to the old-age sample were made, and cross-sectional analyses of sexual activity and interest were made and reported (Pfeiffer, 1972).

The Duke University data confirm Kinsey's findings of lower sexual-activity levels in females than in males at every age and suggest that declines in female sexual activity occur somewhat earlier than those among males. Because female sexual capacity shows less age-related change, nonphysiological variables must be examined to explain these differences in activity.

In a cross-sectional study of over 500 middle aged males and females[*] from forty-five to sixty-nine, Pfeiffer (1972) reported that the percentage of women at each age level who reported "no current intercourse" was considerably greater than the percentage of men. Four-

[*] Ninety-eight percent of the male sample were married at the time of the study compared with 71% of the female sample. This variable may have contributed in part to age-related male/female differences observed.

teen percent of the women under fifty but no men of this age group said that they were currently not engaging in intercourse. In the late fifties and sixties, the proportions of men who were totally inactive were 7% and 24%, respectively; these figures for females of the same age groups were 42% and 73%. Sixty-two percent of the males and 39% of the females under fifty reported having intercourse once a week; in the late sixties, these figures were 26% and 11%. Very active subjects (those who engaged in intercourse more than three times a week) were rare in the middle-aged sample (under fifty) and nonexistent in the groups over fifty years of age.

An analysis of longitudinal data indicated a marked sex by marital status interaction, although there were no consistent age-related changes in the incidence of sexual activity among males. The sexual activity criterion did not include amount of activity but merely incidence—presence of absence of any activity at the time of interview. Subjects were interviewed at three different times; the average ages at the times of Studies I, II, and III were sixty-nine, seventy-three, and seventy-six (Verwoerdt, 1969). There were gradual declines in the proportions of active married men with increasing age. The proportions of active unmarried men were inconsistent over time. At the time of Study I, a higher proportion of married (57%) than unmarried males (35%) were sexually active. By the time of Study II, the incidences were 53% for married and 80% for unmarried men, and by Study III, 36% of the married men and 55% of the unmarried men were active. There was very little systematic change with age among females as a function of marital status. At the time of all studies, married women (42%) always were more active than unmarried women (5%). The proportions of active females stayed about the same across the three studies, although the active proportions of unmarried females increased slightly. By the time of Study III, there was a higher percentage of active married females than of active married males.

Verwoerdt (1969) also looked at the degree of sexual activity in this sample. A cross-sectional analysis indicated that the degree of activity (as indexed by a frequency of intercourse rating scale) decreased significantly with age. The average frequency of intercourse at the time of the first observation was no more than once a month. By the third observation six years later, the average frequency had dropped almost 50%.

Changing patterns of activity in old age were examined (Verwoerdt, 1969). The results again supported the activity differences between males and females. Age-related, intraindividual differences as well as age differences per se were examined by analyzing data from the same group of 154 subjects at two points in time. Patterns of activity were assessed by categorizing differences in self-reported activity from Study I to Study II and looking at the proportions of each age and sex falling into these categories.

Four behavioral activity patterns were classified in the following ways: continual absence of activity in both Study I and II was designated as A(bsent); continually sustained activity (equally active in Study I and II) was denoted by C(ontinued); those less active in Study II than in Study I were labeled as D(eclining), and those more active in Study II than in Study I as R(ising).

The most typical pattern for the sixty-nine females was A (74%), and the most common pattern for the eighty-five males in the study was D (31%). For males, pattern A was reported by 27% and pattern C by 22%. C and D each were reported by 10% of the female sample. Rising activity (R) was relatively infrequent in the female sample (6%) but was much more common for males (20%). These findings from the total sample suggest that the changes in sexual activity patterns had already occurred for females but were in the process of changing for males.

When patterns by age were examined cross-sectionally, the largest increases in proportions of activity pattern A came between the early (sixty to sixty-five) and the late sixties (sixty-six to seventy-one), 6% and 30%, respectively and the early to mid-seventies (seventy-two to seventy-seven) and the late seventies (seventy-eight and older), 29% and 50%, respectively. For females, the percentage increases in pattern A were fairly constant from the sixties through the late seventies. The percentage of sample classified as A were 50% at ages sixty to sixty-five, 77% from ages sixty-six to seventy-one, 90% at ages seventy-two to seventy-seven, and a full 100% at ages seventy-eight and above.

When patterns by age at the time of Study II were examined, the largest increases in pattern A occurred in the sixties and seventies. The percentage of the total sample reporting pattern A at ages sixty to sixty-five was 6% compared with 30% of those ages sixty-five to seventy-one. During the early and mid-seventies, 29% reported this pattern with a 50% incidence in the late seventies (seventy-eight and older). For women, the largest proportion increase was in the early sixties (50%); this figure grew to 90% in the early and mid-seventies and went up to 100% at age seventy-eight. Only one-half of the male sample at age seventy-eight and older reported continually absent activity.

From the age changes in pattern A for females, it is obvious that some other patterns decrease with the increasing age of the sample. The most marked shift in declining activity (D) occurred between the early (18%) and late (4%) sixties. Ten percent of the women in their early seventies (and no women past age seventy-eight) reported D. For males, the percentage of sample classified as D was roughly the same (between 28 to 30%) at all age levels.

The proportion of the total sample who exhibited Rising activity showed the largest drop between the early (33%) and late (15%) sixties. In fact, at age seventy-eight, 20% of the males actually reported R.

The number of females of all ages showing R was low (6%). The proportions remained constant in the sixties (14%) and dropped to 0% from age seventy-two up.

In Verwoerdt's sample, 13% of the males and 57% of the females were unmarried. In the total sample, almost three times as many unmarried (46%) as married men (16%) reported pattern R. Unmarried women (92%) showed a much higher incidence of A than did married women (50%).

These data on activity patterns again support the finding that women are less active than men.

In the sample which included younger individuals (ages forty-five to sixty-nine), Pfeiffer (1972) examined subjects' assessments of changes in their own sexual-activity levels. At the time of interview, 50% of the men and 42% of the women under fifty said they did not notice any decline in their sexual activity relative to their "younger years." The largest drop in proportion of respondents unaware of change was between the late forties and early fifties. Only 29% of the men and 22% of the women said that they detected no decline. By the late sixties, only 4% of the women and 12% of the men reported no awareness of change.

Almost three times as many women (40%) as men (14%) had stopped having sexual relations at the time of the interview. When asked when sexual relations had stopped, answers ranged from within the past year (2%) to twenty years ago (2%). Sixty-four percent of the women reported having stopped more than five years ago. Reasons for termination were given by almost all respondents. Women overwhelmingly blamed someone other than themselves (80%), usually their husbands, and men often blamed themselves (71%). Forty percent of the men compared with 4% of the women said that they themselves were unable to perform sexually. For females, "death of spouse" was the most frequently cited reason for a change in sexual activity (36%). When death as a cause was eliminated, reasons most frequently cited were illness of spouse (20%) and spouse's inability to perform sexually (18%). Loss of interest by spouse was reported by 9% of males and 4% of females, but loss interest by self occurred with a frequency of 14% for males and 4% for females.

Activity is only one measure of sexuality. The Duke University researchers also conducted several studies on sexual interest and interest patterns as part of the large longitudinal study.

Pfeiffer (1972) asked subjects to relate the strength of their current sexual feelings; their responses were categorized as absent, weak, moderate, or strong. Only 6% of the male sample stated that they had no current sexual feelings; 26% reported mild, 56% moderately strong, and 12% reported strong feelings. A much higher percentage of women (33%) reported no current sexual interest, 27% reported mild, and 37% reported moderately strong feelings. Only 3% of the women said that they had strong feelings. When male and female samples were broken down into five, five-year age groups, there was an age-related decline in interest, except for the very oldest age group (sixty-six to seventy-one). There was a similar finding for the activity data. The lack of decline in the very oldest group led the Duke researchers to speculate that the individuals who had survived so long may have represented a biological elite. This hypothesis was supported in a special piece of research which will be discussed later (Pfeiffer, 1969b).

Overall, there was a significant decline in sexual interest with age. The proportion of males with strong sexual feelings was greater at every age than the corresponding proportion of females. The percent of females reporting no sexual interest was always greater than the respective proportions of males. As age increased, there was a tendency for the proportion of males reporting moderate sexual interest to be greater than the proportion of females.

In a more complete and older sample of subjects (ages sixty to seventy-eight and older), Verwoerdt (1969) specifically asked respondents about their interest in sexual intercourse (not sexual feelings) in each of three observations. Responses were put on a four-point rating-scale going from 0 (none) to 3 (strong). Sixty-five subjects participated in all three studies. A significant negative correlation between age and interest was observed in all three studies. The mean interest scores for the studies were 1.08, 0.83, and 0.91—low for each sample. "Strong" interest in intercourse was "exceptional after the age of seventy and was practically nonexistent after 75," Verwoerdt et al., 1969,

p. 145). However, moderate and mild interest were not unusual at any age. There was a slight rise in the interest score in the very oldest age group (Study III).

Subjects then were classified not in terms of degree of interest but simply in terms of presence or absence of this attribute. In Study I (ages sixty to seventy-eight and above), 47% of the subjects (69% of the males and 29% of the females) reported some interest. In Study II, the incidence of interest was 56%. Age-related declines within each sample were observed and decline in incidence was seen as greater for females than for males. By the time of Study III (age range from sixty-six to seventy-eight and above), the total sample incidence figure was 53%. In all three studies, incidence of interest was higher among unmarried than married men. In the first two studies, unmarried women had a lower incidence than married women did but in Study III, the frequency was slightly higher than among married females.

Interest patterns were analyzed in the same way that patterns of activity were (see p. 134). Each respondent was categorized within the four basic patterns based on his or her interest in Study II relative to interest in Study I. Of the sixty males and fifty-eight females, 36% reported A (continually absent interest); D(eclining) (31%) and sustained interest (23%) were less common but R(ising) interest was relatively infrequent (18%).

In males sustained (C) and declining (D) interest were most common (31% each) and continually absent interest (A) was least frequent. For females, this pattern was reversed. A (57%) dominated the sample with R least common (9%). For males in their sixties, C was most common (42%), but men in their early and mid-seventies reflected a high rate of D (50%). At age seventy-eight and above, A was the most typical pattern (37%). An interesting observation, however, was that a relatively high percentage of males in this oldest age group reported R (25%).

Among females, A and D occurred with highest frequencies and earlier than they did for males. In the early sixties, 70% of the females interviewed said that their interest in intercourse was absent or declining (35% each). By the late sixties, this figure had risen to 76%. There was no consistent, age-related increase in A among the female sample—in fact, after age 72 the incidence of A decreased. There also was no age-related decline in R for females, although this may have been an artifact of initially low levels throughout both studies. The age at which females showed the largest incidence of A and the lowest incidence of R was the late sixties (sixty-six to seventy-one).

Marital status seemed to differentiate patterns of interest among males. For unmarried men, R occurred the most frequently (43%) but among married men, C was the highest (34%). A was the most common for all women regardless of marital status but occurred more frequently in unmarried (64%) than in married (45%) men. There was no difference in the proportion of married and unmarried women reporting R.

The degree of interest in sexual activity (intercourse) appeared to be related more to aging than to incidence of interest. The degree of interest correlated negatively with age but incidence did not. Sexual activity per se in terms of frequency of intercourse also showed age-related declines. For men, activity pattern A occurred more frequently than interest pattern A and the decline in activity pattern C was greater than the corresponding decline in interest pattern C. The differences in activity levels between males and females were greater than the differences in interest levels. Among females, the decline in interest and activity occurred earlier (sixty to sixty-five) than it did for males (seventy-two to seventy-seven). Single women showed the lowest activity levels, but differences between married and single women in interest were much smaller than differences in activity, suggesting that availability of a partner and his sexual capability are important variables in determining activity. Verwoerdt (1969) has stated that it is not reasonable to assume that sexual intercourse is the only outlet for these older unmarried women. Married and unmarried men had closely linked levels of activity and interest. Unmarried men, however, were more likely to report patterns of increasing activity and interest.

For both men and women, interest was greater than activity. Although this activity-interest gap remained approximately the same for women, it widened for men with increasing age. Pfeiffer (1969b) reported interest and activity data for a special sample of thirty-nine subjects from four observations over a ten-year period. The average age of these respondents at the time of observation I was sixty-seven and at observation IV was seventy-seven. There was no decline in the incidence of sexual interest in this sample. In fact, the proportions of the sample who had continued active sexual interest for observations I through IV were 56%, 61%, 64%, and 56%, respectively. The incidence of activity declined progressively with age from 44% at the first observation to 28% at the last observation. The so-called activity-interest gap widened with age from 12% to 36%. Examination of demographics of this sample relative to the larger full sample led these investigators to conclude that this group represented a biological elite.

In an effort to determine why females were consistently less active as well as less interested in sexual activity than males were, subjects were asked to rate their interest in sexual activity in earlier years. These retrospective self-report data were compared with self-reported current levels of interest. As expected, men reported higher levels of previous interest than women did. Eighty percent of the males (compared with only 32% of the females) reported strong previous interest. Twenty-six percent of the women and 5% of the men reported weak interest.

HOMOSEXUALITY AND AGING

There is no reason to believe that the physiological effects of aging are any different for homosexuals than for heterosexuals. No replicatable study has demonstrated that homosexuals have a hormonal status different from that of heterosexuals, nor do these groups differ from each other in any other physiological way. All of the physiological factors which influence and result from human aging (functional and capacity changes) naturally characterize all individuals regardless of their object of sexual preference. If there are differential effects in aging, they are the psychological adjustment and responses to the symbolic meaning of growing older as it relates to the homosexual and heterosexual cultures.

In Kinsey's samples (1948, 1953), the accumulative incidence of sexual, same-sex contact among women was 28%, slightly more than half as great as among men (50%). Thirty-seven percent of the single males compared with 13% of the single females reported homosexual contacts to orgasm.

Among single males, 25% of the total sexual outlet from the ages of twenty-one to twenty-five was in homosexual activity. The comparable figures for the late thirties and late forties were 42% and 54%, respectively. The active accumulative incidence among single males went from 25% in the teens to a maximum of 41% in the late thirties. Among males who were single until age thirty-five, 50% had had some homosexual experience.

Among women, the accumulative incidence rose gradually from age ten to age thirty. By age thirty, 17% of the Kinsey sample had had some homosexual experience and by age forty, 19% had had some sexual contact with another woman. By age forty, the accumulative incidence for single (never married) females was 24%, substantially greater than for married (3%) or previously married (9%) women.

As for extent of homosexuality, 2 to 6% of the females and 5 to 22% of the males were exclusively or primarily homosexual (5- or 6-point ratings on the Kinsey scale). In every age group, only one-half to one-third as many women as men were primarily or exclusively homosexual.

The Kinsey data on male incidence figures from ages eight to forty-five* suggest a curvi-

linear relationship between age and incidence of homosexual behavior. These cross-sectional data for ages thirteen, twenty-four, thirty-six, and forty-five show the number of men engaging in homosexual activity at these ages to be 13%, 37%, 27%, and 23%, respectively. In the active sample, 22% of the single males in their late teens had had homosexual contact resulting in orgasm. The comparable figures for males in their late thirties was 40%.

Single-female incidence figures for contact to orgasm were 2 to 3% in the teens showing a gradual increase with age to a maximum of 10% at age forty.

Both single males and single females showed drops in incidence of contact to orgasm by the late forties, suggesting possible age-related declines in sexual activity. Females showed a 60% drop (to 4%) from the late thirties, but males showed a drop of only 10% (to 36% incidence) for the comparable age period.

In Kinsey's active sample of single women, most (51%) had had one partner only. Twenty percent had had two partners, and only 4% had had more than ten partners. The single male experience was quite different, with 22% of the active sample males having had more than ten partners.

Frequencies of homosexual contact to orgasm were not higher than the frequencies of intercourse reported for heterosexual samples. Median frequency of contact to orgasm showed no decrement with age and was about .9 times per month for single women from ages twenty-one through forty. For the active sample of women, the mean frequency went from about once per week in the twenties to about twice per week in the thirties. No active sample data were available for women over forty.*

Among single males, the mean frequencies to orgasm showed a slight age-related increment from 1 to 1.5 times per week in the twenties to about 2 times per week in the early thirties. The mean frequencies of homosexual contact rose from about one per week in the teens to

---

* Total population, U.S. corrections.

* Kinsey's figures from the total sample suggest an average of less than once every two months in the fifties—certainly an underestimate for the active sample.

almost two per week from the ages of thirty-one to thirty-five. They remained at more than once per week through age fifty.

The frequency of contact to orgasm for respondents did not decline in Kinsey's data, and the percentages of respondents engaging in homosexual activity actually increased with age into the forties. Because Kinsey presented very little data on old-age subjects, there is no way to assess changes in activity after mid-life. The maximum frequencies within age groups among males suggest, however, a slowdown which is probably age-related. Kinsey reported maximum frequencies in the late twenties as high as fifteen times per week. By age fifty, the most active person was averaging only five times per week. The age-related increase in proportions of homosexually active respondents may be an artifact of the culture at the time of the Kinsey study. Societal pressures may have introduced a latency for resolving the homosexual orientation which would have resulted in submitting to homosexual inclination later in life.

Weinberg and Williams (1974) in their large sample study* utilizing self-administered questionnaire data, found that older male homosexuals were less involved than younger homosexuals in the social aspects of the gay life style. They associated less often with other homosexuals and attended bars and clubs much less frequently, making access to sexual partners more difficult. Fifty-six percent of the respondents under the age of twenty-six went to bars more than once a month compared with 23% of respondents over the age of forty-five. Thirty percent of those under twenty-six lived alone while 57% of older males did not have a roommate.

In frequency of sexual contact, younger respondents (under age twenty-six) and older respondents (over age forty-five) were more similar to one another than to those in intermediate age groups. The proportions of respondents who reported a high frequency of homosexual sex were 46%, 59%, 55%, and 41% for the age groups under twenty-six, twenty-six to thirty-

five, thirty-six to forty-five, and over forty-five, respectively.

Weinberg's and Williams's study did not support the common view that, because the homosexual subculture values youth, older male homosexuals generally are poorly adjusted psychologically. On a number of psychological measures, older homosexuals compared with younger ones showed no differences in self-acceptance, degree of anxiety, depression, or loneliness. In fact, older respondents tended to have better self-concepts and were more stable. Weinberg (1970, 1974, p. 219) has suggested that the belief may have been perpetuated in part by "falsely attributing to the older homosexual the perspectives and expectations of the persons who hold these beliefs." Younger people observing the sociosexual situations of the elderly view it from a perspective of their own needs and desires, and fail to realize that expectations change with age. Weinberg (1970, p. 535) goes on to say that "the relatively good adjustment of our older subjects is not peculiar to the homosexual but is probably associated with characteristics of the aging process in general."

Research reported by Francher and Henkin (1973) indicates that the "role change" experienced by male homosexuals is qualitatively different from that experienced by most heterosexual males. Generally relatively early in life, homosexuals go through a crisis which heterosexuals do not—the recognition and management of a socially unconventional and largely unaccepted sexual orientation and lifestyle. Once this has been faced, usually in early or mid-life, the response to a later life crisis—aging—differs. Absence of family responsibilities characterize the homosexual lifestyle at every age; changes in family involvement (often representing a role crisis for heterosexual) do not occur. Further, these authors suggest that homosexual narcissism may help in coping with the role changes and declining sexuality associated with aging. There is a hint that some characteristics of the homosexual subculture may provide support for aging later on in life.

Saghir and Robins (1973) in an in-depth

---

* The sample had 1,117 respondents from the United States, 24% of whom were over forty-five years of age.

study of eighty-nine male and fifty-seven female homosexuals found that 28% of males were anxious about growing old. Thirty-eight percent said that when they grew old they would probably pay for sex, but over 25% were hoping for a stable homosexual relationship or several prolonged relationships. Only 12% of the female homosexuals expressed strong fears of growing old alone. More women (40%) than men (28%) hoped for a stable relationship in old age. A large percentage of both men and women in this sample indicated that they would participate more and more in nonsexual activities and relationships as they grew older.

These data suggest that homosexuals experience the same general age-related changes in behavior as heterosexuals do. In the homosexual samples reported, females were less sexually active than males, not in frequency of behavior but in incidence, and seemed to be more interested in long-term relationships. Interestingly, female homosexuals were less anxious than males were about growing old. This may reflect a juxtaposition of heterosexual male and female concerns about changes with age and may reflect basic male/female differences in perceiving the importance of human attributes in interacting with a social-sexual partner.

Homosexuals are as aware as heterosexuals are of changes occurring with aging. For the homosexual and particularly for the homosexual male these changes may require an altered life style. But the heterosexual also must change life style. There are different kinds of changes, but there is no evidence that the ability to adjust to them varies dramatically because of sexual orientation.

TWO ATTITUDINAL STUDIES

Attitudes towards one's own sexuality and perceived age-appropriate aspects of sexual behavior certainly are important determinants of activity levels at every age. The cultural stereotype of old people as sexless probably contributes to depressed sexual activity (Rubin,

1968). Pfeiffer (1969a) commented that he found it quite difficult to obtain old-age subjects for studies of sexual attitudes and activity, mainly because younger members of their families felt that it was inappropriate for them to participate!

A survey by Harris (1976) indicates that both old people (over sixty-five) and younger people have similar views on sexuality for people over sixty-five. Although 41% of the general public (all ages) saw most people over sixty-five as very physically active, only 5% saw them as very sexually active. When asked how they perceived themselves, males were more likely than females to say that they were very sexually active. Fifty-one percent of the respondents from eighteen to fifty-four and 27% from ages fifty-five to sixty-four characterized themselves as having a high level of sexual activity. After the age of sixty-five, this figure declined to 11% (16% for males and 7% for females).

Snyder and Spreitzer (1976) investigated attitudes of 1,020 respondents under sixty-five and 235 sixty years and older toward so-called nontraditional sexual behavior (premarital and extramarital sex and homosexuality). Responses to questions on these topics were put on a four-point scale ranging from *always wrong* to *not wrong at all*. The percentage differences between age groups on the *always wrong* response (indicating the highest degree of intolerance) were tabulated for six demographic variables: sex, education, occupation, number of children, marital status, and church attendance. In general, older people were less permissive and less approving than younger people for all behaviors. The difference in proportion of respondents disapproving of premarital sex was greater (30%) than for either of the other two behaviors (extramarital sex and homosexuality were 19% and 18%, respectively). Age was a stronger predictor of attitudes than any of the other variables, but age did not account for all of the intersubject variability. There were wide variations among people sixty-five and older which could be explained by social background characteristics. As in any cross-sectional study, some of the differences which appear to be age-related may in fact be generational.

DETERMINANTS OF SEXUAL BEHAVIOR ACROSS THE LIFE CYCLE

Activity, as measured by frequency of sexual contact, shows more age-related decrement than interest. Males typically demonstrate high levels of interest; when partners are available to them, activity follows fairly closely. With age, physical capacity changes are accompanied by activity and interest declines, although interest is affected less than activity. Sexual interest among males of all ages is considered to be socially desirable. Before old age, relatively strong levels of interest and general availability of partners lead to sexual contact. These contacts in turn reinforce interest which again motivates contact. This general interest-activity feedback mechanism presumably also operates in older males. Interestingly this seems to be less characteristic of females at every age. For older women, the lower levels of interest in sexual activity and fewer culturally acceptable sexual partners, do not usually motivate sexual contact, and lower activity levels result.

Why there are differences in male and female patterns of sexuality in adulthood and old age has not been answered. Variables affecting sexuality at all ages can be categorized as physical (general health, state of the nervous system, hormones) and psychosocial (experience, learning, and societal factors). Many researchers have suggested that experiential antecedents are important in determining sexual behavior for both males and females in old age. The level of sexual activity and interest of the older person is strongly related to his or her activity and interest in earlier years. Men who were sexually active as young and mature adults tend to be sexually active in old age (Newman and Nichols, 1960; Freeman, 1961; Rubin, 1965). Women who have regular sexual activity before

old age are likely to enjoy sexual activity in old age (Masters and Johnson, 1966). Those who as young and middle-aged adults are more sexually active than their same-age cohorts also will be more active than their cohorts in old age.

Kaplan and Sager (1971) suggest that as early as puberty and throughout the mature years, males are more dependent than females upon physical factors. Males probably also need less specific learning for fully functioning sexual responsiveness or at least they have earlier opportunities for learning. The fact that males are most sexually active and responsive in adolesence but females are, in their thirties and forties (Kinsey, 1948, 1953; Masters and Johnson, 1966) lends some support to this hypothesis.

Young males are extremely sexual; they are highly genitally oriented and masturbate earlier than females do. The male peer-support system in adolescence reinforces early sexual experimentation, and societal mores suggest that seeking sexual satisfaction with a variety of partners is not only permissible but desirable. Parents are less restrictive with sons than with daughters in dealing with adolescent sexual experimentation (Wake, 1969). Parents also are more likely to emphasize to daughters than to sons that love is an integral part of sexual relationships (McCary, 1973).

There are basic differences in the perception of sex early in development which continue throughout life. Females tend to view sexual activity as it is associated with romantic relationships. For females, sexual involvement is preceded by emotional or romantic attachment, but for males sexual attraction precedes emotional involvement (Calderone, 1966; Ehrmann, 1959, 1961; Kronhausen and Kronhausen, 1965). Females at puberty are less interested in sex per se than in boys and romantic relationships (Kaplan and Sager, 1971). Females at all ages tend to be more interested in relationships than in genital sex, and sexual contact represents the meaning of a relationship. Females are more likely to measure the success of a marital relationship by factors other than sexual satisfaction (Adams, 1966), but males place more importance on sexual gratification. In one study (Bell and Bell, 1972), when married females were asked from which aspect of sexual activity they derived the most satisfaction, the most frequent response was closeness or feeling of oneness with the partner.

Marriage offers females the opportunity for extensive sexual experience and provides the framework within which sexual responsiveness can develop. This period may be a time during which there is positive reinforcement of sexual functioning and extinction of adolescent inhibitions (Kaplan and Sager, 1971). Most evidence suggests that males set the tenor of sexual activity within marriage, especially in the early years. Since they tend to be more active than females, it is reasonable to suppose that in early years much of the marital sexual activity is dictated by the level of the males' sexual arousal. In later years, married females' activity levels and married males' activity levels are fairly close but are lower than the activity of single males (see Verwoerdt, 1969), suggesting that in late-middle and old age, the locus of control of marital sexual activity may swing to females. However, the generally lower levels of activity for both men and women may be part of declining male responsiveness. (See Pfeiffer, 1972, for reasons for terminating sexual intercourse).

Compared to earlier years, men in their thirties are less preoccupied with sexual thoughts and fantasies but are still highly responsive to sexual stimuli. In the forties and fifties, sexual expression among males becomes less intense genitally, and men of this age group often require more psychic stimulation for effective sexual functioning (Kaplan and Sager, 1971).

Male declines in sexual capacity often result in frustration over ability to perform sexually. This often leads to avoidance of sexual functioning which, in a marriage, can lead to feelings of neglect by the wife. This perceived neglect may be interpreted by the wife as evidence of her waning attractiveness. If this coincides with menopause, it can reinforce the so-cietal stereotype of the menopausal female as unattractive and unfeminine. Negative behavioral changes by the wife then can precipitate negative responses by the husband.

In an effort to reverse age-related changes, frustration also may lead the male to seek out erotic stimuli in the form of new sexual partners. This frustration and fear of failure to perform adequately also may lead to an attempt to recapture the sexual functioning of earlier years. Interestingly, the strong motivation to perform combined with a new partner can result in short-term improvement.

It is not clear whether monotony precedes or follows changes in sexual functioning. Masters and Johnson (1966) suggest that monotony in the marital relationship is one of the primary causes of loss of responsiveness in middle-aged men. Many middle-aged males' familiarity with their wives combined with lack of interest by the wives themselves (as well as generally greater female appearance changes with aging) may lead to waning interest by these men. Often these declines in interest are reinforced by the older female's negative attitudes towards sex. On the other hand, changes in ability to perform sexually and accompanying decrements in sexual responsiveness may require more erotic stimulation. By definition, the newer the sexual partner is, the more stimulation value is possible.

Although there is no definitive experimental evidence with humans, the cultural stereotype suggests that males are more directed toward variety and novelty than are females. There is some indirect evidence in male/female differences in the sexes versus relationships. These differences are probably tied in part to the fact that men concentrate more on sex, and women emphasize relationships. A very high percentage of male homosexual relationships can be characterized as transitory; these changing attachments presumably reflect a desire for sexual (genital) satisfaction, an important part of which is the new sexual partner. Female homosexual relationships, on the other hand, tend to be more stable and less physical. Heterosexual relationships fall somewhere in between, and sexual monotony as a reason for marital failure is cited much more frequently by males than by females.

If it is true that males are more interested in variety than females are, this difference may have arisen because males traditionally have operated in a more complex and changing environment. Whether this is because of temperamental differences or whether it resulted in temperamental differences is an open question. But if it is true, the double standard has allowed males to experiment sexually with a variety of partners and has imposed severe sanctions on females for similar actions (McCary, 1973). It is possible that years of socially approved sexual experimentation among males have cultivated their desire and need for novelty.

Declining activity in older females appears to be related only secondarily to the change of life. Physical symptoms of menopause, many of which are tied directly to steroid deprivation, may interfere with sexual activity. Adverse feelings about self caused by the symbolic meaning of menopause also may depress sexual inclination and activity. An unflattering self-image may produce frustration and anger which then may lead to avoidance of sexual relations or to behaviors perceived negatively by sexual partners which also may depress activity levels. Women, who probably depend more heavily than men on external reinforcement, would be unlikely at such a time to experiment sexually by seeking out a new partner. If the husband or partner shows a lack of interest, it is likely to be internalized by the woman, with behavioral effects. There is no evidence to presume that males, because of their histories of sexual experimentation, are more likely than females to seek new partners in middle-life but from observation this hypothesis seems reasonable.

Because women often outlive men, they often do not have a suitable sexual partner. The double standard enforced since early adulthood suggests that it is inappropriate for females actively to seek out sexual partners. The cultural stereotype of appropriate partners (men with younger women) compounds this problem. There are social pressures against selecting a younger male, and the pool of peers or older men is limited.

Needless to say, there are always individual differences. Many of the stereotyped generalities may be changing as a result of women's new self-concepts. Traditional roles of behavior seem to be changing. If the cultural stereotypes do influence behavior, the degree to which these stereotypes change will be accompanied by behavioral change.

It is interesting to speculate on the evolutionary significance, if any, of male/female differences in sexual activity as a function of aging. The human female, although losing her ability to reproduce in mid-life, has full sexual capability into old age. Activity levels, however, are low. In the human male, reproductive ability declines only very gradually and for most of the aging population, is never lost completely. The capacity for sexual functioning changes much more with age and activity and although it slows with age, is still present in very old men.

The differences in activity levels between males and females can be attributed on the average to different primary variables. For females, external support is probably most important and is absent for a large percentage of older women. For males, declines are due primarily to changes in capacity inasmuch as environmental support is available throughout life.

If one accepts the premise that the *raison d'être* of a species and every individual in that species is reproduction and therefore survival, male/female differences in sexual activity and interest at every age can be tied to differences in strategies of reproduction. High levels of interest and activity among males increase their chances of contributing to the gene pool. Females, on the other hand, should be more selective and discriminating because of their great biological investment in procreation.

In strictly evolutionary terms, it is clearly

more adaptive for males (who have reproductive ability) than for females to maintain interest and activity in old age. Females who are no longer reproductively capable have no real need for continued interest and activity.

For many nonhuman mammalian species, death marks the end of reproduction/reproductive ability. In the human, technology has altered the course of selection. Great control of the environment has probably increased the life span; this artificial longevity may have occurred in the absence of selective pressures. If this is so, behavioral differences between aged males and females may represent artifacts which have no evolutionary significance whatsoever!

REFERENCES

ADAMS, C. R. 1966. An informal preliminary report on some factors relating to sexual responsiveness of certain college wives. In *Sexual behavior and personality characteristics*, ed. M. F. DeMartino. New York: Grove Press.

ALBERT, A.; RANDALL, R. V.; SMITH, R. A.; and JOHNSON, C. E. 1956. Urinary excretion of gonadotropins as a function of age. In *Hormones and the aging process*, ed. E. T. Engle and G. Pincus. New York: Academic Press.

BELL, R. R., and BELL, P. L. 1972. Sexual satisfaction among married women. *Med. Aspects Human Sexuality* 1972 (December), 136–44.

BENJAMIN, H. 1959. Impotency and aging. *Sexology* 26: 238–43.

BLOCK, E. 1952. Quantitative morphological investigations of the follicular system in women: variations at different ages. *Acta. Anat.* 14: 108–23.

BURCH, P. R., and GUNZ, F. W. 1967. The distribution of the menopausal age in New Zealand: an exploratory study. *N. Zealand Med. J.* 66: 6–10.

CALDERONE, M. S. 1966. Contraception, teenagers and sexual responsibility. *J. Sex Res.* 2: 37–40.

COLEMAN, J. C. 1972. *Abnormal psychology and modern life.* 4th ed. Chicago: Scott, Foresman.

DORFMAN, R. I., and SHIPLEY, R. A. 1956. *Androgens: biochemistry, physiology and clinical significance.* New York: Wiley.

EHRMANN, W. 1959. *Premarital dating behavior.* New York: Holt, Rinehart & Winston.

———. 1961. Premarital sexual intercourse. In *Encyclopedia of sexual behavior*, vol. 2, ed. A. Ellis and A. Abarbanel. New York: Hawthorn Books.

ENGLE, E. T. 1952. Male reproductive system. In *Cowdrey's problems of aging.* 3rd ed., ed. A. I. Lansing. Baltimore: Williams & Wilkins.

FRANCHER, J. S., and HENKIN, J. 1973. The menopausal queen: adjustment to aging and the male homosexual. *Amer. J. Orthopsychiatr.* 43: 621–74.

FREEMAN, J. T. 1961. Sexual capacities in the aging male. *Geriatrics* 16: 37–43.

GHERONDACHE, C.; ROMANOFF, L.; and PINCUS, G. 1967. Steroid hormones in aging men. In *Endocrines and aging*, ed. L. Gitman. Springfield, Illinois; Charles C Thomas.

HARRIS, L. 1976. *The myth and reality of aging in the U.S.* Louis Harris and Associates for the National Council on Aging, Washington, D.C.

JOHNSEN, S. G. 1959. A clinical routine method for the quantitative determination of gonadotropins in 24 hour urine samples. II: normal values for men and women at all age groups from pre-puberty to senescence. *Acta. Endocrinol.* 31: 209–27.

KAPLAN, H. S., and SAGER, C. J. 1971. Sexual patterns at different ages. *Med. Aspects Human Sexuality* 5: 10–23.

KELLY, G. L. 1961. Menopause. In *Encyclopedia of sexual behavior, vol. 2*, ed. A. Ellis and A. Abarbanel. New York: Hawthorn Books.

KINSEY, A. C.; POMEROY, W. B.; and MARTIN, C. E. 1948. *Sexual behavior in the human male.* Philadelphia: W. B. Saunders.

———; and GEBHARD, P. H. 1953. *Sexual behavior in the human female.* Philadelphia: W. B. Saunders.

KRONHAUSEN, P., and KRONHAUSEN, E. 1965. *The sexually responsive woman.* New York: Ballantine.

LYNCH, K. M. JR., and SCOTT, W. W. 1950. The lipid content of Leydig cells and Sertoli cells in the human testis as related to age, benign prostatic hyperplasia, and prostate cancer. *J. Urol.* 64: 767–76.

McCARY, J. L. 1973. *Human sexuality.* 2nd ed. New York: Van Nostrand.

MAGLADERY, H. W. 1959. Neurophysiology of aging. In *Handbook of aging and the individual,* ed. J. E. Birren. Chicago: University of Chicago Press.

MASTERS, W. H. 1957. Sex steroid influence on the aging process. *Am. J. Obstet. Gynecol.* 74: 733–42.

———, and JOHNSON, V. E. 1966. *Human sexual response.* Boston: Little, Brown.

MOLNAR, J. 1965. Testicular activity in old age. In *Proceedings, International Conference on Gerontology,* ed. A. Balazs. Budapest: Akadémiai Kiadó.

MOORE, R. A. 1952. Male secondary sex organs. In *Cowdrey's problem of aging.* 3rd ed., ed. A. I. Lansing. Baltimore: Williams and Wilkins.

NEUGARTEN, B. L. 1963. Women's attitudes towards the menopause. *Vita Humana* 6: 140–51.

NEUGARTEN, B. L., and KRAINE, R. J. 1967. Menopausal symptoms in women of various ages. *Endocrines and aging,* ed. L. Gitman. Springfield, Illinois; Charles C Thomas.

NEWMAN, G., and NICHOLS, C. R. 1960. Sexual activities and attitudes in older persons. *J.A.M.A.* 173: 33–35.

PASCHKIS, K. E.; RAKOFF, A. E.; CANTAROW, A.; and RUPP, J. J. 1967. *Clinical endocrinology.* 3rd ed. New York: Harper & Row.

PEARLMAN, C. K. 1972. Frequency of intercourse in males at different ages. *Med. Aspects Human Sexuality* 92–113.

PFEIFFER, E. Sexual behavior in old age. 1969a. *Behavior and adaptation in late life,* ed. E. Busse and E. Pfeiffer, pp. 151–62. Boston: Little, Brown.

———, and DAVIS, G. C. 1972. Sexual behavior in middle life. *Amer. J. Psychiatr.* 128: 82–87.

———; VERWOERDT, A.; and WANG, H. 1968. Sexual behavior in aged men and women. I. Observations on 254 community volunteers. *Arch. Gen. Psychiatr.* 19: 753–58.

———. 1969b. The natural history of sexual behavior in a biologically advantaged group of aged individuals. *J. Geront.* 24: 193–98.

PINCUS, G. 1960. Steroid hormones and aging in man. *Amer. Ass. Advance. Sci.* 65: 189–97.

RIEDMAN, S. R. 1961. Change of life. *Sexology* 808–13.

RUBIN, I. 1968. The "sexless older years"—a socially harmful stereotype. *Ann. Am. Acad. Political & Soc. Sci.* 376: 87–95.

———. 1963. Sex over 65. In *Advances in sex research,* ed. H. G. Beigel. New York: Hoeber-Harper.

———. 1965. *Sexual life after sixty.* New York: Basic Books.

SAGHIR, M. T., and ROBINS, E. 1973. *Male and female homosexuality—a comprehensive investigation.* Baltimore: Williams and Wilkins.

SHARMAN, A. 1962. The Menopause. In *The ovary, vol. 1,* ed. S. Zuckerman. New York: Academic Press.

SNYDER, E. E., and SPREITZER, E. 1976. Attitudes of the aged toward nontraditional sexual behavior. *Arch. of Sex. Behav.* 5: 249–54.

STEWARD, V. W., and BRANDES, D. 1961. The accessory male sex glands and their changes with age. In *Structural aspects of aging,* ed. G. H. Bourne. New York: Hafner.

TALBERT, G. B. 1968. Effect of maternal age on reproductive capacity. *Am. J. Obstet. Gynecol.* 102: 451–77.

TILLINGER, K. G. 1957. Testicular morphology: a histopathological study with special reference to biopsy findings in hypogonadism with mainly endocrine disorders and in gynecomastia. *Acta. Endocrinol.* (supplement) 30: 1–192.

TIMERAS, P. S. 1972. *Developmental physiology and aging.* New York: MacMillan.

VERWOERDT, A.; PFEIFFER, E.; and WANG, H. 1969. Sexual behavior in senescence. II. Patterns of sexual activity and interest. *Geriatrics* 24: 137–54.

WAKE, F. R. 1969. Attitudes of parents towards the premarital sexual behavior of their children and themselves. *J. Sex. Res.,* 5: 170–77.

WALKER, K. 1964. The critical age in men. *Sexology* 30: 705–707.

WEINBERG, M. S. 1970. The male homosexual: age-related variations in social and psychological characteristics. *Social Problems* 17: 527–37.

———, and WILLIAMS, C. J. 1974. *Male homosexuals—their problems and adaptations.* New York: Oxford University Press.

EIGHT

Personality Development and Sexuality

TAGHI MODARRESSI

The question of how sexuality influences the development of personality has become a central focus for many clinicians, investigators in the field of human behavior, and developmentalists. It has become more important during the last three or four decades, as the role of early experiences in the final shape of the personality has become better understood. It also has been recognized that early individual differences among infants have a lasting effect throughout life (Escalona, 1968).

The civil-rights movement of the sixties, started by black Americans and other oppressed minorities more conscious of their conditions and seeking to remedy them, renewed interest in the nature of the social forces influencing the development of personality. Investigators were impressed by the devastating impact of isolation, poverty, and chaotic family situations.

In the seventies, women and those with different sexual orientations, such as homosexuals, began to examine sexuality within the culture and to re-examine some of the accepted concepts of the development of both normal and pathological sexuality. They questioned particularly the stereotypic definitions of what is masculine and what is feminine. This in turn stimulated research on the roots of sexuality and sexual identity from the cultural, psychological, biological, and developmental points of view. In addition, clinicians began to examine the causes of atypical gender-identity development among their child patients. All this research activity still has not settled the controversy over the role of sexuality in personality development but has greatly softened some of the rigid and dogmatic attitudes towards sexuality.

THEORETICAL CONSIDERATIONS

There is no doubt that Freud's pioneer study on the relationship between infantile sexuality and adult personality (1905) was truly revolutionary. For the first time, the seemingly bizarre and incomprehensible sexual preferences and activities of the adult neurotic could be traced to the individual's long-forgotten infantile sexuality. In short, the neurotic was repeating his or her childhood sexuality in the pattern of his or her adult life, despite the inability to retrieve the memory of the childhood sexuality.

Freud's main contribution to a theory of the development of the ego came more gradually. He defined the formation of personality as based on the defensive identification with and introjection of the lost libidinal object. Beginning with his study of *Leonardo* (1910), whose homosexuality was explained by Leonardo's identification with his mother in response to his loss of her, Freud began to differentiate between anaclitic identification (primary identification) and secondary identification, which was a reaction to separation and loss. In his study of *Mourning and Melancholia* (1917), Freud applied the same categories of identification to explain the clinical manifestations of depression. During normal mourning, Freud stated, the source of pain is the loss of the love object in the object world; during melancholia, the patient is concerned with the loss of an ambivalently attached, internalized object. Finally, in *The Ego and the Id* (1923), Freud formulated the developmental origins of personality, based on the three divisions of personality: id, ego, and superego. The formation of the superego depends upon the child's identification with the parent who has been his or her rival in the Oedipal struggle. This identification is the root of the child's value system, pattern of social conduct, and aspirations. The process and motives for both primary and secondary identification are largely unconscious and unknown to the child. There might be apparent similarities between the child's personality and the personalities of those with whom he or she has identified, but these similarities are not based primarily on conscious imitating, role modeling, or social learning, even though all these are important and do contribute. The most decisive reason for giving up the Oedipal conflict and substituting the superego by way of identification is fear of castration at the hands of the aggressor parent. Boys' sexual desire for the mother increases their anxiety of being castrated by the father. For girls, a feeling of having been already castrated augments their feeling of penis envy and identification with their father; they then give up this masculine striving and adopt a feminine identification, substituting their wish for a penis with the wish to have a child by the father. It is because the female develops her "genitality" by a more complicated method, that Freud believed that her Oedipal struggle rarely is resolved completely. He felt that the female's superego was not as stable as that of the male and that she always carried the vestiges of infantile sexuality in her personality.

The processes of identification during childhood have become the most important element in the formation of personality. Because the central issue in the struggle for identification is sexuality and the loss of the love object, the psychoanalytic theory of personality formation is tied closely to psychosexual development.

Bronfenbrenner's (1960) examination of the concept of identification showed that identification is a condensation of at least three components. First is behavior, especially observable behavior, as a means by which the child can relate to the person with whom he or she identifies by emulating that person's behavior. Second is motivation, Freud considered the motive for identification to be defensive, an attempt by the child to deal with the loss of the love object, through incorporation, introjection, and identification. In other words, he or she comes to possess the love object internally. Kohlberg's (1966) and Kagan's (1964) views stress even more the child's wish to be similar or to possess the person to whom he or she feels deeply attached. Recent developments in psychoanalytic ego-psychology also emphasize the conflict-free aspects of identification, especially the role of

object relationships in this respect. The third component of identification is the process involved. As we have mentioned, the process is a shift of cathexis by which the child gives up his or her tie with an infantile love object, either early in life through anaclitic (primary) identification, or later during the Oedipal struggle in response to castration anxiety and guilt for hostile fantasies about the ambivalently regarded parent.

Another major theory of behavioral differences among sexes is the social learning theory, which relies not upon identification but upon the imitation concept. Using imitation as a prototype of social learning, this theory does not single out sex-type behavior and sexuality as central. To social learning theorists, the same principle governs all social learning, regardless of sex. In fact, childhood sexuality is not considered at all, and sex-typed behavior is not examined as related to sexuality but more as a prototype of certain social conduct. In the works of social learning theorists, there are very few references to such behavior among children as masturbation, inquiries about sexual functions or portrayals of various erotic relations between parents (Issacs, 1946; Malinowski, 1949).

Despite the major controversies among investigators over identification versus imitation, there seem to be many similarities between the two concepts. Often, the opponents seem merely to be describing the same concept in different terms (Bandura and Walters, 1963), referring to the child's development of attitude, behavior, and emotional patterns as similar to those of significant people in his or her life.

Most social learning investigators today emphasize the importance of observation and information processes to social learning based on imitation, as compared with an earlier emphasis on reward and punishment. According to the former view, the child becomes aware of sex differences in personality around four to five years of age and begins to emulate one parent in particular because of the power attributed to that parent (Kohlberg, 1966). Recently, however, many social theorists have been able to bridge the gap between the psychoanalytic concept of identification and the social learning concept of imitation as based on the model's power and status. Whiting (1959, 1960), in anthropological studies of six cultures, explained sexual identification not solely as an outcome of the Oedipal struggle but also as a part of the cultural context, in which the child envies the status of the more influential and powerful parent and thus is apt to identify with that parent. For example, in cultures in which the father is frequently absent and the mother sleeps with the child, the predominant identification in boys is feminine, because of the mother's presence and the control she exercises over him.

SEXUALITY AND CHILDHOOD

Since Freud's exploration of childhood sexuality, there has been a number of clinical and developmental studies in this area. These include the clinical observations of normal and pathological behavior in children and adults, experimental studies of sexuality and patterns of behavior among children and animals, and some longitudinal studies of children who early in life displayed sex-type behavior not congruent with their biological sex assignment.

There is considerable controversy as to what constitutes "sexual behavior" during childhood, since childhood sexual behavior, no matter how closely it imitates the adult sexual experience, does not lead to the orgasm which is the goal of sexual relationship during adulthood. Freud defined sexuality in much broader terms. To him, sexual behavior is motivated by the libidinal drive or its derivatives, and the goal is to discharge energy, as a result of which the individual experiences pleasure and avoids the pain of undischarged energy. The gradual organization and transformation of the libidinal drive's source, objects, and aims, in the course of development, finally lead to genital sexuality as observed among normal individuals—namely, the capacity for a heterosexual and affectionate relationship with a nonincestuous love object.

Because there is no orgastic experience dur-

ing the first five years of life when the major organization and transformation of libidinal drives occurs, many investigators have looked for a manifestation of sexuality in male and female differences in children's behavior. Animal studies among mammals and primates (Beach, 1951) show that animals frequently display specific sexual behavior such as mounting and stimulating genitals before they reach adulthood and become capable of sexual intercourse. It seems that these early sexual experiences are crucial for the mature animal to become sexually competent. Inexperienced adult male monkeys often are incapable of sexual intercourse even with a receptive female. Harlow's study (1962) with monkeys has demonstrated clearly the relation between early maternal experiences and sexuality during adulthood. Monkeys raised by wire surrogate mothers during infancy were incapable of sexual intercourse. The females rarely became pregnant and even when they did succeed in giving birth, their maternal behavior was atypical. Instead of exhibiting the usual maternal behavior such as holding, feeding, grooming, and protecting their young, they showed aggressive and assaulting behavior aimed at the destruction of their offspring.

Sex-type behavior can be differentiated much more readily in young animals than in human children. The behavior of the male infant rhesus monkey is visibly aggressive, and the female infants display more "passive" behavior such as sitting quietly and allowing other animals to approach them. The preadolescent male monkey plays mostly in a group of the same age and sex. His play consists largely of aggressive, rough-and-tumble chasing. The female preadolescent, especially if she is small and weak, is excluded from the male group. There seems to be some similarity between the preadolescent monkey's social behavior and that of preadolescent humans in Western societies. Boys and girls lean toward exclusive homosexual grouping at around eight to twelve years of age (Thumpson and Horrocks, 1947).

Prepubertal sex play is common among most mammals (Beach, 1951). This includes not only the display of behavior usually leading to sexual contact among adults, but also direct genital stimulation. In humans there also is evidence (from everyday observation by parents and nursery and kindergarten teachers) of different sex-play roles and sexual activities among the very young (Issacs, 1946). In societies and cultures in which the expression of sexuality is not repressed as it is in Western cultures, there are reports (Malinowski, 1949) that there often is sexual play among children that does not violate the kinship taboos of the culture.

Galenson and Roiphe (1976) suggested that one can differentiate between two types of autoerotic activities during the early childhood period. One is autoerotic activity proper, which does not include masturbatory fantasy and is objectless. These autoerotic activities belong to the early months of development, in which the process of separation-individuation (Mahler and others, 1975) is not complete and therefore the infant is not capable of fantasizing. The second type of autoerotic activity begins to develop sometime between the ages of sixteen to eighteen months and is apparently accompanied by some form of fantasy by the child. According to these investigators, the child at this stage of development seems to be aware of anatomical differences between boys and girls and is more in touch with a significant caretaker during the autoerotic activities. Not only is the locality of the genitals discovered by the infant at this time, but also he or she is able to reach the genitals more easily. Moreover, the manipulation of the genitalia is closer to adult masturbatory activities. Squeezing, pinching, and rapid rhythmic movements of the hand are usually accompanied by signs of autonomic excitation such as flushing, rapid respiration, and perspiration. In addition, the infant seems to focus on the mother and derives pleasure from touching her and smiling at her. The significance of Galenson's and Roiphe's investigation is that they have found convincing evidence of sexual activity during a very early period of life, and that they suggest that psychosexual development, like many other lines of personality development, is subject to stage-bound and phase-specific transformation and discontinuity. Furthermore, they suggest that variation in any line of development, and specifically in the pattern of development of sexual organization, has repercussions on other aspects of the personality. Both Galenson and Roiphe (1974) and Kleeman (1971, 1975) have demonstrated that the line of development of genital-drive organization shows a difference between males and females that can be documented as early as the seventh month of life. Although during their first years both sexes seem to go through the same stages of objectless autoerotic activities, during the second year, differences appear in the timing of masturbatory activities as well as in the patterns of these activities. In this regard, Kleeman's investigation of five children closely agrees with Galenson's and Roiphe's investigation of seventy children. Boys appear to start genital play several months earlier (seven to ten months of age). The pattern of sexual play also seems to differ between girls and boys. Sexual activity among boys appears to be more focused, more intentional, and more frequent, although the discovery of the anatomical differences seems to come at the same time (fourteen to fifteen months). At around this age, there also appears to be a branching-out of the psychosexual developmental lines for boys and girls. For example, the choice of toys and play activities begins to show differences. Boys usually choose "masculine" toys such as cars and balls. They exhibit a mild degree of hyperactivity and an increase in genital activities. On the other hand, girls display a mild and transitory depressive mood. They become subdued and less zestful. This change of behavior is attributed by the investigators to an early form of castration anxiety in girls as a response to the discovery of the missing penis. Mahler and others (1975) observed a "low-key" period among both sexes at the same stage and suggested that it might be related to the child's sense of loss of the symbiotic tie with the mother, while going from practicing into the rapprochement subphase of separation-individuation.

The important point in this discussion is the

relation that seems to exist between sexual drive organization and other personality functions. The choice of a particular toy or play activity might foreshadow a particular interest or even a pattern of symbolic projection of certain inner articulations of life experiences into the outer world. This was stressed rather cogently by Erickson in his study of the development of psychosocial identity in children (1963, pp. 92–108). Erickson's approach to the development of sexuality emphasized that the "inborn instincts" in man are drive fragments that gradually must be organized and integrated during the course of the child's development, in such a way as to echo his or her modes of adaption. To Erickson, the development of sexuality in boys and girls is not only determined by anatomical differences, sexual interest, and sexual activities, but also by the modes of activity and adaptation reflecting the patterns of sexual experience among sexes. For example, in one study (1963, pp. 102–103), he found the most significant differences between boys and girls were in the manner of their constructing and staging play space. Boys showed a tendency to "erect structures, buildings, or streets." Girls were interested mostly in creating "the interior of a house, with simple, little, or no use of blocks." It appeared that the variable of "high-low" is masculine and the variable of "open-closed' is feminine. These modalities are patterned after the feminine and masculine genital forms and functions. It brings to mind Leonardo da Vinci, who once said that shape of the body tells of its function. Freud himself talked about this relation between anatomical configuration and personality development. He said that "the morphological distinction is bound to find expression in differences of physical development. 'Anatomy is Destiny,' to vary a saying of Napoleon's" (1924, p. 178).

The above studies and other similar studies suggest that there is an intimate tie between psychosexual development and major modes and styles of personality functions, and that there are ways to identify the differences of adaptational approach between boys and girls even in the earliest period of life in normal development.

SEX-TYPE BEHAVIOR DURING CHILDHOOD

Sexual differences in the behavior of children have been studied from several angles. The most traditional are those studies carried out by Sears (1963, 1965) and Beller and Neubauer (1963). These focused on children's behavior, that which is observable and measurable, and omitted childhood sexuality. The differences between boys and girls were studied for the level of aggressive behavior and dependency. According to Sears, boys consistently showed more physical aggression and negative behavior than girls did. In Sears's study this difference in the level of aggressive behavior was detectable as early as age three. In Beller's and Neubauer's study, the difference in the amount of aggressive behavior was apparent between the ages of two and five. The problem with these and similar studies is that they reflect the cultural bias of the examiners and the different patterns of child-rearing practices used by parents according to the sex of the child. The same is true of those studies examining the difference between sexes with respect to dependency behavior. It is interesting that there is no appreciable difference in dependency behavior between sexes early in life, short of more negative attention-seeking behavior among boys (Sears, 1963), which Mischel (1970, p. 5) attributes to boys' greater physical aggression rather than to their psychological differences. As children's ages increase, there is increasing incidence of dependent behavior in females (Beller and Turner, 1962; Beller and Neubauer, 1963).

With the advent of the women's movement during the last few years and the more independent and assertive roles that women are assuming in Western cultures, the validity of these early-sixties studies has become more questionable. Abstract concepts defining masculine-feminine by dichotomies such as aggressive-friendly, rational-emotional, extroverted-introverted, are oversimplifications that attempt to reduce personal confusion and cultural anxieties (Michael and others, 1968). Aggressive or dependent behavior is complex and may express a variety of motivations, tendencies, and styles of adaptation.

CLINICAL STUDIES DURING CHILDHOOD

The clinical study of children who early in their lives show evidences of faulty or deviant gender identity formation is another area of recent exploration. We owe much to the pioneer work done by Money, Hampson, and Hampson (1955), Money and Erhardt (1972), Green and Money (1969), and Stoller (1968). Because of these and similar studies, there now are new ways of looking at sexual development and its fundamental and prevailing influence upon the development of personality.

These investigators began their studies from a clinical perspective. They attempted to understand those individuals with anatomically ambiguous genitalia, such as hermaphrodites, whose condition is due to gonadal, hormonal, and genetic factors. This line of inquiry has its counterpart in the study of transsexualism, the extreme form of gender reversal in which the anatomical male believes he is inwardly female, or the anatomical female considers herself psychologically a male. It appears now that in the development of sexuality and personality, certain influences are responsible for the final patterns of personality functioning, the nature of affectional affiliations, and the individual's personal identity. A most important question is what influences are responsible for one's gender identity or, as Stoller (1976) puts it, for "one's sense of masculinity and femininity" (p. 182), regardless of the individual's anatomical and biological sex assignment. It would seem that the individual's gender identity is not based wholly on his or her biological and genetic imprint. Environment, culture, and parents exert a very important and, at times, crucial influ-

ence. Children born with anatomically ambiguous genitalia will act, feel, and desire as males or females depending upon their sex assignment by the parents, independent of their genetic sexual make-up. In fact, these individuals in adulthood are not distinguishable from those with an absolutely clear sexual/gender identity. Some whose gender identity is based on the sex role assigned by the parents early in life despite their genetic and biological sex assignment, function normally. Others exhibit gender identity, confusion, and conflicts similar to those observed in neurotics. These conflicts, however, seem to be related to various traumas and early frustrations that are the basis of many neurotic behaviors, rather than to specific disorders of core gender-identity development.

It appears that core gender identity is formed early in life, and that once formed it will endure throughout the individual's life, highly resistant to environmental or psychotherapeutic intervention. Since the formation takes place over an extremely short period (the first eighteen months of life), many theoreticians use the process of imprinting (borrowed from ethologists) to explain not only the speed of the formation but also the later resistance to modification.

The question of how environment influences gender identity is of particular interest to those developmentalists who are exploring the roots of individuality and the determining forces behind it. There are several character traits that each culture assigns predominantly to either of the sexes. Of course, it is an oversimplification to talk about these traits as either male or female. Observation shows that what is called a male or female trait by the culture is usually present in both sexes, but often a cluster of "feminine" or "masculine" traits tend to predominate in a particular sex. These traits include such behaviors as manner of talking, pattern of postures and expressive body movements, preference for certain toys or tools, and style of grooming and clothing. In other words, it seems that each culture has a way of classifying feminine and masculine behavior, and that in most instances the members of the culture adopt these behaviors according to their sexual and gender identity. There are a number of individuals within most cultures who for various reasons display behavior normally assigned to the opposite sex. These children with atypical sex-role behavior (Green, 1976), by their rigid attachment to the opposite sex's patterns of clothing, peer-selection, and mannerisms once again provide strong evidence for the link between gender-identity formation and personality-trait development. The scant information about the later development of these children indicates that these early traits have an impact on their adult gender-role and sexual-orientation behavior. For example, Green (1976) reports that adult transsexualism could be an extension of early femininity in boys. Bieber (1962) reports that two-thirds of a group of adult homosexuals had some history of feminine behavior during their childhood. In another report (Prince and Bentler, 1972) there were episodes of cross-dressing during childhood among one-half of all adult transvestites.

To summarize, the development of core gender identity seems to depend upon genetic, gonadal, and early environmental influences. Once it is formed, gender identity and self-concept remain stable throughout life, resisting modification by environmental influences.

SEX-TYPING AND COGNITIVE STYLES

Numerous researchers have examined the differences between the sexes in the field of sense perception, using both children and adults as subjects. Although one would expect to find differences between the sexes in preference of sensory modalities, in sensitivity, and in patterns of perceptual organization of various experiences, there is, in fact, little support for such an assumption. Aside from some evidence that females are "more sensitive and more variable in their response to taste and smell cues" (Maccoby and Jacklin, 1974, p. 37), both sexes show remarkable similarities in their preferences and in the level of sensitivity of their

sensory modalities. This includes audition (Kagan and Lewis, 1965, p. 26), vision (Friedman and others, 1970; Kagan and Lewis, 1965), taste (Nisbett and Gurwitz, 1970; Kaplan and Fischer, 1964), smell (Lipsitt and Jacklin, 1971), and touch (Bell and others, 1971; Lipsitt and Levy, 1959).

Turning our attention to the possible differences that may exist between sexes in intellectual abilities, there is an overriding issue to be considered when judging the evidence provided by the research. It appears that the intellectual functioning of an individual cannot be considered in a vacuum (any more than other lines of personality function can). There is ample evidence that intellectual functioning varies among individuals due to genetic endowment and to biological, psychological, and environmental influences on the mother and her child during the perinatal and postnatal period. For a complete review of this subject, the reader may consult an excellent summary provided by Maccoby and Jacklin (1974, pp. 17–167). There is no compelling evidence so far that suggests that there is a difference between sexes in intellectual functioning and performance.

The controversy over the impact of sex hormones on spatial and verbal abilities is important enough to be mentioned here. Vandenberg's twin study (1968) suggested that both verbal abilities and spatial abilities are closely related to heredity. Spatial ability in particular seemed to be less influenced by environmental, educational, and cultural factors. Vandenberg's findings have been supported by recent studies (Bock and Kolakowski, 1973) which demonstrated a cross-sex correlation between parent-child spatial abilities. On verbal ability, information is limited, but it appears that as early as three to eighteen months of age, girls are superior to boys in verbal abilities, such as "speech quotients" (Moore, 1967), and comprehension and vocabulary (Clarke-Stewart, 1973).

The obvious question is, to what extent do hormonal influences account for these differences? For example, the findings of Ehrhardt and Baker (1973) suggested that fetally androgenized girls have higher-than-average IQs, implying that an increase in the male hormone is responsible for the higher intellectual functioning, which supports the findings of an earlier study by Ehrhardt and Money (1967). However, the same study found that normal sisters of these children also had higher-than-average IQs. Comparing the level of performance, simple, over-learned, and repetitive tasks (set A) with more complex tasks requiring information-processing, reorganization of stimulus, and the inhibition of initial response (set B), Broverman and others (1968) found that females were superior in performing set A, but males were superior in performing set B. This finding has been challenged by Maccoby and Jacklin (1974, pp. 121–24) with some justification, but the matter is not settled and awaits further investigation.

There is a vast area of cognitive style that has been studied since Witkin's and others' (1954) pioneer study of adults' field-dependent versus field-independent patterns of scanning. Studies on stable cognitive styles among individuals have been extended to children. The concept of cognitive style also has been widened to include not only field dependence-independence, but also reflection versus impulsivity (Kagan and others, 1964; Kagan and Messer, 1975), breadth of categorization (Gardner, 1953), and style of conceptualization (Kagan and others, 1973). The results of research on the nature of sex-type differences in cognitive styles among children are promising but not conclusive, for a number of reasons. First of all, children are not as verbal as adults—especially very young children. In addition, most studies on children's cognitive styles lack methodological sophistication and therefore are usually the reflection of the investigators' individual differences rather than the children's.

Children are required to respond to certain limited stimuli provided by the investigator, rather than to behave autonomously and spontaneously, and except for a very few (Block and Block, 1973), most of these studies are carried out in research laboratories and do not take into consideration the actual performance of children in classrooms. Nevertheless, a general survey of the literature (Kogan, 1976) provides convincing information about the cognitive style differences among sexes. In one study Coates (as reported by Kogan, 1976, p. 14) using the Articulation of the Body Concept (ABC) Test, based on the child's ability to articulate an embedded figure, found that girls scored higher than did boys. It was concluded, with some misgivings, that not only field independence, but other cognitive styles appear earlier in females (four to five-year-olds) than in the control group of boys. In Oltman's study (1968), based on the responses of one hundred males and one hundred females between four and thirteen years of age to the Portable Rod and Frame Test, there was a significant increase in the field-independent functioning for both sexes as they became older. Within the *preschool* population of children, similar studies have detected a difference between the sexes in the developmental pattern of field-independent perceptual ability. It seems that girls are ahead of boys in this ability up to age four to five years, but boys surpass girls by the age of five to six years (Coates, 1972; Dermen and Meisner, 1972). This stability of field-independent function in boys over a period of time, as compared with its discontinuity in girls, is puzzling. It might have some relation to other variables, such as girls' tendency to be more socially oriented and boys' tendency to be more task-oriented, as suggested by some investigators (Coates and others, 1975).

None of these studies takes into account issues related to the psychosexual development of children, especially the role of infantile anxieties, the nature of the child's relation to significant individuals in his or her life, and motivational factors. This is unfortunate, because most research on cognitive styles suggests that a difference between the sexes in this area might be related to the nature of the child's relation to important individuals in his or her life. Investigation of the relation between cognitive style of reflection versus impulsivity suggests a greater impulsivity among boys than among girls, although the difference is not significant and is variable (Ward, 1973; Wright, 1972 p. 47). In breadth of categorization, which is based on the child's pattern of sorting when asked to group objects according to some differentiating attributes, there is a developmental shift away from finding perceptual attribute differences toward finding conceptual differences based on abstraction and synthesis. Furthermore, there seems to be a developmental pattern that shifts from over-discrimination (narrow) to breadth of categorization (Saltz and others, 1972). The question is whether the breadth, consistency, and accuracy of categorization bear any relation to the child's observable behavior in the nursery school. Teachers' ratings of children's behavior in the classroom in Block's and Block's (1973) study indicated that four-year-old girls who characteristically "stretch limits" also were broad in their categorization. They also were described as having a number of psychological and interpersonal difficulties such as reacting poorly under stress, feeling jealous, displaying low resiliency, and being undependable. The study did not discriminate significantly for boys. This suggests that the breadth of categorization is inversely related to consistency-accuracy (ego resiliency) in girls at the four-year age level. However, Nelson and Bonvillian (1973) studying eighteen-month-olds, found the reverse pattern. In this study, girls generalized concept words to previously unnamed examples, indicating a much advanced functional level. The same proved true when the style of conceptualization was studied. In this study the child is asked to select from among a few pictures one that is like or "goes with" a standard picture. Evaluation is based on whether the child's style of conceptualization is descriptive part-whole, descriptive-global, relational-contextual, or categorical-inferential (Siegel, 1972). The results of these studies suggest that there is a correlation between the child's style of conceptualization and the child's sex. Boys who score high on descriptive part-whole conceptualization also score high on emotional control. In contrast, girls scoring high on descriptive part-whole,

score high on items such as carelessness, daydreaming, and inattentiveness. These differences also were true for boys and girls who scored high on relational-contextual style of conceptualization.

It is clear that the research on cognitive styles during the early period of life generally and on cognitive style and sexual development specifically, has a long way to go and needs conceptual and methodological clarification. The little that has been done has given us a glimpse of its potential and possibilities.

The field is burdened by controversy and emotionality and is colored by the current cultural trend toward redefinition and re-evaluation of long-accepted stereotypic sexual roles in Western societies. We may predict with some confidence that future patterns of child-rearing, their emphases, and values will be modified as a result of this trend. We also should be mindful that the hierarchy of values, the division of responsibility, and the modes of social and familial participation are defined not only by social and economic forces, but also by biological necessities nourished by genetic, hormonal, and biological roots, whose value is inspired by the survival of the individual and its species. For this reason, overlooking the individual differences between sexes or insisting that equality means an absence of difference, is not productive to our long search to understand ourselves.

REFERENCES

BANDURA, A., and WALTERS, R. 1963. *Social and personality development.* New York: Holt, Rinehart & Winston.

BEACH, F. A. 1951. Instinctive behavior reproductive activities. In *Handbook of Experimental Psychology,* ed. S. S. Stevens. New York: Wiley.

BELL, R. Q.; WELLER, G. M.; and WALDROP, M. F. 1971. Newborn and preschooler: organization of behaviors and relations between periods. *Monographs of the Society for Research in Child Development* 36.

BELLER, E. K. and TURNER, J. L. 1962. A study of dependency and aggression in early childhood. In *NIMH progress report*. Berkeley: University of California.

———, and NEUBAUER, P. B. 1963. Sex differences and symptom patterns in early childhood. *J. Child Psychiatry* 2: 414–33.

BIEBER, I. 1962. *Homosexuality*. New York: Basic Books.

BLOCK, J., and BLOCK, J. H. 1973. Ego development and the provenance of thought. In *NIMH Progress Report*. Berkeley, University of California.

BORVERMAN, D. M.; KLAIBER, E. L.; LOBAYASKI, Y.; and VOGEL, W. 1968. Roles of activation and inhibition in sex differences in cognitive abilities. *Psychological Review* 75: 23–50.

CLARKE-STEWART, K. A. 1973. Interactions between mothers and their young children: characteristics and consequences. *Monographs of Society for Research in Child Development* 38.

COATES, S. 1972. *Preschool Embedded Figures Test*. Palo Alto, Ca.: Consulting Psychologists Press.

———; LORD, M.; and JAKABOVICS, E. 1975. Field dependence-independence, social-non-social play and sex differences in preschool children. *Perceptual and Motor Skills* 40: 195–202.

DERMAN, D., and MEISSNER, J. A. 1972. Preschool embedded figure test. In *Disadvantaged children and their first school experiences*, ed. V. C. Shipman. Princeton, N.J.: Educational Testing Service.

EHRHARDT, A. A., and BAKER, S. W. 1973. Hormonal aberrations and their implications for the understanding of normal sex differentiation. Paper presented at meeting of the Society for Research in Child Development, Philadelphia.

———, and MONEY, J. 1967. Progestin-induced hermaphroditism: IQ and psychosexual identity in a study of ten girls. *J. Sex Research* 3: 83–100.

ERICKSON, E. H. 1963. *Childhood and society*. New York: Norton.

ESCALONA, S. K. 1968. *The roots of individuality*. Chicago: Aldine.

FREUD, S. 1916. Leonardo da Vinci and a memory of his childhood, pp. 57–137. *Standard Edition*, vol. 11. London: Hogarth Press.

———. 1910. Mourning and melancholia, pp. 237–58. *Standard Edition*. vol. 14. London: Hogarth Press.

———. 1905. Three essays on sexuality, pp. 123–245. *Standard Edition*, vol. 7. London: Hogarth Press.

———. 1924. The dissolution of the Oedipus complex, pp. 171–79. *Standard Edition*, vol. 19. London: Hogarth Press.

FRIEDMAN, S., NAGY, A. A.; and CARPENTER, C. C. 1970. Newborn attention differential response decrement to visual stimuli. *J. Experimental Child Psychology* 10: 44–51.

GALENSON, E., and ROIPHE, H. 1974. The emergence of genital awareness during the second year of life. In R. C. Friedman, R. M. Richart; and L. Van de Wieldeds, *Sex differences in behavior*, pp. 223–31. New York: Wiley.

———. 1976. Some suggested revisions concerning early female development. *J. of the American Psychoanalytic Assoc.* 24: 29–57.

GARDNER, R. W. 1953. Cognitive styles in categorizing behavior. *J of Personality* 22: 214–33.

GREEN, R. 1976. Atypical sex role behavior during childhood. In *The sexual experience*, ed. B. J. Sodack, H. I. Kaplan, and A. M. Freeman, pp. 196–205. Baltimore: Williams and Wilkens.

———, and MONEY, J. 1969. *Transsexualism and sex reassignment*. Baltimore. Johns Hopkins University Press.

HARLOW, H. F. 1962. The heterosexual affectionate system in monkeys. *Amer. Psychologist* 17: 1–9.

ISAACS, S. 1946. *Social development in young children: a study of beginnings*. Routledge.

KAGAN, J. 1964. Acquisition and significance of sex typing and sex role identity. In *Review of child development research,* ed. M. Hoffman and L. Hoffman, pp. 625–36. —: Russell Sage. New York, New York.

——, and LEWIS, M. 1965. Studies of attention in the human infant. *Merrill-Palmer Quarterly* 11: 95–137.

——, and MESSER, S. B. 1975. A reply to "some misgivings about matching familiar figures test as a measure of reflection-impulsivity." *Developmental Psychology* 11: 244–48.

——; Moss, H. A.; and SIGEL, L. E. 1963. Psychological significance of styles of conceptualization. In *Basic cognitive processes in children,* ed. J. C. Wright and J. Kagan. Monographs of the Society for Research in Child Development 28: 73–112.

——; ROSMAN, B. L.; DAY, D.; ALBERT, J.; and PHILLIPS, W. 1964. Information processing in the child significance of analytic and reflective attitudes. *Psychological Monographs* 78.

KAPLAN, A. R., and FISCHER, R. 1964. Taste sensitivity for bitterness: some biological and clinical implications. In *Recent advances in biological psychiatry,* vol. 8, ed. J. Wartis. New York: Plenum Press.

KLEEMAN, J. 1971. The establishment of case gender identity in normal girls. *Arch. Sexual Behaviors* 1:117–29.

——. Genital self-stimulation in infants and toddler girls. In *Masturbation from infancy to senescence,* ed. I. Marcus and J. Francis, pp. 77–106. New York: Internal Universities Press.

KOGAN, N. 1976. *Cognitive styles in infancy and early childhood.* New York: Halsted Press.

KOHBERG, L. 1966. A cognitive-developmental analysis of children's sex role concepts and attitudes. In *The development of sex differences,* ed. E. E. Maccoby, pp. 82–173. Stanford, Ca.: Stanford University Press.

LIPSITT, L. P., and JACKLIN, C. N. 1971. Cardiac deceleration and its stability in human newborns. *Developmental Psychology* 5: 535.

——, and LEVY, N. 1959. Electroactual threshold in the human neonate. *Child Development* 30: 547–54.

MACCOBY, E. E., and JACKLIN, C. N. 1974. *The psychology of sex differences.* Stanford, Ca.: Stanford University Press.

MAHLER, M.; PINE, F.; and BERGMAN, A. 1975. *The psychological birth of the human infant.* New York: Basic Books.

MALINOWSKI, B. 1951. *Sex and repression in savage society.* London, Eng.: Routledge and Kegan Paul.

MISCHEL, W. 1970. Sex-typing and socialization. In *Carmichael's manual of child psychology.* 3rd ed., ed. P. H. Mussen, pp. 3–72. New York: Wiley.

——; COATES, B.; and RASKOFF, A. 1968. Effects of success and failure on self-gratification. *J. Pers. Soc. Psychol.* 10: 381–90.

MONEY, J., and ERHARDT, A. A. 1972. *Man and woman/ boy and girl.* Baltimore: Johns Hopkins University Press.

——HAMPSON, J. G.; and HAMPSON, J. L. 1955. An examination of some basic sexual concepts: the evidence of human hermaphroditism. *Bull. Johns Hopkins Hospital* 97: 301.

MOOR, T. 1967. Language and intelligence: a longitudinal study of the first eight years, part 1, patterns of development in boys and girls. *Human Development* 10: 88–106.

NELSON, K. E., and BONVILLIAN, J. D. 1973. Concepts and words in the 18-month old. In *Acquiring concept names under controlled conditions* 2:435–50.

NISBETT, R. E., and GURWITZ, S. B. 1970. Weight, sex, and the eating behavior of human newborn. *J. Comparative and Physocological Psychology* 73: 245–53.

OLTMAN, P. K. 1968. A portable rod and frame apparatus. *Perception and Motor Skills* 26: 503–506.

PRINCE, V., and BENTLER, P. M. 1972. Survey of 504 cases of transvestism. *Psychol. Report* 31: 903.

SALTZ, E.; STOLLER, E.; and SIGEL, I. E. 1972. The development of natural language concepts. *Child Development* 43: 1191–202.

SEARS, R. N. 1963. Dependency motivation. In *Nebraska symposium on motivation*, ed. M. R. Jones, pp. 25–64. Lincoln: University of Nebraska Press.

———. 1965. Development of gender role. In *Sex and behavior*, ed. F. A. Beach, pp. 133–63. New York: Wiley.

SIGEL, I. E. 1972. The development of classificatory skills in young children: a training program. In *The young child: review of research*, vol. 2, ed. W. W. Harteys. Washington, D.C.: National Association for the Education of Young Children.

STOLLER, R. J. 1976. Gender Identity. In *The sexual experience*, ed. B. J. Sadock, H. I. Kaplan, and A. M. Freedman, pp. 182–96. Baltimore: Williams and Wilkens.

———. 1968. *Sex and Gender*. New York: Science House.

THOMPSON, G. G., and HARROCK, J. E. 1947. A study of the friendship fluctuations of urban boys and girls. *J. Genet. Psychol* 70: 53–63.

VANDENBERG, S. G. 1968. Primary mental abilities or general intelligence? Evidence from twin studies. In *Genetic and environmental influences on behavior*, ed. J. M. Thoday and A. S. Parkes, New York: Plenum Press.

WARD, W. C. 1973. Development of self regulatory behaviors. Princeton, N.J.: Educational Testing Service.

WHITING, J. W. M. 1969. Resource mediation and learning by identification. In *Personality development in children*, ed. I. Iscoe and W. H. Stevenson, pp. 112–26. Austin: University of Texas Press.

———. 1959. Sorcery, sin, and the superego. A cross-cultural study of some mechanisms of social control. In *Nebraska symposium on motivation*, ed. M. R. Jones, pp. 174–95. Lincoln: University of Nebraska Press.

WITKIN, H.; LEWIS, H.; HERTZMAN, M.; MACHOVER, K.; MESSINER, P.; and WAPNER, S. 1954. *Personality through perception.* New York: Harper.

WRIGHT, J. C. 1972. Technical report on the Kansas Reflection-Impulsivity Scale for Preschoolers (KRISP). Lawrence: Kansas Center for Research in Early Childhood Education.

2

SEX AND SOCIETY

NINE

Relationships and Sexuality in Contexts and Culture: The Anthropology of Eros

LAWRENCE E. FISHER

INTRODUCTION

Throughout its history anthropology has been more interested in human sexuality than any other social science, save psychoanalysis. The conventional ethnography, a theoretically-motivated description of human life ways, places emphasis precisely on those aspects of belief and action that are given emphasis by people themselves. This chapter explores the richness of variety of this sexual symbolism by drawing on ethnographic reports from diverse parts of the world. It emphasizes the systems of knowledge and belief on which action is based, sexual or otherwise, and it follows a cultural point of view (cf. Schneider, 1968). Additionally, this chapter analyzes the theoretical positions of several of the most influential anthropologists to have written on sexuality, finding an ironic movement away from the study of sexual ideology in each of them.

Culture is here thought to be an infrastructural design for life, not usually expressed in direct propositional form (Dolgin, Kemnitzer, and Schneider, 1977) but part of the natural and given. Through ethnography this paper explores sexuality and its context in societies.

There are enough anthropological tidbits about sexuality to fill volumes. We know, for example, that *Pilaw! Kule!* are Mehinaku onomatopoetic words for the sounds of sexual intercourse (Gregor, 1973, p. 250). It is known that young Marquesan girls masturbate with bananas and that the Marquesan sex act seldom takes more than five minutes (Suggs, 1966, pp. 45, 73). However, this essay is not a survey of sexual customs; rather, it is about general issues in cultural analysis and theory.

TRADITIONAL METHODS OF STUDYING SEXUALITY

The ethnographic sex researcher first is faced with the fact that most sexual behavior is conducted in private; observation is difficult, and all one can do is ask about the topic. Reo Fortune is the earliest to comment on this methodological limitation. He was forced to do so after realizing that traders in New Guinea knew more about indigenous sexual activities than he did. Recognizing the access to information that the trader had through sexual intercourse with native women, Fortune proposed a semi-fantastic "through-Trader's-eyes methodology," designed to discover sexual doings:

> The Trader is usually entirely correct and gets to know more than the anthropologist can about such doings. He also discovers from the woman or women of his own how a Dobuan woman may teach her daughter that the way to keep a man faithful is to keep him as exhausted as possible (1932, p. 244).

By implying that the "with-the-native-living Trader," to use Fortune's phrase, had opportunities routinely denied to anthropologists, Fortune acquiesed to past and current ethical and scientific limitations on anthropological propriety.

With the exception of archaeologist Suggs who monitored the sexual talk of large gangs of men excavating sites in the Marquesas (1966, 1971, p. 176), basic research strategy has been simply to ask questions about sexuality, within the bounds of propriety. These bounds may be a severe obstacle in some societies, but not in others. Anthropologists seldom can check the accuracy of what they are told, and only a few will even speculate on the veracity of verbal reports. Berndt is an exception when he suspects "an element of exaggeration" in the tales of sexual conquest told by highland New Guinea men which add to their prestige in sexual matters (1962, p. 151, note). Likewise, Suggs is aware that in the Marquesas, "Females . . . tend to underplay the extent of their sexual activities, while men tend to exaggerate" (1971, p. 176). Such exaggeration is itself valuable data for constructing culture theory.

A related matter is the literalness of speech about sexual matters. For example, Marquesan men prefer to have intercourse with women who are not overly pregnant. They say, however, that men must do so "to make the baby strong" (1966, p. 23). We do not know if this statement is to be taken at face value, or whether it is something of a joke or hedge. Note that in comparison, Mangaian men in referring to this jokingly express fear that "baby would bite" (Marshall, 1971, p. 108).

Marshall reports that his study of sexuality on Mangaia was relatively easy to investigate; people would readily talk with him about sexual matters (p. 105). In contrast, Bailey felt compelled to give special thanks to the Navajo "who have shared their lives with us and permitted unusual intrusions into their privacy" (1950, p. vii). No wonder material on sexuality from Polynesia is so much richer than that available on native Americans!

The strength of the traditional anthropological approach to sexuality is best represented by Margaret Mead in her classic comparative study, *Male and Female* (1949). The complexity and diversity of our own way of life and our uncritical involvement in this life style, obscures our vision and impairs our objectivity. By looking instead to the Arapesh, Balinese, and Iatmul for examples, Mead is able to make a reasonable comparison of maleness and femaleness in her own society.

In that work Mead comments on the tendency of Westerners to move away from the body itself. Closeness to the body is dangerous; one may lose control and behave irresponsibly, thereby jeopardizing decency:

> The solution for the peculiar difficulties of a puritan society does not lie in a series of pin-up girls whose breasts, tailored for love, are explicitly *not* meant for the loving nourishment of their children. It lies rather in developing greater ease with our clothes on (1949, pp. 79–80).

Given the erotic breast/nourishing breast alternatives, as well as other Western cultural fantasies, it is no wonder that the description of human sexuality in other cultures has been so uneven and devoid of analysis. Mead addresses several Western assumptions, such as our sexual understanding of adult nakedness, which she ascribes to many exotic peoples as a climatic adaptation and not a simple erotic custom.

Moralizing about sexuality is a widespread, indeed universal, phenomenon. For rural blacks in the South, it is something of a disgrace and a failure for a young woman not to know the paternity of her child, so that he or she later will not, unwittingly, commit incest (Dougherty, 1978, p. 90). Because Ashanti men expect their brides to be virgins at marriage, women who are not have been known to put stinging ants into their vaginas just before their wedding day so as to bleed during the first sexual intercourse (Herskovits, 1938, p. 284). Selby (1974, pp. 81–87) reports that rules of sexual continence for Zapotecs are not absolute; whether behavior is moral or not depends on if it violates the best interests of the kindred group, or if it can be taken as an affront to the moral order. Among the Gahuku of the New Guinea highlands, Read found that natives tended to blame all violations of sexual rules entirely on women, rather than sharing the blame with the involved men (1965, p. 144). A final example comes from central Brazil where short Mehinaku men are saddled with a moral failing. An adult male is not tall or short in stature due to genetics or diet, as we know. Rather, the Mehinaku believe that the loss of seminal fluid during a critical adolescent period weakens males and retards growth. Men suspected of having violated the rules of adolescence, including a ban on contact with women, have only themselves to blame if their adult stature is short (Gregor, 1977, p. 198).

HIGH AND LOW ENERGY SYSTEMS: COMPETITION AND BALANCE

Anthropological reports document exaggerated emphases on sexuality in certain societies, primarily in Polynesia, Melanesia, and native South America. "Sex, in the modern Marquesas, is something of a national sport," is one such statement (Suggs, 1966, p. 170). Another ethnographer reports that Marquesans of both sexes name parts of the body, "honorably" naming the genitals (Linton, 1939, p. 149). Marquesans have sacred songs with erotic lyrics believed to stimulate the sexual passions of the gods, thus promoting fertility (Suggs, 1966, p. 30). On the Polynesian island of Mangaia it is said that "copulation is a principal concern of Mangaians of either sex" (Marshall, 1971, p. 116). Adolescent boys will "race" with each other in a contest to see which age-mate can copulate with the most women, providing the most sexual pleasure for the females (Marshall, 1971, p. 151). Inquisitive about the local Catholic priest, the islanders asked, "Are his privates sewn up?" Similarly, Mead reports that the concept of celibacy is "absolutely meaningless" to Samoans (1928, p. 98). Closer to home Dougherty finds that among rural black southerners, "sexual feelings are human nature and cannot be totally controlled" (1978, p. 77).

At the other end of the ethnographic spectrum one finds communities like Inis Beag (Messenger 1969, 1971), an island of the Irish Gaeltacht. Messenger was amazed at the minimal attention to and knowledge about sexual matters: "Lack of sexual knowledge and misconceptions about sex among adults combine to brand Inis Beag as one of the most sexually naive of the world's societies" (1971, pp. 14–15). When Messenger asked one woman to compare the sexual proclivities of Inis Beag men and women, she responded, "Men can wait a long time for 'it,' but we can wait a lot longer" (1969, p. 109).

The extreme cases of Polynesian islanders and Irish peasants are difficult to explain. In an exceptionally provocative paper in this regard, Heider (1976) argues that the level of sexual energy is culturally determined, not innately fixed as the Freudians have it. The Dani of New Guinea invest an extraordinarily low amount of energy in sexual pursuits. In fact, Heider finds that the Dani do not invest much energy in anything. They engage in intercourse just frequently enough to maintain the population.

Coincident with this low interest in sexuality, Heider finds low intellectuality, impoverished art, and low levels of affect, for example, in their casual attitude towards death. Heider finds five lines of evidence:

1. sexual abstinence four to six years postpartum. The Dani told Heider that parents should refrain from sex from the time of birth to the time the child is five years old (approximately, since the Dani do not reckon time in years). Whatever the actual period is, it contrasts notably with the period reported for couples in other societies, such as Tahitian parents who continue intercourse until two or three weeks before birth and commence again one or two months after birth (Levy, 1973, p. 125).

2. The period of postpartum sexual abstinence is invariably observed. The Dani assert this (and Heider believes them) and furthermore, no Dani full siblings are less than five years apart in age.

3. The norm of long postpartum sexual abstinence is neither supported by powerful explanation nor enforced by strong sanctions. Heider understands the sanction as a somewhat casual, *pro forma* sanction. They do not abstain from sex for fear of death, ghosts, or any other moral imperative. Rather, sexual abstinence is easy; it is not an issue.

4. Most people have no other sexual outlets. Although one Dani man apparently had nine wives, only a minority had more than one (43 of 148 total males had more than one wife). Heider rejects the possibility of two wives bearing children for the same man within a few years of each other; wives tend to live in separate compounds, and men are likely to stay in the compound with the new infant for the first year or so of its life, effectively restrained from sexual visitations with other wives. Heider eliminates other possible sexual outlets for men: coitus interruptus with a wife, extramarital sexual intercourse, masturbation, homosexuality, and bestiality. According to Heider, none of these is practiced by Dani men, although they are not specifically prohibited by the regulations of postpartum sexual abstinence.

5. No one shows any signs of unhappiness or stress during the period of abstinence. Heider tried to get Dani men to talk about how they

felt about celibacy. None of them reported much of a problem, and Heider could detect no anxiety or discomfort.

Considering all the data, Heider argues that Dani culture is in a steady state, lacking climax or motion, and is in a low-energy field. He contrasts it with the Balinese reported by Bateson (1972), also in a steady state, this a high-energy one.

Heider found two possible causes for the low energy level of Dani cultural forms, including sexuality. One is ecological: Dani receive low stimulation from the environment (the Dani are rather isolated socially). The other is developmental: the infants are reared in low stress conditions. Recently Pontius (1977) has suggested a third hypothesis, this one medical. Dani subfertility, a subject Heider did not explore, may be caused by a combination of two factors: (1) tight scrotal strings which may rupture the epididymal ductus, and (2) a low protein diet.

The Ik are another group with a reportedly low interest in sexual activity. This small hunting group in East Africa is on the verge of starvation (Turnbull, 1972). In documenting the social decay of the Ik, Turnbull reports that although these "loveless people" do in fact engage in intercourse (which implies at least a degree of mutuality and cooperation), they do so somewhat as an extension of masturbatory practice, consistent with the Icean emphasis on "excessive individualism," rather than as an interpersonal event (pp. 243, 253). Turnbull suggests that sexual activity can occur without involvement; it does not need much cooperation nor much affection. Such is the sad case of the Ik, who apparently can engage in sexual intercourse without violating the "cardinal Icean maxim, which is not to love anyone" (p. 125). Certainly the Ik orientation to sexual intercourse is radically divergent and lacks the considerations found in other societies, such as the Mangaian (Polynesian), in which men attempt "orgasmic timing" with their partners, having received explicit instruction in this regard (Marshall, 1971, p. 154.) In matters of Mangaian sexual performance it is believed that, "the

man who only goes a short time does not love his wife" (Marshall, 1971, p. 154).

Bateson's analysis of Balinese culture is an excellent example of the need to move away from narrow definitions of sexuality and crude measures of it. Bateson's article can be easily overlooked by sex researchers, as it usually is, because it is not written ostensibly about Balinese sexuality. Rather, it addresses the different construction of the Balinese cultural system, which is in a steady state, as contrasted with the Iatmul (New Guinea) and American cultural systems, geared toward cumulative interaction and climax. Bateson writes of Balinese children who learn to avoid cumulative interactions: "It is possible that some sort of continuing plateau of intensity is substituted for climax as the child becomes more fully adjusted to Balinese life" (p. 113). The resulting Balinese adult is under tension, not in a competitive, climactic sense, but in a never-ending struggle to achieve balance and interpersonal stability: "The individual Balinese is forever picking his way, like a tightrope walker, afraid at any moment lest he make some misstep" (p. 120).

Bateson documents the "lack of climax" in Balinese quarrels, which are not resolved or concluded, but rather are "pegged at a state" (p. 113), another example of the substitution of plateau for climax. Likewise, during Balinese oratory things happen, but nothing develops. Interruptions which are both tolerated and accepted cause any tension that might be building to break under the stabilizing effect of the irrelevant interaction (p. 113). Bateson also suggests that both the caste system and the village hierarchical structures remove contexts for competition, again replacing them with contexts that express natural order, stability, and balance.

To follow Bateson, we need to realize that social organizations usually contain multidimensional value systems of tremendous complexity and scope. Sexuality, in a system such as this, provides an organizing construct that elevates and identifies one value as governing social interaction on a given occasion. In other words, there are contexts in every social system which define the scope of interaction, by temporarily reducing the multidimensionality of culture to one dimension. In Iatmul, American, and many other societies, sexuality is such an organizing, reductive construct, providing a competitive context by selecting one value system out of many.

Bateson contrasts sexuality, as one of many competitive contests in Iatmul and American societies, with stability, the important organizing construct in Balinese social life. The Balinese emphasize performance and balance in their dance and in their appreciation of an activity as a process to be valued for itself, not because it is aimed at some distant goal. The implication is that this value system, with its emphasis on stability and process, will be expressed in the sexual life of Balinese. Sexual activity is a performance rather than a contest. It is not an activity with winners and losers, best represented in American society when one sexual partner can claim superior sexual ability and attractiveness vis-à-vis the other. Rather, it is a balancing activity in which economic and competitive considerations are replaced by ceremonial and artistic expression. In this way Bateson finds Balinese sexual life consistent with the value emphasis and emotional tone (he calls this "ethos") found throughout the culture. Presumably, the focus of sexual activity remains on the balancing of relationships during an aesthetic experience, itself part of a process without a beginning with foreplay and an end in orgasm.

Lovemaking for the Balinese is an aesthetic confirmation of balance as a value in Balinese life. It is not a cumulation of interaction, leading toward climax, definition and conquest, as evident in American (and Iatmul) sexuality. In the American cultural system, sexuality is a value which focuses and assigns behavior; in Balinese culture sexual activity is aesthetic behavior which itself is governed by a larger value of stability and the noncompetitive personhood which accompanies it. Instead of focusing and limiting the parameters of the interaction, as does the imposition of "sexuality" as a value in American life, the Balinese value system addresses the issue of balance during lovemak-

ing, quarreling, and orating. Because the Balinese view sexual intercourse as a station on the continuing plateau of intensity, it is not relegated to self-contained behavior during an artificially restricted occasion. This is the difference between Balinese and American sexual culture according to the general pattern of Bateson's formulations. This analysis explains findings such as Belo's (1935), that sexual involvement between an upper-caste Balinese woman and a lower-caste man was treated severely as a case of bestiality. Balance and definition, even on the social level, must be maintained.

It is also known that because of the high level of tension in which each Balinese life is lived, Balinese performers expect and receive audience attention and involvement. Balinese performers do not need to work to command the attention of an audience, then, for this attention comes automatically from the audience's equal concern for balance and continuity.

THE CULTURAL APPROACH: CRAFTSMEN AND PATERNITY

To the Marquesan master craftsman, the building process is regarded as a sexual act (Linton, 1939, p. 146). Linton's report does not indicate whether such building is to be taken as literally sexual (though this is the impression one gets) or metaphorically sexual. Even if the building/sexuality relationship is metaphoric, it still can be understood as fully sexual, to the extent that anything based on the sexual act is itself necessarily sexual. Linton suggests that the craft-building process is conceptualized by Marquesans as similar to the male role in intercourse. If Linton is correct in stating that women are treated primarily as sex objects by Marquesan men (1939, p. 164; but Suggs, 1966, p. 3. disagrees), then the details of the metaphoric extension from male/female to craftsman/craft object should be relatively easy to work out.

The "problem" of paternity is an issue in ethnography which can be traced back to Australian observations in the 19th century and to the pioneering works of Malinowski (1926, 1927, 1929) in the Trobriands. In this matrilineal society the husband is not regarded as the father of his wife's children. Trobrianders are ignorant of "physical fatherhood" (Malinowski 1927: p. 23). Linton's Marquesan informants would admit to understanding paternity ("physical fatherhood," in Malinowski's terms) but preferred to connect their genealogies to those of household heads, who were not necessarily "blood" relatives (Linton, 1939, p. 156). The Trobriand theory of maternity without paternity is diametrically different from that of the Mehinaku child who has many fathers, as many as mother will acknowledge having had sex with during pregnancy, and the child will relate to these men, more or less, as "fathers" (Gregor, 1977, pp. 292–93). Through "multiple paternity" the Mehinaku believe that pregnancy is a sort of "collective labor project." When a child is born, every man who regularly had sexual intercourse with the mother may be regarded as the father.

The consequences of this for the social organization of the Mehinaku are considerable, for "multiple paternity" requires children to acknowledge the paternal status of certain men in the village, even if they are instructed to address them as "papa" only when the husband is not within hearing distance. Likewise, the incest taboo generally is extended to prohibit sexual contact between persons related through maternal affairs, just as persons related through marriage are prohibited as sexual or marriage partners (Gregor, 1977, p. 293). Apparently the Mehinaku are not rigid about all this and allow that if a certain man had sexual relations with a child's mother only "a few times," he is only a "little bit" the child's father, and the child may be allowed to have sexual relations with and even marry this person's children (Gregor, 1977, p. 293).

The area of fertility and infertility is one of the few in the cross-cultural literature that seems to be controlled primarily by women. Even among the sexually repressed Irish islanders of Inis Beag, men are thought to be more naturally libidinal than women (Messenger, 1971, p. 16). However, assuming that a woman is in some control over the men with whom she has intercourse, she can either increase or decrease the total number of instances of sexual intercourse, the number of various partners in intercourse, or the number of occasions of intercourse allowed any one partner. The perceived consequences of these strategies all will be different, given the ideology of the group, but at least in this domain a woman has the upper hand. She hypothetically can control her fertility and equally important to people like the Mehinaku, she can extend her children's kinship system to include men and their relatives, who will relate to these children at the expense of her designated husband.

Malinowski's title, *Sex and Repression in Savage Society* should read *Sex in Savage Society and Repression in Western Society*, to aptly reflect his comparative orientation. In this work Malinowski attempts to demonstrate his theory of culture, with its definite emphasis on the nuclear family, this with regard to the Oedipal Complex, the issue of the day.

Malinowski shows the Trobriand matrilineal social structure to be fundamentally different from family form in modern society. Trobrianders reckon kinship through mothers only; in fact Trobriand children do not have "fathers" as we know them. Fathers have a friendly, "dutiful" relationship to their wife's children. Much of the authoritarian "fathering" of Western societies is accomplished by the Trobriands by the mother's brother, with whom the child is never intimate. The child's relationship to the mother's husband (the "physical father"), on the other hand, is anxiety-free and friendly. As Malinowski says, "father is always there as helpful adviser, half playmate, half protector" (1927, p. 48). This "affection-without-authority" relationship contrasts strikingly with Malinowski's understanding of the neurotic, authoritarian relationship between a Western father and child (especially a male child).

The Trobriand child grows up almost completely independent of adult authority, partly because of the pattern of patrilocal residence which has the children and mother living in a community removed from the mother's brother. Malinowski surmises that children in this pristine condition, running around naked and free, physically distant from the primary authority figure, and whose sexual and excretory functions are treated matter-of-factly, do not think in terms of decent-indecent, or pure-impure (1927, p. 56). The pattern of Malinowski's comparative treatment of social life and cultural form in these two groups shows them to be opposed on practically every measure. In its treatment of sexuality, Western culture is complex and veiled, but Trobriand culture is simple and direct. Western culture creates repressed persons (in a Freudian sense); Trobrianders are in touch with their sexuality and are basically un-repressed. Although Westerners are forced out of the "natural" course of development, Trobrianders are in almost total agreement with their biological systems.

Applying these findings to the original issue, that of "Oedipal conflict" in the Trobriands, Malinowski concludes that the Trobrianders do in fact have complexes, but not Oedipal complexes. Unlike the Western male child whose wishes are to destroy father and marry mother, the Trobriand desires the destruction of the maternal uncle and a marriage with his sister. Brother-sister intimacy is strictly taboo for the Trobriands, and this is the point at which the sexual energies are thwarted, not between child and parent as is the case in the West. Malinowski thus restricts "Oedipal complex" to the particular form of psychological dynamic found in the early-infancy stages in patriarchal societies. Malinowski found the Trobriands to have a different form of nuclear family complex, namely, the "matriarchal complex." In comparison with the Oedipal complex, the Trobriand complex is formed later in life, entails fewer shocks for the child and extends in scope beyond the confines of the "family circle" (1927, p. 83). Consequently it is presumed to leave the Trobrianders practically neurosis-free.

Malinowski's theoretical framework is evident in his response to criticisms raised by the psychoanalyst Ernest Jones (1925). Jones had argued that the Trobrianders do know the facts of paternity, but that this knowledge is unconscious or repressed. For Jones the Oedipal complex is basic; the matrilineal organization of the Trobrianders is a response to Oedipal drives, a way of dealing with the same sexual issues dealt with in the West. Culture does not create or channel the complex but rather is built in terms of the complex. The mother's brother in the Trobriands is simply a substitute for the father, according to Jones. Likewise, the incestuous wishes toward the mother are redirected to the sister.

Note in Malinowski's formulation that the culture structure which he views as primary and determining does not include "sexuality," which he treats instead as a biological impulse. It was important for Malinowski to insist on this point in order to work out his comparative project, for if the biological sex drive were fundamentally different in Trobrianders and Westerners, he could not advance his cultural argument. Culture, for Malinowski, consists of institutions that satisfy biological and psychological needs in appropriate ways. Sexuality is one of those needs that is governed by culture; it is not a part of culture, even in his argument with Jones about the relative merits of psychological vis-à-vis cultural approaches to the Trobriand data. Sexuality, for Malinowski, is regulated by the institutional system; it is not part of the system. By treating something as an "instinct" or biological fact the anthropologist relegates it to an invariable unit in the analysis, one that cannot have a determining effect because institutions are different, but the biological facts are everywhere the same. Again, cultural systems work on sexuality; sexuality is not part of the system. The sad irony is that Malinowski, the anthropological thinker who had the most to say about sexuality, treated sexuality as an instinct which would never become incorporated into a cultural analysis.

MORGAN: THE TRANSFORMATION FROM SEXUALITY TO SOCIETY

Although anthropologists have always been interested in sexuality, they have not always been interested in studying it. A review of the pioneering works of Lewis Henry Morgan, the unilinear evolutionist, and Robert Lowie, an early critic of evolutionary theory, demonstrate this.

Morgan proposed a fifteen-stage evolutionary "in part hypothetical" sequence (1878, p. 498) from a prefamilial stage of "promiscuous intercourse" to the "Monogamian Family," the ultimate culmination of mankind. The hypothetical "Promiscuous intercourse" stage is low on the evolutionary scale, and it is not clear from Morgan's account if he is talking about humankind, or a lower animal form:

> *Promiscuous Intercourse*—This expresses the lowest conceivable stage of savagery—it represents the bottom of the scale. Man in this condition could scarcely be distinguished from mute animals by whom he was surrounded. Ignorant of marriage, and living probably in a horde, he was not only a savage, but possessed a feeble intellect and a feebler moral sense. . . . Were it possible to reach this earliest representative of the species, we must descend very far below the lowest savage now living upon the earth (1878, p. 500).

In contrast to "Promiscuous Intercourse," a stage which "lies concealed in the misty antiquity of mankind" (1878, p. 502), is Morgan's modern "Monogamian Family," the final accomplishment in his history of human progress from savagery to civilization. At this stage, the paternity of children was assured, the joint ownership of real and personal property was introduced, and the inheritance by children was guaranteed. All known advances and institutions are related to this ultimate advance, for in Morgan's own words, "Modern society reposes upon the monogamian family" (1878, p. 505).

Morgan's theoretical goals included the refutation of the "degradation hypothesis" explanation of barbarian and savage populations found to be both physically and mentally below the standard of the supposed original man (1878, p. 506). Although Morgan treated sexuality as part of his larger argument, he did not set out to explore human sexuality as an important topic among contemporary peoples.

According to Morgan, the lowest conceivable stage of savagery was a stage of promiscuous, uncontrolled, unchecked sexuality. Such a stage of sexuality provided a theoretical counterpoint to the modern family, not to modern sexuality. Unrestrained sexuality among persons with a "feeble moral sense" (1878, p. 500), interacting in a prefamilial mode, is ultimately replaced by the institution of the modern, monogamian family. Morgan's unmistakable point of departure is an attempt to document the transformation of raw animal sexuality into a multifaceted modern human social form. Progress is at the expense of sexuality; it does not incorporate it. For Morgan, the "facts of the human experience" (1878, p. 508) are facts which show the institutions of family and government to have evolved from an earlier stage of unbridled sexual license.

One consequence of this reasoning is that anthropologists should study the family instead of sexuality, or ideas about sexuality. To the extent that modern theorists assume that sexuality is "under control" in every known society, the family and/or the mechanisms of control demand study, not sexuality itself. This seems to be a serious error in logic and a potentially serious deterrent to competent ethnography.

This epistemology which opposes or transforms sexuality into social organization is not easily relegated to the writings of one outmoded theorist; Morgan's legacy is still with us. It is evident in the beginning sentence of Fox's chapter on "The Incest Problem" in *Kinship and Marriage:* "If primary kin were allowed to mate, then many of the elaborate arrangements we are going to explore in this book would be unnecessary" (1967, p. 54). The implication is that kinship as we know it and study it would not exist, were sexual relations allowed in the family unit (outside of husband-wife). Stated in another way, the management of sexuality generates the primary structures of kinship and social organization which anthropologists have made as the core of their discipline. With or without tacit acknowledgment of the preempted role of a suppressed sexuality, anthropologists usually tend to address themselves to what sexuality hath wrought (kinship and social organization), rather than to how sexuality operates in a symbolic world, and how it perseveres as an important element of interpersonal relationship and ideology. This oversight finally was noticed in the important work of Schneider (1968, 1969) and Kemnitzer (1977).

Lowie's (1920) critique of unilinear evolutionary theory as promoted by Morgan is based on the replacement of erotic considerations by domestic and economic ones. Briefly, Lowie argues that polygyny should be understood in terms of economic and domestic advantage—men gain prestige and women gain household helpmates—and that anthropological analysis should not emphasize erotic considerations that polygynous natives themselves do not emphasize (1920, p. 43). Lowie's approach attempts to abolish the erotic component of sexuality. That Lowie may be incorrect, at least in one case, is the impression one gets from the explicitly erotic advantage of polygyny, as expressed by a male Kgatla (an African group studied by Schapera):

> I have laid down the rule that I shall sleep with each one for four days in succession, and then go to the other. I find them [my wives] both equally desirable, but when I have slept with one for three days, by the fourth day she has wearied me, and when I go to the other I find that I have greater passion, she seems more attractive than the first, but it is not really so, for when I return to the latter again there is the same renewed passion (1941, p. 193).

Lowie similarly treats Morgan's hypostatized "group marriage" stage of evolution. By rephrasing "group marriage" as "sexual communism," Lowie first demotes the stage from the social organizational to a sexual level and then shows that when it occurs it is temporary, sometimes existing simultaneously with marriage. Lowie's demonstration is designed to show that the institution of "sexual communism" has nothing to do with unrestricted sexual license but is a native notion of reciprocal hospitality. Because some sexual partners overshadow others, Lowie concludes that the husband "enjoys an undisputed preemptive right over his wife" (1920, p. 53). Again, Lowie emphasizes considerations of reciprocity and obligations, while systematically denying the relevance of erotic dimensions in this so-called communism.

Morgan and Lowie reach similar conclusions about erotic sexuality, but for different reasons. Morgan assumed that sexuality had been transformed in all existent societies of his day, since societies are by definition social and not sexual, but Lowie completely disregarded sexual/erotic considerations in his criticism of Morgan's unilinear evolutionary theory. In both cases, the study of the sexual/erotic is not relevant to larger theory. Followers of Morgan's *Ancient Society* (1878) or of Lowie's *Primitive Society* (1920) will equally disregard sexual matters in cultural analysis.

This side-stepping of the cultural study of sexuality, as it were, has at least two ramifications for contemporary studies. The first is a generally conservative approach to sexuality, treating it in the context of marriage, if at all. The second consequence is more subtle, as it stems from the decision to treat sexuality as a universal physiological phenomenon which everywhere is limited in certain ways by social constraints. Suggs and Marshall, for example, view the relationship between physiological sex drive and society as universal. Again, as in Morgan and Lowie, there is an implicit shift from sexuality to sociality. Should we follow Suggs and Marshall, we would attempt to compare societies as social controlling mechanisms, that is, we would ascertain the ways in which the same physiological drive was contained and cathected cross-societally. We would learn, for example, that adult male sexual drive is distributed differently in marriage in polygynous as opposed to serial monogamous societies, and we would seek the mechanisms which regulate men in these two societal types. These mechanisms, often called "institutions," then become the focus of a comparative study. Although this general approach can be useful, the system of meanings attached to sexual symbolism is equally important; we should look at the symbolic dimensions of social action, not just the variation of constraints on behavior.

MEN'S SEXUALITY AND WOMEN'S SEXUALITY

One of the most striking aspects of the anthropological literature on sexuality is the near-universal concern that men have about pollution or contamination resulting from contact with women. The Kaluli men of Papua New Guinea repeatedly warned anthropologist Schieffelin against sleeping with his wife and pointed to Schieffelin's clumsiness on the trail as a result of such indiscretion (Schieffelin, 1976, p. 123). The Kaluli men share the same concern as the men of the Central Highlands of New Guinea, as reported by Read: "In their view of the world, too close and constant an association with the opposite sex, even with one's own wife, could impair a man's vigor or retard his growth during the critical years of adolescence" (1965, p. 97). Mead generalizes that for all of Polynesia, "all women, and especially menstruating women, are considered contaminating and dangerous" (1928, p. 81). Suggs found this to be the case in the Marquesas; men would refuse sex during menstruation for a variety of reasons. Impotence might result, and they also voiced complaints against the practice on aesthetic grounds (Suggs, 1966, p. 20, 26). Tahitian males consider menstrual blood dangerous (Levy, 1973, p. 126). The Fulani of Upper Volta designate menstruation with a phrase which, literally translated, means "to see dirt" (Riesman, 1977, p. 87). Fulani women cannot pray during their menstrual periods. Menstruation and its associations seem to stand as the basis for the Fulani's radical separation of male and female spheres, women being naturally weaker. Navajo women of the American Southwest cannot conduct a chant while menstruating (Bailey, 1950, p. 9). The Navajo have an interesting paradox: although it is dangerous to have intercourse with a menstruating woman, to do so increases the likelihood of pregnancy (Bailey, 1950, p. 11). In native South America, we find Mehinaku men

who see menstrual blood as especially dangerous, capable of causing sickness and cramps in men (Gregor, 1973, p. 243).

Schieffelin observes from Kaluli:

> That women are weaker and less dynamic than men, that they are slow and clumsy and know less, is part of the same general condition of debility they manifest in menstruation. And this condition is dangerous to men because it is capable of destroying their manhood. The man who spends too much time in the woman's section . . . who touches his wife too often, or who eats food a woman has stepped over is likely to become emaciated, develop a cough, or lose his endurance on the trail (1976, p. 123).

The implication here is that menstrual blood or menstruation is not dangerous per se; it is symbolic of the weakness or danger that men more generally attribute to women. That Schieffelin's clumsiness on the trail could be attributed by the Kaluli to his sharing a bed with his wife indicates a more general cultural separation between strength and weakness and agility and clumsiness that ascribes success to men but places blame on women. After all, a man should be able to negotiate a trail smoothly by nature; should a man falter, he is suspected of female contamination. Schieffelin, who knows he is clumsy by nature, sees the irony and sexism in the Kaluli men's comments, and states: "It struck me as poignant irony that the person on whom a man most depends in his domestic household and whom he usually holds in his affections is also the one most dangerous to his vitality" (1976, p. 123).

Because the pattern is so pervasive and consistent in male/female antagonism, one might conclude that there are important, cross-societal universals about men and women. Although such a claim can be substantiated, to do so would be to miss the point about context. Many of these societies seem to be built on a "we/they" male opposition; the "we" is generally the male domain, and the "they" consists of women, who some of the time are incorporated into "we" but usually are treated as a weaker, more dangerous "they."

Freeman's (1970) observation of a Castilian

hamlet superficially seems to address a basic division between farmers and shepherds. However, in sexual matters and capacity, the shepherd is far more feared than the farmer, as Freeman reports:

> The shepherd is forced, by definition, out of the ken of the community which depends upon physical presence for social control. The farmer, on the other hand, continues to live in the bosom of that community. The sexual morality of the bachelor farmer is not subject to the same implicit doubt as that of the bachelor herder who may be his brother. Because the farmer is in constant view of his neighbors, keeping the same schedule that they keep, his movements are known. More important, because he lives continually among others, even though celibate, he is not thought to suffer from lack of sexual satisfaction. Here emerges the notion that strong sexual needs grow out of a life of isolation and are not the necessary product of bachelorhood. The single person who lives among others is thought not to experience sexual desire to the same degree as the person who lives in isolation. Thus the shepherd's sexuality is more exaggerated also than that of the priest and constitutes the greater threat —hence the peculiar apprehension with which herders and other migrants are regarded when they pass through town (1970, p. 183).

Freeman correctly identifies the important symbolic dimension of this interaction. Briefly, she finds an important inside/outside relationship between the farmer and the shepherd. This makes good sense, because farmers are generally of and from the community, but shepherds are more frequently marginal. Shepherding excludes people from the village who may not have been excluded formerly. The farmer is thought to be social in his orientation to others, but interactions with the shepherd are feared as primarily sexual. Here we have a polarization of a sexual and hazardous presence on the outside, contrasted with a social and controllable one on the inside. One does not need to inquire into the sexual behavior of farmers or shepherds to appreciate the symbolic message. Sexual drive (at least for men) grows out of isolated living conditions;

sociality and sociability are substitutes for sexuality, which is important to these people in marking the difference between inside and outside.

Although sociality and sexuality are defined as different by the hamlet dwellers, they address the same issues. Certainly sexuality will be pertinent to many issues of definition and development for villagers, such as male/female, young/old, kinsmen/non-kinsmen, and good/bad. The investigation of how sexuality participates in these larger cultural constructions is the anthropological contribution to the study of sexuality and society.

Because of this orientation to cultural constructions, one might wonder about the place of behavioral analysis in cultural sex research. Although the anthropologist is interested in behavior, he or she is not interested in the behavior per se but rather, in a cultural system of symbols and meanings. Gagnon and Simon state:

> The physical sexual activity of two males when one of them is defined as *berdache* among the Western Plains Indians is identical with the sexual activity of two men in ancient Greece or in a modern Western society; but the meanings attached to the behavior and its functions for the society are so disattached to the behavior and its functions for the society are so disparate in these cases that seeing them as aspects of the same phenomena except in the most superficial way is to vitiate all we know about social analysis (1973, p. 6).

In fact, not all anthropologists agree with Gagnon and Simon, and some would prefer to treat homosexuality, for example, as a unit of or category of behavior that can be analyzed as a phenomenon across cultures.

If the meaning of a sexual act does vary in different cultures, a recent report from the New Guinea highlands demonstrates that the "same" physical act can have a different meaning and lead to different consequences within one cultural system. I refer to Berndt's analysis of adultery among New Guinea mountain people (1962, p. 147). Berndt finds three crucial contexts for adultery: (1) within the lineage, (2) outside the village but within the district, and (3) outside the district. If the partner in adultery were a covillager (context 1), the affair would have only minor repercussions if discovered; in fact Berndt found intravillage adultery was often condoned. However, when persons from different villages were engaged in adulterous activity (context 2), the episode could lead to fighting, and in cases in which district boundaries are crossed (context 3), outright warfare could ensue.

These New Guinea people have a different tolerance for such activity, depending on these crucial contexts. Berndt finds that interdistrict adultery is generally viewed in the idiom of warfare, that is, as an act of one political unit asserting its supremacy over another. Although stealing or enticing a woman away for sexual purposes is viewed as a "legitimate" activity, it risks the retaliatory reprisal of an entire political unit, since many men in addition to the husband will feel that they have been wronged and that their sexual prowess has been questioned. When faced with adultery (or even what in our terms might better be called "forced sex," but for which the New Guinea men nevertheless held the female responsible), men take these contextual issues into account, determining whether or not they themselves personally have been injured and assessing just what kind of an injury they have suffered.

Likewise, "rape" as a universal behavioral concept must be put into context. Gladwin and Sarason, for example, described copulation with a sleeping woman on Truk (1953, p. 113), but ethnographic evidence did not ascertain whether it was rape. A Mehinaku male might seize the wrist of a female and demand sex (Gregor, 1973, p. 251), which poses the question of boundary between forceful coercion and rape. Murphy uncovered a certain case of rape when Mundurucu men gang raped a recalcitrant female who had failed to submit to male authority (1959). Gregor reports a Mehinaku female who had been bold enough to enter a man's house suffered a similar fate (1973, p. 243).

If Marshall is correct in stating that "rape

does not carry the serious social connotation on Mangaia that it does in European society" (1971, p. 152), then what point is there to hypothesizing about rape in the Polynesian case at all? In answer to this question I refer to Carroll's (n.d.) observation that the natives of the Polynesian island of Nukuoro themselves hypothesize about rape. To Nukuoro rape is important conceptually, because it marks the logical obverse of the inherent balance in sexual relationships. Additionally, rape is intrinsically unsatisfying from the male Nukuoroan point of view, since the persuasive/attractive dimension would be totally lost.

The domination of male over female symbolized by and enacted through rape in Western culture may be joined to other forms of political action elsewhere in the world. In certain South African groups a man can face vindictive charges of rape after sex with consent of the woman, should he renege on his promise to give her a gift (Laubscher, 1937, p. 82). Hockings found a comparable political definition in India: "From a male Toda point of view a Toda girl who has given herself to a Badaga has probably been raped by him, and the offender is lucky if he escapes a serious beating at the hands of the woman's husband or husbands" (n.d., p. 64).

The forceful assertion of one person's sexuality on another, that is, rapacious sexuality, is an extreme form of domination. Statutory rape is one of our more paradoxical legal concepts, with the age of the victim replacing consent. The legal definition is consistent, however, with an implicit aspect of American culture which denies responsibility to children. Young girls below the age of consent are not presumed mature enough to exercise consent, even if they have willfully engaged in sexual conduct. The law argues that it is not within their powers as persons to agree.

Because rape is defined as a special crime and a special issue in American culture, it is somewhat difficult to realize that this brutal attempt to engage persons sexually can be understood more generally as an extreme example of strategy in sexual encounter. One strategy similar to rape is the *moetotolo* (or *moe dolo, moo-toro*) "sleep crawling," or "night crawling" attempt at sexual intercourse reported in several Polynesian settings (Suggs, 1966, p. 58; Marshall, 1971, p. 128; Carroll, n.d.; and Mead, 1928, p. 89), as well as among the Cayapa of the lowland region of Ecuador (Altschuler, 1971).

Although each of these reports is somewhat different, Mead and several others depict "night crawling" generally as a rough and risky way to go about seeking sexual relations. The practice is to visit the female lover in her house at night, generally with a quorum of her kinspeople sleeping in the same room. Samoan boys will plan such an adventure to retaliate against girls who have stood them up or have chosen other boys over them. *Moetotolo* is not a delicate courtship maneuver, and Mead prefers to treat it as though it were out of the realm of proper courtship altogether, although such meetings occasionally are mutually satisfying. Girls can pretend that their lover's presence was not sanctioned, should commotion awake parents, family, and dogs. Support for Mead's conclusion that *moetotolo* is a "curious form of surreptitious rape" (1928, p. 89) comes from Nukuoro, where Carroll found much of the "night crawling" attempted by drunken men and boys (n.d., p. 2).

Ethnographic literature often refers to female strategy in sexual relationships, generally as a response to the constraints of domination. Dougherty (1978, p. 81) reports that black women in the rural South are careful not to terminate a relationship with one man until they are certain of the sincerity and commitment of a new lover. Kgatla women will falsely pretend they are menstruating to ward off an unwelcome lover (Schapera, 1941, p. 98). A Yanomamö woman who does not want to be bothered by her husband can tell him to take his drugs into the forest and chant to the forest spirits (Chagnon, 1977, p. 75), which apparently works as a culturally standardized distancing mechanism. Dougherty (1978) and Gregor (1977, p. 203) report that a wife will withdraw sexual and domestic services as a symbolic form of disappointment with the marital relationship.

In sexual approaches, both Mehinaku men and women manipulate kinship terminology to their advantage. A male will ask a female to have sex, but she may refuse, arguing that she is a "real" sister. Since cross-cousins are available for sexual encounters, Gregor finds that among the Mehinaku the attractive girls are usually cross-cousins and not sisters (1977, p. 291). The Tuareg are also reported to use their kinship domain to this same end.

Do the Mehinaku and the Tuareg violate the terms of their own kinship systems in order to make these sexual approaches? Or are we to understand these definitional strategems as part of a larger cultural system? The answer lies in how the Mehinaku and Tuareg themselves conceptualize relationships.

MARITAL AND EXTRAMARITAL SEXUALITY

In American culture, according to Schneider, sexual intercourse is "exclusive to and distinctive of the husband-wife relationship" (1968, p. 38). Schneider knows full well that sexual intercourse as behavior occurs outside of marriage, but his point is that it never occurs outside of the marital context. In an important footnote Schneider supports his contention and demonstrates the broad scope of husband-wife sexuality in defining the impropriety, illegitimacy, and immorality of other forms of sexual activity:

Sexual intercourse between persons who are not married is fornication and improper; between persons who are married but not to each other is adultery and wrong; between blood relatives is incest and prohibited; between persons of the same sex is homosexuality and wrong; with animals is sodomy and prohibited; with one's self is masturbation and wrong; and with parts of the body other than the genitalia themselves is wrong. All of these are defined as "unnatural sex acts" and are morally, and in some cases, legally, wrong in American culture (1968, p. 38).

With this reasoning Schneider could define the symbolic system of American kinship, consisting of and in terms of the central symbol of sexual intercourse. In later publications Schneider widened his study to additional cultural domains grounded in the same symbolic process (1969 and elsewhere).

Schneider's argument allows a cultural approach to such topics as adultery. If we expand upon Schneider's argument, we learn that adultery is wrong because it extends to outsiders the order of law, which unites individuals through marriage. Americans also reckon relatives through tracing "blood" ties. The conjugal love of marriage is opposed in the cultural system by the cognatic love between persons related "by blood." Schneider points out that the product of conjugal love provides the actors who partake of the "blood" relationship. Sexual intercourse, therefore, is instrumental and symbolic in both conjugal and cognatic love.

Adultery, in this analysis, breaks the symmetry and threatens the entire system. Because it is a pivotal symbol, sexual intercourse outside of marriage not only threatens that marriage but threatens personal relationships defined by the "blood" with which it is dynamically associated. Note that the epithet "homewrecker" used to disparage the proverbial "other woman" refers to the total damage done to relations defined both by blood and by law.

Of particular interest to anthropologists are the arrangements of polygamous marriages. Herskovits was somewhat surprised to find that Dahomean polygynyous marriages were not necessarily tense or jealousy-arousing. Cooperative cowives make adjustments among themselves, should a husband's four-day cohabitational visit coincide with a wife's menstrual cycle. She will exchange places in the rotation with a cowife and not be deprived (1938, pp. 340–41).[1] Herskovits concludes: "In essence, the great mass of Dahomean matings, either because of complacency, or of human ability to make the best of a situation, are permanent ventures which in terms of human adjustment cannot be called failures" (1938, pp. 340–41).

Schapera, reporting on the Kgatla, is not as impressed with the way the system works for them, finding jealousy, suspicion and unhappiness among a Kgatla's many wives. His conclusion differs from Herskovits's: "Many women grow reconciled and manage to lead a tolerable existence with husbands who are not unduly inconsiderate, others find some sort of relief by being unfaithful themselves, and some are acutely miserable" (1941, p. 212).

We have a similarly indefinite perspective from the literature on polyandry. Linton reports that jealousy among cohusbands in the polyandrous Marquesas was considered "very bad manners" (1939, p. 175). This report is contradicted, however, by Suggs, who reports that "sexual jealousy is, and was, pronounced in the Marquesas" (1971, p. 171).

Little light will be shed on the topic of jealousy in marriage, plural or otherwise, unless some consideration is given to the larger context provided by native conceptions and explanations. One start in this direction is offered by Firth (1957) who finds that among the Tikopia, jealousy is something engendered by marriage and is a natural extension of the marital relationship:

> Jealousy is a definitely recognized type of behaviour in Tikopia, characterized by a special linguistic expression, *masaro*. It is particularly evident in newly-married people, the natives say, and they regard it as a kind of accompaniment to the recently-wedded state. One of the young pair excites jealousy of the other . . . [Firth asks, "Over what?"] We don't know; there it is, the co-habitation of a newly-married pair. They dwell together, they become jealous (1957, pp. 119–20).

For the Tikopians, jealousy is an expectable part of marriage, especially in its earlier stages. It stems from the marriage and not from the predispositions of either mate, either to incite jealousy by behaving in certain ways or to become jealous easily because of personality.

[1] Evans-Pritchard, however, reports that among the polygynous Zande, it is the men who determine the sleeping arrangements. Thus husband should know which wives are menstruating, so he can plan to sleep with another (1973, p. 174).

As might be expected, people in various societies seek evidence to substantiate their suspicions of infidelity about a marital partner. Evidence may be as highly conspicuous as the love scars Trukese inflict upon one another (Gladwin and Sarason, 1953, p. 111), or as subtle as a change in eating habits, as among the Tapirapé (Wagley, 1977, p. 162). Tapirapé men are known to get ill if they eat soon after an adulterous tryst, so a woman would know if her husband had been adulterous if he should eat sparingly on mornings. A recognizable footprint or buttock-print left in the forest surrounding a Mehinaku village can spell trouble for an adulterous couple (Gregor, 1973, p. 249). Suspicious Dobuan men will time their wives when they leave the compound to urinate or defecate. Extremely suspicious husbands will insist on accompanying their wives to the bush just to make certain (Fortune, 1932, p. 247). Tapirapé husbands carefully watch the fathers of newborn infants, for these men are liable to consort with other men's wives, owing to the postpartum sexual prohibition which denies them access to their own (Wagley, 1977, p. 141).

Because of anthropology's emphasis on marriage and social control, there has been a general de-emphasis on the study of extramarital sexuality. Also lost in the shuffle is the view of sexuality as a component of culture, since it has been assumed to be a component of marriage. Despite this obvious and continuing orientation to sexuality only as it prevails in marriage, some anthropologists have recently begun to report on extramarital relations, mostly in Africa, native South America, Polynesia, and New Guinea.

Wagley, for one, had no choice but to recognize sexual activity outside of marriage, for Tapirapé Indian men take six- or seven-year-old girls as wives, a custom they refer to as "raising your own wife" (1977, p. 157). These men have to find sexual satisfaction surreptitiously; their marriages are, at least initially, asexual. After doing field work among the Fulani, a pastoral people of Upper Volta, Riesman offered this important critique of the standard anthropo-logical understanding of marriage and sexual control:

> It is a commonplace in anthropology to say that marriage, as an institution, channels man's sexual impulses so that they contribute to the maintenance of social structures rather than their subversion. But in reality, in the case of the Fulani at least, the effect of marriage is much more complicated than that. On the one hand, instead of channeling sexual impulses, so that they flower within limits defined as legitimate, marriage, in its beginnings, makes this flowering very difficult. Instead of being a honeymoon, in which the young people can satisfy their passion and begin to become a unit which will present a common front to others, this period in Fulani marriage prevents the couple from being together and, especially, prevents them from becoming a unit. On the other hand, the ease of divorce and the possibility of polygamy are a positive encouragement to men to be interested in other women. In the same way, this interest on the part of men is an encouragement to women to remain in a way available, whatever their matrimonial situation at the present (1977, p. 211).

Riesman criticizes the "sexual channeling" function of marriage identified and emphasized by Malinowski (1929). Malinowski assumed a universal function in marriage, based on his Trobriand data, which in effect focuses emotional and sexual feelings and behavior in one direction, on one person (in monogamous unions). Riesman also cites a statement made by Bohannan, that "marriage and the resultant family is, everywhere, one of the main modes by which sexual activity within the society is controlled" (1963, p. 83). Bohannan is aware, however, of periods of relative sexual freedom in various societies and of the nonfamilial institutionalization of sex, prostitution being the obvious example in our own society.

Work such as Riesman's indicates the mistake of studying sexuality exclusively within the context of marriage and the family for the Fulani case, and it warns against similar assumptions and oversights in work on other societies. Riesman may be aware, however, that Malinowski's focusing effect in marriage may still operate for Fulani women, if not the men. "Being available" and being free to have additional and various sexual partners are different.

Several anthropological reports indicate an important difference in the quality of sexual activity inside and outside of marriage. Gladwin's and Sarason's male Trukese informants say that "love for your wife is not the same as love for your sweetheart" (1953, p. 101). "Coitus with a mistress is said to be considerably more pleasurable than with a wife," is a similar report on the Mehinaku. In fact, Mehinaku men report to Gregor that they have intercourse with their mistresses four to five times more often than with their spouses (1973, p. 244).

Following in the tradition of Oscar Lewis, Rainwater (1971) compares marital sexuality in four "cultures of poverty," and finds a general axiom for each: "Sex is man's pleasure and woman's duty" (1971, p. 189). From the four lower-class systems studied (Puerto Rico, England, United States, Mexico), Rainwater concludes that the low value placed on compatibility and harmony in sexual relations is a function of the more general distance between men and women in the marital relationship (p. 198).

Victor Turner and Paul Riesman have approached the marital/extramarital sexual distinction in symbolic terms. In Africa, Turner finds a symbolic congruence between the color black and (female) sexual attractiveness: "Women with very black skins are said by Ndembu men to be very desirable as mistresses, though not as wives" (1967, p. 73). Riesman details the importance of place as well as of partner in the Fulani symbolic system:

> adultery always takes place in the bush and that only the sexual act of a married couple occurs in the *wuro* in the *suudu* of the woman. As a result, to the extent that women in their huts symbolize legitimate sexuality, hence the right to progeny, they are in fact a necessary cause of the dispersal of men (1977, p. 58).

Fulani symbolism would have to differ from peoples like the Baktaman of New Guinea (Barth, 1975) for whom marital sexual intercourse takes place in the forest near gardens, because of enforced sexual segregation at night. Yet in all these cases there is an unmistakable separation of marital sexuality from passionate sexuality.

What might account for the fact that men in so many societies find extramarital sex more attractive than marital sex? In Trukese marriage the joint interests of husband and wife are subordinate to the lineal ("kinship") commitment each spouse has to his or her own people. If a dispute should develop, a wife must side with her brothers, even if it means she must oppose her husband. Goodenough (1949) contrasts this with the basically exclusive and dyadic relationship between sweethearts. One of the ways that sweethearts are able to express their attraction for each other is through their willingness to run great risks in order to be together. In support of this, Mead offers a convincing example of the danger and risk in love-making in her description of *moetotolo*, "sleep crawling:" "As perhaps a dozen or more people and several dogs are sleeping in the house, a due regard for silence is sufficient precaution" (1928, p. 93).

Schieffelin (1976) explains the political nature of marital sexuality in his ethnography of the Kaluli of Papua/New Guinea. Only after a husband has begun having sexual relations with his new wife does he initiate presentations—in this case giving meat to his wife's relatives (p. 61). Schieffelin reports that this might not commence for as long as a month or two after marriage. The concurrence of (marital) sexuality and presentation suggests that wifely sexuality is part of what the husband is reciprocating. We are not told what, if any, effect this has on sexual performance in marriage, but we do know that it is certainly missing in sexual relations outside of marriage. This feature of apolitical sexual expression, coupled with the contingent opportunity to engage in a veiled but rebellious gesture against the marriage (or its politics), places extramarital sexual activity in the realm of an "intriguing lascivious achievement," rather than the merely foolish, to paraphrase the Dobuans (Fortune, 1932, p. 242).

Ideological issues are also important to our understanding of "alligatoring," a Mehinaku courtship technique in which a male suitor hides behind a female's house, waiting for her to appear so he can solicit sex (Gregor, 1977). As Gregor explains, "The term is a reference both to Mehinaku mythology, in which the alligator . . . is highly sexual, and to the animal's famous ability to lie motionless in wait for its quarry" (1977, p. 142). A Mehinaku male will have a set of "alligator spots" from which he can surreptitiously view a girlfriend's house and await her appearance. Upon making visual contact, sometimes with the aid of a lip-pursing call, the male will lead his friend down an "alligator path" which in turn leads to "alligator areas," where the couple hastily has sexual intercourse, usually in a standing position. The Mehinaku, it turns out, are strongly segregated by gender during the day. They work apart; they even have separate ceremonies, all of which enables "alligatoring" to work relatively smoothly.

If one assigns primacy to the social organizational component, the analysis goes something like this: the social organizational fact of segregation during the day allows, or contributes to, the phenomenon of "alligatoring" observed by Gregor. On the other hand, the approach through ideology recognizes the cultural structure underlying an individual Mehinaku's relationships to persons of the same and opposite sex, both in everyday and in "alligatoring" contexts. One is not social organization, the other "custom." Both are contexts in which ideology comes into play. This ideology, in turn, is predicated on cultural premises.

In many societies, ideas about sexuality assume more concrete form. In fact, the pronounced nature of sexuality in other societies has taken some anthropologists by surprise. For example, Harold Schneider writes of his work with the Turu, "I did not set out to study sexual behavior, but became acquainted with an important dimension of sexual roles in the normal course of a predominantly social anthropological study" (1971, p. 60). Schapera made much the same transition upon contacting the Kgatla: "I was continually struck by the open importance they attached to the sexual aspect" (1941, p. 180). In addition to these comments from Africa, the openness of sexuality has left impressions on researchers working in Polynesia, South America, the Caribbean, and Melanesia.

However, that which takes the ethnographer by surprise—sometimes requiring her or him to re-think the focus of a project—comes as no surprise to the native. "Alligatoring" makes sense to the Mehinaku. Sexual segregation at work and in ceremony makes sense to them too. It is this sense that the symbolic anthropologist hopes to reveal and understand. With this approach symbols are investigated as the basic building blocks of the ideological system. Symbols stand in relationships; they do not stand for something else.

Returning to the matter of Mehinaku extramarital sexual activity, we find that Gregor resorts to a Durkheimian notion of mechanical social cohesion in his explanation. Mehinaku affairs create relationships which keep the community together, though one wonders how. "Extramaritality," to coin a workable expression, is also an important basis of economic distribution, according to Gregor. Women receive "modest but regular amounts of fish throughout the year" if they are sexually active (1973, p. 246).

There is yet a third component in Gregor's analysis. Extramaritality engenders what Gregor calls an "underground kinship system," "wherein the relationships engendered by extra-marital affairs are performed discreetly so as not to embarass or anger the cuckolded spouses" (p. 257). Crocker, studying the Canela Indians of Brazil (1974), reports on an "underground kinship system" that goes one step beyond the Mehinaku system. The Canela (or at least the men) appear to speak to their "underground kinsmen," the consanguinal relatives of their "classificatory wives" or mistresses' with the appropriate affinal term of address. He will even refer to their children as "my children," and assume other aspects of the paternal role (1974, p. 190).

The Mehinaku and the Canela provide examples of systems in which the form of kinship relationships is extended to persons (and to persons related to persons, in the Canela case) understood to share paternity through sexual acts. In one case from Africa, however, the political dimension is constructed somewhat differently. Harold Schneider's analysis of *mbuya* ("lover," or "paramour") among the Turu of Tanzania argues that the Turu family organization is based on productive cooperation, not romantic love. Apparently the Turu have learned that the political dimension of marriage is complicated enough without adding to that burden the emotional peaks and valleys of romantic love. In short, Turu love and marriage do not go together. Marriage is a "lease of rights in a woman to her husband in return for bridewealth" (p. 67). A smart husband would hesitate to divorce a productive wife, so presumably the fact that they have romantic affairs outside of marriage is tolerated by the husbands. Wives show similar tolerance. Schneider argues that "this tenuous marriage . . . would be endangered by romantic love, with its ups and downs" (p. 67). Whether or not Schneider is correct, that is, if romantic love would indeed contribute serious instability in a basically political relationship, he has directed our attention to a group whose ideology places marital relationships (I hesitate to call them sexual) and extramarital sexual relationships in tension and opposition.

The opposition appears to be somewhat differently structured among the Mehinaku and Canela for whom it has been reported that "kinship" is extended through the possibility of "multiple paternity." For these people we probably will not find a sexual/political opposition as with the Turu; instead, they have achieved levels of kinship structure—the so-called underground and above-ground system of ratified kinsmen—that contribute to the tensions of social life. Although a Mehinaku or a Canela may have scores of kinsmen, groups of kinsmen are set off through an opposition between those who are related to ego through ego's mother's husband, and those whom ego knows to be related to him or her as partial fathers through their sexual activity with ego's mother during her pregnancy. Acknowledgement of this latter group of kinsmen, on the instructions of ego's mother, is a recognition of the multiple sexual relationships of the mother, in which case we can say that her sexuality contextualizes the child's social world.

This cultural structure contrasts with the ideological universe of the Turu, who live in two worlds, a body politic and a body sexual, as it were. The important point here is that sexual symbolism can form part of the structure of a bisected world, the other world being political (e.g. the Turu case), or it can provide an overarching structure in which ratified and surreptitious kinsmen are identified and opposed (e.g., Mehinaku, Canela). These two contrasting cases illustrate the insight into cultural systems possible when sexuality is studied within a framework of ideology, rather than separately.

ACTIVE AND PASSIVE SEXUALITY; HOMOSEXUALITY

The anthropological material on homosexuality is uneven and deficient by most disciplinary standards. We find ethnography to report homosexuality to be "common throughout Polynesia" (Suggs, 1966, p. 173), which contradicts Marshall's inability to find a trace of homosexuality on the Polynesian island of Mangaia (1971, p. 153). Gladwin and Sarason inquired about homosexuality on Truk and were met, first by puzzlement, then denial (1953, p. 115). Such findings can only weakly encourage cultural inquiry.

Many reports which discuss homosexuality at all treat it as an alternative to heterosexual intercourse, a second-best option used when women are scarce (e.g., Suggs, 1966, p. 83; Herskovits, 1938, p. 288; Evans-Pritchard, 1970, p. 1429; and Levy, 1973, p. 134). There are similar explanations of lesbianism as a "stopgap" when men are not around (e.g., Schapera, 1941, p. 183, and Evans-Pritchard, 1970, p. 1431). With regard to male homosexuality, one male Azande told Evans-Pritchard: "What man would prefer a boy to a woman? A man would be a fool to do so. The love of boys arose from lack of women" (1970, p. 1429).

Evans-Pritchard speculates that the custom of taking boy-wives arose from a combination of factors, especially a shortage of marriageable women, who were monopolized by rich noblemen able to maintain large harems through extravagant bridewealth payments. Kinsmen of boys who were taken as boy-wives were compensated with bridewealth. They assumed women's roles and did women's work in camp while their husbands were out fighting. Evans-Pritchard finds in all respects, "They were like wives. Their lovers did not approve of their laughing loud like men, they desired them to speak softly, as women speak" (1970, p. 1431).

Levy provides us with a comprehensive analysis of the *māhū*, the Tahitian male who assumes a female role. He may or may not engage in homosexual behavior (although Levy was unable to determine a definitive answer for this). The *māhū* in Levy's district (apparently each district has its *māhū*) generally wore standard male dress, although Levy came across a picture of him, prominently displayed in the *māhū*'s foster-mother's house, dressed in a girl's dancing costume. As a youngster he performed girl's duties, such as cleaning house, braiding palm leaves, and babysitting. His primary associations were with girls, with whom he would share gossip and walk arm-in-arm, something seen otherwise only among same-sexed adolescents.

When *māhūs* are engaged in homosexual acts, they are cast in the active role. Similarly, males emphasize their passive participation in their contact with *māhūs*. Levy's informants were well aware of the asymmetry in the relationship: "You just take it easy while he [the *māhū*] does it to you," and "you just don't take it seriously" (1973, p. 135). Tahitian men who have been "done" by *māhūs* report rather matter-of-factly to others that they have been fellated, much as they would recount any other sexual escapade. The standard story Levy heard was of a young man who had been drinking, and unable to find female companionship, settled for service by a *māhū* (p. 153).

In his discussion of sexual identity Levy develops the importance of the *māhū* role (pp. 232–39). In Tahiti there is relatively less sexual differentiation than the Westerner might expect. Gauguin observed this, describing Tahitian man as "androgynous," and remarking that "there is something virile in the women and something feminine in the men" (cited in Levy, 1973, p. 232).

Additional evidence of low sexual dimorphism in Tahiti comes from linguistic analysis. Levy describes Tahitian as a completely gender-free grammar. This means that pronouns do not carry semantic information about the sex of the person or object to which they refer. Levy reports that it is possible to listen to entire descriptions of interactions without knowing the gender of persons being discussed (p. 232).

Levy concludes that the *māhū* as a sexual partner is simply a "substitute woman" and "it is not a threat to the definition of a man's masculinity if he utilizes the substitution" (p. 235). Tahitian men will dance with men when there are no female partners, even getting unthreatening erections when they rub against one another. "We would laugh because our penises became stiff," Levy is told (p. 235).

Levy's claim that Tahitians subscribe to a "doctrine of sexual equality" (p. 236) can certainly be substantiated, but other important conclusions emanate from this work as well. The Tahitian self is not contingent on sexual dimorphisms—that is, on the presence of distinct "species" of persons, one male and one female—when compared with the importance of gender in the construction of the American self. Because of this, homophobic reactions are reduced to almost nothing, and homoeroticism is nonthreatening to the sense of self. The self is defined to be primarily erotic, with a healthy attraction to persons of the opposite sex but without the strong opposition to homosexual eroticism that Americans have.

Both American and Tahitian identities are largely sexual. However, American culture is motivated largely by an erotic field charged with an inherent and natural dimorphism, domination, and complementarity between two very different sexes. Tahitian culture may be thought to be eroticized by those elements believed to be shared by both sexes, though exclusive to neither. Both the American and Tahitian identities are responsive to the erotic elements in their cultures, but the former has an additional, countervailing, homoerotic force contributing to the shape of the self which is lacking in the latter.

There may be some confusion over Levy's comment that homosexuality is the covert part of the *māhū* role (p. 472), which sounds as though there were some social force preventing its expression at a more public level. Although some Tahitians do indeed disapprove of the *māhū* role, it does not follow that the sexual element of the role is covert because of community disapproval. Rather, it is important to realize that sexuality is the covert part of every role Tahitians engage in, with the possible exception of prostitution. Allowing that the *māhū* has undergone a role reversal, there is no reason to postulate an additional inversion of the overt/covert which apparently has nothing to do with the dynamic.

The asymmetry of the *māhū*-male relationship looms as something of a paradox, given the "doctrine of sexual equality" between the sexes. I think the passivity of the male engaged with a *māhū* is a function of his utilitarian relationship to the individual. The goal for the non-*māhū* is to achieve immediate sexual gratification, not to establish a relationship with the *māhū*, who provides a service, rather than a person. For the *māhū* the interaction has a different meaning, manifested primarily in performing fellatio. The *māhū* is the performer; the non-*māhū* is the erotically-stimulated audience. From this perspective the non-*māhū's* passivity can be understood as a distancing mechanism, not from homosexuality but from "active" participation in an activity. Furthermore, it is possible that the passivity of the non-*māhū* role is attractive to some non-*māhū* males who are unable to interact with women with the same detachment.

An additional definition of homosexual activity comes from American prisons, in which Spradley finds even homosexual relationships are defined in the idiom of hustling—a man "peddles his ass" to someone in jail in order to receive food and cigarettes (1970, p. 235). Here the peddler is not a homosexual though his activity is. The peddler acts not for erotic experience in itself, but as a means to an end.

EDUCATION, EXPLOITATION AND CULTURAL SYSTEMS

The amount and quality of sex education for children varies widely from society to society. At one extreme we find Dahomean girls who, under the supervision of instructresses, learn the "language of love" or "adultery," and later, the eleven positions of sexual intercourse (Herskovits, 1938, p. 281). The Irish girls of Inis Beag who are unprepared for and traumatized by their first menstrual period, occupy a place near the opposite extreme (Messenger, 1969, 1971).

Programs of formal or informal instruction are one measure of children's and adolescents' sexual knowledge. They also indicate the didactic and emotional relationship between generations and the relationship adults have to their own sexuality. Reports such as Schapera's for the Kgatla that "from an early age children are familiar with the nature of copulation" (1941, p. 180) suggest that these adults have a relaxed and direct relationship to their own sexuality. Wagley saw Tapirapé boys and girls imitating or "playing" at copulation in full view of adults who made no move to stop the children or reprimand them (1977, p. 145).

Trukese men's transition from adolescence to a fully adult male marital role is eased by legitimate sexual outlets (Goodenough, 1949). A man can sleep with his wife's sister or his brother's wife. Goodenough implies that men later in life are in fact faithful, but he does not demonstrate this. On the contrary, Goodenough found Trukese men's interests in sex "surprisingly like those of American adolescents, or of men working in lumber camps, or in the Army, or in other places where women are relatively unavailable . . . Indeed, what might be called adolescent behavior in this respect lasts in the case of men into the late twenties and early thirties" (1949, p. 616). Goodenough comes close to suggesting that Trukese men do not achieve a mature sexuality until relatively late in life, a suggestion that many other ethnographers might have wanted to make about other peoples but do not.

What is it that children, adolescents, and even adults are learning? Although explicit sexual "technique" is taught in some societies, everywhere people learn about relations, definitions, and contexts. Although Dahomean girls learn sexual technique, apparently in much detail, the girls of Inis Beag, caught by the surprise of their first menstruation, learn of the inherent weakness and imperfection of their own bodies. Adults could hardly provide a better lesson for these girls through formal instruction.

Mead has addressed the "educational" dimension of sexual knowledge in Samoa (1928). She laments that Samoan boys and girls do not interact with each other sufficiently "to give boys or girls the real appreciation of personality in members of the opposite sex" (p. 87). Mead recognizes that the Samoans' emphasis on sexual technique is advanced at the expense of a regard for relationships. For Samoans, "sex is an end in itself, rather than a means, something which is valued in itself, and deprecated inasmuch as it tends to bind one individual to another" (1928, p. 222). Samoans do not reserve sexuality for important relationships that produce sexual satisfaction. Perhaps it is correct to say that Samoans reserve sexuality for important occasions, rather than for important relationships, and that Samoans do not tend to value or especially appreciate relationships that produce sexual satisfaction. Apparently Samoans enjoy sex, but not the relationships in which sexuality is experienced, a finding which troubles Mead.

As Herskovits's Dahomean ethnography demonstrates, differential treatment of girls and boys vis-à-vis education and knowledge affects male-female relationships in later life. Unlike Dahomean girls with female instructors to teach them sexual knowledge and the specific techniques of intercourse, the boys have no such educational program. They seem to learn from the girls. One Dahomean man told Herskovits, "Among us Dahomeans it is always the woman who teaches the man" (1938, p. 282).

Dahomean girls are incompletely prepared for marriage; they need to be groomed, developed, and fulfilled in marriage by coupling with a male. Boys, on the other hand, are naturally designed and prepared for marriage, so it is thought. This leads to yet another question Herskovits might have asked of his data. If the girl has been educated, then will the responsibility for marriage failure be assigned to her, since, after all, she is the "educated" party?

The emphases on sexual technique found in Samoa and Dahomey, and the subordination of females to males in Dahomey and in so many other places, have analogues in American culture. Kemnitzer's analysis of American culture focuses on the development of the "new sexuality," a recent move toward liberalization and popularization of sexuality, primarily among young professionals and white-collar workers. Kemnitzer finds that persons who subscribe to the "new sexuality" regard sex as a domain unto itself; sexual performance is emphasized at the expense of other matters. By contrast, in mainstream American culture, the sex act is part of an essentially exploitative institution, marriage. Kemnitzer argues that the "new sexuality" maintains the old forms of social relations in a new guise, even though sexuality is no longer submerged in and encapsulated by broader social relations (e.g., husband-wife, boyfriend-girlfriend).

The argument follows Polyani, finding it necessary in capitalist societies to develop standards by which work can be valued. Sexual intercourse, for these people, is work, which can be judged on a performance scale, rating the degree of competence with which the actors execute their assigned duties. The uniqueness of the action is lost to the extent that the person is lost to the action. Sexual activity becomes, if you will, a labor of love; the world of work has invaded the world of home. As Kemnitzer points out, the technical expertise of the work place is a sorry substitute for the sensitivity and intersubjectivity associated with ideas of the home.

Kemnitzer represents his approach to the "problem" of modern sexuality as a contradiction in culture. This he contrasts with Rollo May's analysis (1969) which attributes "normal anxiety" to a confrontation between the cultural order and human psychic nature.

The paradigm through which May understands sexuality is a modified version of the standard popularization of the Freudian model of hostile opposition between instinctual needs and the repressive forces of culture (Freud, 1961, [orig. 1930]). Freud could trace the development of the anal erotic child into an anal retentive adult, an adult whose loss of happiness is commensurate with his or her heightened sense of guilt. If, as Freud asserts, it is the aim of civilization to bring individuals together in social units, it is at an unfortunate and often unhappy cost; the individual's aggressive and sexual impulses become frustrated in the process. Thus the struggle is on; primary, self-serving, egotistical drives are thwarted by culture, which is both an extension of the basic psychodynamic as well as its natural opposition.

Easily overlooked because of the wide acceptance of this model as the keystone of Freudian theory (which is essentially true to Freud), is the model of the dialectic which Freud saw at the level of culture itself. Less well developed in Freudian theory than the antagonistic relationship between instinct and culture, the dynamic of the cultural system as postulated by Freud in *Civilization and Its Discontents* (1930) will perhaps ultimately prove more important to anthropology than the former model, which has served long and well as the basic structural perspective for culture-and-personality study. Freud reports his astonishment when he realized that both human suf-

fering and its relief can be traced to the same system, which he termed civilization:

> we come upon a contention which is so astonishing that we must dwell upon it. This contention holds that what we call our civilization is largely responsible for our misery, and that we should be much happier if we gave it up and returned to primitive conditions. I call this contention astonishing because, in whatever way we may define the concept of civilization, it is a certain fact that all things with which we seek to protect ourselves against the threats that emanate from the sources of suffering are part of that very civilization (1961, p. 33).

I do not intend to diminish or rephrase the central argument of Freud's seminal book; he was indeed concerned with the tension between the individual and civilization. Specifically, Freud focused on the mechanics of the system by which civilization reflects the individual's aggressive and sexual instincts back onto the individual—processes which he called introjection and internalization—thus rendering aggression and sexuality innocuous, at least to the larger society. Freud thus concluded that civilization can persevere by establishing an agency, a sense of guilt, within the individual, "like a garrison in a conquered city" (1961, pp. 70–71).

Freud postulates a dynamic within a dynamic. There is the well known tension between individual and culture. Psychoanalysts will readily agree that there is this "garrison" creating tension and control within the individual. The passage that I have quoted at length suggests much the same dynamic operating at the cultural level. Culture, in Freud's view, is not a monolithic structure, forever bearing down on individuals and creating the complex structures we know as personalities.

Freud's culture is this, but it is also the solution to those pressures; it is the set of strategies we devise (consciously or unconsciously) to address our unhappiness. The contradiction is in culture; culture is both problematic and remedial. It is a symbolic unity which provides the domain for human action. That Freud envisioned it as a primarily unconscious and personally unknowable domain has prevented all but a few anthropologists from taking more than a fleeting look. The systemic, double-binding power of Freud's civilization anticipates and contributes to current advances in symbolic anthropology, understood somewhat paradoxically as a fundamentally non-Freudian development in cultural anthropology.

With the dialectics of the cultural symbolic and Freudian models in mind, we can return to the issue of "sex" education which began this section. Children learn the facts of life, sexual, and other, and ways of succeeding in that life. This may require tutelage in love songs, courtship techniques, and the like, as well as guidance in the general area of "personhood." The point is, they learn a structure for contemplating both problems and solutions; "education" in this sense is much more than a simple how-to-do-it course.

For example, Levy (1973) reports that he finds no impotence among Tahitian men. Within their total "education," these men have learned that a nonerect penis does not necessarily represent a failure in performance:

> The lack of reported impotence is partially due to the concept of the interrelations of the "self" and the sexual act. In a casual relationship, if a man starts to caress a woman and finds that he does not have an erection, he will decide that the woman is not attractive to him and make some excuse to avoid proceeding. This is not considered a failure, nor is it considered that in spite of this desire for intercourse he cannot perform. He simply concludes that he does not want to have intercourse (1973, p. 129).

The Tahitian man knows what to look for in a woman (much as he knows what not to look for in himself). An attractive woman should be clean, with smooth skin and hair and a pleasant smell (Levy, 1973, p. 129). During nonperformance, one of her attributes of attractiveness is deficient; it has nothing to do with his performance. The "solution" involves diagnosing a problem, determining a strategy, and managing a situation, all of which are in turn contingent upon the symbolic world in which Tahitians live. It is a sexual world, but like every world that anthropologists have investigated, it is a world of relationships and contexts.

CONCLUSION: THE ANTHROPOLOGY OF EROS

Anthropological awareness has not always been well served by precedents set by our intellectual ancestors. From Lewis Henry Morgan we received the option of studying family form instead of sexuality. Modern anthropologists can elect this option, even though they no longer subscribe to the unilinear evolutionary argument that the first is a transformed form of the second.

From Malinowski came a perspective which introduces into anthropology the notion that sexuality is equivalent to instinctual biological drive. Even though Malinowski ostensibly argued against a Freudian position which would give primacy to psychological over cultural systems, he accepted the Freudian view of sexuality. Consequently, Malinowski focused on cultural institutions which mediate between biological structure and sexual behavior; he did not consider sexuality as part of the symbolic structure of culture.

Similarly, Lowie's theorizing allowed the popular anthropological alternative to which economic and political considerations take precedence over erotic considerations in understanding cultural systems. Lowie's work emphasized these social elements of cultural form, without realizing that erotic considerations are inherently social and can, indeed must, contribute to investigations of cultural systems.

All together, Morgan's transformation of sexuality, Malinowski's institutionalization of sexuality, and Lowie's analytic substitution for sexuality, have contributed to a trend in anthropology away from the study of ideas about sexuality as they operate in larger cultural systems.

Despite this trend, there is a growing body of ethnography which takes a cultural approach to sexuality. The ethnological goal becomes one of comparing entire cultural systems, rather than behavioral facts regarding sexuality. This requires more than documenting the richness of sexual life in certain societies (although such documentation was a necessary contribution to anthropology in its infancy); it requires analysis of cultural systems which alternatively do and do not delineate sexuality as an organizing construct of independent status. One hopes that anthropological accounts will be consulted in the future, by anthropologists and nonanthropologists alike, not only for their wealth in accurate and detailed accounts of sexual behavior, but also because they advance our knowledge of people, including ourselves, as cultural thinkers and actors.

REFERENCES

ALTSCHULER, M. 1971. Cayapa personality and sexual motivation. In *Human sexual behavior*, ed. D. S. Marshall and R. C. Suggs, pp. 38–58. New York: Basic Books.

BAILEY, F. L. 1950. Some sex beliefs and practices in a Navaho community. *Papers of the Peabody Museum of American Archaeology*. Cambridge, Mass.: Peabody Museum.

BARTH, F. 1975. *Ritual and knowledge among the Baktaman of New Guinea*. New Haven: Yale University Press.

BATESON, G. 1972. *Steps to an ecology of mind*. New York: Ballantine Books.

BEAGLEHOLE, E., and BEAGLEHOLE, P. 1941. *Pangai, village in Tonga*. Wellington, N. Z.: The Polynesian Society.

BELO, J. 1935. A study of customs pertaining to twins in Bali. *Tijdschrift voor Indische Taal-, Land- en Volkenkunde* 75: 483–549.

BERNDT, R. M. 1962. *Excess and restraint: social control among a New Guinea mountain people*. Chicago: University of Chicago Press.

———, and BERNDT, C. H. 1951. *Sexual behavior in western Arnhem land*. New York: Viking Fund.

BOHANNAN, P. 1963. *Social anthropology*. New York: Holt, Rinehart & Winston.

CARROLL, V. n.d. "Rape" on Nukuoro. Unpublished ms.

CHAGNON, N. A. 1977. *Yanamamö*. 2d ed. New York: Holt, Rinehart & Winston.

CROCKER, W. H. 1974. Extramarital sexual practices of the Ramokomekra-Canela Indians: an analysis of socio-cultural factors. In *Native South Americans*, ed. P. J. Lyon, pp. 184–95. Boston: Little, Brown.

DOLGIN, J. L.; KEMNITZER, D. S.; and SCHNEIDER, D. M. (eds.) 1977. *Symbolic anthropology*. New York: Columbia University Press.

DOUGHERTY, M. C. 1978. *Becoming a woman in rural black culture*. New York: Holt, Rinehart & Winston.

DuBOIS, C. 1944. *The people of Alor*. Minneapolis: University of Minnesota Press.

EVANS-PRITCHARD, E. E. 1970. Sexual inversion among the Azande. *American Anthropologist* 72: 1428–34.

———. 1973. Some notes on Zande sex habits. *American Anthropologist* 75: 171–75.

FIRTH, R. 1957. *We, the Tikopia*. 2d ed. Boston: Beacon Press.

FORTUNE, R. F. 1932. *Sorcerers of Dobu*. New York: E. P. Dutton.

FOX, R. 1967. *Kinship and marriage*. Harmondsworth, Middlesex, England: Penguin Books.

FREEMAN, S. T. 1970. *Neighbors: the social contract in a Castilian hamlet*. Chicago, University of Chicago Press.

FREUD, S. 1961. *Civilization and its discontents*, trans. and ed. J. Strachey. New York: W. W. Norton.

GAGNON, J. H., and SIMON, W. 1973. *Sexual conduct, the social sources of human sexuality*. Chicago: Aldine.

GLADWIN, T., and SARASON, S. B. 1953. *Truk: man in paradise*. New York: Wenner Gren.

GOODENOUGH, W. H. 1949. Premarital freedom on Truk: theory and practice. *American Anthropologist* 51: 615–20.

GREGOR, T. 1977. *Mehinaku, the drama of daily life in a Brazilian Indian village.* Chicago: University of Chicago Press.

———. 1973. Privacy and extra-marital affairs in a tropical forest community. In *Peoples and cultures of native South America,* ed. D. R. Gross, pp. 242–60. Garden City, N. Y.: Doubleday.

HANSON, F. A. 1970. *Rapan lifeways, society and history on a Polynesian island.* Boston: Little, Brown.

HEIDER, K. G. 1976. Dani sexuality: a low energy system. *Man* (N.S.) 11: 188–201.

HERSKOVITS, M. J. 1938. *Dahomey, an ancient West African kingdom,* vol. 1. New York: J. J. Augustin.

HOCKINGS, P. In press. *Sex and disease in a mountain community.* New Delhi, India: Vikas.

JONES, E. 1925. Mother-right and the sexual ignorance of savages. *International Journal of Psycho-Analysis* 6: 109–30.

KARDINER, A. 1939. *The individual and his society: the psychodynamics of primitive social organization.* New York: Columbia University Press.

KELLY, R. 1974. *Etoro social structure.* Ann Arbor: University of Michigan Press.

KEMNITZER, D. S. 1977. Sexuality as a social form: performance and anxiety in America. In *Symbolic Anthropology,* ed. J. L. Dolgin, D. S. Kemnitzer and D. M. Schneider. New York: Columbia University Press.

LAUBSCHER, J. F. 1937. *Sex, custom & psychopathology.* London: Routledge.

LEVY, R. I. 1973. *Tahitians, mind and experience in the Society Islands.* Chicago: University of Chicago Press.

LINTON, R. 1939. Marquesan culture. In *The individual and his society: the psychodynamics of primitive social organization,* ed. A. Kardiner, pp. 137–96. New York: Columbia University Press.

LOWIE, R. H. 1970. *Primitive society.* New York: Liveright.

MALINOWSKI, B. 1926. *Crime and custom in savage society.* London: Routledge & Kegan Paul.

———. 1927. *Sex and repression in savage society.* Cleveland: World Publishing.

———. 1929. *The sexual life of savages.* New York: Harcourt, Brace & World.

MARSHALL, D. S. 1971. Sexual behavior on Mangaia. In *Human sexual behavior,* ed. D. S. Marshall and R. C. Suggs, pp. 103–62. New York: Basic Books.

———, and SUGGS, R. C., ed. *Human sexual behavior.* New York: Basic Books.

MAY, R. 1969. *Love and will.* New York: W. W. Norton.

MEAD, M. 1928. *Coming of age in Samoa.* New York: William Morrow.

———. 1949. *Male and female.* New York: William Morrow.

MERRIAM, A. P. 1971. Aspects of sexual behavior among the Bala (Basongye). In *Human sexual behavior,* ed. D. S. Marshall and R. C. Suggs, pp. 71–102. New York: Basic Books.

MESSENGER, J. C. 1969. *Inis Beag, isle of Ireland.* New York: Holt, Rinehart & Winston.

———. 1971. Sex and repression in an Irish folk community. In *Human sexual behavior,* ed. D. S. Marshall and R. C. Suggs, pp. 3–37. New York: Basic Books.

MORGAN, L. H. 1878. *Ancient society.* New York: Henry Holt.

MURPHY, R. F. 1967. Tuareg kinship. *American Anthropologist* 69: 163–70.

PONTIUS, A. 1977. Dani sexuality. *Man* (N.S.) 12: 166–67.

RAINWATER, L. 1971. Marital sexuality in four "cultures of poverty." In *Human sexual behavior,* ed. D. S. Marshall and R. C. Suggs, pp. 187–205. New York: Basic Books.

READ, K. E. 1965. *The high valley.* New York: Charles Scribner's Sons.

RIESMAN, P. 1977. *Freedom in Fulani social life,*

an introspective ethnography. Chicago: University of Chicago Press.

SCHAPERA, I. 1941. *Married life in an African tribe.* New York: Sheridan House.

SCHIEFFELIN, E. L. 1976. *The sorrow of the lonely and the burning of the dancers.* New York: St. Martin's Press.

SCHNEIDER, D. M. 1968. Abortion and depopulation on a Pacific island. In *Peoples and cultures of the Pacific,* ed. A. P. Vayda. Garden City, N. Y.: Natural History Press.

———. 1968. *American kinship: a cultural account.* Englewood Cliffs, N. J.: Prentice-Hall.

———. 1969. Kinship, nationality, and religion in American culture: toward a definition of kinship. In *Forms of symbolic action,* ed. V. Turner, pp. 116–25. New Orleans: American Ethnological Society.

SCHNEIDER, H. K. 1971. Romantic love among the Turu. In *Human sexual behavior,* ed. D. S. Marshall and R. C. Suggs, pp. 59–70. New York: Basic Books.

SELBY, H. A. 1974. *Zapotec deviance.* Austin: University of Texas Press.

SPRADLEY, J. T. 1970. *You owe yourself a drunk: an ethnography of urban nomads.* Boston: Little, Brown.

SUGGS, R. C. 1966. *Marquesan sexual behavior.* New York: Harcourt, Brace & World.

———. 1971. Sex and personality in the Marquesas. In *Human sexual behavior,* ed. D. S. Marshall and R. C. Suggs, pp. 163–86. New York: Basic Books.

TURNBULL, C. 1972. *The mountain people.* New York: Simon & Schuster.

TURNER, V. 1967. *The forest of symbols.* Ithaca, N.Y.: Cornell University Press.

VAYDA, A. P. 1961. Love in Polynesian atolls. *Man* 61: 204–205.

WAGLEY, C. 1977. *Welcome of tears, the Tapirapé Indians of Central Brazil.* New York: Oxford University Press.

TEN

Sex, Power,
and
Human Relations

BENJAMIN B. WOLMAN

The fear of enemies and the need for allies seems to be a valid reason for hostile and friendly feelings. In the past and in the present, the male-female relationship has been both economic cooperation and sexual attraction, but the dynamics of this relationship have been influenced greatly by the relative power positions of the sexes, their display of force, domineering, dependence, aggression, alliance, and occasional tenderness. There is little if any evidence for the Upanishad myth quoted by Freud in *Beyond the Pleasure Principle:*

> The first human being on earth, Atman, felt no delight. Therefore a man who is lonely feels no delight. He wished for a second. He was so large as man and wife together. He then made this his Self to fall in two, and hence arose husband and wife. Therefore Yagnavalkya said: "We two are thus (each of us) like half a shell! Therefore, the void which was there, is filled by the wife" (Freud, 1920, p. 58).

Neither biology nor anthropology confirm such a complementarity, though there is no reason to exclude the possibility that some men and some women may relate to one another in such a manner. Moreover, according to the Indian myth, it was the man Atman who needed a companion, thus male superiority was assumed.

The Hebrew myth of Adam and Eve also sounds like a man-made story. The Bible states that Adam was created first, despite the obvious fact that all men were borne by women. Eve was a part of his body. Medieval Christian philosophers argued that women have no soul, for the Old Testament conveniently does not say that the good Lord gave a soul to Eve; Adam was the sole recipient of the anima. When the Lord expelled Adam and Eve from the Garden of Eden, He told Eve "He shalt rule over thee." Apparently, poor Adam could not assert himself without the Lord's help, and since that time all religions have perpetuated the idea of male supremacy.

It was Freud who observed:

> From the earliest times it was the muscular strength which decided who owned things or whose will shall prevail. Muscular strength was soon supplemented by the use of tools; the winner was the one who had the better weapons or who used them more skillfully. From the moment at which weapons were introduced, intellectual superiority already began to replace brute muscular strength; but the first purpose of the fight remained the same (1932, pp. 272–75).

With rather infrequent exceptions described by Evans-Pritchard (1967), Mead (1949), Murdock (1949), and others, as far back as human history goes, men have always subjugated women. Women were treated as pieces of live property, taken by force or purchased, used or abused. In the underpopulated areas of the ancient world, women were badly needed producers of offspring. The brave Roman males raped Sabinian women and held the *ius vitae necisque* law (the right of life and death) over their women and children. In ancient Hebrew the word *baal* stands for both the owner and the husband, for the Biblical men bought their wives.

The fact that survival has always been the main preoccupation of mankind explains many aspects of the male-female relationship. Hunting and fighting against other human beings required maximum physical strength. It is small wonder that many ancient tribes killed weak, sickly, and deformed neonates, and in many instances eliminated the old and infirm. It has been proved by historical and anthropological studies that men assumed or usurped leadership roles in primitive societies whenever physical prowess was the most important factor in the struggle for survival.

In the struggle for survival female fertility was almost as important as plowing or hunting or fighting. In a primitive economy based on the number of working hands, one's wealth largely depended on the number of children one had. Needing labor power, the production of children was fundamental to the economy. With the advent of mass-slavery during the decline of the Roman Empire, the size of the family shrank and the incidence of homosexuality rose sharply.

In earlier times, in the shepherd-ing and early farming economies, having children was one of the most productive aspects of an economy. In the poorly populated lands, only those who had many children had enough workers to tend the herds, till the soil, and fight off the neighbors. According to the Bible, the Lord promised Abraham that his progeny (the Chosen People) would be as numerous as the stars in the sky and the sand on the seashore. Today this would be a mixed blessing.

BIOLOGICAL CONSIDERATIONS

There are clear biological differences in the role men and women play in the process of re-production. A woman can produce ten to twenty children in her lifetime, but hardly any woman can provide adequate care for all her children. A man can fertilize several women and if he impregnates a large number of women, he can produce an army. Thus polygamy was not determined by male superiority or other alleged differences between the mentality of men and women, but mainly by the difference in their respective roles in the reproductive process. Moreover, mothers and expectant mothers necessarily depend on their male partners for food and protection against enemies. So the subjugation of women by men was not a product of psychological differences, but rather a product of a particular socioeconomic system in which physical force was at a premium and child-bearing women could not provide food and shelter for themselves and their offspring.

Power thus became the symbol of masculinity, and prophets and poets praised the virtues of being a male. The Latin word *virtus* (virtue) is derived from *vir* meaning man. The Hebrew *gibbor* (hero) and *g'vurah* (courage) are derivatives of *gever* (male). In practically all languages *homo* (human being) is synonymous with an adult male. Wisdom, courage, leadership, and responsibility have been ascribed to men, despite the obvious fact that such a generalization flies in the face of evidence. Rationalization (distortion of reality in defense of self-esteem) is probably older than rational thinking, and cowardly, sheepish, submissive, and stupid men by far outnumber the brave, leading, self-assured, and wise men.

The innumerable cases of heroic women have been understated, partly silenced and often totally denied by male-dominated historiography. The very same virtues praised in men were discouraged and ridiculed in women: brave, aggressive, and wise women were branded as being pushy, arrogant, competitive, and therefore unfeminine. Cowardly men have been ridiculed as being "feminine," and brave women have been ostrasized for being "masculine." The owners of slaves have always preferred submissive, subservient, and dull slaves (Wolman, 1974; 1978).

THE PHALLUS—THE SYMBOL OF POWER

The male sexual organ is the most obvious sign of masculinity. Besides being a source of sensual pleasure comparable to the tongue and palate, the erected penis has become a symbol of masculine power. Although penises have never played any significant role in the struggle for survival, they have enjoyed a unique status related to the feeling of power. The so-called virility, he-man feeling, male pride, and other terms referring to the man's ability to sleep with women and produce children have been glorified as most spectacular symbols of power. It is small wonder that men took such a pride in this child-producing tool. One may doubt whether male dogs, horses, bulls, and apes derive much pride from their mounting, inserting, and copulating proficiency, but human males, thanks to their ability for symbolic thinking, have accepted the penis and its potency as symbols of power, courage, health, and creativity. Such a correspondence has never been proved (Mead, 1949).

In its earliest gloomy, hungry, and danger-fraught origins, the human species had good reasons for fostering the myth of male pride and male supremacy. Eunuchs, impotents, and sexually passive males were ridiculed and ostrasized, because they were of little help to their tribe which badly needed the speedy and abundant production of workers and warriors. Troubadours and poets described the hero who fought bravely against enemies and conquered (that is, fertilized) many women. Sexual achievements were praised for economic and military reasons, and many primitive religions adored the Gods-Fathers with erected penises ready for action.

BRAINWASHING

The ancient Romans knew that they could defeat their enemies in combat, but they could not rule them by sheer force. Male domination also has always depended on brainwashing female slaves. Men, the *Herrenvolk,* have for millenia enjoyed all freedoms, especially sexual freedom. In peace or at war men felt free to "conquer" (physically) any woman they could find, but women were supposed to be faithful to their permanent or temporary users. Promiscuity in men was hailed as a virtue and a sign of virility. Poets and troubadours glorified the splendid conquests of Don Juans, and every king and ruler was surrounded by a host of courtesans and ladies-in-waiting.

Women were not only subjugated but also brainwashed into a docile acceptance of their subordinated role. They were told that to be feminine meant not to compete with men in intelligence, industry, initiative, maturity, and courage. The "ideal woman" as prescribed by men was supposed to represent a strange mix-

ture of infant and mother. When men were in one of their artificially fanned domineering or heroic moods, their women were expected to be as soft, gentle, submissive, and obedient as infants. When men were tired, defeated and hurt, their women were expected to be sympathetic, affectionate, soothing, ever-present and ever-caring mothers.

This brainwashing encompassed every aspect of a girl's life from cradle to grave. A little girl was told she must not act in the free, self-expressive manner as her brothers did. As she was growing up, the male-controlled educational systems trained her for her future role as the man's toy and joy, or nurse and caretaker. She was not allowed to express her own desires and ambitions, and her thinking was as constricted as the toes of Chinese girls; obviously the ruling class of men feared that free-thinking and ambitious slaves might rebel and run away.

Woe to the woman who dared to express sexual desires! Pious medieval monks who secretly masturbated, invented perversely sadistic tortures for "women-witches" who were believed to have slept with Satan himself. The famous "Malleus" (The Witches' Hammer) is an infamous historical document of masculine perversions, combined with pornography, perversions, and saintly rationalizations.

PENIS ENVY: FACT OF ARTIFACT?

In Freud's prudish and bigoted Vienna, many a little girl wished she were a boy, for this was the only, though imaginary, way of escaping discrimination. Young men could do whatever they pleased and choose an occupation they liked, but girls were their father's possession until he agreed to transfer them to their future husbands. Marriage was, therefore, the only way of escape from the father's tyranny, but the marital oath committed women to love, cherish, and obey their new masters. Most women preferred new masters to old ones, and some of them slyly outsmarted their marital bosses.

In the Victorian era, marriage was the only

acceptable social role for women. Unmarried women were called "spinsters." They were ridiculed and blamed for remaining single. When a girl preferred an active and independent life, she was called a "tomboy," "amazon," or monstrosity. To be feminine meant to become a hybrid of infantile dependence and motherly protectiveness. Women were expected to practice and enjoy the three great "feminine" K's— *Küche, Kirche, Kinder* (kitchen, church, and children).

In Freud's time masculinity and femininity could have been described as follows:

> When you say 'masculine' you mean as a rule 'active,' and when you say 'feminine' you mean passive. . . . The male sexual cell is active and mobile; it seeks out the female one, while the latter is stationary and waits passively. This behavior of the elementary organism of sex is more or less a model of the behavior of the individuals of each sex in sexual intercourse. The male pursues the female for the purpose of sexual unity, seizes her and pushes his way into her (Freud, 1932, p. 156).

Freud did not invent penis envy but discovered this culturally determined phenomenon. The more restrictions were imposed on girls, the more frequently they wished to escape their yoke.

Penis envy was never a general feeling common to all women at all times; certainly the Tschambuli or Arapesh women never had the reason for such an envy. In Arapesh, men and women shared household and child-rearing responsibilities, and among the Tschambuli, women were the dominant sex. (Murdock, 1949)

Freud's observations of penis envy in women who were reared in an atmosphere of discrimination and subjugation must be interpreted in light of another hypothesis brought forward by Freud, namely, the tendency of the child to identify with the "strong aggressor." In patriarchal families, the father was the absolute ruler, and the male and female children were proud to identify with the father rather than with the mother. It is small wonder that

Freud noticed the preference for a masculine, father-based superego (Fenichel, 1945; Freud, 1938).

One therefore must interpret penis envy in girls not as an envy directed to the male organ of their playmates or brothers, but rather as a wish for the possesssion of the father's penis and with it, father power. Penis envy does not seem to be a general and universal element of female psychology but must be interpreted as the feminine protest against male domination. The penis, as a cherished symbol of power, was envied by women not because of its sexual significance, for vaginas undoubtedly can procure as much and often more sensual pleasure than penises; it was the penis as the power symbol which elicited the justifiable envy (Horney 1950; Kelman, 1967; Millet, 1970; Unger and Denmark, 1975).

THE MOTHER-WHORE COMPLEX

One can easily understand the socioeconomic reasons for the subjugation of women in the past and explain their current rebellion in terms of technological development. There is, however, an important aspect of the male-female relationship which defies such an interpretation, namely, the mother-whore complex, that is, the idealization and debasement of women by men.

The reasons for this ambivalent attitude go beyond the economic exigency.

All men, whether they like it or not, were carried and fed by women through the periods of conception, pregnancy, birth, infancy, and many years thereafter. Not all men resent this fact, and what will be said below concerning the mother-whore complex is not a generalization.

To every human being, male and female alike, the mother is the prototype of a friendly power. The mother is the main if not the only source of life and bulwark of survival. The adoration of the mother is ontogenetically typical in all infants and phylogenetically typical in periods of oppression and despair. The adoration of the Holy Mother is a case in point.

One seeks support of a friendly power as

long as one feels weak and expects to receive unconditional support, but such an ideal relationship may not last long. Infants "love" the "good" mother who unconditionally satisfies their wishes, but they hate the same mother when she refuses to meet their demands. Ambivalent feelings toward powerful protectors are an inevitable product of dependence, and they often carry the seeds of a rebellion against weakness and dependency. Welfare recipients do not waste love on their benefactors, and poor relatives often resent their wealthy supporters.

The ambivalent feeling toward the mother is shared by little boys and little girls, and this attitude has been perpetuated throughout generations taking on various forms and shapes. Rarely if ever can a woman resolve completely her antimother feelings. In Freud's times, it was acceptable for young women to direct hatred toward their mothers-in-law. Freud interpreted this phenomenon as a residue of the castration complex; be it, as he wrote, the symbolic loss of a penis representing a loss of power and of the privileged male status.

Boys' ambivalent feelings toward their mother often have been channeled into the "mother-whore" complex. Even most cowardly and ineffectual men can play the role of a strong man and discharge brute force toward someone weaker than themselves. Women were the choice target, and male-controlled public opinion has been and perhaps still is in favor of "masculine assertion" towards women and children (Wolman, 1975).

The possession of a penis has given the men an additional tool for the humiliation of women and for self-aggrandizement. The sexual act as such is neither beautiful nor ugly and, like almost everything else in human life, it can be performed in either lofty or base manner. However, the allegedly aggressive and domineering sexual insertion was often represented as a way of debasing women.

Discrimination against women follows the same rationale as any other discriminatory behavior. All those who descriminate, abuse their power against some people, and they usually choose their targets carefully. The history of humanity, with its conflicts, clashes, international wars, and fratricidal murders, shows that people discriminate against and persecute only those who cannot defend themselves. In the time of the Crusades, Christian nations fought Moslem nations, and the Crusaders, on their way to the Holy Land, persecuted the Jews. The Turks had a great many wars with other nations, but they discriminated against the Greeks and Armenians. Persecution is a particular type of hostility related not to competition and fighting among equals, but related to the desire to destroy those who can be destroyed easily. There was never persecution of majority groups, of powerful individuals, or of strong political organizations. The persecution was always directed against those who could be easily and safely persecuted. In the United States not the WASPS but the Blacks were persecuted. In Europe not the Protestants but the Jews were persecuted.

The fact that somebody is powerful does not protect him or her against hostility. People can love and hate each other; nationalities and organizations can fight one another. But persecution always has been directed toward those who cannot fight back. Defenseless victims, scapegoats, and innocent bystanders are easy targets for discrimination and persecution.

Whoever intends to deal realistically with discrimination against women must be aware that in most instances those who discriminate try to overcome their inferiority feelings not by fighting their equals but by an unfair use of power against those who cannot defend themselves. There is another issue which is no less important and certainly more realistic: defenseless people invite persecution. Weakness invites discrimination, and those who cannot defend themselves are easy targets for prejudiced people and oppressors. The increasing rate of crime against children in our times is perhaps one of the signs of our *Zeitgeist*, when so many people suffer from feelings of inadequacy and lack of purpose; they act out their phony superiority feelings against innocent children. A great many children have been beaten and tortured by irresponsible, drunken, and drug-addicted individuals, many of them parents of the victims. The abuse of children is largely determined by the fact that they cannot defend themselves.

CHANGING SOCIAL ROLES

The industrial revolution pulled out thousands of women from behind the hearth and crib and forced them into the labor markets of the budding capitalist economy. Women's participation in national economy has changed their social roles. The privileged role of provider which was the backbone of the traditional, male-dominated family structure, began to crack, and currently it is heading toward an unprecedented crisis (Ackerman, 1958).

The erosion of the traditional male-female relationship took place first in the lowest and then in the highest social classes. The middle classes have been the notorious bulwark of conservatism, and Freud's patients came from highly conservative, middle-class families in which fathers exercised absolute power and penis envy was probably an almost general phenomenon among Freud's female patients.

The current family constellation has deprived the father of his authority but has not replaced it by any other. One cannot help wondering what is going to happen in our times to the Oedipus complex, latency period, and the whole area of male-female relationships. Modern women have destroyed the myth of their intellectual inferiority and denied, in vivo, the assumption of either cherub or witch personality (Wolman, 1974; 1975).

THE MALE-FEMALE CONTEST OF POWER

Not all men love women, nor do all men hate them, nor does the one attitude exclude the other. There has been a good deal of speculation and little factual knowledge concerning the characteristics of the two sexes and their interaction, though this area of behavior is secondary in importance to bread-winning behavior only. From the inception of sexual reproduction, that is since females began to bear children, the child-versus-mother relationship has been the first social and emotional experience in everyone's life. The first prenatal impressions are intrauterine: the first serious shock of separation is childbirth; the first sensations of hunger, thirst, satiation, comfort, warmth, and security are experienced in the context of child-mother relationships. But the respective parent roles are changing rapidly, and these changes must have affected the personalities of the offspring.

These sociological changes in family dynamics have produced new psychological phenomena. The neonates need today, as never before, tender love and care, and their feelings of security (and power) depend on being accepted by the parents. Today's toddlers and preschool children fear their fathers much less than the previous generations did. Rarely does a mother threaten the child with "telling on him" to the father; in a great many contemporary families maternal authority has become equal to or greater than the paternal.

It is therefore not surprising that breast envy has become a phenomenon. Some of my male patients have had dreams indicating their wish to be a woman. In some dreams the breasts have appeared as a cherished possession, and the confusion of penis and breast has been quite frequent.

On the basis of my clinical observations, I venture to hypothesize that neither men nor women can completely resolve their Oedipal involvements, whether the positive ones (with the parent of the opposite sex) or the negative (with the parent of the same sex). Some residuum of the "first love" for the parent or the parent substitute seems to remain forever in almost all people.

Although there is a good deal of evidence for the universality of the Oedipal involvement (though it is necessarily different in different cultures), one may doubt the universality of penis envy. In over twenty-five years of clinical practice in this country, I have had a great many women patients. Going through my case reports, I noticed that the penis envy was more frequent among the older generation, brought up in traditional father-controlled families with clear male supremacy, than in the younger generation of women brought up in families with tenuous or nonexistent father supremacy. Freud's observation of identification with the stronger parental figure seems to have been corroborated by my cases.

The male wish to be a woman was noticed by a few psychoanalysts a long time ago. Some men who are not homosexual at all, identify with their mothers and later with their girlfriends. In some cases, feminine men deny that becoming a girl may mean the loss of the penis, and they emphasize that they actually do have a penis, but they act as if they were girls clearly identifying themselves with the powerful mother.

This gradually increasing incidence of breast envy requires further analysis in a sociocultural perspective. It seems that many ideas, theories, and even empirical studies have been influenced by the sociocultural setting. For instance, Terman and Miles found in 1936 that men are self-assertive and aggressive while women are compassionate and sympathetic. But these were the ideas of the thirties. Today, several studies indicate that aggressiveness is not limited to one sex only. Women emerge not as infants or mothers or both, but as people displaying as many diversified personality types as the other sex does (Wolman, 1978).

COLONIALISM OR ALLIANCE?

Self-assertion of women and their distinct gains in economic, political, and cultural life combined with sexual freedom have undermined the foundations of the traditional marriage and family. A great many people experiment with various forms of male-female coexistence ranging from permanent singlehood to various forms of cohabitation, trial marriage, and group marriage.

It is impossible at the present time to predict the future of male-female relationships. One thing is obvious: the traditional subjugation of women in marriage which so closely resembled colonialism is dead. One may project a type of relationship based on a reevaluation of the distinct roles of males and females. Most probably the differences between men and women in economic, political, and cultural life will disappear as women enter all areas of life hitherto monopolized by men. With the growing self-respect and mutual respect of men and women, the one-to-one relationship may prevail, for no man and no woman would accept a subservient role. This new type of relationship based on equal rights and equal expectations will resemble an alliance of two independent countries. Each country is free to lead its own life and follow its own interests, but at the same time each pledges full support to the well-being of its ally. Instead of the old contest of power within the colonial government that tries to exploit the colony, and the efforts of the colonial people to rebel against or to outsmart their rulers, a new relationship may evolve based on genuine friendship and cooperation.

The women's movement against discrimination must encompass all aspects of life, such as the upbringing of children, equal opportunities in education, and equal rights in sexual life. So far only men have enjoyed sexual freedom because, biologically speaking, men are in a privileged position. When a man and a woman have sexual relations, only one of them can become pregnant. The pill must be regarded, therefore, as a major step toward equal rights for all human beings paving the road toward a new era in human relations between men and women. If one of them transgresses these rights, this entitles the other person to transgress them, too. Usually, when people have a strong affection and respect for each other, they prefer to stay away from other involvements, and they keep their relationship clean and honest. Honesty is a two-way street and must be binding on both sides. The double standard is a remnant of the past era when women were enslaved to men. The new era of equal rights for both sexes must be based on genuine equal rights and equal respect for each other.

One need not, however, be naive and expect an era of perfect love and ideal relationships. Human beings compete with one another, and they often are involved in contests of power. This contest of power among various groups frequently includes the male-female relationship. Cooperation and competition are fundamental aspects of social life, and it would be impossible to exclude the male-female relationship from all other social patterns of interaction. But competition and cooperation are not discrimination.

REFERENCES

ACKERMAN, N. W. 1958. *The psychodynamics of family life.* New York: Basic Books.

EVANS-PRITCHARD, E. E. 1965. *The position of women in primitive societies.* New York: Free Press.

FENICHEL, O. 1945. *Psychoanalytic theory of neurosis.* New York: Norton.

FREUD, S. 1920. *Beyond the pleasure principle. Standard Edition,* vol. 18, pp. 7–64.

FREUD, S. 1933. *New introductory lectures on psychoanalysis.* New York: Norton.

FREUD, S. 1939. *An outline of psychoanalysis.* New York: Norton.

HORNEY, K. 1950. *Neurosis and human growth.* New York: Norton.

KELMAN, H., 1967. *Feminine psychology.* New York: Norton.

MEAD, M. 1949. *Male and female.* New York: Morrow.

MILLETT, K. 1970. *Sexual politics.* New York: Doubleday.

MURDOCK, G. 1949. *Social structure.* New York: Macmillan.

UNGER, R. K., and DENMARK, F., eds. 1975. *Woman: dependent or independent variable?* New York: Psychological Dimensions.

WOLMAN, B. B. 1974. On men who discriminate against women. *International Journal of Group Tensions* 4: 45–52.

WOLMAN, B. B. 1975. Between men and women. *Woman: dependent or independent variable?* ed. R. K. Unger and F. Denmark, pp. *able?* New York: Psychological Dimensions.

WOLMAN, B. B. 1978. Psychology of women. In *Psychological aspects of gynecology and obstetrics,* ed. B. B. Wolman. Oradell, N.J.: Medical Economics.

ELEVEN

Sex
and
The Law

JANET L. DOLGIN

BARBARA L. DOLGIN

The study of "sex" and the "law" immediately taps a Pandora's box of social, philosophical, and political conundrums.[1] Merely providing preliminary definitions of the two terms may not adequately delineate the domain of study. Indeed, each concept compels the analyst to consider a world of discourse and of human interaction.

"Law," when restricted in its connotations to those entailing legal forms and systems can be at least minimally demarcated for analysis. Yet even when "law" is reified as an explicitly enacted or habitual set of rules for behavior, its conceptions will vary. (On one level, of course, it is that very variation which strengthens the processes of American jurisprudence.) Although the law is generally presumed to serve the "good" of the community, the puzzle which Swift posed in *Gulliver's Travels* continues to be true: "How . . . should [it] come to pass, that the law, which was intended for every man's preservation, should be any man's ruin."

Gulliver notwithstanding, in sociological investigation, a society's codified law does provide an arena within which to consider a people's notion of itself and of others. Most obviously, laws speak about and express sanctioned behavior and specify other, less tolerable, or intolerable (illegal) activities and interactions. Law separates that which should be from that which should not be. More significantly, law is built upon and contains implicit assumptions about the nature of things as they are. Undergirding the formalized prescriptions and prohibitions of a legal system lie pervasive, taken-for-granted conceptions of and about reality.

Law is created and enforced by particular groups of people who may not represent the interests of all a society's participants, some of whom may, as Swift put it, face their ruin through the law's hand. Correspondingly, laws frequently become the subject of dispute; the very founding of the American nation was represented, if not actually caused by revolutionary dispute over the proper application of British laws of taxation. The obviousness of refutation and protest can, however, conceal fundamental similarities in the way disputing groups understand nature or conceive the limits and possibilities for action. Legal cases and court decisions tend to frame areas of divergence, to focus on issues of disagreement. Equally significant to sociological study are unspoken agreements and shared assumptions; such assumptions often remain tacit, precisely because they are so "obvious," yet they provide a ground on which conflict can be created, shifted, or resolved.

We are concerned here with the application of law to and the interrelation between law and sex. If it is discomforting to attempt definitions of law, it may be impossible to define sex. Even the most immediate definition—"two divisions of organic beings distinguished as male and female respectively" (*Oxford English Dictionary*)—has ramifications. If one takes "sex" to imply modes of behavior, the connotations amplify and spread almost unendingly. Since Freud's work, the forms and referents of sex appear to practically everyone, practically everywhere. Shulamith Firestone suggests that Freud merely said it; he constructed an important theory based on notions of sexuality, because he described a key characteristic of his era: "Freudianism is so charged, so impossible to repudiate because Freud grasped the crucial problem of modern life: Sexuality" (Firestone, 1971, p. 43).

The application of law to sexual activity is at least as old as the codes of Hammurabi and the

[1] We would like to express our appreciation to Lida Orzeck and to Laura Jones for their many insights and for their help in conceptualizing the problem. We are also grateful to Gitelle Seer for her invaluable scholarly assistance in providing us with source material.

Judeo-Christian Bible. Certainly the latter crucially informed moralities behind the constitution of English law. In the Old Testament, rules pertaining to sexual behavior were part of a wider comprehension of ritual purity and sacred wholeness which included interrelated sanctions ranging from the impurities of semen and menstrual blood, to the impurity of certain food categories and combinations of classes of people, animal slaughter, body desecration, and activities in the Temple. Contrastingly, contemporary American law pertaining to explicitly sexual behavior, is not primarily understood through complex and generalized notions of purity and impurity. Sin and crime, posited as existing within the individual, have displaced notions of ritual impurity, posited in reference to the group and to relations between groups. In our post-Freudian universe, in which sex provides metaphors for almost any realm of activity from the political to the religious, sex laws can be isolated somewhat. We do not mean to imply that laws about sex are, in fact, unrelated to other laws. The opposite is the more apt characterization. Rather, we note the presumption within our society that domains of social behavior are objectively separate from one another. What are, from one point of view, taken to be separate domains (e.g., religion, economics, politics, kinship) may, from another perspective, be part of one domain of activity (Dolgin, Kemnitzer, and Schneider, 1977). The irony rests on contradiction, and this contradiction between the presumption that sexuality is pervasive and the relative boundedness within the legal codes of sex laws is important to understanding changes in laws relating to sexual activity.

In general, sex laws constitute a legal arena in which basic principles seem, at least until quite recently, to have been accepted through past implication and precedent but without express attempts on the part of legislatures or courts to re-evaluate and re-examine the fundamental assumptions behind legislation and court decisions. The law comes closest to explicit definitions of sex terms within the framework of the penal law. New York State adopted a new penal law in 1965, after study by a commission appointed by the governor to revise and consolidate extant penal law. The new penal law was drawn in large part from the Model Penal Code, itself drafted in 1962 after approximately ten years of study by the American Law Institute. Appendix I contains the statement of purpose in Article I of the New York Penal Law as well as definitions from Articles 130 and 235.

Sex laws have been characterized as relatively unique because the crimes they define are frequently without victims or involve "victims" who are themselves consenting participants to the criminal behavior. The concept of crimes without victims has been raised in controversy about the benefits and disadvantages of decriminalization in these areas; clearly the task of deciphering which crimes do not have victims, at least in a prototypical sense, and of determining the exact components of victimization is complex. Edwin Schur (1974), illustrating the concept with abortion, homosexuality, and drug addiction, notes that in the last decade the scope of substantive law in these three areas has been reduced. What one commentator takes to be a victimless crime, may appear to involve victimization in another's view. In rebutting Schur's explications of victimless crime, Hugo Adam Bedau stresses the conceptual difficulties inherent to the idea of crimes without victims and summarizes divergent identifications of criminal offenses said to lack victims:

> The criminologist Jerome Skolnick mentioned private fighting and crimes of vice, such as gambling and smoking marijuana . . . narcotics, abortion, homosexuality . . . and prostitution. . . . The jurist Herbert Packer identified fornication, gambling, and narcotic offenses as victimless crimes . . . but he also mentioned bribery and espionage in this category. . . . Norval Morris, criminologist and jurist, cited drunks, addicts, loiterers, vagrants, prostitutes, and gamblers . . . as persons who commit crimes without victims; he explicitly excluded abortion from his list . . . although in his book with Gordon Hawkins, abortion was equally explicitly included

among the crimes which "lack victims" (Schur and Bedau, 1974, pp. 59–60).

Surely from a particular perspective, almost any activity categorized as criminal also can be defined as including a victim, even if that victim be the criminal himself or herself. The question again becomes: Who differentiates victims from consenting participants? Who may determine which domains of activity are criminal? What are the underlying assumptions on the basis of which such determinations are made or rendered reasonable? How, that is, does law or a set of laws relate to a society's more pervasive forms through which the world is understood and through which those understandings are articulated.

In America, as in the West more generally, the individual person is considered to be the autonomous agent of action, valuable in and of himself or herself, and the unit through which larger groups are comprehended (c.f., Barnett, 1977; Dolgin, 1977; Dumont, 1970; MacPherson, 1962). The significance of this particular construction, which seems perfectly natural to us whose own social order is based on its implications, can be compared to other societies in which alternative constructions pertain. American law is based explicitly on the presumption of the autonomous individual who should, ideally, be treated as equal to all other individuals. For instance, the dictum, basic to Americans, that individuals should receive equal treatment is absent in the world of traditional-caste India, which relies on its own fundamental dictum that people are unequal because created unequally (Barnett 1973, 1977). For the sociologist, contemporary efforts in the United States, by both judicial and legislative means, to rectify actual inequalities provide a particularly apt place within which to examine the society's conception of itself. The contradiction contained in "separate but equal" is now patent and such separation is illegal. Other contradictions remain implicit. Programs such as affirmative action, first effected through executive orders during the Johnson administration and based on legislation in the 1964 Civil Rights Act, entail official recognition of extant inequalities and governmental efforts toward rectification. The inclusion of sex in the legislation, along with race, color, religion, and national origin, may well have been a contingent and not particularly well thought out addition. However, for the legal situation of American women in the past decade, the consequences have been vast.

While the above is intended to illustrate a general connection between a society's notion of the person and its substantive law, the examples of discrimination, specifically of sex discrimination, speak more directly to the interrelation between sex and law. Legislation relating to sexual discrimination may seem legally peripheral to laws constraining sex acts. Yet, prescribed or prohibited treatment of women as a group (in contrast to men) must, from within a sociological point of view, be related to more general understandings of both social and sexual ties between men and women. Surely, a basic aspect of personal identity in American society is sexual identity. Gender identity (the fact of being male or female) is fundamental to, though not inclusive of, sexual identity. Social roles and definitions, insofar as they pertain to or limit the behaviors appropriate to men and women, encompass conceptions of "proper" and "improper" sexual relations between people. Obviously sexual relations occur between members of one sex; until recently homosexual relations have been illegal in most of the United States. In large part, views of homosexual relations have been defined through their contrast with "proper" sexual relations. The prototypical example of proper sex in America is sex between men and women married to each other. Images of sex intertwine with images of women, men, and the family.

It is useful to look at American notions of the family and of sex within that context before turning to legislation concerning sex and to recent changes in that body of law. The paradigmatic relation of sexual love in American culture is that between spouses. Sex is not only presumed proper within the context of the marital bond but is presumed necessary. This presumption has legal as well as more general consequences, and within this context, sex has traditionally been considered proper primarily for the purpose of procreation. The bond of marriage is defined by the law and allows the legal reproduction of people in the form of the family. David Schneider, in his study of American kinship as a cultural system, has identified sexual intercourse as the key symbol of American kinship (1968, 1969). This is so, in that sexual intercourse combines the two aspects of kinship as it is understood by Americans: "blood" (or substance) and code-for-conduct or law. Through intercourse, the archtypic relation in law, marriage, is expressed and relations in "blood" (child/parent) are created. The duality of relations in blood (or substance) and in code-for-conduct or law is predicated upon more general notions of nature and culture, respectively. In this frame, relations in law include not only those which are the explicit content of legislation but also relations based in lawlike, ordered sets of interactions. Schneider (1969) suggests that in American culture a similar structure of relations in "blood" or substance and relations in law underlies the cultural construction of nationality and religion as well as of kinship.

Sex and sexual relations are variously understood by Americans through shifts in the respective stress given to the order of nature and the order of culture (or law). Sex may be posed as animalistic. Equally, "proper" sexual relations entail ritualization, order, and control. Even for groups within the population that accept forms of sexual relations more generally viewed as deviant, sex involves ritualized behavior and technique. Within American society, mainstream understandings of sexual relations as an exclusive intimacy enjoyed between wife and husband seem increasingly to be complemented by alternative notions of what sex is or should be. David Kemnitzer (1977) writes about a new cultural construction of sex among young professional and white-collar workers. In analyzing the fact that there is a crucial stress on sex-as-technique among this group, Kem-

nitzer notes the wide popularity of Masters' and Johnson's *Human Sexual Response* "despite its turgid prose, outlandish price, and lack of pictures" (1977, p. 307). Although sexual how-to-do-it books proliferate, the essence of the new sexuality may well be not what it initially appears. Kemnitzer concludes: "For sex to be a matter of technique, a form of *work* an arena for competence, the partner . . . must be rendered a *thing*, rather than a *person*" (1977, p. 308). Precisely among the very groups which mainstream society sees as most animalistic in their sexual behaviors, "technique" and "competence" commandeer sexual relations.

Such alternative sexual patterns notwithstanding, notions of "proper" sex would seem to be predicated largely upon images of sex within marriage and certainly of sex between two adult partners of different gender. Though this image may be of shifting consequence to constraints imposed by law or enacted in behavior, it is sustained as the one sexual relation which receives legal prescription: nonconsummation is grounds for annulment or divorce. Until recently sex within marriage was the only form of sexual relation not explicitly prohibited in at least some states. For the most part, the constraints of law within the United States have restricted legal sexual relations to those between particular sorts of people (related in law but not in blood), to particular (private) places, and to particular forms (genital-to-genital contact). "Indeed it has been said," writes Schur, "that all unmarried adolescents and adults in our society—male and female, heterosexually inclined as well as homosexually oriented—are forced to choose between abstinence and 'criminality'" (1965, p. 78). Almost every sexual act not contained within the rigid definitions of person, place, and form has been defined as criminal. Criminal sexual activities with the wrong person have included incest with relatives (a category which itself is variously defined from state to state), homosexuality with a member of the same sex, fornication or adultery if the partners are unmarried or are married to others, masturbation if with oneself, and sodomy if with an animal. Sex in the wrong place may constitute the criminal act of public lewdness. Perhaps most surprising, even when the partner and the place do not contravene the bounds of legality, the mode of enactment may open the partners to criminal accusation. Anal sex or oral-genital sex, variously defined as sodomy or as the "crime against nature," offer accused parties long jail terms and heavy fines. (Most convictions for this last crime have not involved married partners; however, sodomy, including anal or oral intercourse, has been formally illegal in the United States even between husband and wife.)

These three sorts of limitations on sexual behavior (with whom, where, and how), though changing over time and in their specific content and application, allow classification of legislative enactments and judicial decisions pertaining to the legality of sex. Each separately and the three together are part of more pervasive cultural contrasts within American society. The category, spouse, as the most appropriate sexual partner, is based on a classification which separates family from nonfamily and within the family, a particular relation-in-law (that of spouse) from other relations-in-law and from relations-in-blood (c.f., Schneider 1968, 1969). In defining the bedroom or other similar place as that appropriate for sex, a domain of private space is distinguished from one of public space. The third limitation on sexual activity—how—is perhaps the most tricky; on the one hand, culture or law (ordered, prescribed, or prohibited activity) is separated from nature (unordered, even animalistic, activity); the first has been considered appropriate, tolerable, or legal; the second has not. This division is complicated precisely because culturally created notions of proper sexual forms frequently have been justified through the admonition that they are natural. The term "crimes against nature" has served as a euphemism for sodomy (itself a term variously referring to any or all of mutual masturbation, oral intercourse, anal intercourse, and sex with animals). The confusion can be put to rest at least minimally in a cross-cultural perspective. One might note simply that the sexual form upheld as most respectable within

the West has elsewhere been tagged the "missionary position" (Bullough 1976). To the extent that proper sex has been conceived as natural, the intent has been not to define natural in opposition to cultural or lawlike, but rather has been based on an equation between that which is natural and that which is approved by the Divinity.

SEX DISCRIMINATION

We turn to a brief consideration of substantive and procedural law in the area of sex discrimination, in order to define the terms for our more general discussion of sex and the law. Changes in this area of law during the past decade, reflecting and reflected in more general shifts in the social and political status of women, are particularly significant to the legal alterations pertaining to matters of sex. Models employed by feminist groups seeking to effect legal and other changes have been appropriated by groups working toward equality for homosexuals and lesbians.[2] Further, we must emphasize the link between social and legal understandings of sex as well as classifications of approved or objectionable sexual forms to social conceptualizations of "women" and "men."

As for changing notions of "men" and "women" as groups, related to particular sets of social roles, one might note the history of early twentieth-century social welfare legislation for women. That legislation, designed to protect women in the labor market and intended to protect both genders in a judicial climate tending to deny the state's right to erect such protective legislation, has become the rule of American society; but the special protections offered women protected them right out of the competitive labor market. Only now, under the impetus of women's movements has an understanding developed of the problems created by classifying women separately from men.

[2] As we note below in somewhat more detail, many of the models taken up by feminist groups were themselves appropriated from the civil rights struggle. The full consequences of women and homosexuals or lesbians defining themselves through "ethnic" models are the subject for another paper.

In the field of property rights, women were long treated as inferior, weak and incapable of protecting their own rights. The common law defined a married woman out of legal existence by creating the legal unity of husband and wife, with the husband given power to control the family economy.

In fact, under early common law, the husband was the natural guardian of the children. In America most property restrictions disappeared by the late nineteenth century, and the role of the father as natural guardian was replaced by an idealized view of the mother as natural provider to the young child. This, too, expressed social views of the role of women as limited to, or at least most naturally played in, the home. The role of both parents in the custody of children has been subject to serious reconsideration in the last ten years.

It was less than a decade ago that, in 1971, the United States Supreme Court first used sex discrimination as a viable reason for the invalidation of a statute. In *Reed* v. *Reed,* the Court declared unconstitutional an Idaho statute which gave males preference to females as administrators of estates. This case was one of two landmark decisions in 1971 which agreed on the matter of sex discrimination; the second, *Sail 'er Inn Inc.* v. *Kirby,* held invalid a statute restricting female bartenders to women who themselves held the liquor license for the particular establishment in which they worked or were married to the license holder, while making no similar requirement for male bartenders.

In the history of similar cases testing the constitutionality of sex discrimination, the fact of being female routinely had been judged ample reason for denying equality with other persons (males). In a penetrating review of the history of constitutional issues relating to sex discrimination, Ruth Bader Ginsburg begins with the case of *Bradwell* v. *Illinois* (1873), in which the United States Supreme Court supported the Illinois Supreme Court in denying, on the basis of her sex, Myra Bradwell's application to practice law (Davidson, Ginsburg, and Kay, 1974). Although characterizing the case as a "museum piece," Ginsburg notes that for "a century after

Bradwell, equality of opportunity for women in the legal profession remained unfinished business" (1974, p. 8). It is instructive to compare the language and forms of argument used in 1873 to deny Ms. Bradwell a legal practice with the message and models used ninety-eight years latter in the California Supreme Court's decision that women should have equal opportunity with men to serve as bartenders.

In 1873 Mr. Justice Bradley and two colleagues presented their alternative reasons for concurring with the Illinois court's decision to prohibit Ms. Bradwell's right to be a lawyer:

> [T]he civil law, as well as nature herself, has always recognized a wide difference in the respective spheres and destinies of man and woman. Man is, or should be woman's protector and defender. The natural and proper timidity and delicacy which belongs to the female sex evidently unfits it for many of the occupations of civil life. The constitution of the family organization, which is founded in the divine ordinance, as well as in the nature of things, indicates the domestic sphere as that which properly belongs to the domain and functions of womanhood. . . .
>
> It is true that many women are unmarried and not affected by any of the duties, complications, and incapacities arising out of the married state, but these are exceptions to the general rule. The paramount destiny and mission of woman are to fulfil the noble and benign offices of wife and mother. This is the law of the Creator. And the rules of civil society must be adapted to the general constitution of things, and cannot be based upon exceptional cases (*Bradwell* v. *Illinois*).

In apparently sharp contrast to Bradley's concept of the "divine ordinance" and the "nature of things," stand the models and metaphors invoked in the 1971 California decision that women, equal to men, should have the right to tend bar (*Sail'er Inn Inc.* v. *Kirby*):

> Sex, like race and lineage, is an immutable trait, a status into which the class members are locked by the accident of birth. What differentiates sex from nonsuspect statuses, such as intelligence or physical disability, and aligns it with the recognized suspect classifications is that the characteristic fre-

quently bears no relation to ability to perform or contribute to society. . . . Where the relations between characteristic and evil to be prevented is so tenuous, courts must look closely at classifications based on that characteristic lest outdated social stereotypes result in invidious laws or practices.

Another characteristic which underlies all suspect classifications is the stigma of inferiority and second class citizenship associated with them. . . . Women, like Negroes, aliens and the poor have historically labored under severe legal and social disabilities. Like black citizens, they were, for many years, denied the right to vote and, until recently, the right to serve on juries in many states. They are excluded from or discriminated against in employment and educational opportunities. Married women in particular have been treated as inferior persons in numerous laws relating to property and independent business ownership and the right to make contracts.

Laws which disable women from full participation in the political, business and economic arenas are often characterized as 'protective' and beneficial. Those same laws applied to racial or ethnic minorities would readily be recognized as invidious and impermissible. The pedestal upon which women have been placed has all too often, upon closer inspection, been revealed as a cage. We conclude that the sexual classifications are properly treated as suspect, particularly when those classifications are made with respect to a fundamental interest such as employment.

The above quotations from two judicial decisions, separated in time by almost one hundred years, illustrate well the manner in which the law reflects wider notions of the "person" (here, male and female persons, respectively) within the social order. Mr. Justice Bradley, we may assume, had support within the society of his time for the suggestion that the "divine ordinance" and "the nature of things" placed women in an exclusively domestic arena. What had changed by 1971 was at least some part of the very "nature of things." Legally not full persons in 1873, women were conceptualized in Bradley's argument as essentially belonging to another species than men. By 1971 the models used were quite different; women, by

1971, are compared to "racial and ethnic minorities." The dissimilar dictates of law in the two cases accord with different understandings of women as persons. The legal advantages to women apart, it is significant to note the continued importance of categorizations initially based on and continuing to carry the connotations of a biological base: sex, race, and ethnicity. Although recent court decisions argue against the legislation of inequalities based on such classifications of people, the classifications themselves remain salient. The stress given to classifications based on sex, ethnicity, or race by courts affirming the importance of disregarding such differentiations is essential; the categorizations per se receive sustenance even in court decisions mandating their disregard.

Despite the preservation of such categorizations, the shift in intent of the meaning of these categories for the law contrasts Bradley's 1873 decision and that handed down by the California court in *Sail'er Inn Inc.* v. *Kirby*. Since *Bradwell* v. *Illinois*, a plethora of decisions (at least until the 1970s) continued to employ language and explanations reminiscent of Bradley's conception of the proper state of things, though appeals to the assumed concurrence of the divine ordinance tended to drop away. In 1961 the United States Supreme Court (in *Hoyt* v. *Florida*) upheld a Florida statute which exempted women from jury lists unless they specifically requested inclusion of their names by writing to the circuit court clerk. Mr. Justice Harlan, delivering the Court's opinion wrote: "Despite the enlightened emancipation of women from the restrictions and protestations of bygone years, and their entry into many parts of community life formerly considered to be reserved to men, woman is still regarded as the center of home and family life." In a similar vein, a Pennsylvania Superior Court decided in 1967 that a state statute, providing different forms of sentencing men and women offenders did not violate the equal protection of law dictate of the Fourteenth Amendment. Justice Jacobs, writing for the court, outlined reasons on the basis of which the legislature justifiably might have acted in enacting the statute by which female, but not male, criminals were given indeterminate sentences (in *Commonwealth* v. *Daniels*):

> This court is of the opinion that the legislature reasonably could have concluded that indeterminate sentences should be imposed on women as a class, allowing the time of incarceration to be matched to the necessary treatment in order to provide more effective rehabilitation. Such a conclusion could be based on the physiological and psychological makeup of women, the type of crime committed by women, their relation to the criminal world, their roles in society, their unique vocational skills and pursuits, and their reaction as a class to imprisonment, as well as the number and type of women who are sentenced to imprisonment rather than given suspended sentences. Such facts could have led the legislature to conclude that a different manner of punishment and rehabilitation was necessary for women sentenced to confinement.

A dissenting opinion argued through analogy to examples of racial or ethnic discrimination. Justice Hoffman wrote: "In my view, the imposition of an especially severe criminal sentence on a particular individual or group impinges on his liberty as substantially as legislative action which denies him the right to vote . . . or the right to attend an unsegregated school" (*Commonwealth* v. *Daniels*). Thus we find at least one line of decisions in which courts support the legality of specific differentiations between persons on the basis of sex, appealing to innate psychological and physiological variations between the sexes, while another line of decisions declares such differentiations illegal and frames them through reference to similarities between situations of women and other groups whom discriminations have occurred.

We have included a consideration of sex discrimination because sex, as a physical interaction, cannot be separated legitimately in sociological study from sex as a relationship between members of the two genders—a relation of relative equality or relative domination. We do not claim that shifts in law concerning sex

roles (in the sense of gender roles) or shifts concerning the legality or illegality of differential treatment accorded to men and women directly determine shifts in law relating to sexual activity, nor do we claim the reverse. Rather, we suggest that underlying forms of comprehension within the social order are pertinent to both sets of legal doctrines and concomitantly, to alterations in those doctrines. We further suggest that such underlying cultural forms (such as the basic notion of the "person") are not always consciously recognized by legislators, judges, or the people about or for whom the law is encoded. Such forms are often not consciously recognized, precisely because they are considered "natural." Thus, alternatives are not envisioned.

With this in mind, we consider the character of specific laws and judicial decisions concerning activities understood as sexual or as relating to sex. The history of laws concerning sex in the United States does not have a clear set of linear stages in which the laws are erected and re-defined. Various areas of activity understood as sexual have received relatively more or less stress through time; some areas of sex law have seemed particularly crucial, have been made more rigid, or have been declared unconstitutional. In the same period, other laws have received opposite or different treatment. For instance, laws restricting the use of, or even discussion about, methods of contraception were declared unconstitutional by the Supreme Court in 1965 (*Griswold* v. *Connecticut*), and birth control (though not abortion) is not now a significant issue of legislative debate nor of outspoken social controversy. Legislation on homosexuality—but less so, for example, on premarital sex—remains indecisive and subject to intense disagreement. Two recent instances: in April 1978 an Oklahoma bill, already cleared in that state's House, was unanimously passed in the senate; the bill made public homosexuality by personnel within schools, grounds for dismissal (*New York Times*, April 7, 1978, p. 16A). Without disputing that law's possible rationale or its implications per se, one might ask why the bill was designed to prevent public homosexual acts without simply banning public sexual acts (whether homosexual or heterosexual). Two and one-half months earlier, in another state, the mayor of New York City issued an executive order banning discrimination against homosexuals working or applying for jobs in mayoral agencies (*New York Times*, January 24, 1978, p. 1). Soon after the order's issuance, the president of the Patrolmen's Benevolent Association suggested that the "paramilitary nature of the [policeman's] job," which fostered and necessitated "closer working and personal relationships than [among] people in other fields," would be endangered by retaining homosexuals on the police force. He wrote:

> The predominant attitudes of this latter group ["the vast majority of the present force"] toward homosexuality, which are characterized by refusal to develop any close personal relationships with homosexuals, were formed and hardened over the years. They are part of a morality whose origins date back to pre-Biblical times" (*New York Times*, February 10, 1978, p. 25).

Not only do sex laws vary over time—often not in apparent concert with other laws concerning sex existing at the same time—but there are a diversity of laws and exactions for their infringement among the fifty states. Obviously Supreme Court decisions may entail constitutional objections, resulting in similar legislative changes within many states. Yet large variations from state to state remain in laws concerning sex. A 1972 summary of punishments within each state and Washington, D.C. for consensual sex offenses reveals a variety of offenses and an array of dissimilar punishments for similar crimes from state to state (*Playboy*, August 1972, p. 188–89). According to extant law in 1972, twenty-three states and the District of Columbia punished fornication with fines and/ or prison terms ranging from up to $10 in Rhode Island to imprisonment, up to three years or fines up to $300 in Massachusetts, and imprisonment up to five years or fines up to $300 in Maine.[3] "Crimes against nature" (vari-

ously including any or all of oral intercourse, anal intercourse, sex with animals, and sex with the dead) were punishable in forty-seven states (but not in Oregon, Illinois, Colorado, and Washington, D.C.). Prison sentences which could be imposed ranged from up to six months, in Utah (where a fine of $299 was alternately or concomitantly imposable) to a maximum of twenty years in several states (and up to twenty-one years in one state). In Maine, cohabitation was made punishable by up to five years in prison or up to $300 in fines; at the same time, twelve states did not punish cohabitation at all. Although adultery was punishable in the vast majority of states and in Washington, D.C., definitions and punishments varied; in Minnesota, imprisonment of up to one year and/or fines up to $1,000 were exactable, but not in cases in which the female partner was unmarried.

To describe more adequately the character of sex law discussed above and to introduce a more detailed consideration of that law, we shall at this point summarize those aspects of New York's Penal Law which deal with sex. (The Act was enacted in 1965, and subsequently some revisions have been made.) This review focuses our argument by presenting one state's considered recognition of the law's concern with sex. The following Articles are particularly pertinent:

Article 125: Homicide, Abortion, and Related Offenses. (The provisions of this statute dealing with abortion are discussed below).

Article 130: Sex Offenses (the offense of rape, consensual sodomy, sodomy and sexual abuse).

Article 230: Prostitution Offenses (prostitution and patronizing a prostitute, promoting prostitution, and permitting prostitution).

Article 235: Obscenity and Related Offenses. (Related offenses include the dissemination of indecent material to minors). Definitions from this article are found in Appendix I.

Article 240: Offenses Against Public Order. (This Article includes riot, unlawful assembly, criminal anarchy, public intoxication, and similar offenses; sections 240.20 and 240.25 include

---

[3] It should of course be remembered that the existence of a particular law in and of itself implies little about the extent of enforcement by police or within the courts.

disorderly conduct and harassment, respectively, which in turn include the use of abusive or obscene language and obscene gesturing. Section 240.35 defines a person as guilty of "loitering" when, among other things,[4] he loiters in a public place for the purpose of engaging or soliciting another person to engage in "deviate sexual intercourse or other sexual behavior of a deviate nature").

Article 245: Offenses Against Public Sensibilities (public lewdness, defined as intentional exposure of private and intimate parts).

Article 255: Offenses Against Marriage (unlawfully solemnizing a marriage and related offenses such as bigamy, adultery, and incest).

Article: 260: Offenses Relating to Children and Incompetents (abandonment and nonsupport which include the crime of acting in an injurious manner to the physical, mental, or moral welfare of a male child under sixteen or a female child under seventeen, and the crime committed by a parent, guardian, or other person charged with the care of a child under eighteen, who fails to exercise reasonable control of such child).

Article 263: Sexual Performance By a Child (Using a child in a sexual performance, promoting an obscene sexual performance by a child, and promoting a sexual performance by a child all are classed as felonies).

Article 125 on abortion, amended in 1970, is worth special mention. Abortion in the first degree, a class D felony, which was retained unchanged, entails the commission of an abortional act after the twenty-fourth week of pregnancy. Before that date, commission of an abortional act continues to be defined as criminal if performed by a nonphysician. The primary change effected in New York's 1970 amendment was the legalization of abortion performed before the twenty-fourth week of pregnancy by a physician. An abortionist who is not a physician continues to be guilty of abortion at any time and of manslaughter if death to the female results. After the twenty-four-week period, a licensed physician may perform an abortion only

on condition that such physician believes that procedure to be reasonably necessary to preserve the life of the pregnant woman. Other sections of Article 125, on abortion, make self-abortion a crime, unless done within the first twenty-four weeks of pregnancy on the advice of a licensed physician believing that act necessary to preserve the mother's life.

Even ideally, the construction and review of law is complex. The actual workings of legislatures and of the judiciary subsume the involvement of a host of individuals and groups whose intentions, social relationships, and comprehensions of the law and the reality a law is intended to effect, vary, and often conflict. Resulting formal laws are often vague, sometimes incomprehensible, and often enough contradictory.

Broad shifts in sex (or other) laws can be effected through amendment to the Constitution, independent legislative revision at the state or federal levels, and constitutional objections (by legal action) to existing law. The latter recourse, although presented by Brown and others (1971) as the method of choice in respect to eliminating legal modes of discrimination, is less relevant to most current issues relating to sex. It is of course conceivable, particularly should the Equal Rights Amendment achieve Constitutional status, that it would become a model for decriminalizing homosexual or other presently illegal sexual behaviors. The relatively cohesive arguments encompassed in and under-girding the ERA make Constitutional amendment an auspicious avenue toward legal change. While piecemeal legislative changes within each state may tend to militate against pervasive and rapid legal change, as Brown and others (1971) suggest in proposing strategies for repeal of sex discriminatory laws, relatively coherent legislative changes from state to state often occur simultaneously with, as well as subsequent to the specification of constitutional objections raised in judicial review. Modifications of abortion law in many of the United States in the late 1960s and 1970s provide an apt illustration. (See Lader 1966, 1973 for a detailed history of abortion laws and their revocation).

[4] The statute employs the male pronominal form throughout.

Faced by an increasingly vociferous movement for the legalization of abortion, two crucial judicial decisions in 1969 held existing abortion laws to be unconstitutional. The Supreme Court of California defined abortion to lie within a woman's "fundamental right" of liberty and privacy. Two months later, in November 1969, the United States District of Columbia declared that city's relatively liberal abortion law unconstitutional on the grounds that the law was vague, resulted in discrimination against poor women, and infringed on the basic rights of liberty and privacy.

These two judicial decisions gave support to the campaigns to reform or repeal abortion law within state legislatures. A reform bill was voted down in New York in 1968 and again in 1969. In 1970 the New York Senate and Assembly passed a bill which fully legalized abortion until the twenty-fourth week of pregnancy if performed by a licensed physician. Abortions (prior to the twenty-fourth week) were soon legalized in many states. In 1966 there had been 8,000 legal abortions in the United States. In 1972, 600,000 legal abortions were performed (Lader, 1973). In 1973 the Supreme Court of the United States (in *Roe* v. *Wade*) held unconstitutional a Texas statute which held most abortions to be illegal. Writing for the Court, Justice Brennan summarized the argument: "A state criminal abortion statute of the current Texas type, that excepts from criminality only *a life saving* procedure on behalf of the mother, without regard to pregnancy state and without recognition of the other interests involved, is violative of the Due Process Clause of the Fourteenth Amendment." (The due-process clause reads: ". . . nor shall any State deprive any person of life, liberty, or property, without due process of law.") Although controversy about the specifics of abortion law continues, *Roe* v. *Wade* provided a key decision for effectuation of abortion law reform or repeal throughout the country.

At this point it is not amiss to add a brief note about the history of abortion law in the United States during the nineteenth century. This history underscores the significance of the time-frame in interpreting any given law or body of law. Not the law per se but its implications and its historically determined and historically situated comprehension, is socially significant. The rigid antiabortion laws, widely modified within the last decade, were enacted in the middle of the last century. In sharp contrast is the earlier common-law position on abortion. Common law, which had prevailed in the United States until that time, permitted abortion until "quickening" (movement of the fetus).[5] Lader (1973) attributes the new nineteenth-century laws to a combined attempt to stimulate population growth, to protect women from the danger of abortion in that century, and to punish the "sin" of unwed mothers by preserving its fruits.

Laws against birth-control were similarly motivated: "In its long struggle to suppress sin by legislation, the Puritan mind considered abortion and birth-control laws the ultimate triumph in the use of fear—particularly fear of pregnancy among unmarried girls—to uphold morality" (Lader 1966. p. 90).

A key personnage in the enactment of such legislation was Anthony Comstock, "morality's most fanatical warrior" (Lader 1966, p. 90). The Comstock bill, passed by both congressional houses and signed into law by President Grant in 1873, was primarily aimed against what Comstock saw as instances of obscenity attacking the moral fiber of society. Mary Ware Dennett, writing in 1926, summarized Comstock's understanding of a proper moral code: "some perverts use contraceptives, therefore the law should not allow any one at all to secure them or know anything about them, and besides, as most of those who are not perverts can't be really trusted anyhow, hearing about or seeing contraceptives would be pretty sure to make them go to the devil, especially young people, so the complete prohibition is after all the safest" (1970, p. 43).

---

[5] "As late as 1879," writes Lader, "a Kentucky court ruled that 'it was never a punishable offense at common law to produce with the consent of the mother an abortion prior to the time when the mother became quick with child (*Mitchell* v. *Commissioner*)" (1966, p. 86).

Dennett notes that her recapitulation does not capture Comstock's telling adjectives and fierce descriptions. Whatever else they may indicate, Comstock's activities and legislative successes suggest the importance of recognizing historical interrelations between and express legislative origins of laws aiming to restrict or contain assorted domains of sexual behavior. Dennett argues that the inclusion of the phrase "preventing contraception" in the 1873 anti-obscenity bill framed by Comstock was, if not accidental, certainly not the primary intent of the bill. Yet, for many years thereafter it became a crime for anyone, single or married, adult or child, physician or patient, to use or circulate information about the prevention of contraception.

The history of legal issues relating to birth control and abortion can be outlined fairly concisely (c.f., Lader, 1966, 1973; Dienes 1972). For both, though less so for abortion, the last twenty years have witnessed a widespread repeal of laws laid down a century ago. The two issues have, moreover, been related legally, as well as by common sense. The 1965 landmark decision regarding contraception in *Griswold* v. *Connecticut* has served explicitly as a precedent for subsequent abortion decisions. In *Griswold*, Justice Douglas, writing for the Court, found within the constitutional guarantees a right which he delineated in terms of a "zone of privacy older than the Bill of Rights—older than the political parties, older than our school system" as applying to the marriage relationship. Both birth control and abortion have been tied expressly within the wider society to issues of female equality and the rights of women to maintain control over their bodies. The connotations of "birth control" and "abortion" have altered concomitantly with changes in the connotations of "privacy," "woman," and "marriage," to name a few.

The right of "privacy," so crucial to the judicial decision in *Griswold* is not guaranteed explicitly by the Constitution. The construction of a basic right to privacy is explained in *Griswold*. Justice Goldberg, concurring with Justice Douglas's decision for the Court, wrote: "To

hold that a right so basic and fundamental and so deep-rooted in our society as the right of privacy in marriage may be infringed because that right is not guaranteed in so many words by the first eight amendments to the Constitution is to ignore the Ninth Amendment and to give it no effect whatsoever." The Ninth Amendment states: "The enumeration in the Constitution, of certain rights, shall not be construed to deny or disparage others retained by the people." The social and cultural frames of these new connotations were created largely outside the legal system per se. New connotations have become explicit and have become part of an articulated comprehension of personal relationships (to self and to others) primarily through the activities of more or less organized social movements such as feminism (and its opposition).

Modes of social and specifically legal protest within the feminist movement have sometimes included and have more often provided models for groups concerned with homosexual rights. Gay liberation groups have been formed and have demonstrated publically and actively for the end of discriminations against homosexuals, whether by churches, by legislators, judges and police, by employers, or by psychiatrists. Like feminist groups and so-called ethnic movements, homosexuals brought actions to the courts and demonstrated in the streets, donning T-shirts and buttons announcing their particular identity. A vocal opposition has developed, signaled, among others, by the name of Anita Bryant. In April 1978, 54,096 people voted to repeal a homosexual rights ordinance in St. Paul, Minnesota. Following Anita Bryant's rhetoric, if not her explicit model, arguments for repeal invoked God and nature alike. One local resident is quoted as having said: "If God had meant for men to go with men or for women with women, he would have made us alike" (*New York Times*, April 27, 1978, p. 20). The Reverend Ron Adrian, president of the Concerned Citizens for Community Standards, a group opposing a homosexual rights ordinance in Wichita, Kansas, denied the issue to be one of civil rights, adding, "We think it's an effort on the part of a small group of people to ask us to approve of their criminal lifestyle" (*New York Times*, April 27, 1978, p. 20).

Broadly, two sets of legal issues, interconnected but distinguishable, are important: the legality of homosexual acts per se and the rights of homosexuals to other liberties, including nondiscrimination at work. Although laws against sodomy may not explicitly mention homosexuality, the sexual acts which are mentioned (including, typically, anal and oral intercourse) make nongenital sex illegal and thus effectively legislate against homosexuality. These laws, suggests Walter Barnett, discussing American sodomy legislation, "manage to bar all sexual expression between homosexuals because no alternative exists for them which is licit" (1973, p. 261). The roots of English common law regarding sodomy would seem to be of Biblical inspiration. In the Middle Ages, sodomy was termed the "unspeakable crime." Thomas Aquinas, in delineating sins of sex, placed, in descending order of seriousness, bestiality, homosexual sodomy, heterosexual sodomy, and masturbation. In contrast, adultery, seduction, and rape, being merely crimes against people and not against God and the law of natural procreation, were judged as lesser sins (Barnett, W., 1973, p. 79). When, under Henry VIII, the sins of sex were designated crimes, the "detestable and abominable vice of Buggery" (anal intercourse) was "adjudged Felony" (quoted in Barnett, W., 1973, p. 80). American law has retained common law language and "its religious flavor and fervor: the 'infamous' or 'abominable' or 'detestable' *crime against nature* as it is referred to in the laws of thirty-seven states. No other offense, not even murder is prefixed with such judgmental choice of words—words which cannot help but influence 'impartial' courts and juries as well as those legislators who are being called upon today to repeal these laws" (Martin and Lyon, 1972, p. 39).

In the United States harsh penalties for homosexuality have been justified on the basis of purported consequences of legal toleration for homosexuals. As listed in a *Yale Law Journal* Note and Comment ("Private Consensual Homosexual Behavior") the justifications have included: "(1) the danger of children being seduced, (2) the harmful impact on marriage relationships, (3) the prevalence of tension among homosexuals, and (4) the possibility that such persons will not seek psychiatric aid without the incentive of criminal sanctions" (1961, p. 70). This article debunks each justification. A careful de-mystification of similar rationales for antihomosexual legislation is provided in the report of the Wolfenden Committee to the British Parliament. That committee, appointed in 1954, concluded that private, consensual homosexuality between adults should be decriminalized because, unless a society patently equates "the sphere of crime with that of sin, there must remain a realm of private morality and immorality which is, in brief and crude terms, not the law's business (1963, p. 48). The committee suggested that the terms "private," "consensual," and "adult" should be interpreted in the context of homosexual relations as they would be in reference to heterosexuality. In 1967 the British law, passed during the reign of Henry VIII, was repealed; private homosexual behavior between consenting adults was decriminalized.

Correlative to its severe treatment of those engaging in homosexuality, American law has denied homosexuals equal access to employment. In the latter regard, more than in the former, lesbians have been at jeopardy. In England and in the United States there has been a tendency in fact, if not always in theory, to avoid prosecuting homosexual women. The reasons include a generally greater tolerance for the expression of emotional and physical affection between women that between men; the traditional relegation of women to a domestic sphere, in which they cannot become competitors at or for work and therefore need not be taken seriously in this regard; and a peculiar belief that women are incapable of homosexuality. It is said that when Queen Victoria had it brought to her attention that England's laws against homosexuality excluded lesbians, she "decried the suggestion, dismissing the thought as impossible. 'Two *ladies* would never engage in such despicable acts!' " (Martin and Lyon, 1972, p. 40). Within the American world of work, lesbians, like male homosexuals, have been, and in many places of employment remain, liable to dismissal (c.f., Martin and Lyon, 1972). In the early 1950s, under the instigation of Senator Joseph McCarthy, the Civil Service Commission and the Armed Forces became adamant in barring homosexuals from employment. In 1950 a United States Senate subcommittee admonished against hiring homosexuals because those "who indulge in such degraded activity are committing not only illegal and immoral acts, but they also constitute security risks in positions of public trust" (as quoted in Churchill, 1971, p. 216). A 1955 issue of the *Bulletin of Atomic Scientists* decried homosexuals and "perverts" as security risks because they would be especially open to blackmail (Churchill, 1971, p. 217). Were homosexuality not a crime, blackmail attempts would be easier to resist. As W. Barnett (1973, p. 19) suggests, an individual would be less apt to report blackmail attempts to police if, as a result, he or she faced arrest for homosexuality.

In the last several years homosexuality has been at least partially decriminalized in a number of states, and homosexual rights ordinances have been enacted in several dozen cities. In March 1978, what may be the first judicial decision on the right of homosexuals to be admitted to the bar was written by the Florida Supreme Court. That court ruled that admission of homosexual preferences by an applicant does not disqualify that person from the right to practice law (*New York Times*, March 21, 1978, p. 20). In indicating that its decision might not apply to individuals who acted out their stated homosexual preference, the court affirmed a possible differentiation between homosexuality as a passive state and the manifestation of that state in actual homosexual relationships. Such a differentiation echoes the distinction suggested by the Wolfenden Committee, following Kinsey and certain psychoanalytic theorists, between "the condition of homosexuality (which relates to the direction of sexual preference) and the acts or behavior resulting from the preference"

(*The Wolfenden Report*, 1963, p. 29). The committee report goes on to suggest that individuals are differentially aware of their own propensity to homosexuality, which on some level may exist in all or almost all persons. "Some [homosexuals] are, indeed, quite unaware of it, and where this is so the homosexuality is technically described as latent, its existence being inferred from the individual's behavior in spheres not obviously sexual" (*The Wolfenden Report* 1963, p. 30). A complex set of not fully explicit assumptions is being made about the connections between biology (or biopsychology) on the one hand and action and belief on the other. The distinction, assumed to exist for all individuals, is posed as being alternately mediated or mediatable by a complicated interaction (within the person) of intention and control.

Legally, these issues are intricately connected with that of a right to privacy. Although the separation between public and private domains is presumed within American society and connected with the notion of a distinction between home and work ("love" and "money") (c.f., Schneider, 1968, 1969), no express right to privacy is included in the United States Constitution nor the Bill of Rights. As noted above, a constitutional right to privacy was explicitly acknowledged in *Griswold* v. *Connecticut* (1965), in the context of the marital relationship. The doctrine was extended in subsequent cases to cover other arenas of privacy, including the right to use contraceptives outside the marital relationship (*Eisenstadt* v. *Baird,* 1972), the right of unmarried pregnant women to abortion (*Roe* v. *Wade,* 1973), the private right to possess obscene materials (*Stanley* v. *Georgia,* 1969), the right of minors to nonprocreative intimate relations (*Carey* v. *Population Services International,* 1977).[6] In the decision of the Florida Supreme Court referred to above, which held

[6] In this case (*Carey* v. *Population Services International,* 1977) Justice Brennan, delivering the opinion for the Court, held unconstitutional a New York Education Law which made it a crime for any person to sell or distribute contraceptives of any type to persons under sixteen, for anyone other than a licensed pharmacist to distribute con-

that a professed homosexual could be admitted to the Florida bar, the right of privacy was defined as being subject to limitation in cases in which a "substantial connection" could be shown between the private behavior and the ability to serve as a lawyer (*New York Times*, March 21, 1978, p. 20). "The major problem with expanding this constitutional right of privacy," suggests W. Barnett, "is to determine where it stops" (1973, p. 58). The legal designation of a right to privacy coexists in the broad sense with a common-sense division of space and time into public and private spheres; the genesis of the right to privacy achieves legal credence through a set of related rights such as:

> The right of association contained in the penumbra of the First Amendment. . . . The Third Amendment in its prohibition against the quartering of soldiers 'in any house' in time of peace without the consent of the owner is another facet of that privacy. The Fourth Amendment explicitly affirms the 'right of the people to be secure in their person, houses, papers, and effects, against unreasonable searches and seizures.' The Fifth Amendment in its Self-Incrimination Clause enables the citizen to create a zone of privacy which government may not force him to surrender to his detriment. The Ninth Amendment provides: "The enumeration in the Constitution, of certain rights, shall not be construed to deny or disparage others retained by the people" (Justice Douglas, writing for the Court, *Griswold* v. *Connecticut*, 1965).

---

traceptives, and for anyone to advertise or display contraceptives. Population Planning Associates Inc., engaged in mail order sale of contraceptives, regularly advertised its products. The Court accepted the standing of that organization to bring the case.

The Court, finding the New York statute to be unconstitutional and in conflict with a right to privacy, held that the issues germane to the case entailed decisions an individual should be allowed to make without government interference, matters of a personal nature, relating to marriage, procreation, contraception, family relationships, child rearing, and child education.

In a particularly telling aspect of this decision, the Court held that the relevant statute was unconstitutional even with respect to minors and thus decided against the contention that the statute was justified in furthering the state's interest in limiting promiscuous sexual intercourse among minors (persons under sixteen in this case).

At base, however, issues concerning the extent of a right to privacy (who exactly has this right, when, where, and to what degree) reflect a more fundamental contradiction between liberty and equality which sits at the heart of the American social order. Each right conflicts with another right—the rights of each individual always conflict somewhere at their outer limits—with the rights of another individual or of the group. In specific cases, this contradiction can be treated as conflict: a particular conflict can be settled through a particular resolution. The essential contradiction remains. It effects, and in specific resolutions is effected by, wide-ranging areas of life and law beyond those concerned with behaviors deemed sexual.

A rather extraordinary ruling by Judge Taylor of the New York Family Court (*In Re P*) contains a detailed consideration of the right to privacy in regard to "deviate" sexual acts, including sodomy, but more surprisingly, perhaps, in regard to prostitution. It must be noted that the family court is a lower court of limited jurisdiction and therefore the case is not of importance as a precedent. It is important because it contains an unusual discussion of the rationale behind a sex law and by open discussion, forces attention to the laws which are generally accepted without real consideration being given to their basis and their results. Judge Taylor dismissed a sexual misconduct charge against a fourteen-year-old girl. The bill of particulars stated that at 8:30 P.M. in March 1948, the defendant (referred to by this court as the respondent) accosted the complaining witness on the street; for ten dollars she was said to have offered to engage in sexual relations with him; they went together to a New York City hotel, at which he paid four dollars for a room. "It should be noted," stated the judge, "that the complaining witness was not charged with the violation of patronizing a prostitute. . . . Nor was he charged with any other crime applicable to these facts." The respondent was additionally charged with having participated in forcibly stealing thirty dollars from the same witness. (One might assume this latter charge to be not unrelated to the witness's motivations for having brought the charge under consideration here—that the girl performed "deviate" sexual acts with the complaining witness for a fee.) The case is worth reviewing in greater detail.

Discussing the New York statute concerning consensual sodomy, Judge Taylor employed the above-mentioned precedents for setting forth a right to privacy: "this court states at the outset the premise that private, intimate, consensual sexual conduct not harmful to others, even if it violates the personal moral code of many, does not violate public morality and is protected by the right of privacy" (*New York Law Journal, In Re P*, January 23, 1978, p. 12). She further notes the lack of any evidence that "deviate" sexual acts are harmful to public health, safety, or welfare. The claim is supported by an underlying inconsistency in relevant New York State law; since 1966 consensual sodomy has been permitted in New York between married persons who thereby may engage legally in "deviate" sexual acts. There is no indication that such acts might harm unmarried persons any more than they harm married persons which, after ten years of decriminalization, would seem to be not at all. However, the law against "deviate" sexual acts by unmarried persons cannot be justified as an effort simply to prevent sexual relations between single people, in that fornication is not a crime in New York.

The remaining question in this case is whether the New York statute, which defines as criminal the performance for a fee of certain sexual acts ("deviate" or otherwise), can be declared unconstitutional in New York. The ruling held just this. Initially, the discriminatory application of prostitution laws is held to violate the equal protection clause of the State Constitution, despite the fact that New York State's prostitution legislation was made sex-neutral in 1964 (before which time a prostitute was defined as a "female person"). The present case illustrates the selective enforcement of prostitution laws against women. Courts in several states previously had voided convictions of prostitutes on the basis of the discriminatory character of the laws and/or their enforcement.

In 1976 Kate Millett pointed out that the unfairness of this discrimination had at least a limited advantage in framing the legal strategy of one accused of prostitution:

> until the great decision is handed down that women have the right to dispose of their bodies as they see fit and that prostitution is not a transaction in the public domain—that police interference here is an invasion of privacy—the strategy followed has been to underline the *discriminatory* manner in which laws against prostitution are enforced (1976, p. 12).

Judge Taylor's ruling includes and goes beyond the decision that prostitution laws are used to discriminate against women. After discounting a set of arguments suggesting that prostitution harms the public, she notes that should it be legislative paternalism which inspires the law, the intent is poorly activated: "Women are not protected [by prostitution laws] but rather are penally punished" (*New York Law Journal, In Re P*, January 23, 1978, p. 12). Prostitution, she concludes, like any consensual sexual act between adults, is protected by the right to privacy.

Judge Taylor's decision does not purport to rule on the question whether solicitation by prostitutes is legal. Such behavior, she suggests, may be a public disorder; if so, the public act of solicitation and not the private one of sex for a fee should be the object of the law's concern. (This is in fact covered by New York's Penal Law, Article 240, Offenses Against the Public Order.)

In Re P was an action in family court because the alleged violator was a minor. In that regard, it should be noted that a minor cannot be labeled and treated as a juvenile delinquent by the courts if the behavior in question would be legal if carried out by an adult. The minor status of the respondent, however, does raise other issues, including the responsibility of the state for protecting children. Apropos of this problem a footnote to the ruling suggests that: "Paternalism might dictate. . . . some charge against the patron, such as endangering the welfare of a minor, attempted statutory rape or criminal solicitation" (*New York Law Journal, In Re P*, January 23, 1978, p. 12).

Consideration of paternalism draws attention to a curious pattern in which dominant groups in a host of societies and periods have attempted to provide protection to "weak" groups from members of the same dominant group: the protection of women from men, children from adults, colonizer from colonized. A retrospectively poignant, and significant comment on this process was made by Golda Meir in the following anecdote: "Once in a cabinet meeting we had to deal with the fact that there had been an outbreak of assaults on women at night. One minister suggested a curfew; women should stay home after dark. I said 'But it's the men who are attacking the women. If there's to be a curfew, let the men stay home, not the women'" (quoted in Berger, 1977, p. 43).

Paternalistic legislation might seem to reach a justification of sorts in cases of rape. Although paternalism is not absent from rape legislation, the actual process of prosecuting alleged rapists and the concomitant treatment of rape victims is typically paternalism's nemesis turned against the victim herself.[7]

Rape often has been viewed as an almost unique crime. Among crimes of sex, it is one which is decidedly not victimless. The legal definitions of rape, interpretations of relevant statutes, and indeed the entire criminal process

pursuant to a rape charge, are a myriad of practical and theoretical conundrums. In the Model Penal Code, "a male who has sexual intercourse with a female not his wife is guilty of rape if":

> (a) he compels her to submit by force or by threat of imminent death, serious bodily injury, extreme pain or kidnapping, to be inflicted on anyone; or
> (b) he has substantially impaired her power to appraise or control her conduct by administering or employing without her knowledge drugs, intoxicants or other means for the purpose of preventing resistance; or
> (c) the female is unconscious; or
> (d) the female is less than 10 years old.
> Rape is a felony of the second degree unless (i) in the course thereof the actor inflicts serious bodily injury upon anyone, or (ii) the victim was not a voluntary social companion of the actor upon the occasion of the crime and had not previously permitted him sexual liberties, in which cases the offense is a felony of the first degree. (Section 213.1) (See Appendix II which sets forth the somewhat different provisions of Article 130 of the New York Penal Law).

Only in a minority of cases do rape victims report the crime; rape has a bizarre "halo" effect, bestowing on the victim a sense of degradation and often an implied responsibility for the crime. Although the FBI reports 55,000 rape cases per year (Gager and Schurr 1976) that figure—of reported rapes—is estimated to represent between five percent and twenty percent of actual rapes. Furthermore, a relatively high proportion of rapes reported to the police have been classified as false reports, as "unfounded."

However rape may be defined in a specific, legal sense, understandings of the crime and its implications have shifted through the ages. In Biblical, as in early English law, rape was comprehended as an act akin to theft, robbing a woman's male guardian of her virginity. Earlier assumptions and ambiguities "as to whether the crime was a crime against [a man's] own estate" (Brownmiller, 1975, p. 15) have not vanished totally. The laws of rape continue to be linked with those of marriage. In most states of the United States, though not in other coun-

---

[7] Most current United States rape statutes are not sex-neutral. Only men can be rapists; only women their victims. Although this might seem to be a necessary correlate of the facts of the matter, were rape not defined as "penile penetration" only, sex-neutral legislation would make sense. Obviously, women as well as men are capable of sexual assault involving force and of rape involving sodomy. (A woman who is an accessory or who instigated the conduct, can in fact be convicted of rape; see New York Penal Law, Article 20, which makes a party to the offense criminally liable for the offense itself.) When the act involves a party under the age of consent (or an incompetent), there appears to be no reason why rape legislation should not be sex-neutral and in fact, as this article goes to press, the *New York Times* of 6/6/78 (p. 14A) reports that the Supreme Court refused to review a Circuit Court holding that the New Hampshire statutory rape law is unconstitutional on the grounds of sex discrimination. The case under consideration dealt with a sex act in which the female was under the age of consent. The New Hampshire statute has already been made sex-neutral, as have the rape statutes of Maine and Massachusetts.

tries (e.g., Sweden, Denmark, the U.S.S.R.), rape by legal definition cannot occur between spouses; a woman cannot be raped by her husband, for in establishing the marital bond, she effectively gives up the legal right to withhold consent from what otherwise might be deemed rape.

The law's and the wider society's suppositions about what constitutes the crime of rape may be revealed in comparing rape laws with other statutes. In particular, rape bears certain similarities to incest; that comparison becomes especially striking when comparing statutory rape (rape with a victim below a specified age) to incest committed by a father or legal guardian with his young daughter. In a different sense, rape can be compared with robbery. The first comparison, between rape and incest, becomes significant in regard to dissimilar penalties tending to be exacted from the victimizer; the second comparison, between rape and theft, is important in light of differential treatment typically accorded the respective victims by police and in the courts. What is or should be implied by the victims' consent, crucial to rape trials, and by the rapist's use of "force" becomes the crux of the matter in both comparisons.

Consent by a rape victim is a defense to a prosecution for rape. Consent, however, is irrelevant—being legally impossible to grant or to refuse—when the victim is below a certain age (set at ten in the Model Penal Code) or is incompetent. Penalties for statutory rape of a girl presumed too young to be able to offer reasonable consent, are among the severest handed down in cases of convictions of rape. In contrast, a man charged with "raping" his young daughter (termed incest) tends to be treated with more leniency by the courts than is the convicted rapist. In this regard, the effect of the law, if not its explicit intent, would seem to have a protracted history. The codes of Hammurabi, which condemned a man to death for raping a betrothed virgin, dealt with one found to have committed incest with his daughter by simply expelling him beyond the city walls (Brownmiller, 1976, p. 9).

Particular difficulties in trials of rape with respect to definitions and demonstrations of consent or its absence on the woman's side are further framed through comparison to crimes of theft. All too typically a rape victim's acquiescence to the act has been established in court and thus charges against the alleged rapist have been dismissed, because it could not be established that she spent her last breath warding off the attack: thus has a woman's consent been shown. On another, though not unrelated side, the victim's demeanor, her class, her heritage, and her intimate sexual history have been examined intricately or implied subtly as germane by defense attorneys, attempting to portray her as fundamentally receptive to acts of rape. Recently a New York appellate court overturned a verdict of rape; the conviction had been previously overturned in a 1976 appeal on the grounds that the judge had not informed adequately the jury that proof of rape in the first-degree demands demonstration that the victim "oppose[d] the perpetrator to the utmost limit of her power by genuine and active resistance" (*New York Times*, May 14, 1978, p. 30). That reversal was itself overturned by the New York Court of Appeals. Most recently, the Appellate Division overturned the original conviction a second time on the grounds that the victim's lack of consent was not shown adequately. The ruling, involving an alleged rapist and victim who had known each other for a week before the alleged rape occurred, suggests it is unlikely that a conviction for rape in the case of a dating couple could be sustained.

Obviously, the issues are complex. Not all men on trial for rape are guilty. The right of the victim to be protected from humiliation during trial must be balanced against the right of the defendant to a fair trial (c.f., Berger, 1977). Although the supposition seems strong in many trials for rape that certain victims "had it coming to them," similar sentiments are less frequently and less explicitly expressed toward victims of theft. That a person, while being robbed, did not use all force at his or her command to repel the offense generally is seen to indicate common sense rather than a discreditation of the victim's testimony. Personal blame for the robbed's own misfortune is not presumed to follow from his or her amassed wealth, expensive jewelry, or previous tendency to give away money in the form of philanthropy.

At base, as has been remarked by several commentators (e.g., Brownmiller, 1976, Berger, 1977), rape law and the treatment of rape victims within the criminal system, at least until recent years, have been directed by a view of women as categorically chaste or unchaste; in this view, at the extreme, rape becomes a moot issue. The first kind of woman does not allow herself to get raped but neither does the second, since she consents (and thus the act is not definable as rape).

Brownmiller identifies the above categorization of women in regard to rape with that found in pornography. Females, she suggests "are depicted in two clearly delineated roles: as virgins who are caught and 'banged' or as nymphomaniacs who are never sated" (1976, p. 443). In a broader sense, obscenity, including its legal proscription and definition, offers an arena for examining comprehensions of sex by legislatures and the judiciary. Not only does pornography exploit, while perverting, wider society's notions about sex but jurists, in deciding obscenity cases, must face definitions of sexuality and must differentiate various stances—obscene, educational, honest, scientific, degrading—toward the discussion and presentation of sexual matters. Substantively, the courts have tried to map a path between the constitutional rights of free speech and due process and a presumed right of the state to protect the public from obscenity and pornography.

In *Roth* v. *U.S.* (1957), the Supreme Court upheld the constitutionality of a statute making punishable the mailing of "obscene, lewd, lascivious, or filthy" material. Justice Brennan, writing for the Court, described the current test for obscenity to entail a decision about "whether to the average person, applying contemporary standards, the dominant theme of the material as a whole appeals to prurient interest." Justice Brennan's description of a legal test for ob-

scenity indicates as adequately as more extended legal debate and judicial consideration that comprehensions of sex (including those of the sociologist and the lawyer) cannot be objective or based in value-free understandings of reality. Sex and sexuality are part of a wider sociocultural order. All stand within that wider order and share at least some of its assumptions. Alternatively, of course, one stands elsewhere, sharing other assumptions, prone to other responses and analyses. Neither is fully subjective, neither fully objective. "Coitus," writes Kate Millett, "can scarcely be said to take place in a vacuum although of itself it appears a biological and physical activity, it is set so deeply within the larger context of human affairs that it serves as a charged microcosm of the variety of attitudes and values to which culture subscribes" (1971, p. 43).

LAW AND SOCIAL RULES

Law comprises a set of rules and rules for the use of those rules which, themselves an object of study, allow investigation of the larger sociocultural order. Legal trends appear and shift in concert with other social alterations. There is, however, a tendency for law and judicial decisions to express the specific, concrete concerns and the social policies of a generation past. Judges are generally prosperous, male, members of the bar, over sixty. In addition, the fundamental importance of precedent as the operant principle of the judiciary explicitly demarcates previous decisions as a basis for current ones. Even on the heels of alterations resulting from legislative acts, judges are inclined to provide interpretations which sustain the courtesies of their own experience. In this respect, the landmark decision, *Griswold* v. *Connecticut*, defining a right of privacy (here, in relation to contraception) might appear relatively in advance of law's own time. Cases like this (and succeeding decisions relying on the notion of privacy, e.g., *Eisenstadt* v. *Baird, Roe* v. *Wade*) would appear to rattle a society which had held women to be inferior, weak, and needing protection, and to loosen that society's restrictions on sexual behavior. Although we do not expressly dispute this suggestion, we claim that from a somewhat different perspective these decisions work to reinforce another basic feature of the American polity and society, the division between private and public spheres. We further suggest that that reinforcement may be ultimately of at least equal significance to concomitant changes concerning when and where people have a right to declare particular behaviors private. The state maintains its right to determine who may have sexual relations with whom and to fix the laws of marriage, divorce, property rights, and custody prerogatives. Certain arenas including the marital bed—and now the nonmarital bed—have been declared private. But the declaration may itself create an illusion of sorts. The state continues to set the terms of marriage and to determine which aspects of that legally defined relationship may be generalized to other contexts. The law continues to establish and to limit a private domain, differentiating it from a public one. The state, through law, explicates proper and improper patterns of sexual behavior and, in that lawmakers embed or redefine wider notions of paternity, maternity, spouse, and childhood, which notions, in turn, bear heavily on matters of divorce, inheritance, property ownership, and tax obligations.

Eli Zaretsky (1976) argues that nineteenth-century capitalism brought two interrelated changes which re-defined the notion of "family." Labor was taken effectively outside the family unit and placed in factories and centralized corporate settings. Women continued to "work" in the home, but that work was defined as a marital and maternal obligation rather than as labor. At the same time, a sphere of activity, the activity of "private" life, was separated from public activity, including work, and came to represent those spaces and times preserved for "leisure," for personal creativity and entertainment: "As a result 'work' and 'life' were separated. . . . Just as capitalist development gave rise to the idea of the family as a separate realm from the economy, so it created a 'separate' sphere of personal life,

seemingly divorced from the mode of production" (Zaretsky, 1976, p. 30). Laws concerning sex and sexuality must be understood in light of this history.[8] The state maintains its interest in laws of marriage, and the society maintains a comprehension of sex as ideally represented in and representative of the family (Schneider 1968). Yet, laws concerning sex have been altered and generalized in accord with notions of the increasing importance of "private" life (as opposed to "working" life). Sexuality itself has become another commodity, one through which the individual attempts to underscore and sustain a personal meaning to life.

However poignant—or annoying—Biblical stories of sexual encounter may seem, we learn relatively little about contemporary sex law from their example. It is not the metaphors of Dinah, raped by Shechem, nor of Potiphar's wife, who falsely accused Joseph of the same crime, which are basic to this analysis. Rather, the analogies and comparisons of importance to the consideration of current sex laws are those of the consumer and of the structures and assumptions underlying corporate law.

APPENDIX I

GENERAL PURPOSES AND DEFINITIONS FROM NEW YORK PENAL LAW

§ 1.05 GENERAL PURPOSES

The general purposes of the provisions of this chapter are:
1. To proscribe conduct which unjustifiably and inexcusably causes or threatens substantial harm to individual or public interests;
2. To give fair warning of the nature of the conduct proscribed and of the sentences authorized upon conviction;
3. To define the act or omission and the accompanying mental state which constitute each offense;

[8] See Barnett and Silverman (forthcoming) for an excellent analysis of the complicated inter-relations between the domains of work and home (public and private life), presumably separated and yet each able to be substituted for the other (e.g., personal marriage contracts which, through the use of legal—contractual—form, presume to set the terms of personal relationships).

4. To differentiate on reasonable grounds between serious and minor offenses and to prescribe proportionate penalties therefor; and

5. To insure the public safety by preventing the commission of offenses through the deterrent influence of the sentences authorized, the rehabilitation of those convicted, and their confinement when required in the interests of public protection.

§ 130.00 SEX OFFENSES; DEFINITIONS OF TERMS

The following definitions are applicable to this article:

1. "Sexual intercourse" has its ordinary meaning and occurs upon any penetration, however slight.

2. "Deviate sexual intercourse" means sexual conduct between persons not married to each other consisting of contact between the penis and the anus, the mouth and penis, or the mouth and the vulva.

3. "Sexual contact" means any touching of the sexual or other intimate parts of a person not married to the actor for the purpose of gratifying sexual desire of either party.

4. "Female" means any female person who is not married to the actor.

5. "Mentally defective" means that a person suffers from a mental disease or defect which renders him incapable of appraising the nature of his conduct.

6. "Mentally incapacitated" means that a person is rendered temporarily incapable of appraising or controlling his conduct owing to the influence of a narcotic or intoxicating substance administered to him without his consent, or to any other act committed upon him without his consent.

7. "Physically helpless" means that a person is unconscious or for any other reason is physically unable to communicate unwillingness to an act.

8. "Forcible compulsion" means physical force that overcomes earnest resistance; or a threat, express or implied, that places a person in fear of immediate death or serious physical injury to himself or another person, or in fear that he or another person will immediately be kidnapped.

§ 235.00 OBSCENITY; DEFINITIONS OF TERMS

The following definitions are applicable to sections 235.05, 235.10 and 235.15:

1. "Obscene." Any material or performance is "obscene" if (a) the average person, applying contemporary community standards, would find that considered as a whole, its predominant appeal is to the prurient interest in sex, and (b) it depicts or describes in a patently offensive manner, actual or simulated: sexual intercourse, sodomy, sexual bestiality, masturbation, sadism, masochism, excretion or lewd exhibition of the genitals, and (c) considered as a whole, it lacks serious literary, artistic, political, and scientific value. Predominant appeal shall be judged with reference to ordinary adults unless it appears from the character of the material or the circumstances of its dissemination to be designed for children or other specially susceptible audience.

2. "Material" means anything tangible which is capable of being used or adapted to arouse interest, whether through the medium of reading, observation, sound or in any other manner.

3. "Performance" means any play, motion picture, dance or other exhibition performed before an audience.

4. "Promote" means to manufacture, issue, sell, give, provide, lend, mail, deliver, transfer, transmute, publish, distribute, circulate, disseminate, present, exhibit or advertise, or to offer or agree to do the same.

5. "Wholesale promote" means to manufacture, issue, sell, provide, mail, deliver, transfer, transmute, publish, distribute, circulate, disseminate or to offer or agree to do the same for purposes of resale.

6. "Simulated" means the explicit depiction or description of any of the types of conduct set forth in clause (b) of subdivision one of this section, which creates the appearance of such conduct.

7. "Sodomy" means any of the types of sexual conduct defined in subdivision two of section 130.00 provided, however, that in any prosecution under this article the marital status of the persons engaged in such conduct shall be irrelevant and shall not be considered.

§ 235.15 OBSCENITY; DEFENSE

In any prosecution for obscenity, it is an affirmative defense that the persons to whom allegedly obscene material was disseminated, or the audience to an allegedly obscene performance, consisted of persons or institutions having scientific, educational, governmental or other similar justification for possessing or viewing the same.

§ 235.20 DISSEMINATING INDECENT MATERIAL TO MINORS; DEFINITIONS OF TERMS

The following definitions are applicable to sections 235.21 and 235.22:

1. "Minor" means any person less than seventeen years old.

2. "Nudity" means the showing of the human male or female genitals, pubic area or buttocks with less than a full opaque covering, or the showing of the female breast with less than a fully opaque covering of any portion thereof below the top of the nipple, or the depiction of covered male genitals in a discernable turgid state.

3. "Sexual conduct" means acts of masturbation, homosexuality, sexual intercourse, or physical contact with a person's clothed or unclothed genitals, pubic area, buttocks or, if such person be a female, breast.

4. "Sexual excitement" means the condition of human male or female genitals when in a state of sexual stimulation or arousal.

5. "Sado-masochistic abuse" means flagellation or torture by or upon a person clad in undergarments, a mask or bizarre costume, or the condition of being fettered, bound or otherwise physically restrained on the part of one so clothed.

6. "Harmful to minors" means that quality of any description or representation, in whatever form, of nudity, sexual conduct, sexual excitement, or sado-masochistic abuse, when it:

(a) Considered as a whole, appeals to the prurient. Interest in sex of minors; and

(b) Is patently offensive to prevailing standards in the adult community as a whole with respect to what is suitable material for minors; and

(c) Considered as a whole, lacks serious literary, artistic, political, and scientific value for minors.

APPENDIX II

RAPE, NEW YORK PENAL LAW

§ 130.20   SEXUAL MISCONDUCT

A person is guilty of sexual misconduct when:
1. Being a male, he engages in sexual intercourse with a female without her consent; or
2. He engages in deviate sexual intercourse with another person without the latter's consent; or
3. He engages in sexual conduct with an animal or a dead human body.
Sexual misconduct is a class A misdemeanor.

§ 130.25   RAPE IN THE THIRD DEGREE

A male is guilty of rape in the third degree when:
1. He engages in sexual intercourse with a female who is incapable of consent by reason of some factor other than being less than seventeen years old; or

2. Being twenty-one years old or more, he engages in sexual intercourse with a female less than seventeen years old.
Rape in the third degree is a class E felony.

§ 130.30   RAPE IN THE SECOND DEGREE

A male is guilty of rape in the second degree when, being eighteen years old or more, he engages in sexual intercourse with a female less than fourteen years old.
Rape in the second degree is a class D felony.

§ 130.35   RAPE IN THE FIRST DEGREE

A male is guilty of rape in the first degree when he engages in sexual intercourse with a female:
1. By forcible compulsion; or
2. Who is incapable of consent by reason of being physically helpless; or
3. Who is less than eleven years old.
Rape in the first degree is a class B felony.

REFERENCES

BARNETT, S. 1977. Identity choice and caste ideology in contemporary South India. *Symbolic anthropology*, ed. J. Dolgin, D. Kemnitzer, and D. Schneider. New York: Columbia University Press.

———. 1973. Urban is as urban does: two incidents on one street in Madras City, South India. *Urban Anthropology* 2.

BARNETT, S., and SILVERMAN, M. G. In press. The person in capitalist ideology. Ann Arbor: University of Michigan Press.

BARNETT, W. 1973. *Sexual freedom and the constitution*. Albuquerque: University of New Mexico Press.

BERGER, V. 1977. Man's trial, woman's tribulation: rape cases in the courtroom. *Columbia Law Review* 77: 1–103.

BROWN, B.; EMERSON, T. I.; FALK, G.; and FREEDMAN, A. E. 1971. The Equal Rights Amendment: a constitutional basis for equal rights for women. *Yale Law Journal* 80: 871–985.

BROWNMILLER, S. 1976. *Against our will*. New York: Bantam Books.

BULLOUGH, V. L. 1976. *Sexual variance in society and history.* New York: Wiley.

CHURCHILL, W. 1971. *Homosexual behavior among males.* Englewood Cliffs: Prentice-Hall.

DAVIDSON, K. M.; GINSBURG, P. B.; and KAY, H. H. 1974. *Text, cases and materials on sex-based discrimination.* St. Paul: West Publishing.

DENNETT, M. W. 1970. *Birth control laws.* New York: DaCapo Press.

DIENES, C. T. 1972. *Law, politics, and birth control.* Urbana: University of Illinois Press.

DOLGIN, J. 1977. *Jewish identity and the JDL.* Princeton, N.J.: Princeton University Press.

———; KEMNITZER, D.; and SCHNEIDER, D. 1977. As people express their lives so they are . . . In *Symbolic anthropology,* ed. J. Dolgin, D. Kemnitzer, and D. Schneider. New York: Columbia University Press.

DUMONT, L. 1970. *Homo hierarchicus,* trans. Mark Sainsbury. Chicago: University of Chicago Press.

FIRESTONE, S. 1971. *The dialectic of sex.* New York: Bantam Books.

Forcible and statutory rape: an exploration of the operation and objectives of the consent standard. 1952. Comment. *Yale Law Journal* 62: 623–35.

GAGER, N., and SCHURR, C. 1976. *Sexual assaults confronting rape in America.* New York: Grosset and Dunlap.

KEMNITZER, D. 1977. Sexuality as a social performance: performance and anxiety in America. In *Symbolic anthropology,* ed. J. Dolgin, D. Kemnitzer, and D. Schneider. New York: Columbia University Press.

LADER, L. 1966. *Abortion.* Boston: Beacon Press.

———. 1973. *Abortion II: making the revolution.* Boston: Beacon Press.

MACPHERSON, C. B. 1962. *The political theory of possessive individualism.* Oxford: Clarendon Press.

MARTIN, D., and LYON, P. 1972. *Lesbian women.* New York: Bantam Books.

MILLETT, K. 1973. *The prostitution papers.* New York: Ballantine Books.

———. 1971. *Sexual politics.* New York: Avon Books.

Model Penal Code. 1962.

New York State Penal Law. 1965.

Private consensual homosexual behavior: the crime and its enforcement. 1961. Note and Comment. *Yale Law Journal* 70: 55–83.

SCHNEIDER, D. M. 1968. *American kinship.* Englewood Cliffs: Prentice-Hall.

———. 1969. Kinship, nationality, and religion in American culture: toward a definition of kinship." In *Forms of symbolic action,* ed. V. Turner. American Ethnological Society. Seattle: University of Washington Press.

SCHUR, E. 1965. *Crimes without victims.* Englewood Cliffs: Prentice-Hall.

———, and BEDAU, H. A. 1974. *Victimless crimes.* Englewood Cliffs: Prentice-Hall.

SWIFT, J. I. *Gulliver's Travels.*

The Wolfenden Report. 1963. Report of the Committee on Homosexual Offenses and Prostitution. New York: Stein and Day.

ZARETSKY, E. 1976. *Capitalism, the family, and personal life.* New York: Harper Colophon Books.

CASES CITED

Bradwell v. *Illinois.* 83 US. (16 Wall.) 130, 1873.

Carey v. *Population Services International.* 45 U.S.L.W. 4610, June 4, 1977.

Commonwealth v. *Daniels.* 210 Pa. Super. 156, 1967.

Eisenstadt v. *Baird.* 405 US. 438, 1972.

Griswold v. *Connecticut.* 381 US. 479, 1965.

Hoyt v. *Florida.* 368 US. 57, 1961.

In Re P. New York Law Journal, January 23, 1978: 11–12.

Mitchell v. *Commissioner.* 78 Ken. 204, 1879.

Reed v. *Reed.* 404 US. 71, 1971.

Roe v. *Wade.* 410 US. 113, 1973.

Roth v. *United States.* 354 US. 476, 1957.

Sail'er Inn, Inc. v. *Kirby,* 5 Cal. 3d 1, 1971.

Stanley v. *Georgia.* 394 US. 557, 1969.

State v. *Hall.* 187 So. 2d 861, 1966.

TWELVE

Sex Discrimination

MADELINE E. HEILMAN

Key statistics reveal that women still are not fully integrated into the mainstream of the American work force. Although they now comprise nearly half of all wage earners, they continue to be grossly under-represented in occupations associated with power or status. As recently as 1970, for example, only 5% of all lawyers and judges, 6% of all industrial managers, and 9% of all physicians were women (Council of Economic Advisors, 1973). Thus, despite federal legislation, consciousness-raising activities, and women's caucuses, disparities persist.

Obstacles to women's advancement in nontraditional areas derive both from forces within women themselves and from forces outside them. Women's fear of success (Horner, 1972), limited self-confidence (Lenney, 1977), low achievement motivation (Veroff, Wilcox, and Atkinson, 1953) and role conflict (Hall, 1972) are some of the internal factors detrimentally affecting their own achievement. Discussion of these phenomena, although they act to support and maintain sex discriminatory practices, is not within the scope of this essay. It is designed to explore only the externally imposed barriers that thwart women in their quest for equality.

Because they are so central to the issues of women's advancement, the focus of our concerns will be the experiences women encounter in the work world. When considering work-related discrimination it is necessary to distinguish between its two different forms (Levitan, Quinn, and Staines, 1971; Terborg and Ilgen, 1975). One is the nonjob-related limitations put on members of a subgroup influencing their attempts to enter an organization. This is called access discrimination. Funneling of women to some jobs and not others, failing to hire women applicants for certain positions, and offering a lower salary to women as compared to men all are examples of access discrimination on the basis of sex. The other form of discrimination, treatment discrimination, is the differential treatment of members of a subgroup once they have gained access to a position and are at work on the job. Promoting women more slowly than men, giving them fewer opportunities to learn new skills, or giving them lower or less frequent salary raises all are examples of treatment discrimination involving sex.

In the following pages we will review research detailing the existence of and the potential explanations for sex discriminatory behavior. We will discuss separately research concerning elements of access discrimination and of treatment discrimination. Sex differences with respect to sex discrimination also will be considered briefly. A concluding section will explore the action implied by the research findings and the theoretical ideas presented.

Before delving into research investigations about discrimination per se, it is critical to examine the stereotypes about women shared within our culture. For whatever the dynamics operative in a given situation, the basis of sex discrimination is the beliefs held about women—beliefs about what they are like and beliefs about how they should behave.

SEX STEREOTYPES

Because beliefs about women and how they compare to men are widely shared within our culture and are assumed to apply to nearly all men and women as members of their respective groups, these beliefs are called stereotypes. According to Terborg (1977), sex stereotypes have two components. First, they specify the characteristics of each sex. Second, they dictate which behaviors are appropriate to men and women. Either of these can form the basis of sex discrimination, one based on faulty beliefs about what women are like and the other based on normative expectations about what women should be like.

HISTORY

Although thorough examinations of how women were regarded throughout history can be found elsewhere (Bullough, 1973; Taylor, 1973) it is nonetheless instructive to consider briefly a few central points. Stereotypes about women have had a long tradition in our culture, and it is important to view current events not as isolated happenings but as part of a historical progression. Particularly germane to the discriminatory treatment of women is the age-old image of women as inferior to men and the long-standing image of women as both physically and emotionally frail.

The idea that women are inferior to men has been accepted throughout Western history. The Greeks excluded women from any political, intellectual, or social activities, and gave them no legal status or education. Women were viewed as equipped only to bear children and to maintain the home, and they often had no contact with anyone outside their immediate households (Arthur, 1973). Aristotle perhaps best articulated the Greek image of women when he wrote, "We should look on the female state as being . . . a deformity". Plato, although more diplomatic, was no less biased in his view, "All the pursuits of men are the pursuits of women also, but in all of them a woman is inferior to a man".

Religious teachings also espoused this point of view (Hunter, 1976). In the creation story in the Book of Genesis, Eve is essentially an afterthought, created from Adam. Elsewhere in the Bible, women are depicted as property, first of their fathers, then of their husbands. Christianity, although ostensibly more liberal in its conception of women, largely through the writings of Paul, also has relegated women to a secondary status, allowing them no important role in the church. The Judeo-Christian tradition thus perpetuated the negative view of women so prevalent in antiquity.

An alternative view of women began to emerge in France in the eleventh century. Chivalry came into being. Now a woman no longer was a man's inferior but his inspiration to excellence and his duty to protect. Even so, women were confined to passive roles, waiting for knights to perform brave deeds to win their love. Although different, this also was a belittling role for women. Again their dependence upon men was highlighted, suggestive of a fundamental weakness and inability to cope with life's realities.

These views of women, women as inferior and women as weak and dependent, have predominated through the centuries. The consequence has been the legitimization of the differential treatment of women. Even the courts, until very recently, accepted womanhood as a condition warranting different treatment by the law (Agate and Meacham, 1977). Using the commonly accepted cultural conception of women, United States Supreme Court Justice Bradley in 1873 explained why a state could constitutionally ban women from practicing law: "The natural and proper timidity and delicacy which belongs to the female sex evidently unfits it for many of the occupations of civil life" (*Bradwell* v. *Illinois*, 83 U.S. (16 Wall) 130, 141). It was not until almost a hundred years later that the Supreme Court first ruled that sex was not a permissible basis for differential legal treatment.

Stereotypes about what women are like are part of our heritage. Our legacy is the teaching that men and women are fundamentally different not only in the roles they have played, but also in their capabilities and talents. The specifics of these different conceptions are described below.

SEX-STEREOTYPIC ATTRIBUTES

If asked to describe a "typical man" or a "typical woman," you probably would be able to do so. It also is likely that your descriptions would match those given by others. Whether subjects have differed in sex, age, religion, mental status, or educational background, researchers consistently have found substantial agreement in the beliefs that people have about the traits characteristic of men and women.

Studies of sex stereotypes have demonstrated repeatedly that men and women are viewed very differently; in fact, they are viewed as polar opposites in many personality attributes (Broverman, Vogel, Broverman, Clarkson, and Rosenkrantz, 1972). In achievement-oriented traits men are thought to be competent and strong, and women are thought to be incompetent and weak. Whereas men are described as independent, active, competitive, self-confident, and ambitious, women are described as dependent, passive, uncompetitive, unconfident, and unambitious. Men and women also are described differently in qualities of warmth and expressiveness, with women being rated more positively: they are described as tender, understanding, concerned with others, and comfortable with their feelings, whereas men are described in opposite terms.

It seems that little has changed since 1957 when McKee and Sherriffs found that when subjects were asked to generate images of men and women, males were characterized by (a) rational competence and ability and (b) vigor, action, and effectiveness. Women, on the other hand, were characterized by (a) social skills and (b) warmth and emotional support. Then, too, characteristics most commonly ascribed to men were those essential to achievement but those most commonly ascribed to women were those associated with nurture and affiliation.

The traits associated with women and men are not only different, but they are seen as differentially desirable. Although each is credited with a number of positive traits, subjects of both sexes concur that those associated with men are more valued than those associated with women (Rosenkrantz, Vogel, Bee, Broverman, and Broverman, 1968). Simply put, achievement seems to be more highly valued in our society than nurture or affiliation. A great deal of evidence supports this point. Smith (1939) found that as age increased, children of both sexes increasingly indicated a preference for the traits of males rather than of females. Fernberger (1948) found that college students cast

male rather than female characters in fictional situations requiring intelligence and "all-around superiority." Finally, McKee and Sherriffs (1959) found that a typical man is believed to possess a greater number of desirable characteristics than a typical woman.

Looking at the world around us it is apparent how stereotypical views are passed on and maintained. The images of men presented in children's textbooks, for instance, are consistently active, curious, and independent; girls, however, are depicted as dependent, showing little initiative, and constantly in need of help from boys (Weitzman, Eifler, Hokadin, and Ross, 1972). Similarly stereotyped presentations of men and women can be found in television commercials. In a recent study in which the roles of men and women in these commercials were compared, only 14% of the women were found to be in authoritative positions as compared to 70% of the men. Moreover, when they agreed to buy a product, men were shown to be motivated by potential social and/or career advancement, but women were shown to be motivated by the increased satisfaction of their families or men in their life (McArthur and Resko, 1976).

It is not difficult to see how stereotyped conceptions of what women are like are transmitted. But to what extent are these conceptions accurate reflections of reality? Are men and women actually as different as is commonly assumed?

Until recently it was generally accepted that the biological differences between men and women were paralleled by distinct psychological differences. In fact, several reviews of the literature focused on the nature of these sex differences (Garai and Scheinfeld, 1968; Maccoby, 1966; Tyler, 1965). The areas in which functioning was thought to differ was broad: intellectual ability, dependency, passivity, self-esteem, cognitive style, and perception. In some cases reported findings depicted males more favorably; in others, they depicted females more favorably, but the notion of differences was upheld.

However, in 1974, Maccoby and Jacklin, in

their exhaustive book, *The Psychology of Sex Differences,* carefully examined the available data and concluded that many of the presumed differences between males and females are based on myth, not on reality. They found no support for the view that women lack the motivation to achieve nor that they are less intelligent than men. Patterns of task persistence and risk-taking behavior were found to be quite similar to both sexes. Also challenged were the alleged differences in the social needs often attributed to men and women. According to Maccoby and Jacklin, females have not been found to be more sociable, more dependent on others, or more oriented toward social stimulation and reinforcement than have males.

Additionally, a considerable body of literature examines women's feelings toward and behavior at work. Results from many of these studies also contradict the notion that women are different from men. Women have been reported to have similar vocational interests (Diamond, 1968), leadership abilities (Day and Stogdill, 1972), and problem-solving abilities (Matthews, 1972) to men's. In many areas directly related to achievement men and women are more alike than different. Yet, despite this fact, the view that crucial differences exist between the sexes persists.

SEX-STEREOTYPIC ROLE NORMS

Sex stereotypes denote not only the differences in attributes between men and women, but also the behaviors suitable to each. If, for instance, an irate student were to scuffle physically with a same sex roommate, observers' reactions would differ greatly if the students were women or men. Similarly, if the same student were to burst into tears after a particularly stressful episode, reactions to him or her would again take gender into account. These examples illustrate the fact that there are behaviors deemed "appropriate" to one sex and not the other. Inappropriately engaging in cross-sex behavior can result in social sanctions.

Norms governing the approved masculine or feminine stereotypic image are clearly defined and widely held (Lunnenborg, 1970; McKee and Sherriffs, 1959; Steinmann and Fox, 1966). They specify behaviors that are thought to be not only characteristic of each sex but also desirable and therefore to be encouraged. (Although we may expect women to be catty, we do not demand that they be so; therefore cattiness would be a sex-stereotypic attribute, but not a sex-stereotypic norm.) By and large the norms specify that passive, emotional, and socially sensitive behavior is appropriate to women, but tough, rational, and aggressive behavior is appropriate to men. Consequently "feminine" little girls are preferred to "tomboys," and "masculine" little boys are preferred to "sissies," both by their peers and by adults. Similarly, women who display "womanly" traits and men who display "manly" traits are more favorably evaluated and judged more psychologically healthy than those who do not (Costrich, Feinstein, Kidder, Marecek, and Pascale, 1975).

Because stereotypes dictate what behavior is appropriate to males and females, they have a self-renewing quality: they influence the way in which children are reared. Socialization proceeds according to our assumptions about the sexes: what children "should" be like, and what they "naturally" are like. Many parents protest this idea, vigorously claiming that they treat their sons and daughters identically, that their sons play with dolls as well as with guns, and their daughters with guns as well as with dolls. But researchers and other objective observers disagree.

Even when newly born, parents of girls and boys view their children in accordance with sex-role norms. When asked to describe their infants on an adjective checklist while still in the hospital, the girls were rated by both fathers and mothers as softer, smaller, finer-featured, and less attentive than the boys were (Rubin, Provenzano, and Luria, 1974). They did so despite the fact that doctors reported no objective differences in either size or activities level. Clearly expectations about how happy and healthy little girls and boys should be influenced their judgments.

Parents also have been shown to treat children differently when they are male or female, always cultivating appropriate masculinity and femininity in their progeny. Girls by and large are treated as if they were more fragile than boys and do not as frequently engage in rough-and-tumble games and activities (Kagan, 1971). The message communicated is one of appropriateness—little girls should not be as aggressive as their brothers. A myriad of other behaviors also become designated indirectly as appropriate or inappropriate to girls and boys—through the clothes they wear, the toys they play with, and the television programs they are encouraged to watch.

By the time most children are school age, they already have developed sex-appropriate behaviors. This can be verified by observing them at play. Boys prefer to play with blocks, trucks, and carpenter's tools, and girls prefer playing house and dress-up (Nadelman, 1974). This tendency is reinforced in school. Observation of nursery school classrooms indicated that boys received rewards and attention for disruptive behavior and girls did not; boys were encouraged to experiment on their own more often than girls were. Although the teachers in this study reported being unaware of their differential treatment of girls and boys, they clearly were encouraging boys to be active and independent, and discouraging these behaviors in girls (Serbin, O'Leary, Kent, and Tonick, 1973).

The learning and incorporating of sex-appropriate behaviors is a powerful force during socialization. It also becomes a critical dimension along which others are evaluated. It is in this way that sex stereotypic norms feed discriminatory practices. There are some tasks and job responsibilities seen as unsuitable to women, and their engaging in them or even expressing a desire to do so is unfavorably viewed.

In summary, stereotypes about women have both descriptive and normative components. The former characterizes women in a manner undermining their competence and effectiveness. The latter casts as deviants those women whose behavior seems inappropriately mascu-

line. Each can have potentially detrimental consequences for an achievement-oriented woman.

ACCESS DISCRIMINATION

Both when a woman selects a nontraditional career goal and when she attempts to pursue it, powerful discriminatory forces can come into play. First we will consider the factors inhibiting the choice of nontraditional career goals, then the barriers impeding the realization of these goals.

DISCRIMINATORY PRESSURES INFLUENCING CAREER CHOICE

Which career to choose, or what to do when one "grows up" historically has been a critical question for males within our culture. But the cultural assumption about females is that they will not, if they can possibly help it, work outside the home but rather will care for house and children. If they are to venture out into the work world, there are only certain occupations suitable to their sex. These expectations are operative no matter how educated a woman or how extraordinary her talents.

It has become increasingly evident that not all women share the assumption that a woman's "place" is in the home. Although most women do marry and have children, many also work. In fact, the proportion of working women has risen from 20% in 1900 to 45% in 1974 (Troll, 1975). By 1980, the number of women in the work force is projected to be greater than the number of men.

A great deal of data has been accumulated, however, demonstrating that women still are largely confined to traditional women's occupations. In the sixties, for instance, there was a disproportionately small growth in numbers of women in professional and technical fields, in skilled trades, and in managerial capacities, but a disproportionately large increase in the number of women clerical workers (Hedges, 1970).

Thus, while the numbers of women in the labor force have increased, the scope and range of their activities has not. Even the small number who do enter professions seems to wind up in the specialties considered lowest in status (Gross, 1967). In law, women are found far more frequently in practices involving juvenile, divorce, or welfare cases than in practices involving tax law and corporate litigation. Similar patterns have been found in medicine in which women typically are pediatricians, dermatologists, or psychiatrists, rather than surgeons, internists, or neurologists. In academia this tendency also has been found to predominate with women comprising a far larger proportion of the state teachers college faculties than of the faculties of wealthier and more revered schools.

Although these statistics may well reflect the hesitancy of women to break new ground, they also suggest the existence of decriminatory forces within our educational and work institutions that discourage women from entering nontraditional fields. Two such forces are the vocational counseling process and the paucity of visible role models.

The vocational counseling process. Almost from the time they enter school, girls seem to restrict the range of occupations they consider. Looft (1971), for instance, found that first- and second-grade boys named more than twice as many occupations as the same-aged girls when asked what they wanted to be when they grew up. Furthermore, more than 75% of the girls questioned named the traditionally sex-appropriate occupations of nurse or teacher as their primary career choice. The results since have been replicated (Siegal, 1973).

Even if a girl does choose a nonconventional career objective, she is apt to run up against powerful obstructions. Vocational guidance perpetuates the notion of occupational distinction between the sexes. Research evidence suggests that both male and female counselors respond most positively to those women who hold traditional career goals (Thomas and Steward,

1971). There also is evidence suggesting that professional personnel consultants generally agree that a four-year college is less advisable for women than for men (Cash, Gillen, Burns, 1977). In a recent study it was discovered that the counseling given men and women who were not accepted into medical school differed. Men rejectees were urged to persevere in their career objectives or to substitute others that were of nearly equivalent status; women rejectees, however, were encouraged to reconsider and/or abandon their career goals in favor of those that were more traditionally appropriate to a woman (Weisman, Morlock, Sack, and Levine, 1976). Therefore women often are pressured to set traditional career goals and receive little support for deviating from the pattern deemed appropriate to their sex. Consequently, because of their power and authority, those in a position to counsel can create insurmountable obstacles for women hoping to fulfill nonconventional career aspirations. Such behavior is one of the most pernicious forms of sex discrimination. Unfortunately, its effects most often are not recognized until it is too late to undo them.

A Department of Health, Education, and Welfare regulation prohibits discrimination within educational institutions in counseling materials, aptitude tests, and also in the counseling process itself. Some curriculum packages have been developed for counselors to use to help girls examine various careers and lifestyles (e.g., Hansen, 1972). At the elementary school level, OCCUPACS enables boys and girls to experiment with a variety of occupations. At the junior high school level, counseling tools have been developed to stimulate girls' awareness of the potential and challenge of work. Further information about new developments and counseling techniques can be found in Wirtenberg and Nakamura (1976).

It should be remembered that the vocational counselor is in a unique position to intervene in the socialization process by challenging the assumption underlying sex-typed occupational choices. Training of counselors must emphasize this if these individuals are to become instrumental in facilitating rather than in blocking achievement-oriented women.

The absence of role models. There are many discussions in the literature pointing out the importance of female role models to women with nontraditional occupational goals (e.g., Brenner, 1972; Buchanan, 1969). It has been proposed that the absence of females who successfully function in traditionally male occupations discourages other women from considering them (Shein, 1972). However, the number of women role models still is quite limited.

The term "female role model" usually is used to refer to a woman who has combined marriage and career, and has effectively achieved in the work world without sacrificing her womanhood. In many studies the influence of nontraditional mothers (who combine family with career), on their daughters (who also tend to be nontraditional), is considered the influence of a role model (Almquist and Angrist, 1971; Tangri, 1972). However, the term role model also can be used in a more general sense. It can simply connote the presence of other members of one's subgroup in positions of power and prestige. It is in this sense that the absence of female role models can be a source of sex discrimination.

By not placing women in visible and important positions, organizations and professional groups may be ensuring that they do not attract the interest of women making career decisions. Data supporting this point of view recently have been collected (Heilman, in press). When told that a moderate rather than the traditionally meager proportion of women would populate a given occupation during the next decade, female high school students expressed a greater interest in that occupation. They also indicated a higher estimate of their probability of success. These results attest to the fact that the number of women within an organization or professional group communicates important information to women actively seeking career paths.

Number is not necessarily the only issue; visibility may be very critical. Anecdotal evidence supports this contention. After this author had been a member of the faculty for several years, she was appointed the director of her undergraduate program at Yale College. Immediately following this appointment there was a sudden and dramatic increase in the number of women who "signed up" for that major. Similar trends have been evident in female course enrollments when women rather than men faculty members are instructors. Although causation obviously cannot be attributed in these cases, they nevertheless provide food for thought.

The reasoning implied here appears to be rather circular. If a woman's career choices are determined by the conspicuous presence of successful women already in that career, then occupations currently without women would never shift in sexual composition. Of course this is not so. Many other factors besides the existence of role models enter into career decisions. But the perceived absence of women within the occupational ranks may deter the entry of women and/or slow down the rate at which they seek access to a given career.

Nontraditional career choices can be inhibited both by the stereotypical beliefs of vocational counselors and also by the tacit messages conveyed by the sexual composition of an occupational group. Despite these potential deterrents, some women do select nontraditional career paths. What happens to them then?

GAINING ACCESS TO NONTRADITIONAL OCCUPATIONS

If a woman chooses a nonconventional career, she then has to acquire a position enabling her to pursue it. She "applies" for a job. It is at this point that the most obvious and concrete examples of access discrimination can occur. The fact of discriminatory treatment in selection decisions has been documented widely. Before presenting these data, however, it is important to consider why such processes are so prevalent.

Because of the lack of competing information, when an individual first seeks to enter an organization, sex stereotypes are apt to be a predominant element in decision making. One of the functions of such stereotypes is a cognitive one—to make the world less complex and less ambiguous and thus more manageable. By treating an individual woman as merely one member of a large and well defined subgroup, "women," and ascribing attributes to her that presumably are characteristics of that group, a great deal of information about that individual is generalized. Whether true or not, assumptions about any one woman and what she is like are likely to be made on the basis of her subgroup identity when little other information is available.

Without exception, the attributes ascribed to females are not those believed essential to work success. As we already have seen, achievement-oriented traits are sorely lacking in the stereotypical profile of women's attributes. Consequently, work success, especially in occupations not traditionally feminine, is associated only with males.

Schein (1973) empirically demonstrated this by asking male management personnel in insurance companies to describe either women, men, or successful middle-level managers. She found that "men" and "successful middle manager" were described in very similar terms but "women" were described quite differently. Apparently, those attributes characterizing a successful manager are not at all those typically acribed to women. Success at managerial work is indeed considered to be a "male" phenomenon.

The pervasiveness of this point of view was documented in a study conducted by Feldman-Sumners and Kiesler (1974). In the course of designing the procedure for their experiment, these researchers administered a pretest survey to approximately eighty-five male and female undergraduates at the University of Kansas. Each was shown descriptions of people and was asked to indicate how successful he or she believed them to be. The following professionals were described: pediatrician, writer, child psychologist, surgeon, dancer, diagnostician, clinical psychologist, and biographer of famous women. For each subject, half of these were presented as male and the other half as female. The results were dramatic. In no instance was a woman expected to be more successful than a man! The authors also report that in later work with additional professions and work categories they were unable to find even a single occupation in which women rather than men are expected to be more successful. This was found even when the traditionally female occupations were used, such as nursing and elementary school teaching. This is indeed very compelling evidence that success at work is generally associated with men more than women.

Sex-stereotypic norms also are likely to have a detrimental effect on women's access to jobs. The demands of traditionally masculine jobs, such as managerial ones, are incongruent with the behavior thought to be appropriate to women. Dealing with subordinates, competing for resources, and making hard-nosed decisions are not activities consistent with the view of women as the gentle sex. Women interested in positions with these job descriptions are apt to be seen as "out-of-line" and to be penalized for their violation of sex-related expectations no matter what their background or qualifications. The result: steering the woman applicant to less challenging positions or not considering her for employment at all.

A related point is that concerning the persistent notion that women are unreliable workers, lacking commitment to their work. Starting from the view that a certain type of lifestyle is appropriate to a woman, many personnel decision makers are likely to assume that a woman would be pursuing a nontraditional career only because she either has nothing better to do (has not as yet any family obligations or has a bad marriage) or she is doing so out of economic necessity. Each of these can neatly explain her unconventional behavior. They foster the belief that if the woman in question should "find a man and settle down," "divorce and remarry" or "get her hands on some money" she no longer would be interested in working. Taking this point of view, it is easy to understand the argument that the company should not make an investment in such an individual.

Some women are, of course, exempt from these allegations. Generally they are the "masculine" women who fit into "old maid" or "asexual" categories. Because they seem to have clearly rejected their femininity they are less suspect. Their motives for working appear to be clear, their role conflicts minimal, and the risk in hiring them less grave than in hiring a more feminine woman.

How true is the overall analysis of women's motivation for work? Crowley, Levitan, and Quinn (1973) tested the validity of some commonly held beliefs regarding women in a large national survey. Their findings indicated no support for the belief that women work only for economic rewards nor that they are less concerned than men that their work be self-fulfilling. Furthermore, the idea that women are more content with dull and intellectually undemanding jobs also proved to be unfounded. The assumptions typically made about the motivations of women in the work force have been contradicted by data. Women's images of appropriate behavior for themselves has come to include employment as an important component. This unfortunately does not stop more traditional assumptions from influencing the way women are treated when they seek employment.

Sex stereotypes are the basis for access discrimination, both because they characterize women as less equipped to handle effectively nontraditional occupational demands and because they specify that such jobs are inappropriate for women. Some examples of the consequences follow.

Selection. Sex discrimination has been repeatedly demonstrated in employee selection processes. Although a few studies found no differences in how men and women applying for masculine jobs were treated (e.g., Terborg and Ilgen, 1975), the majority do indicate a tendency toward sex discrimination. When rating predetermined résumés for suitability to a managerial position, males were found to be judged preferable to comparable females by both male college students and professional interviewers (Dipboye, Fromkin, and Wiback, 1975). In another investigation, the lowest acceptance

rates and poorest evaluations for managerial positions were of female applicants (Rosen and Jerdee, 1974). Shaw (1972) demonstrated that sex bias prevailed among college recruiters whether the applicant's résumé indicated an MBA degree or a degree in mathematics. This tendency to discriminate against women in hiring decisions has been found to be as true of female subjects as of male subjects (Dipboye, Arvey, and Terpstra, 1977).

In many of the studies documenting discrimination in hiring decisions, perceived characteristics of the applicants also have been recorded. A look at these data makes clear the fact that sex stereotypes were used in formulating conception of applicants. Dipboye and others (1977), for instance, found female applicants to be less experienced, decisive, informed, competitive, motivated, logical, and assertive than male applicants. Female applicants also were rated as friendlier, warmer, and more emotional than males. Although such data do not provide conclusive evidence that this type of discrimination is mediated by sex stereotypes, it strongly supports this idea.

Role norms are violated by the inconsistency between the gender of a female job applicant and the nature of the job in question. One might thus expect that the more feminine a potential female employee is perceived to be or the more nontraditional the job is, the more inappropriate her work interests would appear, and the more discrimination she would suffer. There is, in fact, some indication that sex bias in selection is more likely when traditionally masculine jobs rather than neutral or traditionally feminine jobs are in question (Cash, Gillen, and Burns, 1977). Results of several studies have additionally indicated that more attractive women (also, according to Bem (1974), considered to be more feminine women) are at a disadvantage when they seek nontraditional positions. In one study, professional personnel consultants judged attractive women to be less qualified than unattractive ones with identical qualifications for low status masculine jobs (Cash and others, 1977). In another investigation, college students recommended that attractive women be hired less often for managerial positions but more often for clerical positions than their unattractive counterparts (Heilman and Saruwatari, in press). When the degree of inappropriateness of fit between the woman and a job is exaggerated, either by the definitively masculine nature of the job or the femininity of the woman, the likelihood of sex bias appears to increase.

Starting salary. Levitan, Quinn, and Staines (1973) reported that 95% of the American working women sampled at that time earned an average of $3,458 less than men with the same educational backgrounds and qualifications. This may be because men and women have very different jobs. There are instances, however, when a woman is offered a lower starting salary than a man for the identical position. This type of differential treatment on the basis of sex is yet another aspect of access discrimination.

Using an in-basket exercise, Terborg and Ilgen (1975) asked subjects to indicate a starting salary for each of four job applicants. The female applicant was given a significantly lower starting salary than a male counterpart. The authors suggest that this type of access discrimination can influence the applicant, even if she has received a job offer, to decide against taking the job. Thus it can be a subtle but nonetheless effective way of discouraging entry.

As Terborg (1977) has pointed out, some (e.g., Treiman and Terrell, 1975) have argued that lower salaries for women are justifiable for economic reasons. Generally the argument is that hiring women is not cost efficient; they yield fewer long-range payoffs but cost no less to train than men. This assertion is not borne out by facts. Although this is true under some circumstances, in the aggregate women have not been found to take more sick leave and/or terminate employment sooner than men (Hoffman and Nye, 1974). Given recent social trends, this is apt to be even less true in the future than it is now.

Impediments to women's access into nontraditional careers often are substantial. They derive from the clearly delineated sex stereotypes that not only prejudice our views of women's capabilities but also influence our beliefs about what women should be and most desire to be.

What happens when women do manage to attain access to the career paths of their choice? The on-the-job treatment of women is the subject of the next section.

TREATMENT DISCRIMINATION

The core issue in treatment discrimination centers on women's performance evaluations in work settings. Such evaluations form the basis of decisions about pay raises, promotions, employee utilization, and training opportunities. First we will consider the differences shown to occur in evaluating the work of men and women. Second, we will consider the discrepancy in how male and female success is interpreted. Last, we will explore reactions to women in nontraditional careers and their potential implications for the treatment of these women.

Sex Bias in Evaluation of Performance

One result of our society's unfavorable stereotyping of women is the prejudicial evaluation of their work. That is, their achievements are viewed in a way that fits with our beliefs; consequently their work is devalued simply because they are women. Inquiries in the past several years have been designed to examine the scope and parameters of this sexually based bias.

A study by Goldberg (1968) explored prejudice toward women in areas of intellectual and professional competence. College women were asked to evaluate published professional articles representing several disciplines: linguistics, law, art history, dietetics, education, and city planning. For each article, half the subjects believed the author was a male and the other half, a female. Goldberg hypothesizd that when confronted with an identical work product, women would value the work of men more highly than that of women. The results confirmed this hypothesis; subjects tended to rate all of the articles more highly when they were attributed to male authors than to female authors.

Using the same experimental procedure, however, Pheterson (reported in Pheterson and others, 1971) found sex bias to be absent in a group of uneducated middle-aged women. In contrast to Goldberg's findings, these women evaluated the professional work of women to be equal to and in some instances even more favorable than the professional work of men.

A subsequent study (Pheterson, Kiesler, and Goldberg, 1971) attempted to reconcile the divergent results from these two investigations. Speculating that differences in the respective subject populations may provide the clue to the differing results, the authors suggested that as contrasted to the college students in Goldberg's study, the uneducated women in Pheterson's study may have viewed the very fact that an article is published to be an indication of success. It thus was postulated that when a work product has uncertain status, the man's rather than the woman's would be valued more highly, but when it is perceived to be of definitively high quality, the woman's would be judged equal to or even superior to the man's. To test these ideas, women college students judged paintings which were (a) attributed to men or women creators and (b) depicted as either entries or prize winners in art competitions. The data supported the major hypotheses: when the paintings were thought to be entries, male work was judged superior, but this did not occur when the painting was thought to be a prize winner. The authors thus conclude that sex-bias does not exist when a woman's success has been proved by the acclaim of others.

Another study expands this notion. Heilman (1974) asked both high school students and undergraduates to evaluate the intellectual value and general popularity of two different course offerings when the instructor was presented as a male or female. Results indicated that when the course described was highly technical, requiring extensive knowledge of quantitative skills, no sex bias was evident. However, when the course described was not highly technical and more qualitative, it was differentially evaluated depending upon the sex of the instructor, with those taught by women severely devalued. The interpretation used reasoning similar to that used by Pheterson and her colleagues. It is argued that the fact that a woman has accomplishments in a field ordinarily populated only by men may in and of itself conclusively confirm the quality of her work, thus precluding discrimination on the basis of sex. A similar explanation can be made of studies by Hamner, Kim, Baird, and Bigoness (1974) and Bigoness (1976) in which women were rated as superior to men when they performed equivalently doing the heavy physical chores of a grocery store stock clerk.

These data, taken together with those provided by Pheterson and others (1971) suggest that not under all conditions are women and their work subject to prejudice. It appears that information about the quality of an individual's work, whether implicitly or explicitly derived, eliminates sex-linked biases in its evaluation. When ambiguity exists, as is far more frequent, prejudicial evaluations seem to abound.

This thesis can account for the repeatedly demonstrated occurrence of sexual discrimination in performance evaluations conducted early in an employee's tenure or by individuals who do not have continuous contact with her. It is only in rare instances that there is no ambiguity about effectiveness in either of these situations. But how can one account for the discriminatory treatment of women who have been on the job and for whom concrete evidence of their success is available? It appears that high performance evaluations are not sufficient to ensure fair and equal treatment. Other dynamics are at work.

SEX BIAS IN CAUSAL
EXPLANATIONS OF SUCCESS

One might question whether, even when equivalently evaluated, performances by males and females are attributed to equal skill. In view of the sex-role expectations fostered during the socialization process, it would hardly be surprising to find that they are not. Attributions of causality are very much affected by prior expectations of behavior. (For more complete coverage of this point, see Deaux, 1976.)

According to attribution theory, when a person performs in a fashion consistent with prior expectations, the outcome is attributed to a stable phenomenon, either of the individual or the situation, one which is enduring and consistent over time. However, when a person performs in a fashion inconsistent with prior expectations, the outcome is attributed to a variable phenomenon, either of the individual or of the situation, one which is unreliable and subject to change from one time to another. Since expectations of the likelihood of success on various tasks are sex-linked, if one adheres to an attribution framework, the consistency or inconsistency of a performance outcome with sex-role stereotypes should affect whether the causal attribution given for that outcome is stable or variable.

Following this reasoning, Deaux and Emswiller (1974) conducted an experiment in which subjects evaluated the identical performance of either a male or female on a "masculine" task. Although rated as equally successful, their success was explained quite differently. By both male and female subjects, a woman's success was attributed to luck (variable phenomenon) rather than to ability; a man's success was attributed to ability (stable phenomenon) rather than to luck. Explanations of causality were indeed strongly affected by the fit between the sex of actor and expectations of the task.

Feldman-Sumners and Kiesler (1974) also explored this issue. In two separate studies subjects had the opportunity to decide the extent to which each of four factors—ability, motivation, task difficulty, and luck—determined another's performance. Again it was demonstrated that the success of women was attributed to a different cause than was the success of men. Subjects attributed greater motivation (variable phenomenon) to females for the identical performance as that of males, and at least in the case of male subjects, successful professional women were viewed as less capable and as having an easier task than their male counterparts did. These results, along with those from Deaux and Emswiller, were interpreted as supporting the idea that female success (an unexpected event) is most often causally explained by variable phenomena (motivation or luck), and male success (an expected event) is explained by a stable phenomenon (skill).

These studies and others as well (e.g., Feather and Simon, 1975) demonstrate that identical performances are not always explained as resulting from equal skill: women's skill tends to be downgraded as compared to that attributed to men for the same performance. Attributional processes work to confirm the stereotypical conception of men and women. Even objective evidence of a woman's competence does not necessarily counteract its effects.

Building on these findings, some have considered the possibility that the different causal attributions arising from sex differences provide the basis for sex discrimination within organizations (Terborg and Ilgen, 1975). The fact that sex biases the formation of causal attributions does not, by itself, establish the importance of attributional processes in mediating discriminatory behavior. Different attributions must be shown to result in differential allocation of organizational rewards.

In a recent study the relationship between causal attributions and reward allocation was directly tested (Heilman and Guzzo, 1978). Subjects, who were MBA students, decided about the appropriateness of various organizational rewards, a raise and a promotion, for those whose successful performance was thought to be because of luck, effort, task difficulty, or skill. They also indicated what their preferred personnel action, if any, would be. The types of causal explanations attributed to successful women were shown to deter from the degree to which organizational rewards were viewed as appropriate personnel actions and if a reward were indeed seen as fitting, to deter from the scope and magnitude of the reward viewed as preferable. It appears that even if they are both judged to be successful, the difference in explanations ordinarily made about the success of males and females can result in their differential treatment in work settings.

We now have considered the ways in which the presumed characteristics of women can create barriers to their career advancement. The normative aspects of sex stereotypes also can present grave problems for them.

REACTIONS TO OUT-OF-ROLE BEHAVIOR

Rosen and Jerdee (1975a) found that women were thought to be out-of-role when they took a threatening approach in filing a job grievance. These same authors (Rosen and Jerdee, 1974) found that employees' requests for released time from work because of family problems were perceived to be more acceptable coming from a woman than a man. There also is some evidence that the sex of a manager influences how descriptions of different managerial styles are evaluated (Bartol and Butterfield, 1976; Rosen and Jerdee, 1973). Generally, these studies suggest that both women and men are evaluated more favorably when their leadership activities consist of sex-appropriate behaviors, e.g., a female manager showing consideration and a male manager initiating structure.[1] Evidently, conformity to traditional sex role standards is regarded favorably in work as well as in other settings.

Most jobs that carry with them authority and responsibility are thought to require behavior that is explicitly male. What are the consequences for women who take such jobs? How do others react to them and how might their performance be affected by these reactions? What are the implications of these reactions for their careers?

Costrich, Feinstein, Kidder, Maracek, and Pascale (1975) investigated the reactions to women's out-of-role behavior in a series of

laboratory studies utilizing three different experimental procedures. The results indicated that women who violate norms of feminine passive-dependency were penalized by the undergraduates serving as subjects. They were rated both as less popular and as more poorly adjusted than women who abided by the behaviors appropriate to their sex. These findings suggest that, paradoxically, women in nontraditional fields may be evaluated negatively if they do their jobs well.

Such reactions, if they occur in work settings, can impair the advancement opportunities of women. There have been a number of field studies that examined the reactions to females in previously male-dominated roles; however, they have focused on the reactions of subordinates to female and male supervisors. Although the reactions of subordinates clearly are not as critical for our purposes as are the reactions of those who have the power to take personnel actions, these studies are nonetheless instructive in understanding the by-products of incongruency between sex and job in actual organizational settings.

Two separate research investigations (Petty and Lee, 1975; Petty and Miles, 1976), investigated the correlations between subordinate perceptions of leader behavior and subordinate satisfaction. Both in the nonacademic divisions of a university and in a social service organization, the correlation between consideration behaviors and satisfaction with supervisors was greater for female supervisors than for male. In the social service organization study the correlation between initiating structure behaviors and satisfaction also was greater for male supervisors than for female. In fact, men with women supervisors had negatively correlated satisfaction scores and ratings of initiating structure. Satisfaction was thus found to be linked with perceptions of sex-role-consistent behavior.

Rousell (1974) conducted a field study in which, as Terborg (1977) has pointed out, greater care was taken to control adequately for factors in addition to sex, thus allowing for a more precise statement about supervisor sex and subordinate reactions than in the Petty

[1] These dimensions of leadership come from the Ohio State Leadership Behavior Questionnaire (Stogdill, 1963). These two dimensions in addition to "production emphasis" and "tolerance for freedom" frequently have been utilized in leadership research.

studies. The effects of department-head sex on teacher ratings of department climate in ten high schools was investigated. The teachers were randomly selected from the four largest departments in each school. The twenty-five men and fifteen women department heads had few differences in background and virtually no differences in teacher ratings of professional knowledge, aggressiveness, or power—all potentially confounding variables. Results indicated that departments headed by men were rated as having a far more favorable climate than those headed by women.

The data from these studies have several pertinent implications. First, they suggest that women in supervisory positions are limited in the extent to which they can adapt a variety of supervisory styles to do their jobs effectively. Their flexibility is constrained and their ultimate performance may suffer. Second, they suggest that negative reactions to women in nontraditional roles are confined not only to the woman herself but influence the perceptions (and perhaps the realities) of the climate of the work setting. Each of these can have costly consequences for the woman striving to move up in the organizational ranks.

An additional and not unimportant point is the fact that the anticipation of negative reactions by organization members can prevent decision makers from placing women in nontraditional positions. Results of a 1965 Harvard Business Review survey of 1,000 men and 900 women executives indicated that over two-thirds of the men and almost 20% of the women said they would not feel comfortable working for a woman. Very few of either sex (less than 10% of the men and approximately 15% of the women) felt that men employees feel comfortable working for a woman. Beliefs of this sort make the prospect of placing women in high-level jobs seem risky. Surely this must enter into decisions about who to put in what position and who to put in charge of whom.

In reviewing the literature pertinent to on-the-job sex discrimination, it again is apparent that sex stereotypes are the basis for the differential treatment of men and women. There is indication that if a woman were to perform well on the job her success might not be acknowledged or even if it were, it might be interpreted as a result of temporary conditions. There also is indication that a woman, simply by her presence in an out-of-role position, can create low morale and dissatisfaction among others at the work place, thereby limiting her effectiveness and others' perceptions of her potential. It seems clear that when competing with men in the work world, women face a tremendous disadvantage.

SEX DIFFERENCES

There is a commonly held notion that women are tougher on other women than men are. The evidence supporting this assertion is only fragmentary. In general, women and men have been shown to share the identical sex stereotypes, to have the same differential standards for men and women, and to be equally sex-biased in their behavior. However, there is a style among professional women that gives rise to and perpetuates such ideas.

The "queen bee" syndrome (Staines, Tavris, Jayarante, 1974) is that in which successful women who could assist the careers of other women prefer not to do so. Queen bees choose not to be mentors and to teach new women "the ropes" and, despite the power to help women advance, they do not support them. There are a number of reasons for this behavior.

First, being a member of a minority often causes people to identify with those in power and to dissociate themselves from those in their own social category. In this way, there is the possibility of being hailed as an exception and being accepted into the ranks of those with power. Second, these women may enjoy their uniqueness. They may relish their positions in male-dominated fields and be unwilling to open the door to additional women who not only will lessen their unique status but also might make them compete for it. Third, these women often have made their ways up the career ladder with great hardship and sacrifice, and they may resent what they perceive to be the "special treatment" and "premature advancement" of younger women who are seen as capitalizing not only on their own talents but on the pressures of the women's movement.

There might well be resistance by established women to the advancement of new young women. But there is no evidence that similar prejudices are harbored by the younger or less established women who usually are the participants in research studies. On the contrary, the overall degree of sex bias evidenced by men and women, whether in the experimental laboratory or in the field, has not been shown to differ dramatically or consistently.

REDUCING SEX DISCRIMINATION

It has been suggested throughout this discussion that sex stereotypes are at the heart of sex discrimination. If one accepts this proposition, it follows that changes in the stereotypes themselves should act to reduce or eliminate discriminatory practices. It also should be possible to decrease sex discrimination by altering contexts regulating the importance of sex stereotypes. Each of these strategies for change will be considered below.

CHANGING STEREOTYPES

Direct evidence of the relationship between stereotypes and discriminatory behavior is rare; most often it simply is inferred from "post-hoc" explanations of research results. In unequivocally establishing that stereotypes mediate discriminatory behavior, one problem has been the development of a reliable instrument to measure stereotypical attitudes toward women at work. In the Attitudes Toward Women Scale developed by Spence and Helmreich (1972) only a few of the fifty-five items deal directly with attitudes toward women at work. An instrument developed by Bass, Krusell, and Alexander (1971), designed specifically to measure attitudes about women managers, is faulty in its construction, e.g., items are double-barreled

and all item stems are unfavorable in valence. In 1974, however, Peters, Terborg, and Taynor developed the twenty-one-item, *Likert*-type Women as Managers Scale (WAMS). Although it has its critics (see Rosen and Jerdee, 1975b), it since has been validated (Terborg, Peters, Ilgen, and Smith, 1977) and used in a number of investigations.

Garland and Price (1977) demonstrated that favorable attitudes toward women in management (as measured on the WAMS) were positively correlated with personal causal explanations and negatively correlated with situational-causal explanations of a woman's work success. These results, together with those of the previously discussed Heilman and Guzzo study (1978) suggest that stereotypical attitudes about women at work can result in the discriminatory allocation of their organizational rewards. Also, Terborg and Ilgen (1975) found that the higher the score on the WAMS, the higher their subjects rated the desirability of hiring a female. Selection processes also indicate that stereotypes about women are related to how fairly they are treated in work settings.

Additional support for this idea can be found in a study by Mischel (1974). She demonstrated that in Israel, a far less sex-typed society than our own, the biases so often shown here in the United States were not apparent. Israel is a country with a policy of sexual equality in many more areas than ours (e.g., women are required to serve in the military). With this equality one might expect sex stereotypes to be less prevalent. Using Israeli students in an experiment fashioned after Goldberg (1968), Mischel in fact found little evidence of evaluation discrimination. Therefore it appears that the lack of traditional stereotypes facilitated the more equal treatment of men and women.

There are findings that verify the relationship between sex stereotypes and sex discrimination. But how does one go about changing such stereotypes? Two very different types of change are conceivable. One is cultural change, the changing of the forces that produce biased conceptions of women. The other is individual change, the changing of the current stereo-typical attitudes and beliefs held by a specific man or woman.

Most investigators have found little evidence that in recent years sex stereotypes have changed within the culture. Even today's college students seem no different than their predecessors in their attitudes and beliefs about women. This lack of change was particularly evident when researchers took precautions to limit the pressures on subjects to give socially appropriate responses (see Spence, Helmreich, and Stapp, 1977). However, there is some evidence suggesting that current societal changes ultimately may alter views of women. If a person's mother has worked, for instance, that individual has been shown to have a less stereotyped view of women than one whose mother has not (Vogel, Broverman, Broverman, Clarkson, and Rosenkrantz, 1970). Exposure to a woman in a nontraditional role (a working mother) can influence one's general view of women. Extrapolating from this finding, one might expect that changes in the way women are portrayed by the media, in the way they are depicted by our educational institutions, and in their visibility and importance in the work force will contribute slowly to an evolved view of women in the coming generations. There is therefore some room for optimism about the future. But what about the present?

Changing the attitudes and beliefs of an individual who has accepted a traditional view of women is no easy task. As Rosen and Jerdee (1975b) have pointed out, there are many potential motivations for holding sex stereotypes. They suggest, for example, that past costly experiences with women, perceptions of women as a potential threat, commitment to traditional values, or needs for clarity in our complex world all are reasons for the maintenance of stereotypes and rigid adherence to them. Depending upon which of these (or other) motivations support stereotypic belief systems, the most effective change-strategy would differ.

It also should be remembered that, as Terborg (1977) first suggested, sex stereotypes have two separate although often overlapping components. Different dynamics may underlie each, and thus different change processes may be needed to change them. It is conceivable furthermore that both have to be changed if certain forms of sex discrimination are to be eliminated. Even if one's stereotypes about women's attributes are altered successfully, and women are viewed as equally competent as men, it may still seem inappropriate for them to take positions of authority. Or conversely, even if one views a position as suitable to a woman, assumptions about her lesser competence can prevent her from obtaining it. At least in some cases, it would be essential to change both normative expectations and stereotypic perceptions of attributes if women are to be treated in an unbiased manner.

For the most part, the programs developed in recent years have been built upon the implicit assumption that the basis of the stereotyping of women is ignorance—ignorance of what women really are like and ignorance of what women's life experiences are. Consequently, their focus is on raising awareness of stereotypical conceptions and on transferring information about the realities of sex discrimination.

Human-relations training and other workshops dealing with these issues have become common within organizational settings. A host of exercises have been developed for individuals and groups to explore personal and societal prejudices and misconceptions. (see Sargent, 1977, for examples.) Techniques such as role-playing have been utilized to encourage men and women to experience the other's dilemmas. Educational programs have become widespread. To fill in the presumed knowledge gap, facts, theory, and research findings are presented and discussed.

Unfortunately, the effects of these programs are rarely assessed systematically, so no conclusions about their effectiveness can be made. It is likely that such programs are successful only when an individual's assumptions about women have been sustained as a convenience, or because they simply have never been put to the test. In these cases, forcing people to confront their stereotypes about women and to come to grips with the consequences of them should be sufficient to bring about change. But when stereotyped views are deeply rooted in value systems, such programs are likely to fail. Information by itself has little impact on value-laden convictions.

An incidental but nonetheless important point about implementation should be mentioned. Kanter (1977b) warns of the consequences of using mixed-sex group techniques in change efforts. The very activities necessary to explore sex stereotypes fully—expressing one's emotions, being open and honest, being concerned about the welfare of others, and collaborating rather than competing—are those consonant with the stereotypic attributes women are assumed to possess. Although Kanter's concerns were related to the lack of opportunities for skill development available to women in such groups, the point she raises is no less important when one's concern is the altering of sex stereotypes. Participation in such groups conceivably can reinforce rather than change men's images of women, unless care is taken to ensure that women also have the opportunity to display behaviors that contradict and challenge the stereotypes men are likely to have.

Changing individuals' sex stereotypes can be a very complicated process, and it is likely to be an expensive one. The training and development needed to accomplish such a change, if indeed it can be accomplished, are not realistic in terms of the money and time required. What then, if anything, can be done to limit the negative consequences of these stereotypes?

ALTERING CONTEXT

Although orientations toward women have roots in socialization processes, and sex stereotypes are often firmly decided at a very early age, some of the unjust consequences of these stereotypes can be limited without actually changing them. Here the issue is not the elimination of the stereotypic belief system but the control of its consequences. Such control requires an understanding of environmental fac-

tors facilitating or hindering the pertinence of sex stereotypes and thus the degree to which they are used. Two such factors will be considered here. Both can regulate the extent to which stereotypic attributes are assumed to characterize one specific woman.

Information. It already has been mentioned that stereotypes about women in general are most likely to be employed when ambiguity exists. Specific information about the woman in question often is more compelling than beliefs about sex-stereotypic attributes. This suggests that consideration be given to revising current personnel decision-making procedures.

If résumés could be supplemented by extensive background information, if performance appraisals were to specify the reasons behind performance, and if concrete evidence of success could be supplied whenever possible, stereotypical assumptions could be prevented from dominating decision processes. Drawing from Kelley (1967), it would seem that information about consistency of successful performance and degree of consensus among evaluators would be particularly important. If, for example, it is known that Ms. X has repeatedly succeeded in the past, has succeeded admirably in various tasks, or has been judged to be greatly talented by many evaluators using many measures, her potential and ability would be very difficult to discount. Structuring both the richness and the specificity of the information given to decision makers conceivably could preclude the ill effects of sex stereotypes without actually altering stereotypical beliefs.

Sex composition. In her recent book, *Men and Women of the Corporation,* Kanter (1977a) claims that the proportional representation of women in work settings not only influences their feelings and attitudes but also influences the way in which they are treated by others. When there is a great disproportion in the size of the minority and majority groups, she believes there is cause for concern. When tokens (the members of that piddling minority) are isolated from informal social networks, they are viewed as alien and different, and their characteristics are distorted to fit stereotyped conceptions. According to Kanter, tokenism is deadly, fostering reliance on stereotypes no matter what the personal characteristics of the individuals are.

The implications of this point of view are simple. Whenever possible, group-hiring and not individual hiring of women for male-dominated positions should be the rule. When a number of women are to be brought into positions held by few other women, clustering, not dispersing is suggested. Women should be bunched in numbers large enough so that they are not tokens even if it means that some units have no women at all. Simply by avoiding numerical scarcity, and providing evidence of the variety and differences among women, reacting to them all as if they were the same becomes unjustifiable.

These are only two examples of contextual factors which can regulate the degree to which sex-stereotypic attitudes affect decisions made about any one woman. Discovering others is of paramount importance. The capacity to control discriminatory behavior may be, at the moment, the only option we have.

CONCLUDING COMMENTS

This article has taken the point of view that sex stereotypes are the rudiments of sex discrimination. It has argued that once these culturally shared conceptions about women are called into play, discriminatory action is very likely to occur. It thus has suggested that the key to reducing sex discrimination is combating these stereotypes either by directly attempting to change them or by controlling their importance and their influence on behavior. Only by undermining the underlying basis for sex discrimination can its consequences be averted.

Readers are reminded that only the external barriers to women's achievement have been considered here. There are, of course, many barriers that reside within women themselves that hinder and sometimes preclude their advancement. For a total picture of how sex affects behavior, such internal barriers also must be explored. Reviews by O'Leary (1974) and Terborg (1977) discuss these intrapersonal barriers to achievement.

Although our discussion has been limited to examining sex discrimination as it pertains to women, it would be erroneous to leave readers with the impression that women alone suffer from sex stereotypes. Men who violate sex roles by exhibiting feminine skills or attributes also have been found to be evaluated less favorably than those who do not (Costrich and others, 1975). There is evidence suggesting that men who select traditionally female careers are suspected of homosexuality (Etzkowitz, 1971). It also has been found that men are treated more harshly when they fail (Feather and Simon, 1975). Thus stereotyping can have negative consequences for both sexes and sex discrimination can be against men as well as against women.

Lastly, it should be noted that although this article has focused on discriminatory treatment in the work world arising from sex stereotypes, the theory and research findings presented apply to any negatively stereotyped group. Assumptions of incompetence or of unsuitability for responsible positions are not unique to women. Others, also regarded as representatives of negatively viewed groups rather than as individuals in their own right, are equally susceptible to the discriminatory consequences of stereotypes, be they ethnic, racial, or religious in origin.

REFERENCES

AGATE, C., and MEACHAM, C. 1977. Women's equality: implications of the law. In *Beyond sex roles,* ed. A. G. Sargent. St. Paul: West Publishing Co.

ALMQUIST, E. M., and ANGRIST, S. S. 1971. Role model influences on college women's career aspirations. In *The professional woman,* ed. A. Theodore. Cambridge, Mass.: Schenkman.

ARTHUR, M. B. 1973. Early Greece: the origin of the Western attitude toward women. *Arethusa* 6: 7–58.

BARTOL, K. M., and BUTTERFIELD, D. A. 1976. Sex effects in evaluating leaders. *Journal of Applied Psychology* 61: 446–54.

BASS, B. M.; KRUSELL, J.; and ALEXANDER, R. A. 1971. Male managers' attitudes toward working women. *American Behavioral Scientist* 15: 221–36.

BEM, S. 1974. The measurement of psychological androgyny. *Journal of Consulting and Clinical Psychology* 42: 155–62.

BIGONESS, W. J. 1976. Effect of applicant's sex, race, and performance on employers' performance ratings: some additional findings. *Journal of Applied Psychology* 61: 80–84.

BRENNER, M. 1972. Management development for women. *Personnel Journal* 51: 65–69.

BROVERMAN, I. K.; VOGEL, R. S.; BROVERMAN, D. M.; CLARKSON, T. E.; and ROSENKRANTZ, P. S. 1972. Sex-role stereotypes: a current appraisal. *Journal of Social Issues* 28: 59–78.

BUCHANAN, E. 1969. Women in management. *Personnel Administration* 32: 21–26.

BULLOUGH, V. L. 1973. *The subordinate sex*. Urbana: University of Illinois Press.

CASH, T. F.; GILLEN, B.; and BURNS, D. S. 1977. Sexism and "beautyism" in personnel consultant decision making. *Journal of Applied Psychology* 62: 301–11.

COSTRICH, N.; FEINSTEIN, J.; KIDDER, L.; MARECEK, J.; and PASCALE, L. 1975. When stereotypes hurt: three studies of penalties for sex-role reversals. *Journal of Experimental Social Psychology* 11: 520–30.

Council of Economic Advisers. 1973. *Economic report of the president*. Washington, D.C.: U.S. Government Printing Office.

CROWLEY, J. E.; LEVITIN, T. E.; and QUINN, R. P. 1973. Seven deadly half truths about women. *Psychology Today* 6: 94–96.

DAY, D. R., and STOGDILL, R. M. 1972. Leader behavior of male and female supervisors: a comparative study. *Personnel Psychology* 25: 353–60.

DEAUX, K. 1976. Sex: a perspective on the attribution process. In *New directions in attribution research*, vol. 1, ed. J. Harvey, W. J. Ickes, and R. F. Kidd. Hillsdale, N.J.: Lawrence Erlbaum Associates.

——, and EMSWILLER, T. 1974. Explanation of successful performance on sex-linked tasks: what is skill for the male is luck for the female. *Journal of Personality and Social Psychology* 29: 80–85.

DIAMOND, E. E. 1968. Occupational level versus sex groups as a system of classification. *Proceedings of the 76th Annual Convention of the American Psychological Association* 3: 199–200.

DIPBOYE, R. L.; ARVEY, R. D.; and TERPSTRA, D. E. 1977. Sex and physical attractiveness of raters and applicants as determinants of resume evaluations. *Journal of Applied Psychology* 62: 288–94.

——; FROMKIN, H. L.; and WIBACK, K. 1975. Relative importance of applicant sex, attractiveness, and scholastic standing in evaluation of job applicant resumes. *Journal of Applied Psychology* 60: 39–43.

ETZKOWITZ, M. 1971. The male sister: sexual separation of labor in society. *Journal of Marriage and the Family* 33: 431–34.

FEATHER, N. T., and SIMON, J. G. 1975. Reactions to male and female success and failure in sex-linked occupations: impressions of personality, causal attributions, and perceived likelihood of different consequences. *Journal of Personality and Social Psychology* 31: 20–31.

FELDMAN-SUMNERS, S., and KIESLER, S. B. 1974. Those who are number two try harder: the effect of sex on attributions of causality. *Journal of Personality and Social Psychology* 30: 846–55.

FERNBERGER, S. W. 1948. Persistence of stereotypes concerning sex differences. *Journal of Abnormal and Social Psychology* 43: 97–101.

GARAI, J. E., and SCHEINFELD, A. 1968. Sex differences in mental and behavioral traits. *Genetic Psychology Monographs* 77: 169–299.

GARLAND, H., and PRICE, K. H. 1977. Attitudes toward women in management and attributions for their success and failure in a managerial position. *Journal of Applied Psychology* 62: 29–33.

GOLDBERG, P. A. 1968. Are women prejudiced against women? *Transaction* vol. 5: 28–30.

GROSS, E. 1967. *The sexual structure of occupations over time.* Paper presented at the meeting of the American Sociological Association, August.

HALL, D. T. 1972. A model for coping with role conflict: the role behavior of college educated women. *Administrative Science Quarterly* 17: 471–86.

HAMNER, W. C.; KIM, J. S.; BAIRD, L.; and BIGONESS, W. J. 1974. Race and sex as determinants of ratings by potential employers in a simulated work-sampling task. *Journal of Applied Psychology* 59: 705–11.

HANSEN, L. S. 1972. A model for career development through curriculum. *Personnel and Guidance Journal* 51: 243–50.

HEDGES, J. N. 1970. Women workers and manpower demands in the 1970's. *Monthly Labor Review* 93: 19–29.

HEILMAN, M. E. 1975. Miss, Mrs., Ms., or none of the above? Effects of an instructor's title on course desirability. *American Psychologist* 30: 516–18.

———, and GUZZO, R. A. 1978. The perceived cause of work success as a mediator of sex discrimination in organizations. *Organizational Behavior and Human Performance.* 21: 346–57.

———. In press. High school student's occupational interest as a function of projected sex ratios in male-dominated occupations. *Journal of Applied Psychology.*

———, and SARUWATARI, L. In press. When beauty is beastly: the effects of appearance and sex on evaluations of job applicants for managerial and nonmanagerial jobs. *Organizational Behavior and Human Performance.*

HOFFMAN, L. W., and NYE, F. I. 1974. *Working mothers.* San Francisco: Jossey Bass.

HORNER, M. S. 1972. Toward an understanding of achievement related conflicts in women. *Journal of Social Issues* 28: 157–76.

HUNTER, J. E. 1976. Images of women. *Journal of Social Issues* 32: 7–17.

KAGAN, J. 1971. *Change and continuity in infancy.* New York: Wiley.

KANTER, R. M. 1977a. *Men and women of the corporation.* New York: Basic Books.

———. 1977b. Women in organizations: sex roles, group dynamics, and change strategies. In *Beyond sex roles,* ed. A. G. Sargent. St. Paul: West Publishing Co.

KELLEY, H. H. 1967. Attribution theory in social psychology. In *Nebraska symposium on motivation,* vol. 15, ed. D. Levine. Lincoln: University of Nebraska Press.

LENNEY, E. 1977. Women's self-confidence in achievement settings. *Psychological Bulletin* 84: 1–13.

LEVITIN, T.; QUINN, R. P.; and STAINES, G. L. 1971. Sex discrimination against the American working woman. *American Behavioral Scientist* 15: 238–54.

———; QUINN, R. P.; and STAINES, G. A. 1973. A woman is 58% of a man. *Psychology Today* 6: 89–91.

LOOFT, W. R. 1971. Sex differences in the expression of vocational aspirations by elementary school children. *Developmental Psychology* 5: 366.

LUNNEBORG, P. W. 1970. Stereotypic aspects in masculinity-femininity measurement. *Journal of Consulting and Clinical Psychology* 34: 113–18.

MACCOBY, E. E. 1966. *The development of sex differences.* Stanford, Calif.: Stanford University Press.

———, and JACKLIN, C. N. 1974. *The psychology*

of sex differences. Stanford, Calif.: Stanford University Press.

McArthur, L. Z., and Resko, B. G. 1975. The portrayal of men and women in American television commercials. *Journal of Social Psychology* 97: 209–20.

McKee, J. P., and Sherriffs, A. C. 1957. The differential evaluation of males and females. *Journal of Personality* 25: 356–71.

———. 1959. Men's and women's beliefs, ideals, and self concepts. *American Journal of Sociology* 65: 356–63.

Matthews, E. 1972. Employment implications of psychological characteristics of men and women. In *Women in the work force,* ed. W. E. Katzell and W. C. Byham. New York: Behavioral Publications.

Mischel, H. 1974. Sex bias in the evaluation of professional achievements. *Journal of Educational Psychology* 66: 157–66.

Nadelman, L. 1974. Sex identity in American children: memory, knowledge and preference tests. *Developmental Psychology* 10: 413–17.

O'Leary, V. E. 1974. Some attitudinal barriers to occupational aspirations in women. *Psychological Bulletin* 81: 809–26.

———. 1977. *Toward Understanding Women.* Monterey, Calif.: Brooks/Cole.

Petty, M. M., and Lee, G. K. 1975. Moderating effects of sex of supervisor and subordinate on relationships between supervisor behavior and subordinate satisfaction. *Journal of Applied Psychology* 60: 624–28.

———, and Miles, R. H. 1976. Leader sex-role stereotyping in a female dominated work culture. *Personnel Psychology* 29: 393–404.

Pheterson, G. I.; Kiesler, S. B.; and Goldberg, P. A. 1971. Evaluation of the performance of women as a function of their sex, achievement, and personal history. *Journal of Personality and Social Psychology* 19: 114–18.

Rosen, B., and Jerdee, T. H. 1974. Effects of applicant's sex and difficulty of job on evaluations of candidates for managerial positions. *Journal of Applied Psychology* 59: 511–12.

———. 1975a. Effects of employee's sex and threatening vs. pleading appeals on managerial evaluations of grievances. *Journal of Applied Psychology* 60: 442–45.

———. 1973. The influence of sex-role stereotypes on evaluations of male and female supervisory behavior. *Journal of Applied Psychology* 57: 44–48.

———. 1975b. The psychological basis for sex role stereotypes: a note on Terborg and Ilgen's conclusions. *Organizational Behavior and Human Performance* 14: 151–53.

Rosenkrantz, P. S.; Vogel, S. R.; Bee, H.; Broverman, I. K.; and Broverman, D. M. 1968. Sex-role stereotypes and self-concepts in college students. *Journal of Consulting and Clinical Psychology* 32: 287–95.

Rousell, C. 1974. Relationship of sex of department head to department climate. *Administrative Science Quarterly* 19: 211–20.

Rubin, Z.; Provenzano, F. J.; and Luria, Z. 1974. Social and cultural influences on sex-role development. The eye of the beholder: parents' view on sex of newborns. *American Journal of Orthopsychiatry* 44: 512–19.

Sargent, A. G. 1977. *Beyond sex roles.* St. Paul: West Publishing Co.

Schein, V. E. 1973. The relationship between sex-role stereotypes and requisite management characteristics. *Journal of Applied Psychology* 57: 95–100.

Serbin, L. A.; O'Leary, K. D.; Kent, R. N.; and Tonick, I. J. 1973. A comparison of teacher response to the preacademic and problem behavior of boys and girls. *Child Development* 44: 796–804.

Shaw, E. A. 1972. Differential impact of negative stereotyping in employee selection. *Personnel Psychology* 25: 333–38.

Shein, V. 1972. Fair employment of women through personnel research. *Personnel Journal* 51: 330–35.

SIEGAL, C. L. 1973. Sex differences in the occupational choices of second graders. *Journal of Vocational Behavior* 3: 15–19.

SMITH, S. 1939. Age and sex differences in children's opinions concerning sex differences. *Journal of Genetic Psychology* 54: 17–25.

SPENCE, J. R., and HELMREICH, R. 1972. The Attitudes Toward Women Scale: an objective instrument to measure attitudes toward the rights and roles of women in contemporary society. *JSAS Catalog of Selected Documents in Psychology* (Ms. No. 153).

———; and STAPP, J. In press. Likability, sex-role congruence of interest, and competence: it all depends on how you ask. *Journal of Applied Social Psychology*.

STAINES, G.; TAURIS, C.; and JAYARANTE, T. E. 1974. The queen bee syndrome. *Psychology Today* 7: 55–60.

STEINMAN, A., and FOX, D. J. 1966. Male-female perceptions of the female role in the United States. *Journal of Psychology* 64: 265–76.

TANGRI, S. S. 1972. Determinants of occupational role innovation among college women. *Journal of Social Issues* 28: 177–99.

TAYLOR, G. R. 1973. *Sex in history*. New York: Harper & Row.

TERBORG, J. R. 1977. Women in management: a research review. *Journal of Applied Psychology* 62: 647–64.

———, and ILGEN, D. R. 1975. A theoretical approach to sex discrimination in traditionally masculine occupations. *Organizational Behavior and Human Performance* 13: 352–76.

———; PETERS, L. H.; ILGEN, D. R.; and SMITH, F. 1977. Organizational and personal correlates of attitudes toward women as managers. *Academy of Management Journal* 20: 89–100.

THOMAS, A. H., and STEWART, N. R. 1971. Counselor response to female clients with deviant and conforming career goals. *Journal of Counseling Psychology* 18: 352–57.

TREIMAN, D. J., and TERRELL, K. 1975. Sex and the process of status attainment: a comparison of working women and men. *American Sociological Review* 40: 174–200.

TROLL, L. E. 1975. *Early and middle adulthood*. Monterey, Calif.: Brooks/Cole.

———. 1965. *The psychology of human differences*. New York: Appleton-Century-Crofts.

VEROFF, J.; WILCOX, S.; and ATKINSON, J. W. 1953. The achievement motive in high school and college age women. *Journal of Abnormal and Social Psychology* 48: 108–19.

VOGEL, S. K.; BROVERMAN, I. K.; BROVERMAN, D. M.; CLARKSON, F. E.; and ROSENKRANTZ, P. S. 1970. Maternal employment and perception of sex-roles among college students. *Developmental Psychology* 3: 384–91.

WEISMAN, C. S.; MORLOCK, L. L.; SACK, D. G.; and LEVINE, D. M. 1976. Sex differences in response to a blocked career pathway among unaccepted medical school applicants. *Sociology of Work and Occupations* 3: 187–208.

WEITZMAN, L. J.; EIFLER, D.; HOKADA, E.; and ROSS, C. 1972. Sex role socialization in picture books for preschool children. *American Journal of Sociology* 77: 1125–50.

WIRTENBERG, T. J., and NAKAMURA, C. Y. Education: barrier or boon to changing occupational roles of women. *Journal of Social Issues* 32: 165–80.

THIRTEEN

Pornography: A Review of Research

ROBERT ATHANASIOU

The decade of the 1970s has seen a virtual explosion in the amount of research data on erotic material. While the social issues of communism and water fluoridation generated social and political action in the 1950s, and the Vietnam War occupied our attention in the 1960s, the "porno plague," as a *Time* magazine cover story titled the problem, has generated considerable concern in the 1970s.

Millions of government dollars have been spent funding research on the effects of pornography, on the one hand, and millions have been spent legally prosecuting distributors of allegedly obscene material, on the other hand. This not all-together logical approach by our government was set into motion in the late 1960s when the Congress of the United States declared "that the traffic in obscenity and pornography is a matter of national concern . . . [and that] . . . the Federal Government has the responsibility to investigate the gravity of this situation and to determine whether such materials are harmful to the public" (Public Law 90–100).

Wilson (1973) has commented with regard to Public Law 90–100: "This act, asserting that a phenomenon is a social issue, raising the question of causal relationships, directing an agency to study these relationships, and . . . authorizing . . . behavioral science research to collect scientific data relevant to the issue, is perhaps unique. Indeed, there is a strong possibility that the Congress did not really know what it was doing" (p. 15). when it created and funded the Commission on Obscenity and Pornography.

The Commission on Obscenity and Pornography (COP), made up of several highly qualified scientists, legal experts, clergymen, and a representative of an antipornography group, has funded studies and collected data in the United States and abroad. After surveying the results of millions of dollars of research and considering previous (Cairns, Paul, and Wishner, 1962) and current findings, "The Commission recommend[ed] that federal, state and local legislation should not seek to interfere with the right of adults who wish to read, obtain or view explicit sexual materials" (COP, 1971, p. 58). When Congress and President Nixon chose to reject the recommendations and the scientific findings of the commission and proceeded to suggest restrictive legislation, it became quite clear that one of the responses to pornography is to arouse strong political reactions.

DEFINITIONS

The definition of the terms "pornography" and "obscenity" are difficult because they reflect sociocultural standards which vary by education, religion, political preference, locale, age, and other variables. The Supreme Court of the United States has grappled ineffectively with the problem of a definition over the last several decades. The most recent definition (at this writing) may be found in the case of *Miller* v. *California* in which the court majority agreed that an object was obscene if a jury found that:

1. the average person, applying contemporary community standards would find that the work taken as a whole appealed to the prurient interest, and

2. the object depicted or described in a patently offensive way sexual conduct specifically defined by the applicable state law as written or construed, and

3. that the object taken as a whole lacked serious artistic, literary, political, or scientific value (see Fleishman, 1973).

The Court's use of the term "prurient interest" seems to be based on the term used in the

Fanny Hill, "Memoirs" decision. In a subsequent decision, prurient interest (from the Latin *prurire,* to itch) was defined as a sick or morbid interest in nudity, sex, or excreta. It is clearly distinguished from a normal erotic interest.

As currently stated, the first test of obscenity requires that the average person, applying contemporary community standards and considering the work as a whole, find that its predominant appeal is to the prurient interest. This test implies that the standards of what is sick or morbid in a community may change. Moreover, the work *as a whole* must appeal to the prurient interest. A single paragraph, photograph, or chapter presumably would be insufficient to cause a work to flunk the pruriency test.

What is not clear is to whose prurient interest the work must appeal. The Court seems to assume that within each normal average person there is a prurient maniac waiting to be released by an appropriate stimulus. There are scant data in psychology to support such an hypothesis, although some psychoanalysts might contend that some or most normal persons have a pathological interest in sex.

As a few plain examples of what a state statute could define for regulation under the second part of the standard announced in the *Miller* opinion, the Court suggested: (a) patently offensive representations or descriptions of ultimate sexual acts, normal or perverted, actual or simulated. (b) Patently offensive representations or descriptions of masturbation, excretory functions and lewd exhibitions of the genitals" (Fleishman 1973, p. 101). The reference to the ultimate sexual act is perhaps a bit confusing, and Mr. Justice Burger did not enlighten the plaintiffs regarding his definition of ultimate. It may generally be assumed, however, that he meant some sort of sexual intercourse. This essay will deal with the material that may be subsumed under the examples given in this paragraph.

The court's definition of obscenity omits any relationship between exposure to an obscene work or object and behavior. The definition is solely for attitudes and opinions (prurient interest), taste (patent offensiveness), and values

(literary, artistic). For scientists concerned with the behavioral effects of social stimuli, this exclusive focus on the cognitive and value aspects of obscenity might seem peculiar. For the empirically testable question of a connection between obscenity and antisocial behavior, the Court, in the case of *Paris Adult Theatre I* v. *Slaton,* stated:

> It is not for us to resolve empirical uncertainties underlying state legislation. . . . We do not demand of legislatures "scientifically certain criteria of legislation." . . . Although there is no conclusive proof of a connection between antisocial behavior and obscene material, the . . . [state legislature] could reasonably determine that such a connection does or might exist. . . . Nothing in the Constitution prohibits a State from reaching such a conclusion and acting on it simply because there is no conclusive evidence or empirical data (Fleishman, 1973, p. 33–36).

EFFECTS OF EROTICA: SURVEY STUDIES

Despite the legal communities' lack of interest in the behavioral and social correlates of exposure to erotica, scientists have spent considerable time and effort looking for empirically valid connections between these variables.

One of the first approaches to studying the effects of erotica was simply to ask people what they thought the effects were on themselves and others. Athanasiou, Shaver, and Tavris (1970) reported on a sample of 20,000 *Psychology Today* readers who indicated rather high levels of exposure. It is generally accepted that four out of five Americans between puberty and senility have been exposed one or more times to explicit sexual materials (Abelson and others, 1971, in COP).

It is interesting to note that the majority of Americans, when surveyed, accepts the display of erotica to adults who choose to see it. Most people report that their own response to erotica has been neutral or mildly positive and quite transient. There is much ignorance because (1) each person seems to feel that he or she is more tolerant than the average and (2) that although he or she himself or herself is not troubled by erotica, there are some undefinable "others" who would be (Abelson and others, 1971, COP; Abelson and Wilson, 1973).

The large sample (2,486 adults) survey data of the Abelson and others study have been re-analyzed (Merritt, Gerstl, and LoSciuto, 1975) to clarify those characteristics of the subgroups who felt erotica was beneficial versus those who felt it was not. The most striking finding was an age gradient. This age gradient persisted despite controls for gender, education, and levels of exposure. As might be expected, the authors found that "younger age groups tended to attribute solely desirable and/or neutral effects to erotica. . . . those who believed that pornography has largely or solely undesirable effects on its consumers were the oldest" (p. 605). It is not at all clear whether these age-related changes in attitude are developmental or generational. Because the major technological changes in our society have affected sexual behavior (e.g., birth control and abortion techniques), it does not seem unreasonable to postulate generational differences as a major factor in the observed age gradient.

Other variables which often have been found to correlate with judgment of erotica and the effects of exposure to it are authoritarianism, religious preference, and church attendance.

Zurcher and others (1973) studied two towns in which antipornography "crusades" had been mounted. They found that the "conporns" tended to be individuals who were satisfied with what they perceived to be the social status quo, rather authoritarian, dogmatic, intolerant of others' political views, with traditional and restrictive views on sexual matters. They also favored censorship to service and protect those views. Conporns associated the use of pornography with sexual deviance, crime, violence, drugs, family disruption, organized crime (87%) and/or a communist conspiracy (61%). Proporns by contrast tended to be far less disturbed by the topic and tended to oppose censorship.

Kirkpatrick (1975) is less kind than Zurcher in describing antipornography crusades. Writing in the *Psychoanalytic Review* he states:

"Antipornography crusading is a result of repressed sexuality and resultant moral indignation among the petty [sic] bourgeois. . . . We feel that sexual repression is the most fundamental category and that it in turn leads to repression in general and to the motivation for social movements which oppose pornography, and the ideologies of moral indignation which accompany these forms of social control" (p. 48). Kenyon (1975) in a brief but entertaining and thought-provoking review of censorship up to 1974 notes:

One underlying fear is that the advocacy of too much sexual license will lead to the decline of family life, thus undermining the whole fabric of society, with resultant anarchy. Frequently quoted in this context is the decline and fall of the Roman Empire. However, if Gibbon's famous account is to be believed, a powerful influence in bringing this about was the disastrous effect of the introduction of Christianity, with its misogyny and unhealthy preoccupation with sexual intercourse, chastity, mortification and flagellation (p. 227).

One's response to erotica and the labeling of erotic material as obscene is a complex and interactive process. Colson (1974) has shown that when subjects with low tolerance of erotica were given false Galvanic Skin Response feedback suggesting they were sexually aroused by the presentation of pedophilic material, they labeled the material unfavorably and called it obscene. It would seem that an operational, if totally idiosyncratic, definition of obscenity for an individual would be sexual arousal in response to material one is not supposed to like.

Byrne and others (1974) have proposed that an individual's response to erotic material (that response being the final outcome of long-term socialization, experience, value judgments, and the like) is attributed to the object itself.

Thus, an erotic depiction is not just pleasing or displeasing to oneself, the depiction itself is good or bad. Next there is an attempt to justify such judgments and to vindicate them by attributing a general benefit or harm to the object. . . . What begins as a personal affective response can end as an elaborate belief system . . . it is not surprising that research data which are relevant to such systems tend to be accepted or rejected not on their own merits but on the basis of the justification or vindication which they provide (p. 115).

EFFECTS OF EROTICA: LABORATORY STUDIES OF PHYSIOLOGICAL RESPONSES

Almost a decade ago, Zuckerman (1971) made a very thorough and interesting review of the state of the art of measuring sexual arousal. His general conclusions were that there were virtually no reliable, specific, sensitive, and objective criteria for determining sexual arousal other than erections in men and vaginal blood flow changes in women. In addition, the invasive techniques required to monitor these changes might often produce false positive and false negative results.

Since that time, a number of researchers have attempted to find a reliable, specific, and relatively noninvasive technique for measuring sexual arousal and physiologic response to erotica. The logical first choice for such an indicator might be changes in sex hormone levels. From a group of male volunteers Lincoln (1974) sampled venous blood from a catheter every ten to forty minutes and attempted to correlate changes in testosterone and luteinizing hormone levels with exposure to an erotic film. Levels were obtained for several hours before and after film viewing. He concluded that "There were no changes in blood levels of LH or testosterone which could be definitely related to the films. . . . it seems possible that a single skin puncture has a greater impact on the hypothalamic/pituitary axis than a 30 minute sexually stimulating film" (p. 233).

Contrary to Lincoln's findings, Pirke and others (1974) demonstrated different results. In their study, plasma testosterone was measured before, after, and during the showing of an explicit sexual movie. Relative to the control group who saw a nonsexual movie, the experimental group showed an average increase of 35% in testosterone levels peaking sixty to ninty minutes after the film.

A resolution of these conflicting results is not immediately apparent. It would seem that at the present time the best that can be said is that plasma testosterone levels are not reliable indicators of response to erotica.

The correlation of arousal and hormone levels in women is even more difficult to demonstrate than in men. Money and Ehrhardt (1972) have theorized that it may not be a "female" hormone which is responsible for arousal in women—it may be an androgen or "male" hormone.

Abramson and others (1976) collected self-reports from 133 women of sexual arousal to an erotic story. The independent factors were hormone levels controlled by birth control pills versus no pills, and phase of menstrual cycle. They found that the greatest degree of sexual arousal and genital sensations were experienced by women on the pill while they were in their menstrual phase. The least arousal was shown by women on the pill during their premenstrual phase. There were no significant differences in response to erotic stimuli between menstrual phases for women who were not taking the pill. These data are not wholly consistent with other studies (Money and Ehrhardt, 1972) which have found that sexual interest and arousability in women peaked during the secretory and luteal phase of their cycle.

In females as with males, the exact nature of the connections among arousal, hormone levels, and erotic stimuli is not yet known.

Ray and Thompson (1974) have demonstrated an interaction between personality traits and physiologic responses to erotica. They found that although all subjects responded with increased GSR to scenes of coitus, low sex-guilt subjects exhibited significant cardiac deceleration during viewing. High sex-guilt subjects failed to show significant deceleration.

Cardiac deceleration is not thought to be a measure of sexual arousal but rather, a correlate of attention. Fixing one's attention on something usually will cause a slowing of the heart beat. Ray and Thompson have probably demonstrated that low sex-guilt subjects pay more attention to sexual stimuli, and high sex-guilt subjects, even though aroused, may not pay such close attention to sexual scenes.

This finding is intuitively consistent with the data collected by the COP, which show that conporns generally have seen less erotica than have proporns. One might question whether they see less because they are conporns or whether they are conporns because they see less erotica. The Ray and Thompson study may suggest that they see less because they are conporns.

Geer, Morokoff, and Greenwood (1974) have described a vaginal photoplethysmograph used to measure pulse and vaginal blood volume during sexual arousal. They found highly significant changes in vaginal pulse pressure and total blood volume in the vaginal walls to be associated with exposure to sexually explicit films but not to be correlated with self-reports of arousal. Since Masters and Johnson (1966) have shown these variables to be present during sexual arousal, we may tentatively assume that some women may not be aware of, or may not be willing to report their aroused state when viewing explicit sexual material.

Wincze, Hoon, and Hoon (1976) modified the device used by Geer and others (1974) to make it both more sensitive and specific, and then investigated the arousal responses of sexually well adjusted women and clinical subjects reporting sexual dysfunction. Their study included attitudinal, demographic, physiological, and sexual activity measures. The sexual stimulus consisted of a video tape of a couple engaging in foreplay and leading up to but not engaging in coitus.

Responses of the clinical group of women to the erotic stimulus differed markedly on a number of variables from those of the normal women. When covariance analysis was performed on the physiological data, the normal subjects showed increased diastolic pressure changes and increased vaginal blood volume.

The covariates included prestimulus physiologic baseline measures, frequency of intercourse, age, number of partners, and last year of schooling.

The data showed significant and consequential correlations between vaginal blood volume during the erotic stimulus phase and frequency of intercourse (+.62), sexual arousability index (+.71), and awareness of physiologic change (e.g., nipple erection, sex flush, etc., +.41). Heart rate was negatively correlated with present frequency of intercourse (−.28) and sexual arousability index (−.38) (cf. Ray and Thompson, 1974). Vaginal blood volume was also positively correlated with day of menstrual cycle (+.64). That is, the later in the cycle and the closer to the next menstrual period, the greater the vaginal blood volume was during the viewing of erotic stimuli. This is consistent with Money and Ehrhardt's contention that arousability is greater in the luteal phase.

The authors state, "Increases in diastolic blood pressure and vaginal blood volume for the normal group relative to the clinical group are consistent with the interpretation that normal women were sexually aroused by erotic stimulus exposure, whereas clinical women were only slightly aroused" (1972, p. 450). This vaginal capillary engorgement took place within the first sixteen seconds of stimulus exposure and remained consistently high throughout the experimental period. These data and the correlations mentioned above "suggest that women who are more aware of physiological changes during sexual activity, who rate erotic experiences as more arousing and who engage in intercourse more often, become more physiologically aroused during erotic stimulation" (1972, p. 451). These findings obviously are important to the diagnosis, treatment, and evaluation of sexual dysfunction.

Differences in physiologic response to erotica among heterosexuals, homosexuals, and transexuals may be used in treatment and diagnosis. Barr and Blaszczynski (1976) have shown that homosexual and heterosexual males in their sample had sex-object-choice appropriate GSR and penile volume responses when shown erotic pictures of males and females, but transexuals (genetic males) showed positive GSR responses to photos of females although their stated object-choice was males. The relatively small sample and lack of adequate specificity of this test does not recommend it for use as a diagnostically certain criterion for distinguishing homosexuals from transexuals, but it may provide useful circumstantial data in diagnostic conundrums.

Physiologic measures of arousal in males have generally focused on either chemical measures such as testosterone levels or urinary acid phosphatase (Barclay, 1970) or mechanical measures such as penile volume.

Schaefer and others (1976) used a strain gauge to measure penile volume and correlated it with subjects' estimates of degree of erection. Overall, degree of erection was underestimated. The authors concluded that men attended more to psychological rather than physiological cues when estimating their degree of tumescence in response to erotic literature.

Kercher and Walker (1973) compared the physiologic responses of rapists with those of nonsex offender criminals in response to slides depicting sexual themes. Their results were quite consistent with other research in this area (e.g., Goldstein, 1973) indicating that these stimuli were unpleasant for rapists. The rapists showed higher GSR measures and gave negative ratings to the sexual themes presented, although changes in penile volume were the same as those in the nonsex offender group. Something which is arousing but not liked is judged as unpleasant.

Howard, Liptzin, and Reifler (1973) have demonstrated that repeated exposure to erotica results in much lowered interest in and much less response to it. They exposed subjects to erotica for ninety minutes per day for fifteen days. They found that persistent exposure lead to self-reports of boredom and decreases in urinary acid phosphatase excretion over time. They also state that "no detrimental changes of any kind were produced in human behavior and attitudes by extensive exposure to pornography" (p. 144).

EFFECTS OF EROTICA: STUDIES OF SOCIAL BEHAVIOR

The behavioral effects of exposure to erotica have been difficult to demonstrate despite the oft-voiced concerns of conporns that such material leads directly to social, moral, and mental decay. There are no studies in the literature surveyed which document adverse behavioral effects of pornography on general or specific population groups. Social behavior is a complex outcome of a complex interaction of almost innumerable variables. To argue that a single factor, such as exposure to pornography, can have a profound effect on such a complex set of behavioral responses is simplistic sophistry.

Most scientific studies have attempted to isolate specific types or instances of behavior and to relate them to exposure to erotica, or they have tried to assess the relative contribution of erotica, in concert with other factors, to predict categories of behavior.

The question of the relationship between erotica and antisocial behavior is an important one. It is, however, difficult to research because of the very high levels of exposure in the general public and the relatively low levels of antisocial behavior. Retrospective analysis is highly vulnerable to ascertainment bias, and prospective studies would require unacceptable levels of surveillance of unwieldly numbers over excessive lengths of time.

Despite the difficulties of defining a relationship between antisocial behavior and erotica, both laboratory and survey studies have provided interesting data.

Kutchinsky (1973, 1976, 1973a) has made several careful survey studies of the effects of easy availability of pornography on the incidence of sex crimes in Denmark. Very substantial decreases in four specific categories of sex crimes—exhibitionism, peeping (voyeurism), physical indecency towards women, and physical indecency towards girls—were noted in Copenhagen after 1964. Some detractors of Kutchinsky's data have stated erroneously that the number of crimes decreased because dissemination of pornography was no longer counted as a sex crime; others noted that sex crimes had been declining before 1964. The first objection is patently false, since only four specific categories of crimes were considered both before and after the change in availability of pornography. The second objection has more merit, but the decline before 1964 was irregular and gradual, and the decline afterwards was steady and substantial—the data clearly show two different slopes.

The decreases in exhibitionism and voyeurism found in Kutchinsky's data could, in part, be attributed to changes in police attitudes or in the victims' motivation to report such crimes. The change in public attitudes toward exhibitionism, as assessed in a representative sample survey of Copenhagen residents, was sufficient to account for any change in the reported incidence. Therefore, one cannot conclude that the reduction in this category was solely because of the availability of pornography. Changes in police attitudes could have accounted for the decreased incidence of reporting voyeurism.

The decline in reported incidence of physical indecency towards women also could be due to changes in attitudes toward "nonserious" incidents. No change in reported incidence of rape was found. One should keep in mind, however, that there are fewer rapes in Copenhagen in one year than there are in one weekend in New York City.

The category of crimes against children showed a fifty-six-percent decrease (from thirty-six to sixteen) in 1965, the first year in which hard-core pornographic picture magazines appeared in Denmark. This change could not be attributed to changes in public or police attitudes, to changes in methods of reporting nor to local changes since the figures for the country as a whole dropped from 220 crimes in 1965 to 87 by 1969.

Kutchinsky concluded that "the high avail-

ability of hard-core pornography in Denmark was most probably the very direct cause of a considerable decrease in . . . child molestation" (1973, p. 179). Perhaps more importantly, the number of recidivists for all sex crimes has decreased as much as the number of first offenders.

Davis and Braucht (1973) in a retrospective study, used data from 365 subjects from seven different types of social groups, from jail inmates to clerical students. In a psychometric tour de force, self-report measures of sexual deviance, sexual experience, exposure to pornography, character, and peer associations were constructed and statistically interrelated. The measure of character had four components: 1) ability to recognize the necessity of a moral decision, 2) inclination to act on a moral rather than on a selfish basis, 3) level of moral reasoning, and 4) interpersonal character evaluated by peers. The sexual deviance measure counted frequencies of behaviors such as voyeurism, rape, and tranvestism. Moral character showed a modest negative correlation ($r = -.25$) with sexual deviance.

Davis and Braucht found that the amount of exposure to pornography correlated negatively with the overall index of character for subjects first exposed to pornography *after* the age of seventeen years. The amount of exposure was positively correlated with sexual deviance and with early heterosexual experience, homosexual, and deviant sexual practices. Exposure was also correlated with social—peer, neighborhood, and family—deviance. This latter finding suggests that exposure to pornography may not be a causal variable but rather an extraneous one which tags along with the deviant peer/deviant behavior relationship. When deviant family and deviant peer circumstances are statistically eliminated from the correlation, the relationship between age of viewing and character is not different from zero at the ninety-five-percent level of confidence. Similarly, when one calculates the partial correlation between exposure to pornography and sexual deviance, eliminating the effect of peer pressures, the result is not different from zero.

Their own analysis, plus that of the reader,

suggest that Davis and Braucht have found exposure to pornography to be an extraneous variable in the relationship between individual sexual deviance and social environment. As Davis and Braucht acknowledged, there is "the possibility that exposure (to pornography) is merely part of or a product of adopting a sexually deviant life style" (1973, p. 183).

Goldstein (1973) reported a retrospective study in which samples of rapists, pedophiles, homosexuals, transexuals, heavy users of pornography, and a control group sample from the community at large were interviewed regarding their experiences with erotic material. The striking finding consistent across types of exposure (photos, movies, books) and samples was that:

> Adolescent exposure to erotica was significantly *less* for all nonheterosexual and offender groups compared to the controls. During adulthood, the sex offenders and transexuals continued to report *less* exposure to erotic stimuli than controls. [emphasis added] . . . The control groups sampled had significantly *greater* exposure to erotic materials during adolescence than the deviants, convicted sex offenders, or heavy . . . users of pornography (p. 197).

These data are in rather sharp distinction to those of Davis and Braucht (1973), since they suggest that sexual deviance significant enough to result in criminal conviction or psychiatric treatment is associated with a low degree of exposure to erotica. Moreover, the relatively high levels of exposure in the community at large were not related to significant sexual deviance.

Both male- and female-object pedophiles reported less exposure to erotica than controls did. When one considers the sharp drop in attacks against children, related to the easy availability of pornography as reported by Kutchinsky (1973), one wonders whether pornography might have a therapeutic and/or prophylactic effect if used for the treatment of American sex offenders.

Rapists and pedophiles reported very little or no discussion of sex in their homes during childhood. Both groups held very conservative,

uptight attitudes toward sex and were uncomfortable talking about it. Pedophiles had very low levels of adult sexual experience, but rapists reported high frequencies of intercourse. Both groups reported very little satisfaction with sex. Although Goldstein reports other significant differences between rapists and pedophiles and between male- versus female-object pedophiles, the repressive and inhibited character of sexual emotions is common to both groups and is consistent with low exposure to and low interest in pornography.

Homosexuals and heavy users of pornography in the sample were reported by Goldstein to have liberal and tolerant sexual attitudes, low levels of adolescent sexual activity and high levels of adult activity. The author suggests that for the "user" group, interest in pornography may be a symbolic way to make up for lost time or an augmentation of infantile fantasy life which has persisted into adulthood. Other studies have found relationships among data for both groups which are somewhat supportive of both these hypotheses (see Money and Athanasiou, 1973).

Laboratory studies of the effects of erotica on behavior are more limited in the ranges of behavior monitored but more exact in the manipulation and measurement of dependent and independent variables.

Griffitt, May, and Veitch (1974) reported that "sexually aroused subjects of both sexes were found to attend visually more to opposite-sex than to same-sex targets and to look more at heterosexual targets than did nonaroused subjects. Sexually aroused subjects who responded negatively to sexual stimulation were found to . . . avoid heterosexual persons in . . . seating proximity. Only those who responded positively to sex stimulation evaluated more favorably or looked more at opposite-sex targets" (p. 367). It is important to note that the subjective evaluation of the sexually arousing stimulus was the thing which differentiated behavior rather than the stimulation per se.

Abel and others (1977) studied the erectile response of rapists and nonrapists to sexual scenes (audio presentation) of rape and found that the rapists tended more often than non-rapists to respond with erections to this material. Rapists with the highest frequency of rape, those who had injured their victim and those who chose children as victims also were distinguished. Some rapists also developed erections to nonerotic violent descriptions indicating a commonality—for rapists—between purely violent and sexually violent scenes. Erectile response to nonviolent, mutually enjoyable intercourse scenes was minimal for these rapists.

These data suggest that normal individuals are not turned on by sexual violence or by violence alone, and that response is a characteristic of the viewer rather than of the material per se. Advocates of censorship take an antithetical viewpoint and assume that, for example, sadomasochistic material can produce arousal in anyone, contrary to the findings of Abel and others and Goldstein (1973).

The question of whether sexual arousal is a general state facilitating many types of behavior or a specific state facilitating only sexual behavior is somewhat open. There are few persuasive data for the general arousal hypothesis, although psychoanalytic theory might support such a position.

Three studies discussed below examined the inhibiting and instigating effects of sexual arousal. The data seem to suggest that sexual arousal does not lead to aggressive behavior in normal adults. Baron (1974), for example, found that "heightened sexual arousal was highly effective in inhibiting subsequent aggression by [angered] subjects but failed to influence significantly the strength of such behavior on the part of subjects in the non-angered condition" (p. 318). Donnerstein and others (1975) found "that mildly erotic stimuli had an inhibiting effect on aggression . . . whereas highly erotic stimuli tended to maintain aggression at a level similar to non-erotic exposure" (p. 237). What would seem to be required is an experimental design which included a variety of conditions such as 1) varying order of presentation of erotic and aggression inducing stimuli, 2) varying levels of stimuli and, most important, 3)

varying the choice of available responses to subjects.

Jaffe and others (1974) conducted a laboratory experiment in which sexually aroused subjects were required to deliver electrical shocks to an experimental confederate. They found that under these conditions, aroused subjects, both males and females, delivered more intense shocks than nonaroused subjects. Jaffe (1975) has supplied as yet unpublished data on a similar experiment in which subjects were allowed to choose whether or not to deliver shocks. Under these conditions, Jaffe found that "when the sexually aroused person has the option of performing positive, prosocial responses or negative aggressive ones, he will, probably, act less aggressively and more positively than will the non-aroused individual. It is suggested then, that under conditions of choice between aggressive and nonaggressive . . . social action, sexual stimulation will be associated with less rather than more aggression. . . ." (personal communication). These findings may be viewed as consistent with social facilitation theory rather than with a theory of general arousal. In general, it seems that exposure to erotica may lead to increased sexual activity immediately following exposure, if and only if there is an established pattern of sexual behavior.

There are many circumstances for which that generalization does not hold. For example, boredom with erotica may set in very rapidly Howard, and others (1973) exposed normal healthy males to pornographic materials for ninety minutes per day for fifteen days and found that "pornography is an innocuous stimulus which leads quickly to satiation and that public concern is misplaced" (p. 133).

In a study which had married couples view erotic movies once per week over a twelve-week period, Mann, Sidman, and Starr (1973) found that a relatively high level of sexual activity occurred on movie-viewing nights, although the average amount of sexual activity over the three months changed only slightly: "Completing daily checklists [of sexual behavior] appeared to facilitate sexual activity more than viewing erotic films. Results appear[ed] most concordant with social learning theory and fail[ed] to support the position that viewing erotic films produce[d] harmful social consequences" (p. 113). Mann and others (1974) reanalyzed these data to determine if there was a satiation effect with repeated exposure to erotic films. "The findings indicated that these movies had become less and less effective elicitors of sexual reactions with successive presentations" (p. 729). These data agree with a limited but somewhat similar study by Brown, Amoroso, and Ware (1976), which showed similar transient increases in normal sexual behavior.

A brief report by Diener and others (1973) of a study using noninvasive observation methods and the "dropped-wallet" technique measured altruism and honesty in relation to exposure to erotica. The authors compared returns from a pornographic bookstore and a general bookstore. More patrons returned wallets discovered while leaving the stores than did those who discovered a wallet while entering the stores. The authors concluded that "these data do indicate that exposure to erotic stimuli did not lead to an increase in the antisocial behavior of stealing" (p. 226).

In summary, the variation of methods and study designs limits the conclusions one may draw from currently available studies. It is safe to say, however, that there are no data which suggest that erotic arousal per se leads to antisocial behavior and many data which suggest its effect is minimal, benign, and transient.

EXPOSURE TO EROTICA: PERSONALITY, SOCIAL DIFFERENCES, SEX DIFFERENCES

Some of the personality and social variables related to viewing or not viewing erotica have been detailed above. Athanasiou and Shaver (1971) have reported a long list of correlates of viewing erotica which include differences in political preference (Democrats versus Republicans), age, attitude toward social issues such as abortion, and other variables. In general, there is little surprise in these correlations, since they make sound social psychological sense.

One of the personality variables which seems central to response to erotica is guilt. Donald Mosher (1966) has developed a well validated measure of sex guilt, a "generalized expectancy for self-mediated punishment for violating or for anticipating violating standards of proper sexual conduct" (p. 26), and demonstrated that high sex-guilt subjects rated erotic films as more pornographic, disgusting, and offensive, and more often saw oral-genital sex as abnormal than did low sex-guilt subjects.

Sex guilt was positively correlated (correlations usually > 0.3) with the following variables in Mosher's (1973) study: religiosity, political conservatism, the belief that the government should enforce sex laws, the belief that homosexuals should be excluded from society, that love and sex are inextricably linked, that extra- and premarital sex are not good ideas, that abortion should be difficult to obtain or illegal, and that conservative standards of sex behavior are best. Additionally, sex guilt was positively correlated with preventing respondents from expressing their sexuality because of social disapproval, guilt feelings, and religious or other moral training.

Sex guilt was negatively correlated with number of sexual partners, intercourse frequency, oral-genital activity, and the belief that sex is fun.

Sex guilt, then, may be seen as a central psychological variable in predicting sex attitudes and sex behavior. Love and others (1976) used Mosher's Forced Choice Guilt Inventory to predict the time spent viewing erotic slides. They found that "the viewing time of the low sex guilt group increased linearly as a function of increasing pornographic content. There was no significant increase in viewing time for high sex guilt subjects. Subjects with a moderate degree of sex guilt displayed a curvilinear pattern" (p. 624). The three groups were referred to as the profligate, the priggish, and the prudent.

Ray and Walker (1973) reported that low sex-guilt female subjects rated masturbation, coitus, and petting stimuli as more sexually arousing, better, more pleasant, safer, and more appealing than did high sex-guilt subjects.

Based on the above, one would expect censorship, condemnation of material on the basis of its explicit sexual content, to enhance viewing of the material on the part of low but not high sex-guilt subjects. Schill and others (1975) conducted such an experiment and found that when material was labeled as "porno junk," viewing time was highest for both high and low sex-guilt subjects. When the experimenter used the phrase, "I really enjoyed that porno stuff" (p. 104), high sex-guilt subjects viewed it for an average of 2.55 minutes relative to the low guilt subjects who viewed it for an average of 0.79 minutes.

It would seem from these data that the "banned-in-Boston" effect served to increase viewing time for both groups, but the approval condition affected only the high guilt subjects' viewing. In retrospect this is an intuitively satisfying outcome but clearly raises the question of the value of censorship to inhibit behavior. Fromkin and Brock (1973) and Zellinger and others (1975) have applied commodity theory analysis to the effects of restrictions on pornography and have found results which confirm "the commodity theory prediction that the imposition of age restrictions upon porngraphic materials increases their desirability" (p. 94). They conclude that "making erotic materials more difficult to obtain, harassing and punishing pornographers and purveyors of pornography, and restricting certain materials . . . may increase interest in the materials and render them more desirable than would have been the case without the restriction, harassment, or difficulty" (p. 219).

SEX DIFFERENCES

Sexual differences in response to erotica might better be labeled sexual similarities. Until fairly recently it was assumed on the basis of self-report, that women were less responsive to various forms of erotica imagery. All current laboratory data, including many of the studies cited above, indicate that women respond with arousal to many or most of the stimuli which arouse men. In fact, Byrne and others (1973) found that "husbands and wives exhibit greater than chance similarity in responding to erotica . . . spouses were found to be similar in their reported sexual arousal, in their judgments of pornography and in their attitudes about censorship following exposure to erotic stimuli" (p. 392). They also found that authoritarianism was an important mediator of these responses.

Englar and Walker (1973) reviewed the literature on sex differences and reported in their study that men and women responded equally to erotica. Izard and Caplan (1974) found small differences in male and female response to a passage from a book dealing with exploitative sex in which a virgin was seduced by a sexually experienced man. Men reported more sexual arousal than women did.

Herrell (1975) attempted to replicate their study and included a passage from (a book known to be not obscene) *Lady Chatterly's Lover*. He found that the type of literature made a significant difference in reported levels of arousal. He concluded, in essence, that men may become aroused independently of the interpersonal content of erotica, but women may become aroused and angry after reading passages in which women are sexually exploited. He states, "Sex differences in response to erotic literature are complex and depend on the interpersonal as well as the erotic content of the passages" (p. 921).

In summary, we find that the dominating evidence suggests that when normal adults view depictions of "ultimate sex acts," their response, which is usually a quite normal degree of sexual arousal, is modulated by personality and social variables. Their reaction to their response is similarly related to experiential, personality, and social variables. There are virtually no data in the scientific literature which suggest a causal link between exposure to erotica and antisocial behavior, and there are many data which suggest the opposite. It may even be that a normal reaction of arousal to pornography may be able to separate sexually functional people from those with sexual dysfunctions.

There are no data which even hint that pornography represents a clear and present danger to society in the way that, say, alcohol or tobacco do. The debate over censorship therefore must continue to be based on attitudes, taste, and values. In a pluralistic and open society such as ours attempts to be, it is not likely that this debate will end soon.

REFERENCES

ABEL, G. G.; BARLOW, D. H.; BLANCHARD, E. B.; and GUILD, D. 1977. The components of rapists' sexual arousal. *Arch. Gen. Psychiatry* 34: 895–903.

ABELSON, H.; COHEN, R.; HEATON, E.; and SLIDER, C. 1970. Public attitudes toward and experience with erotic materials. *Technical Reports of the Commission on Obscenity and Pornography*, vol. 6. Washington, D.C.: U. S. Government Printing Office.

ABRAMSON, P. R.; REPCZYNSKI, C. A.; and MERRILL, L. R. 1976. The menstrual cycle and response to erotic literature. *J. Consulting and Clinical Psychol.* 44: 1018–19.

ATHANASIOU, R., and SHAVER, P. 1971. Correlates of heterosexuals' reactions to pornography. *J. Sex Research* 7: 298.

———; and TAVRIS, C. 1970. Sex. *Psychology Today* 4: 39–52.

BARCLAY, A. M. 1970. Urinary acid phosphatase secretion in sexually aroused males. *J. of Experimental Research in Personality* 4: 233–38.

BARON, R. A. 1974. The aggression-inhibiting influence of heightened sexual arousal. *J. Pers. and Soc. Psychol.* 30: 318–22.

BARR, R., and BLASZCYNSKI, A. 1976. Autonomic responses of transexual and homosexual males to erotic film sequences. *Archives of Sexual Behavior* 5: 211.

BROWN, M.; AMOROSO, D. M.; and WARE, E. E. 1976. Behavioral effects of viewing pornography. *J. Social Psychology* 98: 235.

BYRNE, D.; CHERRY, F.; LAMBERTH, J.; and MITCHELL, H. E. 1973. Husband-wife similarity in response to erotic stimuli. *J. of Personality* 41: 385–93.

———; FISHER, J. D.; and LAMBERTH, J. Evaluations of erotica: facts or feelings? *Journal of Personality and Social Psychology* 29: 111–16.

CAIRNS, R. B.; PAUL, J. C. N.; and WISHNER, J. 1962. Sex censorship: the assumptions of the anti-obscenity laws and the empirical evidence. *Minnesota Law Review* 46: 1009–41.

Psychological assumptions in the censorship: an avaluative review of recent research 1961–1968. *Technical Reports of the C.O.P* 1. Washington, D.C.: USGPO.

COLSON, C. E. 1974. The evaluation of pornography: effects of attitude and perceived physiological reaction. *Archives of Sexual Behavior* 3: 307.

Commission on Obscenity and Pornography. 1970. *Report* and *Technical Reports,* vols. 1–9. Washington, D.C.: U.S. Government Printing Office.

DAVIS, K. E., and BRAUCHT, G. N. 1973. Exposure to pornography, character and sexual deviance: a retrospective survey. *J. Soc. Issues* 29: 183–96.

DIENER, E.; WESTFORD, K. L.; FRASER, S. C.; and BEAMAN, A. L. 1973. Selected demographic variables in altruism. *Psychological Reports* 33: 226.

DONNERSTEIN, E.; DONNERSTEIN, M.; and EVANS, R. 1975. Erotic stimuli and aggression: facilitation or inhibition. *J. Pers. Soc. Psychol.* 32: 237–44.

ENGLAR, Z. C., and WALKER, C. E. 1973. Male and female reactions to erotic literature. *Psychological Reports* 32: 481–82.

FLEISHMAN, S. 1973. *The Supreme Court Obscenity Decisions.* San Diego: Greenleaf Classics.

FROMKIN, H. L., and BROCK, T. C. 1973. Erotic materials: a commodity theory analysis of the enhanced desirability that may accompany their inavailability. *J. Applied Social Psychol.* 3: 219–31.

GEER, J. H.; MOROKOFF, P.; and GREENWOOD, P. 1974. Sexual arousal in women: the development of a measurement device for vaginal blood volume. *Archives of Sexual Behavior* 3: 559.

GOLDSTEIN, M. J. 1973. Exposure to erotic stimuli and sexual deviance. *J. Social Issues* 29: 197–219.

GRIFFITT, W.; MAY, J.; and VEITCH, R. 1974. Sexual stimulation and interpersonal behavior: Heterosexual evaluative responses, visual behavior, and physical proximity. *J. Pers. and Soc. Psychol.* 30: 367–77.

HERRELL, J. M. 1975. Sex differences in emotional response to erotic literature. *J. Consult. and Clinical Psychol.* 43: 921.

HOWARD, J. L.; LIPTZIN, M. B.; and REIFLER, C. B. 1973. Is pornography a problem? *J. Social Issues* 29: 133–45.

IZARD, C. E., and CAPLAN, S. 1974. Sex differences in emotional responses to erotic literature. *J. Consult. and Clinical Psychol.* 42: 468.

JAFFE, Y. 1975. Sex and aggression: an intimate relationship. *Dissertation abstracts international* 35: (9-B): 4709.

JAFFEY, Y.; MALAMUTH, N.; FEINGOLD, J.; and FESHBACH, S. 1974. Sexual arousal and behavioral aggression. *J. Personality and Social Psychology* 30: 759–64.

KENYON, F. E. 1975. Pornography, the law and mental health. *British Journal of Psychiatry* 126: 225–32.

KERCHER, G. A., and WALKER, C. E. 1973. Reactions of convicted rapists to sexually explicit stimuli. *Journal of Abnormal Psychology* 81: 46–50.

KIRKPATRICK, R. G. 1974. Moral indignation and repressed sexuality: The sociosexual dialectics of antipornography crusades. *Psychoanalytic Review* 61: 141–49.

KUTCHINSKY, B. 1976. Deviance and criminality: the case of a voyeur in a peeper's paradise. *Disease of the Nervous System* 37: 145–51.

———. 1973. The effect of easy availability of pornography on the incidence of sex crimes. *J. Soc. Issues* 29: 163–82.

———. 1973a. Eroticism without censorship: sociological investigations on the production and consumption of pornographic literature in Denmark. *Int. J. of Criminology and Penology* 1: 217–25.

LINCOLN, G. A. 1974. Luteinizing hormone and testosterone in man. *Nature* 252: 232–33.

LOVE, R. E.; SLOAN, L. R.; and SCHMIDT, M. J. 1976. Viewing pornography and sex guilt: the priggish, the prudent, and the profligate. *J. Consult. and Clinical Psychol.* 44: 624–29.

MANN, J.; BERKOWITZ, L.; SIDMAN, J.; STARR, S.; and WERT, S. 1974. Satiation of the transient stimulating effect of erotic films. *J. Pers. Soc. Psychol.* 30: 729–35.

———; SIDMAN, J.; and STARR, S. 1973. Evaluating social consequences of erotic films: an experimental approach. *J. Soc. Issues* 29: 113–32.

MASTERS, W., and JOHNSON, V. 1966. *Human sexual response.* Boston: Little, Brown.

MERRITT, C. G.; GERSTL, J. E.; and LoSCIUTO, L. A. 1975. Age and perceived effects of erotica-pornography: a national sample study. *Archives of Sexual Behavior* 4: 605.

MONEY, J., and ATHANASIOU, R. 1973. Pornography: review and bibliographic annotations. *Amer. Journal of Obstetrics and Gynecology* 115: 130–46.

———, and EHRHARDT, A. A. 1972. *Man and woman, boy and girl: differentiation and dimorphism of gender identity from conception to maturity.* Baltimore: Johns Hopkins University Press.

MOSHER, D. 1966. The development and multitrait-multimethod matrix analysis of three measures of three aspects of guilt. *J. Consulting Psychology* 30: 25–29.

——. 1973. Sex differences, sex experience, sex guilt, and explicit sexual films. *J. Soc. Issues* 29: 95–112.

PIRKE, K. M.; KOCKOTT, G.; and DITTMAR, F. 1974. Psychosexual stimulation and plasma testosterone in man. *Archives of Sexual Behavior* 6: 577.

RAY, R. E., and THOMPSON, W. D. 1974. Autonomic correlates of female guilt responses to erotic visual stimuli. *Psychological Reports* 34: 1299–1306.

RAY, R., and WALKER, C. E. 1973. Biographical and self-report correlates of female guilt responses to visual erotic stimuli. *J. Consult. and Clinical Psychol.* 41: 93–96.

SCHAEFER, H. H.; TREGERTHON, G. J.; and COLGAN, A. H. 1976. Measurement and self-estimated penile erection. *Behavior Therapy* 7: 1–7.

SCHILL, T.; EVANS, R.; MONROE, S.; and DRAIN, D. 1975. Effects of approval or disapproval on reading behavior of high- and low-guilt subjects. *J. Consult. and Clinical Psychol.* 43: 104.

WILSON, W. C. 1973. Pornography: the emergence of a social isssue and the beginning of a psychological study. *Journal of Social Issues* 29: 7–17.

WINCZE, J. P.; HOON, E. F.; and HOON, P. W. 1976. Physiological responsivity of normal and sexually dysfunctional women during erotic stimulus exposure. *Journal of Psysomatic Research* 20: 445–51.

ZELLINGER, D. A.; FROMKIN, H. L.; SPELLER, D. E.; and KOHN, C. A. 1975. A commodity theory analysis of the effects of age restrictions upon pornographic materials. *J. Applied Psychology* 60: 94–99.

ZUCKERMAN, M. 1971. Physiological measures of sexual arousal in the human. *Psychological Bulletin* 75: 347.

ZURCHER, L. A.; KIRKPATRICK, R. G.; CUSHING, R. G.; and BOWMAN, C. K. 1973. Ad hoc antipornography organizations and their active members: a research summary. *J. Social Issues* 29: 69–94.

3

SEXUAL DISORDERS AND THEIR TREATMENT

FOURTEEN

Gender Identity Role: Normal Differentiation and its Transpositions

JOHN MONEY

CLAUS WIEDEKING

GENDER IDENTITY/ROLE

DIFFERENTIATION

Most people do not question their own or others' established gender identity and role as male or female. They are readily accepted at face value. What is said and done by men and women in different societies varies and may overlap, since dimorphic norms of gender role are culturally and historically determined. But once an individual's identity and role as a male or a female become differentiated, they remain stable and are unlikely to be shaken even by major crises in life, physiological, social, or accidental.

The greater proportion of gender identity/role differentiation takes place after birth. It develops on the basis of prenatally programmed sex differences in body morphology, in hormonal function, and in central nervous system (CNS) function, but is not preordained or preprogrammed *in toto* by prenatal determinants. Prenatal antecedents lay down a predisposition to which postnatal influences are added. A prenatal defect, skew, or bias may be either augmented or counteracted by postnatal influences.

The dimorphism of gender identity/role as male or female begins (Figure 1) with the genetic dimorphism of the sex chromosomes, XY for the male, XX for the female. It is followed by the differentiation of the gonads with H-Y antigen on the Y bearing sperm governing the differentiation of the testes. Fetal hormonal functioning then programs differentiation of the internal reproductive anatomy, and the external genital morphology. Then follows differential sex assignment at birth, rearing as a boy or a girl, and differentiation of the childhood gender role and identity. The differentiation process is continued through the prepubertal and pubertal phase with, in adolescence, a sexually dimorphic response or, more accurately,

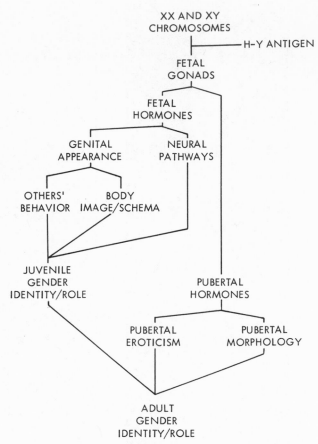

Figure 1. Sequential and cumulative components of the program of gender identity/role.

threshold of response manifested in erotic attraction, falling in love, courtship, mating, and parenthood.

Figure 1 is a framework for a descriptive catalogue of conditions and events necessary for normal gender identity/role differentiation. It also may be used for a descriptive catalogue of biogenic factors and living conditions harmful to the differentiation of an intact, functioning, normal, or healthy gender identity.

DEFINITIONS

Gender identity: The sameness, unity, and persistence of one's individuality as male, female, or ambivalent in greater or lesser degree, especially as it is experienced in self-awareness and behavior. Gender identity is the private experience of gender role, and gender role is the public expression of gender identity.

Gender role: Everything that a person says or does to indicate others or to the self, the degree that one is either male, female, or ambivalent. It includes, but is not restricted to sexual arousal and response. Gender role is the public expression of gender identity, and gender identity is the private experience of gender role.

Gender identity/role: The term used to express the unity of gender identity and gender role which are opposite sides of the same coin. Gender identity and gender role both belong to the self. One's own gender role is not synonymous with a socially prescribed or conventional gender role stereotype, even though it in some greater or lesser degree reflects this stereotype.

Gender identity/role differentiation: The differentiation of gender identity/role is the product of the interaction of prenatal (phyletically prescribed) and postnatal (social-environmentally prescribed) determinants or events, the latter outweighing the former in their overall influence.

Psychosexual differentiation: A term which historically antedates the term, gender identity/role differentiation, and which is sometimes used synonymously, despite the confusion of its also being used as a synonym for gender identity differentiation.

Genotype: An abstract term referring to the hereditary or gene-determined contribution to individual development. The genotype interacts with the envirotype to produce the uniquely individual phenotype.

Envirotype: An abstract term referring to the environmentally determined contribution to individual development. It interacts with the genotype to produce the uniquely individual phenotype. The term recognizes the fact that substances and events from the environment enter the cells of the body, including the cells of the central nervous system (CNS). There is an intrauterine, antenatal environment as well as a postnatal, extrauterine one.

Phenotype: The product of the interaction of genotype and envirotype. Both set limits on each other. The genotype, in order to express itself, depends on a favorable envirotype, and the envirotype cannot process what the genotype does not supply.

Critical period: A time-limited phase, specific to a given aspect or phase of individual development, during which a state of sensitivity or readiness of the organism must be met by phyletically specific external stimuli in order to permit that aspect or phase of development to progress optimally. For example, speech cannot be acquired until the sensitive stage is reached, at which time there must be stimulation from hearing other people talk. At the conclusion of the critical period the development which has taken place is likely to remain permanent.

Identification and Complementation: In the differentiation of gender identity/role, identification signifies that an individual establishes a mental schema in the brain by imitating and copying or modeling the behavior of members of one's own assigned sex. Complementation signifies the mental schema through learning the behavior of members of the opposite assigned sex and through reciprocating with gender-appropriate responses of one's own assigned sex.

DISORDERS OF GENDER IDENTITY/ROLE

Gender identity/role disorders occur most frequently in people with normal external and internal reproductive anatomy. Sexual pathways of the central nervous system (CNS) do not show gross morphological changes to which gender identity/role disorders might be attributed. This is not surprising, since one would expect CNS functions mediating such disorders to be related to the dynamics of neurochemistry, specifically of neurotransmitters, and thresholds of arousal and inhibition in neurosexual pathways. Identification and measurement of these functions is not technically possible at the present time.

Transpositions Versus Intrusions or Displacements

Some clinicians use the term disorder in connection with gender identity/role, to refer only to male-female transpositions. Sometimes known as gender dysphorias, these transpositions contain the syndromes of transexualism and transvestism. They also may include homosexualism and bisexualism, though neither of these need be considered pathologies or disorders (see below).

Other clinicians include in the category of disordered gender identity/role all the paraphilias. Paraphilia refers to a condition in which sexual arousal and performance is dependent on highly specific imagery, perceived or remembered, other than imagery of the erotic partner. A paraphilia may be benign or noxious. The imagery of a paraphilia, as in fetishism, for example, may be in the nature of an imagistic intrusion, to be associated with the erotic image of the partner, or it may be rather a displacement or substitute for the erotic image of a partner, in whole or in part. A paraphilia can be regarded as a part of gender identity/role in that it is essential to the person's masculine or feminine erotic functioning. Thus for the male sadist, his masculine gender identity/role in its erotic manifestation is dependent on remembered or enacted sadistic imagery.

The list of the paraphilias is long. It includes, for example, masochism and sadism, rape and lust murder, voyeurism and exhibitionism, pedophilia and gerontophilia, amputeephilia (apotemnophilia), zoophilia, klismaphilia, coprophilia, urophilia, necrophilia, fetishism, and so on.

The transposition syndromes generally are classified along with the intrusion or displacement syndromes as paraphilias. There is not total professional consensus, however, especially in those cases of homosexualism (and by extension, bisexualism) in which the perceived or remembered imagery of erotic arousal and performance is concordant with the body and the person of the same-sexed, pair-bonded partner, the latter itself being the only unorthodoxy. Transvestism, because of its associated fetishistic dependency on clothing, qualifies as a paraphilia. So also does transexualism, for the transexual person can function erotically only by reason of having, or imagining having a body reassigned and transformed from that of the sex of birth.

The distinction between transposition and intrusion or displacement paraphilias having been made, the transposition syndromes are the focus of the remainder of this chapter, after the examination (section 2.2) of what constitutes pathology.

HARMLESS VERSUS NOXIOUS;
NORMALCY VERSUS PATHOLOGY

A paraphilia is not, by definition, a pathology. Rather, it becomes pathological when it becomes too severe, too insistent, and too noxious to the partner, or to the self. In mild form, paraphiliac imagery and the behavior it engenders may be simply a part of love play. For example, a playful degree of biting, slapping, or pinching qualifies as sadistic but is harmless when the play is between consenting partners.

In medicine generally, and in sexology in particular, there are many occasions when one is confronted with the issue of how to establish criteria of pathology. When, for example, does an elevation in temperature become a fever? Or a shortness of stature, dwarfism? Or an insufficiency of food, malnutrition? The criterion point adopted in answer to such questions may have great practical significance. In Peking, for example, Westerners in the diplomatic corps recently may have been denied a Chinese driving license because their blood pressure, judged normal at home, would be elevated according to the norms of the Chinese who have a lower average blood pressure.

There is always something arbitrary about the choice of a criterion of normalcy. It is arbitrary even to choose the statistical norm—it may be normal to be infested with hookworm or schistosomiasis in certain locales, but it is not healthy. The criterion of health versus pathology involves a chain of logical reasoning that sooner or later brings one into direct confrontation with a value judgment. The personal criterion of pathology may be too much pain, suffering, and loss of the feeling of well-being. The social criterion may be too much harm to, or threat of endangering the health or well-being of others. The well-being of others may be covertly or implicitly defined as their political, legal, moral, spiritual, or religious well-being.

In matters of sexual health, as in behavioral health in general, social criteria have traditionally dominated personal ones. They have been powerfully religious and legalistic, but politically and ethnically arbitrary. This arbitrariness is presently under fire, and to some extent there is today a social re-examination of criteria and standards. In their 1974 referendum, for example, the membership of the American Psychiatric Association confirmed the action of their committee on nomenclature in changing the status of homosexuality from disease to non-disease.

The mood of society today is toward the greater tolerance of the principle of live and let live sexually, provided both partners are consenting adults or, if young, of like age. There is no fixed dividing line between the tolerable and the intolerable, socially, and no criterion for establishing one. A workable criterion, which is both expedient and pragmatic, is the criterion of mutual consent between erotic partners, up to the point of noxious injury to health and well-being. This criterion rules out lust murder, rape, abusive sadism, a masochist's self-arranged torture and death by homicide, enforced amputation of the partner by an amputee fetishist, enforced celibacy or erotic deprivation of the partner by a transexual, and the like. Other forms of erotic expression, subject to the proviso of mutual consent, are not ruled out. Any individual whose form of erotic expression engenders too great a loss of well-being is, however, eligible for whatever therapy sexological medicine may be able to offer.

Greater Vulnerability of the Male

Sexologists agree that the incidence of gender identity/role disorders is greater in males than in females, though there are as yet no fixed statistics. The embryology of prenatal hormonal regulation of sex differentiation clearly shows that nature's first choice is to differentiate the morphology of a female. The differentiation of male morphology requires that something be added (the "Adam principle"). This something

is, for the most part, androgen released by the fetal testes. A second substance, known only as mullerian inhibiting substance, suppressses development of the mullerian ducts which otherwise would form a uterus in the male. By inference from animal experiments to human beings, androgen also influences brain pathways or thresholds that mediate erotic and mating behavior. Apart from some rodent studies, the neuroanatomy and neurochemistry of this influence still must be demonstrated.

It is, by hypothesis, likely that prenatal androgen has a masculinizing effect on brain thresholds subserving the relationship of visual signals and images to erotic attraction and arousal. In lower mammals, including primates, an odor or pheromone from the ovulating female's vagina serves as a sex attractant. In man, the sense of sight overrides smell as a sex attractant. Both sexes respond to visual erotic signals, but woman is more dependent on touch for complete arousal, according to present evidence. In man, the visual stimulus prompts the initiation of an erotic approach. Nature demonstrates the primacy of the visual image in male eroticism in the phenomenon of the pubertal orgasm dream (wet dream) for which there is no exact counterpart in the female.

The actual image that is erotically stimulating is not phyletically programmed so as to be identical in all human males. If it were, any two males and females could pair-bond, that is, fall in love with each other. But nature, in its own wisdom, has designed us as a species rich in the diversity of individual differences, erotic individual differences included. Thus, the image of erotic arousal is no more innate than is native language. Like native language, the image of erotic arousal is established in response to early life experience, and it becomes engramed or imprinted. The so-called errors of imagery, manifested as transpositions of gender identity/role, or as the intrusion or displacement paraphilias, also become engramed or imprinted. The infant and juvenile male appears more vulnerable to such an imprinting error than is his female counterpart, probably because of the greater importance of the visual image to erotic arousal in nature's design of the human male.

GENDER IDENTITY/ROLE TRANSPOSITIONS

As shown in Table 1, gender identity/role transpositions may be classsified in a 3 × 2 scheme of: chronic and episodic versus total, partial, and arbitrary. In this scheme, transexualism represents the most extreme transposition in terms of time and completeness, and also of prognosis and therapy. Transvestism may appear equally complete, except that the transposition is time-limited, that is, cyclic or episodic, alternating between male and female. Homosexualism in its extreme forms of effeminate homosexuality in the male and virilistic homosexuality in the female shows itself not only in erotic but also in nonerotic everyday behavior. The less extreme and more frequent manifestations of homosexualism may not be detectable except in erotic imagery and practice. This type of homosexualism may not, in everyday activities, be distinguishable from bisexualism. Bisexualism as here defined refers to homosexual behavior which alternates with heterosexual behavior as manifest primarily in eroticism and the sex of the partner.

The transpositions classified as arbitrary in Table 1 do not pertain to erotic behavior itself, but to behavior in general that is culturally and historically sex-stereotyped. This applies to vocational sex-stereotyping as related to economic and legal rights of equality. It applies also to recreational and decorational sex-stereotyping. Vocational, recreational and decorational sex-stereotypes represent historically determined options. Nonetheless, many people think of them as eternal verities of sex difference, not subject to personal option and caprice. So great is the conviction of gender identity/role, once it becomes differentiated and built-in, postnatally!

TRANSEXUALISM

Transexual, the adjective, means simply going from one sex to the other. Thus one could have a casual transexual thought or dream, one's hermaphroditic baby could have a transexual change of the birth announcement, or as a hermaphrodite, one could undergo a transexual reassignment of one's sex. A person of nonhermaphroditic, nonambiguous genital anatomy may also seek and qualify to undergo a legal, hormonal, and surgical sex reassignment. This is the person who, in today's nomenclature, is known as a transexual.

DEFINITION AND DESCRIPTION

The transexual is genitally an anatomical male or female who expresses with strong conviction that he or she has the mind of the opposite sex, who lives as a member of the opposite sex part-time or full-time, and who seeks to change his or her original sex legally and through hormonal and surgical sex reassignment.

The actual demand for hormonal and surgical intervention has been dependent historically on the patient's knowledge of the availability of such procedures. The personal sense and conviction of having the wrong-sexed body, however, predates such knowledge. Typically, a transexual dates in childhood the onset of his or her sense of belonging to the other sex. The age at which sex reassignment becomes an *idée fixe* varies. It may be prepubertal or adolescent, or it may be delayed until, in young adulthood or early middle age, the obsession finally can be postponed no longer.

Table 1.   3 X 2 REPRESENTATION OF THE TRANSPOSITION OF GENDER IDENTITY/ROLE.

	Total	Partial	Arbitrary
Chronic	Transexualism	Homosexualism	Sex-coded work, schooling, and legal status
Episodic	Transvestism	Bisexualism	Sex-coded play, manners-grooming, and decoration

INCIDENCE

Public health statistics in the United States do not include incidence figures on any sexological problems, including the incidence of birth defects of the sex organs. Voluntary registration of sexological problems would fail statistically, owing to the social penalties of self-disclosure.. Therefore, there are no authentic estimates of the incidence of transexualism in the United States or anywhere else. However, it can be said that postoperative transexuals in the United States now number in the thousands, but almost certainly not in the tens of thousands. In a total United States population of just over two hundred and twenty million, the condition is far more common than most physicians might think, but not so common that every physician should expect to treat several cases in the course of his or her career. Some will see no cases, and some will miss cases because the patient is too apprehensive to state his or her chief complaint.

ETIOLOGY

In the etiology of transexualism, as of other gender identity/role disorders, there is no demonstrable evidence of a hereditary factor, either in the family tree or as a spontaneous mutation. Transexualism has been recorded in some males with the 47, XXY chromosomal condition (Klinefelter's syndrome), but most XXY individuals are not transexuals.

By inference from experimental animal studies, prenatal hormonal history may be etiologically significant. There is as yet no directly demonstrable human evidence to implicate a prenatal hormonal effect, chiefly because there are no retrospectively retrievable records of the prenatal hormonal history of transexuals. If hormones do play an etiologic role, however, then it is almost certainly in the prenatal period, and not at puberty or later. It is very rare to find a hormonal abnormality in an untreated postpubertal transexual.

In cases of hermaphroditism with a known prenatal history of hormonal abnormality, transexualism is not a subsequent sequel, except in the presence of ambiguity of gender assignment and rearing postnatally. Such cases indicate that prenatal hormonal history alone is not capable of determining the subsequent differentiation of gender identity/role. Postnatal history is proportionally more important. It has not yet proved possible to find a formula from which to predict transexualism on the basis of early childhood history, even among children who overtly wish to change sex. These same children have proved to develop as adolescent homosexuals or bisexuals rather than transexuals. In some families, it is possible to recognize a covert collusion of the parents and the child with respect to the child's repudiation of his or her anatomic sex.

DIAGNOSIS

The diagnosis of transexualism is based initially on the presenting complaint, namely the need for sex reassignment. It is necessary for legal and ethical reasons to check the anamnesis against other informants and social records. It is in the nature of transexualism to give a revised or edited biography. The best diagnostic test is the "real-life test" for a minimum of two years, during which time social, emotional, and economic rehabilitation in the new sex role is achieved.

Usually the physical examination yields nothing contributing to the diagnosis, but it should not be omitted. In a few cases, other unrelated pathology may limit the therapy for sex reassignment. Very rarely, the EEG may show a temporal lobe epileptic focus requiring neurosurgery after which the sex problem may remit. Hormonal evaluations, useful for the research information they provide, are typically noncontributory.

DIFFERENTIAL DIAGNOSIS

The check list for the differential diagnosis includes:

Temporal lobe epilepsy with transexualism or transvestism as a related symptom.

Schizophrenic disorder with transexual gender identity confusion as a symptom.

Transvestism with a strong element of transexualism that emerges, especially in middle life.

Female impersonation in an extremely effeminate male homosexual (drag queen) or male impersonation in a virilistic lesbian.

The above diagnoses do not, in and of themselves alone, rule out the possibility of rehabilitation by means of sex reassignment, but they do require caution and unhurried decisions. Much the same applies also to transexuals who are pathologically depressed, for sex reassignment alone does not reverse depression.

THERAPY

Sex reassignment is a rehabilitative form of therapy, not a cure. It is used because other forms of therapy capable of ameliorating the transexual's suffering have not, to date, been proved effective.

Initially the therapeutic goal is for the patient to achieve success in the two-year, real-life test. During this period, hormonal reassignment is instituted. With the exception of deepening of the voice in the female-to-male transexual, hormonal changes are reversible if the test proves to the patient that his or her transexualism does not warrant further pursuit of reassignment.

The following male-to-female hormone dosages have been found satisfactory: Estinyl (ethinyl estradiol) 0.02 mg. daily, or Premarin (conjugated equine estrogens) 0.6 to 1.25 mg. daily. Before gonadectomy, the treatment would be every day for a minimum of four to eight months. Following surgery, treatment should be cyclic, for the first three weeks of each month, missing the fourth week.

An alternative to the foregoing would be a commercial product combining estrogen and progestin, for example: Lo-Ovral 1 mg. (norgestrel 0.3 mg. and ethinyl estradiol 0.03 mg.), or Ovral (norgestrel 0.5 mg. and ethinyl estradiol 0.05 mg.). The dosage of those preparations is one tablet daily for the first three weeks of each month.

If the patient prefers not to accommodate to a daily oral therapy, but to an intramuscular one instead, then the following could be prescribed: Delestrogen (estradiol valerate) 5 mg. plus Delalutin (hydroxy-progesterone caproate) 62.5 mg. every two weeks. Another intramuscular combined treatment could be: Depo-Estradiol cypionate 1 mg. plus Depo-Provera 25 mg. every two weeks.

After four to eight months of biweekly therapy, the same dosages could be given once every three or four weeks.

If in the preoperative state, the above dosages prove insufficiently effective after four to six weeks, then the dosage could be doubled. Otherwise, the rule is to use the dosage that is thought presently to be replacement therapy for normal women.

Hormonal feminization of male-to-female transexuals promotes a female appearance insofar as it brings about a feminine redistribution of subcutaneous fat. It also stimulates breast enlargement (gynecomastia), and may somewhat retard the growth of facial and body hair.

Hormone dosage for female-to-male transexuals which has provided satisfactory results is: Delatestrel (testosterone enanthate) 400 mg. intramuscularly once a month.

Hormonal masculinization of the female-to-male transexual induces suppression of the menses, but breakthrough bleeding may eventually occur. Permanent suppression requires castration (ovariectomy) or hysterectomy, preferably both. Other effects of hormonal masculinization include deepening of the voice and growth of facial and body hair. The shrinking effect on the breasts is minimal. The clitoris enlarges, but not sufficiently to permit masculinizing surgical reconstruction as even a very small micropenis. Its erotic sensitivity increases. The feeling of orgasm is reported as increased with no loss of the female capacity for multiple orgasm.

The above hormonal dosage does not prevent menopause-like symptoms following ovariectomy. Control of such symptoms may require additional estrogenic therapy with gradual withdrawal over a period of three to six months.

During the period of the real-life test, male-to-female transexuals may take voice retraining. They may also begin electrolysis for removal of facial hair and perhaps body hair also. These services are provided by trained and certified experts, usually in private practice, not in a hospital.

In some cases of female-to-male transexualism, mastectomy is necessary during the period of the real-life test, especially if the patient works as a male in a job in which exposure of a female chest contour, however disguised, is incompatible with continued employment.

A few patients need cosmetic and etiquette counseling, but most are masters of these arts without special help.

To a variable extent, local legal advice may be needed during the period of the real-life test, especially if a divorce is necessary, and also with regard to change of name and sex on documents. Complete legal recognition of the change of sexual status, in the form of a reissued birth certificate, varies according to legal jurisdiction. Usually a medical statement is needed for the legal change, after the sex reassignment has been completed.

The amount of counseling needed during the real-life test varies according to individual need and traveling distance. Patients from far away need a local counselor working in collaboration with the main center.

Some transexuals disown their families, and others are disowned by their families. The ideal of rehabilitation is to have the reassigned transexual acceptable to the family, however limited the personal contact. Therefore, family counseling is also a prerequisite. The siblings, especially the young ones, should not be overlooked in the overall plan of counseling. Nonfamily members, including the lover, personal friends, teachers, and employers also may be given information and advice on how to contribute to the transexual's total rehabilitation.

Sex reassignment surgery is too highly technical a procedure to be discussed here in detail. Male-to-female surgery has been reasonably well perfected, though in some cases there are residual problems of contracture and constriction of the vaginal canal requiring an additional operation. The end result can be convincingly feminine in appearance and function. Female-to-male surgery of the external genitalia presents insurmountable problems as great as in the case of congenital aplasia of the penis or accidental amputation of the penis. A plastic surgeon can make a penis of grafted skin, but it requires from five to fifteen surgical admissions, and the end result is a penis that is numb, unable to erect, and subject too easily to urethral constriction and urinary infection. For sexual intercourse, such an organ can penetrate the vagina only if supported, as in a hollow dildo. Thus, there is very good reason for the female-to-male transexual to settle for a strap-on prosthetic penis and to avoid the expense, pain, and poor result of very time-consuming surgery.

Female-to-male transexuals who undergo genital surgery do not lose the clitoris and so retain the capacity for orgasm. In fact, the orgasm is enhanced under the influence of androgen therapy. Male-to-female transexuals lose the kind of ejaculatory orgasm they once knew, but without regret, for it is replaced by a climactic feeling which, even though more diffuse, satisfies them all the more because they are able to satisfy a male partner.

PROGNOSIS

The number of known cases of sex reassignment followed by a second reassignment to the original sex are few (four known and probably no more than ten) and the number of such cases published, fewer still. The transexual with such a history apparently rushes into the initial surgery prematurely, impulsively, and even against psychological advice. In contrast, for those sex-reassignment applicants who pass the two-year real life test, surgery confirms the status they have already achieved, and they continue to do well. They do well according to the criteria of earning a living, not being arrested, settling down with a partner, not needing a psychiatric referral, and saying that they are contented in their new status and do not regret the change.

The surgical prognosis is guarded. Male-to-female transexuals may need follow-up surgery to keep the vaginal canal functional and patent. The end result, however, only rarely is persistently unsatisfactory. Female-to-male transexuals may have problems, eventually correctable, of urethral stricture, and they always have the problem of impotence for which no successful surgical technique has yet been devised.

The hormonal prognosis is satisfactory for both male-to-female and female-to-male transexuals. Some male-to-female transexuals, particularly those few in show business, are unsatisfied with hormonally induced breast growth. They seek and obtain either augmentation mammoplasty or silicone injections. The latter are dangerous to health and are absolutely contraindicated.

TRANSVESTISM

Transvestism means cross-dressing, that is, dressing in the clothes of the other sex. On the stage, it may be done as a dramatic device, as in a play by Shakespeare. For Halloween, it may be done as a gag or joke. A professional impersonator may cross-dress for a living, but such a person is likely to have more than a salaried interest in dressing up. He may be a drag queen, or she may be a butch lesbian, or either may be a would-be transexual. In the case of the male, he may be a clinically diagnosed transvestite; clinical transvestism has not yet been recorded in the female.

DEFINITION AND DESCRIPTION

As clinically defined, tranvestism is a condition in which a male has a sexual obsession for or addiction to women's clothes, such that he episodically experiences intolerable psychic stress if he does not dress up. In addition, he is handicapped in getting erotically aroused and performing sexually, regardless of being either heterosexual or homosexual in partnership, unless he is wearing female garments, as though wearing a fetish, or at least imagining himself as

doing so. Some transvestites discover their proclivity at puberty by discovering that they can masturbate to orgasm only if wearing or handling some article or articles of female apparel. Many eventually try to find or educate a partner with whom to practice their transvestism. A few, especially as they advance in age, are erotically inert, but cross-dress permanently or as often as expediently possible. They do not request transexual surgery, but they may take female hormones. The typical transvestite, however, wants no female hormones and no feminizing surgery. He simply dresses and wears makeup episodically as a female, and then returns to his male garb, until irritability, restlessness, and inner agitation demand relief again by impersonating a female and having an orgasm. Almost all transvestites have a female name to go with the female wardrobe. There is also a female personality. Like the male personality, it is in the literal sense unwholesome. The two personalities, if they can be put together, would make a whole. The female personality by itself is a travesty of a conventionally stereotypic woman and likewise the masculine personality.

INCIDENCE

The incidence of transvestism is unknown. There are no public health statistics, nor are there satisfactory statistics of transvestites arrested by the police, nor of those seen by psychiatrists. There are some transvestite organizations with their own magazines or newsletters. The syndrome is probably more frequent than is generally assumed.

ETIOLOGY

The precise etiology of transvestism cannot be formulated on the basis of today's knowledge. Most evidence points to the early years when gender identity/role is being differentiated as critical to the beginnings of transvestism. A few tranvestites recall being dressed in girls' clothes as a punishment—the so-called petticoat punishment of the older literature.

DIAGNOSIS

The diagnosis is made primarily from the patient's account of his chief complaint and its history. As in the case of transsexualism, it is necessary to get corroborative evidence from family members or others and from available records. The physical examination is a routine necessity, even though it can generally be counted on as being noncontributory.

DIFFERENTIAL DIAGNOSIS

The diagnoses to be ruled out parallel those for transsexualism (see above). There may be some confusion with transsexualism in the case of the patient who wears women's clothes, but with a full unshaven beard, with or without taking estrogen, and with no demand whatsoever for genital surgery. Until the last few years this variant of transvestism was unknown, through lack of public disclosure. A corresponding female condition is that of the woman who wears men's clothes and who requests only a mastectomy, but no other treatment.

A tricky problem of differential diagnosis occurs in those cases of transvestic transsexualism that sit on the fence, so to speak, of both diagnoses. Typically the patient is fortyish, and has been a covert transvestite throughout adulthood. Finally the compulsion for public appearance as a woman and for total sex change demands expression, despite personal commitments to wife and family. Without a real-life test of two years or longer, such a patient cannot get his affairs in order and himself rehabilitated. Some of them, however, are past masters at clinic shopping. They maneuver from one doctor to another, editing the information given to each, until they finally implement their plans, despite contradictory advice. Some of them become adequately rehabilitated. The burden imposed on their dependents may be excessive.

THERAPY

Some transvestites live for years before they seek therapy or before an incident with the law requires them to do so. Others undoubtedly never seek therapy. Some associate with other transvestites, sometimes in bars where they congregate, or by joining a society formed for the purpose of sociability and self-help.

Transvestism is closely related to the hysterical, dissociative phenomenon of dual personality. It is to be expected, therefore, that the symptom of cross-dressing may in some instances undergo spontaneous remission, or that it may go into remission under the influence of some form of psychotherapy, including hypnotherapy, behavioral modification (aversive conditioning), or even religious exorcism. It has been known also to remit, at a time of formidable personal crisis, to a combined therapy of antiandrogen (medroxy-progesterone acetate) plus counseling. However, since transvestism is also a form of addiction—addiction to female clothing—it is not surprising that it has proved singularly resistant to today's known methods of therapy.

For the most part, the treatment of transvestism is ameliorative and supportive. Often it is necessary as well as wise to include the family in the counseling program. In the case of the married transvestite, effective counseling can ameliorate a separation, if separation is inevitable, and equally well ameliorate continuance of the marital relationship.

PROGNOSIS

The prognosis for complete and permanent remission of symptoms is poor, but not totally negative. The possibility of relapse is such that, in any instance of remission, the patient should be kept in followup at least four to six times a year, indefinitely.

Most patients with transvestism will not have a remission of symptoms. They can be helped in rehabilitation, however, to find a modus vivendi as transvestites.

HOMOSEXUALISM

Homosexualism is the same as homosexuality. Professional opinion is currently divided as to whether homosexuality should be considered a syndrome or simply a socially sanctioned erotic alternative analogous to left-handedness. In the American Psychiatric Association the majority opinion, as expressed in the referendum of early 1974 (see p. 273), supported a change in official nomenclature, so that homosexuality per se is no longer classified as a mental disease or illness. In the religious law of former times, homosexuality was a crime synonymous with treason and heresy. In the civil law today, in many states, homosexuality is classified as a crime against nature, with penalties that are brutally severe. In other states, homosexuality is considered a matter of private morality, provided it takes place between consenting adults.

Definition and Description

In current usage, there are those who define homosexuality mentalistically as a trait, state, or disposition emanating from the personality, and those who define it behaviorally as something that happens between two people with similar sex organs. The mentalist says that a person can be homosexual, even though his or her only sexual practices have been heterosexual, provided the erotic imagery is consistently homosexual. To the mentalist, a single homosexual act by itself does not make the person homosexual, because homosexuality is defined as a continuing state of mind or personality. The behaviorist says that a single homosexual act makes a person homosexual for the duration of that act, but from that one act alone it will not be possible to predict more of the same in the future, nor what the person will say or do to indicate a trait, status, or disposition toward homosexuality.

The only evidence that both a behaviorist and a mentalist have about homosexuality is behavioral, that is, what the ostensible homosexual says or does. Thus, it makes sense to define homosexuality in terms of two people each with a penis, or two each with a vagina in an erotic partnership. Anything further about the fortuitousness of the event versus its replication, and anything about the imagery and thoughts of the partners, will need extra in-

formation. Only then can an inference be made about whether either partner is an obligative versus a facultative (situational) homosexual, the latter being in fact a bisexual. Homosexuality is extensively, though quite wrongly, used as a synonym for bisexuality in today's literature.

Extra information, over and beyond that of erotic performance, also is needed before an inference can be made regarding the extent or pervasiveness of the gender transposition in homosexuality. There are some male homosexuals who manifest negligible femininity vocationally and recreationally. Even in erotic performance, they may be more masculine than feminine in what they do, except that it is usually considered a feminine trait to have a male copulatory partner. The same applies, vice versa, in the case of the female homosexual.

A male homosexual who manifests little gender transposition, except for entering into an erotic activity or partnership with a male, is often said to have a male gender identity, but to prefer a male partner. For the sake of precision, one should say more restrictively that his gender identity/role is predominantly male, though not completely so. Sexual practice and partnership are components of gender identity/role and must be included in its definition as masculine or feminine in any given case.

Incidence

There are no public health statistics on the incidence of either male or female homosexuality or bisexuality. The figures most commonly quoted are those of Kinsey, since subsequent smaller-scale studies confirm them. Kinsey rated homosexuality on a seven-point scale (0—6). A rating of six signifies exclusive or obligative homosexuality of long duration, most likely a lifetime. A man with a rating of three will have had more than incidental homosexual participation off and on for several years during adolescence or later, not necessarily for a lifetime, and not to the exclusion of heterosexual participation. Kinsey estimated a rating of from three to six for 10% of the adult male population, and of five or six for 3%. The figures for the female population are less definite but are estimated at one-half to one-third those for males. On the basis of these estimates, the predominantly homosexual male population in the United States today is approximately three million plus, and the female, one million or more.

ETIOLOGY

There is disagreement, sometimes acrimonious, among experts as to the etiology of homosexuality, as there is also of heterosexuality and bisexuality. Theories range from loose assumptions of voluntary choice, through psychodynamic determinants in the personal biography, to hereditary predestinarianism. There is a good possibility based on experimental animal studies, that an anomaly in prenatal hormonal function may influence sexual pathways in the central nervous system to remain sexually undifferentiated or potentially bisexual. In human beings, an individual so affected would be vulnerable, or easily responsive to additional postnatal influences, primarily social influences that enter the brain through the eyes, ears, and skin senses, that might favor perpetuation of bipotentiality or its resolution in a homosexual differentiation of gender identity/role. Once differentiated, a strongly homosexual gender identity/role tends to persist without changing.

There is not enough knowledge yet to formulate a rational program of prevention. Nonetheless, there is strong presumptive evidence that lifting the taboo on infantile and childhood sexuality, and responding positively to normal heterosexual rehearsal play in the early years, strongly favors heterosexuality at puberty and in adulthood. This evidence comes from anthropological studies and from experimental studies of psychosexual development in nonhuman primates.

DIAGNOSIS

To apply the term diagnosis to homosexuality raises the same problem as applying it to red hair, left-handedness, or limb amputation, all of which are conditions not usually considered syndromes. All are conditions that are self-declared and do not need a diagnostic workup. In consensual homosexuality the evidence may be observed or the person may report it verbally. Without such direct evidence, there may be no way of inferring it from other aspects of behavior.

When homosexuality is not expressed in action, the only evidence may be the person's report of homosexual imagery in dreams, daydreams, and fantasy, or of responding erotically to homosexual images and percepts. In some instances, the only evidence, initially, may be symbolic and disguised; overt homosexual imagery, under the inhibiting pressure of guilt, embarrassment, or shame, may be unable to manifest itself directly. Its place is taken by erotic apathy, inertia, or depression, or by some symbolic sexual substitution.

There are no known or measurable somatic correlates of homosexuality which are important diagnostically. In particular, measures of circulating hormonal levels are noncontributory. However, homosexuality may occur in the presence of other syndromes such as hypogonadism, Klinefelter's (47,XXY) syndrome, and others.

DIFFERENTIAL DIAGNOSIS

Extreme cases of effeminate male homosexuality or virilistic lesbianism need to be differentiated from:

transexualism
transvestism

The most common error in differential diagnosis is to confuse homosexuality with:

bisexualism

The next most common error is to confuse homosexuality with accompanying or derivative symptoms or syndromes of behavioral disability such as:

psychosomatic stress reaction
anxiety neurosis

paranoid schizophrenic reaction

body-image neurosis or psychosis

delinquent or criminal character or conduct disorder

masochism, sadism, pedophilia, or other paraphilia

THERAPY

The incidence of homosexuality is sufficiently high that, on the basis of the simple logistics of health-care delivery, it is economically nonsensical to declare all homosexuals in need of therapy. It would be impossible to supply enough therapists or to meet the staggeringly high cost. Moreover, there is no known form of therapy that can guarantee to change or regulate homosexuality, or bisexuality or heterosexuality, for that matter.

Pragmatically, it makes good sense to conserve society's therapeutic resources for those homosexuals who lack a sense of well-being in the practice of consensual homosexuality. These are the people who seek and who are able to respond to services offered. The only known effective form of therapy is some form of counseling or psychotherapy. If behavior modification therapy is used, it is preferable to use not punishment for homosexual response, but reward for heterosexual response. The reward may be a permitted homosexual encounter, but rewards are so programmed in this form of therapy as to be earned only by an ever-expanding amount of heterosexual involvement.

The goal of therapy should be defined pragmatically, not ideologically. For those homosexuals who are actually bisexual, it may be pragmatic to aim for predominant or exclusive heterosexuality. For others, the goal preferably might be to gain a sense of well-being as bisexual and for still others, a sense of well-being as homosexual.

PROGNOSIS

Provided the goal of treatment is pragmatically set, the prognosis is good, as it is also for those individuals who do not require treatment.

Homosexuality is not a debilitating or life-threatening condition, except for secondary symptoms and reactions which may include even suicide and homicide. The severity of secondary symptoms decreases proportionately as family, friends, and society at large decrease their stigmatization and alienation of the homosexual.

In the course of history, homosexuality has been consistent with the highest levels of achievement and creative originality in the professions of science, art, religion, government, law, and business.

BISEXUALISM

Bisexualism and bisexuality are synonyms. In established usage, one may speak of the morphologic bisexuality of the embryo or of psychosexual bisexuality of the child or adult. In the Freudian and psychoanalytically derived theory of bisexualism, it is implied that a bisexual tendency lurks covertly, if not overtly, in all people. However, by analogy with embryonic development, it is more accurate to conceptualize an undifferentiated stage of gender identity/role which, in the course of a critical developmental period, becomes permanently differentiated as either masculine or feminine, or as a combination of both.

DEFINITION AND DESCRIPTION

The bisexual person has traditionally been stigmatized as homosexual, since specialists as well as society at large overlook the heterosexual component in favor penalizing the homosexual component.

As in the case of homosexuality, bisexuality can be defined either mentalistically or behaviorally. The most workable definition is that a bisexual person is one with a history of performing sexually with a person of either genital sex, separately or in a threesome or group. More broadly, the definition may also include those who have not actually performed but have experienced overt imagery of doing so.

The transitoriness or regularity of either the practice or the imagery needs to be ascertained separately. The definition can then be appropriately augmented or qualified. The qualification may include an estimate of whether the degree and frequency of involvement with each sex is approximately the same (50:50) or disproportionate. Usually it is disproportionate. Falling in love, for example, is usually more intense and less perfunctory with one sex than the other.

Ambisexual, a term not widely used, refers to characteristics shared by both sexes—kissing, for example, as a form of erotic expression.

INCIDENCE

The incidence of bisexuality in American men and women is currently unknown. Except among those who constitute a community of bisexual interest, bisexuality is stigmatized by society and the law. Many people cannot, therefore, overtly admit their bisexuality, even if it occurs only in imagination. Others are not so inhibited, but are among those who can actually practice bisexuality, though only when the homosexual component of their bisexuality is situationally evoked—as among teenaged boys reared in a neighborhood in which hustling with older homosexual teenagers or young men is an acknowledged source of spending money, quite independently of affairs with girlfriends— or among men and women who are able to be homosexual while in sex-segregated jails, camps, or schools, but are heterosexual once released.

In some ethnographically reported societies, sequential bisexuality is a universally prescribed way of life. That is to say, young people at puberty and adolescence are sex-segregated and expected to interact homosexually together until, in young adulthood, their families can negotiate a bride price. After the marriage, the predominant, and usually exclusive form of sexual expression is heterosexual.

In America today, optional bisexuality among consenting adults is openly discussed as a viable and legal life style. In consequence, an increasing number of people admit their bi-sexuality. Some may also dare to express it for the first time. There is no evidence, however, that social permissiveness regarding erotic expression actually increases bisexuality. If such were the case, permissiveness would have to encourage a bisexual differentiation of gender identity/role from infancy onward. In actual fact, permissiveness in the spontaneous sexual rehearsal play of infancy and childhood, and permissiveness in sex education, appear to encourage the differentiation of a heterosexual gender identity.

ETIOLOGY

The etiology or developmental differentiation of bisexuality follows the same general principles as apply to homosexuality. The evidence from embryonic anatomy and neuroanatomy is that nature's primary plan is to differentiate a female. Whereas the female pattern differentiates because the male pattern is not activated by something added (the Adam principle), the male pattern is differentiated by the active suppression of the female pattern. For bisexual behavior, one may speculate on the basis of animal experiments, that the female more than the male retains some of the original bisexual potential. The male, by contrast, may become either totally masculinized or only partially so. If this speculation is correct, then it is easier for women than men selected at random to enter into a casual bisexual encounter—for example at a swinging, group-sex party. Some men will be impotent and erotically unable to respond to any stimulus from a person of the same sex. Others will be erotically versatile with both sexes.

There is no known single determining factor, prenatal or postnatal, that leads to the differentiation of a potentially bisexual erotic component in the gender identity/role. The first bisexual experience may be preceded by bi-erotic fantasy and desire, a decision for sexual experiments, a change of sexual politics as in the women's movement, an awareness and admittance of previously covert bisexual orientation, or an alleviation of some traditional taboos among members of the "swinging" and "group sex" subculture.

DIAGNOSIS

As in the case of homosexuality, bisexuality per se is a condition or way of behaving erotically, not a syndrome. Therefore, in the strict sense, there is no diagnosis. The condition is identified by the history either of sexual practice or imagery, or both. In its most covert form, bisexuality may not be identifiable as such, being manifest only as a failure of complete heterosexual abandon. Physical signs are noncontributory.

DIFFERENTIAL DIAGNOSIS

The issues are the same as in the differential diagnosis of homosexuality (see above).

THERAPY

Of and by itself alone, bisexualism is not a disease and does not require therapy. The vast majority of individuals with a bisexual history never see a therapist. If bisexualism is associated with a lack of well-being, however, or if it is experienced as a source of distress to the person or partner, then either or both will benefit from some form of psychologic counseling or therapy. The goal of treatment most often is to restore a sense of bisexual well-being. Less often and in selected instances, the goal may be one of predominant heterosexual eroticism.

PROGNOSIS

Bisexuality as an optional life style, equally acceptable to consenting partners, is like a vocational life style in not requiring a diagnosis. If a prognosis is required, it is for the sequelae of the life style. For some, overt bisexuality represents a solution to problems of erotic relationships. Then the prognosis is positive. For others, it represents a compounding of problems, with a prognosis that is guarded, but not necessarily negative.

With less social stigmatization, bisexualism could become therapeutically accepted as a variant of human sexuality. For some individuals who otherwise might be victimized by social pressures into becoming patients, bisexuality enlarges the range of their behavioral options in eroticism and love so that they need not become patients.

REFERENCES

GREEN, R., and MONEY, J., eds. 1969. *Transexualism and sex reassignment.* Baltimore: Johns Hopkins Press.

LAUB, D. R., and GREEN, R., eds. 1978. *The fourth international conference on gender identity dedicated to Harry Benjamin, M.D.: selected proceedings. Volume 7, Number 4, Archives of Sexual Behavior.* New York, Plenum Press.

MONEY, J., 1970. Use of an androgen-depleting hormone in the treatment of male sex offenders. *Journal of Sex Research* 6: 165–72.

———, 1971. Prefatory remarks on outcome of sex reassignment in 24 cases of transexualism. *Archives of Sexual Behavior* 1: 163–65.

———, and AMBINDER, R., 1978. Two-year, real-life diagnostic test: rehabilitation versus cure. In *Controversy in Psychiatry,* ed. J. P. Brady and H. K. H. Brodie. Philadelphia: W. B. Saunders.

———, and EHRHARDT, A. A., 1972. *Man and woman, boy and girl: the differentiation and dimorphism of gender identity from conception to maturity.* Baltimore: Johns Hopkins University Press.

———, and MUSAPH, H., eds. 1977. *Handbook of Sexology.* Amsterdam/New York: Excerpta Medica.

———, WIEDEKING, C., WALKER, P., MIGEON, C., MEYER, W., and BORGAONKAR, D. 1975. 47,XXY and 46,XY males with antisocial and/or sex-offending behavior: antiandrogen therapy plus counseling. *Psychoneuroendocrinology* 1: 165–78.

FIFTEEN

Psychoanalysis
and
Sexual Disorders

WILLIAM W. MEISSNER

Psychoanalysis has, from its inception, been inexorably linked with problems of and ideas about human sexuality. From the very beginning of Freud's thinking about the neuroses, particularly at first the hysterias, the problem of sexuality assumed a significant and central role. It was Charcot, with whom Freud had studied in Paris, after all, who had said that hysteria was *une chose genitale*. When Freud returned to Vienna after his Parisian experience, his collaboration with Joseph Breuer deepened his knowledge of hysteria and led him, with Breuer, in the direction of fashioning an effective means of treating hysterical symptoms.

The collaboration with Breuer is interesting, insofar as Breuer himself seemed anxious to avoid, minimize, and even deny the role of sexuality in the causation of hysteria. Breuer, following the lead of certain French thinkers including Janet, preferred to explain hysterical expressions on the basis of hypnoid states, in which the patients were thought to be particularly vulnerable to traumatic experiences that resulted in the characteristic hysterical dissociation within the mind. Breuer's attitude toward sexuality was well displayed in his account of the famous case of Anna O in which his capacity to ignore and deny obvious sexual elements in the patient's history was strained to the utmost. As the patient's intensely erotic transference intensified, Breuer found increasing difficulty in maintaining his treatment of her and finally was forced by his wife's increasing jealousy to break it off. The result was a precipitation of a hysterical pseudocyesis, which Jones (1953) notes was the logical outcome of Anna's highly erotic involvement with Breuer.

If Breuer could shut his eyes to the evidence of sexuality, for interesting transference reasons of his own (Pollock, 1968), fortunately for the development of psychoanalysis Freud did not. In the cases he presented in the *Studies on Hysteria* (1893–1895), Freud was explicit in relating issues of sexuality and sexual conflict to the etiology of hysteria. Freud's thinking led him in the direction of a reactive or defensive theory of neurosis which had at its basis sexual conflicts. More specifically, his clinical experience led him to hypothesize that the roots of hysteria, and presumably other neuroses, lay in an infantile sexual trauma which had been defensively repressed and which was re-expressed in the neurotic symptomatology. As Freud explored the reminiscences of his patients, following Breuer's cathartic principle, he discovered more apparent evidence of such infantile sexual trauma in the recollections of his patients.

The basic hypothesis that Breuer and Freud had advanced in the famous *Studies* (1893–1895) was that "hysterics suffer from reminiscences," and that the cure of the hysterical symptoms lies in the gradual uncovering of those traumatic memories and their re-enactment and reactivation in the present together with the intense charge of emotion connected with those infantile traumatic experiences. It was the cathartic release or abreaction of this emotional charge which allowed the symptom to be relieved and dispelled. Freud and Breuer found in a number of instances that the exact recollection of such early traumatic memories did, in fact, lead to the relief of hysterical symptoms. This allowed them to think of a discharge theory of emotion and to conceptualize their findings in terms of a theory of cathexis and discharge which was based upon economic principles, derived from the scientific culture in which they were thinking and working. Thus, psychoanalysis found its origin in the early dealing with matters of sexual conflict and trauma and the corresponding repression, which led to a dissociation in the mind of the hysteric and a re-expression of traumatic conflicts in neurotic symptomatology.

286

There was, however, a fly in the ointment. Only after several years of convinced application of this traumatic theory of neurosis did Freud begin to question his findings. Not only was he not always able to find the traumatic reminiscence, but the hypothesis that sexual infantile trauma were so frequent such that every neurotic patient would be suffering from such an infantile seduction was a bit hard to swallow—even in turn-of-the-century Vienna. Moreover, Freud had embarked on an interesting exercise that was to change the course of psychoanalytic history. He had begun his own self-analysis, working on his own dreams and discovering in himself the roots of repressed and conflicted aspects in his own psychic development.

The outcome was dramatic. In September 1897, his doubts and uncertainties reached a crisis, and he wrote to his good friend Wilhelm Fliess in the following terms:

> Let me tell you straight away the great secret that has been slowly dawning on me in recent months. I no longer believe in my *neurotica*. This is hardly intelligible without an explanation; you yourself found what I told you credible. So I shall start at the beginning and tell you the whole story of how the reasons for rejecting it arose. The first group of factors were the continual disappointment of my attempts to bring my analysis to a real conclusion, the running away of people who for a time had seemed my most favorably inclined patients, the lack of the complete success on which I had counted, and the possibility of explaining my partial successes in other, familiar ways. Then there was the astonishing thing that in every case . . . blame was laid on perverse acts by the father, and realization of the unexpected frequency of hysteria, in every case of which the same thing applied, though it was hardly credible that perverted acts against children were so general . . . Thirdly, there was the definite realization that there is no "indication of reality" in the unconscious, so that it is impossible to distinguish between truth and emotionally charged fiction. (This leaves open the possible explanation that sexual fantasy regularly makes use of the theme of the parents.) Fourthly, there was the considera-

tion that even in the most deep-reaching psychosis the unconscious memory does not break through, so that the secret of infantile experience is not revealed even in the most confused states of delirium. When one thus sees that the unconscious never overcomes the resistance of the conscious, one must abandon the expectation that in treatment the reverse process will take place to the extent that the conscious will fully dominate the unconscious (Freud, 1887–1902, letter 69).

One can understand Freud's reluctance to abandon the seduction hypothesis, since he had put years of effort into developing it and had accumulated a considerable amount of evidence that seemed to support it, but he could not reconcile the aspects of the hypothesis that did not seem consistent with other undeniable data. The shift in perspective was perhaps the most significant that has ever taken place in psychoanalytic thinking. Freud realized that rather than real parental seductions traumatizing the infant sexually, the possibility now arose that the inherent sexuality of the infant was beginning to express itself in sexual fantasies about the parents. The emphasis shifted in Freud's thinking and in the direction of his investigation of the neuroses from reality factors to sexual fantasies. Freud's abandonment of the seduction hypothesis was also reinforced by the results of his own self-analysis. In analyzing his own dreams and in recovering early infantile memories, he began to discover the elements of infantile sexual wishes and desires in himself. He then realized that what he was dealing with was in some fundamental sense a basic characteristic of infantile experience. The role of infantile sexuality in psychoanalytic thinking had been established.

To explain the phenomenon of sexual wishes in conflict with repressing forces within the mind, Freud postulated a form of sexual energy which was derived from biologically given and biologically elaborated instinctual drives. This sexual mental energy he called "libido." At the beginning of his theoretical enterprise and indeed well on into the later stages of his career, Freud considered the sexual instinct as a basically psychophysiological process, having both mental and physiological or bodily manifestations. Libido came to refer to the force by which this sexual instinct came to be represented in the mind.

In his early thinking about it, Freud regarded the libido as equivalently physiological, even describing it in biochemical terms. The libido which expressed itself in hysterical symptoms, for example, was equivalently a form of transformed sexual substance which because of the damming up of sexual energy due to repressive mechanisms became transformed into a toxic substance. Release of this transformed libido as a toxic substance within the nervous system gave rise to the experience of anxiety. Freud's treatment of anxiety in these quite physical and biochemical terms cast a long shadow over the rest of his thinking. It was really not until the later stages of his career, even as late as the *New Introductory Lectures* (1933) that the hypothesis of anxiety as transformed libido was finally rejected once and for all. Certainly within Freud's thinking the shift in the conceptualization of libido from basically physicalistic parameters to regard it in more strictly psychological terms was long in coming and then only as the result of a slow and progressive evolution in Freud's thinking (Zetzel and Meissner, 1973).

Nonetheless, Freud recognized quite early in his career that the sexual instinct did not spring from the head of Jove, as it were, in some finished or final form, but that it instead arose in a gradual process of evolution and development through the course of infantile experience. While his clinical material drew him inexorably to hypotheses about infantile sexuality, he began to shape a theory of libidinal development, in which at each of the progressive phases the libido could be characterized by specific aims and by relationship to specific kinds of objects. It was only later in this progression that the libido evolved to a point at which these various components of sexual development were integrated into a form of genital primacy.

PSYCHOSEXUAL DEVELOPMENT

Freud's theory of psychosexual development finally came to fruition in 1905 with the publication of the *Three Essays on the Theory of Sexuality*. This was fully a decade after the earlier publication of the *Studies* with Breuer. Even so, the theory of psychosexual development, including the notions of pregenital organization of libido and the libido theory itself, was delayed for another decade until the third edition of the *Essays* in 1915. Thus, the evolution of Freud's basic ideas about psychosexual development had to wait a full score of years after the publication of the *Studies* for their public appearance.

The notion of sexuality which Freud developed in the *Three Essays* was more or less familiar in that it referred in the first instance to the erotic life of the individual. He also used the concept in a more general sense to include sensations and activities that might be described as sensual since they are sources of pleasure and gratification but might not otherwise be regarded as specifically sexual. In his analysis, Freud demonstrated the connection between such sensual behaviors and activities and levels of libidinal gratification connected with the phases of psychosexual development.

The earliest forms of sensual expression arise specifically in relation to bodily functions that are basically nonsexual, such as feeding and the control of bowel and bladder. Freud arranged these stages of psychosexual development into a succession of developmental phases, each building on and successively subsuming the attainments of the preceding phases. The phases he described were the oral phase, the anal phase, and the phallic phase. During these infantile and early childhood stages, erotic sensations arise from stimulation of the mucosal surfaces of particular body parts or body organs. In the oral phase, it is particularly the mucous membranes of the mouth, in the anal phase the mucous membranes of the anus, and finally in the phallic phase the mucosal surfaces of the external genitalia that provide the primary focus of erotic stimulation.

When the adult form of genital sexual integration is achieved, sexual activity is then dominated by the genital zone. Nonetheless, the capacity for sensual arousal and stimulation deriving from pregenital or prephallic erotogenic zones retains a functional place in adult sexual activity, specifically expressing itself in preliminary mating activity or foreplay. When such zones are appropriately stimulated, preliminary gratification or forepleasure can be elicited which usually provides a form of preliminary excitation which leads to coitus. In normal sexual development when mature genital potency has been achieved, the sexual act achieves the full end-pleasure of orgasm.

In Freud's analysis the erotic impulses coming from the pregenital zones were described as component or part instincts. These part instincts can find their expression in love-making activities, in behaviors of kissing, anal stimulation, biting the love object, and the like. The activities of these component instincts may undergo displacement of various kinds so that different kinds of otherwise nonsexual activities become erotized—for example, the derivation of pleasure from looking at or being looked at by a love object. Ordinarily such component instincts are repressed or are expressed in some restrictive fashion in sexual activity such as varieties of foreplay. Such component instincts, however, may come to dominate the libidinal organization and result in various forms of perversion.

At the beginning of his psychosexual development, the young child is regarded as polymorphous-perverse in his sexual disposition. Sexuality and the forms of sexual gratification at this level are relatively undifferentiated and include all of the part instincts. As development progresses toward adult genital maturity, however, the part instincts become subordinated to the primacy of the genital region. In this context the part instincts normally serve as sources of preliminary excitation which lead toward full genital expression. According to this early theory, then, the failure to achieve genital primacy would result in various forms of psychopathology. If the libido became too firmly attached to one of the pregenital erotogenic zones or if a particular part instinct came to predominate in the libidinal organization, forms of perversion such as exhibitionism or voyeurism would come to replace the normal act of sexual intercourse in the libidinal economy, such that orgastic satisfaction and end-pleasure would be derived from that activity rather than from the normal genital expression.

The stages of psychosexual development constituted the basic theory of psychoanalysis, particularly the primary theory of development within psychoanalysis, for most of the early period of Freud's thinking. It was not until the emergence of a structural theory in *The Ego and the Id* (1923) and the subsequent emergence of a more developed ego psychology at the hands of Anna Freud, Heinz Hartmann, David Rapaport, Erik Erikson, and others, that the basic developmental schema provided by the stages of psychosexual development came to be modified to any great extent. The stages of psychosexual development even today remain one of the best understood and most firmly established dimensions of psychoanalytic theory. Although the schema has been considerably modified since Freud's early thinking about it, it nonetheless has remained a fundamental dimension in the psychoanalytic assessment of personality and the pathology of disturbed states of functioning.

In discussing the role of psychosexual development in disorders of sexuality, it is of particular importance to keep clearly in mind the distinction between developmental characteristics derived from the respective psychosexual stages, and the levels of regressive fixation that may characterize one or other form of psychopathological expression. Thus, many aspects of reasonably well-integrated and well-functioning individuals may originate in the respective psychosexual stages, but this does not mean nor can it be used to infer that the behavior in question is an expression of that level of psychological functioning and psychosexual integration, nor that it necessarily reflects a fixation at that particular developmental stage. It is quite a different matter to say that a given individual manifests oral characteristics in his behavior and to say that the organization of his personality reflects fixation at the oral stage of psychosexual development. There has often been a basic confusion in the use of such terms and a failure to distinguish between regressive fixations and developmental attainments.

With these cautions in mind we can turn at this point to a brief description of the psychosexual stages and to a brief specification of some aspects of their implications, both for pathological functioning and for personality development. The following description of the psychosexual stages is based on Freud's early formulations but reflects the contributions of later psychoanalytic thought to the understanding of psychosexual development. Of particular importance in these later contributions are the deepening of the developmental implications of the pregenital stages, the mutual interaction of psychosexual dynamics with object relations, and finally the interplay of psychosexual and psychosocial developmental processes.

THE ORAL STAGE

The earliest of the psychosexual stages Freud described was the oral stage. At this earliest phase of infantile development, the infant's needs, perceptions and behaviors are centered primarily on the mouth, lips, tongue, and other organs related to the oral zone. Pleasurable excitations and affects arise from stimulation of the mucosal surface of these organs. The primary model of oral stimulation and satisfaction is breast feeding, in which hunger pangs give rise to oral sucking movements which are then satisfied by active sucking on the mother's nipple and the consequent feeding.

The oral zone maintains its dominance in the libidinal organization for approximately the first eighteen months of life. Oral sensations would include thirst, hunger, sensations related to swallowing, satiation of hunger, and the pleasurable tactile stimulation evoked by sucking on the nipple or nipple substitute. Libidinal satisfaction at this stage of development, how-

ever, may not be restricted solely to the oral zone but may also arise in connection with the multiple forms of tactile stimulation that are connected with mother-child contact, not only in the feeding situation but in the multiple contexts of infant mothering. There is some evidence, particularly from animal studies, that such maternal contact and tactile stimulation has an important influence on the infant's affective development.

The oral drives are generally regarded as consisting of separate components, the libidinal oral drives and the aggressive oral drives. States of oral deprivation or tension tend to stimulate a seeking for oral gratification which is typified by the state of satiation the infant reaches at the end of a nursing period. Lewin (1950) has suggested that there is an oral triad which consists of the wish to eat, the wish to sleep, and the wish to attain that quiescence and relaxation which occurs at the end of sucking just before the onset of sleep. It is generally thought that the libidinal needs of oral erotism predominate in the early phases of the oral stage, but that they become compounded with more aggressive components later on in the stage of oral sadism. The development of oral sadism can express itself in biting, chewing, spitting, or crying. For many analysts, particularly those of the Kleinian persuasion, such oral aggression is associated with primitive wishes and fantasies of biting, devouring, and destroying. Such fantasies, for example, may be directed against the mother's breast as an expression of primitive incorporative wishes. Although such fantasies can often be recovered in primitive regressive states (in psychotic or border line patients) and may even be elicited in the more regressive associations of even healthier patients, there is no good evidence to substantiate the operation of such fantasies at early infantile stages of development.

In developmental terms, the objectives to be attained in the oral period are among the most important for establishing a well functioning personality and for establishing the rudiments of a significant capacity for an accepted relationship with objects. If the oral period can be carried through successfully, the child should be able to establish a trusting dependence on the nursing and sustaining object and to establish a comfortable expression of oral libidinal needs and to find their gratification without significant conflict or ambivalence from the oral-sadistic wishes to attack, devour, or destroy the object.

The failure to achieve these objectives in one degree or another can lay the foundation for the development of pathological traits. Excessive oral gratification or deprivation can result in significant libidinal fixations. The traits deriving from such infantile fixations can include excessive optimism, narcissism, pessimism, and demandingness. Oral characters are often excessively dependent and require others to give to them and to look after them. Such persons want to be fed and supported and nurtured, and may be selfishly demanding in their attempts to have these wishes gratified; but they may be also exceptionally giving to others as a way of eliciting a return of being given to in kind. Oral characters are thus often extremely dependent on their objects and on a return of support and narcissistic supplies in order to maintain a fragile and often faltering self-esteem. Characteristics of envy and jealousy may often be associated as pathological manifestations of such basically oral traits. Such oral traits are often associated with fairly primitive degrees of narcissism, but these dimensions should be considered separately.

Nonetheless, the oral phase may find a successful resolution and thus provide the basis for character traits positively contributing to personality functioning. Such individuals may develop capacities for giving, for giving to and supporting others, and for receiving from others without a sense of excessive dependence or envy. They may develop a capacity to rely on and trust others and to be capable of relying on themselves and of trusting themselves in their complex dealings with others and in facing the difficulties and challenges of life. The continuing capacity for trust and reliance, either

as an enduring possession of one's own inner life or in one's relationship with the significant others in his environment, rests ultimately on the development of the basic sense of trust during this earliest oral phase of psychosexual development.

Erikson (1963) has characterized these complex aspects of character development deriving from pregenital phases of psychosexual development as phases of psychosocial development. He envisions the phases of psychosocial development arising out of the psychosexual phases as being characterized by certain definitive crises in the development of the individual personality, leading finally to a phase of identity formation. The specific psychosocial crisis associated with the oral phase is the resolution of basic trust versus basic mistrust. The capacity for enduring trust in oneself or in others represents a successful resolution of the early object related crisis in the oral phase, while the failure to resolve that crisis results in a basic and perduring mistrust which provides the basis for a lasting impairment in the capacity to relate to others and to rely on one's own inner resources.

THE ANAL STAGE

The transition to the anal stage is marked by the maturation of neuromuscular control over the functioning of sphincters, particularly the anal sphincters, which thus permits a higher degree of voluntary control over the retention or expulsion of feces. This period extends roughly from about the first to the third year of life and is characterized by a recognizable intensification of aggressive drives mixed with the libidinal compounds in anal-sadistic impulses. The acquisition of sphincter control is also connected with an increased shift from a posture of passivity to one of increasing activity and assertiveness. The classical contexts in which these issues are joined is the struggle with the parent over the retaining or expelling of feces in toilet training. The ultimate issue is one of control: who has the final say as to when and how things will be done. These conflicts over anal control and the struggles with the parent over the retaining or expelling of feces increases the degree of ambivalence. The parent in this period becomes the object of both intensely loving and hating impulses, since the child wishes both to comply with the parent's wishes and thus continue to receive love and affection from the parent as well as to rebel against the parent and withhold the precious fecal gift.

This is also the period of separation and individuation, in which the questions of the extent to which the child can function on his own without continual reliance and support from the nurturing parent are joined. Here again the anal drives are characterized as erotic, referring to the sexual pleasure in anal functioning, both in retaining the precious feces and in presenting them as a precious gift to the parent, and as sadistic, referring to the increased expression of aggressive impulses connected with the discharging of feces as though these were powerful and destructive weapons. These wishes may often be displayed in children's drawings or in play activity in the form of fantasies of bombing and explosion.

The major issue in the anal period is that it is essentially a period of striving for independence and for the child's separation from the continuing support of the parents and from his dependence on them. The issue of control is particularly important here, since in one direction the excess of parental control deprives the child of the opportunity to separate adequately and to gain some foothold for his own stirring autonomy, while the opposite extreme, a failure of parental control, would leave the infant too much at risk of failure and too threatened by the anxieties of separation and the intensification of his still powerful dependency wishes. In this arena, then, the objectives of sphincter control without an excessive degree of overcontrol (fecal retention) or the loss of control (messing) can be matched with the child's attempts to establish and achieve autonomy and independence without an excessive

degree of shame or self-doubt arising from the loss of control. Erikson has characterized this developmental crisis as the tension of autonomy versus shame and doubt.

Certain maladaptive character traits, which often seem inconsistent, arise from the failure to resolve these basic developmental issues and reflect the tensions over anal erotism and sadism and the defenses against it. Thus, one often sees such characteristics as orderliness, obstinacy, stubbornness, willfulness, frugality, and parsimony as characteristics of anal personalities. These characteristics derive from the fixation on anal functions and often assume a highly rigid and controlling quality. When the defenses against anal traits are less effective, either because they have been weakened or have undergone some degree of regression, the anal character then often reveals traits of heightened ambivalence, messiness, defiance, rage, and severe degrees of sadomasochistic behavior. Such anal characteristics and their correlative defenses may often be seen most typically in the obsessive compulsive neuroses and obsessive compulsive character structures.

But the conflict and struggle over anal issues and the difficulties of separation and individuation may also have their successful outcome. The successful resolution of the anal phase and its difficulties is a basis for the development of an increasing sense of personal autonomy, the capacity for independence, and for the exercise of personal initiatives without an abiding sense of guilt. There can result a capacity for self-determination without a sense of shame or self-doubt. In such personalities a healthy degree of independence and the exercise of personal initiative and self-determination can be accomplished without any significant degree of ambivalence. Such individuals, having a firmly established and reasonable degree of personal autonomy, can engage in various levels of willing cooperation with others and even submission of themselves in willing ways to the objectives and purposes of others without a sense of excessive willfulness or rebelliousness on the one hand, and without a sense of self-diminution, defeat, or humiliation on the other.

THE URETHRAL STAGE

A third stage which was not discussed by Freud but has been suggested as part of the psychosexual progression is that of the urethral stage. Some analysts have envisioned this phase of psychosexual development as a transitional stage between the anal and phallic stages. As such, it shares some of the characteristics of the earlier anal phase and by way of anticipation some from the subsequent phallic phase. More often than not, the characteristics of this urethral phase tend to be subsumed under the phallic phase. Urethral erotism can be taken to refer to pleasure in urination and the pleasure in urethral retention similar to the anal erotic pleasure of retention or expulsion of feces. The issues here are issues of performance and control. The classic image of urethral expression is the pride of the little boy in seeing how far he can project his urinary stream. Such urethral functioning can also be contaminated with sadistic impulses, often reflecting the persistance of residual anal-sadistic urges. Similar to the loss of bowel control, loss of urethral control (enuresis) can often have a regressive significance that reactivates and assimilates itself into underlying anal conflicts.

The pathological traits deriving from this period are those of competitiveness on the one hand and ambition on the other, probably connected with the need for compensating an underlying sense of shame due to the loss of urethral control. The conflicts over this issue may be the beginnings of the development of penis envy in connection with a feminine sense of shame and inadequacy in being unable to match the male urethral performance. Successful resolution of the urethral phase builds healthy personality traits, which are somewhat analogous to those derived from the anal period. Urethral competence offers a sense of pride and a feeling of self-competence derived from successful urethral functioning. The area of urethral functioning is one in which the small boy can begin to imitate his father's more adult performance. In this sense then the resolution of urethral conflicts begins to set the stage for and make significant contributions to the shaping of gender identity and the subsequent gender-related identifications.

THE PHALLIC STAGE

The next stage in the progression of psychosexual development is the *phallic stage* beginning some time during the third year of life and extending until approximately the end of the fifth year. The phallic phase is characterized by the focusing of sexual interest, sexual stimulation, and sexual arousal on the genital area. The penis in this stage becomes the organ of principal interest and concern to children of both sexes. In the classic theory, the lack of a penis in the female is thought to be the basis for feminine castration concerns and penis envy. The phallic phase is associated with an increase in genital masturbation in both sexes, usually more predominant in male children in view of the greater availability and utility of the penis, but occurring in females as well. Such genital activity is accompanied by predominantly unconscious fantasies of sexual involvements with the opposite-sex parent. The threat of castration and the related castration anxiety is connected to guilt over masturbation and to such oedipal wishes. It is during this phase that the oedipal involvements and the oedipal conflict are established and consolidated.

During the phallic stage, one of the most significant psychosexual developments takes place, namely, the integration of pregenital instinctual derivatives under the primacy of the genital area. In this way, erotic interest becomes focused on the genitals and their functioning. This lays the foundation for a more specific sense of gender identity and serves to integrate the residues of previous psychosexual stages into a predominantly genital sexual orientation. The establishing of the oedipal situation and its conflicts is essential to the organization and integration of these functions and to laying the basis for subsequent identifications, which not only will consolidate sexual identity but also will serve as the basis for extremely important and enduring dimensions of character organization and functioning.

When the oedipal conflicts fail to be adequately generated and formed or to be adequately resolved, either because of excessive contamination from pregenital determinants or because of failures in the dynamics of the oedipal situation itself, pathological character traits can arise. The derivation of such pathological traits from the failures of phallic-oedipal involvement is extremely complex and is subject to such a wide variety of modifications and influences that it covers the entire range of neurotic and normal development. Neurotic personality development, in fact, is defined in terms of the genesis and resolution of phallic oedipal conflicts. The primary issues are those of castration in males and penis envy in females. The influence of castration anxiety and penis envy, the defenses against both of these, and the patterns of identifications emerging from the phallic phase become the primary determinants of the development of human character.

The phallic phase is also the stage in which the residues of previous psychosexual stages are integrated so that any fixations or conflicts that may be left over from these previous stages can play a continuing role in the modification and resolution of the oedipal situation. The persistance of preoedipal conflict can contaminate the child's experience of the oedipal situation and thus contribute to the manner in which the child's pattern of sexual identification and integration takes place. The male child, for example, who remains excessively close and dependent on the preoedipal mother, cannot sufficiently take her as a love object and cannot adequately separate from her in order to begin to identify with the father as an appropriate object of masculine identification. The pull in the masculine direction, that is in the direction of separation from the mother, assertiveness, and masculine aggressiveness, will prove to be too conflicting and too threatening and drive the child back to a more defensive position of dependent clinging to the preoedipal mother.

In normal development, the pregenital phases tend to be primarily autoerotic, that is, the primary gratification is derived from stimulation of the erotogenic zones so that the object, although it plays a significant role, nonetheless is secondary and instrumental. In the phallic phase, there is a fundamental shift in which cathexis and libidinal investment is directed primarily toward the object. The fundamental task at this phase is the finding of a love object. Establishing genital love relationships and investment of libido in the love object during this period thus lays down a pattern for subsequent and more mature object choices later in life. During this period the child's budding sense of his own gender identity as decisively male or female is based on the discovery and realization of the significance of anatomical sexual differences. The "Oedipus complex" in this context refers to the intense love relationships formed during this period between the child and his parents along with the associated rivalries, hostilities, and emerging identifications along sexual lines.

In the pregenital periods, the child's relationships have been based primarily on one-to-one relationships with each of the parents, separately and individually. In these separate relationships, the child has had the opportunity to develop important aspects of interpersonal relationships, particularly elements of trust, dependency, autonomy, and initiative. His relationships to parental objects move to a new level of complexity in the oedipal situation, insofar as involvement with the parents is no longer one-to-one and separate, but now involves both of them simultaneously in a triadic relationship.

The move from a level of dyadic to a level of triadic involvement gives rise to other significant factors. It involves an increased capacity for differentiation between the internal and external reality, an increased capacity to tolerate the anxiety and uncertainty of oedipal involvement, and an increased capacity for tolerating ambivalence and a new level of complexity of social interaction. The oedipal situation and the Oedipus complex represent the climax of infantile sexual development. The transition from a level of oral erotic development through anal erotic modifications to a phase of genitality and the associated changes in the development of object relations, from simple one-to-one dependency to a more complex triadic oedipal involvement, culminate in the oedipal strivings. The working through of these strivings and their associated conflicts can be replaced later in adolescence by a more mature and adult sexuality. The working through of these conflicts is thus an important prerequisite for further normal sexual development. By the same token, psychoneuroses reflect a continuing and unresolved unconscious fixation in the phallic phase and an unconscious clinging to oedipal attachments.

The Oedipus complex emerges during the phallic period, but there is some discrepancy between the sexes in the pattern of its development. In Freud's view, this discrepancy was the result of genital differences, although contemporary views would see the matter in terms of considerably more complex interactions with social and cultural parameters. Freud felt that the oedipal situation for boys was resolved by the castration complex, that is, because the little boy had to give up his libidinal attachment to his mother for fear of castration (castration anxiety). The situation for the little girl was somewhat different as Freud felt that in her case the Oedipus complex was the result of the castration complex. Thus, the little girl differs from the little boy in that she is already castrated. Consequently, she turns to the father, who has a penis, out of a sense of disappointment in her own lack of a penis and her disillusionment with the mother who also lacks this vital organ. Consequently, the little girl is more threatened by a loss of love, particularly from the father, than by actual castration anxiety.

It should be noted that this classical analytic view has been modified considerably by analytic thinkers since Freud's early formulations, and in the current context represents one of the most vital and dynamic areas of psychoanalytic assessment and reformulation. It seems clear at this point that many of Freud's conclusions

about the implications of the oedipal period can no longer be sustained. Particularly in reference to female development, Freud's implications regarding penis envy, feminine masochism, and the characteristic defects in feminine character development, like impediments in superego development, cannot be supported by the evolving contexts of evidence (Blum, 1976; Schafer, 1974). These matters still are disputed and will be for the foreseeable future.

It seems more than likely, as we have come to realize in so many areas of development of psychoanalytic understanding, that we will be less likely to abandon earlier understandings and more apt to realize their complexity and the limitation of their application. As far as I can tell now, analytic thinking is moving toward a more complex appreciation of the factors in the oedipal involvements, both from our increasing depth and sophistication in understanding preoedipal factors, and from postoedipal influences. The latter would include a variety of learning, educative, social, and cultural dimensions which were only rudimentarily understood in Freud's time and which currently contribute much more significantly to our understanding of the functioning of human beings and their complex interrelationships. Undoubtedly, this dimension of the overall problem will continually yield more knowledge and insights.

Obviously, the psychoanalytic perspective cannot remain isolated from these evolving contexts of understanding, nor is there any need for it to do so. Rather, analysts remain sensitively attuned to the clinical evidences brought to the analytic couch by their patients in the contemporary setting. Thus, the analytic understanding of the processes by which sexual identity, both male and female, are established, consolidated, and reinforced, are continually being revised and expanded. Nonetheless, it is unlikely that the classic concepts, let us say of penis envy or castration anxiety, will be eradicated from this evolving perspective. It seems much more likely that their interplay with other complex factors and their position in the consolidation of healthy personality organization and functioning, in contrast to the more pathological manifestations in various levels and ranges of psychopathology, will be more clearly discriminated and differentiated. At this point in our clinical experience, the classic paradigms certainly cannot be unequivocally applied without carefully considering the patients' individual variance and modifying circumstances.

Undoubtedly, in Freud's thinking, the Oedipus complex served as a central organizing point for his views about personality development and for the organization of various forms of pathology. He saw the Oedipus complex as the nucleus of the development of the neuroses and other forms of symptom formation. In addition, the admixture of libidinal fixations, object attachments, and identifications with which the child emerges from the oedipal situation are important to the development of character and personality. The crucial introjections, for example, accompanying the resolution of oedipal fixations provide the nucleus of the emerging psychic substructure serving as the core of the organization of the superego. The resolution of oedipal conflicts at the close of the phallic period is the basis for the development of powerful internal resources to regulate drive impulses and their channeling in constructive directions. The superego is one such internal source of regulation based on identifications with the parental figures, but it is also accompanied by complex internal acquisitions which contribute to the organization and critical internal integration of the child's emerging personality.

THE LATENCY STAGE

The transition from the oedipal or phallic phase of psychosexual development to the subsequent latency stage is an area of particularly meager psychoanalytic understanding. Only recently have more specific psychoanalytic studies of the latency development yielded an increasing harvest of psychoanalytic understanding of this critical developmental phase. There is much yet to be learned. Latency is often regarded as a stage of relative quiescence or inactivity of the sexual drive in the period following resolution of the oedipal complex and extending through till pubescence at the threshold of adolescence.

Generally at this age there is a general impression of the quieting of the instinctually driven behaviors and the muting of other instinctual derivatives. Certainly the formation of superego at the close of the oedipal period and the further maturation of ego functions during the emerging latency phase allows for much more control of instinctual impulses. Usually sexual interest during this period is thought to be quiescent. In both latency-age boys and girls, one sees the development of primarily homosexual affiliations and the tendency to sublimate libidinal and aggressive energies into learning, playing, exploring the environment, and proficiency in developing skills and techniques which allow the growing child to deal with the world of things and persons.

This is a period for the development of the important skills and capacities that will serve the child during the journey through life. There is often a shift in libidinal organization and a relative predominance of regulatory capacities which produces patterns of behavior that seem obsessive or overly controlled. Such a heightening of defenses and regulatory mechanisms allows more room for the exercise of relatively nonconflicted functions and for the typical latency age expansion in learning and the development of skills. Needless to say, such tendencies to structure and control can easily reach pathological proportions and can lay the foundations for emerging obsessive-compulsive personality organization.

The latency stage is primarily for the further integration of oedipal identifications and a consolidation of sex-role identity and sex roles. The relative muting, quiescence, and control of instinctual impulses encourages development of ego apparatuses and the skills of mastery. There are further identifications which may take place and may be added to the basic oedipal identifications—broadening the organization of the personality through increased contacts with other significant adult figures outside the family, e.g., teachers, coaches, and others.

The latency period also has its risks and dangers. As we have suggested, the inner controls can be excessive and when they are, it may lead to a premature closure of personality development and to the precocious elaboration of highly structured and rigidly organized personality, often found in obsessive character traits. Inner controls may not develop or may fail to consolidate. In such circumstances the child may fail to develop a capacity sufficient to sublimate energies in the interest of learning and the development of skills. This often may be expressed in latency-age children by difficulties in learning or by conflicts over school activities and other involvements with age-mates.

If there has been a tendency to underestimate the importance of the latency period within the developmental schema, more recent efforts have paid greater attention to the latency period and have shown greater interest in the complexities of latency development. There are important consolidations of the basic postoedipal identifications during this period. The previous psychosexual attainments must be integrated and consolidated so that decisive patterns of effective personality functioning and adaptive activity can be established.

It is in this phase that the child can develop a sense of industry and a capacity for mastery of objects and concepts that allows him to function effectively and autonomously with a sense of initiative and competence and without running the risk of failure or defeat or without incurring a sense of inferiority. Erikson has described the psychosocial crisis of the latency stage as one of industry versus inferiority. The latency period is an important stage for the determining and consolidating important dimensions of the organization of personality, particularly those pertaining to organization of ego capacities and skills. When this has been done, the child is then ready psychologically for the regressive upsurge of instinctual drives and conflicts marking the onset of puberty. The more effective the latency consolidation has been, the better able is the developing personality capable of sustaining the regressive pulls

of adolescent development and of resolving them successfully in a more effective and mature direction.

ADOLESCENCE

With the onset of puberty, usually in about the eleventh to the thirteenth year, the child enters the phase of genital psychosexual development or *adolescence*. The adolescent period is variously extended but continues until the individual reaches young adulthood. There is a tendency currently to subdivide the adolescent phase into various substages including the preadolescent, early adolescent, middle adolescent, late adolescent, and even postadolescent periods. Each of these three stages has its characteristic difficulties and conflicts, but we will regard them in a global sense.

The onset of puberty is marked by the physiological maturation of systems related to genital sexual functioning and the accompanying forms of hormonal maturation. This leads to an intensification of instinctual drives, particularly the libidinal drives. The upsurge in intensity of libidinal activity leads to some regression in the organization of personality in which the unresolved conflicts of previous stages of psychosexual development are reopened once again. This provides an opportunity to rework these conflicts and to re-resolve them, now in the present context of achieving mature adult sexuality and identity.

The adolescent crisis has been called a period of "second individuation" by Blos (1967). By this he implies that a primary objective of the adolescent period is the ultimate separation from dependence on and attachment to the parental objects as well as the establishment of mature, nonincestuous, heterosexual object-relationships. Related to this important resolution of the crisis in object-relationships, there is required an achievement of a mature sense of personal identity, an acceptance and integration of a set of adult roles and functions that define the emerging adolescence position vis-à-vis his community and surrounding environment (Erikson, 1959). The individual's personal identity now must be established not merely in terms of the context provided by family and school, but in terms of the broader community.

The reopening of unresolved conflicts and crises from earlier stages of psychosexual and psychosocial development can devastate adolescent development. In our society, the passage through adolescence is often turbulent and troubled. That is not to say that such adolescent disturbances are the modal expression of adolescent development in our culture, but the difficulties are encountered frequently enough so that they become a matter of central concern. If pregenital conflicts and particularly the complexities of oedipal involvements and their related conflicts have been satisfactorily resolved in the earlier life history, the regressive reopening of the adolescent phase often is not so disturbing or troublesome that the adolescent is unable to reintegrate his experience in ways not adequately adaptive and reasonably harmonious.

Undoubtedly, all adolescents feel some degree of regressive tension and difficulty, but the difficulties are sufficiently intense and conflictual in many so that it becomes a matter of pathological deviation. The patterns of pathological deviation are multiple and complex. The defects can arise from any point along the wide-ranging spectrum of psychosexual residues, since the developmental task of the adolescent period is specifically a partial reopening, reworking, and reintegrating of all these aspects of individual development. If the resolution and reintegration of prior psychosexual stages is successful, the development of full genital capacity normally sets the stage for a mature personality with the capacity for full and satisfying genital potency and a self-integrated and consistent sense of identity.

MATURITY

It is important to note that one of the presumptions of the classical psychosexual theory, namely, that the achievement of genital pri-

macy and full genital potency was synonymous with maturity of personality development, is no longer accepted in contemporary psychoanalytic thinking. The psychoanalytic theory of personality development and the theory of the relationship between sexual functioning and personality organization have become considerably more complex since the original propositions were set forth by Freud. Contemporary psychoanalytic thinking would distinguish very carefully between genital capacity and the capacity for love relationships. In fact, the capacity to achieve mature and adult love relationships is influenced more generally by complex dimensions of personality development and psychic development, and is not simply a function of psychosexual development (Kernberg, 1974).

At a minimum one must include the parameters of psychosocial development along with those of psychosexual development in understanding such personality potentialities. The development of the capacities for mature and mutually satisfying love relationships depends on the resolution of basic conflicts on many levels of psychological development. Kernberg (1974) has indicated the importance of such factors:

> The capacity for sexual intercourse and orgasm does not by any means guarantee the capacity for being maturely in love; nor does the capacity for a total object-relation without the resolution of oedipal conflicts and the related freeing from sexual inhibition guarantee the capacity for being maturely in love and for stable relation. The capacity for falling in love indicates the achievement of important preconditions for the capacity for being in love; in the case of narcissistic personalities, falling in love marks the beginning of the capacity for concern and guilt, and some hope for overcoming deep, unconscious devaluation of the love object. In borderline patients, primitive idealization may be the first step toward a love relation different from the love-hate relation with their primary objects. This occurs if and when the splitting mechanisms responsible for this primitive idealization have been resolved and this love relation or a new one replacing it is able to

tolerate and resolve the pregenital conflicts against which primitive idealization was a defense. In the case of neurotic patients and patients with relatively less severe character pathology, the capacity for falling in love should, if and when successful psychoanalytic treatment resolves the unconscious, predominantly oedipal, conflicts, mature into the capacity for a lasting love relation (p. 510).

PERVERSIONS

The range of maladaptive behaviors of particular interest to psychoanalysts has been that of the perversions. The perversions are forms of sexual dysfunction which include such behaviors as homosexuality, fetishism, transvestitism, exhibitionism, voyeurism, and sadomasochism. A perversion may be regarded as a form of sexual disturbance in which sexual gratification can be gained from sexual aims that are fixated at one or other level of infantile sexual development. In the perversions normal adult sexual outlets and sources of satisfaction are not expressed normally but are replaced by more infantile forms of sexual expression. Thus, the perversions are forms of infantile rather than of adult sexuality.

Thus, if we look at fetishism for a moment, the fetishist tends to cathect libidinally an inanimate object that has come to symbolize a part of the body of an ambivalently loved person. Fetishism is consequently a mental state that leads the person to worship or love such a material object which he takes as possessing a magical power or as having a special neurotic interest. This is the fixation of neurotic investment on an object or body part that is inappropriate to normal sexual purposes but is required by the person for the attainment of sexual gratification. Parts of the body such as hair, hands or feet, or even a shoe or handkerchief or other object of personal apparel can serve such purposes. The fetish itself usually is taken to symbolize the female phallus, and its use represents the denial of the danger of castration that might be suggested by the anatomical differences between the sexes. The mind of the fetishist therefore is split; part of his mind is able to assess and accept the absence of the penis in the female, but another part unconsciously adheres to and insists on the idea that the female does, in fact, possess a phallus. Fetishism can be viewed as one deviant resolution of the problem of castration anxiety.

Similarly, the transvestite finds pleasure in dressing in the garments of the opposite sex. For the male this may represent an identification with the phallic mother, and for the female it may serve her wish to deny the lack of a penis. Similarly, the often compulsive exposure of sex organs in exhibitionism may be a defense against castration anxiety because of the shock or fright in the female object at the sight of a penis. Conversely, voyeurism may serve similar defense needs. Sadomasochism early in Freud's thinking was regarded as a partial instinct representing a tendency to seek or inflict physical or mental suffering as a way of achieving sexual arousal or gratification. In masochistic perversion, sexual gratification, even orgasm, is felt as a result of inflicted pain by such practices as beatings, threats, humiliations, or subjugations at the hand of a sexual partner. Similarly, sadistic gratification is derived from inflicting such torment on the sexual partner.

The organization of the perversions may come about either through arrested or fixated development or through a regression from more developed forms of sexual expression. The perversions that come from regression are not typical and tend to substitute aspects of sexual forepleasure for the mature sexual act. Such individuals generally tend to have a more infantile caste to their personality organization in general. The major part of the sexual energies of individuals with perversions are concentrated on one particular partial instinct, so that the dominant role of this partial instinct competes with the individual's genital primacy. These individuals are capable of orgastic release, but the orgasm is usually stimulated by the perverse act rather than by normal heterosexual outlet. The capacity for genital orgasm is inhibited by an obstacle that is overcome or circumvented in the perverse act. Such perverse behavior and sexual expression does not lack organization as is often seen in the sexuality of "polymorphous perverse" children or regressed infantile personalities; rather, it is organized under the primacy of a component instinct whose gratification makes genital orgasm possible in a way that could not otherwise be achieved.

A critical question, then, is what factors inhibit the normal developmental progression to genital primacy. The psychoanalytic answer leans heavily toward the genesis of anxiety and guilt feelings related to the child's oedipal involvement with his parents. The beginnings of genital primacy are established in the phallic phase (in about the third year when genital drives begin to emerge and the differences between the sexes, especially genital differences, become significant) in which the oedipal complex arises. The oedipal complex or situation refers to the complex emotional involvement in relation to both parents as a result of normal sexual development. In his earlier preoedipal years, the child is involved with each parent, mother and father, in separate and different ways. By the third year, he attained a new and more complex level of involvement with the parents. The child must relate to them together as a pair, no longer separately and singly in one-to-one interactions, but now as a member of a triad in which the child is the third, the smallest and most dependent member. This step is important because it is the child's first experience of social interaction, and it sets a decisive pattern for later interactions. This particularly pertains to the experience of himself as a sexual being.

One of the most important contributing factors to the oedipal situation is the upsurge of sexual feelings, directed primarily toward the parent of the opposite sex. Little boys have sexual feelings toward their mothers, along with erections, desires to see mother undressed, to sleep with her, and to get rid of the father who simply gets in the way. The little girl has sexual feelings toward her father, wishes for a baby from him, and the desire to eliminate her rival for father's affections. In both cases, this is re-

ferred to as the positive oedipal complex in that positive loving affects are directed to the opposite sex parent. Consolidation and resolution of the positive oedipal complex leads to normal heterosexuality for both sexes.

There is also a negative oedipal complex. This consists of positive loving (sexual) feelings directed toward the same-sex parent and feelings of rivalry and antipathy toward the opposite sex parent. The little boy wishes for approval and affection from his father and competes with his mother for his father's love. The little girl wishes for closeness, love, and affection from her mother and competes with father for her mother's affection. The negative oedipal complex exists in all children alongside of the positive oedipal complex. When the balance of instinctual forces is shifted toward the negative complex, the likelihood of homosexuality is increased.

The key in this process is castration anxiety. Castration anxiety arises from the fantasized fear that the father will retaliate against the little boy for his sexual wishes to possess the mother and get rid of the father. The balance of oedipal forces may be shifted as a result of this threat to the negative oedipal configuration, in which the son's loving attachment and submission to the father serves to defend against castration fears. In the little girl, the castration complex takes a different form because of her genital anatomy. She has no external organ and may feel envious and deprived on this account. This normally leads her to turn to the father who has a penis. The little girl is more threatened by lack of love than by castration. If turning to the father does not satisfy her need for love and approval, she must cling to her mother—the safer and more infantile love object.

In the perversions, infantile sexuality becomes predominant over adult sexuality. Consequently, there must be something in adult sexuality which is threatening or frightening as well as something that is inherently attractive about infantile sexuality. In the perversions, it is almost universally the fear of castration that interferes with the capacity to express full genital sexuality. Because of such castration fear, the individual regresses to that part of the infantile sexuality at which he is developmentally fixated. At what developmental level, and what parts of the instinctual capacities are fixated, are often influenced by an individual's developmental experience. The dynamic aspects of the genesis of perversion have been described quite succinctly by Fenichel (1945):

> Among fixating experiences at the basis of perversion, one type is prominent: experience of sexual satisfaction which simultaneously gave a feeling of security by denying or contradicting some fear. The pervert, when disturbed in his genital sexuality by castration fear, regresses to that component of his infantile sexuality which once in childhood had given him a feeling of security or at least of reassurance against fear, and his gratification was experienced with special intensity because of this denial or reassurance. To put it schematically, the pervert is a person whose sexual pleasure is blocked by the idea of castration. Through the perversion he tries to prove that there is no castration. Insofar as this proof is believed, sexual pleasure and orgasm become possible again (p. 327).

HOMOSEXUALITY

I would like here to discuss the problem of homosexuality, since it is the primary form of perversion in analytic theory, since it is the area of disordered sexuality receiving the greatest psychoanalytic interest and scrutiny, and since it is an area of particular controversy at this time. Moreover, it provides a paradigm for considerations of the psychoanalytic treatment of sexual disturbances.

In focusing specifically on the dynamics of homosexuality, the general paradigm of the perversions is applicable, but we will have to note the peculiar factors in patterns of homosexual behavior. The first important point is that there is not one form of homosexuality but many forms, so that one can speak more accurately of homosexualities in the plural rather than in the singular. The patterns of homosexual behavior express varying patterns of underlying motiva-

tions that differentiate the early developmental vicissitudes characterizing each individual's early sexual experiences and maturation.

Second, it is important to realize that even relatively normal individuals are capable, under certain forms of stress, frustration, and disappointment, of developing patterns of perverted behavior, for example, an isolated episode of homosexual behavior after a threat to the patient's father's life, or the emergence of homosexual behavior in prison or barracks life. In such circumstances we cannot maintain that the individual has developed a new pathological propensity, but rather that some latent disposition in the organization is the personality has been activated by specific external circumstances or forms of psychic stress. For sexual orientation, it is a basic postulate which Freud embraced and which has been maintained consistently in analytic thinking since, that human beings are essentially bisexual, that is, that they have as inherent components of their libidinal organization both heterosexual and homosexual inclinations. These inclinations are shaped, modified, reinforced, and directed progressively through the years of development by important developmental experiences, particularly those relating to the child's parents.

While analysis has consistently maintained that the normal developmental progression leads toward establishing a mature and mutually satisfying heterosexual relationship, it also has strongly maintained and insisted that homosexual elements even in the most successful development of heterosexual capacity remain as an inherent and abiding component of the personality. This applies equally to both sexes. Consequently, only homosexuality in the homosexual is regarded as reflecting a failure in the essential steps leading toward that heterosexual resolution. In the analytic view, to the extent that heterosexual adjustment is not achieved, it is a form of developmental failure or psychopathology. This does not in any sense infer that homosexuals are incapable of orgastic experience, nor does it mean that they are incapable of affectionate relationships with other human beings. That is to say, the dynamics of perversion simply as such do not exclude these capacities, but the question of how frequently such capacities are actually attained by homosexual individuals remains a matter of doubt and debate.

The available data on the quality of homosexual relations are by no means satisfactory. Certainly the frequency of pick-ups and one-night stands among homosexuals is not reassuring. However, if one chooses to make a comparative argument, the data from the heterosexual side are not altogether reassuring either. The level of casual sexual encounters, the current epidemic of venereal diseases, and the alarming divorce rate all are cause for concern and reflect a general defect in the capacity for enduring, mutually satisfactory, and fulfilling relationships. Those who argue for the normalization of homosexuality tend to emphasize that a homosexual libidinal disposition does not necessarily exclude more mature forms of affectionate involvement and expression. But the fact remains that homosexuality is a perversion and as such, rides on a substructure of some kind of developmental defect. The degree of psychopathology in any given homosexual obviously reflects the extent to which early fixations have come to dominate developmental experience. The earlier such fixations take place, generally the more severe the degree of pathology and the greater the incapacity to sustain satisfactory relationships.

Certainly in nearly all cases of homosexuality, castration anxiety is important. But castration anxiety itself does not exist in a vacuum. The fact of castration anxiety suggests the failure to achieve a healthy resolution of the oedipal crisis, but the castration anxiety may also be riding on a more primitive level of anxiety that relates to the failure of much earlier preoedipal concerns. Consequently, we must be careful about assessing pathological aspects of homosexuals. Clearly there is no uniform pathology, but rather, each case must be individually assessed for its developmental achievements and the level at which the anxiety is operating. We can argue only for the presence of some developmental failure and by inference, some degree

of psychopathology related to that failure. What the degree of failure and the extent of psychopathology may be in any given individual requires specific evaluation and identification.

The male homosexual essentially protects himself from the retaliatory fears of castration by shifting his sexual impulses away from a heterosexual object to a homosexual object. The origin of such castrative fears lies in the oedipal situation in which the child's sexual wish to possess the mother raises the fear of retaliatory punishment in the form of castration from the father. Why a homosexual object in the adult should seem safer than a heterosexual one, however, is not at all clear, but it seems certain from clinical experience that a confirmed homosexual is inordinately afraid of women as sexual objects. The male homosexual is literally fleeing from women. As a neurotic symptom, male homosexuality can be understood as a phobic avoidance of the female genital. Many homosexuals in fact tend to view the vagina with disgust and revulsion. Often such individuals have an intense *vagina dentata* fantasy, that is, the fantasy that the vagina is like a devouring mouth which can somehow consume and destroy the penis.

The castration fear can be related either to the mother or to the father. The typical family configuration in which male homosexuality is fostered generally has a domineering, overpowering, seductive, and excessively intimate mother together with an emotionally detached, hostile, aloof, and rejecting father. The son of such a mother would be expected to have a great deal of anxiety about separating from her and also to fear that she would devour him should he get too close to her or hold on to her for too long. The dependency on the mother, so essential to sustain life and to psychic growth early in the child's experience, becomes associated with aggressive and destructive elements.

The child's dependency on the mother, which is reinforced by the mother's excessive intimacy and overpowering intrusiveness and seductiveness, sets the stage for a primitive fear of engulfment and annihilation stimulated by the child's naturally emerging erotic interest in her during the oedipal phase of development. The anxiety in relationship to the female genital may be of at least two kinds: (1) the anxiety may arise from the awareness that there are "penisless" beings, and this recognition in the child's experience encourages castration fears; or (2) because of a more primitive connection of castration anxiety with previous oral aggressive impulses, the female genitals may be seen as the castrating instrument capable of biting or tearing off the penis—the *vagina dentata* fantasy.

Central to the development of male homosexuality is the identification with the mother. The general unavailability of, distance from, or rejection by the father in such cases makes his availability as a model for developing masculinity somewhat limited. Consequently, the basic identification with the father, which would shape the young male child's emerging sense of himself as a man, is undercut, and the child is drawn with powerful emotional ties to his mother. The tendency of such mothers to be oversolicitous, overprotective and overinvolved —frequently in seductive ways—with these male children contributes to the intense affective coloring of this maternal identification.

It should be noted that such identification generally is not without considerable conflict, and that the degree of anxiety related to it depends largely on the extent to which the child has remained pathologically dependent on the mother and the degree to which he has been unable to establish some degree of separation from her without the threat of loss or abandonment. The basic identification with the mother underlies the homosexual impulse to take a man as a sexual object, since in this way one lives out the maternal identification. One often sees in such cases a combination of impulses which brings the male homosexual to want to be in the position of nurturing, caring, and mothering, usually for a younger male. In this way he can imitate the mother who exercised these functions toward him. It also contributes much conflict about the exercise of more active, assertive, and aggressive masculine propensities. The penis comes to be seen as a powerful, de-

structive, and harmful organ, a fantasy adding to the difficulty in relating to the opposite sex and in achieving genital satisfaction. Clinically a frequent component of this complex is an abiding, unsatisfied, continually frustrated yearning and longing for closeness, acceptance, and loving communication with the father. Often in the course of clinical work with such homosexuals, these wishes can be more or less consciously expressed directly in relation to the father, but more frequently they remain relatively unconscious and tend to be acted-out and expressed as wishes for approval, closeness, and acceptance from other significant male figures in the patient's life. Frequently this dynamic expresses itself in the homosexual inclinations.

It is worth noting that this dynamic also may be part of a religious context. The religious is exhorted to submit himself to the superior in loving obedience. The religious practices which reinforce this submissive and obediential demeanor may serve as a vehicle for essentially homosexual impulses, representing a homosexual submission to a substitute father. Optimally such impulses need not be disruptive and can be effectively sublimated, given adequate strengths of character and the capacity to control and master them. We should not overlook the potentiality for such obedient submission to force a given individual into an equivalent homosexual position either increasing homosexual anxieties (if the wish to submit is ego-alien) or reinforcing such tendencies (if it is not).

Another element germane to the homosexual picture is that of narcissism. Freud once commented that the homosexual is often so intensely narcissistic that he cannot love a being that is other than himself, that is, a being without a penis (in the case of the male). The narcissistic wish often expresses itself as the substitute for oedipal strivings, that is, once the homosexual has identified himself with his mother, he begins to behave as he had once wished his mother to behave toward him. This leads to a choice of libidinal objects such as men or boys who are quite similar to the individual himself and toward whom he then expresses the same sort of tenderness and affection that he had once desired from his mother. While he acts out the maternal identification in this way, emotionally the narcissism plays itself out insofar as the love object is like himself and the psychic situation is equivalent to one in which he is able to enjoy being loved by himself. This particular dynamic may prevail when male religious are in charge of young boys, or females in charge of young girls. This is particularly noteworthy for young adolescents in whom the resolution of gender identity has not been completed and the titre of homosexual impulses runs high.

Often when such narcissistic elements are predominant in the genesis of homosexuality, the character structure tends to be more primitive and pathological. It should be noted that similar mechanisms can be found in heterosexual individuals as well, when narcissistic men fall in love with a woman whom they see as a reincarnation of their own feminine wishes and yearnings. This relates to their own wish to be treated as a little girl by their mothers with results similar to those found in homosexuals, that they then treat these women as they themselves would have wished to have been treated by their own mothers. Consequently, the love relationship is not based on an objective love of the feminine partner as a separate entity in her own right, but rather as a reflection of the repressed feminine parts of the man's own ego.

Certain types of character organization show a tendency or a need to give to others what they did not get themselves and are able to gain the satisfaction of "getting" through an identification to the one to whom they are giving. This is a form of "altruism" in which certain pleasures that the individuals cannot have themselves may be given to others and relished through an identification with these others. But the wish to give and the affection for the other is often intensely ambivalent and mixed with extreme degrees of envy, which may turn into rage and resentment if the one given to is not as pleased as the giver expects him to be.

The identification with the mother may also be mixed with other pregenital components, including an anal fixation. The oedipal wish for sexual gratification from the mother is transformed through the identification into a wish to enjoy it in the same way that the mother does. This dynamic makes father the object of the child's love and leads to a masochistic striving to submit himself to the father in the way that the mother does, in a passive and submissive way. The anal fixation in these cases combines with a maternal identification in the wish for anal intercourse. While patients of this sort may behave in a feminine way with passivity and tenderness, these aspects of their behavior may mask unconscious hostility toward the very father figures to whom they are submitting. In such cases the passive submission to the father or father-substitute replaces a more unconscious intention of stripping the father of his masculinity so that homosexual intercourse can begin to signify active castration.

In this sense, these apparently feminine and passive men have not at all given up their unconscious striving to be masculine and to replace their father. By becoming the feminine part to a more masculine man, they thus can gain the strength and masculine power of the partner. Thus, the retreat from castration anxiety in the feminine identification does not completely replace the wishes for identification with the father. The wish to be like the father, to learn from him, to gain strength and resourcefulness and power by being more like him is always ambivalent, since its ultimate aim is in the oedipal context to replace the father. Once the child places his father in such a position of power and omnipotence, he may try to regain some sense of strength by sharing in the father's power. The tension remains between the extremes of killing and getting rid of the father in order to take his place, and total obedience and ingratiating submission so that the father will grant the son a share in his power and strength.

It should be remembered that narcissistic and passive-anal fixations may occur in the same individual and may express themselves in various combinations in different forms of homosexuality. It should also be remembered that the same dynamics may exist in apparent forms of heterosexuality. Not uncommonly the excessive involvement in heterosexual activity serves as a defense against passive and narcissistic homosexual longings. In situations in which these homosexual inclinations are excessively stimulated, such individuals may be severely threatened and may experience an overwhelming anxiety which has been described as "homosexual panic."

It may be wise to add a word here about the question of feminine homosexuality. Although the origin of male homosexuality lies in castration anxiety, the fear of the penis itself is essential to female homosexuality. Often the penis is seen by such women as a punishing, hurting, destructive, tearing, and biting organ. These fears and thoughts and feelings may impede the capacity for sexual enjoyment, to the extent that there is no sexual pleasure possible if it involves a penis.

For homosexual women, one way in which the male genital can be excluded is by regression. It must be remembered that the first love object of every human being is the mother, so that all women, as opposed to men, begin life with a primary homosexual attachment. When in the course of later development the emergence of normal heterosexuality is blocked, the regression to the homosexual attachment can be revived. Whereas the male regresses from a love of the mother as a sexual object to an identification with the mother, the woman regresses from the love of the father as a sexual object to a love of the mother as a sexual object. Consequently, female homosexuality tends to have two important factors: the first is the rejection of heterosexuality related to the castration complex and penis fear, and the second is the early preoedipal fixation on the attachment to the mother. These factors supplement each other since the attachment to the mother may protect and reassure against the threat of castration.

The normal progression in feminine sexual development is through the little girl's loving attachment to her father. If that attachment is successful, that is, if it is not excessively seductive and if the father is able to respond in positive ways so as to reinforce the young girl's sense of growing feminine attractiveness and worth, she emerges with a more adequate sense of herself as feminine and as capable of attracting, loving, and being loved by a man who is in some way like her father. This dynamic is obviously reinforced when the father's attitude toward the mother is one of loving respect and affection, so that it becomes possible for a little girl to grow up with a positive identification with her mother which then can reinforce her own potentialities for being loved by a man and finding fulfillment and self-esteem by growing into and taking on a feminine position and role in life. The natural outcome of this progression is to lead a young woman to seek fulfillment and life expression through the normal channels of marriage, motherhood, and family life. To the extent that this identification carries with it the positive, constructive, and competent aspects of both parents, the young woman enters life with a sense of her own capacity to strive, compete, accomplish, and produce as an effective and competent human being.

But this process is subject to many vicissitudes. If the father is unable to respond to and positively reinforce the young girl's sense of growing femininity, this disappointment and disillusionment may draw her away from an increasing identification with the mother and toward an identification with the father. This paternal identification may lead her to seek women as love objects resembling her mother. This resolution not only avoids the oedipal competition with the mother but also has an element of continuing hostility toward the father expressed in hostility towards men in general. This form of feminine homosexuality resembles male homosexuality in which identification with the mother leads to a desire to be loved by the father in the same way that he loved the mother. In the female the identification with the father leads to a desire to love the mother in the same way that the father loved her. This pattern is frequent among homosexual women and leads to adopting an active masculine relation to other women. One hears the reverberations of these dynamics in claims from such women that they do not need any men in their lives, or that they can be as good as any man. Such masculine strivings need not be combined with homosexuality but may be, depending on the intensity of the early fixation to the mother as we have suggested, and on the particular outcome of the castration complex.

Frequently for such homosexual women, the retreat from the father is accompanied by an intense longing for acceptance, closeness, and intimacy with the mother or mother-substitute. Loving the mother figure as the father loved her may also be combined with the wish to be loved by the mother in a more infantile way and in a way which has never been satisfactorily realized in the individual's life experience. Turning away from heterosexuality revives elements of the early relationship to the mother and may have a more archaic or primitive character than male homosexuality has. It brings back not only the patterns of behavior, wishes, and gratifications of the early relationship with the mother, but also the fears and conflicts related to that early involvement. In such homosexual relationships there may be a good deal of mothering and infantilization between the partners as well as much kissing, sucking, licking, and other oral components of the sexual experience.

To round out this discussion of the analytic perspective on homosexuality, it may be wise to comment briefly on the analytic attitude toward homosexuality. It should be remembered that Freud was the first to approach homosexuality without condemning it and to see it as a form of psychopathology, which required understanding and treatment rather than condemnation. Perhaps the best expression of this attitude, which has been and continues to be the basic attitude of psychoanalysts, is contained in a letter which Freud wrote in 1935 to a desperate mother who wrote to him

from America requesting help for her homosexual son:

April 9, 1935

Dear Mrs. . . .

I gather from your letter that your son is a homosexual. I am most impressed by the fact that you do not mention this term yourself in your information about him. May I question you, why avoid it? Homosexuality is assuredly no advantage, but it is nothing to be ashamed of, no vice, no degradation, it cannot be classified as an illness; we consider it to be a variation of the sexual function produced by a certain arrest of sexual development. Many highly respectable individuals of ancient and modern times have been homosexuals, several of the greatest among them (Plato, Michelangelo, Leonardo da Vinci, etc.). It is a great injustice to persecute homosexuality as a crime, and cruelty too. If you do not believe me, read the books of Havelock Ellis.

By asking me if I can help, you mean, I suppose, if I can abolish homosexuality and make normal heterosexuality take its place. The answer is, in a general way, we cannot promise to achieve it. In a certain number of cases we succeed in developing the blighted germs of heterosexual tendencies which are present in every homosexual, in the majority of cases it is no more possible. It is a question of the quality and the age of the individual. The result of treatment cannot be predicted.

What analysis can do for your son runs in a different line. If he is unhappy, neurotic, torn by conflicts, inhibited in his social life, analysis may bring him harmony, peace of mind, full efficiency, whether he remains a homosexual or gets changed. . . .

Sincerely yours with kind wishes,
Freud (1960, letter 277).

In more current times psychoanalysts and psychoanalysis have been attacked on more or less political grounds, as adopting a prejudicial attitude toward homosexuals because analysis deals with homosexuality as a form of pathology. It should be clear from the preceding discussion and particularly from Freud's letter that there is no necessary connection between the persecutory or judgmental treatment of homosexuality and the more objective and scientific position that it is a form of psychopathology. Psychoanalysis has solid reason based on clinical experience gathered over many years, to sustain its position and its understanding of the homosexual dynamic. To deal with human psychopathology as pathology, in relation to homosexuality as in relation to all forms of human suffering associated with psychopathology, is neither unfeeling, rejecting, nor judgmental.

I would argue in fact that just the opposite is true: to respond to human distress in terms other than to see it as human psychopathology which can be treated, modified, or alleviated in some degree or manner, is to be less than human and in fact is to condemn such individuals to a lifetime of frustration and unhappiness. The psychoanalytic attitude condemns all prejudicial treatment of homosexuals, but that is not its concern or its business. Its concern is to help to alleviate neurotic suffering and the impediments to self-fulfillment and self-realization. To deny individuals that form of assistance, as is so often the outcome of attempts to deny the pathology of homosexuality, a posture too often adopted by homosexual advocates without sufficient sensitivity or discrimination, is itself a form of cruelty and lack of sensitivity.

It may be appropriate to interject a comment on the current status of the diagnosis of homosexuality according to the Diagnostic and Statistical Manual II. First of all, one would have to decry the method by which the revision was made. To my way of thinking it was a crass example of yielding to political and social pressures in a process of bending scientific statement to expediency. The ultimate step of putting the decision to a vote makes a travesty of any scientific pretext in the formal diagnostic categories of institutional psychiatry. If any demonstration were needed of the unscientific status of psychiatry (even, or should I say especially, at the highest levels of organized psychiatry in this country), little else would be required.

The tragedy of that revision is that it takes homosexuality out of the realm of pathological diagnoses and undermines a long-standing and clinically sound view that homosexual behavior can be regarded as significant symptomatology. Moreover, it does not seem farfetched to argue that it substantiates the view of the most outspoken, and often most disturbed and resistant to treatment, homosexuals and provides a rationalization for avoiding treatment. I have argued here that psychoanalysis is not a specific treatment for such disorders, but I would never infer that homosexuality and other sexual disorders are not diagnosable and treatable disorders. The confusion of legitimate diagnoses with political or prejudicial positions is to my mind unfortunate and unscientific.

TREATMENT METHODS

From the above account, one cannot escape what is most central to and best understood in psychoanalysis, namely, sexuality as a dynamic force in the etiology of various neurotic conditions. This has been one of the most important discoveries of psychoanalysis and is important to all psychoanalytic treatment. However, one should not let this obscure one's view of what psychoanalysis is about and what it is for. I will take the rather strong position here that psychoanalysis is not a specific treatment for sexual disorders. There are other therapies that contend for that honor and perhaps come nearer to filling the bill than psychoanalysis does, although in my judgment we are far from having achieved anything like an effective, therapeutic approach to such difficulties. Even the best of such sex therapy techniques, employed by the most experienced and skilled clinicians, yield results that are less than satisfactory in a large number of cases. We now have only a poor understanding of why such specific therapies are relatively successful in some cases yet seem to fail over the long-run with many.

The implication of my statement that psychoanalysis is not a specific therapy for sexual disorders is that, in my judgment, psychoanalysis would not be indicated simply because a patient suffers from some sexual disorder. That a patient is frigid or impotent or suffers from premature ejaculation is not sufficient grounds for treating such a patient in psychoanalysis. When patients suffer from more deeply engrained and enduring forms of sexual disturbance relating to various forms of perversion, fetishism, transvestitism, homosexuality, psychoanalysis is still not a specific treatment, in my judgment, but in such cases there are almost inevitably other grounds upon which the decision to enter psychoanalysis might be made. In the latter sorts of cases, there are usually long-standing personality defects and impairments, or neurotic conflicts underlying the disordered sexual behavior which call for a deep and thorough analysis of the patient's object-relations, both those in his current life and those in the past, as well as re-examination and regressive reworking of the patient's developmental experience itself. Psychoanalysis is the specific therapy for such an undertaking.

Not only can it be said that psychoanalysis is not a specific sexual therapy, but in implementing its efforts psychoanalysis does not focus on the sexually disordered symptom. Sexual behavior together with its associated wishes, fantasies, attitudes, impulses, dreams, and so on, are subjected to careful examination in an effort to gain a deeper understanding of their meaning in the patient's life and in connection with underlying conflicts and their developmental roots. As analysis progresses, as conflicts are reopened and re-examined and gradually resolved, and as the therapeutic changes begin to occur, particularly those modifying superego dynamics and increasing autonomy and conflict-free operation by the ego, the symptoms begin to wane. Not only do they become less frequent in the patient's experience, but their compulsive and often driven quality seems to become less intense so that the patient gradually becomes relatively symptom-free.

The hysterical female patient who had suffered from frigidity finds her orgastic potential increasing and becoming more readily available, as she is able to work through the underlying oedipal conflicts and to recognize that her symptoms are related to underlying conflicts over sexual impulses towards her father and their gratification. As this aspect of her symptoms becomes more consciously apparent to her and is gradually resolved in the treatment, the symptom of frigidity is also resolved. Similarly, the young man whose difficulties with premature ejaculation have caused him considerable embarrassment and difficulty, finds that as he is able to handle more effectively his conflicts over aggression and self-assertion, and is able to surrender his somewhat infantile position of inadequacy, he too finds that little by little the annoying symptom seems to dissolve and disappear. In none of these cases was the analytic effort directed at the symptom itself, but rather to the underlying personality configurations, conflicts, and developmental issues pervasive influencing the patient's life, of which the sexual symptom was merely one limited expression.

The issues in such symptomatic cases are somewhat different from the more deeply engrained perversions, particularly homosexuality. Recently analysts have directed a great deal of attention to homosexuality and the possibilities for its treatment. Certainly the attitudes toward homosexuality have changed over the last three-quarters of a century. Freud's opinion at the time of the *Three Essays* (1905) was that little could be done for homosexual patients except suppression of symptoms by hypnotic suggestion. The attitude among clinical psychoanalysts toward the treatment of homosexuality has become considerably more optimistic, although at the same time the awareness of the complex personality structure underlying homosexual symptomatology and behavior has deepened.

Socarides (1974) notes that there are two important criteria for selecting homosexual patients for psychoanalysis: (1) the availability of guilt feelings for unconscious wishes underlying the homosexual impulses is an important index of the patient's capacity for therapeutic change. If such guilt is not conscious, this does not necessarily mean that the patient is not suffering from guilt, but the unconscious guilt may be experienced as a need for punishment or as compelling him to self-destructive behavior. Along with guilt we can suggest that some sense of shame may also be important to evaluating the patient's therapeutic potential. (2) The second point Socarides makes is that patients must undertake the treatment voluntarily. If the patient is under any duress or compulsion from others, whether they be parents, superiors, or any other authority figures, the patent's hostility toward parental figures will be readily transferred and will both undermine an effective therapeutic alliance and interfere with positive transference. Positive transference is important to the treatment of homosexuals, since it is through it that the patient ultimately is able to identify with the good father-therapist and thus obtain what he has been unsuccessfully striving to gain through homosexual contacts, namely, the assimilation of masculine strength and identity. This therapeutic gain allows him to begin to free himself from the entangling dependency and enslavement to the mother.

The treatment of homosexuals is complex and difficult and as the preceding discussion suggests, encounters developmental vicissitudes on a number of levels, often of an intensely ambivalent and pregenital character. The difficulty of the therapy and the problems it involves, as well as the likely resolution of underlying conflicts and the possibility of adequate heterosexual adjustment largely depend on the levels of adequate personality development achieved and the extent to which early developmental conflicts and impairments are part of the genesis of homosexual behavior.

Nonetheless, certain critical points are characteristic in the treatment of such patients (Socarides, 1974). Particularly noticeable are the oedipal incestuous and aggressive fears, particularly those relating to the negative oedipal constellation. It is central to the successful resolution of the homosexuality that these oedipal conflicts be resolved and that the nuclear preoedipal anxieties be discovered. These often entail primitive fears of incorporation, particularly of engulfment by the mother, with associated fears of loss of identity and personal fragmentation that may be inherent to any attempt to separate from her or to gain any real individuation.

The male homosexual identifies with his partner in the sexual act, thus gaining a transient sense of pseudomasculinity and masculine identity. Repeated homosexual experiences are constantly necessary to reinforce this sense of masculinity which is often felt to be necessary to avoid more serious decompensation. The understanding and realization that what is sought in the homosexual behavior is essentially masculine rather than feminine is a potent source of reassurance and motivation for change in the direction of heterosexual functioning. The need for seeking such homosexual reinforcement occurs under conditions of mounting anxiety, depression, and paranoid fears. The penis of the male partner is often found to be a substitute for the long-sought but denied breast of the "good" mother and allows the homosexual to compensate for the oral deprivation that may have been suffered at the hands of the real mother.

In the family of such patients there characteristically is found a devaluing, demeaning, and degrading of the father which may be quite open and conscious. This degrading often is done by the mother so that the patient identifies with the aggressive, castrating mother. Along with this there is hatred of the father, intensified by oedipal dynamics, which produces considerable guilt and impedes the patient's ability to feel that he is entitled to be a man. At the same time there is an intense, unsatisfied, and often unconscious yearning for the father's love and protection. The unavailability or unresponsiveness of the father to the boy child's need stands in the way of the child's capacity to gain a masculine identity through identification with the father. The homosexual act thereby becomes an expression of this continually frustrated yearning.

At the same time heterosexual interests or impulses may be continually suppressed or repressed because of unconscious guilt feelings toward the mother created by the intensity of unresolved incestuous and aggressive impulses. In many male homosexual patients, however, the intensity and extent of anger and rage against the mother is strongly repressed and remains unconscious and well defended. Often much therapeutic effort must be expended before a patient can understand the extent of his rage against and fear of women, particularly the mother. A critical part of the therapy of such patients is to overcome such fears, particularly the fear of retaliation by the mother for his attempts to move toward a more consistent and established masculine identity. The mother's hatred and contempt for men (often covering a deeper and pathological envy) must be put in perspective, together with the patient's fears that that hatred would be directed against himself.

Consequently, it can be readily appreciated that the treatment of homosexuality is not a treatment of the homosexual behavior itself, or even a direct attempt to alter the homosexual behavior. One can say apodictically that any direct attempts by the analyst to prohibit, change, judge, or modify the homosexual behavior will be antitherapeutic, will undermine the essential therapeutic alliance, and will more than likely, intensify the patient's sense of guilt and the need to act out destructively or to utilize the homosexual behavior in the interest of a displaced parental rebellion.

The therapist may at times be forced to take a position or be forced to set limits when behavioral acting-out becomes self-destructive. Homosexual behavior can become self-destructive, and it is often useful to draw the patient's attention to the consequences of his behavior. Such an intervention, however, is a recognizable parameter which interferes with the analytic work—however necessary it may be at times with some patients. Most patients are quite able to recognize and acknowledge the self-destructive aspects of their homosexual behavior. The point I am making, however, is that the homosexual symptom itself is not targeted as the element to be treated in the therapy. Rather, other important dimensions of the patient's personality functioning, his conflicts, his developmental impediments, and so forth are the more appropriate object of analytic concern and analytic effort.

Something similar can be said of the full gamut of sexual disorders which we have been considering. Analysis does not and—to my way of thinking should not—direct its efforts to the modification of such sexual disorders. Analysis of such manifestations, whether they be sexual impediments or perversions does not imply change or modification. Rather, it implies an attempt to understand and an attempt to grasp the inner meaning of such symptoms in the fuller context of the patient's life experience and developmental history. The therapeutic presumption of the analytic approach is that the resolution of underlying conflicts and the opportunity for the patient to rework central developmental issues allows for the better integration of the personality and for an inner growth and development making the impairment of sexual functioning and conflicting sexual expression no longer necessary. One can even push the argument to its extreme and maintain that the direct attempt to change sexually disordered or perverted behavior is essentially a judgment about the patient and an attempt to manipulate the patient, which is entirely foreign to the analytic approach and the analytic understanding of the human personality.

REFERENCES

BLUM, H. P. 1976. Masochism, the ego ideal and the psychology of women. *Journal of the American Psychoanalytic Association,* 24: 157–91.

BREUER, J., and FREUD, S. [1893–1895] Studies in hysteria. *Standard edition,* 2. London: Hogarth Press, 1955.

ERIKSON, E. H. 1963. *Childhood and society.* New York: Norton.

———. 1959. *Identity and the life cycle. Psychological Issues.* Monogr. 1. New York: International Universities Press.

FENICHEL, O. 1945. *The Psychoanalytic theory of neurosis.* New York: Norton.

FREUD, E. I., ed. 1964. *Letters of Sigmund Freud.* New York: McGraw-Hill.

FREUD, S. [1923] The ego and the id. *Standard edition,* 19: 1–66. London: Hogarth Press, 1961.

—— [1933] New introductory lectures on psychoanalysis. *Standard edition,* 22: 1–182. London: Hogarth Press, 1964.

—— [1887–1902] *The origins of psychoanalysis: letters, drafts and notes to Wilhelm Fliess.* New York: Basic Books, 1954.

—— [1905] Three essays on the theory of sexuality. *Standard edition,* 7: 123–245. London: Hogarth Press, 1953.

JONES, E. 1953. *The life and work of Sigmund Freud,* vol. 1. New York: Basic Books.

KERNBERG, O. F. 1974. Barriers to falling and remaining in love. *Journal of the American Psychoanalytic Association* 22: 486–511.

LEWIN, B. D. 1973. Addenda to the theory of oral erotism. In *Selected writings of Bertram D. Lewin,* ed. J. A. Arlow, pp. 129–46. *Psychoanalytic Quarterly.*

POLLOCK, G. H. 1968. The possible significance of childhood object loss in the Josef Breuer-Bertha Pappenheim (Anna O.)–Sigmund Freud relationship: I: Josef Breuer. *Journal of the American Psychoanalytic Association* 16: 711–39.

SCHAFER, R. 1974. Problems in Freud's psychology of women. *Journal of the American Psychoanalytic Association* 22: 459–85.

SOCARIDES, C. W. 1974. Homosexuality. In *American handbook of psychiatry III. Adult clinical psychiatry,* ed. S. Arieti, pp. 291–315. New York: Basic Books.

ZETZEL, E. R., and MEISSNER, W. W. 1973. *Basic concepts of psychoanalytic psychiatry.* New York: Basic Books.

SIXTEEN

The Behavioral Approach to Sexual Disorders

HERBERT FENSTERHEIM

JERRY S. KANTER

Most of the currently available methods for the psychological treatment of behavioral disturbances (including sexual disturbances) are one of two models, the psychoanalytic or the behavioral. The psychoanalytic methods range from the orthodox free-association and dream interpretation to the newer methods such as primal scream and bioenergetics. All have in common the "freeing" of unconscious forces and feelings and the consequent change in the behavioral disturbance. The behavioral model provides a completely opposite approach. It either denies, ignores, or minimizes unconscious forces and attempts to change the disturbed behavior directly. To understand fully the behavioral approach to the treatment of sexual disorders, the difference between these two models must be examined.

One clarification of the difference between the two models is provided by Wachtel's (1977) consideration of the unconscious processes. He argues that these processes may be viewed as either independent variables or as dependent variables.

When these unconscious processes are considered as independent variables, it is assumed that they are tendencies within the person, locked in the past and unresponsive to current events in the person's life. They exert a pressure unchanging in quality or intensity. Behavior is the dependent variable in that these unconscious forces influence feelings, perceptions, and actions. Changing the independent variables, the unconscious processes, thus is the only way to change the dependent variables, the behaviors. Insight, conflict resolution, working-through, abreaction, and other methods stemming from the Freudian paradigm are the only means of altering the behavioral disturbance, in a meaningful way.

But when considered as a dependent variable, it is the reverse: the person's action and life-style influence the unconscious processes. Although the unconscious processes originally may have caused the person to act in certain ways, to form a given life-style, it is these actions and their consequences that now perpetuate and maintain these very same unconscious forces. By deliberately changing specific behaviors (now considered the independent variable), not only may various symptoms be made to disappear, but also the (dependent) intrapsychic forces maintained by these behaviors may be changed. Following this line of reasoning, changing behaviors does lead to "deeper" change even in the Freudian sense of these words. The technology of behavior therapy is the most effective means for achieving these behavioral changes.

TARGET BEHAVIORS

From this perspective, the characteristics of the behavioral treatment of sexual disorders differentiating it from the Freudian-based treatments are clear. (1) The behavioral methods are concerned with the maintenance rather than with the origin of the sexual disorder. Origin and history become important only as they reveal what the person does to perpetuate the very things he wants to change. (2) The identification of very specific target behaviors (including such covert behaviors as fantasies, feelings, and desires) that maintain the disturbing condition is the core of the behavioral diagnostic and evaluative procedure. Deliberate and systematic efforts to modify these target behaviors are the core of the treatment. Measurement of change in target behaviors and of disturbed behaviors in the life situation also is an integral part of the therapeutic procedures. (3) Modification of the problem maintaining behaviors is a sufficient goal for treatment, and

314

exploration of intrapsychic dynamics is not necessary for successful and permanent change. As the target behaviors change (assuming the therapist has chosen the correct targets), there will be a feedback into the person's psychological organization that will bring about a "healthier" realignment of the intrapsychic forces.

Indeed, from a behavioral perspective, the consideration of intrapsychic dynamics may often be irrelevant, a waste of time and distract from an efficient course of treatment. This is especially true of those sexual maladaptive behaviors that, whatever their origin, have now achieved functional autonomy from the general psychological organization. These behaviors persist in the present as blind habits.

Premature ejaculation appears to be one such autonomous condition. As long as it is treated as a blind habit and as long as it is treated by the Seman's (1956) method of training, the counter habit of ejaculatory control, good results will be obtained in a large majority of the patients. It is true that some patients do have complications that interfere with treatment. High levels of anxiety (often but not always secondary to the premature ejaculation habit) may impede progress. Specific reinforcers (secondary gains), such as a feeling of vindictive satisfaction in frustrating the partner, may also impede progress. A general attitude of passivity on the part of the patient may make any new learning (including the learning of the Seman's counter-habit) slow and uncertain. However, once these complications have been dealt with, almost invariably the premature ejaculation must be treated as if it were an autonomous blind habit.

Many sexual variant behaviors also appear to have attained a functional autonomy from the general psychological organization. In our own experience this seems to be particularly true of transvestites, exhibitionists, and fetishists. Fensterheim (1974) has already noted that although the Freudian theory of the genesis of these disorders may (or may not) be completely correct, the traditional methods of treatment are remarkably unsuccessful. However,

when they are treated as simple autonomous habits through such behavioral methods as aversion (Rachman and Teasdale, 1969) or thought stoppage (Cautela, 1977; Fensterheim, 1974), a high rate of successful change is attained. Further, instead of the development of substitute symptoms, the removal of the variant behaviors often quickly leads to increased self-esteem and decreased anxiety and depression (cf., Morgenstern, Pearce, and Rees, 1965).

Although the irrelevance of intrapsychic considerations to the treatment of disturbed sexual behaviors that are now blind habits is especially clear, this same behavioral perspective may be applied to all sexual disturbances. Many behavioral therapists take any sexual problem, break it down into its component behaviors, and systematically change each behavior in turn. With this approach they have achieved some excellent results.

Barlow, Reynolds, and Agras (1973), for example, have used just such a behavior-by-behavior approach in the successful treatment of a transsexual young man, an area generally considered to be highly refractory to any kind of treatment. First the patient was trained in "masculine" motor and social behaviors. He was taught to sit, stand, and walk in a male-appropriate (as determined by community standards) role, to deepen his voice, and to converse appropriately. Next, using sexual fantasies combined with social reinforcers, he was trained to identify himself as male rather than as female. Finally, a classical conditioning method known as fading was used to establish heterosexual arousal, and aversive methods were used to decrease homosexual arousal. Through the sequential, successful modification of these component behaviors, the patient changed from a person desiring sex transformation surgery to one on the brink of leading a full heterosexual life. The power and limits of such a completely behavioral approach to complex sexual problems, what it can and cannot do, has not yet been fully tested, but it does have great promise.

In clinical practice, however, there are times when the exploration of intrapsychic processes seems necessary to identify the target behaviors. Even under these conditions, behavioral technology may be used to bring about the actual change. To illustrate this approach, we will describe the treatment of a twenty-four-year-old homosexual man who complained of compulsive masochistic sexual behavior. He was not attracted to lovers who would show him tenderness and consideration but rather to "bastards" who would mistreat and even physically abuse him. He received no pleasure from this and experienced only disgust with himself and a feeling of intense frustration. He rather quickly broke off each such relationship, only to be caught up again just as quickly in a similar one. A variety of behavioral methods was attempted unsuccessfully: desensitization to tenderness, assertive training, aversion to "bastards," and various behavioral assignments.

A series of sessions using quasi-free association methods revealed that he had experienced similar feelings of self-disgust and frustration as a child in relation to his father. The memories of specific incidents, however, were sparse and vague and the feelings were almost conjectural. A nonsystematic desensitization (Fensterheim, 1972) to the vague memories was attempted. The first result of this procedure was more vivid memories and a heightening of the disturbed reaction to them. Eventually the disturbed reactions diminished and then disappeared. At that point, without any further behavioral recommendations or treatment, the masochistic pattern was replaced by a series of more satisfactory relationships. An almost two-year follow-up (he returned to discuss an unrelated career problem) showed this adaptive change to persist.

These illustrations have stressed the importance of identifying target behaviors. It must also be noted that the behavior therapist, as a clinician, is well aware that the sexual problem may not be primary but may derive from other problems. Depression, poor inter-personal relations, a generally high level of anxiety, physiological malfunctions—all may influence sexual behavior.

In these instances, even though the person has a sexual problem, nonsexual target behaviors may have to be selected for change. Many times the modification of these nonsexual behaviors will relieve the sexual problem; other times, further and more sexually-oriented treatment is necessary to resolve the problem.

SEXUAL PROBLEMS AS PHOBIAS

Once the target behaviors are identified, a further step in the behavioral analysis is required: to formulate the psychological organization of that specific behavior. The disturbed sexual behavior may be a blind habit, a product of assertive difficulties, the result of incorrect cognitive patterns or inappropriate learning, or a straightforward phobic response. Each of these requires a different treatment strategy and a different therapeutic technology. The phobic organization is emerging as the most frequent elicitor of sexual disturbance. Masters and Johnson (1970), for example, cite the fear of sexual inadequacy as the greatest single cause of actual inadequacy. Hence, the remainder of this essay will focus on the examination and treatment of sexual phobias.

The word "phobia" is an unfortunate choice. It directs behavior therapists as well as other clinicians to limiting their search to areas of fear or perhaps of anxiety and tension. By so limiting himself or herself, the therapist often misses other clinically important reactions. Actually, phobic reactions may take many different forms.

Following Salter (1948), Fensterheim (1972) defines a phobia as any disturbed reaction of the autonomic nervous system conditioned to a specific stimulus or class of stimuli. Although usually experienced as fear, these reactions may also be experienced as anger, depression, withdrawal, or in many other ways. One patient described his phobic reaction as "a dull feeling of nothing." It is not the quality of the experience that makes it phobic but rather the automatic, persistent, and out-of-control response of the autonomic nervous system.

Once we realize that feelings other than fear or anxiety can constitute a phobic reaction, some otherwise difficult cases become relatively easy to treat. A man complained of intermittent sexual impotency. Periodically he was able to attain and maintain an erection but under those conditions, was usually disappointed in sex. At other times, he was unable either to attain or to maintain an erection. At these times he was aware of feelings of irritability and resentment, and often there were sharp words and fighting between the couple. Closer examination revealed that the more actively the wife behaved in the sexual situation, the more apt the husband was to be impotent. Although such a pattern is usually associated with a fear of premature ejaculation, this did not seem to be true in this instance. Rather, the husband interpreted the wife's level of activity as demands being placed on him, and he responded to these "demands" with resentment. Further examination showed a similar—although a much lower response—to demands in nonsexual situations.

The first treatment attempt was assertiveness training. His rights and his wife's rights were discussed with him. He practiced saying "no" to demands in life situations as well as in role-playing situations with the therapist. He also practiced responses to possible "put-downs" by his wife if he did not meet her expectations. These procedures yielded only a slight and transitory change in the problem area.

The problem was then formulated as a phobic reaction. His wife's activity was the stimulus that set off an automatic and persistent reaction experienced as resentment and irritability. The interpretation of her activity as a demand was, at this point, not an essential part of the reaction but rather an attempt to define this unreasoning, automatic response. Reduction of the phobia through a classic systematic desensitization with relaxation (Wolpe, 1973) made a rapid and apparently lasting change in the sexual problem.

If we consider the sexual phobic reaction to be any automatic, disturbed response of the autonomic nervous system to sexual stimuli, and if we use phobic reduction methods regardless of the subjective experience of this disturbed response, we can markedly increase the usefulness of this behavioral approach. However, the question must now be raised as to whether the phobic response should be limited solely to disturbed responses. Perhaps any out-of-control automatic response, even pleasurable sexual responses, may be considered to be phobic. Rachman (1966), for example, has demonstrated that an automatic sexual response can be conditioned to pictures of boots. If this were so, certain of the sexual variants may be treated by phobic reduction techniques. Three cases, two of them currently in treatment, are examples of this.

1. A nineteen-year-old woman had a sexual response to chewing gum.[1] Whenever she was in the presence of anyone chewing gum (the stimulus could be either visual or auditory), her sexual response was so strong that she would either have an orgasm then and there or she would have to rush to the nearest bathroom to masturbate. She herself traced this reaction to her early adolescence when she had trained her dog to masturbate her by licking her clitoris. The sexual response, however, was limited to the middle range of the phobic stimuli. At a lower level, pictures of a chewing gum pack would set off slight but definite anxiety. At higher levels, the sight of a dog or cat licking itself would set off panic.

This sexual response responded to a phobic reduction approach. Actually, systematic desensitization both to imagined situations and to the therapist chewing gum in her presence had no effect. She did respond to in-vivo-flooding with response prevention (Marks). She exposed herself to situations in which people were chewing gum and remained in that situation while actively inhibiting the sexual response and practicing deliberate muscle relaxation. In a telephone contact six months after termination of treatment, the patient stated that despite repeated exposure to chewing gum situations, only once was there any sign of sexual response.

2. A twenty-eight-year-old man was a fetishistic transvestite. At age thirteen he became attracted to his mother's lingerie, particularly

[1] This patient was concurrently under treatment for other psychological problems with a different therapist.

to the tactile sensations, and he would masturbate with the lingerie as a stimulus. At age nineteen he performed his first cross-dressing with the intent of heightening the tactile sensations. Over time he became more enamored of the visual impact of his appearance, although his greatest thrill was when walking in the street cross-dressed, someone would brush against his clothing. He would always cross-dress alone, never in the presence of his girlfriend with whom there was a normal pattern of heterosexual behavior.

He was treated with phobic reduction methods. A desensitization tape was prepared for him to play at home. With this tape, he first relaxed, then he imagined a transvestite or fetishistic scene. Upon the first feelings of any sexual arousal, he would then relax again. (Detailed instructions for construction of such a tape are given in Fensterheim and Baer, 1977, pp. 308–311.) The tape has eight repetitions of such scenes, takes about twenty minutes to run, and he plays it once a day. A somewhat similar procedure is followed during his office visits.

At the present time he reports a complete cessation of all transvestite thoughts or feelings. This in itself is not conclusive, for on a number of occasions these have spontaneously disappeared for periods of up to two-and-a-half months. This time, however, he reports that there is a different feeling; he has a feeling of being in control. Further follow-up is of course necessary to determine if the phobic reduction method really did work.

3. This patient was a twenty-six-year-old man with a history of sexual exhibitionism. Since age fourteen he has had exhibitionist urges a minimum of three times a week (by his report). He has acted them out on a number of occasions, usually using girls in the six-to-eight year range as targets. On several occasions he moved into actual pedophilic behavior by having the child stroke his penis. He had been arrested twice and is currently on probation. Several years of traditional treatment had no effect on this behavior. He too has a girlfriend and has an apparently normal pattern of heterosexual behavior with her.

The urges tended to come about under similar circumstances, some in actuality, some imagined. He would be bored or would have nothing special to do. There would be an opportunity or a possible opportunity for contact with suitable girls. In the office, when he imagined being in such situations, he would experience a sexual arousal which, by his subjective estimate, went up to a sixty-percent level.

The phobic reduction method used was aversion relief desensitization (Wolpe, 1973). He was given a moderately uncomfortable electric shock to the forearm. When the shock ceased, he imagined being in the excitement-arousing situation. With repetition of this procedure, the intensity of the sexual reaction decreased. After five to fifteen repetitions for each imagined situation, there was no feeling of sexual arousal at all. In other words, pairing an image of the excitement eliciting situation with relief from shock brought about exactly the same kinds of reduction in sexual feeling as we find when we use aversion relief desensitization with fear-eliciting situations and automatic fear reactions.

This conditioning was carried over to the life situation. The patient reported that for the first time in twelve years (his words), he has been completely free of exhibitionistic impulses for as long as one week. At this writing he has had no such urges for six weeks but is being monitored on a regular basis.

In each of these cited cases the variant behavior does indeed appear to be a true phobia. This does not mean that all sexual variant behavior falls into the phobic category. As always, a careful evaluation and formulation is necessary.

THE CONTENT OF THE PHOBIAS

The fear of dysfunction does indeed appear to be the most common phobic reaction in sexual dysfunction. Although it is easily identified, there often are many subtleties involved.

As sex usually involves two people, these fears occur within a social context. Sometimes a critical variable is not the patient's fear of dysfunction but the partner's fear of the patient's dysfunction. One man, with sexual impotence, stated that the fear of dysfunction did not begin to appear until well after the impotence was established. Even at the time of consultation, that fear was not particularly strong. Further exploration revealed that his mate had had a series of experiences with sexually impotent men, that she was phobic to the thought that her current lover would become impotent, that because of this fear she was extremely anxious during sex. It was her anxiety, or rather his reaction to her anxiety, that brought about the dysfunction. Reduction of her fears relieved his impotence without any direct treatment of the man.

Sometimes the fear of dysfunction is combined with an assertive problem. The patient is usually an obsessive male who has great difficulty in saying "no" to a woman in a close relationship. This is especially true in the sexual area. Resentment builds up, and he begins to wish that he were impotent, as a means of gaining freedom. This wish is rapidly converted into a fear and then into an obsessive thought. Dysfunction follows. We have had only fair success in treating patients with this condition, several of whom also failed in couple sex therapy.

Finally, although not inclusive, is the fear of dysfunction as a mask for other fears. The core fear may be the partner's reaction rather than the dysfunction itself, that the partner may become angry, frustrated, contemptuous, rejecting or even more common with women, pitying. In these conditions, even when reduction of the fear of the dysfunction is successful, there is a tendency for the dysfunction to return. Treatment cannot be considered complete until the fear of the partner's reaction is removed.

Although the fear of dysfunction is the most common phobic reaction, many others do exist. Any part of the sex act or situation may become a phobic stimulus. Among phobic stimuli we have seen are parts of the partner's body (especially the genitals), physiological sensations as the person approaches climax such as change in breathing (in several patients with a history of childhood asthma) or rapid heartbeat, fear of performing specific sexual acts (which often include both the fear of being "perverted" and the so-called masturbation guilt), and the fear of not enjoying specific sexual acts (especially among young adults who are afraid of being "inhibited" or "uptight").

Many of these fears are very subtle, and part of the art of behavior therapy is to identify them. One young woman could not have a climax in the presence of another person. The core fear turned out to be the fear of being ugly. She believed that during climax her face became contorted and that even in total darkness her partner might see it. One man had a history of losing all sexual interest in any long-term relationship. After a long investigation the problem turned out to be the fear of boredom. Reduction of this fear appeared to have changed the problem pattern.

Communication between the couple is especially important to attain a good sexual relationship. Hence, special note must be taken of those fears which inhibit such communication. However, regardless of what the specific fears are, usually the most effective method for reducing them is through the assertive training approaches rather than through phobic reduction methods.

Nonsexual phobic stimuli may also disrupt sexual functioning. Fear of darkness is but one example of the many that can be cited. As stated before, part of the art of behavior therapy is the identification of such specific phobias.

THE LAW OF PARSIMONY

The core of the behavioral evaluation is the identification of specific target behaviors. In the sexual area the target behaviors are usually phobias. To those who have not actually seen the dramatic changes in complex sexual problems that may be brought about through the reduction of a simple phobia, such an approach may seem to be simplistic. In actuality, it would be more correct to designate this approach as parsimonious.

The Law of Parsimony is central to scientific thinking. Essentially this law states that "of alternative explanations for a given phenomenon, choose the simplest, that requiring the fewest assumptions, provided it meets the facts adequately" (Schneirla, 1972, p. 34). A corrolary to this law, as it may be applied to the therapeutic formulation, is never to use a complex, higher-level psychological pattern as the core of the formation, when an equally adequate formulation is available using simpler, lower-level behaviors. If the choice is between a simple conditioned response to a specific stimulus and a complex dynamic formulation involving internal conflict and assumptions of repression, instinctual drives, and unconscious fantasies, the logic of science compels us to accept the former—provided it meets the facts adequately.

In sexual treatment, there are several major reasons why therapists do not arrive at the most parsimonious treatment formulation, namely:

1. The confusion between genesis and maintenance. The psychological constellation that produced the sexual symptoms may not be involved in the maintenance of these symptoms. As already noted, the symptom pattern may achieve functional autonomy from the forces that caused it. As also previously noted, the problem behaviors may now be maintaining the original constellation. To arrive at the most parsimonious formulation, the therapist must focus on the psychological variables keeping the problem behavior active in the present, rather than on the variables originally causing it.

2. The failure to distinguish between teleological and automatic behaviors. Symptomatic behaviors often have certain consequences. A sexual dysfunction may result in humiliating the person or frustrating the partner. All too frequently this is interpreted in teleological terms. The purpose of the symptom is to achieve this self-humiliation or frustration of the partner. It is completely true that people are capable of behaving in such a purposive manner. People

also are capable of acquiring automatic conditioned responses to specific stimuli or acquiring certain modes of behavior because of the impact of external contingencies of reinforcement. In those instances self-humiliation or partner frustration may be a by-product rather than a goal of the symptom. The Law of Parsimony requires that we choose the simpler, conditioning explanation over the purposive one, unless compelling reasons exist to do otherwise.

3. The failure to distinguish between precipitating and derivative disturbances. Usually patients with sexual problems come in surrounded by an aura of anxiety, depression, low self-esteem, marital or inter-personal problems, and other disturbances. There is a strong temptation to see the sexual problem as arising out of this disturbed context, as sometimes it does. However, many times these disturbances derive from the sexual malfunction, and to make them part of the therapeutic formulation is to complicate that formulation unnecessarily. Unless there are compelling reasons, it is usually most parsimonious to consider such disturbances as deriving from the symptom rather than as causing it.

A very common error along these lines is made with people with sexual variant behavior. Very common, particularly among fetishists and transvestites, are the derived feelings of "being a monster" or of being found out by other people and being contemptuously rejected. Many times these derived reactions are considered to be precipitating stimuli leading to the variant behavior. Hence, unnecessarily complicated formulations are set forth. Unless there is specific reason to believe otherwise, it is most parsimonious to exclude these reactions from the formulation.

4. The failure to discern when problems are independent of each other. When a person has several problems, the tendency all too often is to see them as being inter-related. Most often they are seen as covarying from a common root cause. Should a woman have a dysfunction of sexual arousal and a fear of authority, both problems are likely to be seen as stemming from an oedipal conflict regarding father. This

often leads to an unnecessarily complex therapeutic formulation and a cumbersome treatment strategy. The most parsimonious formulation may see them as two simple, independent fears: the fear of not being aroused and the separate fear of authority. This conception requires the fewest assumptions. Unless there is specific and definite evidence to show that problems are inter-related, they should be considered to be independent of each other.

Therefore, formulating a sexual problem, even a complex one, in terms of one or several simple phobic reactions is not simplistic. Rather, it is fully scientific in its utilization of the most parsimonious explanation of the problem. Also, it often leads to the most effective course of therapeutic action.

PHOBIC REDUCTION TECHNOLOGY

Having identified the target phobic reactions, the therapeutic task now centers on organized attempts to reduce these reactions. As the phobia disappears, we expect normal sexual behavior (desire, arousal, and orgasm) spontaneously to emerge. There are a number of methods available for this purpose.

The most commonly used methods for the reduction of sexual phobias stem from the desensitization paradigm (Salter, 1949; Wolpe, 1973). This method is a series of controlled exposures to the phobic stimuli and attempts to change the phobic reaction either by reducing its intensity or by increasing the self-control behaviors. With each such exposure, the power of the phobic reaction diminishes until it completely disappears.

Although the efficacy of this procedure has been well demonstrated experimentally and clinically, the theory underlying it is not so clear. It has been explained in terms of counter-conditioning, self-control concepts, extinction, cognitive variables, and in still other terms. The issue is far from resolved. Indeed, Goldfried and Davison (1976) opine that in this area greater confusion exists today than it did ten

years ago. Rather than discussing this, we will present the methods specifically involved.

In its most classical form, systematic desensitization has certain characteristics:

1. The disturbing situation must be approached in a gradual, step-by-step manner. The aim is to keep the elicited disturbance at each step sufficiently low so that the person may learn to counter it. The series of graded situations used in this approach is called a "hierarchy." The situations used may be imagined, may be simulated or may be actual life situations.

2. A counter-anxiety behavior must be applied at each step of the hierarchy. Although deliberate muscle relaxation is probably the most widely used behavior for this purpose, many others are available. Brady (1966) has used medication to counter the tension. Bass (1974) has used the feeling of sexual excitement to counter the anxiety. The aversion relief method has already been mentioned. Wolpe (1973) states that any response-inhibiting anxiety, including assertive responses, can be used in desensitization.

The patient is first presented with the lowest (least anxiety-provoking) item of the hierarchy. When he or she experiences any disturbance, the item is removed and the counter-anxiety element (e.g., relaxation) is introduced. The item is repeated until it no longer elicits any disturbance whatever. At this point, the next item of the hierarchy is introduced.

The self-control method of desensitization (Goldfried, 1971) also utilizes hierarchies and relaxation. Here relaxation is thought of as a coping technique, as a self-control of the physiological reactions of anxiety (Goldfried and Merbaum, 1973). Instead of removing the hierarchy item when an anxiety response is elicited, the person is kept in the situation and is encouraged to cope until the anxiety diminishes.

We have tried both the classical and the self-control methods with the in-vivo-desensitization treatment of vaginismus. Here the hierarchy consists of objects of various sizes to be placed in the vagina. In the classical method, the patient removes the object at the first indication of discomfort and then relaxes. With the self-control method, the patient allows the object to remain while learning to cope with the anxiety. The number of patients involved was far too low to indicate whether one method was superior to the other. However, when both procedures were presented, several of the patients had definite preferences for one or the other.

Desensitization using imagined stimuli has the advantages of convenience, flexibility, and greater control of the stimuli. The stimulus scenes used in imagery desensitization may be very creative, and professional literature abounds with examples. A rather typical hierarchy that we have found useful is the one reported by Lazarus (1968) for the group desensitization of women with the common complaint of frigidity. The items he used were: embracing, kissing, being fondled, undressing, foreplay in the nude, awareness of the husband's erection, intromission, and changing positions during coitus.

Fensterheim has used the classical desensitization (in imagery, with relaxation) for the treatment of ejaculatory incompetence. All of the men so treated were able to ejaculate in the presence of a woman but were unable to do so during intercourse.

The specific scenes used in the hierarchy were tailored to each individual, but all centered on these areas:

a. A series of preintercourse scenes in which the patient wondered whether or not he would be able to ejaculate.

b. A series of scenes depicting longer and longer periods of intercourse in which he was unable to ejaculate.

c. A series of postcoital scenes in which the patient dwelt on the fact that he had been unable to ejaculate and in which his partner made various derogatory comments about it.

This method succeeded in bringing on ejaculatory competence about as often as it failed to do so. However, with several of the failures there was a considerable decrease in the anxiety over the problem. With one such failure, ejaculatory competence was attained in about six months following cessation of treatment. With a second, the anxiety and frustration returned in full force in a short time. It must also be noted that only seven patients were involved, over a period of six years. Hence, these findings are presented merely as an illustration of what may be attempted in a clinical practice.

At times, in vivo and imagery desensitization may be combined or used in tandem. An example of the hierarchies that may be used in such a combination is the case of a twenty-eight-year-old woman with a six-year unconsummated marriage and a fear of penetration.[2] Her history included an episode of actual fainting when seeing female anatomy in a sex-education film shown in high school and an inability to have a gynecological examination (in her two attempts, she literaly jumped off the examining table). When she attempted to put her finger in her vagina, she experienced feelings of nausea and faintness. Imagery desensitization with deliberate relaxation used the following hierarchy (in ascending order of anxiety):

1. Masturbating by rubbing against a pillow (her usual method)
2. Looking at a medical book diagram of female anatomy
3. Looking at her own genitals in a mirror
4. Putting her finger in her vagina
5. Husband putting his finger in her vagina
6. About to be examined by a gynecologist
7. Being examined by a gynecologist
8. Husband inserting his penis into her vagina

The in-vivo-hierarchy contained the following items (in ascending order of anxiety):

1. Masturbating against pillow followed by relaxation
2. Looking at her genitals in a mirror
   a. Just looking
   b. Spreading labia

[2] This patient had been treated by Dr. Paul Menitoff.

c. Looking at her finger placed on the mons
d. Looking at her finger slightly inside vagina
3. Guiding husband's finger into vagina
4. Husband inserting finger without guidance
5. Same as steps 3 and 4 with two fingers
6. Inserting small vibrator into vagina
7. Guiding husband as he inserts vibrator
8. Husband inserting vibrator without guidance
9. Husband on back. She mounts and inserts his penis
   a. Both remain motionless
   b. She moves
   c. Both move

The imagery desensitization was carried out during office visits, and the in-vivo-desensitization was done at home. The latter was discussed during office visits with both husband and wife present. In all, it took fifteen visits over a period of four months for a successful treatment outcome.

The desensitization paradigm can be introduced into a variety of contexts in which other forces may also be operating. Sexual scenarios provide one such context which we have found to be especially useful with people who have only a mild degree of anxiety.

Sexual scenarios, as the term implies, are a sexual encounter planned as if it were a drama improvisation. Each partner acts out a role, and there is at least a vague outline of a plot. The scenario may be based on famous lovers of history or of the theater, on the fantasies of one of the partners, or on just a story acceptable to both. The attempts to remain within the role provide the elements to counter the phobia. We have found that couples who are able to do this often report rapid changes.

With a slight modification, the sexual scenario may be modified into a method called emotive imagery (Lazarus and Abramovitz, 1962). This method first provides a pleasant or an exciting context and then introduces the phobic stimulus (e.g., part of body or specific sexual act) for longer and longer periods of time. After each introduction, the couple immediately return to the exciting part of the scenario role-playing. Fensterheim and Baer (1977, p. 214)

describe the use of such a scenario in removing a woman's fear of performing oral sex.

SUMMARY

This discussion argued that phobic reactions are the most frequent cause of sexual disorders. Therefore, the focus was on the identification and treatment of these phobic reactions. It is important to recognize that we have made no attempt to cover all the behavioral methods available for reducing sexual phobias.

Even more important, we do not hold that all sexual disorders have a phobic core. Should the disorder stem from a blind habit, an irrational cognition, an assertive problem, or some other psychological process, other behavioral modes of intervention must be used.

REFERENCES

BARLOW, D. H.; REYNOLDS, J.; and AGRAS, W. S. 1973. Gender identity changes in a transsexual. *Arch. Gen. Psychiat.* 25.

BASS, B. A. 1974. Sexual arousal as an anxiety inhibitor. *J. Behav. Ther. Exper. Psychiat.* 5: 151–52.

BRADY, J. P. 1966. Brevital-relaxation treatment of frigidity. *Behav. Res. Ther.* 4: 71–77.

CAUTELA, J. R. and WISOCKI, P. A. 1977. The thought stopping procedure: description, application, and learning theory interpretations. The Psychological Record. 2: 255–64.

FENSTERHEIM, H. 1974. Behavior therapy of the sexual variations. *J. Sex Marit. Ther.* 1: 16–28.

———. 1972. The initial interview. In *Clinical behavior therapy*, ed. A. A. Lazarus. New York: Brunner/Mazel.

FENSTERHEIM, H., and BAER, J. 1977. *Stop running scared!* New York: Rawson.

GOLDFRIED, M. R. 1971. Systematic desensitization as training in self-control. *J. Consult. Clin. Psychol.* 37: 228–34.

————, and DAVISON, G. C. 1976. *Clinical behavior therapy*. New York: Holt, Rinehart & Winston.

————, and MERBAUM, M. 1973. *Behavior change through self-control*. New York: Holt, Rinehart & Winston.

LAZARUS, A. A. 1968. Behavior therapy in groups. In *Basic approaches to group psychotherapy and group counseling*, ed. G. M. Gazda. Springfield, Ill., Thomas.

————, and ABRAMOVITZ, A. 1962. The use of "emotive imagery" in the treatment of children's phobias. *J. Ment. Sci.* 108: 91.

MARKS, I. 1975. Behavioral treatments of phobic and obsessive-compulsive disorders: a critical appraisal. In *Progress in Behavior Modification*, vol. 1, ed. M. Hersen, R. M. Eisler, and P. M. Miller. New York: Academic Press.

MASTERS, W. H., and JOHNSON, V. E. 1970. *Human sexual inadequacy*. Boston: Little, Brown.

MORGENSTERN, F.; PEARCE, J., and REES, W. L.

1965. Predicting the outcome of behavior therapy by psychological tests. *Behav. Res. Ther.* 2: 191–200.

RACHMAN, S. 1966. Sexual fetishism: an experimental analogue. *Psychol. Rec.* 16: 293–95.

————, and TEASDALE, J. 1969. *Aversion therapy and behavior disorders: an analysis*. Coral Gables, Fla.: University of Miami Press.

SALTER, A. 1949. *Conditioned reflex therapy*. New York: Farrar, Straus.

SCHNEIRLA, T. C. 1962. Psychology, comparative. *Encyclopedia Britannica*. Reprinted in *Selected Writings of T. C. Schneirla*, ed. L. R. Aronson, E. Tobach, J. S. Rosenblatt, and D. S. Lehrman. San Francisco: W. H. Freeman.

SEMANS, J. H. 1956. Premature ejaculation, a new approach. *South. Med. J.* 49: 353.

WACHTEL, P. L. 1977. *Psychoanalysis and behavior therapy*. New York: Basic Books.

WOLPE, J. 1973. *The practice of behavior therapy*, 2d ed. Elmsford, N.Y.: Pergamon.

SEVENTEEN

A Brief Descripton of the Masters and Johnson Treatment of Sexual Dysfunction

RAYMOND W. WAGGONER

In 1899 Dr. Denslow Lewis read a paper at a meeting of the American Medical Association, entitled "The Gynecologic Consideration of the Sexual Act," at the invitation of the Program Committee. The *Journal of the American Medical Association* refused to publish it because of its "sexual content." Obviously, it was a subject whose time had not yet come. Like Sigmund Freud, Dr. Lewis was criticized for being forthright in his views about sex.

As a result of Freud's work and later that of Kinsey, the subject of sex gradually came out of the closet and became the subject of both psychological and physiological study. In the mid-1950s Dr. William Masters decided to undertake an extensive study of the physiology of sexual function. He was joined in this work by Mrs. Virginia Johnson. Their monumental research project led to the publication of the book, *Human Sexual Response,* which still is the basic text of sexual physiology, and to the development of the successful short-term treatment of sexual dysfunction. Their therapeutic program is described in detail in their book, *Human Sexual Inadequacy,* and the importance of psychological and emotional factors are discussed in their book, *The Pleasure Bond.* As a result of their work and publications, many sex therapy clinics have been established throughout the country. Some of these clinics are staffed by those who are well trained but unfortunately, many of them are staffed by individuals who have no training at all or very insignificant amounts of training, and these clinics may do harm to their patients.

Sexual dysfunction is much more common than is generally recognized, and Masters suggests that at least fifty percent of marriages have experienced sexual difficulty of some sort. Couples with sexual difficulty are very anxious to have treatment and unfortunately, often go to a cozener clinic from which they receive no benefit or may be made worse. As a result, attempts are being made to develop some kind of control for the establishment of sexual therapy programs.

In 1976 a meeting was held at the Masters and Johnson Institute in St. Louis, on the ethics of sexual therapy and research. The success of this meeting led to the development of a congress on ethics which was held in St. Louis in January, 1978. A book incorporating a report of the first meeting has been published by Little, Brown & Co. and the report of the congress will be published later.

Sex therapists should have a basic knowledge of sexual physiology, as well as an awareness of the psychological factors which may be involved. Unless the sex therapist is well trained in these aspects of the problem, it is likely that he or she will do more harm than good.

TREATMENT TEAM

There are arguments for and against a male-female therapeutic team as recommended by Masters and Johnson. The therapist of one sex is best able to describe the reaction patterns of that sex to the patient of the opposite sex. This is a valuable means of improving communication between them. Also, during the therapy session one therapist can take the lead in therapy, while the other watches for verbal and body cues which may be important in the program but might be overlooked by a single therapist. Such cues may be particularly significant and can be used during the therapeutic interview. In the treatment of sexual dysfunction, a transference relationship can be very quickly established and since it is commonly a short period of treatment, there is not time to resolve such a relationship and therefore it should be avoided. On the other hand, the male-female treatment team is more expensive.

When the sexual dysfunction develops as a

symptom of a basic neurotic problem or of a psychotherapeutically treatable psychosis, then a significant period of traditional psychotherapy should be undertaken while at the same time, adequate consideration of the sexual aspect of the patient's problem is necessary. As an aside, it should be noted that oftentimes patients come to the Masters and Johnson Institute after years of psychotherapy, and yet become sexually functional after only ten to twelve days of therapy.

THERAPEUTIC APPROACH

It is always wise to obtain a complete and detailed sexual and background history. At the Masters and Johnson Institute, two histories are taken from each member of the couple: one each by both of the therapists, first, male-male, female-female; then male-female, female-male, with an opportunity for the therapists to discuss the first history with each other before the second one is taken. This gives an opportunity for obtaining additional information by exploring any lead which may have been developed in the first history session.

The next day the therapists meet with the couple to go over the histories and to clarify any misunderstandings which may have occurred. This is described as the "round table." Should any material in the individual history reveal something that the patient does not want the partner to know, then this is red-lined and not disclosed. However, if it seems essential to the therapeutic process for this to be discussed with the other partner, then this is explained to the person concerned, but even then is not disclosed if the individual insists on it even after its importance is explained.

It is believed at the Masters and Johnson Institute that no sexually dysfunctional relationship can exist with an uninvolved partner, even though the presenting complaint is primarily by one partner, such as impotence in the male or a nonorgasmic female. As Masters and Johnson have written, "There is no such thing as an un-involved partner in any marriage in which there is some form of sexual inadequacy" (p. 2 HSI).

Both primary and secondary orgasmic dysfunction, vaginismus in the female, and impotence, premature ejaculation, and ejaculatory incompetence in the male are usually successfully treated by the method developed by Masters and Johnson. The basic approach is that of the history and round-table routine. Each type of dysfunction requires some variation in approach. At the round table after clarification of the history, the couple is instructed to carry out what Masters and Johnson describe as the "sensate focus." In effect, each partner is instructed in ways of caressing the other in order to give the greatest degree of pleasure without involving the breasts or genitals. This is done first by one, then the other partner. The following day these areas may be included in the caressing, but without any attempt to perform sexually, thus obviating performance anxiety. It is emphasized that this should be a sensual, not a sexual activity. Although no time limit is given, it is suggested that the exercise should last for twenty to thirty minutes. The reaction of the couple to this experience is discussed with them, since it is usual in most instances that this type of activity would lead to sexual performance. It does, however, lead to a significant degree of sexual stimulation without performance anxiety, which is an important factor in causing sexual dysfunction. The fear of inability to perform may be a very important factor in causing whatever type of dysfunction exists. The sensate-focus activity is, of course, undertaken with both partners in the nude and in comfortable and pleasant surroundings.

Following the basic approach described above, attention in therapy is directed to the type of dysfunction involved. Thus, the treatment of impotence requires a different approach from that of premature ejaculation, even though such symptoms are quite likely to be closely inter-related. Different procedures are also used in the treatment of the nonorgasmic female or the female with vaginismus. In treating premature ejaculation it is generally conceded that the squeeze technique is the best approach.

This was first described by Semans and more specifically developed by Masters and Johnson. In this approach the female stimulates the male to erection and when the male is aware that ejaculation is about to occur, she is instructed to squeeze the phallus with the first two fingers, one above and one below the corona on the anterior surface of the penis, with the thumb on the frenulum. Considerable pressure can be applied without causing pain when the penis is erect, and if the squeeze is undertaken soon enough it invariably prevents ejaculation. This can be repeated a number of times at each session and after satisfactory reaction has been developed, it should be kept in mind that this procedure should be repeated occasionally. Dr. Kaplan and others recommend this even after the premature ejaculation is under control.

Impotence is often associated with latent homosexual drives, perhaps caused by environmental factors such as early sexual trauma, an adolescent homosexual experience, or some unfortunate sexual failure with a prostitute. Such factors, of course, should always be taken into consideration and discussed in detail with the patient. The support of the partner is important in this situation.

Sexual dysfunction in the female usually is exhibited by an individual either who has never had an orgasm or who has had orgasms only occasionally by some form of noncoital activity. Such problems are primarily psychological and usually the result of early environmental or situational factors. They also may be responsible for the development of vaginismus and dyspareunia, although such symptoms commonly are associated with some type of pelvic pathology. Since many of these problems are psychological, a psychological understanding and approach is basic to dealing with the difficulty.

It is vitally important for the couple to develop both a good verbal and nonverbal communication, since lack of communication is often a major reason for sexual dysfunction. The sensate-focus program is one way of helping to develop good communication.

It is important to emphasize that sexual function is as natural as most other body functions and should not be the source of feelings of guilt or shame, although this is a common reaction in some patients, based on their early life experience. The therapist who has a good knowledge of sexual physiology and psychology is in a position to give adequate instruction in the various phases of sexual function, which is very important as far as the patients are concerned.

In the final analysis, it is vitally important for both partners to understand the psychological factors which so often cause most instances of sexual dysfunction. The need for mutual cooperation must be stressed, with evidence of love and compassion on the part of both husband and wife.

REFERENCES

The Gynecologic Consideration of the Sexual Act Denslow Lewis, M.D. Chicago, 1900. Reprinted by Marc Hollender M.D. M & S Press 1970.

KAPLAN, H. S. 1974. *The new sex therapy.* New York: Brunner/Mazel.

MASTERS, W. H., and JOHNSON, V. E., 1970. *Human sexual inadequacy.* Boston: Little, Brown.

———. 1966. *Human sexual response.* Boston: Little, Brown.

———. 1975. *The pleasure bond.* Boston: Little, Brown.

EIGHTEEN

Helen Singer Kaplan's Treatment Method: an Integrated Approach

MILDRED HOPE WITKIN

HELEN SINGER KAPLAN

OVERVIEW

The rapid treatment of sexual dysfunctions as formulated by Helen Singer Kaplan is psychodynamic and behavioral, and integrates structured sexual experiences into conjoint therapeutic sessions (Kaplan, 1974). Kaplan's treatment method combines behavioral sexual tasks designed specifically for each couple, tailored both to the sexual dysfunction of the individual and the interpersonal functioning of the dyad, with psychodynamic insights and dyadic approaches, including dream interpretations, and gestalt and transactional techniques. Two ways in which the Kaplan method differs from other techniques is that the treatment milieux need not be a sequestered locale but could include performance of the patients in the privacy of their own home, and that a single therapist can be as effective as cotherapists of opposite sexes.

Kaplan states that "all therapeutic maneuvers are mainly at the service of the primary objective of sex therapy: *the relief of the sexual symptoms*" (italics in the original) . . . In the course of sex therapy intrapsychic and transactional conflicts are almost invariably dealt with to some extent" (Kaplan, 1974, p. 187). The latter may be true in a limited sense in other schools of sex therapy; in Kaplan's method it is much more deliberate and prominent. The resistances that arise in response to the structured sexual tasks often must be treated by other (nonsexual) modalities to allow the sexual aspects of the therapy to proceed. On the other hand, if more profound resistances are evoked, their resolution may have a more profoundly therapeutic effect.

In summary, the Kaplan method may be seen as a "task-centered form of crises intervention which presents an opportunity for rapid conflict resolution. Toward this end the various sexual tasks are employed, as well as the methods of insight therapy, supportive therapy, marital therapy, and other psychiatric techniques as indicated" (Kaplan, 1974, p. 199).

THEORETICAL CONTEXT

In Kaplan's view, sex therapy is considered a form of psychotherapy, conducted in an experiential/psychodynamic conceptual framework. It considers superficial and profound causes, and immediate and remote determinants. Treatment focuses on the immediate and the superficial, but the differences among patients demand skill in confronting profound and remote etiology.

Kaplan assumes that sexual dysfunctions have many causes and calls for an eclectic, equally multi-faceted approach. Depending upon whether the primary pathology is intrapsychic or interpersonal, the treatment will emphasize individual or dyadic interventions. The nature of the interventions themselves—the "schools" of psychotherapy used—will depend on the nature of the symptoms as well as on the skills and preferences of the therapist. This, of course, is true in any psychotherapeutic relationship. In practice, both intrapsychic and interpersonal factors are encountered in almost all cases.

Kaplan's treatment does not ignore the total system, the ecology in which the patients' functioning is integrated. No person or couple can escape the effects of a destructive family system; these ecological considerations are confronted and explored when they arise.

Theoretical flexibility extends not only to the treatment offered but also to the definition of the "patient." Although it is traditional in sex therapy to define the patient as a couple, Kaplan feels this is not always appropriate, nor is it necessarily the best procedure. In particular, one type of sexual dysfunction has been addressed by the Kaplan method with only a single person without a partner as the "patient";

lack of orgasm in the female. Since the treatment of the anorgastic woman with or without a partner has the same initial goal—the attainment of orgasm through self-stimulation—the participation of a male is not essential. The step toward having orgasms with a partner and eventually during coitus may or may not require further clinical therapy with a male; whether to seek such therapy is the choice of the individual woman.

In addition to the patient without a partner, it is occasionally considered appropriate to see one member of a dyad alone for a number of sessions. A common situation is for the couple to have bilateral dysfunctions, for example, premature ejaculation or secondary impotence in the male and lack of desire or lack of orgasm in the female. In those cases, a typical treatment schedule would begin by seeing the couple together for one or two sessions, and then seeing the woman alone until she is able to have orgasms by herself through self-stimulation. At that point, work with both partners resumes until the couple has full sexual functioning. Individual sessions might also be indicated when one partner has a special sexual "secret" whose revelation to the other partner might have a deleterious effect on the overall relationship (Kaplan, 1974).

TREATMENT PROCESS

Treatment begins with a thorough evaluation, which has two purposes: to determine whether the patients are suitable candidates for sex therapy and to formulate the erotic sexual tasks appropriate to that couple. The evaluation interview includes a medical and psychiatric history of the patients and a thorough sexual history. The initial aim of the therapist is to obtain as clear a picture as possible of the "target" sexual dysfunction or dysfunctions and of the current sexual relationship of the couple. The patients are asked to describe their latest sexual experience together "as a video picture"; only when the therapist understands both the symptom and the context in which it appears will the

next area be explored. An attempt is made to formulate both the immediate and the remote causes of the patient's problem. To this end the experiential description of the sexual interaction, the "video picture," is supplemented with a description of the history of the dysfunction, including the patient's childhood experiences. The relationships among parents and siblings are explored, and the sexual functioning of each partner in childhood, adolescence, and premarital adulthood is ascertained. The etiology is completed with a discussion of the couple's marital history.

During the initial evaluation interview, if profound intrapsychic or interpersonal difficulties are revealed which might preclude successful sexual therapy, the patients are referred to the appropriate individual or to conjoint therapy and are not accepted at that time for sex therapy. They are, however, encouraged to return, should they still need sex therapy after the resolution of their other conflicts. Contraindications to sex therapy lie in the intrapsychic and interpersonal domains. According to Kaplan, "Sex therapy is indicated only if . . . earlier problems are not insuperable nor screens for psychotic processes. With severely disturbed individuals or couples, sex therapy is usually not indicated" (1975, p. 21). Contraindications include significant medical illness, use of narcotics, or alcoholism, and major active psychopathologies ("florid schizoid reactions, blatant paranoia, and significant depression in either partner"), (p. 21). However, if these are remedied, successful treatment is still possible, "providing the therapist is sensitive to and careful not to tamper with the crucial defense against the emergence of open illness" (p. 21). Interpersonal contraindications are a lack of caring and cooperation necessary to perform the sexual tasks together.

For patients who are marginally suited for sex therapy, the next few sessions are devoted to exploratory exercises intended to clarify their status. The "sensate-focus" exercise (Masters and Johnson, 1970) is frequently used as a "probe"; sometimes the couple is merely instructed to shower together, washing and dry-ing each other (Witkin, 1979). Usually within three sessions, but sometimes requiring as many as four or five sessions, the prognosis is much clearer, and the patients will either continue in sex therapy or be referred to another treatment modality.

Once therapy proper begins, the average course of treatment lasts between six and sixteen weeks. In almost every case, persistance of the symptom beyond twenty weeks is considered an indication that this particular problem is not amenable to rapid sex therapy and calls for other forms of therapy.

The therapy process consists of erotic tasks performed at home, plus weekly or semiweekly meetings with the therapist. At each therapy session, the therapist and patients explore together the feelings and emotions experienced during the erotic exercises, which often are deep and profound. The therapist must be sensitive to the verbal and nonverbal cues that reveal the anxiety beneath the overt and covert responses of the patients and takes great pains to uncover their real reactions to the therapy, if progress is impeded. In this way not only does the therapist help the couple to obtain a clearer picture of their individual functioning and dyadic transactions, but also the partners learn to be frank and open about their emotions in general and their erotic preferences in particular.

Typically, the patients are instructed to perform the exercises more than once during the week. It is common for couples to experience difficulties during the first attempt, and to resolve these difficulties by the last attempt. With these patients, it is necessary only to present the next set of tasks. It is also common for patients to experience initial difficulties that are only partially resolved during the week; with these patients, some exploration of the resistances encountered, with insights and/or interpretations offered by the therapist, is often enough for a complete resolution. These couples also would probably be instructed to go on to the next set of erotic tasks.

These outcomes used to be the most common. However, the population seeking help for their sexual problems seems to be changing. More and more couples are coming with more profound problems that have remote causes. This results in increased difficulties in performing the sexual prescriptions. These resistances and obstacles can occur even before the exercises take place, for example, in deciding which partner "should" initiate the exercises and whether the other partner "must" agree. Other couples can "misconstrue" the instructions or interfere with his or her partner by "sabotaging" the process. Such maneuvers will compound the difficulties normally encountered in performing the actual tasks. Some couples can perform exercises properly and ruin the results—by having intercourse, for example, when intercourse has been proscribed. When these patterns persist or appear deeply entrenched, more intense psychotherapeutic confrontations and explorations are required.

Such psychotherapeutic, as opposed to behavioral interventions are performed strictly in the service of the experiential aspects—the sexual therapy prescriptions. Resolution is attempted only to the depth necessary to allow the tasks to continue; the resolution of intrapsychic or interpersonal conflicts for their own sake is avoided. Similarly, the therapist will tend to avoid offering insights to the couple that may apply to other realms but not to the psychosexual, if they pose a resistance to treatment.

If the resistance seems slight or manageable, it is bypassed, and the couple is instructed to proceed to the next exercises. Bypassing may also be indicated in certain unusual cases, for example, a man with erectile problems may have difficulty assuming the passive role in nongenital sensate focus, but may be much less resistant to genital stimulation. (The former is "womanly," the latter is "manly.") Although the inability to accept affectionate "pleasuring" may imply a severe disturbance, it should not be explored in this case. Instead, the man's resistance to nongenital pleasuring would probably be bypassed, and the couple would be instructed to perform the next exercise, genital stimulation.

If the problems experienced during the sexual exercises appear too severe to be bypassed and are obstructing the sex therapy process, they must be explored jointly by the therapist and the patients. The probable prescription will be a repetition of the same exercise for the next week, which is often enough to solve the problem. When bypassing and repetition techniques are both ineffective or when the resistances seem formidable, they must be confronted directly.

The erotic exercises themselves include those described by Masters and Johnson (1970), in addition to many others which have been developed in the last five years, such as in the treatment of premature ejaculation. In the Masters' and Johnson's technique, the female is instructed in the "squeeze" technique, applying pressure to the coronal ridge area of the penis to inhibit the ejaculatory reflex. Kaplan uses a modification of the Semans technique (Semans, 1956), in which the female aids the male in what is essentially a desensitizing procedure. It is felt that the Semans' technique gives the responsibility for ejaculatory control to the male, to whom it is most appropriate.

The Kaplan method prescribes a unique series of exercises for each couple. Other methods prescribe the same exercises to all patients, with specific exercises for the particular complaint. In Kaplan's technique, the dysfunction, as well as the motivation and assets of each couple, determines the course of the treatment. Using this approach, relief of the symptom will usually take place between six and sixteen sessions, although some patients have reported cures in as few as three sessions.

SUMMARY

The Kaplan method is characterized by the "integrated use of systematically structured erotic experiences together with psychothera-peutic exploration of each partner's unconscious intrapsychic conflicts as well as of the subtle dynamics of their interactions" (Kaplan, 1975, p. 4). The role of the therapist includes education, clarification, and support of the couple as they embark on what is indeed a new way of relating to each other. This integration of experiential and dynamic modes is one of the principal features distinguishing the Kaplan method from other approaches to sex therapy.

The Kaplan method also offers certain advantages outside the strictly sexual domain. The ability to undergo sex therapy while living their daily lives is very important to many patients, who may find it extremely impractical to leave their obligations (business, children) for long periods of time. Kaplan's method invests the responsibility for the therapy in the patients themselves who mostly perform autonomously.

It was stated earlier that the emergence and resolution (if only partial) of more deep-rooted resistances to the sexual therapy also may allow the Kaplan method to have greater benefits which may extend beyond the sexual symptoms.

REFERENCES

KAPLAN, H. S. 1975. *The illustrated manual of sex therapy.* New York: Quadrangle.

———. 1974. *The new sex therapy.* New York: Brunner/Mazel.

MASTERS, W. H., and JOHNSON, V. E. 1970. *Human sexual inadequacy.* Boston: Little, Brown.

SEMANS, J. H. 1956. Premature ejaculation; a new approach. *South. Med. J.* 49: 353–58.

WITKIN, M. H. 1979. The Intimate Shower, unpublished article.

NINETEEN

Sex Therapy: A Holistic Approach

MILDRED HOPE WITKIN

TOWARD A HOLISTIC THERAPY

Sex therapy as a field can be considered in many ways. It is a therapeutic discipline, usually requiring rather extensive training for proficiency. It is a rapidly growing body of knowledge, techniques, and modalities within the general realm of psychotherapy. It is a speciality within the broad area of dyadic and family therapy, with significant implications for both.*

Since sex, dyadic, and much of family therapy center on the treatment of dyads, it is logical that there should be relationships among the three. Theoretically, the resemblances are clear, but in practice the three areas of therapy have only recently begun to move together. The reason is that each arose and developed not only at different times but also in different ways.

Dyadic therapy (usually called couples or marital therapy) was preceded by pastoral counseling and became recognized as a field of therapy in the 1930s (Bowen, 1975). Early counselors, in addition to the clergy, were social workers who had to improvise techniques for dealing with the dyadic problems. Later, psychiatrists and psychologists entered the field, with a variety of theoretical and dynamic formulations explaining what they observed. There is no central figure in dyadic therapy that occupies the place dominated by Sigmund Freud in individual therapy. This also applies to family therapy. More recent than dyadic therapy, family therapy arose in the 1950s among psychiatrists, particularly those treating patients with highly disturbed, neurotic family backgrounds, or patients institutionalized for schizophrenia. With the former, progress or insights

---

* In this essay, except when otherwise stated, dyadic therapy is therapy involving two patients who have an intimate relationship with one another and who may or may not be married. Family therapy adds children and significant others to the dyad.

in the office seemed to dissipate. With the latter, cures in the hospital could be effected, but in most cases once the patients returned home, the schizophrenic symptoms reappeared. To obtain more lasting cures and to help dysfunctional family constellations, the psychiatrist began to try to modify the family environment, and family therapy was born. Ackerman (1958) was one of the first to publish in the field; he was followed by many others, including Whitaker (1958), Wynne et al (1958), and Weakland (1960).

Sex therapy can be traced largely to the work of four people. The first was Dr. Alfred C. Kinsey. Though never addressing the relief of sexual dysfunctions, Dr. Kinsey's dispassionate, scientific inquiry into sexual practices made the entire subject intellectually and socially reputable. Dr. William H. Masters and Mrs. Virginia Johnson initiated sex therapy per se in 1970 with the publication of *Human Sexual Inadequacy*. Their approach was and remains rather stringently behavioral. In 1974 Dr. Helen S. Kaplan extended the therapy of Masters and Johnson by adding psychodynamic and interpersonal modalities to the behavioral techniques, describing her approach in *The New Sex Therapy*. This is the approach generally followed by the author in referring to sex therapy. Unlike sex therapy, family and dyadic therapy does not have major nucleal figures. As Hogan (1975) states, "The way in which the family system is approached differs markedly from one therapist to another. Some family therapists . . . think primarily in terms of the family structure. . . . Others emphasize the interplay between . . . individual dynamics and the larger family system. Still others emphasize the communication aspects" (p. 23). Similar words could be written about dyadic therapy.

In considering the relationship between sex

therapy and dyadic and family therapy, it might be asked, to which of the many types of dyadic and family therapy is sex therapy related? The answer is, to all of them and to individual therapy as well.

The reasons lie in the centrality of sex (discussed later) and in current trends in psychotherapy. Psychotherapy as a whole may be looked at in two ways, in terms of techniques or schools—psychoanalytic, gestalt, behavioral, Rogerian, existential—and in terms of fields or areas of application—individual, dyadic, family, sex, children, geriatric, drugs. What seems to be happening is that distinctions among schools and distinctions among areas of applications are blurring, as the practice of therapists and the fields in which they practice begin to merge into each other. In the words of Martin (1976), "It is clear that the fields of individual, marital, and family therapy have overlapping boundaries and that distinguishing one from the other is, to some extent, an artificial process" (p. 3). There are similar amalgams in psychotherapeutic techniques. But a mere union of techniques and/or fields does not necessarily equal a holistic approach, for even with these amalgams it is possible to view the patient partially, to split the patient into sections treatable by one's specialty. That is, the person practicing individual psychotherapy tends to split the patient from his or her family, but the dyadic or family therapist tends to split the family member from his or her unique intrapsychic problems. Holism insists on the integrity of the patient: the patient is seen as a whole, as part of a dyad or family (or even, as Auerswald * says, as part of a neighborhood, community, or country), and as an individual. Holism also implies that the therapist can vary his or her approach depending on the needs of the patient, dyad, or family. "Man is autonomous," says Bowen, "yet not separated from family and multigenerational past" (1975, p. 370).

* R. Auerswald, Ecological Perspectives in Family Therapy. Lecture in program on marital and family therapy, New York Medical College, Flower and Fifth Avenue Hospitals, May 23, 1973.

It is theoretically possible to cure one member of a family by treating another. Freud, in the notable "Little Hans" case (1909), did just that, curing a phobia in a small boy through work with the boy's father. Some people claiming to be family therapists never see families, only individuals, basing their claim on the "ripple" effect of successful individual therapy. Similarly, some family therapists treat all individual intrapsychic problems as family problems, amenable to family therapy techniques. It is true that the resolution of family problems often eases the intensity of the intrapsychic difficulties of family members. Still, these seem inefficient ways of doing therapy: while the individual is being treated, the overall family can deteriorate (such cases are known to the author), or while the family is being treated as a unit, the intrapsychic problems of some members can be slighted or repressed. It would certainly appear to be true, and it has been my own experience (Witkin, 1975, 1977, 1978) that the most efficient individual, dyadic, or family therapy is when all of the significant people in the problem are treated in therapy at an appropriate time.

Holistic therapy, then, is primarily distinguished not by utilizing a variety of modalities but by the therapist's attitude toward the patient. "What is transpiring in any therapeutic setting is not determined by whether it is distinguished as individual, marital, or family therapy. It is determined by the needs of the patients and the capabilities, versatility, and training of the psychotherapist" (Martin, 1976). In brief, the patient is treated as a whole person, the dyad is treated as two whole people trying to maintain a rewarding relationship, and the family is treated as several whole people in various stages of development with various, mutually dependent needs and satisfactions. Many treatment modalities may be required, since techniques sufficient for treating individuals may not be appropriate to treating families.

It seems likely that holistic therapy will develop along the lines of family and dyadic therapy, that is, a host of approaches and techniques deriving from the myriad backgrounds of the practitioners. It also seems likely that the holistic therapist will need a variety of skills and modalities and that among these will be those associated with sex therapy.

THE HOLISTIC EFFECTS OF SEX THERAPY

If psychotherapy in general is evolving toward a holistic approach, where does sex therapy fit in? The immediate answer is that it is a subspecialty within dyadic therapy, since it deals with a special class of dyadic problems. This classifies sex therapy by the symptoms treated and not by the effects of the therapy—a classification with which most sex therapists would probably agree. However, to narrow sex therapy to symptom removal alone is to ignore the significant role of sex in human functioning. Poor sexual functioning wrenches individual, dyadic, and family functioning into distorted, painful shapes; good sexual functioning can restore inner and outer harmony.

Successful sex therapy has a very strong "ripple effect"; the resolution of sexual problems usually resolves or moderates other problems, interpersonal and intrapsychic. Indeed, the ripple effect is really threefold—a triple ripple, so to speak.

The first ripple is the effect on the formerly dysfunctional patient. In helping a woman achieve orgasm or a man overcome impotence or premature ejaculation, the therapist has usually helped that person gain a whole new self-concept.

One woman, about thirty years old, visited her physician complaining of severe headaches and menstrual cramps which had started many years before and persisted ever since. The physician, a highly sensitive man with a superb ear for unexpressed problems, inquired about her sex life. It turned out that she was anorgastic and her husband was "all right," but "very fast." (This bilateral dysfunction, failure to reach orgasm in the woman and premature ejaculation in the man, is very common.) The physician referred the couple to sex therapy.

They were highly motivated people, and it was decided to address both dysfunctions together. (Usually, the orgasmic difficulties are treated first, then the premature ejaculation.) Results were surprising even for the experienced therapist: the woman had several orgasms after only the second therapeutic session, and the man achieved substantial ejaculatory control after the fourth session. This couple was seen a total of six times; by the end, the woman's headaches had disappeared, and she had had one menstrual period with no cramps at all!

The relief of physical symptoms is not the only effect of sex therapy on individual functioning and usually is not the most important effect. An extremely gratifying case had no physical effects at all, in a sense.

A man in his early fifties, an important executive in a major corporation, appeared for sex therapy with one wish: to have at least one firm erection, one penetration, and one thrusting experience before he died. Describing himself as impotent, he had been examined by a "famous doctor" when he was twenty years old and was told that he would never have an erection as long as he lived. Although the man later married and had two children, he never had a firm erection and of late, having an erection and full-scale intercourse had become an obsession with him.

Although successful at his job, this man almost always had lunch by himself, never went out after work "with the boys" for a drink and some "man talk," and never told—and could barely listen to—risqué, off-color jokes: they reminded him of his problems and aroused the fear that his reactions would reveal that he was less than a man. Socially, he and his wife merely fulfilled their obligations, entertaining others and going out as a matter of duty rather than of pleasure.

The first step in therapy was to send this man to an endocrinologist, who found nothing physiologically wrong with him; in fact, his testosterone level was slightly above normal. The man received this information, from the therapist, with complete neutrality; it took, in fact, several weeks for him to internalize and accept its implications. During this time initial sex exercises were prescribed. When the man, by his comments, indicated a readiness for more intensive work, exercises were given aimed at helping him achieve firm erections. He was told, however, not to attempt intercourse with his wife until he did have a firm erection and then to avoid using their bed, since that had been the scene of many disastrous attempts at intercourse and had depressing associations. In the course of the exercises the man for the first time in his life had a firm erection; he and his wife of twenty-seven years piled blankets on the floor and had successful, thrusting intercourse for the first time in their marriage. During the weekend, this was repeated several times.

The couple now enjoys sexual intercourse regularly. At his work the man now goes out with his colleagues, tells and listens to any kind of sexual joke, and has become, as he reports, not only more liked but also more respected. On that first weekend he and his wife went to a party at which, as they gleefully reported, they astonished everybody by dancing every dance and generally leading the festivities. Since then their social life has been much richer and more enjoyable.

The second ripple effect of sex therapy is on the dyad itself. It is true that many dyads relate all their problems to sex, attributing deep-rooted interpersonal and intrapsychic difficulties to an unsatisfying sex life; it is also true that some couples have what they describe as "great sex" embedded in an otherwise destructive relationship; and it is finally true that some couples have generally good (untroubled) relationships with unsatisfying sex lives. This is to say that good sex and a good relationship are not always linked. But in most cases they are: poor sex is at once a cause and a symptom of a painful relationship, and if the sexual problems are alleviated, the relationship usually improves immediately and markedly.

A couple in their mid-twenties, both teachers, was referred to sex therapy as a last resort. Their referring therapist was seeing them individually and as a dyad, and yet could not help them break through the hostility and coldness they felt for each other. They were planning to divorce, but on the urging of their therapist they decided to try sex therapy.

The woman was orgasmic, the man im-

potent—but had not been before their marriage. At the initial evaluation session, their anger toward each other was expressed not only in words and intonations but also in posture; they never touched and sat half-turned away from each other. The distrust, indignation, and defensiveness were almost palpable.

With some trepidation, the therapist began with simple "pleasuring" exercises. Although everything else had failed these succeeded: within three sessions the man had an erection, he achieved full penetration, with thrusting, after nine sessions. At the twelfth and final session the couple sat together, holding hands and crying as they related how they had regained their original loving feelings. A later check with their referring therapist indicated that their remaining problems had been solved quickly, and the relationship was now secure and functioning well.

The third effect devolves from the first two, and that is the effect of sex therapy on the family.* With a change in the self-concept and ego-functioning of at least one of the parents, and with a further change in the behavior and attitudes of the parents toward each other and the children, it is hard indeed to imagine that changes will not occur in the children themselves. When the children are living with the dyad under treatment, these changes almost inevitably occur.

The problem for one couple was premature ejaculation of the husband. The initial interview revealed that the entire sexual relationship was hampered by their ten-year-old son. An angry and difficult child, the boy would burst into their bedroom at unexpected times; the resulting apprehension did nothing to help the already troubled sex life of the parents.

When the first sexual exercises were prescribed, the parents declared their fear that their son might interrupt them. They were

---

* Although "family" can clearly include parents, grandparents, children, cousins, aunts, and so on, in this essay it is limited to parents and children living together. However, the healing affects of sex therapy can extend to all communicating family members; in one case, successful sex therapy with a dyad resulted in a greatly improved relationship between the dyad's children and the wife's parents.

advised simply to lock the door on those occasions and allow their son to lock his when he wanted privacy. After some reassurance that this would not harm their son psychologically, they agreed.

On first encountering the locked door the boy became very angry and kicked it. Subsequently he would stand outside and shout, "What are you guys doing in there—screwing?" But the couple persisted in keeping the door locked and in doing the exercises. In about ten weeks, the dysfunction was cured.

The experience of joining together to defend their own interests (locking the door) and to enhance their own satisfaction (improving their sexual functioning) pulled the couple closer together and eased communication with each other. The father was able to transfer this ease to dealing with his son, and for the first time they began to have long talks with each other. The boy was finally able to reconcile himself to the loss of his Oedipal fantasies. He became less angry and is no longer a serious problem. The couple returned to the referring family therapist with renewed enthusiasm.

Accompanying the removal of symptoms, then, are behavioral and attitudinal changes so profound and so pervasive as to justify a place for sex therapy (when appropriate, of course) in the holistic approach to patients. First, it is useful to explore the reasons for the strength and dependability of the ripple effect. But it must be emphasized that these effects do not occur in isolated cases but in almost all cases; they are not erratic but predictable, arising from the centrality of sex in human functioning.

THE CENTRALITY OF SEX

In restoring "good sex" to a person or dyad, three aspects of sex therapy are noteworthy. One is the area of treatment: sexual functioning. Another is the treatment process, the way in which the therapy is practiced. The third is the nature of psychotherapy itself, the way in which it works, the goals it attempts to achieve.

To begin with sexual functioning, it may simply be stated that one's sexual self-concept is almost always basic to one's entire ego-concept,

and the sexual relationship within the dyad is almost always crucial to the overall dyadic relationship. This is true even of dyads with good relationships in spite of bad sex; when they come into sex therapy, and their sex life improves, the rest of the relationship typically blossoms and intensifies in ways previously unimaginable to them. For most people and certainly for most dyads, satisfactory sex is the nucleus of the successful, intimate, holistic relationship.

It is the goal of sex therapy to help the couple achieve satisfactory sex, and this makes the definition of "satisfactory sex" critical. To a great extent, the therapist's view of what makes sex satisfactory will determine his or her attitude toward the patient.

It is worth summarizing here the definition of satisfactory sex given by or implicit in Masters and Johnson and in Kaplan (with which the writer agrees). Sex consists not only of desire, excitement, and good performance in intercourse—erection of the penis, engorgement of the vagina, penetration, and orgasm for both partners—but also of the mutual "pleasuring" of the partners, and may include all, none, or some of the "performance" factors. In giving and receiving pleasure, the goal, sex, spreads physiologically away from the primary sex organs to encompass the entire body, and psychologically away from the sensations connected with those organs and nothing else, to the sensations and emotions connected with the entire pleasuring experience. In brief, sex as pleasuring involves more of the total being of the participants than does sex as performance, and sex therapy addressed to pleasuring will address a larger portion of the patient's personality. Further, as the dyad learns to accept pleasuring as a goal, they learn to exchange, for at least a portion of their sexual experiences, the strong sensory excitement of intercourse for the perhaps lower sensory excitement but stronger emotional responses of mutual pleasure-giving. In pleasuring, then, the emotional aspects of the dyadic sexual relationship assume greater importance.

It is these relational (as well as intrapsychic)

aspects that are addressed by the sex therapist. Kaplan makes explicit the need for the modern, effective sex therapist to depart from performance therapy as necessary to help the dyad achieve the better relationship from which better sex can grow, and deliberately to incorporate nonbehavioral, nonsexual modalities in the treatment approach.

Thus, when sex therapy is successful, two results are obtained. First, good functioning has been restored to a central part of the human personality. Second, some of the broader intrapsychic and interpersonal aspects of the relationship have been treated, the aspects touched by the "ripples" of the therapy.

But these do not wholly account for the ripple effects nor their power—in a sense, the effects are not really ripples but upheavals, major shifts in personality structure. No claim is made that successful sex therapy and the resultant good sexual functioning are the be-all and end-all of psychotherapeutic treatment. Like every other significant, therapy-induced change, the results of sex therapy need time and work to become fully integrated into the functioning of the individual and the dyad. As with other therapeutic results, successful sex therapy often leaves much work still to be done on other dysfunctional aspects of the self. Still, sex therapy is a powerful instrument for psychological change and to account for its power, consideration of the general nature or goals of therapy is necessary.

A patient brings into the therapeutic (and "real life") situation at least three major aspects of himself or herself: a current sense of self (an ego-concept or ego-awareness), a way of relating to others, and underlying both, a history as a person, starting from the beginning and continuing to the moment before the present. The dysfunctional person, or dysfunctional relationship, is usually dysfunctional in all three areas even if the awareness of the dysfunction is suppressed, and it is the goal of therapy to improve functioning in all of them. Obviously, the past cannot be improved, but one's attitude toward his or her own past can be altered for the better.

In both inner instinctual drives and external societal expectations, few aspects of the human personality are as strong as sex, or as pervasive in all three areas. The sexually dysfunctional man or woman has a damaged ego-concept and impaired awareness, has (usually) overcompensated relationships in one way or another, and cannot assimilate the past. With the sexual dysfunction resolved a central rupture has been healed; the improvement is not on the periphery, to trickle down, but at the core, to affect everything else. The power of the ripple effect derives from both the strength of sex among the determinants of human behavior and its omnipresence in the functioning of the individual or dyad.

One final "ripple" should be noted: successful sex therapy facilitates other therapies. It helps the dyad or individual to accept more easily other therapeutic modalities, being less rigid and more aware of the necessity for change. The improvement in sexual functioning (which is usually accompanied by increased self-confidence and decreased anxiety) helps to create a belief in the therapeutic process and the expectation of a successful outcome. With successful sex therapy as described, in usually not more than sixteen weeks the therapy is terminated, and the dyad feels—in the word most frequently used—marvelous. Dyads in this state of mind approach other problems with zest and determination and a readiness to try anything. Linked with the better ego-concept and dyadic relationship resulting from improved sexual functioning, this attitude immeasurably eases the task of the next stage of the therapy.

THERAPISTS AND PATIENTS

In regard to the patient entering sex therapy, some of the implications of the process of sex therapy will be discussed, with special attention to referrals by extrasexual therapists. Many different modes of referral, for many different reasons, are possible (Witkin, 1977).* Primar-

---

* Patients have been referred for sex therapy at the start, during, or at the conclusion of extrasexual psychotherapy, with frequent or no consultations between therapists (the choice is generally that of the referring therapist).

ily three questions will be discussed: who should be treated by sex therapy, when should treatment begin, and how should it proceed?

Clearly, the appropriate patient for sex therapy is the person (generally a member of a dyad, though single individuals also are treated) who has a sexual dysfunction: impotence, premature ejaculation, or retarded ejaculation for the man; lack of arousal, anorgasmia, or vaginismus for the woman. It also is important for the individual, dyad, or family to recognize what is now being seen as another dysfunction: lack of sexual desire in either or both partners.

The significance of lack of desire is particularly important to the dyadic or family therapist, because it is not a "natural" state inevitably resulting from long-term relationships or as a consequence of aging, and is not usually a matter of constitutionally "low libido" or some similar, conventionally explained condition. Lack of desire almost always reflects sexual maladaptation, often traced to early childhood.

In interviewing patients with any complaint, it is assumed that the extrasexual therapist will ascertain the patient's (or dyad's) sexual functioning. It is suggested that this be done not by general questioning but by asking the patients whether they suffer from any of the specific sexual dysfunctions including "desire." It is most important to gain some idea of the presence or absence of desire, since this may explain the entire relationship.

If a sexual dysfunction is present—whether or not it is the presenting complaint—when should it be addressed? In other words, at what point in the treatment should the holistic therapist initiate sex therapy or should the extrasexual therapist refer the patients to the sex therapist? It is recommended that sex therapy, by the original or referred therapist, should be undertaken as early in the treatment as possible. The reason is to take advantage of the ripple effects, since this will almost surely facilitate the progress of therapy in other areas.

To propose the early initiation of sex therapy in every therapeutic situation in which any of the patients being seen has a sexual problem, is in some degree to oppose the practice of many psychotherapists. It advocates that the therapist address a particular symptom rather than the underlying constellation of causes determining that symptom, and to many psychotherapists this reverses the order of therapy. In their view, symptomatic relief follows successful general therapy and indicates profound changes in the patient's personality structure.

Sex therapy exercises generally can be divided into two major categories. One is relaxation exercises, such as sensate focus, aimed not at the target dysfunction but at easing tension and anxiety, improving communication, expanding the dyadic concept of sensuality, and removing the demand element from sex. The other is intensive exercises aimed at alleviating the sexual dysfunction and are much more organ-specific with stronger sensory stimulation.

Dyads who present themselves only for sex therapy often have an otherwise good relationship. When they do, it is usually very evident and intensive exercises often can begin immediately. Other dyads and most dyads who come initially for dyadic or family therapy, may have severe relational problems and may not be ready for sex therapy even in its relaxation phase. The combination of hostility, anxiety, and defensiveness is usually so strong as to preclude any approach to physical and emotional intimacy. In these cases, usually caused by communication difficulties, the therapist will work in dyadic/family modalities to help the dyad achieve the minimum of communication skills and mutual trust that allow sex therapy to proceed.

Occasionally a dyad referred for sex therapy will show such hostility, such reluctance to approach each other on any level, as to preclude sex therapy entirely. For such patients, sex therapy should begin with a probe. Invariably, the probe shows an unreadiness for sex therapy, and this is reported to the referring therapist. Often the referring therapist has turned to sex therapy as a last resort, although it may be fruitless.*

---

* A question may arise as to the criteria for returning the dyad to the original therapist for additional therapy or for initiating the "relationship training" aspects of sex ther-

In most referrals, however, the dyad has initial communicative difficulties but has enough motivation to encourage sex therapy. In these cases it is advisable to begin with the probing exercise, to determine the direction of the individual treatment regimen.

The probe used by the author is the prescription that the dyad shower together at least twice before the next session, which is usually the following week. They are to wash each other using only their hands—no washcloths—and then to dry each other. At this time, intercourse may or may not be prohibited, depending on the preliminary evaluation of the psychodynamics.

The results of the probe generally fall into three categories. Some couples enjoy the experience almost from the beginning: typical comments are that it was fun, that they hadn't done that since they were children (or were first married), and that they enjoyed showing each other what to do. Some couples report becoming so excited that they had intercourse in the shower—a resistance if intercourse has been prohibited, a good sign if it has not. For such couples, the sex therapy can proceed to the intensive exercises.

Some couples are obviously not ready for sex therapy as indicated by their resistance to the exercise. Typical responses are to blame the surroundings (it was too cold, too slippery, the shower was too small), or to retreat to personal idiosyncrasy (prefer baths, don't like being touched, don't like to wash anybody). One couple, having been told not to use washcloths, used sponges—an obvious case of resistance.

When the reported results are uniformly negative, and further psychodynamic exploration reveals significant intrapsychic pathology or interpersonal hostility, the couple is usually considered not ready for sexual therapy, and addi-

tional individual or dyadic therapy is needed. When the resistance to shower or relaxation exercises appears to be more a matter of fear of intimacy than hostility toward the partner, it is possible to proceed with sex therapy, bypassing the relaxation phase and proceeding to the intensive exercises.

In many cases, the results of the probe are not clear. Typically, the partners feel awkward, clumsy, and embarrassed, afraid of each other's comments and fearful that they will do something wrong. Usually by the end of the second shower, the situation has eased considerably, but there still may be tension if not outright hostility. In these instances, although intimacy is desired, the tension is so great that intimacy seems threatening. Each has staked out a position in which one is "right" and the other is "wrong," and intimacy can undermine these positions. Such dyads almost always can benefit by starting with the relaxation exercises.

When the therapy is terminated, the sex therapist reports the results to the referring therapist, and these reports, with the permission of the patients, will include discussions of any new material that may have arisen in the course of treatment. The holistic therapist, having incorporated dyadic and family therapy in the process of sex therapy, will reassess with the couple the direction in which they wish to proceed. Even unsuccessful sex therapy can help to clarify the underlying causes of the basic dyadic problem.

In the majority of referrals, treatment proceeds smoothly and there are no unusual complications. In some cases, special problems unrelated to sex therapy itself may arise. Because sex therapy per se encourages pleasure and enjoyment, positive transference to the therapist is sometimes very strong: a dyad still under treatment by a dyadic therapist may wish to leave and continue with the sex therapist; a member of the dyad undergoing individual intrapsychic treatment may wish to discontinue treatment or switch to the sex therapist. In both cases, the dyad or individual is advised to discuss his or her motives with the original therapist.

When does the sex therapist consult other

---

apy. The criteria are based on the definition of sex as pleasuring. If the dyad appears ready for pleasuring exercises, that is, nondemand relaxation, then the couple is prepared to accept sex therapy and becomes the responsibility of the sex therapist. If the dyad cannot deal with even this level of intimacy, then it is the domain of dyadic therapy, and the dyad returns to the original therapist, or the holistic therapist proceeds with dyadic or family therapy.

therapists? The answer is, when it is in the best interests of the patient. This may occur when the sex therapist is only or primarily a sex therapist and the problem is not amenable to sex therapy, or if the dyad wishes to pursue another modality in which the sex therapist does not feel competent.

It may also occur when the patient and therapist have different priorities. Although dyadic therapists place a high priority on the stability of the dyadic relationship, they will not sacrifice the integrity or growth of the individual to the maintenance of the dyadic relationship, but they usually will try to ensure that this growth occurs within the boundaries of the relationship, if possible, and will devote considerable effort to this end. The dyad is indeed "the patient," (as the family is "the patient" for family therapists), and the point of view of the dyadic therapist is that both partners are equally involved in the problem.

The sex therapist, on the other hand, often encounters situations in which only one member of the dyad has a dysfunction and the treatment, although pertaining to both partners, is aimed primarily at that one person. As progress is made and the dysfunction improves, the partner sometimes exhibits change in other areas (the individual ripple effect) that appears to threaten the dyad and may in fact destabilize the relationship. The sex therapist must be very sure whether he or she wishes to encourage the individual to change at the expense of the relational stability, to discourage such change, to work with the dyad on the relational problem, or to refer to another therapist. The sex therapist must be aware of his or her attitude toward extrasexual change if the therapy begins to go, as it often does, beyond the resolution of the sexual dysfunction.

The holistic therapist, by assessing the intrapsychic and interpersonal functioning of each patient, may decide, on concluding sex therapy, to refer one or both members of the dyad or members of the family to another therapist, or may elect to treat any or all members of the family himself or herself. There are no rules. There are, however, advantages in having a single therapist treat all the problems of the couple and family, the advantage of being able to shift emphasis as the need arises and to treat new material and different family members in the most appropriate way. One excellent example is the following:

A couple in their early forties was referred to sex therapy by a psychiatrist treating the woman. The presenting symptom was occasional impotence on the part of the man; the woman was orgasmic. The woman was a compulsive cleaner, vacuuming the house several times a day. She also suffered from severe constipation. They had two daughters, sixteen and twelve years old. It was the psychiatrist's opinion that her constipation was the result of poor sexual function, even though she experienced orgasm every time she and her husband had intercourse.

This couple practiced the very common "Sunday morning sex" ritual, common because that is when couples with children usually have the time for sex, or when excuses for not having sex no longer hold. It was an ordeal for them both, a duty repeated weekly. Even when he was potent the husband found the entire experience unsatisfying; his wife was even more inhibited than he. Neither disrobed in front of the other, nudity was strictly under the cover. Intercourse was quick—and they both felt that sex was supposed to be better than it was for them.

Both partners were virgins when they married, and neither had had any other partner. The woman never initiated the Sunday ritual, a fact that also irritated the husband.

It was clear that this couple was eager to improve their sexual functioning but was in a state of high anxiety. Rather than prescribing even the mild relaxation exercises, it was suggested that they begin by sleeping in the nude (a form of desensitization) together. At the same time, the therapy sessions began to explore the wife's inhibitions and the husband's anxieties, using various extrasexual modalities.

Initially, it appeared that the husband was indeed justified in his irritation with his wife's inhibitions, since she refused to undress in front of him. However, as time went on she was able to remove her outer garments in his presence, to complete disrobing in bed, and finally to undress completely while he watched. At that time the relaxation exercises were prescribed, and the husband's inhibitions appeared in full force.

Extrasexual exploration revealed that he had been hiding behind the Sunday ritual as a protection against his own anxieties about his performance in spontaneous intercourse. Further, while complaining about his wife's failure to initiate sex, he in fact had been discouraging her every time she did initiate, claiming that he needed extra sleep, was tired, and so on.

As the therapy and the relaxation exercises (of the nondemand type) proceeded, the couple gradually grew more at ease with their own needs and desires and bodies. Finally, intercourse was prescribed—for any day except Sunday. The husband was potent; both found the experience the best they could remember. Their sexual functioning continued to improve, the wife's constipation improved, and her compulsive cleaning was markedly reduced.

Many inhibitions and problems remained, however, so the couple elected to continue therapy. Soon they brought up the subject of their daughter. Almost seventeen years old, she had been seeing a boy for a year, and while they suspected that the daughter and her boy friend were having intercourse together, they were not sure. By now they had only two concerns about her: that she use a birth control device and that she have a positive experience; the last thing they wanted, both husband and wife declared, was for their daughter to be as "hung-up" about sex as they were, and for so long a time. They recommended to the daughter that she contact the therapist, which she did.

It turned out that the parents were correct: the daughter was having intercourse with her boyfriend, was not practicing birth control, and was not enjoying sex at all. She was also very fearful of sharing this information with her parents. And she volunteered that most of her friends were in exactly the same predicament.

After several counseling sessions (no real therapy was required), the girl, without telling her parents that she was sexually active, did notify them that she was going to be fitted for a diaphragm and that she wanted to visit the physician by herself. This opened the way to a whole new level of communication between the parents and the girl, who still, however, did not reveal her sexual activity. But the family grew much closer as a

family, and the twelve-year-old daughter began to wonder when she could go into therapy—she had no apparent problems. In her last session with the therapist, the girl reported that she was using the diaphragm, that sex was becoming very enjoyable, and that many of her friends were trying to find the courage to do the same.

A few months later the girl left town to go to college and from the safety of that distance, phoned her parents and mentioned that she had been having sex. She was astonished at their concern for her own welfare and pleasure, and the family has never been closer in an emotional sense. In addition, she altered her original intention of studying education, because "teaching is easy for women to do," to taking prelaw courses, because she had always wanted to be a lawyer but never felt capable until recently. The mother, meantime, was preparing for the absence of both her children by resuming a career in real estate and insurance that she had abandoned eighteen years earlier. The entire household was more relaxed, and the parents report that the younger daughter's friends, who formerly resented the restrictions against messiness, now love to come over.

It should be clear that the holistic therapist can begin as a sex, dyadic, family, or individual therapist. Initial theoretical orientation is not crucial. But any expansion of the scope of practice requires new skills, and it is expected that the therapist entering a new field will obtain them. This granted, the advantages of combining individual, dyadic, sexual, and family therapy in a single therapist are clear and will surely be realized more and more in the future.

HOMEOSTATIC CONSIDERATIONS

A question that might have occurred to the dyadic or family therapist or those familiar with dyad and family dynamics, is the relationship of sex therapy to the dyadic or family homeostasis. In the dyad/family context, homeostasis is the tendency of family members to maintain existing patterns of relationships and to resist change in another family member even if that change is constructive for the entire family or dyad. Homeostatic forces, usually described as "negative feedback" responses,[*] tend to be very strong in dyads and families; the literature[**] offers many examples and management techniques.

To a limited extent, homeostatic forces may appear in the course of sex therapy. They then manifest themselves in two situations, one involving the "healthy" (or at least, untreated) partner of the dysfunctional patient, and the other involving the children of the dysfunctional but improving couple.

Witkin (1977) summarized homeostasis in the dyad as follows:

> With regard to the couple per se, frequently, improvement of the dysfunctional partner is seen as a threat by the "healthy" partner. The most obvious source of the threat lies in the "healthy" partner's sense of his or her own inadequacy and worthlessness. The wife of a premature ejaculating man, for example, may feel that the only reason her husband tolerates her "faults" is that she tolerates his dysfunction and that once he is cured, he may leave her. Men have similar fears. The husband of an anorgastic wife may fear that once his wife can experience orgasms, his own inadequacy as a sexual partner will be revealed. Other men, knowing that some women can be multiorgastic, may fear that if the wife ever becomes able to have a single orgasm, she will become sexually "insatiable" (Sherfey, 1972), he will be unable to satisfy her, and she will seek other partners (p. 27).

Within the family, children may behave in various ways in attempting to maintain the accustomed homeostasis. If the parents have visited a family therapist with the child as the identified patient, that child may tend at first to continue or even intensify his or her disruptive behavior; other children may persist in moderately dysfunctional patterns or adopt new roles aimed at restoring the familiar and therefore nonthreatening, dysfunctional intrafamilial relationships. These occurrences are in every

way consonant with the findings of the dyadic and marital/family therapist.

On the other hand, in sex therapy the homeostatic forces, dyadic and familial, are usually relatively weak. In the dyad, the sex therapist can usually deal with the negative feedback responses as they arise during the normal course of the therapeutic sessions. Similarly with the family: if the relationship between the parents can remain steady, and this is usually the case, the sabotaging efforts of the children almost always fail, and the children readily adapt to the new patterns of behavior.

With regard to homeostasis and sex therapy, Witkin (1977) concludes that: "complications are not the rule. It can be predicted, based on Masters and Johnson's studies as well as personal clinical experience and other clinical studies (Kaplan, 1974), that about 80% of couples entering psychosexual therapy emerge with improved functioning and no undesirable effects" (p. 27). If the homeostasis-maintaining negative feedback is usually encountered in dyadic and marital therapy and generally weak or absent in sex therapy, it is worth speculating on what the reasons might be. There are three reasons, none excluding the others.

First, candidates for sex therapy must have at least a minimally functional relationship, while candidates for dyadic or family therapy can have an almost completely dysfunctional relationship. Whether the pathology is interpersonal or intrapsychic, the most severe cases will be evaluated as inappropriate for sex therapy. To some extent, the relative lack of complications encountered in sex therapy may be attributed to the patient selection process, which presumably leads only relatively healthy patients to the sex therapists, reserving the sick patients for the dyadic or family therapist.

On the other hand, it is unlikely that this accounts for more than a small minority of cases, since the majority of couples visiting a marital or family therapist usually are at least minimally functional also. Sex therapists will occasionally treat extremely disturbed patients (Witkin, 1977). The more plausible explanation for the relatively uncomplicated course of successful

---

[*] Negative feedback tends to inhibit deviations from the family pattern. Given an initial stimulus, negative feedback tends to nullify the effect of that stimulus. Positive feedback would tend to amplify the effects of the stimulus.

[**] Some writers include Bloch, (1973); Boszormenyi-Nagy, (1965); Minuchin, (1974); Haley, (1971, 1967); and Satir (1964).

sex therapy is in two characteristics of the therapy itself, in its speed and the nature of a successful outcome.

It should be noted that negative feedback can come from three sources: from the person being treated for the dysfunction (in which the negative feedback is in effect another name for intrapsychic resistance), from the partner of the person under treatment (dyadic homeostasis), or from the child or children of the couple seeing the sex therapist (family homeostasis). We now must consider how the process of therapy, its speed, and the attributes of success affect these three types of homeostasis.

The process of sex therapy itself considers intrapsychic resistance and dyadic feedback, and attempts to resolve problems as they occur. Not all resistances are resolved, however; many are bypassed in the interests of the rapid alleviation of symptoms. It seems logical that these bypassed resistances would re-emerge later as negative, homeostatic feedback.

In most cases, one reason why they do not is in the result of successful, pleasuring sex. When the treatment is successful, the relationship usually is heightened and intensified to a degree that overwhelms the resistances. It is not merely that new patterns of relating are established; the new patterns receive such powerful reinforcement from the pleasures of the newly rewarding sexual relationship so as to preclude the re-emergence of the old patterns. In brief, dyadic and intrapsychic resistances are dissipated or preempted by the new, sexually heightened relationship.

Within the larger family, the speed of the process is of great importance. The resistant, homeostasis-seeking child seeks to alter his or her behavior so as to reinstate the old family patterns, but this takes time and he or she has not time to experiment with new patterns or work them into the family functioning. In a sense the child is caught unprepared; the change in the parents is so rapid so as almost to present the child with a *fait accompli*. Interference with the process becomes much less likely; the child must now interfere with the results.

But the results usually are a strongly relating, communicating, revitalized set of parents who not only has every incentive to continue in the new patterns and not lapse back, but also has learned that problems are solvable and change is possible. Their tendency now is not to feel helpless in the face of the child's reaction but to do something about it, with professional help if necessary. With parents in a strong relationship, the resistant child will almost always fail to restore the previous homeostasis.

The attempt itself rises out of anxiety. When it fails, it leaves the child no real recourse except to adjust. The adjustment to the new patterns brings such rewards of warmth and understanding that the resistance soon disappears and the new relationship begins. The above case history of the couple with the ten-year-old son is a good example.

In summary, when the couple returns to the dyadic or family therapist or continues with the holistic therapist after having undergone successful sex therapy, homeostatic problems generally will have been understood and will be relatively easy to manage.

DYADS

The sex therapist treats dyads at a peculiarly intense phase of the dyadic relationship and has a unique opportunity to observe the different kinds of dyadic transactions. From these observations, it has been possible to categorize dyads into four general types, based roughly on age and experience. Clearly, a general typology does not mean that the behavior of a particular dyad can be predicted; it can indicate only the consistencies of behavior that experience has revealed.

The four dyadic types are the young unmarried dyad, the young married dyad, the experienced married dyad, and the experienced unmarried dyad.

The young unmarried dyad is seen much more frequently by the sex therapist than by the marital therapist. My impression is that young unmarrieds rarely come for marital therapy. Their sexual problems are the same as those of other patients.

The relationship of the young unmarried dyad is usually centered on sex. Whether they live together or apart (although this is much more pronounced when they are living apart), they tend to have lives separate from the relationship. Because of this, the need for extrasexual satisfaction within the dyadic relationship is diminished, since they can obtain this elsewhere. As a result, as long as sex is good, one partner tends to tolerate behavior by the other that married partners will not. Their perception of their relationship is generally that nonsexual problems "are not a problem."

But if sex is not good, what is the use of continuing the relationship? Just as good sex and strong separate lives can smooth over nonsexual problems, poor sex can cloud otherwise satisfactory aspects of the relationship and interfere with general "good times." That is, after a time the young unmarried dyad comes to feel that if the sexual problem is not resolved the relationship has failed.

Thus the young unmarrieds will seek sex therapy rather than marital therapy. Usually, the therapy proceeds smoothly; there is little "sabotaging" by the nondysfunctional partner and little fear of the outcome. The irony is that it is precisely in the young unmarried dyad that the most drastic changes in the relationship tend to occur. That is, the sexual dysfunction often has been used as an excuse or reason for immobility. The insecurities and fears associated with the failure to achieve good sex have frozen the dysfunctional partner into a practically fixed relationship. With the dysfunction cleared up, that person feels more free to move.

Although many young unmarrieds continue in the same relationship after successful sex therapy, a large proportion does move. This movement can be in two directions: the "cured" partner moves away and begins to explore other relationships, or the dyad gets married. The psychodynamics in the first alternative are evident: the formerly dysfunctional partner, his or her feelings of inferiority cleared up along with the dysfunction, now feels confident to handle sexual situations and eager to see where they might lead. No longer tied down by his or her own sense of inadequacy, or impelled to tolerate the faults of the partner because of his or her tolerance of the dysfunction, he or she elects to move.

The psychodynamics in moving toward marriage are less clear. One possibility is that these partners were planning to marry anyway and wanted to remove an important obstacle to their satisfaction before the relationship became more fixed. Another is that the dysfunctional partner did not want to "inflict" himself or herself on the other with a permanent sexual dysfunction, and a third is that one partner demanded the cure of the dysfunctional one before agreeing to marry. The most likely explanation is that marriage is seen by both partners as a challenging and serious commitment, and that the improved sexual functioning of the one partner and the more satisfactory sexual relationship for both increases their self-confidence individually and together.

The young married dyad with relational difficulties may or may not visit a marital therapist first, but if a sexual difficulty accompanies the relational problem, that sexual difficulty almost always will become the focus of the complaint. The dysfunctional young married dyad with a sexual dysfunction tends to attribute all their problems to the sexual sphere and assumes that once that is alleviated, their basic problems are solved. Clearly, this is far from being always true, although it should be pointed out again that even when other difficulties precede the sexual difficulty, resolution of the sexual problem usually will help greatly in resolving the more general problems.

When sex therapy begins, both partners tend to be equally enthusiastic. As the therapy proceeds and as the results become apparent, covert sabotaging often begins on the part of the nondysfunctional partner.

A couple in their late twenties, married for two years, had not consummated their marriage. The husband would become flaccid upon attempting entrance to the vagina and had never been able to penetrate. After the first six months, he was even unable to obtain the firm erections he had had up until the attempted entrance.

In the first phase of therapy, with intercourse prohibited, the husband was able to sustain long, firm erections. When intercourse was permitted, at the couple's discretion, the couple reported a very strange phenomenon. Even though the wife (not a virgin) was well lubricated, even using the least-threatening (for the male) female superior position, and even with good erections, the husband had not been able to penetrate.

Questioning revealed that the wife was actually dodging the husband's penis; by her movements she was preventing him from entering the vagina. Further discussion helped the wife realize that she was fearful that once her husband became fully potent and functional, he would be unfaithful and then desert her.

This session was enough to dissolve the unconscious sabotaging problem, and four more sessions concluded the sex therapy. Therapy for other problems, however, continued.

As noted earlier, sabotaging usually results from low self-esteem, although more complicated intrapsychic factors may be present. Ironically, as mentioned earlier, it is rare for the cured partner to leave the other partner, either formally or by seeking extramarital sex, or for example, by the newly orgastic woman turning into a nymphomaniac. In almost every case the whole relationship is bolstered by improved sexual functioning; the typical reaction of both partners is to wish that they had had sex therapy when the problem first arose.

It probably has been noted that I did not define "young" in young dyads. The reason is that there is no real line of demarcation between the young and what I have called the experienced. But it is reasonable, I believe, to consider as young those who are in their twenties, who have been married (or have had a strong commitment) to each other for up to five years, and who do not have children past the age of two. When children come, the couple's perception of itself alters radically, but it takes some time for the transformation to be complete. When the baby first is born, the couple remains a young couple with a baby; only after about two or three years does the couple consider themselves a family. At that point they are or may be an experienced couple.

How the experienced married dyad views themselves as individuals and as a couple is reflected in their approach to therapy. Most often, when problems, including sexual problems, arise, the couple's initial visit will be to a marital or family therapist. Even if the patients believe explicitly or tacitly that the sexual difficulty is and has been at the root of their global problem, they still will tend to start out with marital or family therapy.

By the time they do seek therapy, the global problem usually has become severe. Problems neglected before the children came have grown worse. The children, even those without problems, have added new stresses to the relationship, and those with problems have exacerbated the tension and hostility.

Typically, the couple will not go to any therapist until the situation has become very painful. Up to that point, contending with change has seemed too much of a threat. Once in sex therapy the experienced married couple exhibits the same sabotaging behavior and fears of desertion as the young married couple does. Further, the experienced marrieds are much more likely than the young marrieds to have had extramarital affairs. In a sense, they covertly have left the relationship already.

Sometimes one has an affair in order to obtain the sexual (and other) satisfactions missing in the marriage, but often the purpose is to retaliate for the injuries, real or imagined, or to alert the partner that the marriage has reached the breaking point.

In two ways, the extramarital affair can at least temporarily assist the marriage. When it is done in order to obtain otherwise unavailable gratification, it can help that partner to be more generally content and better able to tolerate the other stresses in the family. Clearly, when the unfaithful partner deliberately allows the other to learn of the affair (one man phoned his lover from his home, knowing that his wife usually listened to his conversations on an extension phone), it is a signal that the relationship has become too dysfunctional to be tolerated, and a stimulus for change. Often it is the last stimulus for change before a permanent separation.

Although the early problems of the dysfunctional, experienced married couple may not have been sexual in nature, sooner or later (usually sooner) they reach the sexual sphere. A sexual dysfunction appears or becomes aggravated, or the sex life of the couple begins to suffer in one way or another. From that point on, as with the young married dyad, the experienced married couple usually identifies the sexual problem as the core problem. Although in an etiological sense this may not be true, the therapist may take advantage of this belief by starting sex therapy as early as possible (if hostility between the couple has not progressed too far). With the experienced married couples, the most dramatic extrasexual effects of sex therapy are encountered. Like most couples, they have begun their relationship by being in love and over a period of time have seen all or most of their positive feelings for each other change to or become overladen with tension, hostility, distrust, resentment, and defensiveness, until they seem to themselves to be trapped in a situation at once intolerable and unchangeable. As sex therapy proceeds and as the initial and intermediate results bring both partners not only new sexual satisfaction but also new ways of relating, the incrustation of negative feelings and habits begins to drop off, and the couple experiences again the initial feelings of love, trust, and excitement. Whether or not other problems remain, and usually they do, this recaptured early ardor is almost always enough to propel them through those problems with eagerness and hope.

Of all the types of dyads or couples who come into sex therapy, the quickest and smoothest progress is often made by the experienced unmarried dyad or newly remarried. Usually but not always, these two people have been married before, care about each other, and are committed to a long-term relationship, usually remarriage. Resolved not to repeat the mistakes of the past, they also have learned how to help their partner avoid falling into old, painful patterns.

One middle-aged couple had just been married to each other, the second marriage for both. The presenting symptom was secondary impotence in the man. During their courtship he occasionally had experienced secondary impotence, but after their marriage it seemed to have become permanent. The man suggested to the woman that she see other men for sexual satisfaction, a clear regression to an earlier mode of coping with anxiety. The woman flatly refused and insisted that they go into sex therapy together. Within four sessions, with the wife's full cooperation every step of the way, the secondary impotence was cleared up.

Although the rapidity of this cure was unusual, the general outlines of the case are not. The experienced unmarried couple, or the experienced newly married, are very promising candidates for sex therapy.

OLDER COUPLES

Just as it is impossible to draw a sharp chronological line between the young and the experienced, it is impossible to draw a sharp chronological line between the experienced couple and the older couple. It is true that the sexual functioning of the elderly (especially the elderly man) differs from that of the nonelderly in certain age-related physiological changes (time required for erection, length of refractory period, and so on) (Masters and Johnson, 1966). Sex therapy for the elderly must take these changes into account.

But in their extrasexual functioning elderly couples exhibit all the variations in type, intimacy, and style as do younger couples. Once age-related changes are recognized, sex therapy for the elderly is the same as sex therapy for the younger, with perhaps a stronger attitude on the part of the therapist that "forbidden" normal practices are in fact not merely permissible but even desirable.

The elderly are popularly supposed to be resistant to change, but I have not encountered this phenomenon in my own practice. I have concluded that this resistance of the elderly is not so much inherent as evoked. It is a reaction to two complementary sets of changes experienced by the elderly: those they perceive in their own physical functioning and those they perceive in the way they are treated by others.

The perception of internal change, especially the perception of weakening powers, can provoke anxiety. However, this anxiety can be managed satisfactorily by most of the elderly when they understand that weakening powers do not mean reduced gratification. But when this anxiety is coupled with the attitude of most other people that the elderly person is less competent and less useful than other people are, the elderly feel diminished indeed. This external attitude is harder to fight against because it seems to be confirmed by their own aging bodies. Undermined by the loss of their sense of themselves as accomplished, whole people, they regain a sense of mastery by assuming a rigid posture, by insisting on no-change. When the elderly then are directed to change, this insistence can be defended successfully and a sense of strength is gained.

But only let the therapist encourage the elderly with the same attitude of optimism with which he or she encounters younger patients, and the results are striking. When the external world confirms not the diminution but the sustenance of the elderly, the elderly most often will respond with a mental and emotional (and often physical) vigor that can serve as a lesson to the younger.

THE HOLISTIC THERAPIST

The holistic therapist is the therapist who can treat competently a whole range of problems encountered in the individual, dyad, or family. He or she views the patient as a whole person in a series of relationships and will address the individual and/or the relationships as appropriate. The means by which problems in these areas are addressed—the modalities, schools, techniques—

may be less important than the attitude of the therapist to the wholeness of the patient. Still, certain skills are essential. Again, because sex is so fundamental to the functioning of both the individual and the dyad, because its ripple effects extend to and often include the family, and because sexual functioning is both a reflection and a determinant of other aspects of individual and dyadic functioning, the holistic therapist must be a sex therapist as well as an individual, dyadic, and family therapist.

Theoretically, a psychotherapist can start out in any single area of application and expand in any direction. In practice, it is unusual at this time for a person to begin his or her career as a sex therapist and proceed to individual/dyadic/family therapy; the reverse is much more likely. It is crucial that such a person, no matter what his or her background may be, undertake training at a recognized sex therapy institute.

Sex therapy is simultaneously a theory, a body of behavioral techniques, and an encounter with patients. The theory is easy to grasp. The exercises and their applications are not difficult to learn. The encounter with patients can be devastating unless adequate preparation has been made.

The reason for this is in the difference between sex on a symbolic level in the mind, and sex in the body as organs with sensations. Most psychotherapists of all persuasions have had some sort of training therapy or analysis in which their own sexual history, fears, and fantasies were considered in terms of ideas, symbols, and emotions. Issues of Oedipal conflicts, homosexual impulses, fetishes, fixations, orality, anality—all have been explored. On the ideational and emotional level, most qualified psychotherapists can function very well. This training also is very useful in working with the resistances to sex therapy.

But none of it has the slightest use in, for example, telling a woman how to masturbate her husband being treated for premature ejaculation. One does not speak of impulses, drives, desires; one speaks of organs and parts of organs in the patients' own language, which may range from the formal to the obscene. And one describes, in great detail, exactly what the patient and the partner are to do with those organs. For the inexperienced therapist, this kind of confrontation may be virtually impossible.

> A psychiatric resident was undergoing sex therapy training in a sex therapy clinic. His first actual session as a trainee dealt with an anorgasmic woman. In the course of the session, the woman was helped to overcome her inhibitions against pleasuring herself, and was given detailed instructions on how to stimulate her genitalia, in brief, how to masturbate. Later, in going over the session, the trainee remarked that he was fine up until the point at which the step-by-step physiological instructions began, but from then on he couldn't remember a thing!

Another psychiatric resident, after a few sessions of sex therapy training, left the program with the comment that it had been the most valuable training he had ever had, but that he knew now that he could never be a sex therapist. The exposure to sex therapy training on the organ/sensation level reawakens many of the anxieties associated with sex that were thought to have been resolved or understood but have not been eliminated completely. The typical reaction of the inexperienced sex therapist is to deny (as in the example given) or to avoid. Beginning trainees typically are eager to treat intrapsychic or interpersonal difficulties (which may be very minor), even when these are not resistances to the sex therapy and should be bypassed, postponing their confrontation with the physicality of sex for as long as possible. Working through the trainee's anxieties takes varying amounts of time, but the individual, dyadic, or family therapist who wishes competence in sex therapy should allow for a training period of approximately two years.

Sex is one of the dominant factors in the functioning of whole people with, presumably, greater awareness of the barriers to experiencing one's wholeness. Like everyone else, therapists are not immune to problems in the sexual sphere; like everyone else, their individual and interpersonal lives benefit greatly when sexual difficulties are alleviated. So does their impact as therapists. For the patient, holistic therapy is most effective when it is performed by therapists secure and enthusiastic in their own holistic functioning.

REFERENCES

ACKERMAN, N. W. 1958. *The psychodynamics of family life*. New York: Basic Books.

BLOCH, D. A. 1973. *Techniques of family psychotherapy: a primer*. New York: Grune & Stratton.

BOSZORMENJI-NAGI, I., and FRAMO, J. I. 1965. *Intensive family therapy*. New York: Harper & Row.

BOWEN, M. 1975. Family therapy after 20 years. In *American handbook of psychiatry*, 2d ed., vol. 5, ed. S. Arieti. New York: Basic Books.

FREUD, S. 1955. Analysis of a phobia in a five-year-old boy. In *Standard edition*, vol. 10, ed. J. Strachey, pp. 5–147. London: Hogarth Press.

HALEY, J., ed. 1971. *Changing families: a family therapy reader*. New York: Grune & Stratton.

———, and HOFFMAN, L. 1967. *Techniques of family therapy*. New York: Basic Books.

HOGAN, P. 1975. Creativity in the family. Monograph 2 in *Creative Psychiatry*, ed. F. Flech. Ardsley, New York: Geigy Pharmaceuticals.

KAPLAN, H. S. 1974. *The new sex therapy*. New York: Brunner/Mazel.

KINSEY, A. C.; POMEROY, W.; and MARTIN, C. 1948. *Sexual behavior in the human male*. Philadelphia: W. B. Saunders.

MARTIN, P. 1976. *A marital therapy manual*. New York: Brunner/Mazel.

MASTERS, W. H., and JOHNSON, V. E. 1970. *Human sexual inadequacy*. Boston: Little, Brown.

———. 1966. *Human sexual response*. Boston: Little, Brown.

MINUCHIN, S. 1974. *Families and family therapy*.

Cambridge, Mass.: Harvard University Press.

SATIR, V. 1964. *Conjoint family therapy.* Palo Alto, Calif.: Science & Behavior.

SHERFEY, M. J. 1972. *The nature and evolution of female sexuality.* New York: Random House.

WEAKLAND, J. H. 1960. The "double bind" hypothesis of schizophrenia and three-party interactions. *Etiology of schizophrenia,* ed. D. D. Jackson. New York: Basic Books.

WHITAKER, C. A., ed. 1958. *Psychotherapy of chronic schizophrenic patients.* Boston: Little Brown.

WITKIN, M. H. 1978. Psychosexual counseling of the mastectomy patient. *J. Sex Marital Ther.* 4.

———. 1977. Sex therapy as an aid to marital and family therapy. *J. Sex Marital Ther.* 3: 19–30.

———. 1975. Sex therapy and mastectomy, *J. Sex Marital Ther.* 1: 290–304.

WYNNE, L. C.; RYCHAFF, I. M.; DAY, J.; and HIRSCH, S. I. 1958. Pseudomutuality in the family relations of schizophrenics. *Psychiatry* 21.

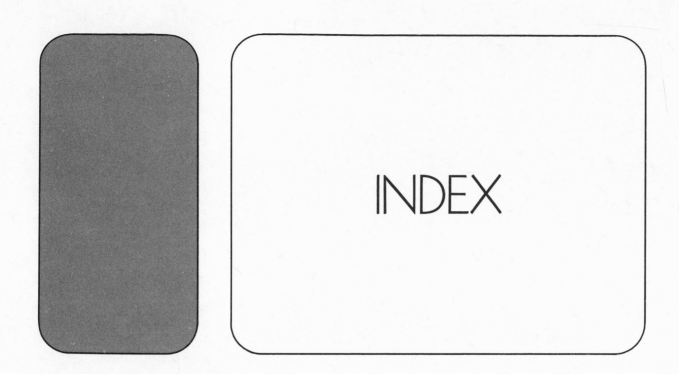

INDEX

357